I0807370

The Essence of the Vast and Profound

FIELD OF MERIT

THE DECHEN LING PRACTICE SERIES

THE ESSENCE OF THE VAST AND PROFOUND

A Commentary on Je Tsongkhapa's *Middle-Length Treatise on the Stages of the Path to Enlightenment*

Pabongkha Rinpoche

compiled and edited by
Trijang Rinpoche

Translated by David Gonsalez

Foreword by Gelek Rimpoche

Wisdom

Wisdom Publications
199 Elm Street
Somerville, MA 02144 USA
wisdomexperience.org

© 2019 Dechen Ling Press. First Dechen Ling edition published in 2014.
All rights reserved.

A previous edition of this book was published by Dechen Ling Press.

No part of this book may be reproduced in any form or by any means, electronic or mechanical, including photography, recording, or by any information storage and retrieval system or technologies now known or later developed, without permission in writing from the publisher.

Library of Congress Cataloging-in-Publication Data
Names: Pha-boṅ-kha-pa Byams-pa-bstan-'dzin-'phrin-las-rgya-mtsho, 1878–1941, author. | Rinpoche, Trijang, editor. | Gonsalez, David, 1964–2014. translator.
Title: The essence of the vast and profound: a commentary on Je Tsongkhapa's middle-length treatise on the stages of the path to enlightenment / Pabongkha Rinpoche as compiled and edited by Trijang Rinpoche; translated by David Gonsalez; foreword by Gelek Rimpoche.
Description: Somerville, MA, USA: Wisdom Publications, 2019. | Includes bibliographical references and index. | Translated from Tibetan. |
Identifiers: LCCN 2019016597 (print) | LCCN 2019981103 (ebook) | ISBN 9781614295419 (hardcover) | ISBN 9781614295594 (ebook)
Subjects: LCSH: Tsong-kha-pa Blo-bzang-grags-pa, 1357–1419. Lam rim chen mo. | Enlightenment—Religious aspects—Buddhism.
Classification: LCC BQ7950.T754 L34437 2019 (print) | LCC BQ7950.T754 (ebook) | DDC 294.3/442—dc23
LC record available at https://lccn.loc.gov/2019016597
LC ebook record available at https://lccn.loc.gov/2019981103

ISBN 978-1-61429-541-9 ebook ISBN 978-1-61429-559-4

23 22 21 20 19 5 4 3 2 1

Diligent efforts were made in every case to identify copyright holders of the illustrations. The author and the publisher are grateful for the use of this material.
The line drawings on pages vi, 7, 14, 29, 82, 122, 139, 161, 228, 232, 252, 293, 327, 371, 539, 549, 581, 618, 635 © 2015 Andy Weber.

Cover artwork: *Tsongkhapa Lobzang Drakpa (1357–1419)*, courtesy Rubin Museum of Art.
Cover and interior design by Gopa & Ted2, Inc. Set in Perpetua MT Pro 12/14.5.

Printed on acid-free paper and meets the guidelines for permanence and durability of the Production Guidelines for Book Longevity of the Council on Library Resources.
Printed in the United States of America..

Contents

Dharmakirti

Foreword by Gelek Rimpoche

KYABJE PABONGKHA, also known as Dorje Chang Dechen Nyingpo, was the preeminent Tibetan teacher, scholar, and adept of the eighteenth and nineteenth centuries. My personal connection with Kyabje Dechen Nyingpo was that he was the most important person who was instrumental in my recognition as an incarnate lama of Tibet. Moreover, my root masters such as Kyabje Ling Dorje Chang and Kyabje Trijang Dorje Chang were disciples of Lama Dorje Chang Pabongkha. My father, who was a great and grand incarnate lama of Tibet, was also a great disciple of Kyabje Pabongkha.

In my personal case, my previous incarnation happened to be the abbot of Gyuto Tantric College while Kyabje Ling Rinpoche was the junior abbot there, commonly known as Gyuto Lama. (Gyuto was headed by the abbot and the deputy abbot, known as "Lama.") Kyabje Ling Rinpoche thus said that "since both of us are disciples of Lama Dorje Chang [referring to Kyabje Pabongkha], all of Gyuto is definitely a follower of Pabongkha." Many earlier Tibetan teachers refer to Kyabje Pabongkha as Lama Dorje Chang, meaning Lama Buddha Vajradhara. Not only Gyuto but almost all Gelug monasteries, individual monks, great incarnate lamas, and members of the huge lay community were Pabongkha's followers.

When my previous incarnation passed away, his personal institute was never planning to have a reincarnation, so they disposed of his belongings in accordance with very traditional Buddhist culture. First and foremost, the most important objects were selected and offered to his root guru, who was Kyabje Pabongkha. Then the remaining items were offered to other well-respected incarnate lamas at that time, including Kyabje Ling Rinpoche, Trijang Rinpoche, and my father, as well as to personal and general monasteries. By the end, almost all the belongings of the late abbot were completely dispersed, except for a single little carpet and one small cabinet throne table. The final distribution again goes back to the root guru, so those who were in charge went back to Pabongkha to make the final distribution and told him there was nothing left except this carpet and cabinet.

Then Kyabje Pabongkha, to everyone's surprise, told the late abbot's manager, who himself was totally devoted to Kyabje Pabongkha, to find this late abbot's reincarnation. I was told as a young boy that as far as that manager was concerned, if Kyabje Pabongkha had told him to jump into a river or throw himself into a fire, he would have done so without a second thought. But when Kyabje Pabongkha told him to find the new incarnation of the previous Tashi Namgyal, the manager prostrated three times and literally cried. With tears dripping down his face he told Kyabje Pabongkha, "I will do anything you say, but please don't ask me to get the reincarnation." He gave the following reasons: "(a) Abbot Tashi Namgyal is not from a long history of incarnation lineages; (b) we disposed of all his belongings sincerely and nothing was put aside, so there is no wealth, and not even one working person is available to go around and search for the new incarnation; and (c) most important of all, if this incarnation becomes someone worthwhile, it may be all right, but if he becomes a wild incarnate lama, then not only will all our efforts be wasted, but I myself will be responsible for creating a lot of harm." The manager then concluded by saying, "All my life I have been doing the best I could, and if at the end I were to become the source of contributing to harm, that would be horrible. As the Tibetan saying goes, 'We eat medicine throughout life and before we die we eat poison.' That won't be good, so please forgive me." Then he started crying again and begged Pabongkha not to ask this of him.

Pabongkha told him to return home and not to make a decision and that they would talk again the next day or thereafter. Then, after a few meetings, Pabongkha assured the manager and the group of searchers that the reincarnation would not be far distant—in fact, he would be found within Lhasa only. As far as the wealth was concerned, Pabongkha said, "When I was studying at Sera Monastery, sometimes I didn't have enough food, and I didn't have money or any resources to get barley flour, so I went to the plains below Sera and picked up sand and filled up my small barley flour bag with about 80 percent sand and then put 20 percent real barley flour on the top, and then I went to the monastery gatherings carrying that and smelled the barley flour and sometimes licked a little bit of it. That's how I lived. Yet today, as you can see, my nephew manager is able to make it appear as though he is managing one of the richest houses in Tibet. It all depends on the individual person, so don't even worry."

He then added, "As far as your third point is concerned, if this were not going to be helpful for a number of people, I would not have bothered you at all, so put a little trust in me and don't talk but go and get ready."

Pabongkha constantly asked what the manager and the group of searchers were doing. They started dragging their feet because they couldn't say no to him. Kyabje Pabongkha very often had to inquire, send people to inquire, and invite them to give updates but heard nothing. Finally, before Pabongkha left central Tibet to go south, he asked the Tag Dag Rinpoche to continue following up on the search for this incarnation. Tag Dag Rinpoche later became the regent of Tibet, so the follow-up on the search came officially from the regent's court.

Meanwhile, before Kyabje Pabongkha left central Tibet, he visited my father and stayed at his house for a while. It is reported that I was put in the seat along with my father and others and received a private Heruka body mandala initiation from him. If that is true, I am very lucky. Lamas handing over young incarnate lamas for others to take care of is not uncommon in the tradition of Tibetan incarnate lamas. In other words, Tag Dag Rinpoche was asked to look after me by Pabongkha, and sure enough, Tag Dag Rinpoche paid very special attention to me when he became the regent.

Kyabje Ling Rinpoche and Trijang Rinpoche each used to joke with us, saying, "You people are unlucky because I was at least able to see, hear, and receive teachings from Kyabje Pabongkha directly. It is too bad you people are unlucky." [But of course they knew that Kyabje Pabongkha had visited my father and given us teachings when I was young.]

Kyabje Pabongkha's collected works alone run into eleven volumes, and his biography is actually in two volumes. He gave a tremendous amount of teachings in public and also in private, both to small groups and to individuals. Kyabje Ling Rinpoche told me personally that Kyabje Pabongkha tried not to disappoint anyone. In the Tibetan tradition, if an incarnate lama such as Kyabje Pabongkha is in the area, he will give an audience to anyone who asks, whether or not they have an appointment. It is early morning when they open the door, and until they shut the door at night there is a constant stream of visitors.

Particularly when a few individuals would come to visit Kyabje Rinpoche, he would enjoy and entertain them and never be in a rush. For example, while he was giving Heruka body mandala teachings in the Tashi Choling retreat area, one f ormer Tibetan government official who had been prosecuted by the government and released from jail came to see Kyabje Pabongkha one day. Kyabje Ling Rinpoche recalled that it was about 11:00 or 11:30 in the morning when the official arrived, so it was about an hour or so before the teaching was to begin. The fellow entered Kyabje Pabongkha's room and did not come out.

Everybody was waiting, including Kyabje Trijang Rinpoche, my father, and about a thousand others. According to Kyabje Ling Rinpoche, an hour went by, two hours, three hours, and then he noticed a tray of food being taken into the room, so he knew it would still be another hour or so. When the teaching finally began, it was dark already. Yet Kyabje Pabongkha never rushed the prerequisite prayers, including the prayer to Heruka known as Sipa Dang Nyam, which he sang tunefully. By the time the teaching was finished, it was long past midnight. There were people who had lanterns to carry at night. Kyabje Ling Rinpoche had one, but many people did not, and some even fell down the rocky mountains, but fortunately no one was actually hurt.

As you can see from the translation itself, this is the transcript of when Kyabje Pabongkha gave Jamgon Lama Tsongkhapa's middle-sized lamrim, along with the Third Dalai Lama's *Essence of Refined Gold* and Panchen Losang Yeshe's *Swift Path*, combined with the *Seven-Point Mind Training.*

The lamrim is a roadmap to buddhahood—a roadmap that draws upon the experience of earlier Buddhist masters and the Buddha's teachings of prajnaparamita (perfection of wisdom). The Buddha's prajnaparamita teachings were commented upon by earlier Indian sage mahasiddhas and great earlier Tibetan teachers, particularly Atisha, who brought to Tibet this style of leading an individual through the path. Jamgon Lama Tsongkhapa himself wrote, in correspondence to one of his teachers, "I am following the basic principles of Manjushri's teaching as the backbone or root of lamrim and find that the sequence and style of Atisha's way is more helpful to individual practitioners in general, especially for the general public who are not following great treatises."

I would also like to add that Jamgon Lama Tsongkhapa emphasized that he himself was not the author of lamrim because the teaching of lamrim came from the Buddha, so this lamrim also originates from the Buddha. Thus, this particular teaching is owned neither by Atisha's followers, known as the Kadampas, nor by Jamgon Lama Tsongkhapa's followers such as ourselves, known as the new Kadampas, though it is one of the main sources of liberation.

In my personal case, many of my difficulties or doubts have been cleared away by the teachings of Jamgon Lama Tsongkhapa in general and particularly by Kyabje Pabongkha's explanations. Despite facing many difficulties with respect to his health, David Gonsalez has been able to translate, publish, and promote these teachings, making a great contribution to Buddhism.

Publisher's Note to the New Edition

It is a pleasure for Wisdom Publications to bring out the *Dechen Ling Practice Series*. Ven. Losang Tsering provided a great kindness to qualified practitioners when he made available in English these incredible texts, which combine the depth of Madhyamaka philosophy with the sophistication of Vajrayana practices, as found in Lama Tsongkhapa's rich tradition.

Some time ago, I expressed to Ven. Losang Tsering that these texts had been helpful in my own practice, and this led to conversations about Dechen Ling Press collaborating with Wisdom Publications. Not long before Ven. Losang Tsering passed, we both agreed that Wisdom Publications would be an excellent place to preserve the legacy of these books and make them available to practitioners throughout the world. I am very happy to see the fruition of our intentions. May this series be a support for practitioners under the guidance of qualified teachers.

Daniel Aitken

Translator's Introduction

Pabongkha Rinpoche's (1878–1941) masterpiece *The Essence of the Vast and Profound* is one of the great "undiscovered" classics that is now being revealed to an English-speaking audience for the first time. This awe-inspiring text is a commentary on Lama Tsongkhapa's (1357–1419) *Middle-Length Treatise on the Stages of the Path to Enlightenment*[1] that will soon find its place as another one of the greatest lamrim commentaries ever expounded. Given over the course of thirty-six days in 1934 in Tibet's capital city of Lhasa, with over a thousand in attendance, *The Essence of the Vast and Profound* covers the entire spectrum of the Buddhist path. Pabongkha Rinpoche masterfully weaves together Tsongkhapa's *Middle-Length Treatise*, the Second Panchen Lama Losang Yeshe's (1663–1737) *Swift Path*, and the Third Dalai Lama Sonam Gyatso's (1543–1588) *Essence of Refined Gold* into a breathtaking discourse that not only informs readers but inspires them to follow the path to enlightenment and reach the supreme state of buddhahood for the welfare of all living beings.

Pabongkha Rinpoche is renowned as one of the greatest teachers in the history of the Gelug lineage. Giving explanations of the stages of the path to enlightenment (lamrim) was considered one of his greatest talents. His teachings brought hundreds or even thousands of attendees who were often greatly affected by his amazing teaching style and the passion and eloquence of his delivery. It is due to the kindness of his heart-disciple Trijang Rinpoche Losang Yeshe (1901–1981), the junior tutor to

1. As indicated in the Tibetan title of Pabongkha Rinpoche's commentary translated here, Tsongkhapa's *Middle-Length Treatise* is sometimes called the *Concise Stages of the Path* because it is a shorter presentation of the lamrim than his *Great Treatise*. However, when Tsongkhapa's *Songs of Spiritual Experience* is taken into consideration, *Songs* becomes the concise lamrim text.

His Holiness the Fourteenth Dalai Lama, that many of these teachings were compiled from various notes and shaped into the masterpieces that we have the good fortune to study today. This text is no exception. Relatively unknown, this commentary on Lama Tsongkhapa's *Middle-Length Treatise on the Stages of the Path* was an oral teaching given by Pabongkha Rinpoche and subsequently compiled and edited into its current form by Trijang Rinpoche.

Although similar in some ways to Pabongkha Rinpoche's renowned *Liberation in Our Hands* (also translated with the title *Liberation in the Palm of Your Hand*), *The Essence of the Vast and Profound* relies more heavily on Lama Tsongkhapa's outlines and contains many teachings, quotes, examples, and headings not found in *Liberation*. Being roughly two-thirds the length of *Liberation,* it will be well received by those wishing for a more manageable yet complete commentary on Tsongkhapa's *Middle-Length Treatise of the Stages of the Path.*

I approached my translation of this work as a retreat, spending roughly seventy to eighty hours a week for five months to complete the initial translation. At the conclusion of the first draft I had a vast number of questions about many of the colloquial expressions, stories, and references. My dear friend Sharpa Tulku graciously spent some twenty hours going over my queries over the course of three months of weekly one- or two-hour phone conversations. Without Sharpa Tulku's assistance, many of the subtleties in the sections in question would have been vague at best. After completion of the initial translation, it took another five months of working two to three hours a day before the draft was ready to be submitted to the editor.

It is my sincere hope and prayer that this text will find its way into the hearts and minds of English-speaking practitioners and inspire them to practice the teachings presented in this book so that they may soon reach the state of complete enlightenment. May those who find the teachings presented in this book meaningful request their own lamas to transmit the lineage of oral transmission and commentary on these amazing teachings, so that this lineage is preserved for future generations.

Acknowledgments

First and foremost, I would like to express my deep gratitude to Gen Lobsang Choephel, who kindly gave me all the transmissions and commentaries to the eight great lamrim texts, including two very lengthy commentaries based on Pabongkha Rinpoche's *Liberation in Our Hands* and Je Tsongkhapa's *Great Treatise on the Stages of the Path to Enlightenment.* I would of course like to thank my other teachers, such as Lama Zopa Rinpoche, Ribur Rinpoche, Geshe Khenrab Gajam, and others who have provided me with invaluable guidance on my spiritual path.

I would like to thank Susan and David Heckerman, whose continued support allows me to spend all my time dedicated to practice, study, translation, and teaching. I am also grateful to the members of Dechen Ling Buddhist Center who assist me in accomplishing my various activities, especially Kirk Wilson, Guru Dorje, Polly Trout, Karolyn McKinley, and others. I would like to extend my gratitude to Sharpa Tulku for his continued support and friendship and for assisting with some of the difficult passages of the present work.

Special thanks to Andy Weber for the line drawings in the text. I would like to thank the staff at the Tibetan Buddhist Research Center (TBRC) as well as its founder, the late and great Gene Smith, for their constant support in providing the texts needed for my various projects and for the invaluable service that they provide. I would also like to thank Art Engle for his help in translating the verses by Gyalwa Yang Gonpa that appear toward the end of Pabongkha Rinpoche's teachings and Joshua W. C. Cutler for his welcome suggestions in several other key spots.

In addition, I thank Chris Banigan for his cover design and my editor, Victoria R. M. Scott, for her dedication and expertise, which have contributed greatly to the readability of this text. I would like to thank Gopa Campbell for her beautiful interior design and Lisbeth Miller for her extraordinary index. I am extremely grateful for their hard work and devotion to this project. I am also very grateful to Vincent Montenegro for contributing his knowledge and talents by proofreading the manuscript and making valuable suggestions.

Special thanks also to Gelek Rimpoche for providing a wonderful foreword to this book.

Special Acknowledgments

Dechen Ling Press would like to express our heartfelt gratitude to Lama Namdrol Tulku Rinpoche and Tekchen Choling Dharma Center in Singapore for generously funding this translation project. Their great kindness will bring immense benefit to English-speaking Vajrayana practitioners far into the future and go a long way in preserving this important lineage.

Dechen Ling Press would also like to extend our deep gratitude to all the other kind supporters of these final four publications. Together we have created something truly meaningful.

Technical Note

The Tibetan titles of the various texts cited by Pabongkha Rinpoche have been placed in footnotes using the Wylie transliteration system. Since this text is intended for practitioners, I have not provided the Sanskrit titles or publication data. Readers skilled in Tibetan can easily enter the titles into the Tibetan Buddhist Resource Center's (TBRC) website and obtain all the related information.

Also, the outline of the text is presented in the same structure that is used in the Tibetan literary system. Although this may not meet the criteria of Western academic standards, the outline system employed by Tibetan authors is meant to serve as a means of memorization. The structure lends itself well to easy memorization while providing very clear access to the entire structure of the text (albeit with some variations, retained here in translation, between the headings found in the text itself and the exact wording in the outline). For these reasons I have retained the Tibetan system for the outline.

One of my goals in translating these texts is to provide the material to English-speaking Dharma practitioners in the same format and style as the original Tibetan, so that they have access to the same material and presentation they would encounter if they were able to read Tibetan. To assist English-language readers in following the outline while reading the text itself, both the text and the outline now include some words and headings in square brackets, supplied for continuity and the reader's convenience.

Many of the pronouns in the Tibetan either are not gender-specific or use the masculine case. This, however, has become increasingly unpopular in modern literature, and many attempts have been made to address this problem. In this book the translator and editor acknowledge women through the use of female pronouns, a gesture of utter and enthusiastic support for the rights of women worldwide. Since the original Tibetan mentions only male yogis/practitioners, the female pronoun has been added in square brackets immediately after the first use in a paragraph of a male pronoun. This has not been repeated each time thereafter in each such passage, however, to avoid distracting from the flow of the original text.

Finally, the line drawings appear throughout in approximate chronological order. The exceptions are Lama Tsongkhapa and Pabongkha Rinpoche; since they are the immediate sources of this particular text, their drawings have been placed toward the beginning of the text.

Losang Tsering (David Gonsalez)
Dechen Ling Press
Translator/President

Lama Tsongkhapa

A Few Scattered Notes Arranged from a Detailed Commentary Given by the Pervasive Lord Vajradhara Pabongkha Palsangpo, Combining Je [Tsongkhapa's] *Concise [Treatise on the] Stages of the Path [to Enlightenment]* and the [Second Panchen Lama's] *Swift Path*, Entitled *The Essence of the Vast and Profound*, [as Compiled and Edited by Trijang Rinpoche]

(Khyab bdag rdo rje 'chang pha bong kha pa dpal bzang pos rje'i lam rim chung ngu dang myur lam dmar khrid sbrags ma'i gsung bshad stsal skabs kyi zin bris mdo tsam du bkod pa zab rgyas snying po zhes bya ba bzhugs so)

[Trijang Rinpoche's Opening Verses of Praise]

WITH GREAT FAITH and devotion, I prostrate and go for refuge to the lotus feet of the foremost holy being endowed with great compassion, the Pervasive Lord Vajradhara Pabongkha Dechen Nyingpo. Please care for me with your great compassion at all times and in every circumstance.

I bow to the lineage gurus,
Shuddhodana's son,[2] the supreme guide of migrating beings including the gods,
Maitreya, Manjushri, Nagarjuna, Asanga,
Shantideva, Atisha, Dromton Je,[3]
And conqueror Losang [Drakpa].[4]

With love and compassion for all migrators,
You are the friend upholding and propagating the stainless teachings of the Buddha;
You are an ocean of enlightened actions of the Conqueror subduing those needing to be subdued;
A treasury of virtue and excellence, you are the supreme agent emanating and retracting.

From the excellent vase of that Protector's mouth issued forth
The heart essence of the ocean of vast and profound scriptures, from which
Emerged this manuscript of a few scattered kusha-grass pieces that embody the two purposes,

2. Shuddhodana was the name of Buddha Shakyamuni's father.
3. Dromtön Gyalwe Jungné (1005–1064), or Dromtonpa, was the chief disciple of Jowo Atisha (982–1054).
4. Losang Drakpa was the ordained name of Je Tsongkhapa (1357–1419).

Which I have arranged here for those who wish to examine them with a mind of joy.

[Trijang Rinpoche's Introduction]

These teachings were given in Kongpo [southern Tibet] at Tashi Dechen Monastery, beginning from the eleventh month of the sixteenth *rabjung*[5] of the Wood Dog Year (1934), to a thousand fortunate attendees, and lasted for thirty-six days. They combined [into a single discourse] Jamgon Tsongkhapa the Great's teaching on the *Middle-Length Treatise on the Stages of the Path*,[6] [the Third Dalai Lama's] *Essence of Refined Gold*,[7] and the [Second Panchen Lama's] *Swift Path*.[8] These were further combined with the teaching on equalizing and exchanging self with others from the *Seven-Point Mind Training* [composed by Geshe Chekawa Yeshe Dorje (1102–1176)].[9] While [Pabongkha Rinpoche] was bestowing these teachings, a few of us composed a rough outline in a few scattered notes.

Initially, [Pabongkha Rinpoche] was led in procession amid a vast assembly of tulkus and lamas, amid a vast offering of incense and the music of *gyalings*.[10] He made three prostrations and sat on the throne. Next, the foremost supreme Guru [Pabongkha] led the recitation of the *Heart Sutra*, which concluded with the mantra of Lion-Faced Dakini and three claps of the hands to dispel a thousand types of interferences. The chant master led the recitation of the entire *jorchö*[11] with a melodious chant. [The chant master] recited up to the end of the passage "arranged on the ground," and everyone recited the verses from the extensive man-

5. A rabjung is a sixty-year cycle.

6. Tib. *Lam rim 'bring po*, composed by Je Tsongkhapa. As already noted in the translator's introduction, Je Tsongkhapa's *Middle-Length Treatise* is sometimes called the *Concise Treatise* because it is a shorter presentation of the same material that is covered in his *Great Treatise on the Stages of the Path*. However, when Tsongkhapa's *Songs of Spiritual Experience* is taken into consideration, *Songs* becomes the concise lamrim text.

7. Tib. *Lam rim gser zhun ma*, composed by the Third Dalai Lama, Sonam Gyatso (1543–1588).

8. Tib. *Myur lam dmar khrid*, composed by the Second Panchen Lama, Losang Yeshe (1663–1737).

9. In addition to providing the commentary, Pabongkha Rinpoche gave the oral transmission of all these texts.

10. These are Tibetan-style trumpets.

11. Tib. *sbyor chos*. This is a preliminary ritual intended to prepare the mind for teachings and meditation. It is especially, though not exclusively, related to the lamrim.

dala. [Pabongkha Rinpoche] loosened the strap on the text cover of Je [Tsongkhapa's] lamrim text, touched it to his head, and led the recitation of the prayers, beginning with three recitations of the verse that begins "Buddha, Dharma, and Supreme Assembly." Next, [Pabongkha Rinpoche] continued with "gods and demigods . . ." and "teaching Dharma from within the divine language."[12]

12. This is a verse that a lama recites at the beginning of a teaching, indicating that he is teaching all the celestial beings as well as human beings.

Maitreya

Day One

He began bestowing the actual teaching on the first day in this way:

Oh, very well.

As it is said in the teachings of the king of the Dharma of the three realms, Tsongkhapa the Great, [entitled *Songs of Spiritual Experience*,]

> This body of leisure surpasses even a wish-fulfilling jewel.
> We will find a body like this only once,
> Difficult to find and easily destroyed, like a flash of lightning
> in the sky.
> Contemplate this, and you will come to realize
> That all worldly actions are like a husk of grain
> And that day and night you must extract its essence.
> I, the yogi, practiced in this way;
> You who seek liberation should do the same.

Thus, we will find only one time a human life of leisure and endowment such as this, which is difficult to obtain and, once obtained, has great meaning; therefore, at this juncture, while we have managed to obtain it, we absolutely must extract whatever pure essence from it we can. Although we have taken countless rebirths as Brahma, Indra, and so forth, we have not had the opportunity to practice the Mahayana Dharma until just recently. From time to time after taking rebirth as a hell being, hungry ghost, and so on, through the force of not obtaining a human form, not meeting the teachings, and not coming into contact with a guru, we did not have even the opportunity to experience the slightest benefit from the Dharma. Therefore, now that we have obtained such an excellent human form and have met the teachings and a guru, we must extract the unique essence provided at this time, which is complete with all the outer and inner favorable conditions to practice Dharma. Moreover, this human life of leisure and endowment that we have found at this moment is more valuable than even many hundreds of thousands of myriads of wish-fulfilling jewels. In dependence upon this life we can also accomplish the physical forms of Brahma, Indra, a chakravartin king, and so on. With this life we can even manage to accomplish the causes for rebirth in a buddha's pure land. Not only that, but in dependence upon this life we can even attain liberation or the state of omniscience.

If we waste this human form it would be much more devastating than wasting even many hundreds of thousands of myriads of wish-fulfilling jewels, yet squandering this human life of leisure and endowment does not cause us even the least bit of regret. This fault stems from not considering the great value of this life of leisure and endowment and how difficult it is to obtain. At the moment, we don't investigate the situation with critical examination and instead assume that we will obtain a human life of leisure and endowment in our future life out the kindness of the guru and the Three Precious Jewels, which is unimaginably foolish! This is similar to planting poisonous seeds in the spring and expecting an [edible] crop in the fall.

In general, it is mandatory for someone who is content with merely obtaining a human life of higher status to protect at least one form of moral discipline completely purely as its cause. In the *Precious Garland*[13] Nagarjuna stated,

> Enjoyments come from generosity, happiness from moral discipline . . .

The vast enjoyments of those in the lower realms with great wealth, such as nagas and so forth, come from their previous acts of generosity, yet

13. Tib. *Rin chen phreng ba*.

their rebirth in the lower realms stems from not safeguarding their moral discipline. [Chandrakirti's (600–ca. 650)] *Guide to the Middle Way*[14] states,

> If the enjoyments of generosity arise in a lower rebirth,
> It is because of your defiled limbs of moral discipline.

We are extremely fortunate to have obtained our present human form, and if we don't take the opportunity to extract some essence from it but instead squander it, it will be extremely rare to obtain such [a human life] again. The previous Kadampas[15] would say that obtaining this life of leisure and endowment is like rolling a copper boulder halfway up a mountain. We strive for the means of this life's happiness, such as amassing wealth, resources, and so on, which is *not* the meaning of extracting the essence of this life of leisure and endowment. Although we may have strength, power, and dominance, like a chakravartin king, this is also not its essence.

Query: Well then, how do I extract its essence?

Response: You must extract its essence by listening, contemplating, and meditating on the stages of the path to enlightenment. Once you train your mind in this, if you then develop the realizations of a being of small scope, you will have extracted its least essence. If you develop the realizations of a being of middle scope, you will have extracted its middling essence. If you develop the realizations of a being of great scope, you will have extracted its supreme essence.

Moreover, since the day of our death is soon approaching, if we don't sincerely apply ourselves to the means of extracting its essence in this very moment, because this human body does not last long at all, we will lose our chance. Moreover, [death] is coming without warning. Presently, we will watch others die as though it is unrelated to us and will treat them as objects of our compassion; yet our turn to die will definitely come. The time is definitely coming when our body will be folded in thirds and bound by a rope, our family members and companions will

14. Tib. *dBu ma la 'jug pa*. This is Chandrakirti's masterpiece on Madhyamaka philosophy.
15. The phrase "previous Kadampas" refers to practitioners belonging to the Kadampa school from the time of Atisha up to Je Tsongkhapa. Subsequent to Je Tsongkhapa they were sometimes referred to as the "new Kadampas."

shed their tears, and everyone will eventually become revolted by our corpse. Moreover, there is absolutely no way whatsoever that this is not currently on its way to greet us. Je Mila[repa (1052–1135)] stated,

> The phrase "that terrifying thing called a corpse"
> Will soon be used for the body of the yogi.

The term "corpse" will soon be used to address our own bodies as well; this is the real situation of this body.

With respect to the time of death, even if you are a great king governing a hundred thousand subjects, you cannot take even one servant with you. A beggar cannot even bring his walking staff and satchel. Although you may be a lama with a hundred thousand disciples, you cannot bring even one disciple with you. You must go on alone, like a hair being extracted from butter. The lineage of instruction of the previous holy beings also states,

> A king must put aside his kingdom and depart;
> A beggar must set aside his staff and depart.

If we could at least bring this body with us, it would uplift our minds a little, but even this must be set aside as we depart for our next life.

[The First Panchen Lama] Je [Losang] Chögyan[16] proclaimed,

> Our body that we have nurtured with care deceives in our time of need.

16. This is the First Panchen Lama, Losang Chökyi Gyaltsen (1570–1662). The quote that follows is from his famous *Supplication for Liberation from [Fear of] the Perilous Journey of the Intermediate State, Entitled "A Hero Liberated from Fear."* For a complete translation of this work and a commentary by Ngulchu Dharmabhadra (1772–1851), see Ngulchu Dharmabhadra, *The Blazing Inner Fire of Bliss and Emptiness: An Experiential Commentary on the Practice of the Six Yogas of Naropa*, trans. David Gonsalez (Seattle: Dechen Ling Press, 2014).

At that time [of death], nothing other than the holy Dharma will be of benefit. Je Gungtang Jampalyang [Rinpoche][17] stated [in his *Advice for Meditating on Impermanence*],[18]

> Dharma is the guide when you don't know your way on the path.
> Dharma is the provisions on the long path.
> Dharma is the captain guiding you along the difficult path;
> From this moment on, practice the Dharma with your three doors.

When the time comes that we must set aside our cup and even our bodies, there is nothing whatsoever other than the holy Dharma that will be of any benefit. No matter how many great skills we may possess, such as settling disputes or having great power and courage, they will not be of benefit at that time. Kadam Kamapa said,

> Right now we are fearless, but at
> The time of death we dig our fingernails into our chest.

[In the *Hundred Thousand Songs*,][19] Je Milarepa proclaimed,

> Repeatedly fearing only the time of my death,
> I trained in the essence of the primordial deathless mind
> And gained conviction in the clear light of emptiness;
> Now I have no fear of either birth or death.

We should train in accordance with this. Currently, we aren't mindful of death, and we may wonder if at the time of death we will be able to apply skillful activities, yet if we can't apply such skillful activities the moment

17. Also known as Gungtang Tenpai Dronmé (1762–1823), he was the third incarnation in the Gungtang lineage of lamas and the twenty-first abbot of Tashi Kyil Monastery in Amdo, eastern Tibet.
18. Tib. *Mi rtag bsgom tshul gyi bslab bya.*
19. Tib. *Mi la mgur 'bum.*

thunder crashes above our head, there is absolutely no chance of [applying them at the time of death]. My guru, my refuge and protector, said,

> If I don't die in a month or two,
> I hope to accomplish the aims of my future life.
> And if I don't die in a year or two,
> I hope to accomplish my lasting aspirations for all lives.

We should practice in accordance with this. Similar statements are also explained in the collected works of Ensapa [Losang Dondrop (1505–1566)].[20] We are like an overconfident man pretending to be brave, who made plans claiming that his death wasn't coming yet didn't make any plans whatsoever for the future life. From this point on, the longest we could hope to live is fifteen years; we certainly won't be able to live more than sixteen more years. Moreover, those [years] are quickly used up, just as the words of a sutra eventually reach their end or the calculations of an accountant eventually reach their conclusion; such is the situation with death and impermanence. This is similar to the way the Teacher passed into nirvana once he reached the end of his numerous amazing deeds, such as the twelve and so forth, and fulfilled the purpose of those deeds.

Yet after death we don't come to an end like the death of a candle flame; instead, we must take rebirth. Moreover, there are definitely [only] two migrations.[21] The nonvirtuous will be thrown into a bad rebirth and the virtuous into a happy rebirth; other than this, it is out of our control. Nagarjuna proclaimed [in his *Precious Garland*],

> All suffering comes from nonvirtue
> [And likewise all suffering migrations.
> All happy migrations come from virtue
> As does the happiness in all rebirths.]

20. Ensapa's collected works can be obtained at Tibetan Buddhist Research Center (TBRC) with resource code W111128.

21. Despite the fact that there are six realms and limitless types of rebirth, they are often reduced to just two: happy rebirths in the upper realms and unhappy rebirths in the lower realms.

Our simultaneously born gods and demons[22] are motivated by our virtue and nonvirtue, which they calculate using black and white pebbles that are measured on a scale. Once they determine whether we have been virtuous or nonvirtuous, they follow us and take rebirth in either the happy migrations or the bad migrations. Furthermore, our transmigration is influenced at the time of death by whether our virtue or our nonvirtue is more powerful, the degree of our familiarity, which was performed first, and so on. For that reason, it is rare for us to practice virtue, and when we do practice virtue, the majority of our time is not spent focusing on our spiritual practices; instead, our mind is constantly distracted by commerce, farming, our sponsors, and so on. In contrast, we have great familiarity with extraordinarily powerful motivating factors, such as attachment, anger, and so on. Eventually we are even considering the way in which we are going to kill lice.

We don't need to request a dice divination to determine whether we will have a good or bad place of rebirth in our next life. The Bhagavan Buddha already explained in the precious sutras that the ripened result of virtuous actions is happiness, [whereas] from nonvirtue comes suffering. Therefore, since the vast majority of our daily actions involve engaging in negative karma and downfalls, we have no other option than taking a bad rebirth. Since we currently can't even bear the suffering of being poked with a stick of burning incense, there is absolutely no way we will be able to bear it if we are reborn in a place such as the hot hells, where the entire foundation is composed of blazing iron and so forth. One day in the Reviving Hell is equal to nine million human years. Thus, there is no way we would be able to bear even the slightest suffering of the hot hells. The only thing separating us from such lower realms is the fact that we can still draw breath. If your breathing were to cease, you would find yourself in your next life having just arrived in the lower realms. [Je] Gungtang [Jampalyang Rinpoche] exclaimed,

22. Tib. *lhan cig skyes pa'i lha*. These are virtuous and nonvirtuous spirits that follow us from life to life.

In the short slumber of an impermanent life comes
The meaningless joy and anguish of a troubling dream.
Yet what will you do when you suddenly awaken
In the pit of the lower realms?

Shantideva explained the situation when you are suddenly reborn in the lower realms when he proclaimed [in his *Guide to the Bodhisattva's Way of Life*],

When you stare with a look of horror on your face . . .

The means of not being reborn in a lower realm such as this is to go for refuge to the Three Jewels. The thought to train in the discipline of the ten virtues is setting your motivation in conjunction with training the mind in the path common to a being of lesser capacity.

Query: Well then, is that much sufficient?

Response: This is not sufficient because training in the moral discipline of abandoning the ten nonvirtues only temporarily frees us from the lower realms and merely accomplishes the attainment of a physical form in a happy rebirth but does nothing to completely liberate us from samsara. [Nagarjuna's] *Letter to a Friend* states,[23]

Once you become Indra as a worldly object of veneration,
[Through the force of karma you will fall once again.
Although you may become a chakravartin king,
You will become a slave on the wheel of samsara].

Occasionally you will experience the happiness of gods and men but then die and transmigrate to rebirth in Avici [Hell] and so forth.

The Great Being of Ngari[24] proclaimed,

23. Tib. *bShes spring*.
24. I believe this is Tib. mNga' ris Pan chen Pad ma dbang rgyal—that is, Ngari Panchen Pema Wangyal (1487–1542), one of the five *tertön* emanations of King Trisong Deutsen.

> Although you may be reborn at the peak of existence,
> It is not different from taking rebirth in a copper pot of the lowest hell.

No matter where you are reborn—whether as a god, human, demigod, or so on—[that existence] doesn't transcend being anything but suffering. Therefore, from this moment on, we need something capable of severing the continuity of rebirth, with its contaminated appropriated aggregates, and gaining liberation from samsara. Nagarjuna stated in his [*Letter to a Friend*],

> Each being has drunk more milk than there is
> [Water] in all four oceans, yet
> By emulating ordinary beings,
> Samsaric beings will drink even more still.

[Nagarjuna's] *Letter Dispelling Suffering*[25] states,

> In hell time and time again . . .

According to these teachings, regardless of whether or not there is an end to samsara in general, we must work to bring an end to our own samsara. The previous Kadampas would say, "We need greater confidence than even someone working at becoming an arhat." Accordingly, at the moment, we perform only nonvirtue yet still act as though we don't have a care in the world, even though, by remaining this way, we are going to have to experience the unending suffering of samsara. For that reason, if we wish not to have to experience suffering, we must be capable of severing the continuity of rebirth in samsara. Nagarjuna stated,

> If your hair should suddenly catch fire . . .[26]

25. Tib. *Mya ngan bsal ba'i spring yig*. This is a collection of advice by Nagarjuna.
26. The verse continues, "cease trying to extinguish it and strive at a means of ending samsara."

To sever the root of samsara, we need to develop the axe-like wisdom realizing selflessness in our mental continuum. To cultivate that [realization] in our mental continuum, we need to train in the shoulder-like higher concentration that blocks even the most subtle mental distractions. To develop that in our mental continuum, we need to apply ourselves sincerely to training in the main-body-like higher concentration whereby we block the coarse mental distractions. All the precious collections of the Conqueror's teachings are included in those three;[27] therefore, don't be fooled by practices such as meditation on the channels and winds, maintaining the essence of mind, and so on. You must work at listening, contemplating, and meditating on the Three Baskets,[28] for these are the general structure of teachings. Thus, by training your mind in the three higher trainings, you are setting your motivation by training your mind in the stages of the path common to a being of middling scope.

By sincerely applying yourself in this way, you will merely liberate yourself from samsara and merely accomplish the state of liberation. Again, simply [accomplishing] that much is insufficient, for you still must work for the welfare of all living beings. The reason necessitating this stems from the fact that since beginningless time in samsara, these beings have been acting as your mother; therefore, you must work for their welfare. Regarding how they acted as your mother, Dharmakirti's *Commentary on Valid Cognition*[29] states,

> [When someone takes rebirth],
> His breath and sense faculties of mind
> [Do not depend on the physical body]
> Independent [of other entities] of a similar type.[30]

27. The previous section outlines the three higher trainings of moral discipline, concentration, and wisdom.
28. The Three Baskets (Tripitaka) are broad divisions of the Buddha's teachings—namely, the basket of moral discipline (Vinaya Pitaka), the basket of discourses (Sutra Pitaka), and the basket of wisdom (Abhidharma Pitaka).
29. Tib. *Tshad ma rnam 'grel.*
30. Here Pabongkha only quoted the verse in part, so I have supplied the remaining sections in square brackets to facilitate understanding. The verse appears in whole further on in the text.

This must be proven through reasoning. Therefore, consider how the moment ordinary beings are born, they begin breathing, their sense faculties become clear, their mind takes on a special luminosity, and so forth. Because it possesses the quality of breath and so forth, when someone takes rebirth, it is in dependence upon an entity of a similar type, not something unrelated. This is analogous to our current process of breathing and so on. The luminous quality of the mind and so forth is developed through familiarity with its own primary cause, which definitely proves its forward and reverse pervasion. If it weren't this way, there would be the extreme consequences and the logical conclusion that there is no cause and effect whatsoever. Thus, I shall establish this with reasoning in accordance with the phrase "because it lacks authenticating logic,"[31] to induce certainty in the way in which all living beings have been one's mother. Moreover, I will explain it so that it is easy to understand for those who haven't trained in the textual tradition of reasoning.

As soon as an ordinary being takes rebirth, he [or she] begins breathing and so on, which is necessarily through familiarity with a previous cause of a similar type; if that familiarity did not exist with that cause of a similar type, there necessarily would not currently be breathing, which is ascertained through valid cognition. If it weren't possible to generate certainty in this way, it would follow that neither the causal breathing and so on nor the effect breathing could exist. [Although one may] think, "There does not exist authenticating logic establishing that these two are cause and effect," such authenticating logic does in fact exist; therefore, these two are cause and effect. Because these two are cause and effect, it necessarily follows that there was a previous state of breathing of a similar type [as the cause of] our current state of breathing. If that exists, we necessarily take rebirth. If that is necessarily the case, [then] this is contradicted by counting the states of rebirth for which you don't need a mother, which are the warmth born and miraculously born.[32] But that is not necessarily the case because this doesn't exclude being born in either a womb-born birth or an egg-born birth, which means that the

31. This means that oftentimes a thesis is put forward without authenticating logic. In this case, however, Pabongkha Rinpoche is going to establish his premise based on the sound reasoning presented in the following paragraph.

32. There are four types of rebirth: (1) womb, (2) egg, (3) heat, and (4) miraculous.

vast majority of living beings need someone to serve as their mother. Therefore, all living beings have served as your mother.

Not only have all living beings served as your mother, but each and every living being has been your mother countless times. Contemplate how they provided you with every type of the greatest kindness in the beginning, middle, and end while serving as your mother. It would be utterly despicable to forsake these kind mothers who are tormented by the suffering of samsara, and for that reason you must accomplish the aims of those kind mothers. When it comes to accomplishing that, even with concerted effort we are incapable of measuring the amount of drinking substance in our teacups. Only a completely perfect buddha can spontaneously and effortlessly accomplish the aims of living beings; therefore, thinking "By all means I must attain the precious state of a buddha to accomplish the welfare of all living beings. For that purpose I am going to listen to Dharma such as this" is setting your motivation by training the mind in the stages of the path common to a person of great capacity. Those holding other tenets don't have this type of preliminary discourse, but it is a distinguishing characteristic of the old and new Kadampas,[33] who hold that even the words of a dedication prayer should contain the entire path to enlightenment.

In short, think, "I am going to listen for the sake of attaining the state of enlightenment for the welfare of all living beings," and receive these teachings while clearly evoking the excellent motivation of precious bodhichitta. While you are listening in this way, I shall give a small section of the oral transmission, starting from the beginning of all three lamrim texts. The explanatory discourse[34] will be offered on the basis of [Je Tsongkhapa's] *Middle-Length Treatise on the Stages of the Path*, while the [Second Panchen Lama's] *Swift Path* and so forth will serve as the practical discourse.[35] Next, I shall begin with the greatness of the author, based on oral instructions of Je Lama [Tsongkhapa's] outline.

Although it has been explained numerous times that the stages of the path to enlightenment are the central focus, you should try your very

33. The term "old Kadampa" refers to what was formerly called the Kadam tradition, founded by Atisha and Dromtonpa, while the term "new Kadampa" refers to the Gelug tradition.
34. Tib. *bshad khrid.*
35. Tib. *nyams khrid.*

best to listen, contemplate, and meditate on this to the very best of your ability, since right now may be the only chance you get. Although you may have seen the face of your personal deity, attained clairvoyance and magical powers, completed a great retreat [of three years], and so on, it requires much greater merit and good fortune to be able to develop a mere understanding of these stages of the path to enlightenment. Do not think, "I am incapable because I have grown old." If you make a sincere and concerted effort to understand as much as you can, it is impossible that you won't understand. In days of old, there was a great pandit in India named Pandita Norbu Ling. He was a stupid old man of eighty years of age when he first met his guru. Afterward, he had a direct vision of Manjushri through his persistent efforts, and he became a pandita. Based on this and other such teachings, if you also try in whatever way you can to sow the seeds of practice with respect to whatever you hear, you will also come under [Manjushri's] loving care. [Therefore, think,] "I will amass whatever [understanding] I can."

The teaching ended [for the day] through the encouragement of the chant master, and we offered a thanking mandala.

Day Two

The second day began as the previous day.

The king of the Dharma Tsongkhapa the Great made the following pronouncement:

> I shall explain to the best of my ability
> The essential meaning of all the Conqueror's scriptures,
> The path praised by all the holy conquerors and the sons,
> The entryway for the fortunate seeking liberation.[36]

The purpose of the subject matter of every one of the Conqueror's scriptures is contained in teachings on the stages of the path to enlightenment. Not only that, but it is also the path praised by the conquerors and their sons. It is also the entryway for the fortunate beings seeking liberation. According to the hidden meaning, "the essential meaning . . ." refers to renunciation, "the path praised . . ." refers to bodhichitta, and "the entryway for the fortunate . . ." reveals the correct view of emptiness. Therefore, these teachings on the stages of the path to enlightenment are the supreme means for those striving to generate these [qualities] in their mental continuum. And thus [these teachings] are indispensable for attaining the state of perfect and complete enlightenment. You should briefly set your motivation by thinking, "Once I listen to this path to enlightenment that is the sole lamp for the three realms, I shall put it into practice."

Regarding the Dharma you shall be listening to, to begin with I shall

36. This is the opening verse of Je Tsongkhapa's *Three Principal Aspects of the Path.*

Atisha

once again give a small portion of the oral transmission of all three lamrim texts while you listen.[37] It is also indispensable that the Dharma instructor covers each of the headings.

37. The "three lamrim texts" are cited in Trijang Rinpoche's introduction and are (1) Je Tsongkhapa's *Middle-Length Lamrim*, (2) the Second Panchen Lama's *Swift Path*, and (3) the Third Dalai Lama's *Essence of Refined Gold*.

The Commentary on the Stages of the Path to Enlightenment has four sections:

1. The Greatness of the Author to Show the Authentic Source of the Dharma
2. The Greatness of the Dharma to Generate Faith in the Instructions
3. How to Listen to and Explain the Dharma Endowed with Those Two Greatnesses
4. How to Sequentially Guide the Disciple with the Actual Instructions

All four of these sections are taught in Je [Tsongkhapa's] *Great* and *Middle-Length Treatises on the Stages of the Path [to Enlightenment]*. They are of prime importance whenever teaching the lamrim. Of the two systems of explanation of glorious Nalanda and Vikramalashila [monasteries], the great monastic seats of India, here we shall use the tradition of Vikramalashila. Moreover, Jowo [Atisha][38] was a scholar of this [institution] and followed this tradition of explanation. [Regarding the etymological explanation of its name,] *vi* means "aspect," *kramala* means "scent," and *shila* means "moral discipline"; therefore, it means "endowed with the scent of moral discipline." And the main temple was endowed with the scent of moral discipline.

The Greatness of the Author to Show the Authentic Source of the Dharma

It is important for a Dharma practitioner to seek out the pure origin of the Dharma by first examining the Dharma instructor. If you happen to encounter a Dharma teaching and practice where neither [the teaching nor the practice] is reliable, you will attain similar [nonreliable] results; therefore, you should perform a critical examination of the Dharma. Sakya Pandita [1182–1251] proclaimed,

38. Throughout this text, Atisha is often referred to by the epithet Jowo (Tib. Jo bo), which means "lord" or "foremost elder"; in many other spots, he is also referred to simply as Atisha. Thinking that Atisha is more recognizable, I have taken the liberty of replacing "Jowo" with "Atisha" throughout the remainder of the text.

I've seen the effort of being involved in
Such petty affairs of this life.
They question and examine every detail
While doing business in trivial things
Such as horses and jewels.

However, when it comes to relying on the holy Dharma
That fulfills the aspirations of all their lives,
I have seen the way they accept whatever they come across
And gobble it down like a dog
Without examining its quality.

Panchen Losang Chögyan[39] also stated,

If you have any self-concern at all,
You should thoroughly examine the holy Dharma
That a guru is teaching, and then either accept or discard it.
Don't accept whatever you happen to encounter
Like an old dog begging for food.

When purchasing the most insignificant things of this life, such as horses, jewels, and tea, we vigorously search for the best possible products and examine them in detail. When it comes to the Dharma, we are like a dog wandering down the road that immediately puts in his mouth whatever impure things he stumbles across, such as bones and hides, without feeling the need to examine them. In the same way we go running to try to get whatever we can when we hear that someone is called "a lama" or that some Dharma is called "ancient." If we sustain a loss through a business transaction with respect to something such as tea, there is no danger whatever that we will sustain any long-term damage from a faulty teacup

39. This is the First Panchen Lama, Losang Chökyi Gyaltsen. Although some claim that he was the fourth Panchen Lama and justify this by adding his three previous reincarnations of Khedrup Je (1385–1438), Sonam Choklan (1438–1505), and Ensapa Losang Dondrup (1505–66), this identification wasn't made until the Fifth Dalai Lama, who claimed that his guru, Losang Chökyi Gyaltsen, was a reincarnation of Khedrup Je, thereby attempting to make him the fourth Panchen Lama. There has been considerable disagreement as to whether or not this should be officially acknowledged. I personally refer to Losang Chökyi Gyaltsen as the First Panchen Lama.

and teapot set. Yet if there is a shortcoming in our activities related to the Dharma, it will cause lasting damage to [our attaining] our future goals.

Query: Well then, what sort of Dharma do we need?

Reply: Just as a river must find its source in a [field of] snow, so the Dharma must ultimately find its source in the teacher Buddha. Furthermore, it must have first been taught by the Buddha; in the interim, it must have been thoroughly discussed by pandits to determine whether it has any faults; and finally, it must have been practiced by powerful siddhas who attained realizations through it.

Previously, when the Kalachakra teachings were first being propagated, the pandits of India debated their doubts and suspicions about whether or not it was pure, through which they came to a definite conclusion about its purity. Previously, although I also received empowerments, transmissions, oral instructions, and commentaries from the Sakya, Gelug, and Nyingma, among them all, none is more beneficial than these teachings on the stages of the path to enlightenment, and when I give teachings on [the stages of the path], it benefits the mind of the disciple. Giving teachings such as empowerments and transmissions and their lineage of instructions is, for the most part, incapable of benefiting [a person's] mental continuum. Here, [while teaching the lamrim,] it is impossible for anyone to grasp at sectarianism. This is the sole path traversed by all the buddhas of the three times. The *Concise Perfection of Wisdom* states,

> Wherever this [perfection of wisdom sutra] currently resides,
> it is as if the Conqueror did not pass away and depart but is
> still with us. This is the path of perfection; there is no other.

This lamrim was not newly fabricated by Atisha or Je Rinpoche [Tsongkhapa] but is the teaching of our teacher the Buddha himself.

Query: How can that be?

Reply: The supreme scripture of the Teacher is the perfection of wisdom sutras, where we find the actual teaching on the profound stages of the path and, implicitly, the vast stages of the path.[40] Their intended meaning is extremely difficult to discover; therefore, the great trailblaz-

40. The lamrim can be divided into the two broad categories of the vast and the profound. The profound addresses the wisdom aspect of the teachings, and the vast addresses the method aspect of the teachings.

ers Nagarjuna and Asanga founded their respective scriptural traditions. The *Jataka Tales*[41] state,

> The trailblazers clear a path on the ground somewhere.
> Likewise, they encourage others to proceed where others have
> not gone before.
> In that way, they initiate a path and forgo the easy way out;
> I am displeased by those who enter erroneous paths.

Thus, although there may have been a convenient, well-traveled path that everyone else comfortably proceeded along, the two great trailblazers [Nagarjuna and Asanga] were establishing their own systems, which are now well-traveled and upon which all the scholars and siddhas of India and Tibet proceed without using any other. The individual tenet systems that they established do not contradict each other. The two heart sons of the Teacher are Maitreya and Manjushri. Nagarjuna relied upon protector Manjushri as his guru. By relying upon the oral instructions of venerable Manjushri, he established the tradition of the profound path and composed his Six Collections of Middle Way Reasoning.[42]

Again, when the vast stages of the Mahayana were declining, a brahman woman with strict moral discipline generated the heartfelt aspiration to propagate the teachings of the Mahayana. She relaxed her moral discipline and gave birth to Asanga and Vasubandhu. Asanga accomplished his meditation to meet with Maitreya and instantly traveled a great distance to the Tushita Pure Land and listened to the teachings of Maitreya and so forth. In his *Ornament of Clear Realization*,[43] [Maitreya] directly revealed the hidden meaning of the vast stages of the path by condensing them into eight states of reality.[44] It was Asanga himself who also wrote down the Five Treatises and others illuminating the vast stages of the path. At that time everyone had sharp intellects, so they were capable of developing an understanding based on the [Six] Collections of Reasoning [of Nagarjuna] and the [Five] Treatises of Maitreya.

After Nagarjuna, there was Chandrakirti. According to the lineage

41. Tib. *sKyes rabs*.

42. Tib. *dBu ma rigs tshogs drug*.

43. Tib. *mNgon rtog rgyan*; Skt. *Abhisamayalamkara*.

44. Tib. *dngos po brgyad*.

supplication for the profound stages of the path, this lineage came to Atisha through Vidyakokila. The lineage of the vast stages of the path came down from Asanga to Vasubandhu to Arya Vimuktisena, and so on. Arya Vimuktisena composed commentaries to the *Perfection of Wisdom in Twenty Thousand Verses* and the *Ornament [of Clear Realization]*. Acharya Haribhadra's *Illuminating the Meaning of the Commentary*[45] is the supreme commentary on *The Ornament of the Three Perfection of Wisdom Sutras*.[46]

With respect to this lamrim being the oral instructions on the *Ornament of Clear Realization*, although in general you must practice something like the generation of the mind of enlightenment at the conclusion of relying upon a preliminary oral instruction, the *Ornament* states, "Generating bodhichitta and the oral instructions . . . ," which states just the opposite. Regarding this, during the lamrim, teachings on bodhichitta are given during the preliminary discourse. Bodhichitta is developed during the preliminary rituals as well, and in particular bodhichitta comes later, during the actual teachings on the lamrim itself. The instructions for the beings of small and middling scope are not autonomous but have a way of transforming into the limbs of the discourse on the Mahayana. Moreover, [the *Ornament*] states, "Faithfully visualize the Buddha and so forth." Therefore, faith in the teachings on the guru, the Buddha, cause and effect, the four noble truths, the path of the three higher trainings, and so on is common to the small and middling scopes. It then states, "Recall the most excellent intention," which is bodhichitta. It continues, "Sincerely apply yourself to the sphere of activity such as generosity," which is training in the general activities [of a bodhisattva], and to "completely nonconceptual concentration and the five aspects of wisdom understanding all aspects of phenomena," which separately reveals the way to train in the final two perfections. Therefore, this is taught for the sake of the abridged wisdom, from either analytical or placement meditation on all the good qualities of the Mahayana, and the actual wisdom, which is the principal way of progressing along the path unifying tranquil abiding and superior seeing. In short, this is the means of teaching the general scope of the Mahayana through skill in the five objects such as faith and so forth.

Subsequent disciples had increasingly dull faculties, so Atisha, Je

45. Tib. *'Grel pa don gsal.*

46. Tib. *mNgon rgyan yum gsum ga'i rgyan.*

Tsongkhapa, and others composed very clear explanations through their texts such as the *Lamp for the Path*, the *Great* and *Middle-Length [Treatises on the Stages of the Path to Enlightenment]*, the *Swift Path*, [the Fifth Dalai Lama, Ngawang Losang Gyatso's] *Manjushri's Oral Instructions*, and so on. Atisha Je combined in a single stream the lineages of the vast and profound. If you develop a good understanding of this text, you will be able to understand the stages of the path with respect to the scriptures and their commentaries. Other than that, the teachings are called "the vast stages of the path" or "the profound stages of the path," depending on whether it is the vast or the profound that are primarily being taught. However, it is not that [the vast and the profound are separate] and don't [each] contain instructions on both the profound and vast. The *Ornament of Clear Realization* states,

> There is nothing whatsoever that should be removed;
> There is not the slightest bit that should be added.

For a teaching on the profound stages of the path, [Nagarjuna's] *Root Text on Wisdom* states,

> Speech and physical actions,
> Unobservable unabandoned actions, [and]
> Unobservable abandoned actions,
> As well as others are similarly asserted.
>
> Merit and nonmerit
> Derived from enjoyment
> As well as intention are maintained to be similar phenomena.
> These are asserted to be the seven types of action.[47]

This teaches ten paths of action together with their results and belongs to the vast path. The statement [by Je Tsongkhapa that "the composer of that is also the composer of this" indicates that the composer of all the stages of the path is Atisha [Dipamkara]. We find a similar statement in the *Swift*

47. This translation is based on that in Tsongkhapa, *The Ocean of Reasoning*, trans. Geshe Ngawang Samten and Jay L. Garfield (Oxford and New York: Oxford University Press, 2006), 349.

Path. The translation equivalent of *Dipamkara* is "producing light,"[48] while *Atisha* means "exquisite." The fact that this type of lamrim spread far and wide here in Tibet is due to the kindness of Atisha coming to Tibet. Since he is the teacher of every lamrim, it is the tradition to begin by teaching Atisha's biography, which contains three sections.

The Life of Atisha has three sections:

1. How He Took Rebirth in an Excellent Lineage
2. How He Practiced and Attained Good Qualities of Realization through Proper Practice
3. How He Worked on Behalf of the Teachings

How He Took Rebirth in an Excellent Lineage

Regarding the country of [Atisha's] birth, [Nagtso Lotsawa Tsultrim Gyalwa's (1101–?) *Eighty Verses of*] *Praise* states,

> In the excellent country of Bengal . . . [49]

His family was from Zahor and their country was Bengal, which these days is called Kalakata. Regarding "Vikrama," this means that "the city in the aspect of steps" was extremely powerful and prosperous. The name Tongkun[50] was mostly used by previous lamas; however, Changkya Rolpai Dorje [1717–1786] said that it was because the Tibetan lamas didn't know Sanskrit. It is said that the King of the East called it Tongku.[51] As soon as Atisha was born he had compassion for all, as is extensively taught in his biography. Once Atisha the Great was born and reached eighteen months of age, he held the teachings on going for refuge and generating bodhichitta as being of extraordinarily great importance, and he attained good qualities in dependence upon those two. He attained good qualities

48. Tib. *mar me mdzad*. This could easily be translated as "maker of butter lamps"; however, it most likely refers to the light produced from a flame.
49. For a complete translation of these verses, see Tsongkhapa, *The Great Treatise on the Stages of the Path to Enlightenment*, vol. 1, trans. by the Lamrim Chenmo Translation Committee (Ithaca, NY: Snow Lion, 2000), 36.
50. Tib. sTong khun.
51. Tib. Tong kus.

of scripture through his abundant knowledge of the first of those two methods. Afterward, upon reaching the age of fifteen, he read *The Drop of Reasoning*[52] once, and afterward was able to defeat the most skilled logicians. *The Drop of Reasoning* is one of glorious Dharmakirti's teachings and is referred to as *The Drop of Reasoning* among the Seven Texts on Valid Cognition.

His parents had already picked out a princess for him by the time he was ten, at which point Tara encouraged him to [practice] the Dharma by proclaiming, "Sole divinity, fortunate one, do not be attached, do not be attached. . . ." The first "do not be attached" refers to this life, and the second one refers to the swamp of samsara. Take an elephant, for example: they have massive bodies, so if a large elephant falls in the swamp, it is much more difficult to remove than other types of living beings stuck in the mud, such as horses, goats, and so forth. Likewise, if the holy beings succumb to impure views and tenets, it damages the teachings and beings of that entire country. The same thing applies to this day and age: if a single lama has noble views and tenets, the country where he lives also becomes pure with Dharma teachings. Just as Tara exhorted Atisha, so those of us who are teachers should also learn the exhortation entreated by the gods of the pure abodes from the *Extensive Sport Sutra*[53] and others.

Atisha's father had great hopes that he would assume the kingdom. As for Atisha, he had no other intention than to leave behind the kingdom and practice Dharma. He grabbed a few belongings and headed off to the mountains in search of a guru. He relied properly upon Bodhibhadra, Rahulagupta, Avadhutipa, and others. His parents tried to postpone his entering the Dharma, but Atisha told them that his only intention was to practice the Dharma and that if they handed him over to the Dharma, in the future they would continue to meet life after life.

When Atisha had the thought that he should remain single-pointedly within the nature of mind through the practices of the central channel, Guru Rahulagupta passed without obstruction through a wall and admonished him to become an ordained monk. Heruka also admonished him, saying, "Son of the lineage, you absolutely must not leave to engage

52. Tib. *Rigs thigs*; Skt. *Nyayabinduprakarana*.

53. Tib. *rGya cher rol pa'i mdo*; Skt. *Lalitavistara sutra*.

in the practices of the central channel. You must ordain! If you ordain now, in the future many disciples will follow your example by ordaining." One night during a dream, the teacher Shakyamuni was at the head of many monks seated in a row and having lunch. When he reached the end of the row, he came across Atisha. Once the Teacher saw Atisha, he wept and asked, "Why have you not ordained?" In this way he admonished him to ordain.

Under the Abbot Shilarakshita, whose name means "guarding moral discipline," it is said that Atisha attained the first section of the path of preparation. There are many ways people explain this, such as "the realization of the selflessness of persons," "the realization of the selflessness of phenomena," and so on; however, this refers to the patience stage of the path of preparation.[54] Furthermore, in the Mahayana there are four sequential stages: (1) heat, (2) peak, (3) forbearance, and (4) supreme Dharma. [Atisha] had the concentration of obtaining visions, multiplying, and simultaneously remaining absorbed in suchness, as well as the immediately preceding concentration. The Seventh Supreme Conqueror [that is, the Seventh Dalai Lama, Kelsang Gyatso (1708–1757)] explains it this way:

> The reason that it is called "simultaneously absorbed in suchness" is because in general there is a distinction between the apprehended and the apprehender. And by being thoroughly apprehended, there is a thorough distinction made on all sides between the side of the afflicted and the side of complete purity. The conception apprehending the afflicted is the heat section of the path of preparation. The conception apprehending the complete purity is the peak section of the path of preparation. Once you have diminished this disparity, you attain the patience section of the path of preparation. The realization of those two conceptions is not generated in a

54. The path of preparation is divided into four parts: (1) heat, (2) peak, (3) forbearance, and (4) supreme Dharma. After the path of preparation comes the path of seeing, which is a direct realization of emptiness.

> way similar to other ordinary beings; therefore, at that time apprehended appearances cease. Because you are incapable of at least diminishing that conceptual grasping, it is called "simultaneously absorbed in suchness." This is the distinction between Madhyamaka and Mind Only and is very difficult to understand.

Under Dharmarakshita,[55] whose name means "protector of the holy Dharma," Atisha gained knowledge of the entire *Treasury of Explanation*[56] and without any partiality was honored by all the scholars in all the eighteen classes of scriptures as their crown ornament. Not only that, but there were five hundred [great scholars skilled] in this teaching; therefore, [Atisha] became like the crown ornament of all the pandits and scholars from a great distance, whereby he was called "the crown ornament of five hundred."

How He Practiced and Attained Good Qualities of Realization through Proper Practice

This explains how [Atisha] attained good qualities of realization through proper practice and understood the necessity of generating the teachings of scripture and realization to attain good qualities of realization.

Although these days the good qualities of realization are clairvoyance, magical powers, and so forth, such things also exist within the non-Buddhist schools, the Bonpo, and so forth. Just as a certain Bonpo named Naro Bonchung held a contest of miraculous powers with Jetsun Milarepa, so a heretic robbed Sapan[57] and the two playfully debated, and when the heretic was defeated he held a competition of miraculous powers. When the heretic began his display of miraculous powers, Sapan enlisted the assistance of the siddha Darchawa and in this way was able to defeat the heretic.

Our Teacher said as well, "Ordinary beings place their hopes in clairvoyance and miraculous powers," and also, "The two activities of the

55. Dharmarakshita was one of Atisha's primary teachers (see note 542 below). His most famous text in Tibet was the *Wheel of Sharp Weapons*, Tib. *mTshon cha 'khor lo.*

56. Tib. *bShad mdzod.*

57. Sapan is a contraction of Sakya Pandita.

ordained are (1) reading, listening, and contemplating, and (2) being a renunciant." We think, "I don't have realization in my mind unless I generate a realization of clairvoyance and miraculous powers"; however, this is not correct. Having the precepts and vows of a novice and a fully ordained monk in your mental continuum *is* a realization. This is also the teaching of the Buddha. Atisha was able to remain utterly unsoiled by any downfalls of the *pratimoksha*. He was only defiled by the most minor infractions of the bodhisattva precepts and a few scattered infractions of the secret mantra commitments. He didn't maintain his affiliation with these faults for even a day but would confess them; therefore, in this way his actions were pure. There were many who appeared and admonished him, stating that if he wished for swift enlightenment, he should train in bodhichitta. A gilded statue spoke to him saying, "Hey, *bhandata*," which is similar to saying, "Hey, you monk." In Sanskrit, the term *dzoki* means "yogi." Previously Atisha had already listened to the instructions on bodhichitta in the presence of Dharmarakshita, who cut off pieces of his own body to benefit a sick person.

[Atisha also received teachings from] Kusali the Younger, or, as he is also known, Guru Maitri Yogi, who when another person struck a dog with a club, cried out "Ah-na" and covered himself as [the dog] was being struck. In that exact same spot [where the dog was struck, Maitri Yogi's] own body swelled up due to the power of actually exchanging self with others. In his presence, Atisha repeatedly accomplished giving birth to bodhichitta in his mental continuum by listening to *The Melodious Vajra Song of Singing Meditation*.[58] However, when he investigated the root of the instructions for training in bodhichitta, his mind was still not satisfied. What he did after learning that Serlingpa[59] was the sovereign lord and protector of bodhichitta is declared in a verse that states,

> I supplicate glorious Atisha,
> Who worked to benefit all beings
> By receiving the medicinal nectar of bodhichitta
> From the protector of the world, King Serlingpa.

58. Tib. *Gyer sgom rdo rje'i glu dbyangs*.

59. Tib. gSer gling pa. This is the Tibetan name of Suvarnadvipai Dharmakirti (tenth century), a key teacher of Atisha.

Thus, he traveled for thirteen long months across the ocean and arrived at the Golden Isle.[60] Obstructive winds and lightning were naturally pacified by Atisha, and after thirteen months in this way he arrived at his destination. Throughout [the entire voyage] up until he arrived, he never let the attire and signs of being ordained decline. This is not like those of us who put on the attire of a householder the moment we step beyond the boundary of the monastery. In general, even just the external attire is extremely important. Even a single ordained person who doesn't allow the attire indicating they are ordained to deteriorate [by not wearing monastic robes] is beneficial to the teachings of the Buddha. Khedrup Je[61] declared,

> The pair of saffron-colored robes
> Beautify the body of the ordained.
> The conduct of a monk wearing the attire of a
> Householder destroys the teachings.

Do not belittle even the mere symbols [of a monk's] garments. Instead, we should have respect for them. Also, the monastic community should have great regard for their own robes even when it comes to something like finding lodging. Also, once you feel it acceptable to wear fine clothing, your mind will become like a silver inkpot.[62] You should not be like wrapping dog feces and pig manure in fine silks. Previously, Lama Losang Sherab told Dorje Chang Losang Jinpa that although it is permissible to wear a shirt with sleeves, he shouldn't do so.

As already mentioned, because the great Atisha kept pure moral discipline of the three sets of vows, he was endowed with the higher training in moral discipline. Although the downfalls of secret mantra poured down upon him like rain, he engaged in confession and restraint immediately, so he didn't retain them for a single day. Through his manner of possessing the higher training in concentration, while he was in Tibet he could hear the devotions of his students in [faraway] Magadha, together

60. Tib. gSer gling. The Golden Isle—possibly present-day Sumatra—was where Serlingpa lived (as his name indicates).

61. Khedrup Geleg Pelsang was one of Tsongkhapa's foremost disciples.

62. This refers to how a silver inkpot looks nice on the outside yet is black on the inside.

with the sounds of cymbals and their supplications, and he called out to Drom[tonpa], "I hear their requests through the power of my auditory clairvoyance." He also said, "By my receiving a crown ornament offered by a dying girl in [the region of] Yorpo Chingru, she has purified her obscurations, and that daughter of the lineage has been born as a god in heaven." In accordance with the supplication that states, "You are the guide of migrating beings . . ." and "endowed with the higher training in wisdom," we can understand that he was endowed with the realization of superior seeing of both the common and uncommon traditions of sutra and tantra.

How He Worked on Behalf of the Teachings has two sections:

1. His Activities in India
2. His Activities in Tibet

His Activities in India

[Atisha] became the jewel ornament of all scholars and took hold of eighteen classes of scripture. In India it was very risky to debate non-Buddhists because the king and his ministers would come to bear witness. The king would sit for the spectacle, and the side that was defeated would have to submit themselves as well as their belongings to the other side, offering their own religious tradition as a trophy. Although Ashvaghosha was previously a non-Buddhist, he lost a similar debate with Acharya Aryadeva. Likewise, Atisha defeated thirteen non-Buddhist pandits. He defeated the non-Buddhists who were ranked by having thirteen layers of parasols, seven layers of parasols, five layers of parasols, and so on, which contributed to the spread of the teachings.

His Activities in Tibet

At first, [Atisha] didn't come to Tibet. The Dharma had first come to Tibet during the reign of Lha-Thothori Nyentsen[63] of the royal heritage

63. Lha-Thothori Nyentsen was the twenty-eighth king of Tibet (dates unknown).

and Songtsen Gampo,[64] who worked to establish the Dharma while Shantarakshita, Padmasambhava, and King Trisong Deutsen caused it to spread.[65] At one point even that [initial spread of the Dharma] began to decline, with Majö serving alcohol and Pajö[66] arriving with a book of tantra, saying he had composed it and initiating many false tantras and commentaries. Langdarma's destruction of the teachings, as well as [his destruction of] even the most subtle signs of ordination, continued for nearly seventy years,[67] after which the great lama Gongpa Rabsal from Tsang and the two Indian bhikshus Yo-ge-chung and Mar Shakyamuni[68] worked to spread the Vinaya in the lower regions [of Tibet]. The Vinaya spread once again in the upper regions from the three border regions of Phala and so forth. After a while, the Indian pandits Blue Skirt and Red Acharya, as well as pandits searching for gold, spread the paths of liberation through [sexual] union, the path of attachment, and so on, causing the teachings to deteriorate.

At that time, the Tibetan king Lha Lama Yeshe Ö [ca. 959–1040] and his nephew [and successor Lhatsun Jangchub Ö] dispatched twenty-one youths of sharp intelligence, such as [the future *lotsawa*] Rinchen Zangpo [958–1055], to train in the Dharma in India. Having forsaken body, life, gold, and so on, they invited Atisha to Tibet, explaining the unbearable difficulties they had endured. Lha Lama Yeshe Ö even gave up his life for the welfare of the Buddha's teachings and passed beyond sorrow in prison. With respect to you and me, forget about forsaking our lives in that way: we cannot even fathom the idea of giving away the worst parts of our barley for the sake of the teachings.

Lhatsun Jangchub Ö gave Nagtso Lotsawa Tsultrim Gyalwa a golden

64. Songsten Gampo (sixth to seventh century) was the thirty-third king of Tibet (605–649?).
65. Shantarakshita was invited to Tibet by King Trisong Deutsen, who was the second so-called Dharma king, with Songtsen Gampo being the first. Trisong Deutsen invited Shantarakshita to establish the first Tibetan monastery, called Samyé. After numerous obstacles attributed to spirits, Shantarakshita suggested that the king invite Padmasambhava to subjugate the spirits.
66. Tib. Ma jos and Pha jos. I was unable to find reference to these two persons.
67. Langdarma only reigned from 838 to 841, but his destruction of the Vinaya lasted for nearly seventy years.
68. These are the three men who preserved the pratimoksha under Langdarma. Referred to in Tibetan as *smar g.yo gtsang gsum*, their full names are 'Jad kyi gyel mi gtsang pa rab gsal, g.Yo dge 'byung, and sTod lung pa smar shA kya mu ni.

hunting weapon and seven hundred *sang*[69] of gold, as well as four assistants. He advised Nagtso to offer once again the seven hundred sang of gold to Atisha in India while again extending an invitation to Atisha, and he instructed Nagtso on exactly how he should [most politely] greet Atisha. Atisha asked his personal deity whether or not going to Tibet would benefit living beings and so on, and was finally received in Upper Ngari [in western Tibet], after which he composed the *Lamp for the Path*[70]—and it was as though the sun of the teachings was shining [at last on the Land of the Snows].[71]

69. Tib. *srang*. This is a coin of either gold or silver weighing approximately one ounce.
70. Tib. *Lam sgron*.
71. For more information, see Alexander Gardner, "Atisha Dipamkara," Treasury of Lives, http://www.treasuryoflives.org/biographies/view/Atisha-Dipamkara/5717.

Day Three

[In *Guide to the Bodhisattva's Way of Life*,] the great bodhisattva Shantideva proclaimed,

> Having found a life of leisure such as this,
> If I don't use it to acquaint myself with virtue,
> Nothing else could be more foolish than this;
> Nothing else could be more ignorant than this!

Cultivate the proper motivation to listen to the teachings by thinking, "Since I have found merely this one time a human life that is difficult to obtain and has great meaning, if I don't use it to accomplish my everlasting aspirations, there could be nothing more unimaginably ignorant than this. Therefore, I am not going to fall under the influence of the affairs of this life but instead strive to extract its unique essence. For that purpose, I am going to listen to the teachings."

After giving this short introduction, Pabongkha Rinpoche covered the headings.

Yesterday we left off at the point of Atisha's biography. Your activities should be practicing the Dharma, and moreover, it should be unmistaken [that is, pure Dharma]. Regarding such a thing, there is nothing superior to this lamrim. Moreover, it reveals both the vast and profound aspects of the perfection of wisdom sutras, whose lineage was sequentially passed down from Maitreya and Manjushri, and from Atisha the lineages of both the vast and profound and the vast activities were combined into a single stream.

Because of the excellent way in which Lhatsun Jangchub Ö requested the Dharma, Atisha's mind was extremely pleased, and he composed the *Lamp for the Path.* Drom[tonpa] Rinpoche returned from Kham and said to the Tibetans, "I will try to invite Atisha to [Lhasa] in Tibet, and you should invite him as well." Atisha was not going to stay in Tibet for more than three years, at which point he would return to India, because his elder at Vikramalashila had made Nagtso promise that he would send Atisha back in three years. [However,] a war broke out between two rival kingdoms along the way, blocking the route and preventing Atisha from returning. [Atisha] sent a letter, along with a copy of *Lamp for the Path*, which was examined by the assembly of pandits of India, and they all sang its praises and compliments. The elder [at Vikramalashila] said it was excellent that [Atisha] had gone to Tibet and permissible for him to stay in Tibet but that he needed [Atisha to compose] an autocommentary.

Next, [Atisha] made his way back [to central Tibet]. Drom[tonpa] wrote a letter inviting Atisha and sent it with Lekpai Sherab and others, clearly stating the names of Tibetan lamas of various statuses and saying that they should set out to welcome Atisha. Kutön Tsondru Yungtrung said, "My name is not listed there." Told that he was included in the "and so forth," Kutön was not pleased. They set off in a greeting procession, according to the general custom. According to the *Swift Path*, [Atisha] was in Nyethang for nine years.

Regarding the "three causes of a composer of commentaries," he [or she] should possess either all three of the following or have them as complete as possible: (1) skill in the objects of knowledge of the five sciences, (2) unbroken oral instructions of holy beings, and (3) a direct vision of his [or her] personal deity and [the deity's] permission to compose. Atisha possessed the complete authentic instructions of this teaching of the Buddha.

Regarding [Je Tsongkhapa's] threefold division of his outline—"How [Atisha] Took Rebirth in an Excellent Lineage" and so forth—and applying it to practice, you must attain a special physical form to be able to accomplish the complete path and in particular to work for the welfare of the teachings and living beings. Next, you must engage in much learning and properly practice its meaning. Once you attain special signs, you should undertake the welfare of the teachings and living beings. Without learning, you won't be able to practice; therefore, there is no way to benefit others by teaching, either. It is extremely important to understand the way the outline of this teaching of Je [Tsongkhapa] is arranged, as well as the essential points of the teachings of practice. You should also understand the way to incorporate the practices of each of the other outlines as well with depth and stability, whereby you will develop an understanding and an honest belief in each one.

The lineage of oral instructions of equalizing and exchanging self with others comes from Manjushri, and its way of practicing is called "the lineage of vast activities." Moreover, there is the lineage of the philosophical tenets, the lineage of blessing, and so on. Regarding the lineages of various instructions, all of the practices that come from the Narthang Gyatsa,[72] our way of making *tsa tsas*,[73] Tara practice, *torma gyatsa*,[74] and so on, all came from the kindness of Atisha. While Atisha was teaching the *Lamp for the Path*, he also disseminated many other teachings, such as those of Malgyo Lotsawa, Lokya Lotsawa, Sakya Bari Lotsawa [1040–1111], [Sachen] Kunga Nyingpo [1092–1158], and others. However, the sole essence of them all is Atisha's *Lamp for the Path*.

From [Geshe] Potowa [Rinchen Sal (1027–1105)] up to Dragor Khenchen are the Kadam Shungpawas. Those belonging to the Kadam Shungpawa [that is, the scriptural tradition] engage in extensive study in dependence upon the great treatises, such as the Six Treatises of the Kadam[75] and so forth. Regarding the Kadam Lamrimpa [that is, the stages of the path tradition], the lineage begins with glorious [Palden] Gonpawa [Wangchuk Gyaltsen (1016–82)], and their teachings are based on the *Supreme Path*,[76] the *Blue Udder*,[77] and others. The lineage of Kadam Managpa [that is, the oral instruction tradition] begins with [Geshe] Chen-nga-wa Tsultrim

72. The Narthang Gyatsa is a collection of approximately one hundred different empowerments and blessing permissions.

73. Tsa tsas are small clay cast images of enlightened beings.

74. Torma gyatsa is a practice where one makes a hundred torma offerings, among other types of offering.

75. The six great treatises are (1) Shantideva's *Compendium of Trainings*, (2) Shantideva's *Guide to the Bodhisattva's Way of Life*, (3) Maitreya's *Ornament of the Mahayana Sutras*, (4) Asanga's *Bodhisattva Levels*, (5) Aryashura's *Jataka Tales*, and (6) the *Collection of Uplifting Sayings*.

76. Tib. *Lam mchog*.

77. Tib. *Be'u bum sngon po*, by Dölpa Sherap Gyatso (1059–1131).

Bar [1038–1103], and their exposition and study relies upon texts such as Atisha's commentary on *The Essence of Dependent Relationship.*[78] In the same way, listening, contemplating, and meditating on the five texts of scriptural instructions and so on is similar to the Shungpawas' exposition and study. Relying upon [Je Tsongkhapa's] *Great* and *Middle-Length Treatises on the Stages of the Path [to Enlightenment]* is similar to the exposition and study of the Lamrimpas. Receiving commentaries in addition to the guru's oral instructions on brief texts such as the [First Panchen Lama's] *Path to Bliss* and [the Second Panchen Lama's] *Swift Path* is equivalent to the Managpas. Therefore, Dagpo Lama Rinpoche [1845–1919] said that these days we also have all three lineages.

In this case, we are Lamrimpas because our explanation is based on [Je Tsongkhapa's] *Middle-Length Treatise on the Stages of the Path.* In general, the teachings of Jetsun Tsongkhapa the Great are not even slightly mixed with the nectar of Manjushri's words.[79] Yet when it came to his trip to Olga to live as a hermit, he asked Manjushri for guidance on almost everything—when to leave and stay, when to arrive, and even who should be his attendant. Previously, when the three great scholars[80] assembled in Tölung at Namse Deng,[81] each one gave teachings. Their disciplinarian was named Karma Konchog Shönu, who, with an extremely pleasant expression, extolled the virtues of Tsongkhapa and had harsh criticisms for the others. While in Tölung, Je Rinpoche [Tsongkhapa] made some inquiries about the Vinaya concerning what should be abandoned and what should be adopted. At that time the Vinaya had reached a state of serious decline, so he worked to make significant improvements. When it came to the teachings of the Vinaya, Je Tsongkhapa was extraordinarily kind. In particular, while staying in the monastery of Ratreng,[82] he made

78. Tib. *rTen 'brel snying po.*

79. This means that despite the fact that Lama Tsongkhapa received numerous teachings from Manjushri, all his writings are based solely on the various great treatises that originate with the historical Buddha Shakyamuni himself. The special instructions of Manjushri are maintained in the Ganden Hearing Lineage.

80. These three great scholars were Lotsawa Kyapchog Palsang, Rendawa, and Tsongkhapa. See Thuken Losang Chökyi Nyima, *The Crystal Mirror of Philosophical Systems*, trans. Geshe Lhundub Sopa with E. Ann Chávez and Roger R. Jackson (Boston: Wisdom, 2009), 254.

81. Tib. gNam rtsed ldeng.

82. Tib. Rwa sgreng. This was the first Kadampa monastery, which lies to the north of Lhasa.

supplications to open the door of the supreme path and composed the *Foundation of All Good Qualities*[83] and others.

In the summer at Ratreng, he taught the lamrim Dharma extensively. With the encouragement of migrating beings, both gods and men, he also composed *The Great Treatise on the Stages of the Path to Enlightenment*[84] at Ratreng. At that point, there were not many who had faith in the Prasangika Madhyamaka viewpoint. Therefore, he thought, "Even if I compose the section on special insight, it will not benefit beings. As a result, I will set aside composing the special insight section temporarily," and he went to ask Jetsun [Manjushri] questions. Jetsun [Manjushri] said, "I am elated. This is most excellent. You should definitely compose the special insight section, and it will be moderately beneficial for beings." This *Great Treatise on the Stages of the Path* is the sole crown ornament of this world. Although [great beings] may compose other teachings, they will never match its significance. Regarding that point, Panchen said,

> Gold is more precious than sandalwood,
> Yet the foolish compare it with charcoal.[85]

Since this is the case, we should not become like that. The teachings of Jamgon Tsongkhapa are blessed, so the fact that they have at least come into our hands makes us extraordinarily fortunate. *The Great Treatise on the Stages of the Path to Enlightenment* was composed when Je Rinpoche [Tsongkhapa] was forty-six, and the *Middle-Length Treatise on the Stages of the Path* was composed when he was fifty-nine. Je's *Great*, *Middle-Length*, and *Concise Treatises on the Stages of the Path*,[86] as well as [the Third Dalai Lama's] *Essence of Refined Gold*, [the Fifth Dalai Lama's] *Manjushri's Oral Instructions*, the [First Panchen Lama's] *Path to Bliss*, the [Second Panchen Lama's] *Swift*

83. Tib. *Yon tan gzhi gyur ma.*
84. Tib. *Lam rim chen mo.* This has been translated in three volumes as Tsongkhapa, *The Great Treatise on the Stages of the Path to Enlightenment*, 3 vols., translated by the Lamrin Chenmo Translation Committee (Ithaca, NY: Snow Lion, 2000–2004).
85. I was unable to locate this quotation, so I am uncertain to which Panchen it is attributed.
86. Here Tsongkhapa's *Concise Treatise* refers to his *Songs of Spiritual Experience*; see note 6 above.

Path, and Dagpo Gomchen Ngawang Drakpa's[87] teaching *The Quintessence of Excellent Explanation* make up the "eight famous lamrim texts." Although we consider secret mantra to be the most extraordinary teaching ever, without the stages of the path to enlightenment, the secret mantra would not even have existed. Therefore, the stages of the path are very important. Je [Tsongkhapa's] *Middle-Length Treatise on the Stages of the Path* is not that much more concise than his *Great Treatise on the Stages of the Path to Enlightenment*. The teachings of Panchen Palden Yeshe state that the *Great Treatise* primarily explains the Scriptural Lineage and the *Middle-Length Treatise on the Stages of the Path* addresses the Hearing Lineage.

The Greatness of the Dharma

The stages of the path to enlightenment have **three unique qualities** and **four greatnesses** that make them vastly superior to other scriptures.[88]

[The Three Unique Features has three sections:

1. The First Unique Feature: It Embodies the Essential Points of Both the Sutras and Tantras
2. The Second Unique Feature: The Stages Are Primarily Composed to Subdue the Mind, Therefore, They Are Easy to Put into Practice
3. The Third Unique Feature: It Is Adorned with the Instructions of the Two Gurus Skilled in the Tradition of the Two Great Trailblazers, Therefore, It Is Superior to Other Traditions]

The First Unique Feature: It Embodies the Essential Points of Both the Sutras and Tantras

The first unique feature [of the stages of the path to enlightenment] is that they embody the essential points of both the sutras and tantras and

87. An important lama of the fifteenth century (dates unknown), Dagpo Gomchen Ngawang Drakpa was a direct disciple of Khedrup Je and Gyaltsab Je. He established Dagpo Shedrup Ling Monastery.

88. Here we follow the system of Tsongkhapa's *Middle-Length Treatise on the Stages of the Path*—namely, that of presenting "The Three Unique Features" followed by "The Four Greatnesses."

are the purpose behind the phrase "by teaching it, the complete subject matter is covered." For subduing the mind or pacifying degenerations, they contain the essential points of meaning of the sutras and tantras.[89] The cycle of Dharma for a person of small capacity is for the trainee who is striving to subdue his [or her] mind for the welfare of just this life, as well as those striving to subdue the mind with the mere wish for a happy migration. The cycle of Dharma for a person of middling capacity is for a person striving to subdue his mind for the sake of the mere happiness of liberation. The cycle of Dharma for a person of great capacity is for a person striving for complete enlightenment for the welfare of all living beings. A sutra states,

> Do not engage in any nonvirtue;
> Engage in perfect virtue;
> Thoroughly subdue your mind;
> This is the teaching of the Buddha.

The first line explains the higher training of moral discipline; the second, the higher training of wisdom; and the third, the higher training of the mind [that is, concentration]. Thus, this presents subduing the mind with every form of abandonment and acceptance, through the complete path of the three types of beings. The *Ornament*[90] declares,

> This path of peace for living beings
> Is abridged in four aspects.

This quote reveals that the teachings are abridged in four aspects that contain all the essential points of bringing benefit and that are the method

89. The following sentences have an obvious error that must have occurred somewhere along the process of printing the Tibetan text. What appears above reflects my corrections made to the following, which originally appeared in the Tibetan text: "The cycle of Dharma for a person of small capacity is for the trainee who is striving to subdue his mind for the welfare of just this life. The cycle of the Dharma for a person of middling capacity is for those striving to subdue the mind with the mere wish for a happy migration. The cycle of Dharma for a person of great capacity is for a person striving to subdue his mind for the sake of the mere happiness of liberation."

90. The Nitartha Online Tibetan-English Dictionary (http://www.nitartha.org/dictionary) states that this is a contraction for the *Ornament of the Mahayana Sutras*.

for pacifying degenerate migrating beings.[91] The cycle of Dharma for beings of small capacity is the means of pacifying the degenerations of the lower realms. The cycle of Dharma for beings of middling capacity is the means of pacifying the degenerations of samsara. The cycle of Dharma for beings of great scope is the means of pacifying the disadvantages of nirvana, the mind wishing for that state, and so on. The subject matter of all the essential points of the scriptures being thoroughly complete [in the lamrim] is the first unique quality. Je Tsongkhapa offered an official letter to Lama Umapa,[92] stating,

> Looking at the instructions of the great being, glorious Atisha, I am amazed at how they reach an unmistaken definitive conclusion about the stages of the path and the mantra vehicle, and I instruct my disciples to rely solely upon these stages. These instructions also have a way of teaching where they combine into a single path all the oral instructions of the scriptures and their commentaries composed by great Indian masters. Developing an understanding through their expositions and an understanding through listening is sufficient to understand not only how to practice the minor oral instructions for practice but all the scriptures as well. Therefore, I teach it as much as possible.

Although there are numerous other insignificant commentaries teaching the preliminary practices, they are unnecessary. The lamrim teaches the utterly complete path from the proper reliance upon your guru up to the attainment of Vajradhara. Regarding the preliminary practices in general, they are not merely going for refuge, prostrations, mandala offerings, and so forth. Instead, the preliminaries such as the jorchö [that is, lamrim ritual preparations] have the actual path of a being of small scope as well as the path of small scope as the preliminary, the actual middling scope as well as the path of middling scope as the preliminary, the actual great path . . . up to the preliminary of the union of no more learning. Although you may merely engage in a scanning meditation on these stages

91. Here the four are not clearly enumerated.

92. Tib. dBu ma pa dpa' bo rdo rje (dates unknown; fourteenth century) was a Karma Kagyu lama who was one of Tsongkhapa's teachers and confidantes.

of the path, it constitutes a scanning meditation on the complete path. Although this may be explained only one time, at the end of the teaching the complete essence of all the world's scriptures will have been revealed. Geshe Tolungpa stated,

> When I teach the stage of this teaching, each of the books and scriptures of this world tremble and think, "This grey-haired old monk just explained all of our meaning."

And when [Geshe Tolungpa] taught, he said, "I slaughtered the great yak of the Dharma." Previously, when Changkya Rolpai Dorje taught the emperor of the Manchu dynasty, he taught the lamrim that contained the complete meaning using very few words. He had in fact given a commentary on the lamrim in dependence upon the lamrim verses composed by Dorje Dzinpa Konchog Gyaltsen.[93]

The Second Unique Feature: The Stages Are Primarily Composed to Subdue the Mind, Therefore, They Are Easy to Put into Practice

Although all the scriptures are nothing other than means to subdue your mind, you will be deliberately causing disturbances if you have decided to forgo the oral instructions and instead blindly enter into the scriptures without relying on the oral instructions of the guru. For example, although it states at the end of the chapter on Sadaprarudita in the *Perfection of Wisdom Sutra in Eight Thousand Lines*[94] that in beginning stages of practice you need to practice, if you begin [your practice] in that sequence, it will not be easy. A beginner in the lamrim does not go from his [or her initial]

93. His dates are unknown; however, his guru Losang Chökyi Gyaltsen lived from 1570 to 1662, so we can assume that he was born sometime after 1570.

94. This story is briefly summarized in Kachen Yeshe Gyaltsen, *Manjushri's Innermost Secret: A Profound Commentary of Oral Instructions on the Practice of Lama Chöpa*, trans. David Gonsalez (Seattle: Dechen Ling Press, 2013), 191: "Furthermore, the bodhisattva Sadaprarudita viewed his guru as superior to all the buddhas and although he directly perceived numerous buddhas, that was not sufficient and he sought out his spiritual master Dharmodgata and relied upon him without any regard for his body, life, and enjoyments whatsoever and through his worship, he progressed in a few short years from the stage of accumulation to the first bodhisattva ground which would have otherwise taken many eons to accomplish."

state right to that of a buddha. [Rather,] you progress along the path like on the steps of a ladder, without making a mess of the teachings. Furthermore, you will not be able to evaluate properly what is to be rejected and accepted, and the [teachings] will not be in their proper sequence. The sutras use the example of polishing a jewel for the sequence of subduing the mind. Initially, you subdue the mind's attachment to the appearances of this life. After that, you subdue the mind's craving for the next life. After that, you subdue the mind's self-cherishing, and so on. The stages are primarily so that the teachings are all easy to put into practice. For example, it is similar to a three-step process of preparation for clothing—bringing it from a state of sheep's wool to processed wool and finally making it ready to wear. If we consider beginners such as ourselves, sheep's wool is like the teachings of the Buddha, processed wool is like the commentaries on that, and [a garment] being ready to wear is like being ready to put [the teachings] into practice; this is the guru's oral instructions on the lamrim.

The *Guhyasamaja Root Tantra* does not teach sutra, and the commentary [on the perfection of wisdom sutras entitled] *Ornament of Clear Realization* does not teach mantra. Although these two are similarly established, they don't teach the principal stages for subduing the mind; therefore, they don't have the complete characteristic of making them easy to put into practice. Not only that, but we undertake famous teachings such as mahamudra and dzogchen, saying how profound they are, but none of them has all the unique qualities in the same way this does.

The Third Unique Feature: It Is Adorned with the Instructions of the Two Gurus Skilled in the Tradition of the Two Great Trailblazers, Therefore, It Is Superior to Other Traditions

Regarding this point, it is adorned with the oral instructions of Serlingpa, who was the guru skilled in the tradition of the great trailblazer Asanga, with his presentation of the sevenfold cause and effect and equalizing self with others for training the mind in bodhichitta. Therefore, it has a unique feature that surpasses the Hinayana and so forth. It is adorned with the oral instructions of Vidyakokila the Younger,[95] who was the guru

95. Vidyakokila the Younger was also known as Avadhutipa. He was the direct guru of Jowo

skilled in the tradition of the great trailblazer Nagarjuna, whose instructions unmistakably and nondeceptively explain how things are merely imputed through corresponding names, signs, and reasons established through logical proofs, with the view of Prasangika as the supreme pinnacle of philosophical tenets. Therefore, it has a unique feature that surpasses other traditions, such as the Svatantrika and so on.

If you don't understand the lamrim, you will not know how to do anything besides meditate on some deity and count some mantras. Sometimes we don't think anything other than "I am Vajrabhairava" or "I am Chakrasamvara." We pretend we are counting the YAMARAJA mantra and so forth. Sometimes we merely think that we are different from others and we have wings like Vajrahumkara, great and glorious Phurpa, Chemchog Heruka,[96] and so on. The previous Kadampas said,

> Everyone has a deity body to meditate on,
> Everyone has a mantra to count,
> Yet no one has a Dharma to contemplate.

Accordingly, if you don't understand these stages of the path to enlightenment as an object of contemplation, you may stay in your meditation house yet do nothing more than paint, count something similar to a mantra, engage in sewing, spin thread, and so on.

The Four Greatnesses [has four sections:

1. The Greatness That You Will Come to Realize That All the Teachings Are Not Contradictory
2. The Greatness of All the Scriptures Appearing as Personal Instructions
3. The Greatness of Easily Discovering the Ultimate Intention of the Conqueror
4) The Greatness of Stopping the Great Misdeed]

Atisha who transmitted the lineage of the profound. His own guru was Vidyakokila the Elder. Although his exact dates are unknown to the translator, since Atisha lived from 982 to 1054, we can surmise that Vidyakokila was born prior to 982.

96. These are various wrathful deities, each of whom has wings as part of its iconography.

The Greatness That You Will Come to Realize That All the Teachings Are Not Contradictory

The first greatness is that you will come to realize that all the teachings are not contradictory. The lamrim of Je [Tsongkhapa] also contains a vast amount of oral instructions of Jetsun [Manjushri] that don't exist in the *Lamp for the Path*. Before Atisha arrived [in Tibet], people did not understand the stages of the path, and migrating beings thought that sutra and tantra were as contradictory as hot and cold and were incapable of understanding that they were in fact noncontradictory. The term "noncontradictory" means they are mutually inclusive. Whatever the Buddha taught was taught as a means for a single person to become enlightened. Moreover, with the exception of a few of the unique teachings, such as striving for the bliss of liberation from the Hinayana, they should all be practiced by a bodhisattva. The common Mahayana [practices] and [the uncommon practices of] secret mantra should all be practiced only by bodhisattvas. The paths of the beings of small and middling capacity are from the collection of teachings of the Hinayana.

To generate bodhichitta, initially a mind of renunciation that is detached from samsara is indispensable. In general, the primary object of desire for a bodhisattva is to work for the welfare of living beings. For that, they must extend their care to the three types of trainees. For that, they must understand the various types of realizations of the three vehicles; therefore, they must master their understanding of all the paths of shravakas, pratyekabuddhas, and bodhisattvas. Apart from the mind striving for the bliss of nirvana for oneself alone, which is unique to Hinayana, all the other teachings from the Hinayana basket are common with the Mahayana and you should meditate on them all. This includes meditating on the sixteen aspects of the four noble truths, such as impermanence and so forth, as well as the twelve limbs of dependent relationship. Relying on the path in this way, you should realize not only that all the teachings are noncontradictory but that all the teachings are noncontradictory in accordance with their result as well.[97]

97. According to the Mahayana, once a Hinayana arhat attains the state of nirvana, the buddhas eventually awaken him [or her] from his meditative equipoise and encourage him to enter

A buddha has eliminated all faults and is endowed with all good qualities. Moreover, there is not even the slightest fault in the Conqueror's teachings, and there is not a single good quality that you are not capable of developing. Therefore, you should practice them all, out of desire to attain enlightenment. Some people think that, other than renunciation, bodhichitta, the four noble truths, and so on, presented in the sutras, they don't need to practice secret mantra; however, this is not the case. The reason bodhichitta is included within whatever meditations there are, such as the generation and completion stages of secret mantra, is that [bodhichitta] is the solitary cause of proceeding to the Mahayana. The mantra vows and other verses state,

> I shall generate the sacred
> Unsurpassed bodhichitta.

And the *Vajra Peak Tantra*[98] proclaims,

> Do not forsake bodhichitta
> Even for the sake of your life.

If you assert that you don't need bodhichitta in the practice of mantra, then you incur [two] faults: (1) there is a bodhisattva who has not generated bodhichitta, and (2) there is a buddha of the mantra vehicle who belongs to the Hinayana. The fact that all the buddhas first generated bodhichitta is also explained in the *Sutra of the Fortunate Eon*,[99] which proclaims,

> First generate the mind of enlightenment . . .

There are also many other teachings that contradict [that mistaken thesis]. For that reason, when you come to an understanding that everything that was taught by the Bhagavan was intended solely for a person's

---

the Mahayana. Therefore, even the shravaka and pratyekabuddha vehicles eventually lead the Hinayana practitioner to the state of full enlightenment.

98. Tib. *rGyud rdo rje rtse mo.*

99. Tib. *mDo sde bskal bzang.*

practice of enlightenment, all the scriptures will coalesce into the stages of the path. Your faith will also greatly increase. There are also many ways of explaining the [colloquial] expression "Carrying all the teachings of a four-sided path . . ." My guru explained it by stating, "Just like carrying the entirety of a square sitting mat, all the teachings should be carried by a single practice for enlightenment." If we understand this point for the stages of the path, we shall know how to "carry them" [that is, put them into practice]. [Vasubandhu's] *Treasury of Abhidharma*[100] states,

> The two aspects of the Teacher's holy Dharma
> Are the nature of scripture and realization.

The definitive number of the Muni's [that is, the historical Buddha Shakyamuni's] teachings is two: scripture and realization. Therefore, Acharya Avalokitavrata[101] stated,

> The transmitted scriptures of the Buddha reveal the unmistaken teachings on the four noble truths for those wishing for liberation.

Accordingly, the valid scriptural tradition is to be understood as a means of assisting a single individual in his [or her] progression to enlightenment, and one must realize that every type of abandonment and realization contained in the subject matter of Hinayana and Mahayana, and all the teachings of scripture and realization, are noncontradictory as complementary factors for a single person's enlightenment. This view prevents speculation that is in opposition to that, as well as the view of whether it exists or doesn't exist and so on. There is no need to realize that all philosophical views are noncontradictory, such as those designated dzogchen, mahamudra, and so on, as well as the Dharma traditions of the Bon. The phrase "all the teachings are understood to be noncontradictory" is not intended to mean that you must realize that all the philosophical views are noncontradictory. In short, although at first glance the language of some of

100. Tib. *Chos mngon pa'i mdzod*.

101. Avalokitavrata was a disciple of Bhavaviveka, the founder of the Svatantrika tradition of Madhyamaka.

the teachings from sutra and tantra appears to be as contradictory as hot and cold, in fact, they teach the means of eliminating all faults; therefore, they are necessarily noncontradictory according to a single individual at various times of their practice. For example, although it may appear contradictory when a doctor tells a sick person to both eat meat and not eat meat, and even though this may apply to the same individual, it is in fact necessary for the sick person to apply [both instructions] at various times during his illness.

The Greatness of All the Scriptures Appearing as Personal Instructions

The king—or, in other words, supreme—oral instructions are the precious spoken words of the Conqueror[102] as well as the commentarial collection[103] such as [the works of] the six ornaments,[104] the two supreme beings,[105] and so on. There is no oral instruction superior to these. Moreover, in this world the oral instructions taught by a guru do not surpass those of the Buddha Bhagavan. The oral instructions also do not surpass the precious spoken words of the Conqueror. The regent Maitreya states in his *Ornament of the Mahayana Sutras*,[106]

> There is no one in this world who is wiser than the Conqueror.
> No one else perfectly understands in every way all there is
> to know about supreme suchness.
> Therefore, do not wreak havoc with the sutras set down by
> the Sage himself.
> By causing harm to the holy Dharma, you will also destroy
> the system of the Muni.

We regard the Kangyur and so on as nothing more than objects of worship and don't understand that they could be meant for far more

102. Tib. bKa' 'gyur (Kangyur).
103. Tib. bStan 'gyur (Tengyur).
104. The six ornaments are Nagarjuna, Aryadeva, Asanga, Vasubandhu, Dignaga, and Dharmakirti.
105. The two supreme beings are Shakyaprabha and Gunaprabha.
106. Tib. *mDo sde rgyan*; Skt. *[Mahayana]sutralankara*.

than ritual recitation. This is the fault of not developing an understanding of the stages of the path. Although the Bon teacher Shenrab[107] and others claim that they are related to the Teacher, there is no evidence of this whatsoever. Although some claim that Dharmakaya Samantabhadra, Vajradhara, and so on are superior to our Teacher, such a thing is simply not possible. Once the Teacher attained the ultimate state of fearlessness, he became enlightened. If there was a buddha superior to that, this would mean that [Buddha Shakyamuni] would not be enlightened and, therefore, that, instead of becoming better, he got worse.

If you understand the lamrim, whenever you assess the scriptures, you will immediately be able to identify them with one of the three types of beings of the lamrim. For example, if you have a small quantity of barley in a container, and you get a little more from somewhere else, you will be able to add it to that. Previously, when the supreme siddha [Drubchog] Losang Namgyal[108] was giving the oral transmission of the *Perfection of Wisdom Sutra in Eight Thousand Lines*, Trichen Ngawang Chogden,[109] the tutor to Gyalwa Kelsang [Gyatso, the Seventh Dalai Lama], said, "When I listen to a commentary to the lamrim in the presence of Jamyang Shepa Ngawang Tsondru,[110] [I realize] that when I undertook my previous philosophical studies, I was in fact undertaking a study of the lamrim."

Thus, all the great scriptures are the lamrim. However, not recognizing them as the lamrim stems from the fault of not developing an understanding of the lamrim. For example, when dancers train in dancing, they should train in whatever dance they are learning. Likewise, you should study and contemplate whatever you are meditating on. You should meditate on whatever study and contemplation you undertake. Je Rinpoche [Tsongkhapa] also proclaimed, "Just as it would be a source of laughter to show a horse track to a horse and then have the race somewhere else, how can it be acceptable to learn and contemplate something and then settle upon something else for your practice?" This is stating that it would

107. Tib. gShen rab. Shenrab was the purported founder of the Bon tradition, according to which Shenrab predated Buddha Shakyamuni.
108. Tib. Blo bzang rnam rgyal (1670–1741).
109. Tib. Khri chen Ngag dbang chos ldan (1697–1751). He was the root guru of the Seventh Dalai Lama, Kelsang Gyatso, as well as Changkya Rolpai Dorje and many others.
110. Tib. Ngag dbang brtson 'grus (1648–1721).

be inappropriate to study and contemplate one thing and then meditate on something else and is the same as studying and contemplating the Five Treatises and then settling upon something else as your object of meditation. If you develop an understanding of the stages of the path, it is utterly impossible that you will not learn how to apply everything you come across to your practice, all the way from the spoken words of the Conqueror to a discarded page in a tsa tsa house.

Previously, while Je Lama Dorje Chang [that is, Pabongkha Rinpoche] himself was staying at a monastic center, he found a page in the tsa tsa house that was a teaching from the Supreme Conqueror Kelsang [Gyatso, the Seventh Dalai Lama], which stated, "The young tiger bee . . . ," and he knew without a doubt that it belonged to a being of middling scope and immediately applied [its import] to the faults [of samsara].

Some people assert that it is sufficient to practice some separate, insignificant oral instruction, such as a small manual, and think that the spoken word of the Buddha is only for performing ritual recitations for hire. Yet if we behave in this way, we will have very little faith in the scriptures and will regard the Kangyur and Tengyur as something not intended for practice, whereby we will accumulate the extremely grave karma of abandoning the Dharma. Those people will have created obstructions to developing faith in the stainless scriptures and their commentaries. For that reason, you should sincerely apply yourself to the stages of the path to enlightenment as a means of developing an understanding and faith in the great scriptures as well. Je Tsongkhapa the Great stated,

> The fault of abandoning the Dharma despite much study
> Is due to the scriptures not appearing as instructions.

Previously, a scholar from Sera Monastery visited a great Nyingma meditator from Kham and requested separate teachings to put into practice; this is the fault of not understanding the lamrim and is due to [not implementing] the two distinguishing features of realizing that (1) all the teachings are noncontradictory and (2) all the scriptures appear as personal instructions. For example, a tangkha painter arranges all his goods necessary for tangkha painting, such as his paint pot for painting the deity, his white, yellow, red, and green paints, his paintbrush, and so on, and doesn't leave even one thing out. This is analogous to realizing that all the teachings are noncontradictory. Likewise, understanding nothing more than the fact that the Conqueror's scriptures and their commentaries are intended for a single individual to put into practice means that you will not discard even a single letter. Thus, not only does the tangkha painter understand that the paints and so forth are indispensable for painting the deity, but he understands how to paint the deity image with a complete set of features, which is analogous to the scriptures appearing as oral instructions. Not only will you understand that all the scriptures and their commentaries are completely necessary for a single individual's enlightenment, but you will see that they are noncontradictory and intended to be put into practice, which is the meaning of "knowing how to put them into practice."

The Greatness of Easily Discovering the Ultimate Intention of the Conqueror

Finishing a tangkha painting is analogous to the third greatness of easily discovering the ultimate intention of the Conqueror, which means "discovering the jewel-like ultimate intention of the Conqueror through practice." In general, the *Three Principal Aspects of the Path* possesses the ultimate intention of the Conqueror, which is within the ocean-like scriptures of the Conqueror. If you rely upon the boat-like stages of the path to enlightenment and the skillful captain-like guru, you will easily be able to discover the underlying intent of the Conqueror. The *Three Principal Aspects of the Path* is the underlying intent of the Conqueror. Also, the words of the *Three Principal Aspects of the Path* from Je Rinpoche [Tsongkhapa] state,

> For as long as you accept the relationship between
> The nondeceptive dependent arising of appearances
> And emptiness as being separate,
> You still have not realized the true intent of the Muni.

This verse is in reference to the correct view of emptiness. And:

> This is the essential meaning of all the Conqueror's scriptures.

This also reveals the Conqueror's underlying intent about renunciation. Regarding bodhichitta, this is the absolute greatest underlying intent of the Conqueror.

The Greatness of Stopping the Great Misdeed

If you give rise to all three of the previous greatnesses of the lamrim, you will automatically stop the great misdeeds of abandoning the Dharma and so forth. This teaching refers to the smallest misdeed of abandoning the Dharma, such as merely [abandoning] its symbolism. In accordance with the hidden meaning of that, through the stages of the path endowed with three greatnesses, you will stop the misdeed in your way of relating to the spiritual guide, such as not having faith in your spiritual guide and so on; this stops the misdeed of wasting your life with what is meaningless and mistaking what is meaningful through "the great meaning and great difficulty of finding this leisure and endowment," and it stops the misdeed that comes from grasping at permanence through the point of view of death and impermanence and so on; [thus, you also need to] apply the same thing to the remaining points. As you undertake listening to and contemplating the words proclaimed with these four greatnesses, you should combine the subject matter of the four greatnesses with your mental continuum.

Day Four

Drom[tonpa] the king of the Dharma proclaimed,

> The wondrous teachings are the Three Baskets,
> Which are beautified by the instruction of the three scopes
> of beings;
> This golden rosary of the precious Kadam—
> Whoever tallies its beads becomes meaningful.

Regarding the supreme means of leading migrating beings along the path of liberation and omniscience, it is the Three Precious Baskets. The meaning of all three of those is contained in the three scopes of beings. Furthermore, because it is a teaching that condenses all the stages of the path, this teaching is not like other teachings, such as secret mantra and so forth; it will bring nothing but benefit to all who practice it, and it is not possible that they will ever sustain a loss. These stages of the path to enlightenment are a Dharma that will benefit anyone with a supreme, mediocre, or inferior mind. Adjust your motivation by thinking, "If I sincerely apply myself to this my human life of leisure and endowment that I have obtained, [my life] will become meaningful; therefore, from this day forth, I shall put it into practice."

After giving this brief introduction to adjust our motivation, Pabongkha Rinpoche restated the topics.

Yesterday we already covered the first two benefits. The third heading is this:

How to Listen to and Explain the Dharma Endowed with Those Two Greatnesses has three sections:

1. How to Listen to the Dharma
2. How to Teach the Dharma
3. How to Conduct Their Common Ending

This outline on how to listen to and teach the Dharma constitutes the instructions for how to effectively listen to the Dharma.

How to Listen to the Dharma has three sections:

1. Contemplating the Benefits of Listening to the Dharma
2. Developing Reverence for the Dharma and the Dharma Teacher
3. The Actual Way to Listen to the Dharma

Contemplating the Benefits of Listening to the Dharma

If you contemplate the benefits of listening to and studying the Dharma, you will develop a desire to listen. These days we think it is sufficient to meditate on the Dharma and not necessary to study. Unless we have very good mental imprints from our previous lives and awaken those slight imprints, it is utterly impossible to generate qualified realizations. Sapan stated,

> Although you apply yourself merely to meditation,
> Without study it is the means of accomplishing the animal state.

Therefore, to practice Dharma you must understand how to practice, for which you must study. Hence it is extremely important that you initially engage in study. The Arhat Chökyab famously compiled the miscellaneous teachings of the Buddha as the *Dhammapada*,[111] which is now included in

111. The *Dhammapada* is a collection of instructional sayings of the Buddha, usually set in some type of parable, that is as useful to the lay community as it is to scholars and monks due to its accessibility.

the Kangyur. If you don't study, you won't know how to go for refuge or even as much as how to make a prostration; you won't even know how to offer a mandala. If you do study, although you may read just a single line in a text, you will develop wisdom eyes that can make a proper estimation of it. Without studying, no matter how intelligent you may be, it will be as if those with eyes have arrived at a place of complete darkness. If you have studied, it will be like igniting a bright flame in a dungeon, and you will clearly understand everything. It is extremely important that you do so now, while you are young. If you do, you will be able to practice Dharma when you have reached a more advanced age. If you don't study, you will be [as dumb] as a donkey when he encounters the Dharma, and whenever it comes to worldly matters you will be as [brilliant] as Manjushri.[112]

When you study, you begin by studying, then contemplating, and then developing wisdom arisen from meditation. Je Tsongkhapa appeared to Panchen Losang Chögyan in a dream and proclaimed,

> For the sake of benefiting yourself and others,
> Do not be satisfied with your learning.
> Be like the bodhisattvas who have attained the third bhumi[113]
> Who are not satisfied with their learning.

Although Drubwang Ngagsur Dorje Chang[114] was in his eighties, he memorized the *Concise Perfection of Wisdom Sutra*, and before he died he recited it from memory a hundred times. If you haven't studied, your view, meditation, and action will be analogous to being unable to distinguish flour, wheat, and baking soda: you will just say, "Everything is the same—white!" In the same way, your entire view and meditation will be greatly flawed. The reason for that was explained by Je Tsongkhapa when

112. Pabongkha Rinpoche is being facetious here.

113. The term *bhumi* means ground or level. In relation to the spiritual grounds and paths, the bhumis begin when a bodhisattva gains a direct realization of emptiness. There are ten bhumis on the bodhisattva path. The third is called "luminous," at which point the bodhisattva attains the perfection of patience. One of the three types of patience is called "definitely contemplating Dharma" and refers to the forbearance attained with respect to the hardships involved in the study and contemplation of emptiness that are required to progress to the higher bhumis.

114. Tib. Grub dbang sNgags zur rDo rje 'chang. I was unable to identify this particular lama; however, "sngags zur" indicates that he was a former abbot of one of the tantric colleges.

he addressed questions to Tibetan scholars and great meditators in *The Questions of Perfectly Pure Superior Intention*,[115] at which time no one was able to answer. Later, Losang Chökyi Gyaltsen offered his services to untie the difficult points of [Je Tsongkhapa's] intention.

Those of you who are young and have sharp minds must complete your studies of the great treatises at the great monastic institutions. If you do that, you will be of great benefit when you return to your homelands. For those of you who are old and not so bright, if you alternate study and contemplation on something concise such as the [First Panchen Lama's] *Path to Bliss* or the [Second Panchen Lama's] *Swift Path*, this will be sufficient to cover the entire journey along the path, from prior [to entering the path] through entering the path [and] up to the ground of buddhahood. Although Je [Tsongkhapa's] *Concise Treatise on the Stages of the Path*[116] has few words, it is well known to contain the abridged meaning; therefore, you should use it as a means of at least grasping the main points and then work your way up to formulating an understanding of the precise meaning of the words.

Through your study, you have the means of training in the Dharma of moral discipline and so forth. Through your study, you have the means of concentration if you [forsake] the meaningless; through your study, you have the means of training in the wisdom [attaining] nirvana. Moreover, through study you have a way of sequentially developing your wisdom of the Dharma, such as listening, contemplation, and meditation. Anyone who has become knowledgeable through completing his [or her] former studies and through these studies has developed the three types of faith, as well as the wisdom of listening, contemplation, and meditation, can even be called "self-realized"; nevertheless, he should never be content with his studies. Moreover, even though you may be called "self-realized," it is appropriate to pay for the opportunity to listen and study even with the weight of your own flesh. Even learning the alphabet—even as many as two thousand letters in a single book—you will develop the wisdom of understanding them all.

Considering this, we should collect learning as our collection of

115. Tib. *Dri ba lhag bsam rab dkar.*

116. This *Concise Treatise* is otherwise known as the *Songs of Spiritual Experience*; see note 6 above.

essential wealth. In particular, we who are ordained should absolutely accumulate it, since faith, study, moral discipline, and so on are the seven jewels of the aryas.[117] If we have them, although we may not have anything other than our robes and a cup, the [seven jewels of the aryas] are the supreme riches. They also cannot be stolen by thieves and so on. In our future lives, and even until we attain enlightenment, we shall pursue them. No matter how much concern we may show toward our worldly belongings, if we don't have the seven jewels of the aryas, we are as poor as a beggar. When we die we must leave behind all our worldly companions and wealth. If we have learning, we have something of value that can never be stolen and that is not as meaningless as a penalty incurred from a government official, for we know that it is an adornment that will eventually transform our suffering into happiness. Study has such kindness.

Previously, Tse[chok] Ling Yongzin Pandita, [Kachen Yeshe Gyaltsen]'s [1713–1793] maternal uncle, pretended at first that he didn't know him. Later, when [Kachen Yeshe Gyaltsen's] good fortune had increased, his [uncle] returned, saying, "I am your uncle!" Also, another person felt the need to say, "I prostrate to you, piles [of wealth]." For that reason, your worldly relatives and all your wealth are deceptive and without essence. Listening and so on is your supreme wealth and the very best of all your relatives, friends, medicine, and so forth. If you are learned, you will be able to give a multitude of eloquent discourses even in the presence of the learned; otherwise, you will be like the disciple of Lama Menkhapa who waited until he was old to become ordained without any knowledge of Dharma, while [the great scholar] Zhog Donyon Khedrup was trying to have a conversation with him.

For those who have studied, when it comes to needing the help of others for gaining certainty, through having analyzed its meaning, they are absolutely self-reliant. If they have fully perfected their practice through meditating on the meaning [of Dharma], they will generate the wisdom arisen from meditation which [realizes that] rebirth is the fortress of samsara.[118] Moreover, if you become someone for whom it is not necessary to

117. They are (1) faith, (2) moral discipline, (3) generosity, (4) learning, (5) shame, (6) modesty, and (7) wisdom.

118. The process of taking uncontrolled rebirth is like a fortress or stronghold of samsara that prevents us from attaining liberation or enlightenment.

take on the contaminated appropriated aggregates, you will be liberated from samsara. Nagarjuna proclaimed,

> Make every effort for the sake of overcoming rebirth.

Although you may be someone who studies and contemplates a mere portion of the futility associated with the difficulties of samsara presented in the stages of the path to enlightenment, complete enlightenment will not be difficult. Even if you merely apply yourself each day from the depths of your heart to the lamrim for the length of time it takes to make a cup of tea, you will most certainly reach progressively higher realizations. Je Lama [Tsongkhapa] also stated,

> In this day and age, those seriously pursuing yoga have done little study . . .[119]

Developing Reverence for the Dharma and the Dharma Teacher

Arrange a high throne for the lama who is expounding the Dharma to sit on, and so forth. It is said that during an oral teaching, when the recipient is someone like the Conqueror Father and Son [that is, the Dalai Lama and Panchen Lama] and the presenter of the offering is someone like one of their tutors, it is permissible that the height of their thrones be equal. When someone is presenting an opposing philosophical position [in a debate], he is called "presenter of the current teaching," and the listener [that is, the Dalai Lama or Panchen Lama] sits on a higher throne. Although it is also the tradition that the expounder who is a simple monk and of lower status sits on a lower throne and "offers it upward,"[120] it is an extremely grave fault not to show respect for the Dharma once he receives it by setting it aside.

Previously, after a lama did just that [that is, had to sit on the ground and offer the teachings "upward" to a person on a throne], the [lama] offering the Dharma [sarcastically] stated, "From the time of the Bhagavan

119. See the opening lines of day six for the remaining lines of this quote.

120. Tib. *yar 'bul.*

Buddha until me, the Dharma has only been offered downward. Yet presently, I am 'the fortunate one who gets to present the Dharma upward.' With displeasure I will offer the teachings while remaining in the lowest possible position."[121] This was taught in the biography of the Prince Agastya Muni.

The Actual Way to Listen to the Dharma has two sections:

1. Abandoning the Unfavorable Condition of the Three Faults of a Vessel
2. Cultivating the Six Recognitions

Abandoning the Unfavorable Condition of the Three Faults of a Vessel

An [**upside-down vessel**] is analogous to an upside-down teacup: although you may pour tea on top of it, not a drop will make it inside. In the same way, although you may be sitting amid the Dharma assembly, if you don't listen with all your attention, you will incur the fault of being like an upside-down vessel.

Although you may have an upright vessel, if the interior is unclean, the tea and so forth that mixes with it will not be appropriate to use, which is like examining the lama and thinking that it is *you* who are a great scholar. With respect to thoughts such as "What use can there be in that famous teaching called the 'lamrim'?," this is like a **defiled vessel**.

With respect to being like a **vessel with a hole in its bottom**, although you may have listened well, you can't remember what was said due to forgetting what you received. This is the case with the majority [of people]. As soon as most of us receive Dharma teachings, we immediately forget what was received and so on. To ensure that that doesn't happen, it would be excellent if you wrote down notes once you heard [the teachings]. You should also reflect on them on your own, and once you establish a foundation of each heading, you should go over each point

121. Because the person giving the teachings should also be seated higher than the recipient of the teachings, he was not pleased in being in a lower position and sarcastically referred to himself as "the fortunate one."

of the outline until you have filled in all the empty sections within each one. It is also acceptable to conjoin them with the oral instructions of the lamrim texts of other lamas and, once you do, compare them with each other and count the number of steps in the outlines. A sutra states,

> Listen well, thoroughly, and retain it in your mind.

This quote is in reference to the way to apply [these three points] to various aspects of the teachings such as the three faults; being virtuous in the beginning, middle, and end; study, contemplation, meditation; and so on. The person listening to the Dharma should not act in such a way as to let his [or her] mind wander from a single portion of the recitation "all sentient beings" to something else. The oral instructions of Choné Rinpoche[122] state that "listen well" is an affirmation and that the term "well" means you are being impartial and straightforward. "Listen thoroughly" means to be wise, and "retain it in your mind" means striving. In terms of what to negate, you should think over the rain falling but not soaking in and so forth, and the sick not relying on medicine, and how we eat food. You should think over the benefits of listening to and studying the Dharma, and once you are uplifted and inspired with bodhichitta and so forth, you should listen.

Relying upon the Six Recognitions as Favorable Conditions has six sections:

1. Establishing the Recognition That You Are a Sick Person
2. Establishing the Recognition That the Dharma Teacher Is Like a Doctor
3. Establishing the Recognition That the Dharma Teachings Are Medicine
4. Establishing the Recognition That Persistent Practice Will Cure the Illness

122. Choné Rinpoche was one of Pabongkha Rinpoche's gurus.

5. Establishing the Recognition That the Tathagata Was a Holy Being
6. Establishing the Recognition That the Dharma May Remain for a Long Time

Establishing the Recognition That You Are a Sick Person

It is not that you think of yourself as a sick person when you are not. The Kadampa Kamawa stated,

> If that were not really the case, then our meditation would be misguided. However, we have in fact been afflicted with the virulent disease of extreme intensity through the three poisons yet have no idea whatsoever that we are ill.

Accordingly, being tormented by the disease of the afflictive emotions, you are in fact ill but don't realize it. You are like a sick person who has been seized by a high fever and doesn't realize he [or she] is ill. This severe illness is extremely intense! You also have the agony of being tormented by anger, attachment, and so forth, which, when generated with extreme intensity, has never before brought you any happiness. Moreover, since beginningless time, you have been tormented by many hundreds of illnesses of afflictive emotions. [Geshe] Potowa proclaimed, "A patient that will never be cured . . ." [Shantideva's] *Guide to the Bodhisattva's Way of Life* states,

> If even someone who is stricken with an ordinary illness
> Should act according to his doctor's advice,
> What need is there to mention someone constantly stricken with
> The illness of a hundred faults such as attachment and so forth?

You will also experience the suffering of the lower realms through the illness of the afflictive emotions. Although [ordinary] illnesses come from wind, bile, phlegm, and so on, the afflictive emotions are not generated in that way.

Establishing the Recognition That the Dharma Teacher Is Like a Doctor

In this way, you are a patient who is tormented by an illness, and you seek out a skilled physician; yet you are extremely foolish if you don't follow his [or her] advice. Just like a sick person who searches for a doctor, listens to his advice, and takes his medicine, you are seized by the illness of the afflictive emotions and therefore seek out a spiritual guide who is similar to a skilled physician. The proper way of relying upon him is similar to the way a patient relies upon a doctor.

Establishing the Recognition That the Dharma Teachings Are Medicine

You should highly value the oral instructions of your teacher the spiritual guide, which are just like medicine that functions to dispel the illness of the afflictive emotions.

Establishing the Recognition That Persistent Practice Will Cure the Illness

In the same way that a patient who doesn't take his [or her] medicine according to the doctor's instruction will not be able to cure his [or her] illness, if you don't put into practice the instructions you listened to in the presence of your spiritual guide, you will not be able to dispel the illness of the afflictive emotions; therefore, you must put them into practice. The *King of Concentration Sutra*[123] states,

> Although I have explained the most excellent Dharma,
> If you don't perfectly apply it upon hearing it,
> You will be incapable of curing your illness
> Despite being given a bag full of medicine.

And,

123. *Ting nge 'dzin gyi rgyal po'i mdo.*

Having received medicine that is plentiful, good, and valuable,
If you don't take the medicine that can cure your disease,
The doctor is not to blame, nor is the medicine at fault;
It is the fault of the patient himself.

Likewise, how can someone who ordains in this teaching,[124]
Who has learned all the powers, concentrations, and sense
faculties,
Yet who doesn't actually apply himself to meditation
Or make a proper effort ever attain nirvana?

This is similar to those here who do not practice once they receive this vast and profound Dharma in the presence of the guru: if they take rebirth in the lower realms when they die, it is not the fault of the guru or the Dharma—it is their own lack of practice that is to blame. From the six recognitions, this fourth recognition [that persistent practice] will cure the illness is extremely important. [Shantideva's] *Guide to the Bodhisattva's Way of Life* states,

I should physically put this into action;
What can I accomplish by merely spouting words?
How can sick persons ever be benefited
By merely reading the prescription?

You should definitely meditate on all the steps in the way they are set forth in the extensive and concise stages of the path. This is similar to how you absolutely must take all ingredients in the medicine for a heat disorder called "camphor twenty-five" to dispel a heat-related illness. For the lamrim, to abandon the afflictive emotions, at the very least you must apply all the different types of meditations in dependence upon the *Swift Path*, whereby you will be able to attain the state of liberation and omniscience. These are also stating that you need to learn to practice Dharma,

124. This reference to being an ordained monk or nun is due to the fact that the vast majority of the Buddha's direct disciples were ordained Sangha at the time.

and to learn you must listen and so on, which is an extremely important and vital point.

With respect to "delighting in discourses yet not putting the meaning into practice," this is delighting in talk without considering the meaning but merely engaging in prayers and recitation. Regarding "observing performances," if we relate this to war, it is like persons who are unable to fight in battle discussing the good qualities of their war heroes, which is analogous to you yourself never practicing in any way whatsoever. If we compare a great deal of expounding the Dharma of the vast and profound to a performance, it is like a theatrical play in which those [expounders of the Dharma] are like an elegant king who is only discussing the actors' roles in its meaning, and we are like a poor person. Once you understand the Dharma, your system of practice should not be merely to act like a practitioner by squatting down and placing your hands in meditative equipoise.

Geshe Chen-nga-wa was reading the Vinaya and came across a line that said [that you should not use] leather skins, so he threw his out. He kept reading, and it said [that it is permissible if you are] sick, so he retrieved it; we should conduct ourselves in the same way. We should apply whatever we hear to our practice to the best of our ability. It is utterly inappropriate to say, "That text is ancient, and it is not possible to conduct ourselves in the way that lama describes in this day and age" while we drink alcohol and so forth, claiming it is beneficial for the winds. If we conduct ourselves in that way, unlike the lamas of the past, we will follow a different path than those "ancient" lamas and those "modern-day" lamas will end up in the hell realms. When we contemplate and meditate on even a fraction of what we have understood when studying the lamrim, we shall experience a great potency that is superior to that [study]. Even more than mere study, our practice of contemplation and meditation should be in accordance with whatever we have studied. Dromtonpa stated,

> When I study, I increase my contemplation and meditation;
> When I contemplate, I increase my study and meditation;
> When I meditate, I increase my study and contemplation;
> I know the way to bring them all into the path of Dharma
> By combining them all together as one.

I am a Kadampa who does not fall into half-measures;
Therefore, a Kadampa is someone who realizes everything
perfectly,
Like an illusory display of a hundred similar replicas.

Regarding illusions, the term "hundred" refers to a ritual of transformation with numerous similar emanated aspects. The *Praises of Confession*[125] [states],

What use could there be for a leper with missing limbs
To rely upon medicine just a few times,
When he has long since been establishing the basis [for his illness]
With a mind that has been perpetually confused?

This is analogous to a person with leprosy who has had his limbs amputated and is not benefited by taking medicine for a day or two. Likewise, it is not enough for us who have been tormented due to having been ill with the afflictive emotions since beginningless time to rely upon the antidote just once or twice; instead, we need something very powerful over a long period of time. Furthermore, we should engage in meditation practice during all our daily actions of walking, moving about, lying down, and sitting. Otherwise, it is not necessary to stay in strict retreat.

Establishing the Recognition That the Tathagata Was a Holy Being

This is also extremely important and does not exist for others such as non-Buddhists. Although it is said that it is not easy to understand a small portion of this fifth recognition, the *Great Commentary to Valid Cognition*[126] states,

125. Tib. *bShags bstod*. I have not been able to discover who wrote this text.
126. Our text lists this as *rNam 'grel tika chen*. However, I believe this is in reference to Khedrup Je's commentary entitled *Tshad ma rnam 'grel gyi tika chen rigs pa'i rgya mtsho*.

> One proves the faultless meaning of scriptural teachings through proving the validity of teachings that are the subject matter of realization. When one proves they are faultless through realizing them, one is an accomplished being of the valid teachings.

We should understand how to correlate how the Teacher became a valid being as the teacher of the unmistaken path for those beings desiring liberation, in accordance with the reasoning set forth in the *[Great] Commentary on Valid Cognition*. [The Second] Changkya, [Rinpoche] Ngawang Chöden [1642–1714] also stated, "By recalling with faith that Dharma was initially taught by the Tathagata, view him with faith."

Establishing the Recognition That the Dharma May Remain for a Long Time

The sixth point is establishing the recognition that the Dharma may remain for a long time for the sake of those wishing for liberation, because it is a valid teaching taught by a valid nondeceptive teacher; therefore, it is absolutely necessary. Je Tsongkhapa also stated,

> May I work for the benefit of the teachings until the
> End of samsara and never be swayed by winds of negative
> conceptions.
> May I eternally discover confidence in the Teacher
> By understanding the nature of the teachings.

In general, whatever Dharma is being taught should be used as a means of critically analyzing the state of our own mental continuum, and we listen to it by using it to benefit our mental continuum. Furthermore, the *Jataka Tales* state,

> When I examine clearly the form of my bad
> Actions in the mirror of the Dharma,
> I develop anguish in my mind
> And turn my mind toward the Dharma.

This is stating that our activities are similar to a face in the mirror of the Dharma, which openly reveals our faulty actions that contradict the Dharma and their defilements. We should listen to the Dharma for the sake of clarifying them. The biography of Saudasa explains that the Dharma is like a mirror and that by not only listening but even reading texts, [it] should also be applied [to our minds], and we should read while we critically analyze the state of our own mental continuum.

Once a lama has proclaimed the stages of the path to enlightenment to the minds of his disciples, they should not dissect the faulty words from the discourse. If both the listener and the expounder of the lamrim carry out their duties properly, the [disciple] should develop his [or her] first type of realization right here, amid the Dharma assembly. We pretend that the mere continuity of blessing for a commentary on the two stages or [for] bestowing empowerment substances is profound, yet in one sense it comes close to being a lie when we pretend to be a bodhisattva and say, "I am a fortunate one of great bliss."[127] The ability to develop realizations amid the Dharma assembly is not a possibility other than in relation to the stages of the path to enlightenment. In the past, [Geshe] Potowa was teaching in Deltse. Geshe Chökyi Öser had a certain way of reaching a definitive conclusion about the object of learning when he taught. Later, Geshe Chökyi Öser went to listen to [Geshe] Potowa teach the Dharma and said that although he didn't learn anything he didn't already know, he came to an understanding he previously had not comprehended. Even if you secretly offer tea to the lama in exchange for teachings in private, it will never be as effective as the teaching you will receive from the lama while he is teaching from the throne. In the same way, even if the disciples try to secretly carry out visualizations, it will not be as effective in transforming their minds as it is while they are attending a discourse.

How to Teach the Dharma has four sections:

1. Contemplating the Benefits of Teaching the Dharma
2. Cultivating Respect for the Dharma and Its Teacher

127. This phrase is repeated during an empowerment ceremony when the initiating lama inquires about your motivation. Through reciting the above response, you are stating that you are in fact a bodhisattva, which for most of us is simply not the case.

3. An Explanation of What Type of Thought and Behavior You Should Have [when Explaining the Dharma]
4. Making a Distinction between Who Should and Should Not Be Taught

Contemplating the Benefits of Teaching the Dharma

Although a simple teacher may be doing as little as instructing his [or her] students in reading texts, he [or she] is teaching the Dharma, so we should contemplate the benefits. Also, when teaching the Dharma there are great faults that we can incur from the afflictive emotions—such as thoughts of being respected and venerated, thoughts of being famous, and thoughts of the benefits that will come to us from within our household—that come from studying texts and teaching the Dharma. The benefits of explaining Dharma should be contemplated in accordance with the twenty benefits of explaining the Dharma as presented in the *Sutra Inciting the Superior Intention.*[128]

Cultivating Respect for the Dharma and Its Teacher

Set out an excellent teaching throne for the Dharma teacher and so forth.

An Explanation of What Type of Thought and Behavior You Should Have [when Explaining the Dharma] has two sections:

1. What Type of Thoughts You Should Have
2. What Type of Behavior You Should Have

128. Regarding the twenty benefits, you will come to have (1) recollection, (2) intelligence, (3) understanding, (4) stability, (5) wisdom, (6) supramundane wisdom, (7) little desire, (8) little hatred, and (9) little ignorance. Also, (10) demons will not find the opportunity to harm you, (11) the Bhagavan buddhas will think of you as a precious, only child, (12) nonhumans will protect you, (13) deities will bestow charisma and power on you, (14) enemies will find no opportunity to harm you, (15) friends will remain steadfast, (16) your words will be trusted, (17) you will attain fearlessness, (18) you will have abundant happiness, (19) you will be praised by the wise, and (20) your gift of the teachings will be worthy of remembrance.

What Type of Thoughts You Should Have

You should adjust your motivation as you make your way from your dwelling to the place where you will be teaching. Prepare by making prostrations and performing the proper visualizations. When you reach the throne, imagine that the [lineage] gurus dissolve into you. When you sit on the throne, recall impermanence by contemplating that sitting on the teaching throne is only momentary and recite, "As fleeting as a shooting star . . ."[129] Geshe Nyugrum stated, "I meditate on impermanence before each [teaching] session [and remind myself that] I have no experience teaching the Dharma." If you don't contemplate in that way, you will develop pride; therefore, meditate on impermanence and contemplate bodhichitta. At the very least, once you have sincerely thought them over, you should make a sincere effort for the welfare of others. You should be clean, hygienic, and so forth; and while you are teaching, if you praise yourself and criticize others, it will appear as though you have your own best interests in mind by either directly or indirectly seeking respect and fame. Atisha said, "In India, they sold their wealth and had much to sell. In Tibet, they sell the Dharma and have much to sell." We must proceed very carefully and examine our innermost thoughts.

Making a Distinction between Who Should and Should Not Be Taught

There are many texts that extensively discuss this point, such as the *Well-Explained Reasoning*.[130] You should follow the tradition of teaching not through considering the size of the offerings and so forth, but [through considering] whether or not [the recipients] are suitable vessels for the Dharma.

How to Conduct Their Common Ending

Both the lama and the disciple should dedicate their roots of virtue from listening to and explaining the Dharma for complete enlightenment.

129. The verse states, "View all compounded phenomena like / Shooting stars, mistaken appearances, lamps, / Illusions, dewdrops, bubbles, / Dreams, lightning, and clouds."
130. Tib. *rNam bshad rig pa*. I have not been able to discover who wrote this text.

Day Five

[In the *Guide to the Bodhisattva's Way of Life*], the great bodhisattva Shantideva proclaimed,

> This leisure and endowment is difficult to acquire;
> Having attained it, accomplish the aims of beings.
> If you don't accomplish its benefit in this life,
> How can you get such a perfect endowment in a future life?

As this states, a human life such as this is very difficult to acquire, and we will only have it this one time. This life that we have acquired also has great meaning. In dependence upon this life, we are capable of attaining the state of temporary higher status and the ultimate goodness of omniscience. If we don't accomplish that here in this life, we will not attain it in a future life. Adjust your motivation by thinking, "Right now I am going to listen for the sake of extracting its essence."

Having given this short introduction, Pabongkha Rinpoche covered the headings.

How to Sequentially Guide the Disciple with the Actual Instructions

How to sequentially guide the disciple with the actual instructions begins with proper reliance upon the spiritual guide. This is the root of the path in dependence upon which you actually train the mind and for which there are two stages. The phrase [from the above sentence] that states "How to sequentially guide the disciple" refers to the commentary itself.

Pabongkha Rinpoche

Even the mere [point in the outline] about "the root of the path" and so forth is of extraordinarily great importance, since every realization, from [that of the preciousness of] our leisure and endowment up to [realization of] the union [of no more learning], stems from this. The phrase "in dependence upon" has its "source word,"[131] which comes from the *Thirty*

131. Tib. *byung khungs kyi sgra.*

Verses[132] [by Vasubandhu]. Whatever its origins, all realizations are generated in dependence upon the spiritual guide.

[How to Sequentially Guide the Disciple with the Actual Instructions] has two sections:

1. A Slightly Elaborate Explanation for the Sake of Attaining Certainty
2. The Characteristics of the Relying Disciple

A Slightly Elaborate Explanation for the Sake of Attaining Certainty

Je [Tsongkhapa] stated, "A disciple generating a single good quality in his [or her] mental continuum . . ."[133] He also stated, "The foundation of all good qualities is the foremost kind [guru],"[134] as well as, "The [source] of mundane and supramundane virtue and excellence . . ." [Geshe] Potowa proclaimed, "There is nothing more important than a guru for accomplishing liberation." Just as we can't know whether we have erred in our travels for even one day on a roadway if we don't have someone [with us] who knows the way, so without a guru to guide us to the state of liberation and omniscience we are like a blind person; therefore, it is extremely important that once we rely properly upon a guru from the beginning, we do so unerringly. The person to follow for that is a fully qualified spiritual guide. When it comes to a guide to liberation and omniscience, if we rely upon any guru that happens to come along, we will be led astray on mistaken paths. Geshe Potowa stated,

> If a disciple relies upon a lama who drinks alcohol, the disciple will also start drinking alcohol. If a disciple relies upon a good and conscientious lama, the disciple will also become good and conscientious.

132. Tib. *Sum cu pa.* Skt. *Trimsikakarika.*
133. This is a direct quote from Tsongkhapa's *Middle-Length Treatise on the Stages of the Path.*
134. This is the opening line of the lamrim prayer entitled *Foundation of All Good Qualities.*

There are also numerous teachings about the power of a fully qualified lama who holds each of the three sets of vows. The *Ornament of the Mahayana Sutras* declares,

> Rely upon a spiritual guide who is subdued, is pacified, is thoroughly pacified,
> Has superior good qualities, is diligent, has a wealth of scriptures,
> Has a realization of suchness, is skilled in speaking,
> Has a compassionate nature, and has abandoned weariness.

Therefore, it is simply not enough to act like a lama without possessing the full qualifications of a lama. Regarding the term "subdued," it is not sufficient that a person have a gentle mode of behavior of body and speech; he [or she] must have subdued his own mind. Although to others on the outside he may seem to have a peaceful and disciplined manner, if the guru's mind is not disciplined, it will be like teaching beneficial instructions to a leper infested with leprosy. Although there is a tradition of subduing the mind, [the mind] must be subdued through the three higher trainings. The term "subdued" refers to the training in moral discipline. "Pacified" is concentration. "Thoroughly pacified" is wisdom. The Vinaya states,

> Directing through constant effort with
> A bridle of a hundred piercing sharp spikes is
> Appropriate for reining in the horse-like mind;
> These are the [vows of the] pratimoksha.

Our mind is similar to an untamed wild horse, and the subduing bridle is the training in the pratimoksha. The thing capable of subduing someone who has come under the influence of the afflictions is also the moral discipline of the pratimoksha. There are various interpretations of "a hundred spikes" and "piercing"; the first term is understood to be "pure," as explained in the commentary to the sutra, and to mean "pacified." Thus, with respect to being properly trained and so forth, this refers to the way of being properly trained in the training of moral discipline. Subduing the horse[-like mind] through the training in concentration is like [the horse] remaining happily within its stable.

Not only should [a spiritual guide] be endowed with good qualities of the realization of training in wisdom, but he [or she] should have good qualities superior to your own. This is also the case for your friends with whom you spend your leisure time, such as your roommates and so forth. The Supreme Seventh Conqueror [that is, the Seventh Dalai Lama] stated,

> The unbearable scent of faults, by which
> We are easily defiled and which are difficult to remove—
> This comes from the bad activities of immoral
> Friends with whom we associate.

Dromtonpa proclaimed,

> An inferior person who associates with a noble person will not reach beyond the ranks of a middling person.
> If a superior person associates with an inferior person, he [or she] will easily become an inferior person.

Previously, there were two monks from the region of Phenpo,[135] one of whom drank alcohol and the other didn't. The first went to Ratreng and the other went to Lhasa. The one who drank alcohol met the Kadampa lamas, due to which he quit drinking. The one who didn't drink alcohol met some bad companions, whereby he became a drinker. This example shows that you must be careful about associating with the "dogs" that are bad friends. Evil friends are like dogs that cause bite wounds to your moral discipline and state of liberation and omniscience; therefore, you must act with the utmost caution. Instead, rely upon a virtuous teacher with pure moral discipline and supreme wisdom who is endowed with the good qualities of scripture and realization. The *Sayings of the Four Extremes of the Kadampas*[136] states,

> I try to emulate those old men of Ratreng.

The old men of Ratreng are Drom[tonpa] Rinpoche and the others. If you don't try to emulate the good qualities of your lama and companions, you

135. Tib. 'Phen po. A place in Tibet a short distance north of Lhasa.
136. Tib. *bKa' gdams pa mtha' bzhi'i zhal nas.*

will not have their good qualities either in this life or in future lives. You should look to the biographies of those qualified beings such as Je Tsongkhapa, your own lama, and so forth for examples to look up to.

With respect to "diligent," this means being endowed with the diligence of intense application and the diligence of constant application. The disciple should be subdued through the transmission of the Dharma; therefore, [the lama] must have "a wealth of scriptures." When a Mahayana guru explains the Dharma, he should skillfully teach through scriptural reasoning and analogies.

Regarding the end of the teaching, you should conclude with advice about the teaching. Regarding realization of the selflessness of phenomena, this is the realization arisen from meditation on the selflessness of phenomena or, alternatively, "suchness" and so forth. Regarding this, when the selflessness of persons has been ascertained "through one's own power," this means it has arisen from your own contemplations. Reaching a correct assumption by relying upon the guru's teachings of scripture and realization is "through the power of others." Ascertaining an inferential cognition through one's own power of analyzing scripture and realization is from your former higher training in wisdom and not through proclamation. Regarding this, it is a special wisdom of realization that is generated from analyzing any appropriate meaning of the scriptures, such as the unique characteristic of the first of the four noble truths. Regarding this, it is either a direct realization of emptiness or an inferential realization of emptiness in dependence upon the reasoning of dependent arising and so forth. Alternatively, if the [lama] hasn't even [attained that degree of realization], [then] he [or she] must have ascertained a correct assumption of emptiness in dependence upon the transmission of teachings and so forth. At the very least, he should be someone who is skilled in explaining it perfectly to others through scripture and reasoning, to develop an unmistaken understanding about the meaning of emptiness in others. Otherwise, he will not know how to guide someone along the complete path. With respect to being "skilled in speaking," which causes [the meaning] to be transmitted into the mind, this means skill in explaining in such a way that it is easy for the disciple to understand. Moreover, with respect to "compassionate" skill in transmitting to the mind, this means compassion for the disciple. Regarding "abandoned weariness," this means being able to withstand the trials of teaching the Dharma.

With respect to five of the ten qualities, the last three refer to the good quality of caring for your disciples. Je Rinpoche [Tsongkhapa] stated,

> Of all activities, teaching
> Is the supreme activity.

Also, the *Collection of Uplifting Sayings*[137] states,

> The munis do not wash away negative karma with water;
> They do not dispel the suffering of migrating beings with their hands;
> They do not transfer their realizations of suchness to others:
> They liberate migrating beings through teaching the truth of reality.

Regarding "the truth of reality," this is the good quality that the Buddha himself attained, which he taught to his disciples. This is the supreme activity of the Buddha. If you combine this with the four noble truths, the munis do not dispel with their hands true causal origins that come from true sufferings and true origins; it is not as though they wash away the negative karma of the resultant true suffering, nor do they transfer their good qualities of the path of cessation to the minds of their disciples, and so on. Among the ten qualifications, the five that are most important to possess are (1–3) the three higher trainings, (4) the realization of suchness, and (5) compassion. With respect to the word "converse"[138] used by [Geshe] Potowa, this is an archaic term. With respect to "discussion"[139] and "loving affection,"[140] these are merely names for compassion.

With respect to explaining their benefits, the teachings of Gyalwa Kelsang [Gyatso, the Seventh Dalai Lama,] explain that the benefits of giving follow from faithfully offering tea and so forth to the assembly of Sangha. Although there are various ways in which the holy beings have explained

137. Tib. *Ched du brjod pa'i tshoms.*
138. Tib. *glang bo.*
139. Tib. *gleng mo.*
140. Tib. *drin du gcags.*

the Dharma, such as skillfully and unskillfully, we should not seek out faults in their presentations but instead seek out their good explanations of the essential points of practice and so forth. Although Chusang Lama [Yeshe Gyatso] Rinpoche,[141] Trichen Khenrab Wangchug,[142] Longdol Rinpoche,[143] and Dorje Chang Kelsang Khedrup[144] were accomplished scholars, they had various ways of teaching, such as gently and roughly as well as quickly and slowly. And although Trichen Jangchub Chöphel[145] was also not a skilled speaker, through his discussions with others about the oral lineage, he subdued the mental continuums of them all. He had a bald head and rubbed snot on his head, and much of what he taught was very difficult to understand.

According to previous reports, when it comes to a lama, it is very important that the person you choose to rely upon is fully qualified and is called "lama" because he [or she] is someone who can guide you along the path to liberation and omniscience. The incomparable Dagpo Lhaje [that is, Gampopa][146] also proclaimed,

> Once you have renounced this life, your activities become nothing but Dharma. For that, you must come into contact with an infallible guru, and you must come into contact with an infallible Dharma. If you come into contact with an erroneous guru, [then] you come into contact with an erroneous Dharma, and you will not generate an unmistaken path in your mental continuum. If you don't generate that, [then] an erroneous result will arise in your mental continuum. Once that happens, you will not become enlightened. Therefore, when you come into contact with an infallible guru, you come into contact with an infallible Dharma. Through coming into contact with them, you will generate an infallible path in your

141. Tib. Chu bzang ye shes rgya mtso (1789–1856).
142. Tib. Blo bzang mkhyen rab dbang phyug (?–1872), the Seventy-Sixth Ganden Tripa.
143. Tib. Klong rdol Bla ma Ngag dbang blo bzang (1719–1794).
144. Tib. Chu bzang dge bshes skal bzang mkhas grub (eighteenth century).
145. Tib. Shar rtse Byang chub chos 'phel, the Sixty-Seventh Ganden Tripa and the first Trijang Rinpoche.
146. Dagpo Lhaje is the proper name of Milarepa's foremost disciple, most commonly referred to as Gampopa (1079–1153).

> mental continuum. By generating that in your mental continuum, an infallible result will arise in your mental continuum.

Although in this day and age, due to the force of the passage of time, it is rare for someone to have a complete set of all the characteristics, it is nevertheless inappropriate to rely upon someone who has either an equal measure of faults and good qualities or a predominance of faults, [because] a qualified lama should at least be someone with good qualities that surpass his faults. You should rely on someone who holds the next life as more important than this life; between the Dharma and the mundane, holds the Dharma as more important; and between self and others, holds others as more important. In India there were traditions such as examining the guru for twelve years. There are charlatans in the extreme border regions who are called "lamas." The Bonpos and so forth who give the empowerments, blessing permissions, and so forth from Jamgon [Tsongkhapa's] Hearing Lineage are creating the causes for everyone involved—both themselves and others—to go to the lower realms. Although the [students] are not at fault because they are destitute of Dharma, they don't examine the spiritual guide, like a thirsty person drinking poisonous water at the moment of death. Once we encounter this sort of thing, if we rely upon such teachers, even the Dharma protectors won't know how to help us.

In general, a unique characteristic of lamas of either the new or old Kadam is that they should keep their good qualities hidden like a lamp inside a vase and devote themselves to the welfare of migrating beings and the teachings. Otherwise lamas may be completely deceitful, and although they may profess to work for the welfare of the teachings and living beings, they are in fact great frauds; therefore, you must examine them carefully.

The Characteristics of the Relying Disciple

Regarding the term "impartial,"[147] this means they are not biased and listen with complete sincerity. The term "biased" means having attachment

147. As before, the terms in quotation marks are directly from Tsongkhapa's *Middle-Length Treatise on the Stages of the Path*.

to your own system and hatred for the systems of others. Once we think "My Dharma tradition is best" and fall into partiality, the teachings that are being explained will not enter into our minds. Regarding the term "wise," this means endowed with the intelligence to distinguish between good and bad. If a disciple is intelligent yet is without wisdom, profound explanations of the oral instruction and so forth will have very little impact, making it very important for them to understand through things such as stories and anecdotes. For example, once, while Gyalwa Kelsang [Gyatso, the Seventh Dalai Lama,] was teaching the Dharma, someone said, "I learned something new: Lhundrub Fortress in Phenpo was also known as Mai-Cha Castle!" We should not let this sort of thing happen to us. If the [students] are not "diligent," although they may have faith in and listen to the Dharma and the lama, his discourses and so forth will be wasted.

How the [Disciple] Properly Relies upon Him has two sections:

1. How to Rely through Thought
2. How to Rely through Action

How to Rely through Thought has two sections:

1. How to Apply It to the Root of Faith
2. Generating Devotion by Recalling His Kindness

How to Apply It to the Root of Faith

In general, faith is the root of all virtuous Dharmas. Previously, someone requested of Atisha, "Give me some teachings," to which he replied, "Hey, hey. My hearing is good—quite good. My oral instruction is to have faith, faith, faith!" [This is like the story that] because others did not understand the indications that [a certain lama] was [actually] a pandita, they called him "Konchog Tala-la" when in fact his name was Konchog Dronmé. [The point is that] it is a great fault if you don't have any faith inside. Previously, in India, a famine arose in a certain country and someone named Ama Genmo recited the mantra of the goddess Chunda as BALÉ BULÉ and so on. Although she pronounced the mantra incorrectly, when Ama cooked stones and ate them [to avoid starvation, due to her faith in the goddess she] became youthful and vibrant. These sorts of things will happen if you have faith. Also in India, a lama said MARI LEDZA to someone, who understood it to be an oral instruction and recited it [faithfully], whereby his benefit to others expanded immensely. With respect to common attainments, despite making mistakes in the oral instructions, if you have faith you will reach attainment. However, for the supreme attainments, you must be unmistaken with respect to the oral instructions. And example of the common [attainments] is that despite the fact that the siddha Darcha mistakenly recited the mantra of Kilaya as VAJRA KYI LI KYI LA, after a competition in miraculous powers, he threw his *phurba* and planted it right into a cliff face.

Although there are many objects of faith—such as faith in the four noble truths, cause and effect, and so on—in this case we are referring to faith in the guru. If you wonder whether or not the guru is a buddha and then come to the conclusion that he [or she] is an actual buddha, you will receive the blessing of an actual buddha through your act of faith. [Geshe] Potowa stated,

> The blessings of the guru are not really
> Great or small; they depend on you.

There is a story of an old woman who had faith in a dog's tooth, whereby it produced relics and so forth. In this case, she received the blessings of an actual tooth of the Buddha. Although the lama may be an actual buddha, if you don't have that perception, you will not receive his blessings, as is related in the historical account of Devadatta and the Teacher. Drom[tonpa] asked Atisha why, despite having so many people practicing meditation, they had not attained any special good qualities, to which Atisha replied, "All the good qualities of the Mahayana, whether great or small, depend on the guru. You Tibetans don't perceive your gurus as anything other than ordinary beings; therefore, how could you develop [any good qualities]?"

Ensapa also proclaimed,

> In short, whether great or small realizations come from meditating
> Depends on whether you have great or small faith.
> Contemplate the good qualities and don't look for faults
> In the kind lama, the source of all attainments.
>
> Hold this instruction as your main practice;
> May there be no obstructions to perfecting this sacred oath.

Once you have the perception of your guru as an actual buddha, you will receive the blessing of an actual buddha. Accordingly, the degree to which you have great or middling faith in him as a shravaka, pratyekabuddha, and so on determines the degree of great or middling blessings. Drikung Jigten Gonpo[148] stated,

> If the sun of faith and devotion does not shine on
> The snow mountain of the guru's four bodies,
> The stream of blessings will not emerge.
> Therefore, put great effort into this mind of faith and devotion.

Although at this point there is usually an outline [topic] that states, "Vajradhara said that the guru is a buddha," this is not taught in [Je Tsongkhapa's] *Middle-Length Treatise on the Stages of the Path* as a method of training. Whether or not you see the guru as a buddha depends on your viewpoint. The Teacher said that acts such as having contempt for the Tathagata, disparaging him, and so forth will lead to rebirth in hell, as a hungry ghost, and so on. This statement is unmistaken when considering beings such a Devadatta, Sunakshatra, and others who looked for faults in the Teacher, whereby they perceived him as faulty. For example, when a teacher doesn't sleep most of the night and does recitations, a student who is fond of sleep will see what is actually a good quality as a fault. If a student who is fond of drinking alcohol has a teacher who is a fully ordained monk and who drinks alcohol, he will see what is actually a fault as a good

148. Jigten Gonpo (1143–1217) was one of the eight main disciples of Phagmo Drugpa and the founder of the Drikung Kagyu tradition.

quality. Serlingpa held the view of the Chittamatra [that is, Mind Only school], whereas Atisha held the view of the Madhyamaka [that is, Middle Way]. Although [the former] is lower than [the latter], through Atisha's faith he treated Serlingpa as the most exalted of his gurus.

Generating Devotion by Recalling His Kindness

Delight and faith are not the same. Faith delights in perceiving the good qualities of the guru. Devotion[149] for him brings an understanding of modesty from contemplating his kindness, and you act with reverence for the guru. Therefore, if you generate these [two] in your mental continuum, it is an individual mental factor. There is a saying that states,

> The guru's kindness is greater than even the Buddha.
> His compassion is greater than all the conquerors.

From the perspective of his kindness, the guru is superior to the Buddha, yet from the perspective of his good qualities he is *not* superior to the Buddha. Although someone might say that he possesses good qualities superior to the Buddha, if he were superior to the Buddha, [then the Buddha] would have faults to overcome, so he would have bad karma and would not be a noble being. The way of recalling [the guru's] kindness that is presented here has its source in the collection of sutras and is inconceivable. [The point in] the outline about the lama's kindness being superior to that of the Buddha is explained during the section on training. Regarding this point, Geshe Chömawa and others were unable to cope with [memorizing] the verses recalling his kindness [but found that] if they could remember them by reciting Phago Rinpoche's verses for recalling [the guru's] kindness from the *Essence of Nectar Stages of the Path*,[150] it became extremely clear [for them]. Whether or not you recite these verses, [be

149. In the preceding two sentences the Tibetan terms *dad pa* and *gus pa* have been translated as "faith" and "devotion," respectively. Here they are being used interchangeably. Although they are not synonymous, they are two qualities of the same mental factor that recalls the kindness of the guru.

150. Tib. *Lam rim bdud rtsi'i snying po*. This text was composed by Yeshe Tsondru (1761–1816), whose full name in Tibetan is Phag mgo Bla ma Ye shes brtson 'grus.

sure to] recall the kindness of the [gurus] who taught you the alphabet [and those who] gave you vows, empowerments, commentaries, and so on. Atisha the Great would make such proclamations as "I have no good qualities. They are this lama's, and they are that lama's . . ."[151] and "They are like wet nurses feeding [us] the milk of good qualities . . ." The above verse[152] is from Sudhana recalling the kindness of his spiritual guide, the meaning of which is clearly explained in the notes on the eight great commentaries on the lamrim.[153]

151. Here Atisha is pointing out the qualities that he has actually belong to various lamas by saying, "This good quality belongs to this particular lama, this other quality belongs to this other lama 'so and so,'" and in this way he attributes all of his qualities to his gurus.

152. I have translated the entire set of verses as presented in Kachen Yeshe Gyaltsen's *Lama Chöpa* commentary, published by Dechen Ling Press as *Manjushri's Innermost Secret*, which reads, "The *Array of Stalks Sutra* states:

> I have come to this place after single-pointedly contemplating,
> 'My spiritual masters who teach the Dharma
> Thoroughly reveal the good qualities of phenomena
> And then reveal the bodhisattva's way of life in its entirety.
>
> Because they generate [these qualities] they are like a mother,
> Because they give the milk of good qualities they are like wet nurses,
> They thoroughly train me in the limbs of enlightenment,
> These spiritual masters expel the aspects of harm.
>
> They are like doctors that free me from old age and death,
> They send down a rain of nectar like Indra, the lord of gods,
> Like the full moon, they cause the virtuous Dharma to flourish,
> Like the illuminating sun, they reveal the way to peace.
>
> Toward friends and enemies they are like mountains,
> Their minds are unassailable like an ocean,
> They completely protect me like a boat.'
> Thinking in this way, I Sudhana have come here.
>
> These bodhisattvas have developed my mind,
> They have produced my enlightenment as a son of the buddhas,
> I praise these spiritual masters as buddhas;
> With these virtuous thoughts, I have come here.
>
> By protecting the world, they are like heroes,
> And have become my captains, protectors, and refuge.
> They are eyes that produce happiness in me;
> With such a mind I honor these spiritual masters."

153. These notes became the basis for Pabongkha Rinpoche's *Liberation in Our Hands*.

How to Rely [upon Your Guru] through Action

"Venerate your guru with material belongings, service, [and practice]": these three ways of venerating your guru are the supreme, middling, and least.[154] To undertake the best way of relying upon him [or her], when you are together with your guru you should not seek out some other visualization for your guru yoga. Do not go to the guru if you have the wish to listen to the Dharma but don't have any idea of relying upon him as a guru. And if you also don't have any idea of listening to the Dharma as it is in monastery rules,[155] the *poshadha* confessional sutra,[156] and the recitation lessons,[157] do not go to the guru.[158] Both the Dharma teacher sitting on a golden throne or a silver throne and the one in your room sitting on a hairless tanned leather seat should be considered equally as gurus. Although you may have a nice way of properly relying upon the Dharma instructor once he sits on a throne, if you don't have a nice way of relying upon the teacher instructing you in texts, you have severed the root of all excellent accumulation of merit. While from the disciple's side, you should be in accordance with [the guru devotion of] Dromtonpa and Geshe Tolungpa, from the lama's side, he [or she] absolutely must not have even the slightest concern for material things. The oral instructions of Geshe Sharawa (1070–1141) state,

> Thus, between two [hypothetical] lamas—one who thinks, "If disciples don't offer material gifts, my prestige will decline," and another who feels, "If I have offerings, it will increase my pride"—despite calling them [both] "lama," the former has only his own interests at heart. We use the term "lama" for someone who is pleased by practice and does not have even the slightest concern for material gifts. Someone who does the

154. The list is inverted in the Tibetan. Practice, service, and material things are in the proper sequence of best, middling, and least.
155. Tib. *dgon gyi sgrigs lam.*
156. Tib. *gso sbyong gi mdo.*
157. Tib. *brtsi bzhag bskyor.*
158. This means don't go to a lama seeking teachings without the proper prerequisites previously listed for receiving teachings.

> opposite of that is not a suitable lama for anyone accomplishing liberation.

These words are extremely to the point. The teaching states, "A lama striving for material offerings is not a lama," which accords with the teachings of Gungtang Jampalyang. Je Marpa [Chökyi Lodro (1012–1097)] stated,

> The Great Magician[159] never has any wealth whatsoever,
> And Ngogtön[160] is my attendant.
> I am not strict and liberal with the oral instructions;
> I act according to the holy Dharma.

With respect to undertaking the essential practice according to the teachings, delighting your guru with the offering of practice or serving is the best. Milarepa stated,

> This practice of voluntarily enduring hardship with fortitude
> Is service to delight my fatherly guru.

The *Fifty Verses of Guru Devotion*[161] states,

> That generosity will always become
> An offering to all the buddhas;
> That offering is the accumulation of merit.
> Through accumulation you accomplish the supreme attainment [of enlightenment].[162]

During a teaching on the way of training, there will also be explanations on the way to properly rely, on not relying, and on the faults of improperly relying. By virtue of properly relying on the guru, his [or her]

159. "The Great Magician" is a term of endearment used by Marpa for his student Milarepa.
160. This is Ngogtön Chökyi Dorje (1036–1106).
161. A translation of this is available in Kachen Yeshe Gyaltsen, *Manjushri's Innermost Secret*.
162. Pabongkha only quotes the first and the last line of this verse; however, I have included the entire verse for the sake of facilitating comprehension.

advice does not become a burden but becomes an ornament, in the same way others proudly bear the burden of mundane ornaments such as the numerous adornments of the head disciplinary monk of one of the great monasteries, with his padded garment, as well as the male and female householders in the marketplace with their ornate jewelry.[163]

A Concise Way of Practicing [the Preliminary Rituals] during the Meditation Session

There is an [instruction on how to practice] during the meditation session and the post-meditation session.[164] The virtuous actions of an entire human life can be reduced to day and night within a twenty-four-hour period. This can be further reduced into meditation sessions and post-meditation sessions. For the first type of session there are (1) the preparation, (2) the actual session, and (3) the conclusion. The actual session depends on whether the preparations are brought into the path. Even when it comes to making a cup of tea, you first need to prepare by assembling many good ingredients such as tea, butter, and so forth. For that reason, sweep your meditation room and arrange images of enlightened body, speech, and mind. The way the six preliminaries[165] are taught in this text is according to the biography of Guru Serlingpa. Next, from Atisha to the new and old Kadampas, it became very widespread. If we combine this with the preliminary ritual from *A Necklace of the Fortunate*,[166]

163. A head disciplinarian has to wear very heavy and uncomfortable garments as an indication of his status, yet he does so proudly and regards it as a sign of his greatness. Laypeople also wear heavy and uncomfortable jewelry with pride. In the same way, we should joyously engage in whatever instruction our lama gives us without considering it a burden.

164. At this point, Pabongkha diverges from the outlines of Tsongkhapa's *Middle-Length Treatise* and inserts the preliminary rituals as presented in the Second Panchen Lama's *Swift Path*, and then he completes the outline of how to rely upon the guru after the explanation of the preliminary rituals.

165. The six preliminaries are listed below but without separate headings. They are (1) cleaning the meditation space and setting out physical representations of enlightened body, speech, and mind; (2) arranging suitable offerings; (3) sitting in the correct meditation posture, going for refuge, and generating bodhichitta; (4) visualizing the field of merit; (5) accumulating merit and purifying negative karma through the seven-limbed prayer and the mandala offering; and (6) requesting the fields of merit for their blessing.

166. Tib. *sByor chos skal bzang mgrin rgyan.*

the power of its blessing will be unlike anything else, and the welfare of migrating beings will also be vastly increased.

The first of the preliminary rituals is **sweeping your room**, which has its source in the *Great Commentary to the Perfection of Wisdom in Eight Thousand Lines*, which states, "The bodhisattvas sit in their clean abodes in the cross-legged position." If we do things such as a great deal of cleaning even when a government official is coming to our house, yet we don't sweep our dwelling when we invite the gurus, the buddhas and bodhisattvas of the ten directions, all living beings, and so forth, then we will definitely incur a great wave of negative karma. In general, obscurations are purified by sweeping. It is also a way of attaining realizations, as taught in the biography of Lamchung. Because of that, there is nothing superior to this for purifying negative karma and obscurations if you take this into consideration while sweeping your dwelling. If you sweep for your own wish to be happy, [however,] it won't be beneficial.

Anathapindika of Jetavana Grove would give alms each and every day while sweeping the grove. One day, Anathapindika was unable to sweep the grove, so the Teacher, out of his great compassion, did the sweeping with his own golden hands that were like outstretched golden limbs. My guru said, "The previous incarnations of the Dalai Lama used to sweep with a broom with a handle wrapped in golden-colored fabric. The ends of the broom were worn down from so much sweeping that they looked like the end of a donkey's tail. [This broom] can currently be viewed in a reliquary box at the Potala." According to Choné Lama Rinpoche's lineage of teaching, "dust" is not dust particles but the dust of attachment and so forth in your way of relying upon the spiritual guide. In a similar way, it means the dust of nonfaith, and [the teaching] continues in this way to incorporate the complete path. Although you may be unable to sweep[167] because of illness, extreme old age, and so on, you should have someone such as your disciple sweep while you recite sayings such as "Dust is not earthly dust . . ." while you contemplate their meaning. If you sweep in this way, you receive five benefits: (1) your mind becomes pure, (2) others' minds become pure, (3) you delight the virtuous gods,

167. Although the term "sweep" is being used, it should be understood to mean any method of cleaning the monastery, temple, your meditation room, and so on.

(4) you accumulate the karma to be beautiful and so forth, and (5) in your next life you will be born in the god realms; these five were taught by the Buddha himself in the sutras. Although it states "the karma to be beautiful," it means pure moral discipline. Also, through sweeping you will go to the pure lands of a buddha.

To **arrange physical representations of enlightened body, speech, and mind**, you should set them out in the appropriate sequence of the lamrim and by considering the quality of the substance from which they are made. If we place Dharma protectors and so forth at the head of the row, we will incur the fault of contradicting our practice of going for refuge and so forth. We will receive absolutely no blessings whatsoever if we merely judge them according to their size and the value of their substance—whether composed of gold, copper, bronze, or clay. The teachings of Keutsang Jamyang Monlam state that if we discard our physical representations of enlightened body, speech, and mind someplace like a tsa tsa house because they are old, dirty, and so forth, we will be throwing away our merit. If we expel physical representations of enlightened body, speech, and mind far away, we will be expelling our merit far away. Instead, you should have the recognition that thinks "Those are the physical representations [of enlightened beings]." When you attain the concentration of the Dharma continuum,[168] the first level [that is, bhumi], and so forth, you will perceive these current physical representations as the actual supreme emanation bodies and enjoyment bodies, respectively.[169] Thoyon Lama was inseparable from a statue of Je [Tsongkhapa] that was only two thumb-lengths tall. This statue would converse with him, whereby he stated,

> Jamgon Lama wears a tall pointed pandit hat.
> His hands are in the mudra of turning the wheel of Dharma
> holding sword and scripture.
> He is not golden in color but appears golden in color.
> He is not made of composite but appears to be made of composite.

168. This is the third stage of the path of accumulation, which is the first of the five Mahayana paths.

169. On the stage of the Dharma continuum, you perceive all physical representations of enlightened body, speech, and mind as the supreme emanation bodies, and when you attain the first bodhisattva level (*bhumi*), you perceive them as the actual enjoyment bodies.

He composed expressions of worship during a retreat of accumulated recitations of Migtsema prayers, as related in his biography. With respect to arranging statues and tangkhas in the four directions of your room, you will accumulate negative karma by not having any concerns about things such as having your feet aimed in the direction of the three physical representations while you sleep.[170] You should repeatedly and respectfully view them and not think, "I am already very familiar with this statue of the Teacher since I am continuously inseparable from it." It is said in the sutras that it is sixteen times more beneficial to encounter a statue of the Buddha than the body of the actual Buddha; therefore, each time we come into the presence of statues of the Teacher, Atisha, Drom[tonpa], Je [Tsongkhapa], your lama, and so forth, we cause the atoms in the pure lands to tremble. Although you may not have a vast collection of statues, it is indispensable that at the very least you have a statue of Shakyamuni for the sake of remembering the Buddha and a statue of Je Tsongkhapa for the sake of remembering your guru.

It is said that for a scriptural support we should have a copy of a perfection of wisdom sutra such as the *Eight Thousand Lines*; therefore, you should definitely at least have an abridged version. If there are times when you can't even afford that, you should at least use the lamrim text that you use for your practice as an object of worship and place it in the row of religious symbols. Once you have these, it is permissible to bring them down from your altar and repeatedly and respectfully read them. If you only have ancient texts as supports of speech, you should use high-quality text covers and place them with your religious symbols.

For supports of mind, set out a stupa or vajra and bell. If you are someone like a simple monk and don't have many other things, it is acceptable to set out tsa tsas as the supports of mind. A scripture is the symbol of enlightened speech; an icon is the symbol of enlightened body; a stupa, a vajra and bell, and tsa tsas are symbols of enlightened mind. Therefore, it is utterly unacceptable for you to set your vajra and bell on the bare ground without a tablemat, and other such actions, as well as for you to disturb the fire in a Vajradaka burnt offering and the burning *gugal* and

170. In Indian and Tibetan culture it is considered extremely rude to point your feet in someone's direction.

white frankincense when you are doing things like village rituals. If you do such things, it will be no different from turning the entire body of the Teacher upside down and using his *ushnisha* to stir up the flames; therefore, you must use a tablemat.

There are two points with respect to **honestly acquiring offerings and arranging them beautifully**: (1) the substance of the offering and (2) the motivation. Regarding the substance of the offering, don't use things such as moldy parts of cheesecake or the yellow parts of your vegetables. At the very least, they should be clean and of good quality, and not inferior to your own enjoyments. You offer them for the sake of your own and others' enlightenment. With respect to "deceitful," there are two types of deceitfulness: (1) deceitful substances and (2) deceitful motivation. Concerning deceitful substances, although they may come from a householder, he or she should not contradict worldly conventions, such as by using the wrong measurements or the wrong amount of currency.

Regarding offerings produced from wealth that comes from things such as working as a butcher and hunting wild animals, although you may offer them, it is best if you don't do so. [For example,] in the past there was an old monk from Lhasa called Kunsang who would put lead weights inside yak meat [before he] put it on the scales; once he received butter in trade for it, he would quickly remove the lead weights. When he traded [the butter] away, he would again insert the lead [before weighing it]. We should not use even a little butter traded in this way. Later, he died, and he resides in the lower realms to this day. [Also,] many fish are killed in the Yarlung and the Kongpo[171] [rivers, and] there are those who burn the forest and plow the empty fields, and even their name comes from the Chinese. Although it is the tradition to affix pleasant-sounding names [to these types of activities], it is in fact an extremely wretched way to make a living. After those who burned the forest died, they went to the hot hells, and I took an oath to free them. [Nevertheless,] if the ordained receive wealth procured with deceptive motivation through the five forms of wrong livelihood, they can present them as offerings.

171. The Yarlung is a river situated 113 miles southeast of Lhasa; the Kongpo is another river near the Yarlung in southeastern Tibet.

Regarding the five [bad motivations]: (1) **Wishing for personal gain** is when you contrive a way of acting so that your bodily activities accord with the Dharma. (2) **Flattery** is speaking very skillfully with the motivation of hoping to get something from someone such as your benefactor. (3) **Hinting** is like telling your benefactor things such as "Last year my benefactor gave me tea that was enormously beneficial" while speaking in a skillful way, thinking that he or she might give you some more this year. (4) **Acquiring gifts through gifts** is when you offer something small in the hope of receiving something larger in return. (5) **Coercion** is forcefully taking something that didn't come to you, such as when someone like an official forcefully takes something. The materials acquired through such bad motivation are not suitable to present as an offering, yet if we have already obtained them in this way, it is best to offer them. According to the lineage of teaching, these come from asking for something merely discretely, therefore, this wrong form of livelihood is extremely pervasive, and both the lama and disciple are in great danger of being defiled by this. Therefore, you should learn about these in detail from the *Well-Explained Reasoning*.

Regarding a good motivation in general, offerings and so forth are very important, as further related in the biography of [the Kadam] Geshe Ben [Gungyal (eleventh century)]. We say, "How can the motivation be the main factor?" But if we don't follow the proper procedure for offerings and act inappropriately, it is a grave fault. Moreover, [the offerings] should beautifully arranged. The way of arranging the torma decorations, the shape of the torma, the offering bowls, and so forth should be as beautiful as possible, and they should have been procured in the purest possible way. Atisha the Great also said that Tibetan water had eight special features; therefore, if we offer water oblations, we attain numerous benefits from offering it. The way of presenting other offerings will also be explained later.

Day Six

[In his introductory verses to *The Great Treatise on the Stages of the Path to Enlightenment,*] the king of the Dharma Tsongkhapa the Great proclaimed,

> In this day and age, those seriously pursuing yoga have done little study, while
> Those who have done much study are not skilled in the essential points of practice.
> They view most of the scriptures with partisanship
> Because they are powerless to discern the meaning of the scriptures through logical investigation.
>
> So I have seen that they are off the path pleasing the wise,
> The supreme instructions on the complete essential points of the teachings;
> Explaining this path of the great trailblazers
> Would bring utter joy to my mind.

In this day and age, although some may engage in practice with the hopes of accomplishing good future lives, because some people haven't studied, they deviate down mistaken paths. Others study their entire lives but do not practice, so they can't accomplish good future lives. There are also some who, despite accomplishing both study and practice, are confused about the limbs of the path and that which merely resembles it. By clinging to refuge in scriptures alone, too many of them stagnate due to lack of the complete essential points of the teaching on the path.

We are extremely fortunate to have something to practice such as this [*Middle-Length Treatise on the Stages of the Path*], which embodies all the aspects of the paths of sutra and mantra. Je Rinpoche [Tsongkhapa] also said that explaining the stages of the path brings extreme joy to his mind. Listen with faith, devotion, and joy to these teachings on the stages of the path that is the sole path traversed by all the buddhas, and put them into practice.

Pabongkha Rinpoche gave the oral transmission of the outlines.

The third section of the preliminary rituals is **sitting on a comfortable seat with the eight essential bodily features**—or whatever way of sitting is most comfortable—and **going for refuge and generating bodhichitta within a particularly virtuous state of mind**. Draw a white swastika[172] under your seat to represent a Dharma wheel. Although it is not permissible in the sutra tradition to generate a boundary marker, you can leave little stones in the four directions of your retreat room and think of them as the four guardian kings.[173] Jointed grass is used for increasing your lifespan and so forth. Kusha grass creates a special auspiciousness exemplified in the Teacher's biography and is for increasing the wisdom to develop realizations of the lamrim and so forth. The back of your cushion should be slightly elevated so that if you meditate for extended periods, your lower back won't become sore. So that your central channel will remain straight, you should sit in the sevenfold posture of Vairochana. When you combine that with the flow of the breath, it becomes eight. These are extremely important. As Marpa proclaimed,

172. Despite its strong negative association since the 1930s, the swastika is an ancient Indian symbol for inner strength, stability, and good luck. Hitler took the symbol and either intentionally or unintentionally recreated it so that it is drawn in the opposite direction.

173. The four great kings are Vaishravana, Virudhaka, Dhritarashtra, and Virupaksha, who have taken oaths to protect the Buddha's teachings. In the practice of tantra, you generate boundary markers as protective deities associated with the particular practice you are engaged in. Since the lamrim is related to the sutra teachings, generating such deities is not permitted. However, it is permissible to generate the four great kings.

> Even if you combined all the profound oral instructions of Tibet, they could not compare to my system of sitting in the sevenfold posture of Vairochana alone!

When these are combined with mantra, each one has a profound, essential point for each part of the completion stage. If your body is straight, your channels will be straight; if your channels are straight, the winds flowing within them will be straight; once those are flowing properly, the meditating mind that is its mount will become serviceable. While doing practices such as restraining the winds during the completion stage, most people's teeth and lips will naturally close. Press your tongue against your palate so that when you are in a deep state of meditative absorption, saliva doesn't drip from your mouth and lead to your mouth becoming dry. Your head should be bent slightly so that it causes a slight pressure on your larynx. In the Nyingma tradition, there is a way of focusing the gaze while saying, "The best is the truth body, the middling is the enjoyment body, and the least is the emanation body"; however, you should focus your gaze at the tip of the nose. The phrase "seven Dharmas of Vairochana" is used because it is the way the Buddha Vairochana sits; therefore, you should set your gaze according to his, which will cause the mind to remain in a state of mental tranquility and in turn stabilize your development of realizations. Although you don't close your eyes, when stabilization occurs you will be incapable of seeing things such as your cup on the table before you.

All your meditations, such as the generation and completion stage, the lamrim, and so on, should not come under the influence of mental sinking and excitement. Thus, upright physical posture has a specification of twelve good qualities, such as being able to sit upright consistently. Sitting on a cushion of grass as well as the ground has other good qualities, which is why it is important that they be carried out in their entirety. For example, although you may be meditating on love, compassion, and bodhichitta for living beings, during the generation of some [emotion] such as strong anger, you will not be able to establish it clearly. For that reason, you need to transform your mind into a neutral state similar to a white woolen cloth. The way to transform it is through counting breaths. It is taught that you can visualize your negative karma and obscurations being expelled with the exhalation and the blessing entering you [with the inhalation] while your breath is flowing in and out; however, this is said to do nothing more than dispel obstructions and enhance [the state of your mind], for the actual meditation consists of counting breaths.

Next, [there] is **how to adjust your motivation**. Your motivation is very important. The *Collection of Uplifting Sayings* states,

> Dharma is preceded by the mind;
> A swift mind is the principal mind . . .

Nagarjuna stated [in the *Precious Garland*],

> That which is produced by attachment, anger,
> And ignorance is nonvirtuous.
> That which is produced by nonattachment,
> Nonhatred, and the absence of ignorance is virtuous.

Je Rinpoche [Tsongkhapa] proclaimed,

> If the thoughts are good, the grounds and paths will also be good.
> If the thoughts are bad, the grounds and paths will also be bad.
> Everything depends upon one's thoughts.

For that reason, in general a good thought is very important, and in particular motivation is the most important factor for Dharma practitioners. The *Kadam Mind Training*[174] states,

> There are two activities at the beginning and end.

This is stating that to begin by adjusting your motivation and conclude with dedication are very important. A good or bad motivation will determine whether or not something becomes the Dharma. This point is exemplified by the account of four persons reciting prayers to Tara or

174. Tib. *bKa' gdams blo sbyong*. This line appears in the *Seven-Point Mind Training* composed by Geshe Chekawa.

going for refuge.[175] Although your merit may be very slight, if you give rise to renunciation and bodhichitta, your virtuous roots will become very strong. Je Lama [Tsongkhapa] asked the great meditators of Tibet how they [thought they] should begin their meditations, and some of them did not know the correct answer other than to say, "By going for refuge." Later, Panchen [Losang] Chögyan replied perfectly by stating,

> You should examine your mind well
> At the very start of every meditation,
> In accordance with the phrase "in the Indian language,"
> As you, the incomparable supreme lama, assert.

You should learn how to properly adjust your motivation in accordance with this narration and know how to perfectly establish it at the beginning of the lamrim. This also explains how to formulate your motivation. At all times you should formulate a good motivation. You should have already accomplished bodhichitta while you are on your way to the assembly at the debate yard, and [if you do so, then] your virtuous roots will arise with such great power that even many thousands of golden coins could not compare to it. Your activities will become those of a bodhisattva and will become a cause for attaining the state of enlightenment.

While **visualizing the objects of refuge**, the Teacher's right and left hands reveal that he himself has destroyed the four *maras*,[176] and [this] is a symbolic gesture that we as practitioners will destroy them. Your root guru's right hand is in the mudra of expounding Dharma, and his [or her] left is in the mudra of meditative equipoise, so that the right is study and the left is practice. Alternatively, the meditative equipoise of the left hand symbolizes that with the meditative equipoise on suchness, [your guru] teaches the Dharma by expounding the Dharma of conventional reality from within that state. This is a unique attribute of a buddha. You should establish a definite number of lamas with whom you have established a Dharma connection. If someone asks us, "How many lamas do you have?" and we have to count from the bottom, this is a sign that

175. These examples are explained in Pabongkha Rinpoche's *Liberation in Our Hands.*

176. The four maras, or "demons," are (1) death, (2) afflictive emotions, (3) contaminated aggregates, and (4) the son of a god. It is only the last of these who is an actual living being.

we don't practice at all! The *General Confession of the Thirty-Five Buddhas*[177] has greater power than other practices for purifying negative karma and obscurations. There are limitless benefits from reciting and hearing the names of the seven sugatas from the *Medicine Buddha Sutra* eight times, a hundred times, and so forth. It is taught that, by hearing the name of Medicine Guru, there is absolutely no chance of going to the lower realms. Atisha the Great stated,

> Merely hearing the name of Guru Medicine Buddha
> Dispels the suffering of going to the lower realms and dispels the illness of the three poisons.

Panchen [Losang] Chögyan also stated,

> Great assembly of Bhagavans, please turn your attention to me.
> Previously, the seven sugatas made pure prayers
> Promising [to protect] Shakyamuni's teachings
> When they are ending at their final five-hundred-year period.

As this states, having previously assembled, the seats of the eight medicine guru sugatas[178] made great prayers, such as the four, the eight, the twelve, and so on, and by making aspirations established their activities during the final five hundred years of Shakyamuni's teachings. The traditional interpretation of the lineage is that we should combine this point [of the preliminary rituals] with the recitation of the names of the eight medicine guru sugatas for the sake of evoking their heart commitment. It is said that due to the thousand buddhas of the fortunate eon coming to this world,[179] it is excellent to visualize as fully as possible at this point, due to their powerful connection with us. We should also visualize the eight close bodhisattvas, the twelve fortunate bodhisattvas, the six-

177. Tib. *lTung bshags kyi sangs rgyas so lnga.*

178. There are seven medicine buddhas—known as the seven sugatas—and Buddha Shakyamuni makes the eighth.

179. The thousand buddhas of the fortunate eon are buddhas who will appear in this world and turn the wheel of Dharma by manifesting the aspect of fully enlightened beings. Buddha Shakyamuni is the fourth of these thousand.

teen incomparable bodhisattvas, the twelve pratyekabuddhas, the sixteen shravakas and so forth, the heroes such as Khandakapala, the heroines such as Partzandi, and the principal protectors of the Dharma of the three types of beings [all] as the supramundane guardians of the Dharma. It is improper to visualize among the field of merit those who, despite being wisdom beings, in an interpretive sense have assumed the aspect of arrogant spirits. Previously, someone showed Tse[chok] Ling Yongzin Pandita a depiction of the field of merit, and he was not pleased to see [the protector] Pehar drawn among the field of merit and remarked that it would have been better to paint a drawing of a jewel as a substitute.

The Dharma of realization appears in the aspect of books as the Dharma Jewel of scripture. This is a significant point of dependent relationship if you visualize the field of merit as being pleased. Although we generally engage in harmful actions, at the moment we are only causing delight in the field of merit. The oral lineage of Je Drupkang[pa Geleg Gyatso (1641–1713)] states that this is analogous to a boy in a certain family who is constantly engaging in bad behavior: if he acts very properly one day, his parents will be extremely delighted.

Surrounding us are all living beings experiencing the suffering of their individual states but appearing in the aspect of human beings so that they are capable of understanding and reciting what is being said. Although you may be counting recitations of going for refuge, the visualization is more important than keeping count. The visualization of purifying nectar that descends while you recite individually each line to the guru, then the Buddha, and so on, is for the sake of developing bliss.

Regarding the negative karma that you [can] create in relation to the guru, endangering his [or her] body would [occur,] for instance, when a teacher reprimands his students, and in response they brandish some sort of weapons. Breaking his speech could be something as small as forgetting to implement his advice. [And] there are four possibilities with respect to annoying[180] and disturbing the mind.[181]

While you are [reciting the line of going for refuge to] the guru, focus primarily on the five groups of lamas, and if you recite the words of

180. Tib. *thugs 'khrugs.*

181. Tib. *thugs dkrugs.* Unfortunately Pabongkha doesn't mention what these four are.

refuge a hundred times, during the first fifty times, [visualize that] white nectar purifies the unfavorable factors. During the next fifty, [visualize that] yellow [nectar] increases your good qualities as favorable conditions.

You should do the same thing during [the line of going for refuge to] the Buddha and so on. During the [recitation] for the Buddha, you should visualize [the buddhas] in the aspect of personal deities of the four classes of tantra and the supreme emanation bodies of buddhas. Although [our present human existence shows that] we can be completely certain that in a previous life we did not experience certain harmful [states of] mind in relation to the Buddha [and hence commit a heinous action] such as drawing blood,[182] we should imagine that everything below that is purified. [Thus,] regardless of the quality of a representation of an enlightened being, [anything] other than commenting on the quality of the artistry, such as saying "The nose of this Buddha [statue] is big," becomes [a case of] critically analyzing his qualities. If there are numerous cracks in a statue, have it repaired. If there is a smudge and so forth, have the color restored very nicely. The previous holy beings have done numerous things such as these [types of restoration]. [Otherwise,] many types of negative karma can be committed in dependence upon the Three Jewels' physical representations.

Discriminating between some of the scriptures as good and others as bad and so forth; criticizing the Hinayana on account of the Mahayana [or] criticizing mantra on account of sutra; and [criticizing] those who act disparagingly toward the Sakya, Gelug, Nyingma, and so forth out of attachment and anger—each [of these] is an act of disparaging [the Dharma]. However, someone such as a lama will not incur any fault by performing acts in relation to his [or her] own tradition such as making corrections to the view, meditation, and action; [making correction to] the basis, the path, and the result;[183] and making evaluations. [In his *Guide to the Middle Way*,] Glorious Chandrakirti stated,

182. One of the five actions of immediate retribution is (1) drawing blood, or causing a buddha to bleed. The others are (2) causing a schism in the Sangha, (3) killing an arhat, (4) killing your mother, and (5) killing your father.

183. The basis, path, and result are three points in time that are sequentially interrelated and transformed through a series of symbioses. The basis is our current body, speech, and mind, which function as the foundation. The path is the means of transforming those three states

Not engaging in analytical debate due to attachment to
commentaries
Yet teaching suchness for the sake of liberation—
There is no fault if that explanation of suchness
Destroys the scriptures of others.

[Shantideva's] *Guide to the Bodhisattva's Way of Life* also states,

With respect to ordinary worldly people,
We are harmed by the yogas of the worldly,[184]
And slowly the minds of yogis are also
Harmed by each preceding one.

It is extremely inappropriate—and it accumulates the karma of abandoning the Dharma—when we do things that are seemingly insignificant such as tearing a small piece of paper from something like a Tibetan block letter and rolling it up; taking some other form of writing and placing it under our cushion; or setting our rosary, eyeglasses, and so forth on top of written letters—or such things as the way villagers set things [such as statues] on top of a text such as the *Perfection of Wisdom in a Hundred Thousand Lines.*

[For example,] previously, in Ngari, a [certain] mantra practitioner wouldn't listen to Je Atisha teach the Dharma and saw a scribe mark a letter with the plaque from his teeth. Atisha couldn't bear it and said, "Alas, this is utterly unacceptable," whereby the mantra practitioner developed faith in Atisha and requested Dharma teachings from him. [Also] previously, someone from central Tibet and some government officials were disrespectfully walking back and forth over some lettering, revealing that they had no regard for them whatsoever. Sera Gyalwang Chöje Trinley Namgyal, the composer of Je [Tsongkhapa's] great biography, was also staying among them, so he moved the lettering out of the way before walking to the outhouse. [Sera Gyalwang Chöje Trinley Namgyal] was so careful that he tucked in the ends of his robes so that they wouldn't

through spiritual practice. The result occurs when the mind becomes the truth body, the speech becomes the enjoyment body, and the body becomes the emanation body.

184. Here "yogas of the worldly" is a mocking reference to worldly behaviors.

cover the lettering [as he walked]. After the ends of their clothing became frayed by their two hands, [the officials] acted with extreme reverence for that type of lettering. [And] Lama Riku Rinpoche said to Thagpu Dorje Chang,[185] "Because you use a few of those letters for a pillow and a few for your mattress, there's no need to protect your precepts of refuge!"[186] Again, when Riku Rinpoche returned, Thagpu was sorting out the scattered pages.

It is inappropriate to place scriptures on the bare ground without a placement mat. Furthermore, [the mat] should be a clean shawl, cloth, or the like. Bartering your scriptures for food is also a very deleterious deed, as related in the biography of Önton Kyerkang.[187] It is also inappropriate for a monk to sell his texts when he is released from the monastery.

There is the Sangha on the sutra side, as bodhisattvas, shravakas, and pratyekabuddhas, as well as heroes, dakinis, and Dharma protectors on the mantra side. When it comes to the Sangha, confession is not the same as it is with respect to the Buddha and the Dharma, for despite how much you may engage in [confession], it is impossible not to experience a small portion of the ripened result [of your harmful karma accumulated in relation to the Sangha]. If there is an assembly of four ordinary monks with pure moral discipline, they are the Sangha Jewel of ordinary beings. After someone who caused disunity among a group of Sangha members died, another person practiced there for twelve years but didn't develop the slightest realization. In the past, when a fight broke out among the group at Samyé, a monk called Gelong Selshé lived among them, so Geshe Potowa said, "What a pity! If he had died three years earlier, he would have died a holder of the Pitaka."[188] If you unwittingly cause a division of

185. I am unable to identify the lamas in this story. Thagpu Dorje Chang was one of the lamas in the line of the Thagpu lineage, but I am uncertain which one this is referring to.

186. Here Riku Rinpoche is being sarcastic and commenting on the disrespectful way that Thagpu Dorje Chang was treating the written letter.

187. Kyerkang was a great Shangpa Kagyu siddha who had constant visions of Chenrezig. When a family fed him a meal with food purchased from the sale of the perfection of wisdom sutras, Kyerkang's vision disappeared.

188. The Pitaka (literally, "basket") is a Sanskrit term for a collection of the Buddha's teachings. This means that if the monk in question had died three years earlier, before becoming involved in a fight among the Sangha, he would have been a scholar upholding the Three Baskets of the Buddha's teachings. Instead, he created horrible negative karma and lost his vows.

four members of the four-part ordinary Sangha, it is also a schism of the Sangha:

> Harmony among the Sangha is happiness;
> The asceticism of the harmonious is happiness.

According to this passage, harmony among the Sangha is the foundation of all reading, study, and contemplation, as well as [the foundation of] renunciant meditators. If you feel that you must talk behind each other's backs, doing so will not only cause you to go to the lower realms but [will send] every Sangha member in your house [there] as well, as though you were anchors [dragging each other to hell]. [An example of this] is related in the biography of Arya Sangharakshita. Sangharakshita perceived those experiencing the suffering of a temporary hell realm in the aspect of [various implements within] a monastery. These beings had created a schism during the teachings of Kashyapa's Dharma, and they were reborn as such until the teachings of Shakyamuni. Not only that, but they had also created the cause to go to the great hell below. Even stealing the general belongings of the Sangha without the Sangha's permission will cause you to be reborn in the temporary hells.

Likewise, if you taste the tea intended for the Sangha to see if it has the right amount of salt in it, you are diminishing the best portions of the tea; and if you pillage something intended to feed the assembly—such as stealing so much as the size of a mustard seed of butter for tea that was intended as a gift and so forth—you will be reborn in hell. Therefore, you must be careful in the way you conduct yourself when in their presence. There is an example given of two monks with varying degrees of miserliness. One is the head of the monk's house and serves generous portions of tea; yet though he may take something as insignificant as a piece of firewood the size of a small stick for making tea, [nevertheless] he has accomplished the cause to be reborn in a temporary hell. Even Sangharakshita saw living beings who were in a temporary hell, where living beings' bodies were like walls, pillars, ropes, a pot, and a mortar and were bound together at a river's edge. Furthermore, the one whose body was deformed [into the shape of] a wall [had that shape] because he had wiped unclean substances, such as snot, on the wall of a temple; and the being [whose body had the shape of] a pillar had wiped [snot] on a pillar. Previously, someone had stolen a rope that belonged to the Sangha and was [reborn in the shape of] a rope. [Another,] because of delaying expenditures even subtly through restraining and distributing them [dishonestly], had a wide upper and lower body and a thin waist bound by a cord; these beings were reborn together at the river's edge. By stealing property intended as food for the Sangha you will be reborn in the Hell without Respite, and through stealing only the general substances you will be reborn in a temporary hell. At the very least, although you appropriate something by thinking, "This is just a patch of cloth; no one will know," the Lord of Death will know!

Karma and its effects are extremely profound, so you must be careful. Even amid the assembly of monks, the row to the right goes for refuge to the left row, and the left row goes for refuge to the right row; therefore, it is utterly unacceptable to call each other bad names, use bad words, and so forth. Je Konchog Yanlag stated,

> When I see my noble friends, the Arya Sangha,
> I recall that they are noble friends escorting me on the path.

Thus, all the Sangha members are mutual friends leading each other to liberation. We must think that they are friends on the path to omniscience. The living being reborn in hell as a mortar was a fully ordained monk who had previously used harsh language toward a novice monk, and that was the result. Although monks may be good friends, it is an extremely wicked and profane custom to call each other things such as "old dog," "useless," "thief," and so on. You should not think, "Others call me that, so it is fine if I call them that as well," for it is an extremely grave fault.

Previously, in India, five hundred fishermen together with their friends were fishing at the bank of a great river, and it took one thousand men to reel in a sea monster with eighteen heads. There was a tribe to which the Buddha made a prophecy. Moreover, he said that this was a result of calling the Sangha bad names in particular.

When going for refuge, we go for refuge to the Sangha, and through this we [also] purify our accumulation of faults. Visualize that the realization of equalizing and exchanging self with others and bodhichitta descend from the bodhisattvas, [and that] the three higher trainings as well as training in the twelve good qualities [descend] from the shravakas and pratyekabuddhas—all in the aspect of nectar that descends [into you]—and that you develop these realizations in your mental continuum. Although it is indeed the fact that you collect the six perfections, such as generosity through refuge and bodhichitta, the main point is collecting (1) the roots of virtue that arise from charity by way of generosity and so forth, (2) the roots of virtue that arise from protection by way of moral discipline and so forth, [and] (3) the roots of virtue that arise from meditation by way of patience and so forth.

For the four immeasurables, immeasurable aspiration is thinking, "How wonderful it would be if all living beings were to abide in equanimity." Immeasurable prayer is thinking, "May they come to abide in it." Immeasurable superior intention is thinking, "I will cause this to happen." Immeasurable supplication is thinking, "Please grant your blessing that this may come to be." This contains all four immeasurables. The four immeasurables of equanimity, love, compassion, and superior intention should each possess a complete set of four.

In particular, during the recitation of bodhichitta, of the two [designated as] "quickly,"[189] the first reveals the need to accumulate merit for three countless great eons during the practice of the perfection vehicle. In this situation that is not necessary, because you can quickly become enlightened in one life and in one body, in dependence upon the secret mantra Vajrayana. Not only that, but the second reveals that [you may] quickly become enlightened in one short life in this degenerate era if you rely upon highest yoga tantra. Alternatively, the first refers to the general system of tenets and indicates that you can quickly become enlightened in one short human life in the degenerate era in dependence upon the secret mantra Vajrayana, without having to rely upon accumulating merit for three countless eons as presented in the sutra system. The second one reveals that you can quickly attain enlightenment in only twelve human years if you rely upon the oral instructions of Jamgon [Tsongkhapa's] Hearing Lineage. This is a unique feature of the new Kadampas.

Furthermore, although some people have the impression that for the

189. In Tibetan it says "may I quickly, quickly . . ."

Gelugpa, other than sutra there is no practice of secret mantra, this is not the case, for it is utterly impossible that there could not be both sutra and mantra in all [four Tibetan Buddhist traditions]. For the Nyingmas and so forth, if sutra doesn't exist, there is no cycle of beings of small and middling capacity or of bodhichitta as well as the activities of a bodhisattva. Since this is the case, there must be both sutra and mantra. In particular, not only does secret mantra exist in these teachings of Je Tsongkhapa, but they have profound pith instructions, which are the most essential points of the Vajrayana that others do not possess and that are like warm water from the mouth of Manjushri and that contain numerous consummate secrets. In fact, this teaching of Je [Tsongkhapa] is a teaching of venerable Manjushri. Not only is there secret mantra, but Tagsang Lotsawa proclaimed,

> The entirety of sutra and tantra is a unique feature of the Vajrayana;
> The entirety of the tantra is the unique meaning of highest yoga tantra;
> The entirety of the two stages is unique to the illusory body;
> I praise this unprecedented unique great treasure of eloquence.

I offer similar praise. In days of old, Acharya Padmasambhava, Sachen [Kunga Nyingpo], and others sat at the head of their doctrines and presented unmistaken systems of view, meditation, and action. Later, there were many who did not understand even a portion of things such as the essence of tranquil abiding, superior seeing, and so forth of sutra; bliss and emptiness, the illusory body, and so forth of mantra; and so on. To begin with, Marpa and Milarepa of the Kagyu lineage had numerous authentic systems of the mahasiddhas of India, yet later mistakes emerged. From Je Milarepa's offering of realization to the trailblazer Marpa, we can tell that [Milarepa] knew the way of progression presented in the lamrim of the Kadampas. [Milarepa's offering of realization] states,

> Due to the initial condition of ignorance, compositional factors emerge through which the twelve links of dependent relationship are embodied. This corporeal body of flesh and

blood, together with its apprehending consciousness, is ripened as a body of leisure and endowment that is a great ship for those desiring liberation. Alternatively, for those with negative karma from harmful actions, it can be a guide that leads you to bad rebirths. Understand that this is an extremely important time in your life, when you can either gain a profit or sustain a loss, and is the demarcation line going upward or downward that will determine your fate, for better or worse, far into the future. Furthermore, it is extremely difficult to gain liberation from the origin of this suffering ocean of samsara; yet at this moment, owing to you, [Marpa,] the foremost captain of living beings, I have a sure chance at being freed. Initially, the disciple properly trains by requesting the lama for refuge in the Three Jewels. Even among those, the guru is the source of all happiness and excellence. It is very important that you not defile your commitments and instead accept and practice whatever you are taught; understand this as the first essential point. After that, contemplate with powerful visualizations death and impermanence, cause and effect, and the faults of samsara, whereby you reflect on the wish for liberation from samsara by subduing your uncontrolled mind, through which you rely upon whichever of the pratimoksha vows you find appropriate. This is similar to foundational support.

Understand that in dependence upon that, you establish the stages of the Mahayana and protect the precepts you have promised to uphold as you would your own eyes, restoring them if they become defiled. You deviate into the Hinayana by striving for your own peace and happiness. Therefore, once you develop bodhichitta by striving to liberate all living beings from the entirety of samsara, cultivate love and compassion to the best of your ability, and generate the mind of the Mahayana dedicated to striving for all other [sentient] beings.

Having abandoned the path of the shravakas and pratyekabuddhas, you enter into the path of the Mahayana. Once you establish a foundation through the completely pure view [of emptiness], enter the path of the unsurpassed Vajrayana. Furthermore, to generate a realization of the completely perfect view, you need a fully qualified guru who is endowed with the method and wisdom to decipher and explain without error the completely pure rituals of the four empowerments. Through the force of the profound view of the four empowerments, meditate now according to the completion stage. Moreover, striving to discover the selflessness of a personal self common to the vehicle of characteristics[190] through many examples and reasons using both scripture and reasoning, you will not find a self and will realize the selflessness of personal self. Thus, you should equally establish the nonfinding of a personal self and the mind. When you establish this through continuous reflection with numerous reasons, the mind stills in a state of nonconceptuality.

You should remain in this state for years, months, days, and so on, without thinking of anything else, and when it occurs in proper measure, you have developed tranquil abiding. By sustaining this with introspection, you will not fall into mental sinking and dullness. By cultivating an intensity of awareness in which the pure nakedness of nonconceptuality and clarity appears yet is without inherent existence, a pure lucidity will dawn that is the experience of tranquil abiding. Yet this is not fit for apprehending superior seeing, since a fully qualified superior seeing will not dawn for an ordinary being,[191] despite the fact that you may wonder whether or not you have attained the first bodhisattva ground and encountered superior seeing. Therefore, in dependence upon this meditation, you are forging the path with specific manifestations. Various other manifestations will emerge through the experience of tranquil abiding, such as the appearance of the deity's body and so forth, yet these are merely signs of meditation, and you should never think that they have any essence.

190. Tib. *mtshan nyid theg pa*. This is synonymous with the sutra vehicle.

191. Here there is a footnote by Trijang Rinpoche that says, "This means that a direct realization of emptiness will not dawn."

> In short, the experience of tranquil abiding, together with eliciting a state of vivid awareness, constitutes the profound wisdom of individual investigation conjoined with analysis, which is indispensable for attaining superior seeing. Understand that, having generated the mind focusing on doing as much as you can for the welfare of others, in the meantime you are training in the nonobjectified[192] through the completely pure view, and finally, make elaborate dedications for the welfare of others while operating within a state of that unobservability; understand [also] that this is the foremost of all paths.
>
> Just [as you] need to understand that food is beneficial to feed hungry people, so you should understand that it is necessary to meditate and that it is not sufficient [only] to understand the meaning of realizing emptiness. In particular, understand that you must strive without distraction in both accumulation and purification, in subsequent attainment, at the means of working toward realizing superior seeing. In summary, understand that the view of the secret mantra Vajrayana is the inexpressible nonconceptuality that coincides with the four empowerments.

There are many more teachings like this in the old edition of the *Hundred Thousand Songs of Milarepa*. To attain the perfect state of union, Milarepa had to engage in immeasurable hardships. However, in these teachings of Jamgon Tsongkhapa the Great, you don't engage in great austerities. Gyalwa Ensapa Father and Sons[193] raised the victory banner of liberation and so forth in one short life and attained enlightenment through the extremely profound oral instructions of Je [Tsongkhapa's] Hearing Lineage. Not only that, but if you earnestly practice the complete path of this

192. Tib. *dmigs med*. This term is sometimes translated as "unobservable" and refers to the "nonfinding" or "imperceptibility" of inherent existence.

193. The term "Father and Sons" refers to a guru and his or her direct spiritual descendants and also to those disciples' students and so on. Thus, it encompasses the lineage of persons who become the holders of that particular lineage or set of teachings. Here Gyalwa Ensapa Losang Dondrup is the "father," while his disciple Khedrup Sangye Yeshe, Khedrup Sangye Yeshe's disciple the First Panchen Lama, Losang Chökyi Gyaltsen, and so on are the "sons."

oral tradition of the Hearing Lineage by taking guru yoga as the life of the path, it will be as Drubwang Longdor Rinpoche [1710–1794][194] stated in his text *Thirty Convictions.*[195] According to Longdor's teachings, a few have manifested extremely great signs of having accomplished the attainment of union through mantra but are not counted among the mahasiddhas and others of the sutra tradition.

194. Tib. Klong rdol Bla ma Ngag dbang blo bzang.
195. Tib. *Yid ches sum cu.*

Day Seven

The teachings of the supreme scholar Dignaga state:

> The best way to practice is to meditate
> Through disciplined study endowed with contemplation.

Thus, our studies should follow the holy beings who appeared in the past. Moreover, we should dwell in a state of listening, contemplation, and meditation on the scriptures of the Conqueror—in addition to maintaining pure moral discipline as a proper foundation in accordance with what is written in [Vasubandhu's] *Treasury of Abhidharma*—by immediately extracting them right now, as initially ascertained by listening in the presence of a lama. Next, we should engage in perfect contemplation, meditation, and so on, which functions as the foundation. Set your motivation by thinking, "Whether the subject matter is the old teachings or all the scriptures, the stages of the path to enlightenment are like the embodiment of their essential points; therefore, once I hear these instructions, I am going to put them into practice."

Once we visualize the field of merit as the fourth preparation, we should (1) make requests to the guru inseparable from the deity to generate the realizations of the grounds and paths in our mental continuum, (2) sincerely apply ourselves to accumulating merit and purifying obscurations, and (3) sustain the practice of the meditations as the substantial cause. If we combine these three, our progress will be extremely swift. The actual meditations occur during the stages of the path, while supplication, purification, and accumulation come from the preliminary rituals. With respect to explaining the field of merit separately, it is like

Trijang Rinpoche

the foundation and earth of performing accumulation and purification, making it important, so it is explained separately.

With respect to blessing the ground, it is not like your cramped little room; it is an environment free from faults that is vast and peaceful, like Sukhavati, and similar in arrangement to the heavenly pure lands. The offerings are also not for the sake of the recipients of the offerings but are offered for the sake of your own accumulation of merit. Therefore, there are [offerings] that are actually set out as well as those that are emanated to the best of your mind's ability. The intensity with which you imagine the offerings is the degree to which you will complete your accumulation of merit. Moreover, imagine them as being similar to the clouds of Samantabhadra's offerings.[196] Moreover, for the most part, the water offerings and water-offering canopies come from the *Avatamsaka Sutra*.[197] There are numerous ways to emanate the clouds of Samantabhadra's offerings, so imagine the offerings according to that [sutra]. If [you offer them] according to mantra, then the exalted wisdom of inseparable bliss and emptiness itself arises in the form of the offerings. Furthermore, that exalted wisdom itself is present in each moment of the beginning, middle, and end, and is virtuous and good; therefore, it is called *Samantabhadra*.[198]

In the tradition of the [First Panchen Lama's] *Path to Bliss* and the [Second Panchen Lama's] *Swift Path* according to Thubten Lundzé, the visualized objects of refuge themselves are the visualized field of merit. In this case, we use the system of Lama Chöpa. Regarding the teachings which state that it is improper to retract the objects of refuge, there are actually three systems for retracting the objects of refuge.[199] Whichever of those three oral instructions you use is permissible. Combining the Lama Chöpa field of merit at this point is not merely for the sake of illustrating its ease in engaging in recitation; [rather,] it is included at this point because of its extraordinarily powerful blessing. Gyalwa Ensapa, Drubchen Chökyi Dorje [1457– ?], and so forth took this as their personal practice and [through it] attained the state of union in that life and body. Inducing an ascertainment of emptiness as the meaning of inseparable bliss and emptiness is the necessary means of arising in the perceived aspect of the deity. Whatever it is that you meditate on—whether your personal deity or the field of merit—imagine that the perceived aspect of the deity arises from emptiness as the ascertainment factor and that the exalted wisdom of bliss and emptiness [arises] as the appearance factor. If you don't understand this essential point, although you may pretend that

196. Samantabhadra was a bodhisattva who was famed for his power of emanating offerings due to the power of his prayers in previous lives.

197. Tib. *mDo phal po che*. A translation of this sutra is available as *The Flower Ornament Scripture*, trans. Thomas Cleary (Boston: Shambhala Publications, 1993).

198. Tib. *kun bzang*. This term literally means "all good."

199. The three systems are (1) raise it up into space, (2) dissolve it into the sphere of emptiness, and (3) dissolve into yourself.

you are meditating on the generation stage with a vibrant green deity, it will not be a system that functions as an antidote to samsara. For that, you must damage self-grasping. For that, you need a system of comprehending the realization of selflessness through wisdom. It is inappropriate to explain the meaning of bliss and emptiness to those who have not obtained an extensive empowerment.

The roots of the wish-fulfilling tree are planted in the ground; the trunk is born from the earth, above which the branches spread out. Regarding the branches, numerous smaller limbs branch out. The petals are completely flat, as in the general case. The leaves emerge from amid the petals and are very subtle, like channels. Regarding the "five-tufted ones,"[200] this is a name that is synonymous with "lions," which are in fact not ordinary beings but great bodhisattvas emanating in the aspect of lions for the sake of accumulating an ocean of learning. Through this method of supporting the lion throne, they listen to whatever Dharma the field of merit teaches. Regarding the principal [deity] of the field of merit, it is Lama Losang Tubwang Dorje Chang.[201]

These four[202] should not be as though they are trampling upon one another; rather, they are instead of a single nature, like a ritual dancer changing numerous hats and masks. Furthermore, each aspect has its own way of teaching, such as the way the Teacher turned the wheel of Dharma and so on. Conqueror Vajradhara himself was the first teacher and then sequentially appeared in various aspects to work for the welfare of the multitude, such as protector Nagarjuna within India and so on and the great Acharya Padmasambhava and so forth in Tibet during the early spread of the Dharma. After many years had passed, he again taught in a multitude of diverse aspects, such as Atisha the Great and Je Tsongkhapa the Great. And, at this very moment, he is appearing in the aspect of your guru, giving teachings. Therefore, these four are one nature. Not only that, but your guru is the nature of all the buddhas and is their embodi-

200. Tib. *gdong lnga pa*.

201. On Lama Losang Tubwang Dorje Chang, see note 202.

202. Here, the "four" contained within Lama Losang Tubwang Dorje Chang are (1) your root guru appearing externally as (2) Losang Drakpa (Tsongkhapa), who has (3) Tubwang (Powerful Able One Shakyamuni) within his heart, who in turn has (4) Dorje Chang (Vajradhara) within his heart. See also the glossary, under "Losang."

ment. If you understand that, whatever guru yoga you meditate on will go straight to the point.

Next, you recite "The embodiment of all the buddhas" and "the universal form of the conquerors of the three times." In short, [your guru] is the very nature of the omniscient exalted wisdom of [all] the buddhas, which reveals whatever subduing aspect is most suitable to a disciple. Furthermore, the *Meeting of the Father and Son Sutra*[203] proclaims,

> Working for the welfare of living beings,
> They appear in the shape of Indra and Brahma;
> Some are in the shape of a demon,
> Yet the worldly are unable to identify them.

As this states, the [buddhas] reveal themselves in a multitude of aspects, such as a demon, a bird, a deer, a woman, and so forth; in this moment, they are revealing themselves in the aspect of your guru. It is extremely important that you perceive your guru as a buddha; therefore, it is essential that you understand very well the meaning of these instructions. Once you attain certain knowledge that your guru is the embodiment of all the buddhas, you will get right to the essential point when you meditate on a form of guru yoga in the space before you. If you don't develop a proper understanding of this, it will not become guru yoga.

For the sake of completing all the essential points, [you therefore need to] (1) outwardly practice the Vinaya, (2) inwardly [practice] bodhichitta, and (3) secretly [practice] secret mantra [so that the guru] appears in the aspect of a fully ordained monk with the colors of Kashmir saffron, which are (1) plain yellow, (2) orange, and (3) red. This is the meaning behind their colors and why he wears the three sets of monk's robes; it is not the meaning behind the color of his face. The white color with a red hue of his face is a sign of being endowed with the unique exalted wisdom of bliss and emptiness. Also, in the *Swift Path*, the yellow color of his face is a sign of his enlightened activities. The yellow color of his hat symbolizes that Je [Tsongkhapa's] teachings on view, meditation, and action are like refined stainless gold. Being in the aspect of a fully ordained monk and

203. Tib. *Yab sras mjal ba'i mdo.*

of the Teacher together represents the commitment being. Vajradhara at his heart is the wisdom being, and the syllable HUM at his heart is the concentration being. This is similar to how when attaining the illusory body all three nested beings are within oneself.

What is presented here is the body mandala of Guhyasamaja and is like revealing the heart of the root and explanatory tantras of Guhyasamaja. The arrangement of the conquerors of the five families and so forth is taken directly from the tantra. Their form aggregates and so forth implicitly reveal the five vajra mothers. Je [Tsongkhapa's] system of teachings of arranging the body mandala is the authentic way to practice the oral instructions that reveal the underlying intent of the root tantra by combining the root and explanatory tantras. The explanatory tantra of Guhyasamaja *Vajramala* proclaims,

> The body of the Conqueror abides in sequence
> Within the body of the vajra master.
> First, the vajra body perfectly
> Dwells within the aggregate of form.

This unravels the underlying intention. The body mandala of the principal [deity] in the well-known field of merit for Lama Chöpa is conjoined with the body mandala of Guhyasamaja. The practice of Lama Chöpa is an oral instruction that comes from the *Emanation Scripture*;[204] therefore, it is unacceptable to arrange it however you like by combining it with Guhyasamaja, Heruka, and Yamantaka and haphazardly placing the deities on the body mandala of the principal [deity]. It is important to understand that this is not merely arranging the deities of a body mandala; each part of the guru's body is the nature of that particular deity, which accords with the teaching from Guhyasamaja. If you are able to visualize this [in this amount of detail], imagine the deities with three faces and six arms; if you are unable, it is permissible to visualize the parts of the guru's form body arising as the deities of the body mandala with one face

204. Tib. *sPrul pa'i glegs bam chen mo*. Often referred to as the "Kadam emanation scripture," this text is said to be the manifestation of Manjushri's omniscient wisdom, which is only perceptible to beings with extremely high realizations.

and two hands according to yoga tantra. Regarding the arhats in his hair pores, they are Mahayana arhats.

In general, the inconceivable bodies of the tathagatas all appear with entire pure lands in the body, and the body pervades all pure lands. [Chandrakirti's] *Guide to the Middle Way* also states,

> The powerful able ones, at one time, corresponding solely to
> that cause
> In a single form body [reveal] birth, abiding . . .[205]

Thus, this is stating that the bodies, pure lands, and the activities of turning the wheel of Dharma of innumerable buddhas are revealed simultaneously in each hair-pore of a buddha's body. The world in the region of a single atom reaches the realms of space, and the world pervades limitless directions while being revealed in an atom, without the atom becoming larger or the world becoming smaller. Accordingly, they enact the deeds of an eon within the span of a single moment, which is referred to as "the seat for the feet of the worldly beings." It is reasonable to merely understand this as the seat of the worldly deities, or it is also acceptable to visualize them as empty lotus surfaces.

It is a teaching of my guru Yab Rinpoche[206] that you should visualize five rows for the lineage of blessed practice: (1–3) Guhyasamaja, Heruka, and Yamantaka, (4) the sixteen drops of Kadam, and (5) the system of oral instructions for the Ganden Hearing Lineage. Khedrup Je's intention was that we should reject the sixteen drops [of Kadam], but you shouldn't have any doubts because he had other reasons for stating this. There have been many valid texts composed by others according to the visions of many great beings who came after Je [Tsongkhapa], such as the Dalai Lamas and the Panchen Lamas. Imagine the faces, hands, and so forth of the deities to the best of your mind's ability. Although it is said that with respect to the performance tantras, other than Vairochana Abhisambodhi they were not

205. This is chapter 11, verse 19 of Chandrakirti's *Guide to the Middle Way*.

206. Yab Rinpoche's personal name was Jampal Tenpa'i Ngodrup (1876–1922/35); he was more commonly known as Thagpu Pema Vajra and was the fourth incarnation of Gargyi Wangpo. More information can be found in Pabongkha Dechen Nyingpo, *Secret Revelations of Chittamani Tara*, trans. David Gonsalez (Seattle: Dechen Ling Press, 2013).

translated into Tibetan, Buton's *Source of Dharma*[207] and other texts state that the *Tantra of Secret Manjushri*,[208] the *Tantra of the Conquering Aspect of the Wrathful Destroyer of the Lord of Death*,[209] the *Vajrapani Empowerment Tantra*,[210] and so forth are classified as performance tantras; therefore, if we know the canonical descriptions of those deities, it is permissible to visualize them as well.

The abodes that are the essence of the five lineages of conquerors are (1–3) the three seed syllables, (4) a yellow SVA at his navel, and (5) a green HA at his secret place. It is the guru's oral instruction to arrange the three nested beings on all the deities of the field of merit, and [this] is a special feature unique to an enlightened being. They are also singular in nature with the guru.

Query: Well then, can't there just be one?

Reply: There most certainly is also a system called "the tradition of the all-encompassing jewel," in which you meditate solely on the guru. However, in this instance we meditate on many in the field of merit, which also has a singular unique state revealing itself in limitless aspects such as a buddha, bodhisattva, personal deity, Dharma protector, and so on, for the sake of recalling [the guru's] kindness. In the future, when you become enlightened you also must accomplish the state of the supreme being of a hundred families and so forth. For example, it is similar to how Arya Avalokiteshvara subdued trainees within Tibet by revealing various emanations.

Regarding the way to **invoke [the wisdom beings]**, although in general you may not invoke them, if you visualize the guru-buddhas, they will abide before you accordingly. There is a quote [from the sutras] that states,

> For those with faith, this serves as the principal factor
> Whereby the Buddha will abide before them.

207. Tib. *Chos 'byung*.
208. Tib. *'Jam dpal gsang ba'i rgyud*.
209. Tib. *gShin rje gshed khro bo rnam par rgyal ba'i rgyud*.
210. Tib. *Phyag na rdo rje dbang bskur ba'i rgyud*.

And,

> For the person who invokes the Buddha upon a moon,
> The Buddha will rest upon a moon before him.

There are similar historical accounts of such instances such as Asanga seeing Maitreya and Chandragomin perceiving Chenrezig. The pervasive wisdom of a buddha thoroughly pervades the objects of knowledge, and whatever is pervaded by that [wisdom] is pervaded by his body. A sutra also declares,

> Whatever extent to which that wisdom pervades
> Is the extent to which his body also pervades.

If we follow the logical path of reasoning, there isn't any location that is not perceived by the valid cognition of a buddha, which can [also] be applied in this instance. A being with pure karma and so forth can perceive the supreme emanation bodies and so forth as needed, and someone on the first bodhisattva ground can perceive the enjoyment body. For that reason, we invoke [the wisdom beings] for the sake of dispelling doubt that wonders, "If I don't see them, maybe they don't exist." Although we invoke them according to phrases such as "The completely pure . . ." and "All living beings . . . ," they definitely appear like for the woman in the *Sumagadha Narrative*.[211] Thus, when we invoke them, we also invoke them from the heart of each buddha together with an entire field of merit, which dissolve into [each one of] the [objects of our visualization]. Establish a well-formed appearance factor of those fields of merit as well.[212] For the ascertainment factor, think, "Those are the actual [fields of merit]." We should think, "The most exquisite shrine of worship is from the point of view of faith."

211. Tib. *Ma ga dha bzang mo'i gtam rgyud*. This is a well-known story of a woman who, although a great distance away from Buddha Shakyamuni, invited him to her home, to which he arrived through the force of his magical powers.
212. Pabongkha Rinpoche is using the phrase "*fields* of merit" to indicate that each being in the field of merit is him/herself a field of merit, whereby there are as many fields of merit as there are beings in the field of merit.

We don't need to make numerous requests for cleansing rituals from others in order to cleanse our obscurations—such as obscurations caused by misappropriated offerings[213]—with the use of cleansing implements, because when we bathe the bodies of the field of merit, it illuminates and clears away our own obscurations. The person offering the bathing ritual emanates three bhikshus, as is done during the abridged great consecration ritual, and offering deities as in the practice of mantra. Although the field of merit doesn't have stains of previous impurities and they haven't created any new impurities, you offer the bathing ritual in dependence upon the true nature of reality of dependent relationship, for the sake of purifying the negative karma and obscurations in your own mental continuum.

You should imagine that through offering the bathing ritual, the fields of merit give birth to the exalted wisdom of great bliss in their mental continuum. While drying their bodies, arrange the five syllables OM, HUM, and so on, which is different[214] from the way they are arranged in the consecration rituals. Here, the five places are sequentially established as (1) the crown, (2) the heart, (3–4) the right and left shoulders, and 5) the navel. Although some people have a way of arranging [the syllables] that is different from this, this is how it is done in our tradition. Once you have completed the bathing ritual, adorn them with the signs and indications of a conqueror and offer them clothes and so forth. Whatever degree to which your mind is capable of imagining throughout this process is the degree to which you will accumulate an equivalent great store of merit. Alternatively, it is also suitable to offer the principal [deity] of each of the six lineages food and antique ornaments. It is also acceptable to imagine you invite each object as a basis of prostration and offering.

Offering the Seven Limbs Together with the Mandala

The fifth preliminary ritual is offering the seven limbs together with the mandala. It is important to (1) make requests, (2) accumulate merit and purify negative karma, and (3) meditate in accordance with the previ-

213. Tib. *dkor sgrib*.

214. Tib. *mi 'dra*. In Pabongkha Rinpoche's *Liberation in Our Hands*, it says "similar to" (*ltar*); however, in the following sentence, Pabongkha explains just how it is that they are different.

ous request to generate the path in your mental continuum. Therefore, accumulation and purification are part of the fifth preliminary ritual as the seven limbs; the request is part of the sixth preliminary ritual; and training in the visualizations is the actual practice. You must ripen your mental continuum to generate the good qualities of realization in your mental continuum. If [your mental continuum] is ripened, it will ripen your faults and expel them like pus. Ripening your good qualities is like fruit that is suitable to enjoy. Therefore, although the cause may be subtle, if you ripen your mental continuum well through supplications, accumulation, purification, and so forth, you will easily develop the good qualities of realization.

Je Tsongkhapa also engaged in practices of accumulation and purification at Olga[215] and so forth to instruct those of us who are his followers. Je Milarepa built Marpa a nine-storied tower, Naropa undertook twelve great hardships, and so on. When they also ripened their mental continuums, they developed realizations without difficulty. Je Tsongkhapa stated,

> When you listen, you don't retain the words; when you contemplate, you don't understand the meaning; when you meditate, you don't develop [realizations] in your mental continuum. When the mind has such little power, the oral instruction is to rely upon the power of the field [of merit].

If you sincerely apply yourself through accumulation, purification, and supplication through the special field consisting of the guru, buddhas, and bodhisattvas, realizations will easily be generated. Geshe Dölpa [Sherap Gyatso] stated,

> If, secondary to your contemplations, you sincerely apply yourself with perseverance to the accumulation of merit, purification of negative karma, and supplication of the deity and guru, since composite phenomena do not remain static,

215. Olga Chölung is located to the southeast of Lhasa. Lama Tsongkhapa did his famous four-year retreat there and had numerous visions of various buddhas, bodhisattvas, saints, and mahasiddhas. See Janice D. Willis, *Enlightened Beings* (Boston: Wisdom, 1995).

> you will generate [realizations] that you thought couldn't be developed in a hundred years.

With respect to accumulating merit and purifying negative karma, it is similar to cultivating a field with manure, water, and sunshine, while meditation is like sowing the seeds. The instruction manuals of previous Tibetans stated,

> If you don't train your mind, it is like drawing with butter;
> If you don't safeguard your vows, it is like treasure without an owner;
> If you don't accumulate merit, it is like seeds without moisture.

If you wonder just how you are supposed to go about doing this, the concise essence of accumulation and purification is the practice of the seven limbs. King Indrabhuti stated,

> If those wishing for swift enlightenment did not become enlightened through meditating on the view of the True Aspectarians and the False Aspectarians of the Chittamatra, they should train in the Dharma practice of the seven limbs.

The incomparable Dagpo Lhaje [that is, Gampopa] also stated,

> The seven limbs are the principal virtuous practice.

As well as,

> There is no practice of Dharma apart from accumulation and purification.
> Through the purification of negative karma, one accumulates merit;
> Through accumulation of merit, one purifies negative karma.

For that reason, accumulating something like four sets of one hundred thousand preliminary practices[216] is not sufficient; you need both accumu-

216. For a commentary on the preliminary practices, see Kachen Yeshe Gyaltsen, *Manjushri's Innermost Secret*.

lation and purification until you are enlightened.[217] A passage in [Chandrakirti's] *Guide to the Middle Way* states, "At that time, this person will see a hundred buddhas," which is in reference to those on the first bodhisattva ground and so forth who engage in immeasurable practices of accumulation and purification with bodies numbering one hundred up to innumerable. If they do that, and we—with nothing more than a short life, one body, and two hands—don't undertake them to the best of our ability, [then] we have closed the door on ourselves to the grounds and paths.

It would be mistaken to think that once we cultivate mere knowledge of maintaining the mind's essence, mere knowledge of meditating on channels and winds,[218] or mere understanding of the view of emptiness, we don't need accumulation and purification. Je Tsongkhapa stated,

> If those great bodhisattvas who have obtained control over material substances emanate many hundreds and thousands of bodies, and each of those emanated bodies also has limbs numbering a hundred, a thousand, and so on, and once they arrive in all the pure lands, they make offerings to the conquerors for numerous eons, we should not be content with just a few partial good qualities. For someone to say "I don't need to do such things to become enlightened" is just speaking nonsense with very little knowledge of the Dharma.

With respect to the term "seven limbs," this is exemplified by considering that if you emanate a carriage with seven limbs yet one piece is incomplete, you won't be able to travel on the path.

[Offering the Seven Limbs Together with the Mandala has seven parts:

1. The Limb of Prostration
2. The Limb of Offering
3. The Limb of Confession
4. The Limb of Rejoicing

217. This means just collecting the hundred thousand sets and leaving it at that, without further accumulation and purification, if sufficient.

218. Tib. *rtsa rlung*. This is a profound meditation on the channels and winds in the Nyingma tradition that lays the groundwork for a realization of the mind's essence.

5. THE LIMB OF REQUESTING THEM TO TURN THE WHEEL OF DHARMA
6. THE LIMB OF MAKING SUPPLICATIONS NOT TO PASS INTO NIRVANA
7. THE LIMB OF DEDICATION]

The Limb of Prostration

For that, the first of the seven limbs is prostration. According to sutra, the translation equivalent of "hand"[219] is *nama* [in Sanskrit] and means "to perfectly bow," "to engage with respect," and "close approach." To bow respectfully with our body is a physical prostration. To proclaim the good qualities of the three secrets of the field of merit with phrases such as "Whoever has such great . . ." is a verbal prostration. Faith and devotion of the mind is a mental prostration. There are two primary forms of prostration: a full-length prostration and a contracted prostration. Full-length prostrations are taught in the *Array of Stalks Sutra* and were the personal practice of Panchen Naropa. Milarepa also made three full-length prostrations near the place of Lama Ngok and offered praises, saying, "This is where a lineage holder of Naropa's Dharma lives." The scriptural basis of the contracted prostrations is the purification and restoration ritual found in the Vinaya, which says, "Prostrate."

If you offer one prostration well, you will obtain the merit to become chakravartin kings equal to the number of atoms within the ground that is covered by your body all the way down to the great and powerful golden base.[220] Therefore, the size of your body is also significant. This full-length prostration is important for accumulation and purification, and it teaches the practice of abandonment and acceptance[221] through the great number of atoms that are covered, the way of conjoining your palms, and so forth. You should properly learn the authentic sources for

219. The Tibetan term for prostration consists of two words, *phyag* and *'tshal*. The first word means "hand," "bow," "reverence," and so on, while the second means to "supplicate," "beg," or "request."

220. According to ancient Buddhist cosmology, the universe is supported by a golden base, as explained in the extensive mandala offering.

221. Tib. *spang blang*. This term is used repeatedly in Tibetan Buddhism and refers the abandonment of nonvirtue and the acceptance of virtue.

these as well, and if you don't understand them, although a few people say you are a lama or a geshe, you will be someone who doesn't even know the tradition of prostration.

By joining your folded hands on the crown of your head, you establish the imprint to accomplish the major mark of an ushnisha; by touching your eyebrows, you establish the imprint to attain the hair treasure; by touching your throat, you establish the imprint to attain the melodious speech of Brahma and [a sound] like a conch; and by touching your heart-orb, you establish the imprint to accomplish the exalted omniscient wisdom. While touching your crown, imagine that you purify the negative karma and obscurations of your body and that the blessings of an enlightened body enter you. Apply the same reasoning to your throat and heart with your speech and mind and enlightened speech and mind. Although it is extremely good to collect a hundred thousand prostrations, it is important that they be done properly. At the beginning of prostrations, conjoin it with the mantra for transforming prostrations, and make at least three prostrations. Other traditions use the phrase "refuge prostrations" and conjoin going for refuge with prostrations, which is also excellent. It is also permissible to recite any number of things such as going for refuge, OM MANI PADME HUM, and so forth. In particular, according to the personal practice of Lodrak Drubchen, the oral tradition of Je Tsongkhapa states that the very best way to [perform prostrations] is to conjoin them with the *Confession of Moral Downfalls.* I shall teach this way of making prostrations conjoined with the *Confession of Moral Downfalls* later, during the confession section of this text, after which we should practice according to this explanation.

The Limb of Offering

This is also quite important. If an ordinary person left a field empty and abandoned for just one year, it would cause them to feel regretful. The supreme field in which to sow all our seeds of merit is the guru, the conquerors, and the bodhisattvas. If we left this field empty, it would be cause for regret a hundred or even a thousand times greater than the previous [example of an ordinary field]. Jamgon Tsongkhapa stated,

As it states in a sutra,

> For example, just like being unable to bear abandoning a fine field without sowing seeds in it, in a similar way, the only thing that will satisfy you is unceasingly sowing the seeds of virtue and excellence with the plouw of faith in the holiest of all fields, which is a source of all happiness and excellence of this life and the next, through which it will be transformed into the most wondrous field.

If we don't make use of [the supreme field of merit,] it would be an enormous cause of regret.

The [above quote] together with the narratives of Arya Gabamyati[222] and the King Mandhata[223] reveal that [the guru, the conquerors, and the bodhisattvas] are the field of accumulation because they bestow great stores of merit; therefore, they are called "field of merit." These sutras explain how a pleasing physical form comes from offering even a handful of flowers to the gurus, buddhas, and bodhisattvas, how limitless benefits come from pure moral discipline, and so on. Even in the amount of time it takes to drink a cup full of tea, we can visualize the field of merit and light a candle, a stick of incense, and so forth. Although a householder may not produce [virtuous] seeds equal to a thousand pack-loads, when he [or she] accumulates merit, purifies negative karma, and makes supplications, he still accumulates incomparable stores of merit.

The supreme field has a special feature, in that it is not possible that our roots of virtue from such acts as making offerings to it will not become a cause of unsurpassed complete enlightenment, even if our thoughts are only of this life and we have yet to embrace bodhichitta. There are extensive quotes from the *White Lotus of Compassion Sutra*,[224] such as [the example of] the field of a householder farmer and so forth. We can further cite the example of preparing an excellent harvest in the spring by sowing seeds of wheat and barley and then praying, "May flowers not grow in

222. Tib. 'Phags pa Ba lang bdag. He was a monk who received ordination from the Buddha and was a disciple of Shariputra.

223. Tib. rGyal po Nga las nu. He was a former incarnation of Buddha Shakyamuni.

224. Tib. *mDo snying rje pad dkar.*

the summer, and may the wheat and barley not bear fruit." Despite such prayers, unless [the seeds] are interrupted by other poisonous conditions, those prayers will not be able prevent the emergence of the wheat and barley crops. For that reason, although offering actual substances such as water offerings and close-enjoyment offerings are surpassable offerings,[225] you should offer as much of them as you can with pure intention. Regarding the unsurpassed offerings,[226] these are offering substances that are transformed from your roots of virtue with respect to the oral instructions of meditating on great compassion and generating bodhichitta.

225. Tib. *bla na yod pa'i mchod pa*.

226. Tib. *bla na med pa'i mchod pa*. Surpassable offerings are those made by ordinary beings; unsurpassable offerings are those emanated by highly evolved beings with miraculous powers, such as bodhisattvas on the first bhumi. See Tsongkhapa, *The Great Treatise on the Stages of the Path to Enlightenment*, 1:96–97.

Day Eight

The teaching of glorious protector Arya Nagarjuna [in his *Letter to a Friend*] states,

> Someone who commits nonvirtue after being born a human
> Is much more foolish than
> Someone who cleans up vomit with
> A golden vessel adorned with jewels.

We have this excellent physical form that is difficult to obtain, so while we have obtained such a physical form, vastly superior to other types of embodiments, we absolutely must extract an essence that fulfills our permanent objectives. For example, it would be extremely foolish to pour filth into a golden vessel. Likewise, while we have obtained a physical form such as this, to use it as a vessel for nonvirtue would be a hundred or a thousand times more foolish than the former example. In order not to allow something like that to happen, contemplate, "I must practice the essential instructions on the stages of the path to enlightenment for the sake of extracting the unique essence of this life."

After this short introduction, Pabongkha Rinpoche restated the headings.

Offering the mandala is a special aspect of the offering of the seven limbs. The most essential point of the mandala is the visualization; therefore, although you are offering one complete mandala, you obtain the merit of offering the four continents, Mount Meru together with its surrounding environment, the seven precious substances, and the sun and moon. The

Vasubandhu

Sutra of the Mandala[227] speaks of the benefits of offering the mandala when it states,

> By making a mandala of the Muni
> You obtain the six transcendent perfections.

227. Tib. *Man da la gyi mdo.*

The extensive explanation comes from the ritual for the mandala composed by master Kampala. Just as Drom[tonpa] rebuked glorious [Palden] Gonpawa,[228] so we should apply ourselves sincerely to making mandala offerings, whereby we will perceive numerous buddha lands. The mandala also finds its source in the *Fifty Verses of Guru Devotion*,[229] which contains the concise meaning of tantra and states,

> With a mandala and flowers in the palms of your hands,
> Respectfully honor your teacher guru
> And prostrate with his feet on your head
> With supreme faith throughout the three times.

The *Sutra of the Mandala* states,

> Present it together with cow urine.[230]
> Smearing it well is moral discipline;
> Clearing it of worms, ants, and flies is patience;
> Fully engaging in these actions is perseverance;
> The mind instantly combining these together as one
> Is a clear image of concentration and wisdom.

This is the way of combining all six perfections with the mandala. The *Sutra of Golden Light*[231] states,

> When I became a chakravartin king,
> At that time I sent forth the earth together with the ocean
> Replete with the four precious continents,
> And I offered it to the previous kings.

It is permissible for the ascetic yogi, who doesn't have even the very minimal substances of value and is without wealth such as silver and cop-

228. Palden Gonpawa was spending so much time in meditation that he felt he didn't have time to make mandala offerings. Dromtonpa rebuked him, saying that Atisha had much higher realizations than Gonpawa and that Atisha made a mandala offering every day.
229. See Kachen Yeshe Gyaltsen, *Manjushri's Innermost Secret.*
230. This is one of the five cow products listed in note 232 below.
231. Tib. *gSer 'od dam pa'i mdo.*

per, to offer substances such as stones and flat wood. The offering heaps can also be grains or jewels. At the very least, it is permissible to offer clean substances such as crushed pebbles. If you are wealthy, the offering [base] should be whatever is best, such as gold, silver, and so forth; if it is, your merit will have great strength. The size is not fixed, but Kampala and others state that it should not be smaller than a full cubit. The oral instructions state that at the very least it most definitely should not be smaller than our drinking cup. It is taught that the shape and color can be whatever you wish and are not absolutely fixed. The biggest it should be is the size of a rice bowl, so that you can carry it. It is inappropriate if you are thus unable to carry your mandala.

When offering [the mandala], hold it with both hands while [each hand also] holds some heaps of grain, and wipe it outward as many times as possible while imagining you are sweeping away your negative karma and obscurations. Wipe it inward three times and imagine you are receiving the blessings of the gurus, buddhas, and bodhisattvas. The best would be to do this every time you offer a mandala. If you are unable to do even that, from time to time you should wipe the mandala with cow products.[232] The top of the mandala and the substances arranged in heaps absolutely must be sprinkled with scented water.

You should learn the way the four continents and Mount Meru were formed, as well as the three abodes and the designation of the world, from the authentic instruction manuals on the mandala. The phrase "in short" means a very concise explanation. In the Kalachakra system Mount Meru is round, but in [Vasubandhu's] *Treasury of Abhidharma* it is square, which is the system we are practicing at the moment. Below the Realm of the Thirty-Three and downward is supported by the earth foundation. The yoke of the first golden mountain has a grade of forty thousand leagues.[233] Next, going outward there are sequential levels that are progressively lower. Videha is white and semicircular. Dzambuling is the shape of a horse, is blue, and its broad side faces Mount Meru. The [continent] in the west is red and circular, and [the continent] in the north is square

232. Tib. *ba byung*. The "five cow products" are five substances of a cow that are collected before they touch the ground. They are (1) urine, (2) dung, (3) milk, (4) butter, and (5) curd. You can obtain pills containing all five substances that are properly prepared.

233. Tib. *dpag tshad*; Skt. *yojana*. This is a measurement of approximately four and a half miles.

and yellow. The subcontinents are the colors of the [continents in their corresponding] directions. The cut faces of the continents face outward.

If you are primarily offering your body, enjoyments, and roots of virtue, then the east faces the recipients of the offering. To receive their blessings inward, the east faces you. Although it doesn't matter which way you do it, it is best if, when offering a mandala [simply as an offering], the eastern direction of the mandala is facing [toward the field of merit], and when requesting, it is offered in your direction.[234] From the Heaven without Conflict[235] up to Bountiful Virtue[236] is supported by a wind and cloud foundation. Bountiful Virtue does not have clouds but is supported by wind. In Harvest Unsown, if you sow seeds at night, they bear fruit in the morning without the need for cultivation.

Regarding the seven precious possessions of a king, imagine that they are perfectly made from the gold of the Dzambu River and so forth. In highest yoga tantra the supreme horse is white, and in yoga tantra he is blue. When you imagine the arrangement of the eight [goddesses, such as the Goddess of] Beauty and so forth, their way of abiding in their blissful abodes and so forth should be according to yoga tantra. In the oral tradition, the sun and moon are to the right and left, the parasol is on the opposite side, and the victory banner is in your direction.

When you recite the lines "The ground sprinkled with perfume . . ." and ". . . perceived as a buddha land . . . ," in the first moment it is the impure worldly realm, and in the second instant it is transformed into a pure land, which is then offered. The term "land" indicates it is a land with special qualities that you imagine when offering it. It is also permissible to relate to the recipients of the offering and offer it to Brahma, Indra, and those who possess vows, [requesting] their assistance. And although it is said that you imagine offering the mandala with the assistance of Brahma, it is the assertion of Ngulchu [Dharmabhadra] Father

234. For instance, when presenting offerings primarily focused on the accumulation of merit, the eastern direction should be facing the field of merit so that the western direction is closest to you. When you pour out the mandala, you pour it toward the field of merit. When requesting blessings, teachings, and so on, the eastern direction is facing you and is poured out toward yourself.

235. Heaven without Conflict is one of the desire realms.

236. Bountiful Virtue is one of the form realms.

and Sons[237] that it is also permissible to offer it as being produced from the shared karma of living beings in this world as well as from a portion of your karma. Although this has been analyzed with reasoning, it would be best if you offer it as being produced from a portion of your own karma.

The thirty-seven-heap [mandala] was the personal practice of Drogon Chögyal Phagpa [1235–1280] and has authentic sources in the sutras, tantras, and their commentaries. The twenty-three heaps was the tradition of Je Tsongkhapa. Although you offer twenty-three [heaps], it has the complete meaning of the thirty-seven. It is extremely important to develop a solid understanding of the lamrim on the basis of all of this. If you are accumulating a count [of mandala offerings], for each recitation of "Buddha, Dharma, and Supreme Assembly," together with "The ground strewn . . . ," you arrange and offer a seven-heap mandala. If you are not keeping count, you can do it any way you like but should establish a clear visualization. Once you have offered many of them in this way, if you repeatedly receive good indications in your dreams, such as perceiving enjoyments as heaps of grain and so forth, this is a sign that your merit is increasing.

The Limb of Confession

The third limb is confession. The act of confession is extremely important. Our mental continuums are like a king's treasury of negative karma and downfalls, so if we don't confess them, even though we may have very little nonvirtue, it will repeatedly double so that it increases to a point where it becomes infinite, after which its ripened effect will propel us into the lower realms. Even the taking of one life: if you do not engage in confession, it will continuously double until, after eighteen days have passed, one act of killing will have increased to the point of being equivalent to taking the lives of 311,072 beings. You can apply this reasoning to all nonvirtues. The mind cannot comprehend the negative karma we have created, whereas the small amount of virtue we have created can be counted on ten counters attached to our rosary beads. Even while I am

237. On "Father and Sons," see note 193 above.

explaining it to people, if they kept count, they necessarily accumulate both virtue and negative karma.

Although we think our negative karma is not that great, from this morning until the present moment we have repeatedly accumulated the negative karma sufficient to be reborn in all three lower realms. In particular, for those of us who have taken ordination, once we wrap ourselves up in the three sets of robes and sit down for something like a session, although we may be sitting still, our thoughts will be nothing but nonvirtuous. Most of what we say is lies, and in particular, we violate the boundaries of the three vows, so that each day faults and downfalls pour down like rain. Our Teacher said that although at the moment an *upasaka* may be protecting his precepts, in the future a fully ordained monk will not be able to protect the vows of a [present-day upasaka]. At a minimum, we try to get our cup filled with as much noodle soup as we can, and we then slurp it down, smack our lips, and blow on it with "hu hu" and "phu phu," whereby we accumulate at least forty or fifty downfalls[238] and our deficit is greater than our profit. [Our Teacher] also stated,

> For some, moral discipline is happiness.
> For some, moral discipline is suffering.
> Possessing moral discipline is happiness.
> Violating our moral discipline is suffering.

If we don't protect our moral discipline, we will accordingly accumulate negative karma. There are many wicked people who have taken rebirth as demons, *rakshas*, and so forth because they accumulated enormous negative karma in their previous lives. Our negative karma is not like our current property, which we will no longer possess once it wears out. The quantity of our negative karma is like the treasure of the chakravartin king that increases bit by bit. For as long as all [our negative karmas] exists, if we also don't engage in confession, we will definitely have to experience the result. For example, no matter how long a bird flies in the sky, eventually he must definitely descend upon his shadow:

238. One of the minor precepts of a bhikshu is not to noisily consume food.

Regarding the karma of embodied beings,
It will not be wasted for even a hundred eons.
Once the circumstances are assembled and the time
Is right, it will ripen as the result.

No matter how much negative karma you have, if you engage in confession and restraint, it can definitely be purified. Once it is purified, it is called "the good quality of purified negative karma."[239] Accordingly, there is absolutely no possibility that your negative karma will not be purified once it is confessed. [Nagarjuna's] *Letter to a Friend* states,

Whoever was once nonconscientious
And later becomes endowed with conscientiousness
Is beautiful like a moon freed from clouds, just like
Nanda, Angulimala, Darshaka, and Udayana.

According to oral tradition, Angulimala had a rosary [made of the] fingers [of people he had killed], but through making extremely powerful confession and restraint, he purified [the negative karma of chopping off people's fingers] and became an arhat. Devadatta gave Prince Ajatashatru, the son of King Bimbisara, extremely bad counsel by advising him, "Once we have killed both the Buddha and the king, I shall act as buddha and you act as the king!" However, [Devadatta] was unable to kill the Buddha. Ajatashatru killed King Bimbisara, who was his own father, whereby Bimbisara attained the result of a never-returner, which [eventually resulted in] Ajatashatru also attaining the result of a never-returner. Because of the great force of the action of immediate retribution of killing his father, [Ajatashatru] engaged in extremely powerful confession and restraint, whereby he attained the state of a stream-enterer. Udayana, also called "Svaka," committed an action of immediate retribution by killing his mother; however, he later developed faith in the Buddha, requested the Dharma, engaged in confession, and through meditating on

239. It is often said that negative karma has only one good quality: it can be purified. Hence, this is called "the good quality" of purified negative karma.

the path was liberated from the effects of his negative karma and attained the fruit [of the stages of the path].

Likewise, we should engage in proper confession and restraint, and [if we do,] we will definitely purify these negativities that we have also spent our entire lives with. If we continuously apply extremely powerful confession over a long period of time and with great force, we will be able to purify all the karma that we would have had to definitely experience otherwise and that would have caused us to go to the Hell without Respite in our next life. These days, nonvirtuous people seem to have long lives, great strength, successful activities, and so on, whereby they think that there is no such thing as actions and their effects; however, this is not the case. Regarding the people who engage in virtue yet receive bad omens, this is a definite sign that their extreme virtue is ripening their negative karma that would result in experiencing the lower realms in a later life. This is a sign that once it is ripened in this life, they will go to the pure lands in their next life.

When Atisha was at the point of passing away, Dromtonpa requested, "Atisha, please care for me again in your next life," whereby Atisha replied, "I am going to Tushita. You should also pray [to be reborn] in Tushita. You will become ill with leprosy at the end of your life. However, you will be reborn in Tushita, so you and I will not be apart." Accordingly, Dromtonpa accepted leprosy at the end of his life, after which he passed away, and went to Yiga Chözin[240] in Tushita. The *Diamond Cutter Sutra* from the perfection of wisdom sutras states,

> Further, Subhuti, the sons of the lineage or daughters of the lineage who accept the words of this sutra and retain it, grasp it, read it, and fully comprehend it will become tormented. They will be extremely tormented. What is the reason for that? Subhuti, those living beings have purified all the nonvirtues from their previous lives that would have resulted in rebirth in the lower realms, and they are tormented in this life. Through this, all of the nonvirtue from their previous

240. Tib. *Yid dga' chos 'dzin*. This is a palace in Tushita pure land where Maitreya gives Dharma teachings.

> lives that would have resulted in rebirth in the lower realms is purified, and they become cleansed, and they will also attain the enlightenment of a buddha.

When nonvirtuous beings have long lives and great success in this life, it is a sign that they are exhausting all the results of their virtue and that after death they will transmigrate to the boundless lower realms.

You should continue with your confession for months or years, until you receive repeated indications that your confession has purified the negative karma that you have accumulated since beginningless time according to dream signs explained in the *Chunda Dharani Scripture.*[241] After that, in this life you will continue to accumulate new negative karma in general, and in particular you will accumulate negative karma in this very day. Therefore, it is important that you confess that negative karma before you go to bed; and since you will accumulate negative karma and downfalls tonight, you should confess tonight's [negative karma in the morning], so that you don't encounter any negative karma and downfalls for a twenty-four-hour period. By doing this every day, if you are not defiled by negative karma and downfalls, that will be enough for you to transfer your consciousness [to a pure land]. A sutra also states,

> Not heard by the ears and not seen before the eyes, as well as
> Protecting the teachings—this person will go to a higher rebirth.

The fact that we engage in all sorts of negative actions without restraint, even in the presence of our gurus, is the fault of not having contemplated actions and their effects. Previously, upon seeing the negative karma accumulated by the Tibetans, Je Atisha stated,

> Old man, old man, it is not right to be so brazen, it is not right to be so brazen; cause and effect is subtle, cause and effect is profound.

241. Tib. *bsKul byed kyi gzungs.*

Also, when Atisha would incur some minor infraction while traveling, he would immediately engage in confession and restraint. Thus, it is important to sincerely apply ourselves to confession and restraint. In addition to being utterly unsoiled by defeats[242] down to the remainders,[243] not encountering them for a twenty-four-hour period is the measure of having the completely pure moral discipline of the ordained. In general, although the Vinaya states that there are three ways of rectifying them, according to Tse[chok] Ling Yongzin Pandita [Kachen Yeshe Gyaltsen], in this day and age the people who can carry them out in that way are rare; therefore, we should make confession each and every day. Although you may be a householder, you should sincerely apply the methods of confessing your negative karma.

To properly perform confession, you need the four opponent powers in their entirety. The first is **the power of reliance**, for which numerous ways are taught; however, in our tradition, we go for refuge and generate bodhichitta in a similar way to how we lift ourselves up from negative karma—[that is,] in dependence upon the object in relation to which we establish it.[244] There are also certain criteria for why we use these two types of power of reliance, since whatever negative karma we accumulate is accumulated in relation to either the objects of refuge or living beings; [hence] we go for refuge for the sake of purifying the negative karma created in dependence upon the Three Jewels and generate bodhichitta in relation to living beings. All the vows of mantra and so forth require both going for refuge and generating bodhichitta.

With respect to **the power of destruction**, develop extremely powerful regret for your previously accumulated negative karma and downfalls, as if [you had ingested] poison, as already covered. Je Mila[repa] also stated,

242. Tib. *pham pa*. There are four defeats for the ordained Sangha: (1) killing a human being, (2) stealing, (3) sexual activity, and (4) lying about one's spiritual attainments.

243. Tib *lhag ma*. For a list of these, see Jamgön Kongtrul Lodrö Tayé, *Buddhist Ethics*, trans. by the International Translation Committee (Ithaca, NY: Snow Lion, 1998).

244. This is explained in the next sentences. All of our negative karma is created either in relation to living beings or enlightened beings. By going for refuge we are relying on enlightened beings, and by generating bodhichitta we are relying on living beings. By going for refuge and generating bodhichitta, we encompass all beings that were the basis of our negative karma.

> Although you may confess your negative karma, if your thoughts
> are pure
> And if you apply regret, it will be purified.

While practicing **the power of turning away from faults**, you may consider that there are certain things, such as killing, that you are able to completely forsake from the root by utterly abandoning them, according to your guru's oral advice; yet even for those that you can't [completely abandon], you should rely upon a mind determined to abandon them bit by bit, for a month or a day. There are still other oral instructions on how to turn away from faults.

With respect to **the power of applying the antidote**, this is related to the previous story about poison and is like relying upon milk churned into butter or a medicine to induce vomiting. Confession is the power of applying the antidote as the model of engaging in virtue for the sake of purifying negative karma. There are six types of this power taught in [Shantideva's] *Compendium of Trainings*.[245] The Hundred-Syllable Mantra [of Vajrasattva] is classified as relying upon a supplication. It is also taught that by reciting eighty thousand of each mantra such as Ushnisha Vijaya, Immaculate Ushnisha, Mitrugpa, Kunrig, or Padmo Ushnisha, you can purify all your negative karma so that none remains. In our own tradition, according to the biography of Je [Tsongkhapa], the very best thing is to recite the *Confession of Moral Downfalls* with a mind of regret and a mind of restraint, and combine it with prostrations. Lhodrak Namkha Gyaltsen did the same thing and had a direct vision of thirty-five sugatas, and his realizations increased. Tse[chok] Ling Yongzin Pandita told Drubchog Losang Namgyal that if you request that the great force of whatever virtue you accomplish will serve to purify your negative karma and combine this with the *Confession of Moral Downfalls*, this is the supreme way to make prostrations.

During the *Confession of Moral Downfalls*, there are nets of pearls and hanging pendants at the corners of the elephant thrones for the assembly of deities of this field of merit, which are set in rows with four-tusked

245. Tib. *bsLab btus*. A famous text by Shantideva, similar to his *Guide to the Bodhisattva's Way of Life*.

elephants of Brahma [supporting the thrones]. Although it is sufficient to have the principal Teacher on a lion throne, you should change it to an elephant throne. I will explain the teachings of my guru concerning the system of recitation of the oral tradition. Once you repeat one section of the thirty-five names, you repeat it several times, which counts as one repetition. In a situation where you are alone, recite their names one by one while recalling the benefits of their names, which counts as one accumulation. This strikes the essential point. You keep collecting repetitions until signs arise that you have purified your negative karma. Confess individually all the negative karma and downfalls caused by the three poisons, whatever negative karma you have incurred through the three doors [of body, speech, and mind], and that which you have caused [others] to engage in or have rejoiced in. The term "individually" implies that we are also confessing with the body those [negative actions] of the body.

Alternatively, [confessing] your negative karma is similar to purifying them through confession in your monk's quarters. With respect to the downfalls being one nature with negative karma, in the pratimoksha you confess them through the restoration and purification ritual[246] in the presence of your abbot, master, and Sangha. Bodhisattva vows are confessed in the presence of the guru, buddhas, and bodhisattvas. In mantra, confessing them to the guru and assembly of mandala deities is indicated by the phrase "individually." Another meaning of "confess them individually" is also to say, "I repeatedly confess them."

At the conclusion, you should think that they are purified so that none remains and seal [the thought] with unobservability. It is a wrong view to have doubts about whether or not [your negative karma] are purified and to lack confidence in the opponent power; therefore, it is inappropriate to think that they are not purified. Because the Teacher said that we have negative karma *and* that it can be purified by confession, both statements are equally true.

246. Tib. *gso sbyong*.

The Limb of Rejoicing

The fourth limb is rejoicing. [Shantideva's] *Compendium of Trainings* states,

> Calculating the measurements and weight of the three thousand [worlds]
> And Mount Meru, then rejoicing in that, is not what it means [to rejoice].

Je Rinpoche [Tsongkhapa] also declared,

> Rejoicing is said to be the supreme way to assemble
> A great wave of merit with little effort.

As it states, [rejoicing] does not require hardships of body and speech. If you mentally project an excellent intention, you create the merit of others and obtain greater [merit] as well. If we are more highly developed and we rejoice in someone lower, we obtain greater roots of virtue. If they are our equal, we obtain equal roots of virtue; if we are lower and we rejoice in someone higher, like a bodhisattva, we definitely obtain a portion of their roots of virtue. There is nothing superior to rejoicing for accumulating merit. [Je] Gungtang [Jampalyang] Rinpoche stated,

> If someone is going to create virtue while lying down,
> He [or she] should meditate on rejoicing in others.

There is also a system of acquiring roots of virtue similar to the previous [explanation] found in the *Golden Rosary*[247] and other scriptures, which state that if the object of reliance is higher, [then] you obtain lesser power, and also that the degree of your rejoicing determines the power you obtain. Meditate with joy, without jealousy or competitiveness, and rejoice in virtues performed by others. This is, for example, similar to the extreme joy that a mother develops when her child performs a noble deed. Thus, you obtain a great force of virtuous roots through rejoicing,

247. Tib. *gSer phreng.*

as related in the story of the beggar.[248] A person with very little mental capacity can obtain powerful roots of virtue through this wondrous method, which is the main practice of the bodhisattvas.

There are two types of shravakas: trainees and nontrainees. The nontrainees are shravaka arhats. For the most part, pratyekabuddhas actualize all five paths in one life; however, they are not called "pratyekabuddha learners" when they don't actualize the remaining paths beyond the path of preparation in one life. Although we pretend to be Mahayanists, these days, although they may be on the path of accumulation of a shravaka, [people] still make proclamations such as "I am a buddha!"

Next, from the Teacher until your guru, rejoice in their deeds by considering what type of body the venerable guru has and so on. The way to rejoice in the roots of virtue of persons who have entered the path is revealed in the phrase "the merit of all living beings." The phrase "the mouth of my guru" refers to oral instructions. At this point, you take a different perspective in rejoicing and practice rejoicing in your own virtue. In the same way, practice rejoicing in the virtue of others, the virtues of both self and others, the virtues of your former lives as well, the virtues of this life, and the roots of virtues performed in previous years. The *Sutra of the Ten Dharmas*[249] states,

> Know smoke from fire;
> Likewise know water from waterbirds.
> Know those endowed with the mind of a bodhisattva
> From the pure signs of their lineage.

Likewise, you obtained this physical form through previously guarding your moral discipline and so forth. Rejoice in [this] by contemplating these [indications of previous virtue]. From this moment onward, you must not be misled:

248. I was unable to locate the source of this story, but it may be in reference to a beggarwoman who went to a vast ceremony conducted by a grand lama. Standing outside, she rejoiced in the great offering being made. At the conclusion of the ceremony, the lama dedicated the merit to her, stating that her act of rejoicing had created the greatest merit of all.
249. Tib. *Chos bcu pa'i mdo.*

> The precious human body you have currently obtained
> Is from a precious rebirth in a former life.
> Do not let the precious bhikshu of this moment
> Throw you into an abyss in your future life.

Rejoicing in the virtues of others is a practice employed exclusively by bodhisattvas. For instance, the father of a household carries the responsibility of providing sustenance for many people [in his household] by feeding and clothing them. Then, if one of the children is able to provide his own food and clothing, the father will be delighted in his actions and think of his great kindness. Likewise, although bodhisattvas carry the sole responsibility of liberating all living beings from samsara, when living beings practice virtue from their own side, the bodhisattvas are especially delighted and rejoice.

The Limb of Requesting Them to Turn the Wheel of Dharma

The fifth limb is requesting [the objects of refuge] to turn the wheel of Dharma. Regarding the "wheel," [Vasubandhu's] *Treasury [of Abhidharma]* states,

> There are two aspects of the Teacher's holy Dharma,
> And these are the nature of scripture and realization.

From the point when the Teacher turned the wheel of Dharma of scripture and realization up until [the time of] your guru, it has been turned by each successive person in the lineage. Moreover, the teaching of scripture consists of explaining them and comprehending through listening and contemplation. The teaching of realization consists of accomplishing them and comprehending them through practice,

> That act of comprehension is only through
> Speaking and practicing.

Moreover, according to the well-known metaphor, an official, a king, and so forth should preserve the teachings of the Buddha through influence and power.[250] Turning the wheel of Dharma of realization also depends upon turning the wheel of Dharma of scripture. Whether or not the lama turns the wheel of Dharma depends upon the disciples requesting him to do so through supplications. It is not like a doctor from the region of Po carrying a bag of medicine and traveling from door to door inquiring whether anyone in the household is ill.

The Teacher arrived in the world for the sake of turning the wheel of Dharma; however, [a sutra states,]

> These beings had faith in Brahma, and when he
> Made the supplication, the wheel of Dharma was turned.

Thus, until Brahma made the supplication, the [wheel of Dharma] was not turned. The same thing applies to us as well; therefore, you should make supplications to whomever exists in the ten directions and so forth. Although [the preliminary prayer] states "the aspect of enlightenment," if you have a mandala, you should arrange nine heaps—four in the cardinal [directions], four in the intermediate directions, and one in the center—after which you imagine it becomes a golden wheel with a thousand spokes. The best would be to imagine that you invoke each and every buddha in the ten directions and emanate [an equal number of images of yourself in the aspect of Brahma] who entreat the [buddhas] to turn the wheel of Dharma. If you do it this way, it creates a very important auspiciousness so that you will not be bereft of Dharma in the future. If your mind can't manage [such a complicated visualization], invoke each being in the field of merit. If even that is too much, simply imagine the field of merit as it is.

250. I have been unable to find the source and exact meaning of this metaphor. Sharpa Tulku surmised that it may mean that it is up to those in a position of power to use their influence to help preserve the Buddhist teachings by supporting practitioners, implementing favorable laws, and so forth.

The Limb of Making Supplications Not to Pass into Nirvana

The sixth limb is to make supplications [to the objects of refuge requesting them] not to pass into nirvana. It is extremely important that you also make supplications to your guru requesting him [or her] not to pass into nirvana. The *Sutra of Golden Light* states,

> The Buddha does not pass into nirvana,
> Nor does the Dharma vanish;
> Yet for the sake of thoroughly liberating beings
> He demonstrates a thorough passing into nirvana.

In general, although [it is best] if the guru and buddhas do not pass into nirvana and the Dharma does not disappear, [they sometimes] reveal the manner of passing into nirvana and the disappearance of the Dharma for the welfare of disciples; the Teacher said the same thing to Ananda three times.[251] The guru and buddhas not passing into nirvana depends upon the disciple making requests for them to remain. Thus, when you make supplications, it becomes the supreme means of accomplishing your own longevity. At this point, if you have a mandala, you should again place five heaps on it—four in the cardinal directions and one in the center—and imagine that they become a lion throne. Furthermore, invoke each being from the field of merit and so forth, and emanate [as many bodies] as you are mentally capable of after offering [the lion thrones] as a supplication. This reveals the way of obtaining eight great benefits from this practice.[252] Even though the [beings in the field of merit] remain silent at this point or when supplicating them to turn the wheel of Dharma, you should nevertheless imagine that each one accepts your request. Master Tsultrim Kyang composed a commentary on some of the detailed points of the Vinaya in which he stated that the term "remain silent" indicates that to

251. Buddha Shakyamuni mentioned to Ananda on three different occasions that it is important to ask enlightened beings not to pass into the sphere of nirvana, but Ananda didn't pick up on the import of what Buddha was stating. Because of this he didn't request the Buddha not to pass into the sphere of nirvana, resulting in the Buddha's passing away.
252. I have been unable to locate these eight great benefits.

give verbal permission is the sign of being an ordinary being. Therefore, the perfect and complete Buddha and the shravakas give permission by remaining silent.

The Limb of Dedication

The seventh limb is dedication. If you don't seal the dedication with emptiness, your roots of virtue will be destroyed through anger. [Chandrakirti's] *Guide to the Middle Way* states,

> Therefore, through becoming angry with the Conqueror's sons,
> You instantly destroy the virtues accumulated
> In a hundred eons through generosity and discipline;
> Therefore, there is no negativity greater than impatience.

[Shantideva's] *Guide to the Bodhisattva's Way of Life* states,

> All the good deeds such as
> Generosity and worshiping the Sugatas
> Accumulated over a thousand eons
> Are destroyed by a moment's anger.

When a person of inferior merit becomes angry with someone of superior merit, he [or she] destroys the virtue of a thousand eons. When one of inferior merit becomes angry with another person of inferior merit, he destroys the roots of merit of a hundred eons. Considering how the force of the superiority or inferiority of the object of reliance [determines the amount of virtue destroyed], you should investigate the way in which merit is destroyed if they are equal to each other.

Some people perform noble actions yet don't dedicate them, and when they get angry, as explained above, they exhaust [their merit] so that it has no opportunity to bear fruit. Some people make dedications [of merit] for mere happiness in a future life, and that is [therefore] the only result. Some dedicate [merit] for merely attaining the state of a Hinayana arhat, and [so their merit] is exhausted upon attaining the sphere of nirvana without remainder. When they dedicate their merit for unexcelled complete enlightenment, [however,] it cannot be destroyed by anger and so forth and will not be exhausted until the attainment of enlightenment. The *Sutra Requested by Sagara Mati*[253] states,

> Just as a drop of water that falls into a great ocean
> Will not run out until the ocean is exhausted,
> So the virtue dedicated as a cause of enlightenment
> Is not exhausted until the attainment of enlightenment.

Some scholars say that [this verse] doesn't exist in that sutra, and that the verse exists in *Inexhaustible Wisdom*[254] and is therefore incorrect. However, it is cited in [Je Tsongkhapa's] *Great Treatise on the Stages of the Path* and others. Although it couldn't be found, or didn't exist, in any editions of the *Sutra Requested by Sagara Mati* other than one, there are limitless scriptures that we haven't seen, and there are definitely transmissions of other [editions] of the *Sutra Requested by Sagara Mati.* Thus, if you mix a drop of water with the ocean, it will not become exhausted until the ocean dries up.

Pabongkha Rinpoche told us a story of two messengers who mixed their bean tsampa and barley tsampa.[255]

The difference between a dedication and an aspirational prayer, moreover, is a function of whether or not there is something being dedicated. When one identifies a thing to be dedicated and then prays, "On its basis, may there be such and such a result!" this is both a dedication and an aspirational prayer. If, without something to be dedicated, one thinks, "In the future, may I be thus!" that is an aspirational prayer but not a dedication. In general, for a dedication prayer, it is extremely important that you also request the holy beings such as your guru, buddhas, and so forth to turn the wheel of Dharma and to engage in extensive activities, just as they prayed to carry them out according to their bodhichitta generated

253. Tib. *Blo gros rgya mtshos zhus pa'i mdo.*

254. Tib. *Blo gros mi zad.*

255. This story can be found in Pabongkha Rinpoche, *Liberation in Our Hands, Part One: The Preliminaries*, trans. Sermey Khensur Lobsang with Artemus B. Engle (Howell, NJ: Mahayana Sutra and Tantra Press, 1990), 219, n. 66.

in previous rebirths. Evil Mara is able to strike numerous living beings with disaster, which is the result of his former mistaken prayers. Further, when it comes to our virtues, they are like raw gold, while the dedication prayer is like using that gold to make ornaments and jewelry. Further, the dedication and prayer are like the reins and the bridle that guide the horse. Arya Shariputra became the foremost of the learned shravakas of the Teacher, which was the result of offering his knife and needle in the past when he was a tailor for the bhikshus' robes. He also had many other good qualities. A sutra states,

> The concordant condition of all Dharmas
> Depends upon the strength of your aspiration.
> Whatever dedication prayers one makes
> Will result in the attainment of just that.

Day Nine

The teachings of the great being Shantideva state,

> In dependence upon this boat of a human life,
> You can be liberated from the great river of suffering.
> This boat will be difficult to acquire in a future life,
> So this is no time to sleep, you fool!

Kyabje Pabongkha Rinpoche began with the following motivation:

We can be liberated from the great ocean of samsara and be guided to the island of liberation with such a boat. Although we have obtained this physical form, if we don't use it to be liberated from the ocean of samsara, such a life as this will be extremely difficult to acquire again in the future. Therefore, do not come under the influence of this life's affairs but strive with all [the determination] you can to be able to travel to the blissful land of liberation; for that purpose, listen to these teachings on the stages of the path.

He then covered yesterday's outline on the seven limbs.

Regarding the nature of dedication, the *Ornament of the Mahayana Sutras* declares,

> The dedication of the stable
> Is an intention accompanied by aspiration.

If the way of dedicating is expanded, there are seven sections. If you entreat the field of merit and so forth to bear witness to your dedication, it has the great distinction of accomplishing your dedication prayers. With respect to the six, prostration and so forth[256] have their objects of dedication, such as the prostrations and so forth. With respect to the necessity [of dedication], [Shantideva's] *Guide to the Bodhisattva's Way of Life* states,

> I dedicate everything for the sake of
> Enlightenment for the welfare of living beings.

A sutra also states,

> The roots of virtue should be dedicated collectively for all living beings.

When we dedicate for our own enlightenment, [the roots of virtue] become [a cause for becoming] a pratyekabuddha. By dedicating them to complete enlightenment, the roots of virtue cannot be destroyed by anger, as explained earlier, and they will not be exhausted. [Shantideva's] *Guide to the Bodhisattva's Way of Life* and [Chandrakirti's] *Guide to the Middle Way* also state that the roots of virtue from bodhichitta can be destroyed by anger. During the dedication, dedicate them by means of unobservable [emptiness]. A scripture states,

> Extraordinary thorough dedication
> Is the supreme activity.
> It has the special aspect of unobservability;
> It has the sign of irreversibility.

If you capture the roots of virtue from reciting even a single verse or one round of Manis[257] with noble dedications, they will not be exhausted until you attain the state of enlightenment. In the meantime, it is impossible

256. The six are (1) prostrating, (2) offering, (3) confessing, (4) rejoicing, (5) requesting, and (6) beseeching.
257. "Mani" is a colloquial abbreviation for the mantra of Chenrezig: OM MANI PADME HUM.

Dignaga

to exhaust them through the happiness of gods and men. It would be excellent if you combined those dedications with meditation on the path.

In short, whatever you dedicate, dedicate for unsurpassed complete enlightenment for the welfare of all living beings. The "substance" is your roots of virtue. A dedication with such an aspect blocks grasping at the true existence of the three circles of the dedication[258] and must be

258. The three circles are (1) the substance of dedication, (2) the act of dedication, and (3) the object of the dedication.

embraced by method and wisdom. It would be difficult for us to replicate this with our slight wisdom; therefore, if you make extremely powerful dedications with verses such as "Just as the hero Manjushri realizes the nature of things . . . ," this will suffice. For example, previously there was an old woman at the Jokhang [temple] in Lhasa who made a very eloquent prayer. A nomad heard her and said, "Although I don't understand the intention of what she said, I also make my dedication prayer in just the same way as the dear old woman." Dedications such as "The [path] of noble deeds upon which the conquerors of the three have gone . . ." and "Through this completely pure white virtue . . ." are great binding prayers of dedication. If in addition to these you recognize the view about the unobservability of the three circles, it will be an excellent way to train yourself in the view. If you dedicate [the roots of virtue] as a contributing factor for the enlightened actions of the buddhas in the ten directions to guide all living beings, they will also be inexhaustible. Although this functions to remove doubts about dedicating the roots of virtue of other living beings, I wonder whether the act of rejoicing in the roots of virtue of other living beings is [also] a dedication of virtue.

There are three great dedications: either (1) dedicate as a cause of attaining the resultant complete enlightenment, (2) dedicate as a cause of comprehending the holy Dharma, or (3) [dedicate] to be cared for by spiritual masters.[259] The prayers "The prayers of the bodhisattvas . . ." and "Whatever merit . . ." are also prayers to comprehend the holy Dharma. There are countless hundreds of thousands of prayers of the bodhisattvas that are included within prayers for comprehending the holy Dharma. Because both of these are dependent upon a guru, both of these [kinds of] prayers are indirect causes to be cared for by the guru. Moreover, so is the prayer "The unsurpassed teaching of the Teacher . . ." Although we have a great wave of virtuous roots, when it comes time to dedicate [them], we dedicate for long lives, freedom from illness, collecting debts, winning lawsuits, and so forth. When we do so, we waste and squander our roots of virtue. Yet if we dedicate even the barely discernible roots of virtue from [offering] a single stick of incense along with a prayer the

259. The third great dedication of virtue is mentioned below, at note 268.

size of a mountain, although it may be small at the time, it will bear an enormous result:

> If this mere portion of virtue had already been transformed
> By the "supreme prayers of skillful means" of the conquerors' sons,
> The inferior results would have swiftly become excellent
> And would never be exhausted.
>
> Whatever virtue exists in the three times
> Should be transformed by a great wave of prayers;
> Since all wise beings engage in this,
> You too should engage in this skillful means.[260]

The first two [great dedications] are included in the verse that begins, "Through this completely pure white virtue . . ."

In the oral instructions of explanation, each of the seven limbs leaves an imprint. For example, prostrations accomplish the major mark of the ushnisha, the vajra body and so forth; offerings attain mastery of the sky treasure of enjoyments during enlightenment; and so forth.[261]

Accomplishing a Definitive Integration between Your Mind and the Supplication

The sixth preliminary ritual is accomplishing a definitive integration between your mind and the supplication. The [First Panchen Lama's] *Path to Bliss* and the [Second Panchen Lama's] *Swift Path* offer the mandala of supplication during the fifth ritual preliminary, and [the Fifth Dalai Lama's] *Manjushri's Oral Instructions* offers it during the sixth. Although it is not taught as being concealed among the three great purposes conjoined with mantra within the preliminary rituals, it is clear within the new arrangement of the Lama Chöpa ritual and so forth,[262] which con-

260. Although this prayer appears in numerous rituals, I have extracted this translation from the extensive dedication prayers of Chakrasamvara.
261. For a full list, see Pabongkha Rinpoche, *Liberation in Our Hands.*
262. This refers to the arrangement of Lama Chöpa with the preliminary rituals (*jorchö*).

tains the three great purposes and the *Foundation of All Good Qualities*;[263] the latter is utilized in this [ritual] as a well-known request for powerful blessings.[264]

The three great purposes state, "Outer and inner obstructions . . ." The outer obstructions are things such as a king not acting in accordance with the Dharma. Inner obstructions are when you have numerous illnesses and so forth. Secret obstructions are not having a stable mind for practicing Dharma and so forth. They depend upon your not making supplications for your guru's blessings. Mochog [Rinpoche] stated,[265]

> It is doubtful you will be liberated through rigorous practice;
> There is no doubt you will be liberated through faith and devotion.

And Gyalwa Götsangpa[266] stated,

> There are many meditations on the generation stage;
> None of them surpasses meditating on the guru.

Tilopa [988–1069] proclaimed,

> Naropa, the foremost of
> All enhancements is the guru.

Recite the supplication "I request you my glorious and precious root guru. . . ." Make the supplication twice, during which a purifying descent [of nectar] and a duplicate [of your guru] dissolve into you, while you [simultaneously make supplications] to the lineage of vast activities down to Atisha, purify obstructions to generating the vast stages of the path, and generate realizations of the vast stages of the path. While [making supplications] to the lineage of profound view down to Atisha, you thus purify obstructions to [developing] realizations of the profound stages of

263. Tib. *Yon tan gzhi gyur ma.*

264. For a translation of the jorchö preliminary ritual, see the appendices in volume 1 of Pabongkha Rinpoche, *Liberation in Our Hands.*

265. At this point the explanation of the third point mentioned earlier begins.

266. Tib. rGyal ba rgod tshang pa (1189–1258).

the path. In a similar way, from Atisha the Great, the vast and profound have been combined as one [lineage]; thus, it is called "the stages of the profound path." Therefore, they don't need to be separated, and you combine this [portion of the request] with purifying obstructions to generating realizations of the stages of the path to enlightenment.

The biographies of the lamrim lineage gurus are in texts such as *Opening the Door to the Supreme Path*,[267] which is like the root of the path. Practitioners of the lamrim should definitely become acquainted with their biographies. According to tradition, the last lines of each of the verses of the *Path to Bliss* and the *Swift Path* are recited twice. The field of merit is [supplicated in] this way as well. In the complete preliminary ritual, you perform scanning meditation in dependence upon the *Foundation of All Good Qualities*. It is also permissible to leave this [prayer] aside when carrying out the visualizations of the lamrim.

When you get to the point of tranquil abiding and superior seeing, it would be the incorrect object to imagine purifying nectar and so forth descending from the lineage of vast activities and so forth; therefore, it should be the lineage of profound view. Regarding the cycle of secret mantra, this should be carried out from the lineage of blessed practice. At this point you can receive the blessings of the four empowerments and the four actions by combining it with visualizations of mantra. I am not going to explain this, however, since many of you have not received an [empowerment] of mantra. It is a great binding factor of prayer to also recite "Throughout all my lives, may I never be separated from the guru. . . ."[268]

While dissolving [the field of merit] into light, five-colored light rays radiate from the heart of the principal [deity] and come into the presence of the three lineages, the gurus, and so forth. Their retinues melt into light and dissolve into the four principal figures.[269] The deities on the lotus tiers dissolve into their lion thrones, which dissolve into the lion throne of the principal figure. Imagine that the wish-fulfilling tree disappears

267. Tib. *Lam mchog sgo 'byed.*

268. The third great dedication of virtue is exemplified by this request.

269. The four principal figures would represent (1) the lineage of the vast activities, (2) the lineage of the profound view, (3) the lineage of blessed practices, and (4) the lineage of your direct gurus.

into emptiness. Evoke a clear image of the five remaining principal figures and their retinues. Finally, Maitreya and Manjushri dissolve into the right and left shoulders of Lama Losang Tubwang Dorje Chang.[270] Continue until Vajradhara dissolves into his heart, so that Vajradhara dissolves in the same way you dissolve the exalted wisdom being and he becomes inseparable [with the Buddha].[271] Regarding the lama before you, regardless of whether or not he is living, you should not dissolve him into light but dissolve him into the heart of the Buddha, as though absorbing butter into butter. The Buddha also dissolves into your root guru on the crown of your head. The throne also dissolves into the principal. Making supplications to the guru on the crown of your head while carrying out your meditations is the way of making guru yoga the life of the path.

The guru on your crown can be utilized as the single principal [deity], appearing as Avalokiteshvara while practicing love, compassion, and so forth; as Manjushri during [practice of] the view [of emptiness]; and as the guru deity in other [meditations]. Make a single final recitation to the Dharma of the stages of the path to enlightenment as well. It is of great importance to make supplications through planting the stake.[272] Dzogchen Patrul Rinpoche [1808–1887] stated,

> What use is listening if you haven't retained even one of the hundred things you have heard?
> What use is contemplating when you need to make further requests although you have already heard it?
> Do away with meditation that does not become the antidote to the afflictions.

The Dharma, guru, and personal deities are not like provisions of salt and flour. If we view them in this way, there will never come a time when

270. On Lama Losang Tubwang Dorje Chang, see note 202 above.

271. When you visualize a particular enlightened being, it is called the "commitment being." When you invoke the actual omniscient mind of that enlightened being, it is called the "wisdom being." You then dissolve the wisdom being into the commitment being. Here, you regard Vajradhara as the wisdom being and Buddha Shakyamuni as the commitment being and absorb Vajradhara into Buddha Shakyamuni.

272. Tib. *phur tshugs*. This is a process of repeating a supplication repeatedly as a means of making your request increasingly firm, much like pounding a stake into the ground.

we cross the threshold of the path. If we have reached complete certainty about whatever practices we undertake, such as accomplishing the Dharma and so forth, even the state of enlightenment will most certainly not be a long way off. Like striking a phurba in one spot, you should make supplications to the guru alone with verses such as the [request from the Lama Chöpa ritual that states], "You are the guru, [you are the *yidam*, you are the *daka* and Dharma protector] . . . ," while imagining him to be the sole embodiment of all objects of refuge such as the gurus, personal deities, buddhas, bodhisattvas, shravakas, pratyekabuddhas, Dharma protectors, and so forth. While meditating on the actual stages of the path, you should make the request correspond with that section and make the changes in recitation as explained above. According to the *Path to Bliss* and the *Swift Path*, at the conclusion of the request [to the guru] as the embodiment of all objects of refuge, you should transform yourself, all living beings, and so forth [into the Buddha and his surrounding pure land]. Otherwise, the conclusions of the various preliminary practices are the same.

The Actual Practice

At this point, the outlines of [Je Tsongkhapa's] *Middle-Length Treatise on the Stages of the Path* state,

[The Actual Practice has two sections:]

1. How to Carry Out [the Meditation] in General
2. How to Carry Them Out at This Point [in Particular]

How to Carry Out [the Meditation] in General has three sections:

1. Identifying Meditation
2. The Faults of Improper Meditation
3. How to Carry Out Proper Meditation

Many of the previous Tibetans asserted that placement meditation was the only type of meditation, and that all types of conceptions and analysis are grasping [at signs of inherent existence], and they therefore did not assert analytical meditation as meditation. Je Rinpoche [Tsongkhapa] stated that in general there are two types of meditation: analytical and placement. In particular, without analytical meditation, you won't be able to develop even the slightest realization of proper reliance upon the spiritual guide, which illustrates the great importance of analytical meditation and grants stark recognition of these two types of meditation. During a certain period of time, other than Je Tsongkhapa, most Tibetan lamas didn't understand that analytical meditation is meditation.

Therefore, you should meditate with both analytical and placement meditation by ascertaining the classifications and the proper order of the Dharma as your object of meditation. For example, if you are not certain about the quantities when it comes to making a full pot of tea, and if [as a result] you don't use enough salt, [then] you will incur the fault of depreciation, whereas if you use too much soda, you will incur the fault of excess, and you will become bloated. Just as [the tea] won't be delicious if you confuse the proper order and mistake its preparation, in the same way, if you don't meditate on the lamrim and instead meditate on the channels, winds, and so forth, there is a risk of going to the vajra hells, whereas if you begin by meditating on the proper reliance upon the spiritual guide, you will reach the state of Vajradhara.[273]

How to Carry Out Proper Meditation

In a similar way to the first training in faith as the root for proper reliance upon the spiritual guide by contemplating the benefits in the outlines by utilizing scriptures, reasoning, examples, and logical arguments, once you have a proper reliance upon the spiritual guide, [apply the same process] to subjects such as wasting your leisure and [precious human] endowment. While training in faith as the root, you should not mix it up with things such as recalling his [or her] kindness with mindfulness. If you are mentally uncertain because you merely neglected the first portion of the lamrim, you won't understand the [following] meditation topics.

273. The first two headings are included in the paragraph above.

Like needing tsampa, salt, and butter when making some food to eat, if you leave out even one section of the lamrim, you will not understand the path. When this happens you won't [be able to] understand how to meditate on the stages of the path by merely reading the text. This is why analytical meditation is more important than placement meditation. You definitely need analytical meditation for renunciation, bodhichitta, and emptiness as well:

> Many are deceived at their time of need
> By those whose knowledge remains solely in the text,
> Those who don't practice secret mantra,
> And those who teach while being absentminded.

When even one word makes it into your mind, that much is sufficient for meditation, yet if the mind is uncertain, you will not be able to access it when you need it; therefore, it will not yield great benefit.

Although there are six sections during an elaborate explanation, when it comes time to meditate, there are four.

Relying upon the Spiritual Guide has four sections:

1. The Benefits of Reliance [upon the Spiritual Guide]
2. The Faults of Not Relying and the Faults of Improper Reliance
3. How to Rely in Thought
4. How to Rely in Action

The four are similar to the outlines for a practical commentary on the lamrim in the smaller texts. Furthermore, the root of whether or not all the excellent accumulations emerge—such as generating realizations of the grounds and paths of all the sutras and tantras and so forth—depends upon how perfect your way of training in faith as the root is. From the outset of that training, you must understand the benefits of relying upon the guru and the faults of not relying upon him [or her] or having a faulty way of reliance. There are eight benefits of reliance.

The Benefits of Relying Properly upon the Spiritual Guide has eight sections:

1. You Will Come Closer to the State of Enlightenment
2. You Will Delight the Conquerors
3. You Will Not Be Harmed by Demons and Bad Companions
4. All Your Afflictive Emotions and Unwholesome Behavior Will Naturally Cease
5. All Your Realizations of the Grounds and Paths Will Continuously Increase
6. You Will Not Be Deprived of Spiritual Guides in All Your Lives
7. You Will Not Fall into the Lower Realms
8. You Will Accomplish All Temporary and Ultimate Aims

You Will Come Closer to the State of Enlightenment has two sections:

1. By Practicing the Instructions Taught to You by Your Guru, You Will Come Closer to the State of Enlightenment
2. By Worshiping and Respectfully Honoring Your Guru, You Will Come Closer to the State of Enlightenment

By Practicing the Instructions Taught to You by Your Guru, You Will Come Closer to the State of Enlightenment

Enlightenment that would otherwise take three countless great [eons] to accomplish is bestowed in one short human life:

> Vajra Holder, my jewel-like guru
> Through whose kindness I am
> Filled with the state of great bliss in an instant,
> At your lotus feet I bow.

From the point of view of the gods above to the hell beings below, one human life is like an instant. This meaning is also contained in *Lama Chöpa* when it states,

> I prostrate to the lotus feet of my jewel-like guru,
> The vajra holder, whose compassion
> Can bestow in an instant even the supreme state of
> The three bodies, the sphere of great bliss.

The *Essence of Nectar [Stages of the Path]* states,

> The great unification, extremely difficult to obtain
> Even through practicing with a hundredfold effort
> Over an ocean of countless eons, can easily be accomplished
> In one short life in [this] degenerate age in dependence upon the guru's power.

Je Mila[repa] also attained enlightenment in one life through properly relying upon his spiritual guide, Marpa. He endured hardships such as building a square nine-story tower. And the primary [practice of] those such as the mahasiddhas of India, though they relied upon the unmistaken path of mantra to attain enlightenment, was proper reliance upon the spiritual guide. Not only mantra but, according to the *Ornament of the Mahayana Sutras*, the perfection vehicle takes two countless [eons to attain],[274] and in the *Great Commentary to the Perfection of Wisdom Sutra in Eight Thousand Lines,*[275] you must accumulate merit for twenty-four countless eons. The bodhisattva Sadaprarudita progressed from the path of accumulation to the eighth bodhisattva ground in the span of one life through his perfect reliance upon [his guru] Dharmodgata. Despite having direct visions of many tathagatas, he [realized that] it was also extremely important to meet and establish a karmic connection with a lama; therefore, he still wasn't satisfied and went in search of Dharmodgata and attained the "acceptance that Dharmas are unproduced."[276]

274. It is generally said to take three countless great eons to become enlightened.
275. This is the commentary by Haribhadra mentioned earlier.
276. This is a type of attainment on the eighth bodhisattva ground.

He came close to surpassing the swiftness that even mantra provides, without any regard for his body or life, so that he could engage in proper reliance upon his spiritual guide. Protector Nagarjuna stated,

> If someone were to fall from the peak of a great mountain,
> Although he might think he will not fall, he would still fall.
> If you obtain beneficial transmission from the kind guru,
> Although you may think you will not be liberated, you will still become liberated.

[The mahasiddha] Padampa [Sangye (d. 1117)] stated,

> When led by the guru, you can reach any place you desire;
> The guide's wages are offered in faith and devotion, people of Dingri.

When a fully qualified guru and a student who is a worthy vessel meet, it is said to be as though it were sculpted by the hands of the Buddha. If you can conduct yourself in that way, you will quickly become enlightened, just like Gyalwa Ensapa and others, as taught in the biographies of the lamrim lineage gurus.

By Worshiping and Respectfully Honoring Your Guru, You Will Come Closer to the State of Enlightenment

> Therefore, because a single hair-pore of
> The master is superior to merit of the
> Buddhas and bodhisattvas in the ten directions,
> The buddhas and bodhisattvas have perceived that
> You should make offerings to the master.

That meaning is expressed in *Lama Chöpa*,

> To all the conquerors in the three times and ten directions . . .[277]

277. The entire verse reads, "I make requests to you, my compassionate refuge and protector; /

The roots of virtue from worshiping the guru for merely one morning overpower the merit from worshiping a thousand buddhas. With respect to the phrase "hair-pore of the guru," this refers to his horse and so forth, as well as pet dog and so forth, and is saying that you should worship things like that, on up. If you worship something such as your guru's pet dog, the benefits are far greater even than worshiping all the buddhas in the ten directions. Once when Geshe Tolungpa understood that his own guru, [Geshe] Chen-nga-wa, was residing in the Phenpo Lo Monastery, he said, "I get much greater benefit from giving food to Lopa's[278] dog than from inviting the monks of Tolung for a Dharma festival," and acted accordingly.

Moreover, among the recipients of the offerings, the pratyekabuddhas are superior to the shravakas, the bodhisattvas are superior to them, the buddhas are superior to them, and offering to one hair-pore of the guru is said to be superior to them. [Protector Nagarjuna's *Five Stages*[279] states],

> You should completely forsake all [other] offerings
> And commence with perfect offerings to the guru.
> By pleasing him, you will obtain the
> Supreme exalted wisdom of omniscience.

Sapan proclaimed,

> The merit accumulated by giving away your head, limbs, and possessions
> Through the means of the perfection vehicle for a thousand eons
> Can be accumulated in a single instant through this path of the guru;
> Oh my, you must honor him with joyous reflection.

When presenting offerings to all the buddhas of the ten directions, although there is the benefit of presenting the offering, it is not certain that you will [also] obtain the benefit of [the buddhas] accepting it. If

---

Even just one of your hair pores / Is praised as the perfect field of merit superior to / All the conquerors of the three times and the ten directions."

278. Lopa is another name for Geshe Chen-nga-wa.

279. Tib. *Rim lnga.*

you present offerings to your gurus such as your personal teacher and so forth, the conquerors will spontaneously enter into his [or her] heart and joyously accept the offerings, whereby you obtain both benefits.

You Will Delight the Conquerors

For example, if a monastery's representative conducts himself well, the monks will naturally be delighted. Likewise, the Buddha emanates as the guru, who then works for the welfare of disciples. Once we understand this fact [and honor the guru properly, the buddhas] naturally enter his [or her] heart with joy. The *Essence of Nectar Stages of the Path* states,

> When a disciple relies properly upon his guru,
> The conquerors are invoked into the body of the guru.
> They remain joyfully and accept all the collection of offerings,
> And also bless the mental continuum of that [disciple].

This is also the final intention of the tantras and mahasiddhas. [The Fifth Dalai Lama's] *Manjushri's Oral Instructions* states,

> For the few endowed with this meaning,
> I will abide in his body and
> Accept the offerings of other practitioners;
> This will delight my mental continuum
> And purify their karmic obstructions.[280]

This comes down to the same essential point. Therefore, this is stating that when a disciple makes offerings to his [or her] guru, Vajradhara also delightfully enters into the body of the guru and, remaining there, accepts the offerings. There is no activity superior to correctly engaging in proper reliance upon your guru as a means of delighting the Conqueror. The *Essence of Nectar [Stages of the Path]* proclaims,

280. The first-person pronoun is being used here by Buddha Vajradhara, who originally spoke this verse. See note 26 in part 2 of Pabongkha Rinpoche's *Liberation in Our Hands* for details about the text quoted here.

> When [disciples] undertake proper reliance upon the holy spiritual guides,
> Like a mother seeing her child accomplish something beneficial,
> All the conquerors become delighted from the depths of their hearts
> And state, "This one will quickly be liberated from samsara."

You Will Not Be Harmed by Demons and Bad Companions

You will obtain great merit through your excellent reliance upon your spiritual guide, and through that acquisition and so forth you will also be invulnerable to obstacles. Bad companions will also be unable to harm you. A sutra states,

> It is difficult for karma and afflictive emotions to get the best of bodhisattvas who are thoroughly cared for by their spiritual guides.

As this states, it will be difficult for karma and afflictive emotions to overcome you. The *Essence of Nectar [Stages of the Path]* also states,

> At that time, all the buddhas bless him, and
> Through the force of entering the crown of the faithful-minded,
> He will not be harmed by demons, afflictive emotions, and so forth.

All Your Afflictive Emotions and Unwholesome Behavior Will Naturally Cease

[The *Essence of Nectar* continues:]

> If you always serve him through constant devotion,
> Afflictive emotions and unwholesome behavior will naturally cease.

If you rely perfectly upon your spiritual guide, you will know to adopt virtue and forsake nonvirtue. Your afflictive emotions and unwholesome behavior will naturally cease; therefore, you will not be harmed by afflictive emotions and unwholesome behavior. For example, the afflictive emotions and unwholesome behavior of those who remain in the physical presence of their guru and in close contact with abbots and good teachers will naturally cease. The primary [reason] is that, through proper reliance upon the spiritual guide, you listen to the stages of the path to enlightenment, whereby you come to recognize afflictive emotions and unwholesome actions, which then naturally cease.

All Your Realizations of the Ground and Paths Will Continuously Increase

If your reliance upon your spiritual guide is proper and good, there will be no difficulty in developing your realizations of the grounds and paths as well. Indeed, your realizations of the grounds and paths will develop and increase!

Atisha's disciples Amé Jangchub Rinchen and [Palden] Gonpawa compared their realizations, whereby [Palden] Gonpawa and Amé had attained high realizations. When Atisha reached an advanced age, Drom[tonpa] was scooping up [Atisha's] feces with his bare hands when he suddenly developed clairvoyance that could read the minds of others and know the thoughts of creatures as small as ants at a distance so great it would take a vulture eighteen days to reach. Jayulwa Shönu Ö [1075–1138] and Potong Lungpa[281] were servants who served [Geshe] Chen-nga-wa. Jayulwa always served [Geshe] Chen-nga-wa skillfully and proclaimed,

> Although the emanated encircling iron mountain of the mandala is established,
> If the teachings of the holy guru come from
> The instructions of previous holy beings,
> [You will receive benefit] even if each letter is only partially written.

When writing the top section, it is as if each letter is an oral prophecy from the speech of the guru, and even if you don't have time to write the middle part [of the letter], it seems as though it is finished.

281. I believe this is the same as Geshe Tolungpa (1032–1116), mentioned earlier.

One day, [Jayulwa Shönu Ö] was carrying out an order and went to the place where you throw the garbage in the trash, and once his feet touched the third step in the flight of stairs, he developed extraordinary realizations.

You Will Not Be Deprived of Spiritual Guides in All Your Lives

Although you may perceive your personal teacher as nothing more than a depraved person,[282] you should not have contempt for him [or her]. Instead, if you rely upon him properly, this will serve as a result corresponding to the cause,[283] so that in a subsequent rebirth you will encounter lamas like Maitreya and Manjushri. The *Essence of Nectar [Stages of the Path]* states,

> The result corresponding to the cause of properly
> Pleasing your guru in this life will transform into
> Meeting supreme spiritual guides in all future lives, and
> Listening to the unmistaken holy Dharma in its entirety.

There are other teachings similar [to those just mentioned].

You Will Not Fall into the Lower Realms

Through your practice of properly relying upon the spiritual guide, the negative karma that would have caused your rebirth in the lower realms will be purified without any remaining. Marpa also caused Milarepa great hardship nine times, and when he did, [Milarepa] attained enlightenment without the remaining aggregates. This being the case, when you engage in properly relying upon the spiritual guide, it severs obstructions that you have created, and its [associated] karma—which would have resulted in a subsequent experience of the lower realms—is exhausted through a scolding or merely a dream. With respect to being scolded, this is being reprimanded by your personal teacher and so forth. [Geshe] Tolungpa did nothing but reprimand his student Lhasowa, and when he did, Lhasowa's

282. Tib. *sdug rul zhig*.
283. For more on this, see the section below on karma and its effects.

own disciple Nyagmowa exclaimed, "This master is extremely angry with my guru and his disciples!" At this Lhasowa stated, "Each time he acts that way toward me, it is just like receiving a blessing of Heruka." Drogon Tsangpa Gyaré stated,

> When I receive a beating, it is an empowerment bestowed;
> If I am going to receive a blessing, I receive it from that.
> A powerful rebuke is a wrathful mantra;
> With that, my obstacles are dispelled.

Although your guru may feel the need to look at you with a disapproving glance or a slightly gloomy facial expression, due to his mind being either pleased or displeased, these are a means of purifying extremely virulent negativity. The *Array of Stalks Sutra* states,

> The bodhisattva who is perfectly cared for by the spiritual guide will not fall into the lower realms.

Not only that, but you will also recall the guru at the moment of death, and if you make supplications, this is the very best of any transference of consciousness. The *Tantra Requested by Subahu* proclaims,

> If any ordinary being recalls just
> One word of the guru at the time of death,
> This becomes the supreme transference of consciousness practice:
> This being will actualize enlightenment.

This tantra is stating that, through the kindness of the guru, you will not go to the lower realms but will be reborn in a pure land and so forth, after which you will become enlightened.

You Will Accomplish All Temporary and Ultimate Aims

This was explained in the *Avatamsaka Sutra*, and Je Lama [Tsongkhapa] also stated,

> The foundation of all good qualities is the kind Lord,
> Having seen that proper reliance upon him
> Is the very root of the path . . .

And,

> The kind Lord is the root of all good qualities
> Of mundane and supramundane virtue and excellence.

And,

> Having seen that the root of corresponding excellent
> auspiciousness
> And of any excellent accumulations in this life and the next
> Consists of striving in thought and deed to rely properly upon
> The holy spiritual guide who teaches the path,
> Do not forsake him even for the sake of your life,
> And delight him through offering your practice according to
> his teaching.

In both India and Tibet, Je Atisha's enlightened actions were as vast as space, which also came from his proper reliance upon his 151 gurus, such as Serlingpa. [Atisha's disciple] Drom[tonpa] Rinpoche became the crown ornament of the Kadampas. Furthermore, while relying upon Lama Setsun from Kham, during the day [Dromtonpa] would take care of Setsun's consort's young daughter and serve as a stool for [Setsun's consort when she] milked the cows, fetched water, and so forth. At night, he would gird himself with three different types of weapons, such as an arrow, a sword, and a spear, and protect his lama's cattle from enemies, bandits, and thieves. All at one time, he would carry a leather pouch of milk on his back, soften leather with his feet, spin wool with his hands, and so on. He relied upon Setsun from age seventeen until he was thirty years old. Within Tibet, he carried out perfect reliance upon Atisha.

Kuton from Yarlung had nothing more than moderate reverence for Atisha. Drom[tonpa] Rinpoche said, "Let's depart to an area called Nyethang that is a happy valley where flowers grow even in the winter," to which [Atisha] acceded. Inviting him to Nyethang was done through skillful means. Later, when Atisha said that there were no flowers in the wintertime, the teacher [Dromtonpa] emanated a garden of lotus flowers on his tongue together with a miniature Atisha and Drom, after which Atisha saw this emanation.[284]

The great mahasiddhas have also conducted themselves in the way that [Dromtonpa] perfectly relied upon Atisha. Even now, [Dromtonpa] is the crown ornament of all. The quality of the auspicious connection in your reliance upon the spiritual guide is also extremely important. Naropa emanated the mandala of Hevajra and revealed it to Marpa, and when he said, "Will you prostrate to the lama or prostrate to your personal deity?" Marpa made a mistake in establishing an auspicious connection and instead of prostrating to Naropa, he prostrated to Hevajra. When Mila[repa] first met Marpa, [Marpa] revealed himself in the aspect of a plowman, and [Milarepa] didn't recognize Marpa. However, [Marpa] commanded [Milarepa] to finish the remaining plowing and gave him some beer to drink that he had also emanated, which established an auspicious connection. [When Milarepa] came into the presence of Marpa offering numerous supplications, from that very day [Marpa] began rebuking Mila[repa], and [Milarepa] offered his body, speech, and mind, which is said to be a good gesture. Again, at a later time, [Milarepa] obtained many bushels of barley from Lhodrag and offered [Marpa] a stainless empty copper vessel, whereby he incurred a good and bad dependent relationship.

According to the teachings in Tse[chok] Ling Yongzin Pandita [Kachen Yeshe Gyaltsen]'s biography, [Kachen Yeshe Gyaltsen] himself received the empowerment of Heruka in Luipa's tradition and others in the presence of Sharchö Namkha Zangpo. In general, it is taught that when the lama is leaving, you do not prostrate behind him. However, [Kachen Yeshe Gyaltsen] subsequently forgot this teaching and when they met in his hermitage, he recalled the good qualities [of his guru] and made prostrations behind him after they met. Also, when Gyaltsab Je [1364–1432] initially met Je Tsongkhapa, he went up to the teaching mound,[285] which established an auspicious connection. During the painting of a mural at

284. This story is related in detail in Atisha and Dromtonpa, attrib., *The Book of Kadam*, trans. Thupten Jinpa (Boston: Wisdom, 2008).

285. Tib. *pur*. A mound of dirt usually covered with grass, which lamas often used for teaching thrones.

Ganden Monastery, Gyaltsab Je and Dulzin Drakpa Gyaltsen [1350–1413] drew the Buddha as the main object [of the field of merit] instead of the lama, and due to this dependent-related connection, even now, from among the three main monastic institutions of [Sera, Ganden, and Drepung], Ganden has limited scholarship and prosperity because of this mistake of inauspiciousness. This is an essential point that comes from the oral tradition. There are numerous such [events]. All the excellent accumulations in this life and the next depend upon the proper reliance upon the guru, which is the root. You should also perfectly rely upon your personal teacher and so forth.[286]

Next, in [Je Tsongkhapa's] *Middle-Length Treatise on the Stages of the Path* this is elaborated with a repeated explanation and a concise teaching on how to train.

286. Tib. *dge rgan*. This is being translated as "personal teacher." It is often contracted with the suffix *lags* added, to render "Gen-la," and is in reference to your own teacher whom you see most often and who is easily and mistakenly overlooked during the discussions of proper reliance upon the spiritual master.

Day Ten

The teachings from the *Interwoven Praises*[287] state, "This bottomless samsara . . ." up to "whoever goes for refuge today." The quotes from this scripture tell us that, since time without beginning, we have wandered within the bottomless and endless ocean of samsara, through which we experience the unbearable suffering of body and life inflicted by the sea monsters of the afflictive emotions. Yet if there was no way of being liberated from this, our suffering in samsara would be endless. Therefore, we definitely need to seek, in this very moment, a refuge to protect us from this. Furthermore, with respect to the refuge that has terminated all faults and is endowed with all good qualities, it is none other than the Teacher, the perfect and complete Buddha, and it is for that reason that we go for refuge in the Buddha. We entrust ourselves to the scripture and realization of Dharma taught by that teacher as our actual refuge through listening, contemplation, and meditation. We embrace the Sangha as our companions who practice that [Dharma] refuge. [Therefore, set your motivation] as before, by thinking, "By every means possible, I am going to gain liberation from this great ocean of suffering; for that purpose, [I am going to listen to the teachings] on the stages of the path."

After giving this short introduction, Pabongkha Rinpoche once again explained the benefits of proper reliance upon the spiritual guide.

We can even attain enlightenment in one life through secret mantra, in dependence upon proper reliance upon the spiritual guide. This is what Milarepa and others did.

287. Tib. *sPel mar bstod pa.*

The Faults of Not Relying upon Your Spiritual Guide

If we become separated from even a single oral precept that the lama taught, we will experience the opposite effect [of the aforementioned eight benefits] such as "We will come closer to the state of enlightenment," and instead there will be eight faults such as the state of enlightenment becoming increasingly farther away and so forth.

The Faults of Not Relying [upon Your Spiritual Guide] has eight [sections]:

1. If You Disparage Your Guru, You Criticize All the Buddhas
2. If You Generate an Angry Mind toward Your Guru, You Destroy the Roots of Virtue Equal in Number to the Instances of That [Anger] and Will Be Reborn in Hell for [That Number of] Eons
3. You Will Not Accomplish Supreme [Attainments] despite Your Reliance on Mantra
4. Although You May Apply Yourself to the Meaning of Tantra, It Will Be as though You Are Accomplishing the Hells
5. You Will Not Develop Your Previous Good Qualities of the Grounds and Paths or Develop New Ones, and Those You Have Developed Will Deteriorate
6. In This Life You Will Be Tormented by Undesirable Things such as Illness
7. In Your Next Life You Will Wander Endlessly in the Lower Realms
8. You Will Be Deprived of Spiritual Guides in All Lives

If You Disparage Your Guru, You Criticize All the Buddhas

The *Fifty Verses of Guru Devotion* states,

> If a disciple comes under the care of such
> A protector and then despises him,
> He will be despising all the buddhas
> And will continuously receive suffering.

The *Essence of Nectar [Stages of the Path]* proclaims,

> The spiritual guides are the enlightened actions of all the conquerors,
> And because your guru is the very manifestation of that,
> If you disrespect him, you disrespect all the conquerors;
> What could have a more severe consequence than that?

As this states, if we engage in criticism of a lama such as our personal teacher, because that guru is the embodiment of the enlightened actions of all buddhas, it becomes a disparagement of all the buddhas.

If You Generate an Angry Mind toward Your Guru, You Destroy the Roots of Virtue Equal in Number to the Instances of That [Anger] and Will Be Reborn in Hell for [That Number of] Eons

The *Root Tantra of Kalachakra*[288] states,

> Count the moments of anger toward your guru.[289]
> You destroy the merit accumulated for that number of eons, after which
> You will have to experience intense feelings of suffering
> Of hell and so forth for that same amount of time.

If you are angry with your guru for the span of one instant, you destroy your roots of virtue accumulated over that length of time, after which you must remain in hell for eons equal in number to those moments.

288. Tib. *Dus 'khor rtsa rgyud.*
289. According to simple Buddhist mathematical equations, a moment or instant is equivalent to 1/65th of the duration of a finger snap.

You Will Not Accomplish Supreme [Attainments] despite Your Reliance on Mantra

[The fifth chapter of the *Guhyasamaja Root Tantra* states,]

> Although sentient beings have engaged in great acts
> Of nonvirtue such as the five heinous actions,
> In this life they will attain siddhis of the supreme vehicle
> Through the great ocean of the Vajrayana.
>
> Those who disparage their master from the depths of their hearts
> Will be utterly without attainments despite their practice.

If we disparage our guru, however much we enthusiastically exert ourselves in dependence upon mantra, it is absolutely certain that we will not develop realizations. Previously, Marpa's esteemed wife secretly arranged for Mila[repa] to receive instructions in the presence of Ngog Chödor, yet despite his attempts in practice [Milarepa] did not develop even the slightest realization. If things such as this happen even when you don't get the lama's approval, there is no need to mention other [more serious] things.

Although You May Apply Yourself to the Meaning of Tantra, It Will Be as though You Are Accomplishing the Hells

The *Vajra Mandala Adornment Tantra*[290] states,

> Anyone who criticizes his perfect master
> Will be accomplishing the hells and so forth,
> Despite properly practicing the supreme
> Sadhanas of all tantras while abandoning
> Sleep and companions.

290. Tib. *rDo rje snying po rgyan gyi rgyud.*

You Will Not Develop Your Previous Good Qualities of the Grounds and Paths or Develop New Ones, and Those You Have Developed Will Deteriorate

If you disparage your guru, although you may be on the verge of developing realizations, you will not be able to develop them. It is said that Jetsun Rechungpa [Dorje Drakpa (1083–1161)] had created the causes to become enlightened in his lifetime without any physical remnants, yet because he broke the advice of Mila[repa] three times, it took him three lifetimes to become enlightened. In general, if we lose faith in our lama, although we may have a karmic connection, it will be impossible to gain realizations.

Two novice monks from Khoton[291] came to see the Dharma king Songsten Gampo, yet because of their mistaken conduct, their realizations of the grounds and paths deteriorated. It is said that in the past there was a certain intelligent disciple who was flying in the sky, yet as soon as he belittled his master of lesser intelligence, he fell to the ground.

In This Life You Will be Tormented by Undesirable Things such as Illness

Regarding this point, we will leave [this world] with bad conditions surrounding our deaths, all our ventures will not meet with success, and so on. The *Fifty Verses of Guru Devotion* states,

> If you are so stupid as to criticize your master,
> You will be plagued with infectious diseases,
> Afflictive illnesses, harm from spirits,
> Epidemics, and poisons, after which you will die.
>
> You will be killed by kings, fire,
> Poisonous snakes, water, dakinis, thieves,
> Harmful spirits, and harmful evil forces,
> After which you will go to hell.

291. Tib. Li yul. This was a Buddhist country beyond northern Tibet.

You will die through any of these thirteen negative circumstances, and even in this life, all sorts of inauspicious things will happen. While master Buddhajnana was teaching the Dharma, he saw his own lama Drubchen Phagtsang walking in the distance, but when he subsequently met with him, [Buddhajnana] lied and said that he hadn't seen [Phagtsang], at which point both of his eyes immediately fell from their sockets. His guru returned one of Buddhajnana's eyes to him and was able to restore [his vision in one eye].

Previously, when mahasiddha Krishnapada asked his guru mahasiddha Dzalandharapa for permission to engage in tantric activities, his guru examined him to see whether or not it was the appropriate time, after which he said, "To be able to enter the tantric activities, you must be able to both protect and destroy through actions of consciousness and exalted wisdom; therefore, you need to be able to both kill and restore life. As opposed to the activity of annihilation, you are unable to protect it; therefore, now is not the time to engage in [the tantric activities]." Despite this, [Krishnapada] didn't listen and broke [his guru's] command. He engaged in the tantric activities and met Vajrayogini in the aspect of an old leper woman on the banks of the Ganges River, yet he didn't recognize her because his preparations were not completed.

This sort of thing happened numerous times. Again, Heruka Father and Mother appeared as emanations of a plowman, a scripture reader, and a woman picking fruit, yet he did not recognize any of them either. Finally, Krishnapada was seized by a virulent illness. His great mahasiddha disciples obtained medicine, but many [nonvirtuous] dakinis [washing themselves] in a pool of flowers confused and distracted them. After these obstacles occurred, [Krishnapada] passed away. The reason he did not attain the supreme attainment [of enlightenment] in that life and body was due to the fact that he had directly disobeyed his guru's command.

Also, Rechungpa insisted on going on pilgrimage to Lhasa although Mila[repa] would not grant him permission. He went to Yarlung and met Lhacham Dembu, who was the daughter of the local ruler of a small estate. Once they met, they were together for only two years and she served him well. Finally, Rechungpa himself had a piece of turquoise that someone else had offered him, which he gave to a beggar, thus establishing a connection with him. Lhacham spread out unwholesome food, such as vegetables without any flavoring as well as the residue from the beer and curdled milk. She beat [the beggar] and chased him from the fortress. She threw the container of bad food at him, wounding him and causing blood to spew profusely from his body:

> In the upper part of his neck and the recesses of his stomach,
> One fatherly lama and a hundred *repas*[292]—
> Even half of a repa—act as servant to the lama;
> Even half of a repa will travel to an isolated mountain.
> The unfortunate Rechung was entrapped by the hand of
>   a demoness
> And suffered at the hand of the shameless demoness.

And,

> I am a repa yogi of the kingdom;
> However many empowerments I have received,
> I am not familiar with the empowerment of the clay pot.
>
> However many oral precepts I have received,
> I am not familiar with the oral precepts of the residual beer.
>
> However many blessings I have received,
> I am not familiar with the blessing of the white stick.
>
> However many baths I have experienced,
> I am not familiar with the bath of curdled milk.
>
> However many clothes I have worn,
> I am not familiar with wearing blue leaves.
>
> However many flowers were scattered,
> I am not familiar with flowers in the palm of your hand.

292. A repa is a type of yogi who emphasizes *tummo* (inner fire) meditation. Because of the bodily heat that tummo generates, they wear a simple white cotton robe. The first syllable *re* in the term *repa* means "cotton"; the suffix *-pa* makes it a personal pronoun. This is sometimes translated as "cotton-clad."

However many blessing cords I have worn,
I am not familiar with requesting the blessing cord of pepper water.

The bad action of a person in samsara familiar with scriptures
Is the harvester of the misery of actions performed
With anger and a lack of gratitude;
I contemplated [my actions], and I, Rechung, have regret.

This is [Rechungpa's] melancholy song of heartfelt regret. Having fled, he was forced to [continue to] run away, which came from the fault of having broken the command of his guru.

Within the lineage gurus of *nyungnä* is Pandita Yeshe Zangpo, who had an extremely virulent skin disease [resulting in lesions]. Venerable Tara spoke to his lama, Pandita Dawa Shönu, and said, "In the past he didn't properly rely upon a guru, and this is purifying that obscuration." Geshe Neusur's disciple was a novice monk who made a mistake in his faith in his guru and was struck with a serious illness. He had a terrifying vision just before he died of a fire bursting forth from Neusur's mountain and monastery that descended upon him, and with a terrified expression he died. [Neusurpa] said that this was a sign that in his next life he would also be reborn in a hot hell.

In Your Next Life You Will Wander Endlessly in the Lower Realms

Fifty Verses of Guru Devotion states,

You should never agitate the minds of
Any of your masters.
And if you are so stupid that you do so,
You will definitely roast in hell.

To quote the *Commentary on the Difficult Points of the Black Enemy*,[293]

293. Tib. *dGra nag gi dka' 'grel.*

Whoever does not accept as a guru someone from
Whom he listened to even one verse
Will take rebirth a hundred times in the abode of dogs
And then be reborn a butcher.

Regarding "a butcher," this means in the lineage of butchers and outcasts. Although there are teachings that state "a scorpion" and so forth, the former [example] is the best system. The *Vajrapani Empowerment Tantra* states,[294]

> Bhagavan, what sort of karmic maturation will there be for those who disparage their masters?
>
> The Bhagavan declared,
>
> Vajrapani, do not ask such things, for it would terrify the world together with the gods [to hear]. Lord of Secrets, I will nevertheless proclaim just a small portion. Hero, listen very carefully:
>
> Any of the unbearable hells that I have taught,
> As a result of actions of immediate retribution and so on,
> Are proclaimed to be their abodes for limitless eons.
> For this reason, never disparage your master at any time.

Thus, if you happen to disparage a lama [in general], the ripened result in your next life will be boundless. What need is there to mention criticizing your own lama? If you have lapsed *samaya* with another lama or even his companions, attendants, and so forth, you will have bad dreams.

You Will Be Deprived of Spiritual Guides in All Lives

Through having an erroneous reliance upon [your spiritual guide] right now, you will absolutely not meet spiritual guides in your future lives, and

294. Tib. *Lag na rdo rje dbang bskur ba'i rgyud.*

for that reason, although you will have obtained a human body, you will not have the opportunity to listen to Dharma and so forth. The *Essence of Nectar [Stages of the Path]* states,

> Even if you obtain life in a happy realm one hundred times,
> As the result corresponding to the cause of disrespect
> You will take birth in a place without freedom,
> Without the chance to even hear the sound "Dharma"
> or "spiritual guide."

You may be motivated with desire to listen to Dharma or to learn Dharma, but you need faith—recognizing your guru as the Buddha—even for something as minor as listening to the alphabet:

> Shakya son, if you don't develop faith after requesting
> a Dharma connection,
> What use is there in having requested a Dharma connection?
> There is no point in practicing because it becomes the cause
> of Hell without Respite
> And is like the blind being led by the tail of a cow.

Although Je Drubkangpa [Geleg Gyatso] meditated unceasingly upon his other lamas with whom he had a Dharma connection, he didn't meditate on the disrobed monk who had taught him the alphabet; therefore, until he visualized him as the principal [deity] of the field of merit, he was not able to develop any realizations of the lamrim. It is also extremely important to forsake nonvirtuous teachers and bad companions. All those who engage in trainings that are in opposition to the Dharma are bad companions; therefore, it is extremely important that you be very cautious around them. Although in [Je Tsongkhapa's] *Great* and *Middle-Length Treatises on the Stages of the Path [to Enlightenment]*, the benefits of reliance and the faults of nonreliance are taught after training in faith and recalling [the guru's] kindness, when carrying out the meditations, you should bring them up [to this section of the outline] and apply them at this point.

The Actual Way to Rely in Thought and Action has two sections:

1. How to Rely in Thought, or Training in Faith as the Root
2. The Way of Recalling His Kindness

How to Rely in Thought, or Training in Faith as the Root

Whether or not you develop all the realizations of the grounds and paths depends upon training in faith in the guru. Previously, Drom[tonpa] asked Atisha, "Why is it that we Tibetans have numerous meditations we practice, yet we haven't attained special good qualities?" Atisha replied, "Developing all the greater and lesser good qualities of the Mahayana arises in dependence upon the guru. You Tibetans don't regard your gurus as anything other than ordinary, so how could you develop [those qualities]?"

For example, whether or not the branches, leaves, and fruit of a tree grow is dependent upon whether or not they are connected to the trunk's root. All the realizations, from the point of the leisure and endowments up to the union [of no more learning], come solely from the guru; therefore, he is called "the root of the path." Of all of the meditations on the lamrim, training in the root of faith [in the guru] and recognizing all beings as your mother are the two most difficult, as previously cited. In short, whether your realizations are great or small is also determined by whether the strength of your meditation on faith is great or small:

> The kind lama is the root of all attainments;
> Contemplate his good qualities and don't look for his faults.
> May I hold this instruction in the palm of my hand
> And perfect this and other such pledges without obstruction.

This is saying that whether or not you develop realizations in your mental continuum ensues from whether or not you have faith and devotion in your guru. Therefore, you should train yourself to perceive the guru as a buddha.

[How to Rely in Thought, or Training in Faith as the Root, has three sections:]

1. The Reason You Must Perceive Your Guru as a Buddha
2. The Reason You Are Able to Perceive Your Guru as a Buddha
3. How to Regard Your Guru as a Buddha

The Reason You Must Perceive Your Guru as a Buddha

> You should see your guru as a buddha
> Because you want a profit and don't want a loss.

This is established from establishing the fundamental reason. Although your guru may be an actual buddha, if you don't see him [or her] as a buddha, you will not gain any profit and will only sustain a loss, like Sunakshatra and Devadatta. Even if your guru is not a buddha, if you view him as a buddha, it will be like the woman with the dog's tooth that she was convinced was the actual tooth of the Buddha, whereby she received the Buddha's blessing and it produced relics. In this way you will receive only a profit with no loss.

The Reason You Are Able to Perceive Your Guru as a Buddha

You are able to see you guru as a buddha if you develop a very powerful mind perceiving his [or her] good qualities; although you may see a few faults, they will be overpowered by your perception of the good qualities. According to the teachings in [Tsongkhapa's] *Great Treatise on the Stages of the Path*, Atisha perceived the incomparable Serlingpa from the perspective of apprehending his good qualities. Alternatively, there is also a system of transforming [the guru's] appearance of faults as an aid to perceiving his good qualities.[295]

295. This is explained in the following four headings and is elaborated on in Pabongkha Rinpoche's *Liberation in Our Hands*. You consider the Buddha's great kindness in appearing to

How to Regard Your Guru as a Buddha has four sections:

1. Vajradhara Said That the Guru Is a Buddha
2. The Guru Performs the Enlightened Actions of All the Buddhas
3. In These Degenerate Times, Buddhas Continue to Work for the Welfare of Living Beings
4. Our Perceptions Are Unreliable

Vajradhara Said That the Guru Is a Buddha

The *Vajra Tent Tantra* states,[296]

> He who is called Vajrasattva
> Himself assumes the form of the master;
> To be perceptible for the benefit of living beings,
> I will abide in the form of an ordinary being.

The *Hevajra Tantra* states,[297]

> During the final five hundred years [of the Buddha's teachings],
> I will abide in the form of the master.
> Develop conviction thinking that I am him.
> At that time, develop devotion for him.

With respect to the phrase "final five-hundred-year period," that also refers to our current era. A sutra also states,

> Listen, Amoghadarshi!
> In the future, when the time has come,
> I will teach through the body of an abbot;
> I will abide in the form of a master.

---

you as an ordinary being with faults so that you have someone on your level whom you can perceive and receive guidance from.

296. Tib. *rDo rje gur.*

297. Tib. *Kye rdor gyi rgyud.*

This is saying that you shouldn't become disheartened, thinking that you didn't meet the Buddha when he was here, because he is saying, "In the future, I will appear in the aspect of the guru and teach the Dharma." For that reason, in this day and age, conqueror Vajradhara appears in the aspect of the guru and has currently arrived; Vajradhara has manifested as all of your gurus. Moreover, Vajradhara also works for the welfare of living beings. When your own guru works for your welfare, you should also realize that Vajradhara is emanating within the position of your guru.

Some people say that that is not so. They think that when Vajradhara says, "He is an emanation," it is a general statement, and that although their guru is an actual buddha, this does not necessarily mean that all gurus are buddhas. Vajradhara has emanated as your own guru, and that is who he is; if you don't recognize this, you must be on guard against the danger of [not recognizing that] all your gurus are emanations of conqueror Vajradhara. Not only should you not have doubts, but you must perceive them all as Vajradhara. When he appears in the aspect of a single one of your lamas, [just that one lama] is not able to teach you everything, such as the alphabet, vows, empowerments, commentaries, transmissions, and so on; he must appear in the aspect of numerous lamas. Although you don't recognize it, conqueror Vajradhara himself said that your guru is a buddha; therefore, as scripture states,

> Although the moon and stars may fall to earth,
> It is impossible for the Great Sage to speak a lie.

Thus, it is not possible for Vajradhara to lie, and [this] is an actual fact [stated] in all the scriptures. Since this is the case, it is absolutely certain that Vajradhara has emanated among your lamas. You need to be on guard against trying to guess [which ones are buddhas] by wondering, "Perhaps this one is, this one isn't?" They are all buddhas!

The Guru Performs the Enlightened Actions of All the Buddhas

This section is accomplished through reasoning. Although this may be sufficient for a disciple with dull faculties, being a disciple with sharp faculties requires reasoning. Furthermore, if you don't have a lama, it will be impossible to receive the enlightened actions of all the buddhas. Therefore, the guru is the closest gateway through which you can receive the blessings of all the buddhas in the ten directions. Sapan stated,

> Although the sun's rays may be extremely hot,
> Without a magnifying glass they will not catch fire.
> Despite the blessings of the buddhas in the ten directions,
> Without a guru, you will not receive them.

The Buddha is like the sun, the magnifying glass is your guru, and the tinder is your mind. Götsangpa Losang Da-ö Rinchen also stated,

> If you purify the obscuring clouds,
> The heavenly orb of the sun will shine
> And alight upon the kindling, through the
> Dependent relationship of a transparent magnifying glass.
>
> If an ordinary being purifies his conceptual faults,
> The blessings of the buddhas of the ten directions
> Will alight upon the mental continuum of the disciple
> Through the dependent relationship of the qualified guru.

There is no other possible way for the blessings of all the buddhas in the ten directions to enter the mental continuum of the disciple so that he [or she] can develop abandonment and realization other than operating indirectly through the guru. In relation to yourself as well, the blessings of the Buddha must be received in that way, so without the guru there is no way of receiving them. For that reason, the guru is the intermediary between you and the enlightened actions of the Buddha, similar to an attendant of a Tibetan [official].

Some may also wonder, "Although I am convinced that [the guru] is the means of receiving [the Buddha's] enlightened actions, that does not necessarily mean that [the guru] *is* a buddha." As a response to this, consider that when the buddhas work for the welfare of living beings, the buddhas themselves emanate as the agent of the enlightened actions of all the buddhas and then perform their actions without relying upon living beings. For example, if a wealthy person breaks a drinking cup, it will only suffice if he buys a new one with his own money; he won't drink from one that has been borrowed from a beggar.

The engagement of the enlightened actions of the Buddha for the disciples must rely upon the wisdom truth body as the dominant condition. Because of that, the wisdom truth body functions as the cause of faith and so forth in your own mental continuum; therefore, the wisdom truth body must exist in the mind of one's own guru to serve as the cause of your faith. Regarding the wisdom truth body, this is a unique quality of a buddha and is not possessed by an [ordinary] living being; therefore, that also resolves conclusively that the guru is a buddha. With respect to the wisdom truth body, that is only [a quality] of a buddha and is not possessed by sentient beings; therefore, it is certain that your guru is a buddha.

In These Degenerate Times, Buddhas Continue to Work for the Welfare of Living Beings

Even in this day and age, the buddhas work for the welfare of living beings. A scripture states,

> The buddhas and bodhisattvas who appeared in the past
> Are still working for the welfare of migrating beings
> When you understand that this is not merely a thesis
> But [that they] have in fact congregated within the qualified guru.

Once the Buddha became enlightened, he didn't remain idle and not work for the welfare [of living beings]. From the very beginning [of his path as a bodhisattva], the Buddha generated the supreme bodhichitta for the welfare of all living beings. In the middle phase, he accumulated merit. Finally, he enacted the welfare of all living beings according to his bodhichitta. He also works for our own welfare. An oral instruction of my guru states that each and every buddha also dwells amid each and every living being within his [or her] visual perception. In this day and age, all the buddhas are working for our benefit. When they do, the being that is doing the emanating must emanate by transforming in a way that will benefit us; therefore, we can be absolutely certain that in this day and age he [or she] has also emanated as someone carrying out deeds for our welfare. Since this is so, if one buddha emanates, because all the buddhas are of a single taste in the Dharmadhatu, it is necessarily a emanation of all the buddhas. For that reason, if one buddha is working for our benefit, all buddhas are necessarily working for our benefit.

Thus, if it is certain that they are emanating to accomplish our welfare, there could be no other way than through our guru. This fact is also expressed in a verse that states, "The munis do not wash away your negative karma with water. . . ."[298] For the sake of liberating us from samsara and the fears of the lower realms, the [gurus] work on our behalf, enacting the deeds of the buddhas by teaching us the Dharma from the alphabet and so forth on up, so that we can eliminate every last fault and cultivate every single good quality. For that reason, we needn't [look] anywhere other than to our guru to find the agent enacting the deeds of the buddhas, in accordance with our fortune. Therefore, we can decide with complete certainty that the guru is a buddha. But he is not only *a* buddha, he is the embodiment of *all* buddhas. *Lama Chöpa* states,

> I prostrate at the feet of the holy refuge and protector.
> As the exalted wisdom of all the infinite conquerors
> Displaying the aspect of a saffron-robed monk,
> Your skillful means appear according to the needs of your
>   disciples.

The *Ornament of the Mahayana Sutras* states that the exalted wisdom of the buddhas has coalesced as one taste in the truth body, just as separate drops of water from each individual country in this world have gathered together within the ocean. Thus, all the buddhas reveal various aspects from the single taste of the Dharmadhatu. The *Meeting of the Father and Son Sutra* states,

> Working for the welfare of living beings,
> They appear in the shape of Indra and Brahma;

298. "The munis do not wash away negative karma with water; / They do not dispel the suffering of migrating beings with their hands; / They do not transfer their realizations of suchness to others: / They liberate migrating beings through teaching the truth of reality."

Some are in the shape of a demon,
Yet the worldly are unable to recognize them.

They act in the shape of a woman, and
They also take birth in the abodes of animals.

The *Kadam Scripture*[299] states,

> Since they reveal various emanations, why wouldn't they appear as
> Arrogant beings who pretend to have knowledge they don't
> possess?

And,

> Since they also reveal themselves in whatever aspect is beneficial,
> Why wouldn't they emanate even as a wise man or a crazy person?

In general, we are incapable of determining that even our father and mother and so forth are not emanations of the Buddha. The Buddha primarily works for our welfare, applying various means to help us generate a single aspect of virtue and overcome a single aspect of nonvirtue, yet this is accomplished primarily through teaching us to adopt virtue and abandon nonvirtue through teaching Dharma. Therefore, since it is our guru himself who carries this out, he is a buddha. Since his deeds have the knowledge and capacity [of an enlightened being], you should decide with utter certainty that he is a buddha.

Our Perceptions Are Unreliable

You may think, "Well then, if my guru is a buddha, I should see him as a buddha; yet I don't see him as such; therefore, he isn't a buddha." It is only [due to] our own current lack of good fortune that we do not see him in this way:

299. Tib. *bKa' gdams glegs bam.*

> As long as we are not free from the obscuring veils of our bad actions,
> Even if all the buddhas appeared directly before us,
> With the exception of what we currently perceive,
> We would not have the good fortune to perceive their
> Supreme emanation bodies adorned with the signs and indications [of an enlightened being].

This being said, what need is there to mention meeting the buddhas face to face? Although they reveal the aspect of higher beings such as Manjushri, we do not perceive them. That being the case, if [the buddhas] appeared in an aspect superior to that of the guru we have right now, we would be unable to perceive them. If they revealed themselves in an inferior aspect, such as that of a bird, dog, or some other type of animal, we wouldn't have any confidence in them. Therefore, it is due to their wondrous skillful means that they emanate in an aspect similar to ours, with the same bodily features. In general, merely perceiving [our guru] as a buddha or not does not mean that he definitely is or isn't [a buddha]. [Chandrakirti's] *Guide to the Middle Way* proclaims,

> Similar to a person with obscured sense powers,
> The mind of a hungry ghost perceives a flowing river as pus.

When the water of this world is perceived simultaneously by a god, human, and hungry ghost, each being perceives a single basis as nectar, water, and pus and blood [respectively]. To a god, it does not appear as pus and blood. Likewise, it does not appear as nectar to the hungry ghost. With the guru as well, even though you don't perceive him as a buddha, you should not think that he is not a buddha. For example, worldly gods, nagas, king spirits, and *tsen* spirits emerge to influence and affect castles and so forth. However, despite the fact that the nagas, king spirits, and tsen spirits definitely exist, we don't see them.

If [I were to explain] this in detail at this point, I would apply the over-pervasion of non-observation[300] from the *Commentary on Valid Cognition* to gain certainty. Moreover, for someone with bile disease, silver and a

300. Tib. *mi snang ba ma dmigs pa'i rtags.*

white conch appear to be yellow. For those with a wind disorder, a white snow mountain will appear blue and so forth, due to being influenced by momentary causes of confusion. Therefore, when we entertain [doubts such] as "Is he or isn't he [a buddha?]," we should realize that the mistake is ultimately being made from within us, whereby we contaminate our perceptions, whereas the guru is actually free from faults. Once we project the blame on the modes of appearance from our confused viewpoint with anger, attachment, and so on, we perceive them as having faults. Although we project [our faults] on the guru and rank him among our companions, we are incapable of determining whether or not he is a buddha. The Bhagavan stated, "Only I or someone such as myself can judge an individual. An ordinary being cannot judge another ordinary being, for they will certainly deteriorate." Not only that, but we are extremely fortunate to even see our guru as a human being. Chen-nga-wa Lodro Gyaltsen said,

> Due to the vast degree of our obscuring bad karma,
> It is a joyful occasion that we can even see our guru as a human being.
> We have great merit to not see him as a dog or a donkey;
> [Therefore] develop heartfelt faith and devotion, son of Shakya.

Most non-Buddhists could not perceive the signs and indications of our Teacher and instead saw him as an ordinary being, yet Buddhists saw him adorned with the signs and indications. Moreover, Panchen Naropa saw mahasiddha Tilopa as someone frying live fish and wondered whether someone like that could really be Tilopa, at which point [Tilopa] said, "I am not, I am not!" and so forth. Tilopa was the actual conqueror Vajradhara, yet all the people in the area didn't see him as anything more than an old beggar. Getsul Tsembuwa saw a leper woman as Vajravarahi. When Acharya Buddhajnana met Acharya Manjushri Mitra, he saw him as an old disrobed monk wearing a turban and so forth, even though he was in actuality Guhyasamaja.

Since such a variety of things occur, we cannot rely upon our perception of external features. Mila also saw Marpa as a plowman. Tilopa saw Shawari as a murderer of pigs. Although Milarepa attained the state of Vajradhara in one life and one body and is the actual Vajradhara, Naro

Bonchung and others couldn't see him as anything more than a vulgar old beggar lying naked on the ground, as is cited extensively. With the exception of a few holy beings such as Kyabchog Palsangpo and others, no one else could perceive the special qualities of Gyalwa Ensapa; [instead, they] called him "the madman from Ensa" and could not see anything other than an ordinary monk. When Ensapa was in Tsang Rong, he heard a few Sakya scholars debating some difficult points and spoke some [verses from] the *Perfection of Wisdom in Eight Thousand Lines* in Sanskrit [causing the Sakyapas to think he was a ghost].

The oath-bound Dharmaraja would disguise himself as a human and come into the presence of Je Tsongkhapa to receive teachings. Je Rinpoche [Tsongkhapa] was on the verge of giving some Dharma teachings on the profound essential points of mantra when [Dharmaraja] stopped him. Although Gungru Gyanzang was not pleased, Khedrup [Je] scolded him and said, "Kachu,[301] don't get yourself so worked up." Maitreya appeared to Asanga as a rotting female dog and so forth and in a variety of other appearances, and despite the fact that [Maitreya] is without faults, [Asanga] perceived him as such. Chen-nga-wa Lodro Gyaltsen proclaimed,

> Those afflicted with bile disease see a white conch as yellow;
> Those with mistaken conceptions see the Buddha as a charlatan;
> The faithful see everyone as the Buddha;
> This is the one you should choose, son of Shakya.

In one way, even though he is without fault, even the Teacher reveals himself as having [faults]. As a scripture states,

> Even though he is without attachment, he reveals himself as being attached;
> Even though he is without fear, he reveals himself as having fear;
> Even though he is without ignorance, he reveals himself as ignorant;
> Even though he isn't crazy, he reveals himself as a crazy person

301. Tib. *dka' bcu*. This is equivalent to a geshe degree obtained from Tashi Lhunpo Monastery and means "ten difficult subjects," referring to the curriculum at Tashi Lhunpo.

> And as a cripple, although he is not crippled.
> He does this to subdue living beings.

Also, the *Great Nirvana Sutra*[302] states,

> Although I reveal complete nirvana in the realm of this world of a thousandfold universe, it is not a final complete nirvana.[303]

[The Buddha] gave extensive predictions such as this. The Teacher himself revealed the form of a wicked person for the sake of subduing a wicked brahman youth. He emanated as a musician to subdue the king of the gandharvas.[304] He emanated as an ordinary bhikshu for subduing Angulimala. If buddhas work for the welfare of living beings in this way—revealing aspects of being attached and so forth when they don't actually have any attachment, anger, ignorance, and so forth—then you can understand how, even though their nature is that of compassion and they are therefore without faults, they reveal the aspect of being extremely wrathful, with their faces revealing bared fangs, such as [is the case with] Bhairava, Vajrapani, and so forth, for the sake of subduing those of us who possess such faults.

Previously, in Lhasa, a wicked man named Golog Arig Topa went to the Jokhang to make a simple butter-lamp offering. However, other than darkness, he was unable to see the Jowo[305] and instead saw the flesh of one quarter of a yak in lieu of the Jowo. While a Kangyur lama from Drepung named Losang Dhonden Rinpoche was giving the oral transmission of the Kangyur, a monk saw a wooden basin full of meat in front of the lama where the texts were placed, from which [the lama] was eating. This illustrates how appearances are uncertain. People even saw Je Tsongkhapa and the great master [Padmasambhava] as ordinary.

If you contemplate how appearances are uncertain, it also has the

302. Tib. *mDo myang 'das chen mo.*

303. This means that the speaker would not remain in a state of solitary liberation but would continue to work for the welfare of living beings.

304. Tib. *dri za.*

305. The Jowo is the most famous statue in Lhasa. It was brought to Tibet in the seventh century by one of the wives of Songsten Gampo. It was destroyed by the Communist Chinese in 1959. In 1986 the torso was retrieved from China and restored by the late Ribur Rinpoche (1923–2006).

special quality of preventing obstacles from occurring. Train in faith as the root continuously, year after year. Begin by training in great faith in one of your gurus. Next, train in faith in all your gurus by sequentially contemplating how they are all one nature. Consider how that one lama appeared as a master to train you in reading when you needed to be subdued through a teacher of the alphabet; how he appeared in the body of an abbot to bestow ordination as a novice and fully ordained monk when you needed vows; and how he revealed himself in the aspect of a vajra master of mantra when you needed to be subdued by entering the gateway of secret mantra—all those lamas were emanations of that single guru. Moreover, as it states, "The guru himself is Mahakala; Mahakala himself is the guru." The same reasoning can be applied to all buddhas by stating, "Vajrabhairava is also your guru, and your guru is also Vajrabhairava," and so on. The *Tantra Equaling the Extent of Space*[306] states,

> This migrating being is the nature of the five buddhas,
> Appearing like an actor in a play or a fine painting,
> Whose sole activity is called "great bliss."
> This singular experience enacts numerous dramas.

For example, the lead ritual dancer himself constructs the ritual dance and will change his hat and clothes numerous times. Although he is labeled in numerous ways, with a variety of names such as Dharmaraja, Black Hat, and so on, they are all in fact the lead dancer himself. No matter how many various mandala deities the Teacher explained from the various classes of tantra, they are all in fact nothing other than emanations of the single truth body of great bliss of the guru. *Lama Chöpa* states,

> I make requests to you, supreme guru of the nature of the
> Three Jewels;
> Your aggregates, elements, sources, and limbs
> Are the nature of the fathers and mothers of five buddha
> families,
> The bodhisattvas, and the wrathful powerful deities.

306. Tib. *Nam mkha' dang mnyam pa'i rgyud.*

The hundred buddha families, the five buddha families, the one, and so forth are also all emanated aspects of the guru's truth body of great bliss. [*Lama Chöpa* also states,]

> I make requests to you, protector of the primordial union;
> You are the ten million circles of mandalas,
> The manifestation of omniscient exalted wisdom,
> The principal vajra holder, pervasive lord of a hundred lineages.

The basis of emanation of all the buddhas is the guru's truth body of great bliss; therefore, we also call him "the pervasive lord of a hundred lineages." The phrase "the body, speech, and mind of all the tathagatas of the ten directions and the three times" is the long wording for it and contains great significance—and is part of the refuge formula that young monks first learn. Although their numbers exceed the hundreds of ten million circles of mandalas, the projector of them all is also your guru. The retractor is also your guru; therefore, they are all not separate from the guru. Geshe Jayulwa [Shönu Ö] stated, "If you assert that Vajradhara or your sole personal deity is separate and superior to your guru, realizations will never occur for that person." While Mochog [Rinpoche] was having a vision, [he] stated,

> Great Compassionate One, you may be white; Hevajra, you may be blue; Vajrayogini, you may be red—but I am never separate from the appearance of the guru; therefore, it is possible that I will become enlightened in one life.

[Hence] the guru is the basis of the emanation of all the buddhas, and if we perceive him [or her] as the ultimate embodiment of all the buddhas, this is also the definitive meaning of guru devotion, which is similar to other sayings such as "the body assembling all the buddhas" and so forth. Thus, the display of various emanations for our welfare consists of emanation bodies of the guru. The emanation of your present guru depends on the complete enjoyment body, which is its foundation. That guru who is the truth body of great bliss arises in a physical aspect; therefore, your ultimate ground of the guru is the truth-body mind of all the buddhas. Therefore, you must understand that the guru is inseparable from the [three] bodies [of all the buddhas]. When we ourselves also become enlightened, we necessarily attain the state of the guru. The tea offering ritual states, "Grant your blessing that my mind may mix as one with his." This also states that you necessarily attain the state of the guru, but it is not like making the lama your friend.

For that reason, when it comes to our guru, according to the estimation of our perceptions, we see nothing more than the external human skin, and although we currently don't have the good fortune to see the buddhas directly, we should cultivate a mindset that has faith that the three bodies of our guru are the embodiment of all the buddhas and that this is the real situation. Continue with repeated meditation in this way for a period of time. For example, if you have something that is semicircular with a yellow cloth cover in your room, when you recall the semicircle, you do not need to think about the yellow cloth cover separately; your recollection of it will occur naturally. In the same way, once you merely recall your guru, you will not need to meditate to recall that he is all the buddhas; it will happen naturally. If the blending of all the buddhas and your guru arises in this way, it is said that you have generated the realization of proper reliance upon your spiritual guide.

While undertaking the other meditations on the lamrim, once you meditate on all the gurus during this proper reliance upon the guru and spiritual guide, you then contemplate the benefits [of proper reliance] and so on. Go over each [point in the] outline until it is complete, without moving on to the others but making sure that you have got the scriptures and meanings in your mind just right and with complete certainty. Think over the scriptures and reasoning, the examples, the verses, the historical accounts, and the biographies of the holy beings. It is also sufficient to divide the four sections and apply one to each session, such as "Vajradhara said that your guru is a buddha," and so on. If you attain absolute certainty by contemplating these from every possible angle, you should then place your mind in single-pointed equipoise.

Next is an explanation of the teachings for continuing our practice as explained above and a concise way of continuing that training.

Day Eleven

The king of the Dharma Tsongkhapa the Great stated in his composition [the *Foundation of All Good Qualities*],

> The kind lord is the foundation of all good qualities . . .

Proper reliance upon the spiritual guide is like the root of all of your temporary higher status and ultimate definite goodness. Furthermore, you must most definitely establish the root of your aspirations by relying upon him with completely pure thoughts and deeds. For that reason [correct your motivation, thinking, "I will listen to the lamrim teachings for the sake of attaining enlightenment for the welfare of all living beings"].[307]

Pabongkha Rinpoche then restated the headings:

The Way of Recalling His Kindness has four sections,

1. The Guru Is Kinder than the Buddhas
2. His Kindness in Teaching Us Dharma
3. His Kindness in Blessing Our Mental Continuum
4. His Kindness in Assembling Disciples through Material Gifts

307. The text merely says "as before" in lieu of ellipses here and expects the reader to apply the motivation from the previous sections.

The Guru Is Kinder than the Buddhas has two sections:

1. He Is Kinder than All the Buddhas in General
2. He Is Kinder than Buddha Shakyamuni in Particular

He Is Kinder than All the Buddhas in General

You should contemplate [the guru's] good qualities to develop faith that sees the guru as a buddha and contemplate his kindness to develop devotion. Therefore, train in faith that sees him as a buddha by way of recalling his good qualities and train in devotion that he is superior to the Buddha by way of recalling his kindness. Furthermore, the guru is kinder than all the buddhas. *Lama Chöpa* states,

> [I make requests to you, compassionate refuge and protector;
> You perfectly reveal the path of the sugatas for those
> Migrators of these degenerate times, so difficult to tame,]
> Who were not subdued by the countless buddhas of the past.

There are countless buddhas who have already come and passed away, and there are also the buddhas of this eon who have already come—namely, Krakucchanda, Kanakamuni, and Kashyapa. And although each one led limitless disciples, we did not have the good fortune to be included within their [disciples] and did not benefit at all from their emergence. Presently, we have met the Conqueror's teachings, heard the Mahayana Dharma, and even discovered the means of attaining liberation from samsara, which is due to the kindness of the guru. From the perspective of good qualities the guru and the Buddha are equal, but from the perspective of their kindness the guru is much kinder than all the buddhas in general.

He Is Kinder than Buddha Shakyamuni in Particular

Previously, when our Teacher took rebirth as the brahman Samudrarenu, the bodhichitta of the other buddhas had abandoned[308] living beings dur-

308. It sounds slightly awkward to say "the bodhichitta of the other buddhas had abandoned." The intended meaning is that the other buddhas who were destined to become the thousand buddhas of this fortunate eon were each taking responsibility for beings of a certain era, and

ing the age of strife when the lifespan was [only] one hundred years. Yet [the brahman Samudrarenu] generated bodhichitta and made five hundred great prayers to tame them, whereby he appeared in India [as Buddha Shakyamuni].[309] He turned the wheel of Dharma and in the brief span of an instant led innumerable living beings [to liberation and enlightenment]; however, he didn't do anything for us, and we also didn't do anything ourselves [because we were not around then]. Not only that, but the successors of his teaching such as Upagupta had [such a vast] number of disciple-arhats that if you used a toothpick [to represent each one], they would fill to the brim a cave twelve cubits in width, six cubits in height, and eighteen cubits in depth. Moreover, during the previous spread of the Dharma [in Tibet] under the great master Padmasambhava, there were numerous holy beings who were actual buddhas, such as his twenty-five main disciples during his lifetime, yet we didn't have the good fortune to be subdued at that time, either. During the later spread of the Dharma, there were the five original great beings of the Sakya [tradition],[310] as well as Marpa, Milarepa, and so on. Again, there were innumerable scholars and siddhas of the Kadam tradition, such as Atisha the Great and so on, as well as the arrival of Jamgon Tsongkhapa Father and Sons, who were innumerable like stars in the sky. At that time as well, we were staying in the lower realms and so forth, so once again we weren't around at the right time.

For that reason, this present guru of ours who is teaching you the Dharma and the lama who is teaching you the unmistaken path to

---

only the brahman Samudrarenu had strong enough bodhichitta to willingly assume the responsibility for beings of this degenerate era of conflict.

309. Kachen Yeshe Gyaltsen gives slightly more detail in his commentary to *Lama Chöpa*, translated under the title *Manjushri's Innermost Secret*, 210–11: "Furthermore, the thousand buddhas of this fortunate eon generated the mind of enlightenment in the presence of the Tathagata Ratna Garbha. When they were laying claim to their various realms, there was no one who was capable of assuming the responsibility for this age of strife when the lifespan is one hundred years. However, the Bhagavan Shakyamuni had taken rebirth as the brahman Samudrarenu and, due to his compassion, was unable to bear this; therefore, he said, 'I alone will subdue these ignoble beings who have been forsaken by all the other buddhas, and I shall attain enlightenment during the age of strife when the lifespan of beings is only one hundred years.' Thus, after generating the mind of enlightenment and making five hundred great prayers, he was born in this world."

310. The five founding fathers of the Sakya school were Sachen Kunga Nyingpo, Sönam Tsemo, Jetsün Drakpa Gyaltsen, Sakya Pandita, and Chögyal Pakpa.

liberation and omniscience are kinder than all the buddhas. [Nagarjuna's] *Five Stages* also states,

> He is the self-arisen Bhagavan,
> One with the supreme deity.
> Because he is the best treasure for instructions,
> The vajra master surpasses [the deity].

For example, the guru is like someone giving food to another on the verge of dying, and the buddhas are like someone giving a mountain of succulent meat to another who is already prosperous.

His Kindness in Teaching Us Dharma

Our Teacher endured great hardships for the sake of the Dharma; he offered his son, his queen, and even drove a thousand iron spikes into his body, [used his body as wicks to] ignite a thousand butter lamps, and so on, for the sake of each verse of the Dharma. A tantra states,

> Set out in search for the holy Dharma even if you must cross
> An ocean of swords and a pit of blazing fire until you reach the other side.

Although we should undertake such hardships for the sake of the Dharma, we can't endure even the prick of a single needle, not to mention a thousand iron spikes. Yet due to the kindness of the guru, we don't need to endure such hardships and instead have the opportunity to listen to the Mahayana Dharma such as this because of his great kindness. Panchen [Losang] Chögyan proclaimed,

> Previously, the Muni underwent hardships such as
> Jumping into a pit of blazing fire,
> Pounding a thousand sharp iron spikes and so forth,
> For the sake of each and every verse of the Dharma.
>
> But these days we don't need such intense perseverance
> For we receive a multitude of vast and profound sutras and tantras

From your great kindness, fatherly [Guru];
I know of no way to possibly repay your kindness.

Previously, Atisha the Great endured extended hardship by traveling for thirteen months across the ocean to the Golden Isle[311] for the sake of receiving the Dharma of these stages of the path to enlightenment. The lotsawas [realized translators] of the past collected whatever gold they could, as well as their possessions [to give as offerings], while forsaking any regard for crossing three narrow river gorges, the difficulty of traveling vast plains, the fear of humans and nonhumans, and the fatigue of heat and cold. Having forsaken any regard for their lives, they traveled a great distance [under such circumstances] all the way to the land of India. At that time, going to India was not like it is now. Those paths were blocked by snow with no escape; therefore, they had to take the roundabout way to Nepal and traveled by foot. Therefore, it is not like the comfortable traveling on our modern roads. There is nothing easier than traveling by train or car!

Although they had arrived in India, the land of Dharma, initially they were not permitted to listen to the Dharma and had to learn the language from the ground up. Next, they had to listen, contemplate, and meditate and so on while enduring great hardship. As it stands right now, we don't have to endure even a small portion of such hardships. The fact that you can easily see the texts in the Tibetan language and so forth is all due solely to the kindness of the guru. Atisha the Great stated,

> It is due to your great merit that you have discovered the essential meaning without having to undergo hardships. Therefore, sincerely apply yourself well.

Je [Losang] Chögyan stated,

> Even the *Sutra Requested by the Wrathful One*[312] states,
>
> > Although you may unwaveringly present offerings with devotion to [the guru] from whom you have received

311. On the Golden Isle, see note 60 above.
312. Tib. *Drag shul can gyis zhus pa'i mdo*; Skt. *Ugrapariprccha sutra.*

> transmissions for as many eons as there are letters in the scriptures, you could not finish.

> In short, this means that even by offering and venerating
> For six eons, you could not repay the kindness
> That comes from receiving even just the Six-Syllable Mantra.

The *Essence of Nectar [Stages of the Path]* states,

> In this way, if a man is suffering in prison
> And someone ransoms him from that prison
> And establishes him in the most wondrous enjoyments,
> This would indeed be an act of great kindness.
>
> In the same way, the gurus reveal to us the means
> Of liberation from the three lower realms
> And kindly bestow the enjoyments of all we desire
> As the temporary leisure and endowment of gods and men.
>
> Next, they teach us the excellent unsurpassed ways and means
> Of pacifying all the misery of samsara and nirvana
> And lead us to the sacred state of the three bodies;
> How could this not be the greatest kindness?
>
> If it is said that we cannot repay their kindness even in as many eons
> As there are numbers of letters in the teaching of even one verse,
> [Then] how could we repay the kindness of
> Teaching the noble path in its entirety?

Therefore, the guru's kindness is greater than that of the Buddha. Further, as I already mentioned, Atisha the Great also said, "I don't have any good qualities; these are my guru [so-and-so's good qualities]. . . ." The fact that you can at least read Dharma books every day is not something that came about all on your own; it is due to the kindness of your guru. Not only that, but your understanding of how to listen to, contemplate, and meditate on the Dharma, such as the stages of the path to enlightenment, is also due to the kindness of your guru. The fact that we currently do not have to experience the suffering of carrying out some obligatory chores for someone such as an older sibling is also due to the kindness of the abbot who bestowed our vows. The fact that we have currently obtained a human life of leisure and endowment is once again due to the kindness of our guru; not only that, but whatever excellence we have is due to the kindness of the lama. Therefore, from the perspective of his [or her] kindness, the guru surpasses all the buddhas. The commentary to Drolungpa's[313] *Stages of the Teachings* also states,

> [Even] if it were appropriate to reduce the wages set
> For the value of the excellent expositions,
> How could you possibly dispute that even
> The price of a kingdom itself would be enough?

His Kindness in Blessing Our Mental Continuum

The guru doesn't merely teach us Dharma, he also blesses our mental continuum. Whatever virtuous mind you develop, such as having the wish to study, contemplate, and meditate on a particular text, this is all due to the guru blessing your mental continuum. When you don't understand the meaning of the lamrim and so forth, or when you meditate but don't develop realizations, if you supplicate the guru with great force, you will come to understand them all without obstruction. Not only that, but all the undesirable things of this life will be immediately pacified by supplicating the guru. Geshe Khamlungpa [1025–1115] was seized by a harmful spirit, and although nothing else was of any help, it was pacified by reciting the name mantra of his guru Drom[tonpa]. In India, Panchen Naropa was the guardian of the northern gateway of Nalanda Monastery and was unrivaled in debate. He engaged in debate with a certain non-Buddhist scholar, and through the line of arguments it seemed as though Naropa was losing ground in the debate. He supplicated his guru Tilopa, whereby

313. Drolungpa Lodro Jungné (eleventh century) was a direct disciple of Dromtonpa and composed a *Great* and *Small Stages of the Teachings.* See Thuken Losang Chökyi Nyima, *The Crystal Mirror of Philosophical Systems*, 105.

Tilopa came to the crown of his head, and he was able to defeat the non-Buddhist in debate.

Dombhipa was also Atisha's guru, and although [Atisha] had not actually met him even once, he made supplications to him. One night, Atisha had a dream in which he met a bhikshu eating the flesh of a human hand, whereupon he thought, "I wonder why a bhikshu is eating human flesh?" The bhikshu said, "Does a buddha make mistakes?" Atisha replied, "A buddha does not make mistakes." "Well, then, you should also eat this," [replied the bhikshu, whereupon] he cut off one of the fingers, and [Atisha] ate it. Although this occurred in a dream, the following day Atisha gave birth to an extraordinary concentration in his mental continuum. Afterward, a mantrika was supplicating Dombhipa, and Dombhipa said, "You and I don't have any karmic connection. I have a disciple named Jnana,[314] and in this very moment I blessed his mental continuum; you and he have a karmic connection, so go to him and make supplications." Accordingly, he went before Atisha, presented a mandala, and made supplications. [Atisha] said, "Who sent you to me?" When [the mantrika] explained the previous events, [Atisha] realized that it was Dombhipa who had blessed him.

Je [Drubkangpa] Geleg Gyatso made Phurchog Ngawang Jampa [1682–1762] memorize *Manjushri's Oral Instructions* [by the Fifth Dalai Lama, Ngawang Losang Gyatso]. [Later, Phurchog] carried some dried yak dung to [Geleg Gyatso's] mountain retreat. His guru gave him some inner offerings to drink that he had blessed. Afterward, while Phurchog was at the Dharma assembly, he developed renunciation and was overcome with a weariness [of samsara] that could not be suppressed, so that all he did was shed tears. [In my own case,] by merely seeing the face of my precious guru [Dagpo Lama Rinpoche], my refuge and protector,[315] I was nearly moved to tears. Previously, the same thing also happened to Chusang Lama [Yeshe Gyatso] Rinpoche.

What need is there to mention actually living with the guru? Although you may not reside in his presence, if you know how to make supplications, you will continuously receive his blessings. Mahasiddha Tilopa said to Naropa, "The very best of all enhancements is the guru." Among all

314. Jowo Atisha's ordination name was Shrijnana.

315. This is Pabongkha Rinpoche's guru Dagpo Jampal Lhundrub.

the means of dispelling obstacles and enhancements for our practice of Dharma, having faith and devotion for your guru and making supplications to him are the very best.

Pabongkha Rinpoche related the following story: When Lama Dorje Chang[316] *himself was thirty-seven years old, he was quite ill. He met Dagpo Lama Rinpoche in a dream, who placed his right hand on [Lama Dorje Chang's] head and recited Ganden Lha Gyama and other prayers. By the evening of the following day he had developed a joyous well-being. Therefore, if anything undesirable happens to you, make powerful supplications to your guru, and you will effortlessly accomplish your desired aims.*

His Kindness in Assembling Disciples through Material Gifts

For a few disciples, you should act in accordance with the following lines:

> Having gathered a circle of living beings through
> Initially giving them material gifts, may I satisfy them with Dharma.

There is a story from the past about a family that sent a person to Dagpo to see my refuge and protector Dagpo Lama Rinpoche in his hermitage, at which time [Dagpo Rinpoche] offered the man excellent provisions, whereby he developed faith [in Dagpo Rinpoche]. In particular, you should recall the kindness of how a teacher cares for his pupils with all their needs and how your own teacher did the same thing by giving you food, clothing, a place to stay, even down to your bedding. Apply this to each and every one of your teachers by considering what each one gave you, thinking, "This lama showed me kindness in this way, and this one in that way. . . ." In short, you should contemplate, "The human body that I currently have obtained, meeting the teachings of the Buddha, being counted among the members of the Sangha, and in particular meeting

316. This note was compiled by Trijang Rinpoche. "Lama Dorje Chang" refers to Pabongkha Rinpoche himself.

the teachings of Je Tsongkhapa and so forth are all due to the kindness of my guru."

You should also recite requests for the kindness of your guru. Furthermore, you should recite the verses from the *Array of Stalks Sutra* where youthful Sudhana recalled the kindness of his spiritual guide as follows:[317]

> I have come to this place after single-pointedly contemplating,
> "My spiritual masters who teach the Dharma
> Thoroughly reveal the good qualities of phenomena
> And then reveal the bodhisattva's way of life in its entirety.
>
> Because they generate [these qualities], they are like a mother.
> Because they give the milk of good qualities, they are like wet nurses.
> They thoroughly train me in the limbs of enlightenment;
> These spiritual masters expel the aspects of harm.
>
> They are like doctors who free me from old age and death.
> They send down a rain of nectar like Indra, the lord of gods.
> Like the full moon, they cause the virtuous Dharma to flourish;
> Like the illuminating sun, they reveal the way to peace.
>
> Toward friends and enemies they are like mountains.
> Their minds are unassailable like an ocean.
> They completely protect me like a boat."
> Thinking in this way, I, Sudhana, have come here.
>
> These bodhisattvas have developed my mind.
> They have produced my enlightenment as a son of the buddhas.
> I praise these spiritual masters as buddhas;
> With these virtuous thoughts, I have come here.

317. Pabongkha Rinpoche only quotes the opening line, but I have included the section in its entirety to facilitate a better understanding of the following commentary.

By protecting the world, they are like heroes
And have become my captains, protectors, and refuge.
They are eyes that produce happiness in me;
With such a mind I honor these spiritual masters.

There is a way of applying these to the side of complete enlightenment. Assembling the "milk of good qualities" refers to the bodhisattva's conduct on the path of accumulation being endowed with a new [quality] of generosity not previously possessed. "Mother" refers to the path of preparation. The "limbs of enlightenment" and so forth refer to the path of seeing. "These spiritual masters" and so on refers to the path of meditation from the first ground up to the seventh. "Free me from old age and death" refers to the eighth ground. "Send down a rain of nectar" refers to the ninth ground. "Like the moon" and "sun" refers to the tenth ground. On the side of nirvana taught by the Buddha, "friends and enemies" and so on refer to the temporary benefits. You should change the "Sudhana" to "I" so that you are thinking, "With such a mind, may I come to be this way." This is a cause for bodhichitta and moreover becomes a means of relying upon your guru. It also becomes a means of relying upon your guru through recalling the resultant enlightenment. If these verses are difficult to understand, you can recite teachings from the *Essence of Nectar [Stages of the Path]* that state,

Having ordained and left home life, which is like a pit of fire,
And abiding in solitude with the conduct of a sage,
I experience the supreme taste of nectar of holy Dharma,
Which is [all] due to the kindness of my venerable guru.

Having searched for many thousands of eons, I have
Met the teachings of the Jamgon Lama, so difficult to find,
And have attained confidence in the system of his teachings,
Which is due to the kindness of my holy tutors.

For that reason, the spiritual masters of mine are protectors
Protecting me from the body of the lower realms,
Captains liberating me from the ocean of samsara,

> And guides leading me to the ground of higher status and
> liberation.
>
> They are doctors curing the chronic illness of the afflictive
> emotions,
> A stream to pacify the great fires of suffering,
> A lamp to dispel the darkness of ignorance,
> Suns of the teachings illuminating the path to liberation,
>
> Liberators from the prison shackles of samsara,
> Rain clouds sending a gentle rain of holy Dharma,
> Friends who produce benefit dispelling harm,
> And parents eternally protecting me with love.

If we recite the aforementioned verses while recalling their meaning, it is very easy to understand, thereby giving great significance to recalling the kindness [of our guru].

Pleasing Him through Action

The *Ornament of the Mahayana Sutras* states,

> You should rely upon your spiritual master by way of
> Veneration, material things, service, and practice.

Thus, for actually offering material belongings, venerating him [or her], or providing service, although you may not be able to actually provide these services due to not being in his presence, you can nevertheless apply yourself sincerely to their sequential application by means of the lamrim ritual preliminaries, Lama Chöpa, and so on. As I explained before, the supreme service is accomplishing your practice. If you realize the meaning through practicing what you have learned, this will be the primary [form of offering]. The *Jataka Tales* state,

> The offering to be made in return for my help is
> To practice in accordance with my instructions.

Je Milarepa stated,

> I repay the kindness of my guru through practice.

Je Drowai Gonpo [1508–1548] also stated,

> Regardless of whether or not a certain dog will stay by my side, when I give him dog food and he gulps it down without chewing, he will remain before its giver staring with wide open eyes. Likewise, when we first meet a lama, although we may damage our commitment to the guru, we still request the lama to compose a more extensive sadhana.[318] From the time we begin learning to write letters, we want to learn whatever is the most difficult and request a religious instruction such as the meaning of "place it in a skull cup" just because it is considered the most difficult. Most people do not understand even those words, yet they ask for the next [ones]. We should first understand the words individually. There is no way of engaging in concentration other than that. Whatever we visualize, that mind should be established in virtue. If you concentrate on a sentence about [the objects of] attachment, from the beginning to end you will be focusing on the mind of attachment. When you are not focusing on any of the afflictive emotions at all, this is called "concentration." Therefore, you should be like a dog that is given food [and gulps it down] without chewing.

Next, if you spend your life engaged solely in practicing and learning Dharma, it will be as the previous Kadampas stated: "A great deal of listening with very little meditation is the cause of becoming insensitive to the Dharma." You should understand that the reason for the lama teaching Dharma is so that the disciple will practice. If we give the concise essential meaning, the *Fifty Verses of Guru Devotion* state,

318. This means that we don't even keep the commitment to recite the sadhana that we currently have, yet fervently request our lama to compose an even longer sadhana.

What need is there to expound on this any further?
You should sincerely apply yourself by
Doing whatever pleases your guru
And forsaking all that causes displeasure.

As this states, you should practice to the best of your ability all that is pleasing to your guru and abandon the things that are displeasing.

A Repeated Explanation and a Concise Teaching on How to Sustain That According to the Previous Explanation

This is from the perspective of meditating solely on the way to rely upon the spiritual guide in a single session. If you are engaging in mere scanning meditation, it is permissible to go over all the headings briefly in each session as a way of performing scanning meditation. If you are striving to attain realizations, you should continue until you gain a thorough experience of each heading. However, the way of carrying this out in combination with placement meditation will be explained extensively later.

Next, complete your recitation of the lamrim preliminary rituals. Moreover, you can add the other sections of the lamrim in the same way and combine them with this practice. It is also permissible to meditate on the actual generation and completion stages and so on. Finally, you and all living beings transform into Buddha Shakyamuni. Contemplating that you have attained the state of Buddha Shakyamuni is similar to the "supreme conqueror of the mandala"[319] in the practice of mantra. Conclude with dedication prayers for whatever you have practiced. In the evening, as you lie down to sleep, you should recite whatever extensive prayers you can, such as The Prayer of Noble Conduct, to dedicate the roots of virtue accumulated on that day. In general, from the very start of your meditation, you should not create bad habits; therefore, it is good to spread out your meditations into numerous short sessions and so on.

319. For an explanation of this, see Ngulchu Dharmabhadra and Losang Lungtog Tenzin Trinley, *The Roar of Thunder: Yamantaka Practice and Commentary*, trans. David Gonsalez (Ithaca, NY: Snow Lion, 2012).

As you gain greater familiarity, it is permissible to extend the length of the sessions.

The Session Breaks

Next, Pabongkha Rinpoche gave the oral transmission of the headings we had completed thus far in addition to the text used as an explanatory commentary, in addition to bestowing the practical commentary. This same reasoning can be applied to the remaining sections.

The session breaks are very important. If you let your mind become engaged in whatever happens to come along during the session breaks, you will demolish what little progress you have so carefully made during the session. For example, although you may meditate on impermanence during the session, if you generate nothing but thoughts grasping at permanence during the session breaks, the careful application you undertook during the session will be undermined. The same thing also applies to the other [topics]; therefore, you must implement methods so that whatever you meditated on during the session does not deteriorate during the session breaks. Therefore, if you read texts taught by the Teacher together with their commentaries that directly relate to your practice during the actual session, the session break will be strengthened and enhanced by the session and the session will be further enhanced by the session breaks.

The term "enhance" means to make progress, [advance, and develop].[320] While [developing] proper reliance upon the spiritual guide, you should focus on presentations of that, such as the teachings on the stages of the path and biographies of qualified beings. The system of restraining the doors of the senses is different from that [taught] during the generation stage. In general, developing an awareness of pleasing objects and displeasing objects causes us to subsequently generate attachment, hatred, and so forth. Therefore, in this practice, we block the generation of attachment for the six pleasing objects and the hatred for the six displeasing objects that is subsequently generated by not allowing the mind to engage in whatever appears to your consciousness. For that, we try not

320. Tib. *skyed thon*. There are several translation options for the Tibetan term, so I have listed three of them to give the reader a broader understanding.

to come into contact with an object, and even if we do come in contact with an object, we rely upon an antidote to prevent us from developing attachment and so forth. It is very important that we don't engage in the object we encounter; therefore, you should also abandon your homeland. [Ngulchu] Gyalsé Thogmé [1297–1371] stated [in his *Thirty-Seven Practices of a Bodhisattva*],

> Attached to friends and relatives, you are agitated like water;
> With hatred for enemies, you blaze like fire;
> In the darkness of ignorance, you forget to adopt and discard;
> Abandoning one's homeland is a practice of the bodhisattva.

It has been repeatedly stated by the previous holy beings that you should abandon your homeland. We will continue to generate attachment and hatred for objects such as forms, sounds, and so on, right down to something as simple as a cup of tea. Therefore, it is extremely important that we don't come into contact with [such] objects.

With the exception of the former lion-like beings such as Jetsun Milarepa, there will be numerous obstacles when we ordinary beings remain in solitude. With that in mind, the conqueror Dromtonpa said, "Prepare an assembly of somewhere between three and five assistants." Thus, it would be good for us to rely upon somewhere between three and five noble friends. It makes no difference whether the objects that increase our afflictive emotions are from another area or our own. However, when we encounter objects, if we don't grasp at characteristics of good and bad, thinking, "This is attractive; this is unattractive," they will not be capable of generating attachment, hatred, and so on.

Regarding the employment of introspection, [Shantideva's] *Guide to the Bodhisattva's Way of Life* states,

> In short, the definition of introspection
> Is nothing more than to
> Repeatedly examine the
> State of your body and mind.

This is a summary of the essential points of something such as the vows of engaging bodhichitta. There is also an extensive presentation on guarding introspection taught in one of the chapters,[321] which indicates how important introspection of the mind is. [Shantideva's *Guide to the Bodhisattva's Way of Life*] also presents a system of introspection when it states,

> What is the use of a multitude of activities
> Other than the courageous action of protecting the mind?

This is in reference to guarding the mind; therefore, you should constantly examine your body, speech, and mind at all times and be relentless with respect to nonvirtuous states of mind. If you let your body, speech, and mind run wild, you will not be aware of whether or not you are engaging in nonvirtue; therefore, it is extremely important that you constantly examine the state of your mind at all times. [Atisha's] *Bodhisattva's Jeweled Garland*[322] also states,

> Examine your speech when you are among many,
> Examine your mind when you are alone.

Furthermore, we should practice according to the example of the Kadam Geshe Ben Gungyal. He stated,

> I have no other task than to hold the spear of the antidote at the castle gates of my mind. When [the afflictions] increase their strength, I also increase my strength. When they relax, I relax as well.

To be on guard in the battle against the afflictive emotions of body, speech, and mind, [Geshe Ben Gungyal would also] place a small white pebble in a pile for each virtuous thought that occurred and a small black pebble for each negative thought that occurred. When a virtuous [thought] arose, he would extend his right hand and say, "Bhikshu victorious in moral discipline," and when a nonvirtuous [thought] arose, he would extend his left hand and [reprimand himself] by saying, "Hey you, Ben Gungyal," and so forth. At another time, when he was staying at his benefactor's home and

321. In Shantideva's *Guide to the Bodhisattva's Way of Life*, "Guarding Alertness" is the fifth chapter, while chapter 4 is "Relying upon Conscientiousness."
322. Tib. *Byang sems nor bu'i phreng ba*.

his benefactor went outside, he put his hand in the tea container and was about to steal some tea when he immediately recalled his [commitment to moral discipline] and yelled out with a loud voice, "You thief!"; this was his way of applying the antidote.

We should also strive to conduct ourselves in the same way as he did, and, when we see that we are about to engage in some nonvirtuous action, protect ourselves against it by applying the antidote. If we don't conduct ourselves in this way and are instead careless in the application of introspection, we will come under the influence of our [negative] mind, as before. Once we have been overpowered by our mind of afflictive emotions, we will engage in a variety of negative actions and will be forever united with our afflictive emotions. [As Shantideva's *Guide to the Bodhisattva's Way of Life* states,]

> A crazy, untamed elephant in this world
> Cannot inflict the same kind of harm as
> The suffering of Avici Hell caused by
> The wild elephant of the mind.

As [stated above], you should guard your speech while you are with your friends and [your mind] when staying alone. For example, if you think, "If the king were to die, I would become the ruler," or "If such-and-such a person in one of these great households in the valley were to die, they would ask me to come perform rituals for his passing," such thoughts create many causes for rebirth in the lower realms; therefore, when such thoughts arise, you must immediately guard your mind. As scripture and a corresponding historical account state,

> If you don't welcome future suffering
> Or you welcome future suffering
> Like the father of the famous moon Chandrakirti.[323]

Thus, when you are alone, you must guard you mind by not letting your mind grasp at the kingdom of samsara and the lower realms. Among the

323. This verse appears to contain some serious scribal errors. One very learned lama I consulted via a translator friend indicated this, saying that, as written, it does not really make any sense in Tibetan.

body, speech, and mind, the body is of least importance, while the two [doors] of speech and mind are more serious. In particular, the mind carries the greatest risk [of incurring negative karma]; therefore, you must infuse the various activities of your body, speech, and mind with virtue. If that happens, that is the real meditation training.

Although you may remain inside your meditation house, if your mind roams around the entire region, this does not constitute being in retreat. When your body is in retreat, the mind of the practitioner should carry out introspection during the sessions and [also] the session breaks. If you complete your strict retreat without having engaged in the three root afflictive emotions[324] or the eight worldly concerns, that is the real retreat. Mahasiddha Ling Repa[325] also declared,

> In the mountain-[like] body composed of the four elements
> Is the blissful cave of the primordial mind;
> Within it exists the wondrous place to practice:
> Gurus, if you are going to engage in a practice, do it there!

Next, we must identify which actions are appropriate and inappropriate, right down to all the activities we undertake in our daily lives with our body, speech, and mind, including the movements of walking, moving around, lying down, and sitting.

You Should Understand the Appropriate Diet

Je Mila[repa] stated,

> If you restrain yourself with respect to food, transference of consciousness will be easy.

As this states, you should not eat as much as you possibly can. Instead, you should eat the correct proportion by dividing your stomach into four sections: (1–2) two sections should be filled with fluid, (3) one portion should be filled with food, and (4) one portion should be empty to allow for the

324. These three are hatred, attachment, and ignorance.

325. Ling Repa Pema Dorje (1128–1189) was the founder of the Drikung Kagyu school. He composed a series of these verses that are directed toward Tibetan gurus in particular.

movement of air [to allow for digestion]. Our compassionate Teacher said that bhikshus and shramaneras should abandon food in the afternoon. It is also important to sleep for a lesser period of time for the sake of maintaining a clear awareness and so forth. We should not eat as much as we possibly can, otherwise food will naturally cause our awareness to become unclear. We should contemplate the faults that come from sleeping too much and so forth, searching for food, partaking of food, begging for food, and so on. We should put an end to our attachment to food by observing its faults. By recalling the negative karma that originates from food and drink, we should purify our thoughts regarding them. Moreover, we should consider food as medicine for the purpose prolonging the life expectancy of our body for the sake of practicing the Dharma. [Nagarjuna's] *Letter to a Friend* states,

> With an understanding that food is like medicine,
> Rely upon it without attachment or hatred,
> Not for the sake of vanity, nor for the sake of grandeur,
> Not for the sake of becoming stout; eat solely for the sake of sustaining your body.

As this citation states, you should understand the correct proportions of foods so that you don't eat far too much or far too little. Do not eat with thoughts of attachment or hatred, do not eat for the sake of conceitedness or vanity, do not eat for the sake of grandeur or attachment to your youthful appearance nor to assume an air of greatness or attractiveness, and do not eat food for the sake of becoming stout and lustrous or for the sake of being well-proportioned. Instead, you should contemplate that you only eat for the sake of remaining in this human body as well as benefiting your benefactor, accomplishing the welfare of all living beings, and so on, thinking, "In this way, may I be able to benefit them by conducting myself perfectly by establishing a beneficial connection with them through food and drink such as meat and so forth." The common [mode of procedure] is to think that the microorganisms you are currently assembling in your body through the material gifts [made through the food that you eat] will be assembled in the future [as disciples to whom you teach] the Dharma. By experiencing them through the practices of secret mantra, through the burnt offering yoga of eating, and through the *tsok* offering, you will not incur a karmic debt from the misappropriation of offerings,[326] and they will instead become a means of completing a great wave of merit. Je Mila[repa] stated,

> Sometimes I eat and eat and meditate;
> When I eat and eat and meditate it is [because]
> I have instructions for making my food portions into a tsok offering.

Machig Labdron[327] stated,

> I have a Dharma that allows me to sleep that
> You, my son disciple, do not know about.
> This makes this old woman concerned.

There is the way in which learners accept the food that has been offered by the faithful, the way in which those who are no-more-learners accept it in the manner of a lord, and the way in which those who are endowed with moral discipline [accept offerings] as well as the way in which a karmic debt is incurred by those who do not possess moral discipline, are not diligent in their practice of Dharma, and are immoral. When such persons [without moral discipline] partake of food given out of faith, it is like eating a blazing-red heap of molten iron and is a cause of rebirth in hell and so forth. There is also the way in which you partake of offerings made out of faith and their faults and benefits, which vary according to the Hinayana and Mahayana. [Thus] we should not be satisfied with merely eating pork, a dish of tsampa, and so forth; instead, we should eat after careful consideration, as explained earlier, whereby we will also complete a great collection of merit. With respect to alcohol, it is not appropriate even for a householder mantra practitioner to drink it. The Teacher himself stated in the Vinaya scripture and the sutras that

326. Tib. *dkor dang bu lon du mi 'gyur.*
327. Machig Labdron (1055–1149) was a Tibetan yogini who originated several Tibetan lineages of the Indian tantric practice of *chö*.

NAGARJUNA

you should recall the Three Jewels as well as engage in the recitation of sutras and so forth while eating and drinking.

You should [also] endeavor [to practice] the yoga of not sleeping. Regarding what to do when you do sleep, Nagarjuna stated [in his *Letter to a Friend*],

> Knowledgeable One, having passed the entire day
> As well as the upper and lower parts of the night in meditation
> session,

> Sleep between those two [periods] with mindfulness,
> So that your sleep does not become ineffective.

The phrase "Knowledgeable One" is a symbol of praising King [Surabhibhadra]. [Nagarjuna] is stating that you should engage in virtue during all parts of the day as well as the beginning and end of the night and that it is permissible to sleep in the middle period of the night. Due to our overindulgence, we try our best to sleep all night and past dawn. However, when the Buddha actualized enlightenment and actualized realizations such as the example and meaning clear lights of the generation and the completion stage, he did so at dawn. Therefore, having [become accustomed] to sleeping in the morning, it will be difficult for us to practice true Dharma. For that reason, it is extremely important for us to also arise early, at dawn. If you sincerely apply yourself to the means of not wasting your life during sleep, you will be able to engage in yoga in which your practice becomes a continuous stream. When your tendency is to sleep face-down, which is similar to [the position of] an animal, you will have a deep sleep, and your awareness will become unclear. When [you sleep] on your left shoulder, like a demigod or hungry ghost, when you awaken from sleep, your mind will be agitated. There are numerous faults taught when you sleep flat on your back and so forth. Therefore, you should sleep in the manner they describe. The final deed of the Buddha revealed the correct manner of sleeping, by lying down on his right shoulder in the lion posture. In general, sleep is a neutral and changeable mental factor; therefore, whatever virtuous or nonvirtuous thought processes you develop just before falling asleep will also transform the nature of your thought processes throughout the entire time you are asleep.

The best way [to accomplish this] is through the completion stage; therefore, Milarepa states,

> Sometimes I sleep and sleep and meditate;
> When I sleep and sleep and meditate, it is [because]
> I have instructions on transforming sleep into the clear light.

If this occurs, even for an ordinary being who has engaged in virtuous practices in one life, these instructions are an incomparable way to practice. Even if such a thing doesn't occur, you should definitely employ the means of transforming sleep into virtue by meditating with certainty upon each virtuous mind, right down to going for refuge. Regarding concentration and so forth, those who meditate on emptiness should meditate with great force upon the view of emptiness as they are falling asleep, whereby when they sleep it becomes a way of directing you toward the realization of emptiness. With respect to mindfulness during sleep, as you recite something such as going for refuge, this will immediately block any nonvirtues you may recall. For the sake of having light sleep, meditate on a white luminosity. Regarding the discrimination you should have upon rising, it is important to set your intention by thinking, "For the sake of sustaining this body, I shall sleep for a short while. Once I get up early tomorrow morning, I shall engage in virtuous actions." If you set your intention in this way, you will definitely awaken from sleep early the next morning. We also know that if we need to do something like a village ritual tomorrow, and we set our intention tonight, we will be able to awaken from sleep early the next morning and so forth. If we are practicing according to mantra and we are able to carry out the yoga of washing, the yoga of dressing, and so on according to the [aforementioned instructions], there is not the slightest chance of such practices not being virtuous.

Day Twelve

The great being glorious Shantideva stated [in his *Guide to the Bodhisattva's Way of Life*],

> If I do not engage in virtue now that I have
> The fortune to be able to practice virtue,
> How will I be able to when I am
> Completely obscured by the suffering of the lower realms?

If we don't take advantage of the opportunity to practice such an authentic Dharma as this while we have found, just this once, our current physical form that is suitable for the practice of Dharma, what need is there to mention practicing an authentic Dharma once we have already taken rebirth in the lower realms? We will not even have the freedom to merely recite the refuge prayer or employ the methods for dispelling our temporary suffering. For that reason, while we have this human body and have encountered a Dharma such as this, we should do everything possible to extract its unique potential. For that reason we should set our motivation as previously explained.

I have already covered [the subjects under the heading] "A Repeated Explanation" and how to conclude [the session,] and then, while going over the meditations on the proper reliance upon the spiritual guide, how to dissolve the gurus emanated in the space before you and dissolve them into the guru on the crown of your head and so on.

During the session breaks, you should examine the stories of how youthful Sudhana properly relied upon protector Maitreya by extracting them from the *Array of Stalks Sutra*, as well as the biography of

Aryadeva

Sadaprarudita by extracting it from the *Perfection of Wisdom Sutra in Eight Thousand Lines* and so forth.

For the actual way to practice, you should employ analytical meditation to [the meditation topics] from the proper reliance upon your spiritual guide up to superior seeing with the exception of tranquil abiding.[328] With respect to placing the mind on a single meditation topic, this is placement meditation, for which we shall use the topic of proper reliance

328. This is because tranquil abiding utilizes only placement meditation. Analytical meditation would be a hindrance to the attainment of tranquil abiding.

upon the spiritual guide, which can then be used as an example for all the meditation topics. Using logic and reason, as well as scriptural references, to repeatedly meditate with analysis on [proper reliance upon the spiritual guide] from all sides and every angle is analytical meditation. Moreover, this is analogous to thinking over the number of times that someone such as our enemy caused us harm, and as we do so our anger and so forth greatly increase. When we do so, we are engaging in analytical meditation on attachment, hatred, ignorance, and so forth. Likewise, when we repeatedly engage in analytical meditation by moving through the proper reliance upon our spiritual guide, [Tsongkhapa's] *Three Principal Aspects of the Path*, and so forth, this analytical meditation greatly increases the power of our mind.

Regarding the procedure for analytical meditation, when the object under consideration is something such as proper reliance upon the spiritual guide and we are training in faith as the root, we establish the assertion with something such as how Vajradhara said that our guru is a buddha, after which we apply scripture and reason as the proof of the reasoning that supports that [assertion] and so forth. When we repeatedly engage in analytical meditation in this way and then develop a powerful ascertaining consciousness that has no other thought than "My guru is an actual buddha," we have elicited an experience [of that subject], whereby we engage in placement meditation on that exact thought.

Pabongkha Rinpoche explained that you should memorize passages from the Path to Bliss *and the* Swift Path *and use them as a support. When you contemplate by thinking over the various headings, this becomes a mental reflection and not analytical meditation.*

The source for the existence of analytical and placement meditation is the *Ornament of the Mahayana Sutras*. In that text it states that initially, on the basis of study, mental investigation into the proper reliance [upon the spiritual guide] comes first. The wisdom [realizing] the authentic meaning of the object emerges from meditation based on mental investigation, and so on. Furthermore, the understanding of the meaning [that is developed] by listening to the lamrim in the presence of your guru is a realization arisen from listening and is called "ascertainment and assumption [developed] through the force of another." For this, if you abandon your premise because someone says, "You are incorrect," then it will change into something else.

Regarding the special ascertaining consciousness that is even clearer than your previous [understanding], which came from repeated meditation on the meanings of what you previously listened to and is like a storehouse, this is called "developing wisdom arisen from thought." It is self-powered and is an ascertainment [developed] through an inferential valid cognizer that cannot be changed into something else. Next, when you gain a direct perception of the meaning through repeated meditation, it is a realization arisen from meditation. The *Ornament of the Mahayana Sutras* states,

> The limb of ascertainment and the path of seeing
> Are the path of meditation itself.
> Repeated reflection, assessment,
> And definite realization are the meditation.

The limb of ascertainment is the path of accumulation, during which one must engage in analytical meditation. The phrase "repeated reflection" refers to the four types of reasoning [applied] to the meaning of what was studied during the path of preparation. Through repeated reflection during the path of seeing, you repeatedly assess the meaning during the path of seeing through the nine [stages] of tranquil abiding. During the path of meditation you employ meditative absorption upon that, through repeated analysis. The *Well-Explained Reasoning* states,

> Employing reflection is for the sake of ascertaining the meaning of what was studied. Employing assessment is for perfecting reasoning, which itself is taught for the sake of utilizing a special object of perception. With respect to employing investigation, it is an aspect of meditation used for the sake of individual realization of the meaning apprehended in that way.

[Shantideva's] *Compendium of Trainings* also explains the existence of both analytical and placement meditation. There is no reason that analytical meditation is not meditation, because no matter how long you employ placement meditation on the mere thought "My guru is a buddha," it will not be possible for this to elicit an experience, and if you have developed strong thoughts such as lack of faith in your guru, you will not be capable of overcoming that lack of faith through merely thinking that your guru is a buddha. Therefore, it is indispensable to employ analytical meditation using scriptures, reasoning, examples, and logical arguments, the meanings of which are also [presented] in this text. For example, the explanation that once you superimpose a defining characteristic of attractiveness upon an object of attachment, [you create a basis for the development of afflictive emotions] and so forth is [explained] here.

Query: Well then, what is engaging in analytical meditation and what is engaging in placement meditation?

Reply: Tranquil abiding and small portions of the generation and completion stages are placement meditation, while you should apply analytical meditation to all the rest. With respect to tranquil abiding and so forth, you engage in placement meditation for the sake of reinforcing a factor of stability. Also, according to authoritative scriptures, both ascetic meditators and scholars need to utilize both analytical and placement [meditation]. Our inability to generate realizations of the lamrim comes from not knowing how to perform analysis and placement. When someone such as a philosopher thinks over the meaning of logical arguments and conclusions and the way to arrange formal arguments, for the most part this is analytical meditation. Although there are some who claim that by engaging in a great deal of thought as analytical meditation you are involved in conceptual elaborations, which is an obstacle to enlightenment, this is utterly incorrect. Regarding concepts creating obstacles for enlightenment, it is the conceptions that constitute inappropriate attention, such as attachment, anger, grasping at true existence, and so on that are creating the obstacles to enlightenment. However, the three principal aspects of the path, going for refuge, action and their effects, and so on, constitute appropriate attention and are correct conceptions and are the cause of enlightenment; therefore, it is impossible that they could be creating obstacles to enlightenment.

The assertion that both good conceptions and bad conceptions are all obstacles to enlightenment and the assertion that it is inappropriate for the mind to engage in them in any way whatsoever were the views of the Chinese abbot Hvashang Mahayana. According to a prophecy, when such bad views as these arose, master Shantarakshita invited master Kamalashila [to debate with Hvashang], and Kamalashila put an end to Hvashang's bad views by refuting them. Furthermore, [Hvashang's] view was the extreme of nihilism; therefore, those meditating on that [view] were going to Avici Hell. With the intention of putting an end to this, [master Shantarakshita invited] master Padmasambhava, who, together with his twenty-five main disciples and so on, had a view that was completely pure.

Afterward, the mistaken view of Hvashang went to numerous areas. Although the Kagyus such as Marpa, Milarepa, and so on had the authentic view of the Prasangika, from the time of Dagpo Lhaje [Gampopa] onward, there were some who had a mistaken view that was reminiscent of Hvashang's view. These days as well, there are many upholders of such views. Moreover, it is said that when Hvashang was sent back to China, he left one of his shoes behind in Tibet. Due to this detrimental inauspiciousness, great harm has been done. Regarding the teaching that states, "With respect to gold and silver, a blacksmith or a blacksmith's apprentice who is skilled and so forth . . ."[329] through repeated analysis with the wisdom of individual investigation on the side of virtue, the mind can be made serviceable with respect to the three principal aspects of the path. Regarding the term "nonconceptual," this refers to a mind set single-pointedly upon an object of observation and also contains the essential points of tranquil abiding meditation.

How to Train the Mind once You Have Relied [upon the Spiritual Guide] has two sections:

1. Encouragement for the Sake of Extracting the Essence of This Human Existence
2. How to Extract Such Essence

329. This is in reference to this section in Tsongkhapa's *Middle-Length Treatise on the Stages of the Path to Enlightenment*, which states that just as a smith can use gold, silver, and so forth and fashion it into whatever jewelry he likes through cutting, burning, washing, and so on, so, through analytical meditation, the afflictions can be transformed into virtuous states of mind.

Encouragement for the Sake of Extracting the Essence of This Human Existence

The fact that, with the exception of our attachment to our belongings, we don't have any desire to extract the essence of our leisure and endowment is the fault of not recognizing this [life of] leisure and endowment. Therefore, so that we don't continue to act that way from now on, we need encouragement to extract the essence of this leisure and endowment, for which there are three sections.

[Encouragement for the Sake of Extracting the Essence of This Human Existence has three sections:]

1. Identifying Leisure and Endowment
2. Contemplating Their Great Value from a Temporary Perspective and Contemplating Their Great Value from an Ultimate Perspective
3. Contemplating the Great Difficulty in Obtaining [a Life of Leisure and Endowment]

Identifying Leisure and Endowment

Regarding leisure, the *Collection of Precious Good Qualities*[330] states,

> Due to a code of conduct, one continually attains leisure by abandoning [the causes of]
> The nature of a multitude of migrations such as animals and the eight states lacking freedom.

If one is a Dharma practitioner with freedom, this is leisure. In fact, it should be divorced from the eight states of nonfreedom.[331] With respect to the eight states of nonfreedom, there are four nonfreedoms of being a human and four nonfreedoms of a nonhuman, making eight in total.

330. Tib. *Yon tan rin po che sdud.*
331. Here the Tibetan terms *khom* and *mi khom* are translated as "freedom" and "nonfreedom," respectively, while the term *dal* is translated as "leisure."

Furthermore, the four nonhuman states lacking freedom are (1) a hell being, (2) a hungry ghost, (3) an animal, and (4) those in the god realm. Regarding the long-life gods, there are the ordinary beings in the formless realm and those without discrimination; there are also desire-realm gods who are constantly distracted by objects of desire [and are considered a type of long-life god]. Of these, the first three are oppressed by ordinary suffering whereby they have no opportunity to practice Dharma, so they are incapable of [practicing] Dharma. Those in the last group are gods, the first of whom are without Dharma to accomplish the path to liberation; therefore, theirs is a state of nonfreedom. The second [those without discrimination] lack the [type of] mind for practicing Dharma; therefore, theirs is a state of nonfreedom. Regarding the third, [the desire-realm gods] are distracted; therefore, they lack the freedom to practice Dharma.

If we don't have anything to eat or drink for even one day, we are tormented by hunger, and if [under such circumstances] we find it extremely difficult to develop the mere thought wishing to practice Dharma, there will be absolutely no opportunity for us to practice Dharma when we must continuously experience the suffering that each being in those states of nonfreedom undergoes. According to *A Commentary on the Eight States of Nonfreedom*[332] composed by Khechog Pawo, for the most part the desire-realm gods are distracted by amusing themselves with happiness and enjoyments of the objects of enjoyment and are therefore not suited for the Dharma. Consider the historical account of Shariputra's disciple, the physician named Youthful Jivaka, who was reborn as a god.[333] If the gods without discrimination don't even have the mind that desires to practice Dharma, how could the [ordinary gods] ever engage in it? In general, the ordinary gods in the form realm have peaceful and coarse aspects that they have attained through the path of meditation merely [with the wish] for a happy migration, yet they are also said to be migrations of nonfreedom. As soon as they are born in those heavenly abodes,

332. Tib. *Mi khom pa brgyad kyi gtam.*

333. When Shariputra was alive, Jivaka had so much devotion for his teacher Shariputra that as soon as he saw him he would immediately stop whatever he was doing and make prostrations. After Jivaka died he was reborn in the god realms, and one day Shariputra went to visit him by means of his magical powers. When Jivaka saw him all he could do is raise a finger in acknowledgment because he was so absorbed in his divine enjoyments.

they have a slight distraction of the mere bliss of samadhi, such as the first two mental stabilizations as well as the access concentration and so forth, and it is not possible for them to practice Dharma in dependence upon the pure conduct of celibacy. Although the lives of those born in these abodes are extremely long, the negative karma that they accumulated in their human lives and some other rebirths causes them to be reborn in hell when they die [in these abodes]. When that lifespan is exhausted and they are free to take a higher rebirth and they once again attain a human body, it is as though they had become enlightened.[334]

From among the four states of nonfreedom as a human, [the first is being born in] a place where the Buddha's teachings do not exist, such as borderlands of non-Buddhists, foreign countries, a land of savages, and so forth. If you are reborn in one of these places, you will not be able to engage in even one word of the refuge prayer during your entire life. Although you may be reborn in a central land, if you are reborn with incomplete sense faculties, such that you don't understand how to practice Dharma although it is explained well, or if you don't understand what is being said because you lack the basic intelligence and so on, it will not be possible to practice Dharma mentally, verbally, and so forth; therefore, we are very fortunate to not have been born in such places. The Bonpos and the non-Buddhists are considered the same thing; therefore, although they may have taken rebirth in the Arya Avalokiteshvara's pure land [that is, Tibet], it is rare for them to bring with them even one virtuous root through the recitation of one complete round of the Mani mantra at the time of their death. Still, the [Bonpos] have a Dharma similar to the Mani that they call "Matri" and "Akar" and so on. They deceive people with their recitations and say that it is no different from the Mani, and they even claim that it has existed for a very long time, which is extensively explained in the historical accounts of the Bonpo teacher Shenrab.

If we had been born with views denying the existence of past and future lives, we would have contempt for actions and their effects; therefore, it would have been much worse than any of the former [examples]. Concerning the barbarians' Dharma, [this is similar to] a person alive

334. This means that the suffering in the hell realms is so severe that taking a human rebirth feels as though they have attained nirvana.

during the lifetime of master Nagarjuna named Pandita Mamathara, who opposed the Dharma and spread his evil tradition by traveling around and turning others away from the Dharma. Although *tirthikas*[335] are not Buddhists, they have a slight appreciation for actions and their effects; therefore, they are better than the non-Buddhists mentioned earlier. We are very fortunate to not have been reborn in any of those human states of nonfreedom. We should think over how it is also extremely fortunate that we haven't taken rebirth as an animal and so forth; how it is also very fortunate that we haven't taken rebirth as someone like a soldier [who battles] with other kingdoms; how it is also very fortunate that we have complete sense faculties, that we are not reborn as a Muslim or a Bonpo,[336] and that we haven't been reborn in a barren land where the Buddha did not appear.

If we briefly sum up the meaning of the phrase "leisure and endowment," we can state it as "leisure is being free from the eight unfavorable conditions for the practice of Dharma, and endowment is having all ten favorable conditions." The *Shravaka Levels*[337] states,

> Being born a human, in a central land, with complete sense faculties,
> Reversible karma, [and] faith in the foundation of the spiritual life . . .

These are five personal endowments that you must have in your mental continuum. [The first is] "Being born a human." Being born "in a central land" is a land where there is a retinue of four types of followers with bhikshus being the principal [retinue] and where pure teachings and practices are being spread. "Complete sense faculties," as well as having complete limbs, fingers, and toes, are so that you are free from all the obstacles to the vows of celibacy. "Reversible karma" means not having

335. Tib. *mu stegs pa*. In the previous sections I have been translating this term as "non-Buddhist"; however, in this instance I have opted for the original Sanskrit term for clarity.
336. This is not a defamation of Muslims but refers to a small community of Muslims who lived in Lhasa. Pabongkha Rinpoche is saying that it would be unfortunate had we been born in one of the groups in Tibet that don't believe in the Buddhadharma.
337. Tib. *Nyan sa*.

committed any of the five actions of immediate retribution. "Faith in the foundation of the spiritual life"[338] means having faith in the teachings on the Vinaya. Here "Vinaya" is faith in all Three Baskets.[339] Regarding downfalls of discipline, this refers to the Vinaya. Regarding the afflictions of the discipline, this refers to the Sutra basket and Abhidharma basket. Therefore, we are very fortunate to also have the five personal endowments for the practice of Dharma.

The five endowments related to others are taught as follows:

> The Buddha has arrived, the holy Dharma is being taught,
> The teachings remain, there are those who follow it, [and]
> They have compassion for others.

The first is "The Buddha has arrived," for which the guru is his representative who is able to substitute for his appearance, making this one complete. The teachings of the guru are able to substitute for the Dharma, making this one complete as well.

Regarding the term "teachings" in the phrase "the teachings remain," this refers to the "teachings of practice." The five thousand years that the Buddha's teachings will remain are divided into sections of (1) result, (2) attainment, (3) scripture, and (4) grasping at mere signs. Of these, this modern era is generally considered the section of scripture, during which if we practice and develop realizations in our mental continuum, this is the teachings of attainment emerging. The previous Kadam masters said, "The general teachings [of the Buddha] are not something we possess in our mental continuum. The teachings we must keep from declining are our own."

Regarding "followers," this refers to having others who have attained realizations whom we can look up to. Although these days they do not reveal extremely conspicuous signs of their attainment, we need to follow holy beings who have generated realizations in their mental continuums by practicing a Dharma such as this.

Regarding "compassion for others," this refers to the existence of

338. Tib. *gnas la dad pa*.
339. The Three Baskets, or "scriptural collections," are those of the moral discipline (Vinaya), discourses (Sutra), and higher knowledge (Abhidharma).

contributors who act as benefactors and so forth, providing favorable conditions for the practice of Dharma such as food, clothes, and so on. [Thus] we have a similitude of the first four endowments related to others and the actual fifth, making [all five of] them complete.

There are eight unfavorable conditions to the practice of Dharma that we are free of and ten favorable conditions; we are very fortunate to have these eighteen. If we should be extremely joyous at having the good fortune to attain even one of these continuously in this life, just think of how extraordinarily rare it is to have found all eighteen of these precious and invaluable jewels assembled at once, now that we have attained this human life of leisure and endowment. For example, if you needed to purchase eighteen different articles from somewhere like Lhasa and were able to get no more than seven or eight of them, [you would be disappointed,] yet this human life surpasses even a hundred or a thousand [collections of] eighteen precious jewels throughout our succession of lives:

> This human existence surpasses a wish-fulfilling jewel;
> We will find one like this just this once . . .

As this states, now that we have attained this human life just once, while we have it we must extract whatever essence we can from it; if we don't there would be nothing more foolish; nothing could be more stupid! Therefore, extract its essence right now! If we develop just this one realization of [our extremely fortunate] leisure and endowment, it will be utterly unlike anything that has previously happened in our mental continuum. At present we are like a destitute person using gold for foundation stones, not realizing their worth. Now we must do whatever it takes to be like someone who recognizes [their value].

Contemplating Their Great Value from a Temporary Perspective and Contemplating Their Great Value from an Ultimate Perspective has two sections:

1. Their Great Value from an Ultimate Perspective
2. Contemplating the Great Difficulty in Obtaining [a Life of Leisure and Endowment]

[Their Great Value from an Ultimate Perspective]

Our text, [Tsongkhapa's *Middle-Length Treatise on the Stages of the Path,*] states,

> If you fail to practice Dharma purely for the sake of lasting happiness and instead strive merely to dispel suffering and attain happiness until you die, you are just like an animal despite having been born in a happy migration.

If you fail to work at a means of lasting happiness, and if you are attached to this life alone, you are no different from an animal. Even an animal knows how to collect provisions; a rat collects wheat, barley, grass, and so on, and a bee knows how to collect honey. Even animals are skilled at subduing their enemies and protecting their loved ones. Snakes and lizards combat each other, and at the time of one of the Kadampas, a raven and an owl in Phenpo had a battle. Also, a magpie and a raven as well as a hornless yak and a horned yak had a battle. When it comes to protecting loved ones, human beings must care for their children for many years, whereas animals stay with their offspring for just a few months. For that reason, the previous Kadampas also said, "Now is the time to distinguish yourself from wild animals." Thus, we must practice a Dharma that distinguishes us from animals; moreover, that type of Dharma that we wish to practice is something we are capable of practicing with this physical form, and for generating the mind of enlightenment, this human physical form is supreme. [Chandragomin's] *Letter to a Disciple*[340] states,

> With a human life you attain great mental strength; it is the basis of the
> Path of the sugatas and equips you to guide migrators.
> Such a path is not attained by gods, nagas, demigods,
> Garudas, knowledge-holders, *kinnaras*, or snakes.

340. Tib. *sLob springs.*

This human life is also the supreme basis for the realization of emptiness. With the exception of gods of the desire realm who have established imprints in dependence upon a former human life, [the rest] are not capable of realizing emptiness. Even those in the form and formless realms cannot newly generate the path of an arya from a realization through a previous human existence. The pratimoksha vows as well cannot be developed in other migrations, such as on the other three continents[341] as a god, in the lower realms, on Kurava, and so on.

Not only that, but [this human life] is the basis for the bodhisattva vows. In particular, a womb birth as a human in this continent is the basis of attaining complete enlightenment in one life through secret mantra, for it is only in dependence upon the six elements of earth, water, fire, wind, and red and white bodhichitta [that enlightenment in one life is possible]; it is not possible even in the buddha lands such as Sukhavati. The bodhisattvas in Sukhavati pray to once again take rebirth in this world. The previous holy beings such as Milarepa attained enlightenment in this human physical form. However, instead we use it as a cause for accomplishing the hells.

Instead of straying into this mistaken purpose, devoid of meaning, let's find out if we can attain our permanent objectives. If we accomplish that, we will surely reach attainments. Even Je Mila[repa] and others didn't have a means of attainment superior to this physical form. Regarding these [attributes of a human life], when considering our ultimate objectives, they are the means of [attaining] great value. For that reason, now that we have this physical form, if we don't extract its extraordinary essence, there is nothing more stupid and ignorant; there could be no greater loss. [Shantideva's] *Guide to the Bodhisattva's Way of Life* states,

> Having found a life of leisure such as this,
> If I don't use it to acquaint myself with virtue,
> Nothing could be more foolish than this;
> Nothing could be more ignorant than this!

341. Ancient Buddhist cosmology states that there are four continents in our world system.

If we use this human life as a means of attaining what is meaningful, even obtaining a hundred thousand wish-fulfilling jewels cannot compare to it. When we possess this life of leisure and endowment, we can attain the state of enlightenment in one life, as well as accomplish our aims. When we don't possess it, even if we have many hundreds of thousands of jewels, there is no way of attaining even a slight liberation from samsara, so what need is there to mention enlightenment? To determine whether or not this is the case, we can observe the difference in knowledge and capacity between Je Mila[repa] and the Naga [King]. Phuchungwa [1031–1106] stated,

> Having obtained a life of leisure and endowment, if you die without have used it for virtuous actions, it would be like finding a priceless gem and throwing it out without having benefited from it. If you engage in negativity, it is like mixing the jewel with poison and trussing it up together as poisonous food.

If we let one day of this life go to waste, it is a much greater cause of devastation than if we dropped a pouch of gold in a ditch. Although we may merely waste some gold, it cannot benefit or harm us beyond this life, whereas wasting even a small portion of this life is a much greater reason to feel a sense of loss. By wasting even a single day of this life, we make the journey to liberation and omniscience that much further off. Even in the time it takes to drink a cup of tea, if we engage in a proper accumulation and purification through practices such as Lama Chöpa, jorchö, and so forth, we will be that much closer to the state of enlightenment. The best of us will attain enlightenment in this life; if that doesn't happen, we can achieve a state of [spiritual] stability in this life; if even that doesn't happen, we will at least not have any regrets at the time of our death. If we don't at least manage not to go to the lower realms after death, we have seriously deceived ourselves, and nothing could be more stupid!

Therefore, at this time when we have obtained an excellent physical form, we have reached the demarcation line between going upward or going downward. Our decision at this juncture marks the turning point that will determine our fate, for better or worse, far into the future. For example, previously someone gave a man an instruction that stated, "The foundation of excellence is virtue; the sphere of reality is the best of all things; respectfully prostrate to all supports of devotion." Yet he did not understand what the person had told him and mistakenly thought that the person had said, "If it is good, it has a good foundation. If it is faulty, it has a faulty foundation. I respectfully prostrate to the good foundation and the faulty foundation." If we accomplish virtue while we have obtained this life of leisure and endowment, we will get off to a good start to lasting happiness through our series of rebirths. If we accumulate negative karma, there is a grave danger of it becoming lasting suffering.

Right now, from this moment onward, you must not be mistaken and instead put all the knowledge you have into striving for virtue. Thus, not only is there great value with respect to the ultimate, but there is great value with respect to the temporary as well. In your next life you will obtain an excellent physical form with a body and enjoyments of high status, have a sublime retinue, and be endowed with the seven qualities of higher rebirth[342] and the eight qualities of karmic maturation.[343] With this current human body you have the means of accomplishing the cause for rebirth in Sukhavati, Abhirati, and so forth. Therefore, in the period until you attain enlightenment you will accomplish all your desired aims with the body, enjoyments, and so forth of higher status. In the ultimate sense, with this human life you can also attain the state of enlightenment. If we don't extract as much essence [from this] as we possibly can, it will be like returning home from a jeweled island empty-handed. If we accumulate negative karma in this life and then go to the lower realms, it will be like going to a jeweled island and instead of leaving with jewels, acquiring as much debt as possible. Although we have already wasted so much [of our life], with whatever little bit of life we still have left, we absolutely must extract its essence to the very best of our ability for as long as we have it. With respect to obtaining just once such an excellent physical form as we have currently, [Geshe] Potowa states in *Jewel Heaps of Teaching*

342. The seven qualities of a higher rebirth are (1) a noble family, (2) a beautiful bodily form, (3) a long lifespan, (4) no illness, (5) good fortune, (6) abundant wealth, and (7) great intelligence.
343. The eight qualities of karmic maturation are (1) long life, (2) excellent features, (3) excellent family lineage, (4) excellent wealth and power, (5) respected speech, (6) renowned authority, (7) being a male, and (8) possessing strength.

through Analogy,[344] "A worm making full-length prostrations . . ."[345] He gives extensive examples with similar meanings and says that you should think, "If I don't extract its meaning right now, when will I extract it?"

Contemplating the Great Difficulty in Obtaining [a Life of Leisure and Endowment]

Not only does this human life have great meaning, but it is extremely difficult to acquire as well. The Teacher gave the following example: "As few as dust particles on the tip of a fingernail . . ." Those beings who transmigrate to rebirth in the lower realms after their deaths in a happy rebirth and those who transmigrate to a lower realm after their deaths in a lower realm are similar to the amount of atoms of this great earth. Those who transmigrate from those two states [of the lower realms] to a happy rebirth are similar to the particles on the tip of a fingernail. This is taught in the *Sutra on the Bases of Discipline*.[346]

[Contemplating the Great Difficulty in Obtaining a Life of Leisure and Endowment has three sections:]

1. The Great Difficulty in Obtaining It by Way of Its Cause
2. The Great Difficulty in Obtaining It by Way of Its Nature or Result
3. The Great Difficulty in Obtaining It by Way of Example, Expanded with the Oral Instructions of the Gurus

The Great Difficulty in Obtaining It by Way of Its Cause

Furthermore, in this world, to get a good crop from a field, if you do not establish a multitude of causes with great effort, such as planting seeds

344. Tib. *dPe chos rin chen spungs pa.*
345. The point is that just as it is extremely rare for an earthworm to stand upright and make full-length prostrations, so it is extremely rare to obtain a human life with a complete set of eighteen qualities.
346. Tib. *'Dul ba lung gzhi'i mdo.*

in the springtime, providing water, manure, warmth, and so on, you will not get a crop. With respect to obtaining a human life of leisure and endowment, you need even more sublime causes that are far superior to that. If you don't assemble them, how will it come about? For that, in general, we must absolutely guard our pure moral discipline even to attain a mere human life of high status. [Nagarjuna states in his *Precious Garland*,]

> From giving comes wealth, through moral discipline comes happiness . . .

We should study authentic scriptures with the three types of incontrovertible analysis about the meaning of this subject matter. In particular, to attain a human body with leisure and endowment such as the one we have now, we must by all means establish the foundation through pure moral discipline, assisted by the six transcendent perfections such as giving and so forth, conjoined with stainless prayers. Therefore, although these causes are indispensable, we are utterly without the complete purity that comes from maintaining the first pure moral discipline. Without even mentioning the others, it is extremely rare to protect purely even one of the four root downfalls [of the Sangha].[347] It is nothing other than next to impossible to also be aided by giving and so forth.

We also need at the very least [to combine pure moral discipline] with stainless prayers by making completely pure prayers striving to attain a human body in our next life. Right from the beginning [of our practice], we come under the influence of craving solely for the things of this life, so it is extremely rare to make even the slightest prayers striving toward our future lives. Therefore, if we don't take the opportunity to extract the essence [of this precious human life] in this very moment, it will be extremely difficult to obtain a human life such as this in the future. It is also extremely important that we consider the way in which it is difficult to obtain leisure and endowment, without looking at the number of

347. The four root downfalls of any ordained person are (1) killing a human, (2) stealing, (3) lying about your level of spiritual attainment, and (4) sexual contact.

people besides ourselves but looking precisely at whether or not we have the complete set of causes of leisure and endowment in our own mental continuum.

The Great Difficulty in Obtaining It by Way of Its Nature or Result

In general, very few beings go to a happy rebirth after migrating to a lower rebirth, those who attain a human rebirth are rarer, those who attain a human life suitable for the practice of Dharma are even rarer, and of those, people who practice Dharma purely are extremely rare. Therefore, consider the least numerous of the three lower realms, [namely, that of] animals. The majority of animals are in the depths of the ocean, in the dark spaces between continents, and so forth.[348] Although the animals that we see scattered about [on the earth] are the fewest of them, in the summertime the number of bugs is the greatest [of these]. Yet if we were to collect the number of people in the upper, lower, and middle parts of this country and double that number, there would still be even more bugs in just a small pool of water. Within each anthill, there are more ants than all the people in this country; and this is just one type of bug. Thus, there are innumerable other animals and other migrations, and since this is the case you should think, "I am extremely fortunate not to be born among them at present; therefore, at this moment I must extract some unique essence of this human life."

The Great Difficulty in Obtaining It by Way of Example, Expanded with the Oral Instructions of the Gurus

[Nagarjuna's] *Letter to a Friend* states,

> Since it is more difficult to obtain a human life from life as an
> animal
> Than it is for a turtle to meet with the opening of a yoke

348. Ancient Buddhist cosmology states that there are oceans that surround the four continents, and in the vast distances between them, they are devoid of light.

Abiding on a great ocean, Your Majesty, make this
[Life] fruitful by practicing the holy Dharma.

[Shantideva's] *Guide to the Bodhisattva's Way of Life* states,

A human life is as extremely difficult to attain
As it is for a turtle to insert its neck into
A yoke adrift on a great ocean.

[Geshe] Potowa's *Jewel Heaps of Teaching through Analogy* states,

Grass on the rooftop, the neck of a turtle,
Loding's son, riding a stallion,
A Tsangpa's food of fish, roasted balls of tsampa,
A worm making a full-length prostration . . .[349]

By conjoining the meaning [of the aforementioned verse] with examples, you get a detailed and extensive way to contemplate the need to extract the essence of this life of leisure and endowment.

349. These analogies are explained in Pabongkha Rinpoche's *Liberation in Our Hands.*

Day Thirteen

The teachings of Jamgon Tsongkhapa the Great state, "You will find this excellent human existence once . . ." Through this quotation we can see that a human life of leisure and endowment such as the one we have found at this moment is something we have not previously attained. The phrase "human existence"[350] serves to identify leisure and endowment. The phrase "extremely difficult to find" indicates that you will not find [a life] such as this in the future. We should extract its essence throughout all times of the day and night, without wasting even one hour of this human life. Regarding the king-like oral instructions of the Teacher for the means of taking the essence of this life, this is called "the Dharma of the stages of the path to enlightenment," as mentioned earlier.

After giving this brief introduction, Pabongkha Rinpoche restated the headings while once again giving a discourse to encourage us to extract the essence [of this precious human life]. He continued:

You should think about how fortunate we are to have the complete set of leisure and endowments and how fortunate we are to have obtained a human life such as this and not to have been born in a place without freedom. Next, you should contemplate by thinking about its great value by considering its temporary and ultimate value. Contemplate how difficult it is to find by way of its causes—how difficult it will be to obtain in the future by analyzing whether or not we have the causes of leisure

350. Tib. *dal ba'i rten*. This can be translated in a number of ways, such as "life of leisure," "fortunate rebirth," and so on.

Buddhapalita

and endowment in our mental continuum—by way of nature, and by thinking how in general there are fewer hungry ghosts than hell beings and even fewer animals. Consider how, in the space occupied by just ten people, there are more animals such as bugs than all the people in an entire kingdom combined and, therefore, how fortunate we are not to have been born among them. Contemplate, by way of example, how it is next to impossible to set a mustard seed upon the tip of an upright needle or throw dried peas against a smooth surface and expect each one to stick. Finding this human life with leisure and endowment is even rarer than those examples. Acharya Kamalashila proclaimed,

> Considering the number of living beings, the difficulty of obtaining a human life
> [Is similar] to the possibility of throwing a pea against a wall and having it stick.

Therefore, you should think about how it is generally difficult to attain a human body. And even if you attain it, it is difficult to be born in a world where the Buddha's teachings exist and in a land of devout persons. And once you are born in such a place, it is rare to repeatedly encounter the teachings of the Buddha. With respect to meeting the teachings of the [Ganden] Hearing Lineage, as [the Second] Panchen [Lama] Losang Yeshe told a Mongolian, this is almost impossible. Since this is the situation, you must use every means possible to extract its essence in this very moment.

Although it is permissible to complete many of the subjects in each session when practicing mere scanning meditation, if you are striving to attain realizations, you would take one subject, such as the value of leisure and endowment, and should [then] continue in this way for a year or a month until you generate experience. You can use scriptural citations such as this:

> Although the lamrim extracts the essence of the excellent scriptures,
> To accomplish happiness depends upon the Dharma; therefore, you should practice the Dharma.
> When you practice the Dharma, take it as your spiritual guide for the sake of gaining the complete set of leisure and endowments;
> If you don't accomplish this, it will be very difficult to attain in the future.

Once you have contemplated well the great value and difficulty of obtaining leisure and endowment, Jamgon Tsongkhapa states, "If you understand how difficult it is to find, there is no way you can sit idly by. Once you see its great value, you will feel devastated if it is lost on the meaningless."

When this happens, you have generated the realization of the great value and difficulty of obtaining leisure and endowment.

How to Extract Its Essence has two sections:

1. Developing Certainty in the General Presentation of the Path
2. The Actual Means of Extracting Its Essence of Leisure and Endowment

Developing Certainty in the General Presentation of the Path

There wasn't anything that our Teacher taught that wasn't a means to guide his disciples to either higher status or definite goodness, all of which can be subsumed within the teachings on the path of the three types of beings. Therefore, the lamrim is naturally different from other systems of practicing Dharma such as counting mantras. Attaining a higher rebirth as a human or god is "higher status." Attaining the state of liberation and omniscience is "definite goodness." With respect to an ordinary person of lesser capacity, he [or she] is only concerned with this life and is not included within the three types of beings.[351] With respect to a being of special capacity, he is not attached to this life, and due to his fear of the suffering of the lower realms, he abandons the ten nonvirtues and practices abandonment and adoption with respect to actions and their effects. Through this, he primarily accomplishes the state of higher status and is considered a being of lesser capacity. [Atisha's] *Lamp for the Path [to Enlightenment]* states,

> Know that those that diligently strive for the mere
> Happiness of samsara by whatever means
> For their own welfare alone
> Are beings of the least capacity.

Regarding a person of middling capacity, after developing aversion for all of samsara, including the happiness of gods, humans, and so forth, he

351. Within the small scope, there are ordinary persons and special persons. The former are not counted as spiritual practitioners since their motivation is only for the sake of this life.

[or she] practices Dharma with a mind striving for liberation. [*Lamp for the Path to Enlightenment*] states,

> Those who turn their backs on the happiness of existence
> And have turned away from negative actions
> While striving for merely their own peace
> Are called beings of middling capacity.

This states that with fear and trepidation of samsara and the lower realms, they strive for liberation by properly training in the path of the three higher trainings. Those who are not concerned for themselves alone but, observing all living beings, strive in the six transcendent perfections, the two stages [of highest yoga tantra], and so on are beings of great capacity. [*Lamp for the Path to Enlightenment* again states,]

> Those who sincerely wish to eradicate
> All the suffering of others because of
> The suffering included within their own continuum
> Are beings of supreme capacity.

The purpose of leading others through the path of the three types of beings is to guide them to the path of the great scope, in the same way you [ascend] a staircase; therefore, "beings of the small and middling scope" is a mere conventional nominal designation. For this reason, if the beings of the small and middling scope were nonexistent, there would be no way of guiding them to the great scope. Furthermore, if we apply the example of three people traveling from here to Lhasa, one going from Brula Khang—where we are now—to Kongpo is like a being of the small scope. Next, one going to inner Maldro is like a being of the middling scope, and then finally the one reaching Lhasa is like a being of the great scope.[352] Thus, the way of establishing the three types of beings is like how three travelers have different thoughts. Therefore, both the beings of great and those of middling capacity must train their minds in impermanence, going for refuge, and actions and their effects. The path of the

352. Using American geography, this would be like going from Seattle to Portland, and finally reaching Los Angeles.

being of least capacity is common to all three. The path of the middling being is common to both the great and middling scope. And the great scope is unique [unto itself].

The Reason Beings Are Guided through the Stages has two sections:

1. The Actual Reason
2. The Need to Lead through the Stages in That Way

The Actual Reason

[Shantideva's] *Guide to the Bodhisattva's Way of Life* states,

> The moment destitute beings bound within the
> Prison of samsara generate bodhichitta . . .

"Destitute" refers to animals such as dogs and pigs. Whether a practice is the Mahayana or not is entirely dependent upon whether or not bodhichitta exists. You should contemplate the benefits of generating bodhichitta in your mental continuum, which has been illuminated in the supreme scriptures of the Teacher as well as [Shantideva's] *Compendium of Trainings* and *Guide to the Bodhisattva's Way of Life*. If I were to state the benefits concisely, the *Prayer to Maitreya* states,

> I prostrate to bodhichitta, which turns one
> Away from the path of the lower migrations,
> Perfectly reveals the path of high rebirth,
> And acts as a guide to a state without old age or death.

If you generate bodhichitta in your mental continuum, there are limitless temporary and ultimate benefits. You will attain the states of happy migrations, and these are just the benefits from now until the attainment of enlightenment.

If you don't train your mind in the path of a being of lesser capacity, you won't have the wish to be liberated from the lower realms and won't develop the wish to attain the state of higher status; therefore, you won't receive the temporary benefits of bodhichitta. If you don't train your mind in the path of a being of middling capacity, you won't have the wish to be liberated from samsara and won't develop the wish to attain liberation; therefore, you won't receive the ultimate benefits of bodhichitta. Therefore, your [meditation] must be preceded by these two [motivations of small- and middle-scope beings]. Not only that, but both of them must precede your meditation on bodhichitta as well. [Shantideva's] *Guide to the Bodhisattva's Way of Life* states,

> If these beings previously didn't
> Even dream of such a mind for
> Their own welfare while dreaming,
> How will they generate it for the welfare of others?

To generate bodhichitta, you need compassion that is unable to bear other living beings being tormented by the suffering of samsara. For that to happen, you need renunciation that is unable to bear the way you are being tormented by the suffering of samsara. My guru Choné Rinpoche said that renunciation and bodhichitta are merely a change of perspective from self to other. You must develop the paths of the small, middling, and great beings by inducing each one with each preceding stage. For example, just as if we are going from here to Lhasa, we need to [first] arrive in Maldro, and to arrive at Maldro, we must first arrive at Kongpo, so to generate bodhichitta of the great scope in our mental continuum, we must generate great compassion through explanations concerning the Dharma of a being of great capacity. To generate that, we need to generate renunciation as a preliminary that has become disenchanted with samsara while [training] in [the practices of] a being of middling capacity. To generate that, we must first generate renunciation that is terrified of the suffering of the lower realms through explanations from [the viewpoint of] a being of the small capacity.

Therefore, it is utterly impossible to develop bodhichitta without [training] in [the practices of] beings of small and middling capacity. If you generate the realizations of a lesser being through training as a being of lesser capacity, you are getting close to the middle scope. If you generate the realizations of a middling being, you are getting close to a great being. Therefore, if you sincerely apply yourself in this way, the path will be very quick. If you understand this way of thinking, it will double the speed of the path of secret mantra; therefore, the stages of the path are the quick path. Some people say that Gedenpas[353] practice the long path, and although they call us "the long path practitioners," they don't understand in the least how we are designating the name "stages of the path to enlightenment." Previously, Changkya Rolpai Dorje was listening to teachings in the presence of Phurchog Ngawang Jampa. Afterward, Changkya Rolpai Dorje said, "Lama Jampa Rinpoche even combines the teachings of the secret mantras with the lamrim. The profound features of secret mantra should be drawn out with the lamrim. His way of teaching is really extraordinary."

Moreover, you will not reach anywhere without the lamrim. There are numerous stories to illustrate this point, such as that of a Hevajra yogi attaining the state of a stream-enterer of the Hinayana and a Yamantaka yogi being reborn as an evil spirit. If you don't understand that the small and middling paths are shared with the great path, there will never be a time when you will practice the complete path and so forth; therefore, their great value will deteriorate. Between method and wisdom, everything from tranquil abiding and below reveals the cycle of teachings about method. From the two types of accumulation, they are the accumulation of merit. From the two truths, they are conventional truths. Likewise, those [teachings] concerning superior seeing extensively explain the cycle of teachings about wisdom, the accumulation of exalted wisdom, and ultimate truth.

Thus, train through stages in such a path. You should also understand, from the teachings on the essential points in the authoritative lamrim texts, how to also train in mantra. From the point of view of secret mantra, purify your defilements of root downfalls through confession, and from the beginning don't let yourself be defiled by a root downfall. This is very much like repairing your two legs through medical treatment once you break them and not breaking them at all in the first place, [respectively].

353. *Geden* was one of the early terms used for what is now known as "Gelug." *Geden* means "endowed with virtue" or simply "virtuous." The Tibetans were struggling to pronounce the term "Gedenpa" so it slowly changed to *Gelug*, which means "virtuous tradition."

The Need to Lead through the Stages in That Way

In general, training the mind in the bodhichitta of the person of great capacity is the actual lamrim, and the paths of the small and middling scopes are preliminaries. They are objects of training that are general activities of training. You may doubt, "If they are practiced by a person of the great scope, it is not necessary to divide them into the three types of persons." [However,] there are two reasons it is necessary [to do so]: (1) it destroys the pride of thinking that you are a Mahayanist despite not having generated the minds of the small and middling scopes, and (2) it is of great benefit for those with minds of highest, middling, and lesser capacity. Even though it is a system of great benefit, without training the mind in stages, you will not develop any of the paths of the lesser persons, no matter how much you try. Thus, the supreme person will not incur the faults associated with [developing] the achievements taught in the paths of the great and middling scopes.[354] Therefore, beings [of all three capacities] should be led through the stages of the lamrim in this way [precisely because these stages] reveal the importance of training in the common paths and how the lamrim is a special feature [that adds] profundity and swiftness even to [the practice of] mantra.

The Actual Means of Extracting Its Essence of Leisure and Endowment

In Je Tsongkhapa's teachings, these sections on the actual means of extracting the essence [of leisure and endowment] and so on have unexcelled profound features, for which there are three headings:

1. Training the Mind in the Path Common to a Person of Lesser Capacity
2. Training the Mind in the Path Common to a Person of Middling Capacity

354. This means that following the stages of the path of lesser, middling, and great scopes, a practitioner of the great scope develops the good qualities of the lesser and middling capacity but isn't affected by their respective shortcomings, such as seeking mere liberation for yourself alone, not overcoming the obstructions to liberation, and so on.

3. Training the Mind in the Path Common to a Person of Great Capacity

Training the Mind in the Path Common to a Person of Lesser Capacity has three sections:

1. The Actual Training of the Mind of a Person of Lesser Capacity
2. The Measure of Having Generated such an Intention
3. Dispelling Misconceptions about That Intention

The Actual Training of the Mind of a Person of Lesser Capacity has two sections:

1. Developing a Mind Striving for Future Lives in the World
2. Revealing the Means of Attaining Happiness in Future Lives in the World

Developing a Mind Striving for Future Lives in the World has two sections:

1. Being Mindful of Death and That You Will Not Remain Long in This World
2. Contemplating How the Beings in the Two Types of Migrations Will Have Happiness and Suffering in Their Future Lives in the World

Being Mindful of Death and That You Will Not Remain Long in This World has four sections:

1. The Faults of Not Cultivating Mindfulness of Death
2. The Benefits of Cultivating Mindfulness of Death
3. How to Cultivate Mindfulness of Death
4. The Way to Meditate on Mindfulness of Death

The Faults of Not Cultivating Mindfulness of Death

If we aren't mindful of death, we will not remember our futures lives; if we aren't mindful of that, we will not remember the beneficial methods of Dharma regarding our futures lives; although we may recall [death], we will not practice due to falling under the influence of postponing it until later; and although we may practice, we will come under the influence of the eight worldly concerns, whereby our practice will be impure—all of these come from not being mindful of death and impermanence. To practice Dharma purely, we need a mind forsaking this life, which comes from being mindful of death. Furthermore, if we expand on a mind renouncing [this life], this means the eight worldly concerns. If we state it concisely, it is attachment to food, clothing, and pleasant conversation related to this life.

Lama Yegonpa stated,

> Cut short the rope of attachment to your homeland,
> Show the back of your head to miserly loved ones,
> Rely upon the antidote for contentment toward wealth;
> These are the first steps of a renunciant.

And,

> Until you separate yourself from the shackles of attachment to the appearances of this life, there is no way you will ever have an authentic Dharma practice; instead you will carry the water of loss to the blazing stake of death.

The king-like precepts for forsaking this life are the "ten innermost jewels of the Kadam," which are the four entrustments, the three vajras, and the three expulsions.[355]

Geshe Chen-nga-wa said, "While initially practicing, if the tsampa ran out, I relied on nettle soup. I couldn't find a patch to mend my lower monk's robe, so I pieced together bits of leather and was known as 'Chenga

355. For an explanation of these, see Yangsi Rinpoche, *Practicing the Path: A Commentary on the Lamrim Chenmo*, trans. Tsering Tuladhar, ed. Miranda Adams (Boston: Wisdom, 2003), 92.

dressed in leather skin.' Now even if I must support every living being in this world, I will be able to support them."

The spiritual guide [Geshe] Ben [Gungyal] said,

> When I was a layman, I fastened myself with three different weapons[356] as though they were thorns, and although I thrust each of those three as well as two knives, I had numerous enemies and few friends. When I was a bachelor, I had a field that would reap forty bushels of harvest and was nicknamed "the Forty Frightener." During the day I was a robber and at night a village thief, yet I still didn't have enough to eat. Now, I have abandoned my weaponry and don't have even one enemy. Having cast away work like spittle, whenever hunger arises, it is related to the deeds of the wealthy.
>
> Previously I could not find food,
> Now the food cannot find my mouth;
> I can't finish the food I have, nor
> Can I consume all the things to drink that I possess.
>
> This mind of the true Dharma has double or tripled them.

Geshe Potowa said, "If someone is a Dharma practitioner, he will become someone different from others. When I was a layperson, I went three times to search for gold but couldn't find even one measure of gold. Now, each day I receive many ounces of gold." In Phenpo Yungwa, there is no one better known for his happiness and comfort than Geshe Khamlungpa. In Lungsho, there is no one happier than [Geshe] Chen-nga-wa. Both of these beings have confidence in the Three Jewels. Such things come from forsaking this life and practicing Dharma.

Je Milarepa said,

> My happiness unknown by loved ones,
> My suffering unknown by enemies:
> If I can die this way in a mountain retreat,
> The wishes of this yogi will be complete.

356. These three are a sword, a spear, and an arrow.

My aging unknown by my friends,
My illness unknown by my sister:
If I can die this way in a mountain retreat,
The wishes of this yogi will be complete.

My death unknown by men,
My rotting corpse unseen by vultures;
If I can die this way in a mountain retreat,
The wishes of this yogi will be complete.

Flies sucking my rotting flesh,
Insects eating my nerves and sinews:
If I can die this way in a mountain retreat,
The wishes of this yogi will be complete.

With no footprints at my doorway
And no tracks of blood inside:
If I can die this way in a mountain retreat,
The wishes of this yogi will be complete.

With no one to surround my corpse
And no one to weep when I die:
If I can die this way in a mountain retreat,
The wishes of this yogi will be complete.

With no one to inquire where I went
And no one to notice when I depart:
If I can die this way in a mountain retreat,
The wishes of this yogi will be complete.

May this prayer to die destitute in
A cave in an unpopulated region
Establish the welfare of migrating beings;
If it is established, my wishes will be complete.

There are numerous teachings such as this that indicate the innermost Dharma focusing on the state of a beggar and the innermost jewel of entrusting yourself to dying in a barren ravine. These are especially important for monks and [indicate] that they are content with their simple monk's quarters, clothes, bedding, and life. They should delight in being a renunciant and meditate while abiding in the four kinds of arya beings.[357] You should forget about this life and recall death and impermanence. Furthermore, it is similar, for instance, to a traveler set to go to Kham: if you recall death and impermanence, not only will your Dharma be pure, but you will not strive for the things of this life. Once you are properly mindful of impermanence, if you abandon this life, [then] even offering one stick of incense or reciting one round of Manis will accomplish the welfare of your future lives.

If you don't abandon this life, then whatever you do will be lost on this life and your Dharma practice will not be pure. If you aren't mindful of death and impermanence, then even though you may practice Dharma every once in a while, most of the time you will be lost in distraction and will be unable to practice enthusiastically; therefore, you will never get around to sincere practice. If you are mindful of [death and impermanence], then no matter how much effort you apply to your virtuous practices such as recitations, meditations, and so on, they will not be difficult. If you recall impermanence each time you engage in a practice such as recitation, it will have the profound significance of bringing the entire time spent on recitations to their essential point.

As soon as you get up each morning, you should set your intention by summoning up thoughts of impermanence. Not only that, but if you have attachment for this life, or anger, then you will act inappropriately in order to subdue your enemies, protect your loved ones, and so on. By engaging in various negative actions you will ruin this life and the next by uniting yourself with numerous unbearable types of suffering. And, although it will definitely benefit your next life if you do practice Dharma authentically, you will not manage to practice in that way; therefore, you will have to die with this regret at the moment of your death and so forth; this is the fault of not being mindful of death.

357. The four types of arya beings are (1) arhats, (2) pratyekabuddhas, (3) bodhisattvas, and (4) buddhas.

The Benefits of Cultivating Mindfulness of Death

There is great meaning in being mindful of death. If you are mindful of death, even your practices such as the six perfections will be carried out without attachment for the things of this life such as friends, wealth, and so on. Being mindful of death is a powerful means of destroying afflictive emotions and bad actions, [similar to] recollecting the view of emptiness, as we will see later on in the text. By being mindful of [death and impermanence], when we see or hear of others dying, we should think, "I too have a nature such as this," and if we then practice Dharma once we are frightened of death, it will serve as a gateway to Dharma. In the middle it will serve as a whip exhorting us to the Dharma. In the end it will cause us to perfect the Dharma. What need is there to mention us beginners? The great mahasiddhas of secret mantra carried around skull cups and thighbone trumpets to remind them of impermanence, selflessness, and so forth. Out of his great compassion, even the Teacher said that among all conceptions, the conception of impermanence and death is supreme, and as he was about to pass away he said, "All conditioned phenomena are impermanent." Thus, his final testament was impermanence, after which he departed.

If we are going to practice Dharma, we need a solid mindfulness of death and impermanence. As the saying goes, "The best Dharma practitioners will die with joy, the middling will die without sorrow, and the least will die without regret." Thus [if we recall death and impermanence], at the moment of death we will die joyously and happily, like a son returning to his father's home. Previously, during an outbreak of smallpox in the local region, a certain lama could not be spared from smallpox and his attendant stated, "How happy I would be if a small portion of this could be averted elsewhere," to which the lama replied, "In the morning I am an old monk, but in the evening I will be reborn as a god in the pure lands; therefore, I have no desire to avert this."

Day Fourteen

Acharya Chandragomin stated,

> Those who desire the blissful worldly sustenance are like
> Elephants that have become attached to a few bits of dried grass
> Growing on the edge of a deep well, who
> Fall into the abyss without ever obtaining any.

The elephant [at the edge of] a deep well is like a baby elephant who becomes infatuated with some grass and so on growing on the edge of a well or a terrifying abyss; if he goes to the edge of the abyss in search of a little grass, he will fall into the abyss and experience unbearable suffering. Likewise, the majority of us also don't accomplish our lasting aims and instead come under the influence of the comfort and happiness of this life. Therefore, from now on we absolutely must practice a beneficial Dharma. We should set our motivation by thinking, "There is no means of accomplishing [enlightenment] superior to the stages on the path to enlightenment; therefore, I am going to listen [to these teachings] and practice them well."

After this introduction to set our motivation, Pabongkha Rinpoche restated the headings. He explained once more how all the scriptures are included in the paths of the three types of beings and so forth and that we should rely upon a means of attaining happiness in our future lives by developing a mind striving for the welfare of our future lives; that we should be mindful of death and meditate on it from the outset; that we need to understand the benefits and faults of that meditation and how there are differences in the outlines for the Great *and*

Middle-Length Treatises on the Stages of the Path [to Enlightenment] *as well as the* Swift Path; *and that we should use whichever is most suitable to elicit a powerful ascertainment of the faults of not being mindful of death, as well as the fault of having to die with regret at the time of our death. He supplemented these with oral instructions from the gurus.*

If we are mindful of death, it will be as the following saying states: "The fox and the weasel at the gateway of the white grouse . . ."[358] Even if someone who is a learned and righteous great meditator becomes lost in the things of this life, his Dharma practice will not be pure. Je Drowai Gonpo said,

> Even a noble scholar and great meditator
> Desires to be scholarly and noble for this life.
> Even the great meditator who writes "I do not
> Meet with people" above the boundary of his door
> Is wishing to be a noble great meditator for this life.
> Although they practice giving, they only desire
> To practice giving for this life.
> This is analogous to adding tsampa to water
> And wishing to offer it to the Three Jewels.
> They even hope that others will see their actions.
> How could they ever gain any profit
> From these wild conceptualizations?
> Whatever virtuous actions they undertake fade away,
> Carried away by the horsemen of all translators and pandits;
> Therefore, all ordinary beings must lance
> The conceptual thoughts of this life with each spear.
> If you don't lance this life with each spear,
> All the noble scholars, teachers, and meditators
> Will not obstruct the door to the three lower realms.
> May the noble scholars and great meditators
> Who are unable to avert the suffering of the lower realms
> Reach the essential meaning of whatever it is they need.

358. I believe this metaphor indicates that death is inevitable, just like the fate of a grouse in a situation where both a fox and a weasel are waiting to eat him the moment he comes out of his burrow.

Thus, the fact that we pretend to be practicing Dharma but it doesn't even become Dharma is due to not being mindful of death. For example, if you don't know that there is a steep cliff along a house and you go out on a long walk exploring the grounds and paths, you will fall off the cliff. The same thing applies to us: although we may do a great deal of investigation into the spiritual grounds and paths, if we haven't forsaken a mind focusing on this life, it will not ever become Dharma practice; therefore, although we may be a noble scholar and great meditator, we will be unable to avert the door to rebirth in the lower realms in our next life even in the slightest. Palden Gonpawa stated,

> Once you see the Dharma of cause and effect and impermanence as insignificant, the listening of the listener will be worthless, the teacher's explanations will be worthless, and even the wise will be shunned.

Gyama Rigpai Wangchug proclaimed,

> Although you have never accomplished even a single Dharma practice,
> You arrogantly think you are a Dharma practitioner. You fool!
> The first Dharma practice is to forsake this life;
> Examine your mind and see if you have done this or not.

Thus, it is important that you forsake this life by recalling death and so forth, so that your Dharma practice does not become some insignificant semblance of Dharma.

How to Cultivate Mindfulness of Death

With respect to your mindfulness of impermanence causing you fear of being separated from your loved ones and wealth, this comes from combining the two thoughts of attachment and craving for this life with a recollection of impermanence.

Query: Well then, how should I be mindful of death?

Response: You should fear death due to feelings of loss about death because you won't have time to practice Dharma. This is the proper way to identify thoughts recalling impermanence.

How to Cultivate Mindfulness of Death has three sections:

1. [The First Root:] Contemplating That Death Is Definite
2. [The Second Root:] Contemplating That the Time of Death Is Uncertain
3. [The Third Root:] Contemplating That, at the Time of Death, Nothing other than Our Practice of Dharma Will Be of Any Benefit

These are the three roots. Each of these has three reasons, making nine reasons in all. Each of the three reasons ends with a determination, making three [determinations] in all. The first root is the contemplation that death is certain, and it has three reasons.

The First Root: Contemplating That Death Is Definite has three reasons:

1. The Contemplation That the Lord of Death Is Definitely Coming and That There Are No Circumstances That Can Turn Him Away
2. Our Lifespan Cannot Be Extended and Is Constantly Decreasing
3. Even While You Are Alive, There Is No Time to Practice Dharma

The Contemplation That the Lord of Death Is Definitely Coming and That There Are No Circumstances That Can Turn Him Away

If we don't extract the essence of our human life that we have obtained this one time, the Lord of Death is definitely coming. It doesn't matter what type of body we have taken, what type of country we live in, or when we were born; there is no situation where we will be unharmed by the Lord of Death. Even the Buddha Bhagavan passed into the sphere of peace. Even among those who have attained the state of a knowledge-holder of immortal life, at present there is no one left to meet. Thus, if there isn't a single person from our compassionate Teacher down to our own father and mother who can remain without being destroyed by death, how can you alone survive? Regardless of what type of body they have assumed or which country they lived in, they all died. [The *Collection of Indicative Verses* states,]

> There is no place on this earth where you could
> Live and not be harmed by death—
> Neither in the sky, nor within the ocean,
> Nor even if you live amid the mountains.

Previously, King Virudhaka incited a war with the region of the Shakyas and killed 77,000 of them. At that point, Buddha hid some of the Shakyas in the mansion of the sun and moon,[359] some inside the crevices of Mount Meru, and some inside the Teacher's begging bowl through the use of his miraculous powers. However, when the other Shakyas were killed, those hidden inside Shakyamuni's begging bowl and the rest simultaneously died due to the force of their karma. Not only that, but no matter what type of rebirth you have in the past or future, you will die as well:

> There is no such place where you can quickly run and hide—
> Not even a place where a great sage with the five types of
> Clairvoyance can go in the distant sky;
> There isn't any place in existence where you can live
> Where you can dwell in the domain of immortality.

No matter how mighty you may be, you will be unable to overcome [death]. When the Lord of Death comes, even a mighty lion draws in his paws and dies. Even a chakravartin king is unable to overcome the Lord of Death by paying him off with wealth. Although you may be very

359. According to ancient Buddhist cosmology, there are mansions in the sun and the moon where gods reside, giving these celestial bodies their luminosity.

intelligent and clever, there will be no way to use your intelligence and cleverness during death.

Our Lifespan Cannot Be Extended and Is Constantly Decreasing

[Shantideva's] *Guide to the Bodhisattva's Way of Life* states,

> This life is constantly decreasing,
> Without remaining day or night;
> Once it declines, there is nothing that can extend it;
> How is it possible that I could not die?

The *Extensive Sport Sutra* declares,

> The three worlds are impermanent like autumn clouds.
> The births and deaths of migrating beings are like watching a play.
> The passage of beings' lives is like lightning in the sky,
> Moving with great swiftness like water falling from a steep mountain.

The Supreme Conqueror Kelsang Gyatso [the Seventh Dalai Lama] proclaimed,

> Once we are born, we are powerless to remain even for an instant;
> We are racing as fast as we can into the presence of Yama, the Lord of Death.
> Although we are called "the living," we are preparing for the great highway of death;
> This is as sad as a criminal being led to his place of execution.

Although we think we are going to continue living a relaxed and comfortable [life], we are not going to remain [that way]. Throughout the day and night we are running full speed ahead in the direction of the Lord of Death, with no time to rest. Je Tuken stated,

> Impermanence and death getting closer and closer, we cannot remain;
> Each day our extra lifespan is getting further and further away;
> A time is coming when body and mind will be separated.

Yama, the Lord of Death, is like the shadow of the sun: you think it is a long way away, but in a time not too far away, pitch blackness will descend upon you. As the *Extensive Sport Sutra* described it above, right now we are like actors playing our parts in a theatrical production; [our lives] are like the swift descent of water, like a burning incense stick being extinguished, like the sun setting with each passing moment, and so on. Consider how human life is similar to all these and how death is drawing ever closer, so that out of fear you feel, "I must extract the essence of whatever little bit of this human life I have remaining."

Even While You Are Alive, There Is No Time to Practice Dharma

From the moment we are born from our mother's womb until we reach the age of twenty, we don't recall the Dharma. From the age of fifty or sixty onward, we are incapable of practicing Dharma, and this is how we get started. For the entire time in between, we say things such as "It is the New Year" and so on. Each day we deceive ourselves by giving such pleasant-sounding names to our work and end up never practicing Dharma. [Je] Gungtang [Jampalyang] Rinpoche stated,

> Twenty years pass without remembering that we should practice Dharma,
> Twenty years pass in a state of thinking, "I am going to, I am going to," and
> The last ten are spent saying, "It never happened, it never happened";
> Such is the biography of a wasted human life.

Geshe Chekawa proclaimed,

> Of sixty years, if we divide the time spent putting it off due to food, clothing, and illness, we are left with no more than five years to put toward the Dharma.

Let's say, hypothetically, that we will live for sixty years; in the interim, we waste our life by letting it slip away due to the influence of such distractions as food, clothes, cooking, sleep, and illness, so that we don't even have five years left to devote to the practice of Dharma. Although we attend a discourse, in general there is the question whether or not it becomes a reason related to the certainty of death. However, this contemplation about the certainty of death and there being no time to practice the Dharma definitely becomes a reason for our own certainty of death without [having practiced] Dharma. Of all three reasons, if we contemplate this well, we will generate the determination that death is definite. The *Jataka Tales* state,

> Alas, afflicted worldly beings,
> There is no joy in unstable things;
> Even the Glorious White Water Lily
> Will become a memory.

Regarding the "glorious white water lily," this is similar to the theatrical performance of Aché Lhamo in Tibet, which in India was previously called "The Autumn White Water Lily," and is being used as an example of a grand dramatic performance. Just like that example, we should consider that we too look like beings in a theatrical performance or the coming together of people at a market gathering: once the evening comes, they fade away and disappear without remaining, to become mere objects of someone's memory. Human life is just like this as well, and once it is exhausted we move on. Thus, at the conclusion of contemplating the three reasons why death is definite, we make the determination that we must practice Dharma.

The Second Root: [Contemplating That] the Time of Death Is Uncertain

This section is extremely important. Although in general we cannot say for certain that we won't die for a long time, once we think that we are going to die today, we will [realize] the necessity of practicing Dharma. Once we think that we will not die today, if we were to sit down and die this evening, then having that assumption even for the length of a single day would have deprived us of the opportunity to practice Dharma for the time of death, which would benefit our future life; therefore, the mind is betrayed by the thought that we won't die.

The Second Root: Contemplating That the Time of Death Is Uncertain has three sections:

1. Contemplating That in General the Lifespan in This World System Is Uncertain
2. Contemplating That the Time of Death Is Uncertain Because There Are Many Causes of Death and Few Causes of Life
3. Contemplating That the Time of Death is Uncertain Because Our Bodies Are Extremely Fragile

Contemplating That in General the Lifespan in This World System Is Uncertain

[Vasubandhu's] *Treasury of Abhidharma* states,

> The lifespan of the beings in Kurava is a thousand years;
> In two others it is progressively reduced by half.

The lifespan of those in Kurava is a thousand years, those in Aparago-daniya live for five hundred years, and those in Videha for one hundred fifty. Thus, [the lifespan of] those living in Kurava is definite. Although the lifespan of those in the other two continents is mostly fixed, we have the least degree of certainty in this world. Regarding this last point, a scripture states,

> Ten years, initially immeasurable . . .

As this states, although the lifespan in this world is indefinite, it was initially immeasurable. The *Collection of Indicative Verses* states,

> Since so many men and women and
> Even those in the bloom of youth die,
> How can those alive say with confidence,
> "This person is too young for that"?
>
> Some die in the womb,
> Likewise, some at birth,
> Likewise, some when they can crawl, and
> Likewise, some when they can run.
>
> Some are old, and some are young,
> Some people are in the bloom of youth;
> They gradually all go,
> Like the falling of ripe fruit.

Our gurus, spiritual guides, and so on die from a variety of causes before their lifespans are finished, as each one suddenly dies. Some die the very moment they are born from their mother's womb, some die as soon as they can crawl, and so on. When you consider it, these days we should live ten years at the longest, for there is no certainty that we won't die when we are young or old. Therefore, in general, there is no certainty about the lifespan of beings in this world.

Regarding the fact that there is no fixed lifespan particularly in this degenerate era, from the moment we are being formed in our mother's womb to a hundred years or less, there is absolutely no chance that we won't die. It doesn't matter whether or not it is our hindrance year[360] or whether or not we are ill. There is no certainty [about the time of death], since a sick person may live as long as a few years or months while someone who was not previously ill may not. In a [given] year, many old and

360. According to Buddhist astrology, there are certain years in a person's life when they are highly susceptible to life obstructions.

young [die], leaving no certainty as to when we will die. Therefore, since this is the situation, it is utterly impossible that the same thing will not happen to you:

> Of the numerous people we see in the morning,
> There are some we won't see in the evening.
> Of the numerous people we see in the evening,
> There are some we won't see the next morning.

Previously, Tastag Yongzin Gendun Gyatso was about to give an explanatory transmission of *The Great Treatise on the Stages of the Path to Enlightenment* once the monks arranged their seating on the first day; he passed away the following day, before he had time to give the lamrim teachings. Although he was both a scholar and an adept, he didn't know when death and impermanence was coming. Likewise, [death] is coming for us all, including the spiritual leaders of others, kings, ministers, monks, and ordinary people; therefore, there is absolutely no way that we can have any confidence that we will still be alive this evening:

> Tomorrow or the next world—
> There is no way of knowing which will come first.
> I shouldn't strive to aid tomorrow;
> I should strive for the sake of my next life.

If we can't be certain which will come first—tomorrow, next month, next year, or the next world—what is the use of accumulating wealth and possessions with the hope that they will benefit us next month and so on? If the Lord of the Death is definitely coming at some point between today and a hundred years from now, we need to be cautious, since we can't be certain if he will arrive today or tomorrow. Once we consider death carefully, we will realize that the time of death is uncertain and this life is fleeting. The oral instructions state that it is very beneficial if you meditate that [death] is coming in that way for yourself as well.

Contemplating That the Time of Death Is Uncertain Because There Are Many Causes of Death and Few Causes of Life

Sickness, harm from spirits, obstructions, calamities, and so forth are like clouds obscuring the sky and like flies surrounding a rotting corpse. Moreover, there are numerous things that are meant to be conditions for life but that end up being conditions for death, such as unsuitable food, intestinal worms, poisonous food, collapsing houses, being thrown from a horse, being killed by thieves and bandits, and so on. [Nagarjuna's] *Precious Garland*[361] states,

> One dwells with the factors of death
> Like a lamp sitting amid a windstorm.

And,

> The conditions for death are numerous
> While the conditions for life are few,
> And even those can cause your death;
> Therefore, always practice the Dharma!

Moreover, say, for example, you place four snakes of equal strength in one container; they will be unable to kill each other. Likewise, if one is very powerful, it will kill the weakest of the three; what need is there to mention the others as well? The same thing applies to this body of ours when the elements get out of balance, providing numerous opportunities for our death. It is not certain that we won't assemble the causes of death today; therefore, it is utterly amazing that we have survived up to this point. We should think, "Right now, from this very moment I must practice Dharma for the benefit of my future lives."

361. Tib. *Rin chen phreng ba*.

Contemplating That the Time of Death Is Uncertain Because Our Bodies Are Extremely Fragile

Nagarjuna stated,

> If even the ashes of the physical world such as the
> Earth, Mount Meru, or the oceans will not remain
> Once they are incinerated by seven suns,
> What need is there to speak of such fragile beings?

Thus, if one day even the four continents and Mount Meru will be utterly destroyed so that not even ashes remain, then the time of death is uncertain because this fragile body can die due to the influence of [minor] conditions, such as being pierced by a thorn, smallpox, and so on. Je Gungtang [Jampalyang Rinpoche] proclaimed,

> There is a great danger that before tomorrow comes
> When you were going to practice Dharma, the time of death may arrive today.
> Now is not the time to confuse yourself;
> If you are going to practice Dharma, start today!

Contemplating in this way should impel you to practice Dharma. If we don't practice now, while we have attained the capacity making us suitable for the practice of Dharma, we will not be capable of practicing Dharma when we come under the influence of illness and so forth later on, and on top of that we will be filled with regret and will be unable to transcend misery. Therefore, we must sincerely apply ourselves right now, while we have liberty and have assembled the favorable conditions. The mahasiddha Mitra Dzöki stated,

> Lord of the Earth, whatever type of body you have on loan,
> Abiding in a state free of illness, without decay, and blissful—
> When you have that very thing, extract its essence.

> When you are fearless about sickness, death, and decay,
> You should also remember that you are a
> Servant to old age, decay, and so forth.

The fact that at the moment we also don't remember to practice Dharma stems from the fault of not contemplating that the time of death is uncertain. As I explained previously, oath-bound Dharmaraja emanated as a human being and came into the presence of Je [Tsongkhapa] and acted as his servant, after which he repeatedly went from Ganden to Lhasa. He usually spoke very little and didn't laugh. However, one day on the way from Lhasa, he said, "Today we can see the footprints left by the boots of a certain person, and tomorrow they are going to die," and then burst out laughing. If we recall the uncertainty of the time of death, we will come to realize that we don't have any free time. If you recall that at the time of your death nothing other than the Dharma will be of any benefit, you will develop the realization of the worthlessness [of worldly pursuits]. Through authentic mindfulness of death and impermanence, you will come to forsake this life. If you think that once you lie down to sleep this evening, you may not wake up in the morning, this is an indication that you have developed mindfulness about the uncertainty of the time of death.

Thus, at the conclusion of contemplating the three reasons for the uncertainty of the time of death, you should come to a determination to practice Dharma from this very day onward.

The Third Root: Contemplating That at the Time of Death Nothing other than Our Practice of Dharma Will Be of Any Benefit has three reasons:

1. Our Wealth and Enjoyments Are of No Benefit
2. Our Friends and Loved Ones Are of No Benefit
3. Even Our Body Will Be of No Benefit

Our Wealth and Enjoyments Are of No Benefit

As a scripture states,

> A king leaves behind his kingdom;
> A beggar leaves behind his walking stick.

And,

> Although you may have enough food for a hundred years,
> The day after your death, you go hungry.
> Although you may have enough clothes for a hundred years,
> The day after your death, you go naked.

Although we may have wealth and resources equal to Vaishravana, at the time of death you cannot take even a particle of it with you and must leave it all behind and move on. We are extremely foolish because we amass as much wealth and possessions as we possibly can, despite the fact that we can't bring it with us when we die; yet we don't amass the seven jewels of an arya and so forth, which are things we can bring with us when we die. Panchen [Losang] Chögyan proclaimed,

> We amass food and wealth out of miserliness, only to leave them behind.

Padampa [Sangye] stated,

> Our illusory-like wealth and possessions are on loan;
> Don't be bound by the bonds of avarice, people of Dingri.

Our Friends and Loved Ones Are of No Benefit

Although someone may be a king, with a prince, a queen, a cabinet minister, a subsidiary minister, an army, and many hundreds of thousands of subjects, when he dies the king must go on alone and can't bring even one of his wives, children, subjects, and so on with him. Mahasiddha Mitra Dzöki stated,[362]

> Sole deity, no matter how much wealth you have,
> When you have departed to the next world
> You'll be alone without your prince or queen,
> Like someone destroyed by his enemy in a wasteland.

Furthermore, Je [Losang] Chögyan stated,

> May I be endowed with delight and confidence as
> [Food and wealth accumulated through miserliness are left behind],
> I am completely separated from my loving and longed-for friends,
> And I go alone to that dreadful abode.[363]

The *Tree Sutra*[364] states,

> Great being, when you lie down to sleep on your bed
> Surrounded by many loved ones and
> Are seized by the messengers of the Lord of Death,
> You will experience death all alone.

A lama may have many thousands of disciples, or you may have numerous family members such as your old father and so on, yet of all your close

362. In the Tibetan text, the same quote stated earlier is repeated at this point, which I believe is an editing oversight. At this point in Pabongkha Rinpoche's *Liberation in Our Hands* there is a more applicable quote, which reinforces my assumption that it is an editing error. Therefore, I have taken the liberty of reproducing what I believe is the appropriate verse. The verse included in this text states, "Lord of the Earth, whatever type of body you have on loan / Abiding in a state free of illness, without decay, and blissful— / When you have that very thing, extract its essence. / When you are fearless about sickness, death, and decay, / You should also remember that you are a / Servant to old age, decay, and so forth."

363. This comes from *A Supplication for Liberation from [Fear of] the Perilous Journey of the Intermediate State, Entitled "A Hero Liberated from Fear."* For a complete commentary and translation of this text, see Ngulchu Dharmabhadra, *The Blazing Inner Fire of Bliss and Emptiness.*

364. Tib. *lJon shing gi mdo.*

friends and relatives, you cannot take even one of them with you but must go on alone, like extracting a hair from amid butter.

Even Our Body Will Be of No Benefit

A scripture states,

> We are deceived in our time of need by this body we have cherished so dearly . . .

At the time of death, our wealth and glory, friends, and relatives are left to others. The most important thing is this physical form. If it were possible to bring this body—which emerged through the door of our mother's womb and which exists simultaneously with our consciousness—with us, that would be one thing, but it functions as a support for our consciousness for just a short while, and we are not at liberty to bring it with us; therefore, it must be left behind in our bed. Our consciousness requires a body of subtle wind for its travel. Therefore, even at that time our [coarse] body is of no benefit. Thus, when we move, a fierce wind pushes this body of wind from behind, while it is being led from the front by a terrifying black being. This is what occurs. Although at present we give instructions for recognizing the intermediate state as the corpse lies with its head on the pillow, and without doing anything else the lama says things such as "Right now the body and mind are at peace; at this moment all favorable conditions have been assembled," once we have been tormented in this way, it is very difficult for it to become Dharma. If you are going to practice identifying the intermediate state, it will be very beneficial if you begin training from this moment on in identifying the intermediate state for yourself. You are going to have to travel along the intermediate state of the four terrifying sounds, the three dreadful abysses, and so on! At that time there won't be any beneficial refuge other than the Dharma. [Je] Gungtang [Jampalyang Rinpoche] stated,

> Dharma is the guide when you don't know your way on the path;
> [Dharma is the provisions on the long path;
> Dharma is the captain guiding you along the difficult path;

From this moment on, practice the Dharma with your
three doors.]

Je Mila[repa] stated,

I have sad news, maiden-disciple Paldar Bum, [so]
Listen, wealthy and faithful one:
Future lives are much longer than this life.
Have you arranged your meals for the journey?
If you haven't arranged your meals for the journey,
Procure them through practicing generosity.

And,

I have sad news, maiden-disciple Paldar Bum:
The next life is more fearful than this life.
Have you arranged an escort to accompany you?
If you haven't arranged an escort to accompany you,
Procure one through the sublime Dharma.

Although we should meditate continuously and with great force in this way on death and impermanence, there is a practice called "seeing the Dharma of impermanence outwardly" where you blink your eyes as though you are so holy, even though it is nothing more than a loud clamor of deception. Yet this is not acceptable as a way of life for us old and new Kadampas. Thus, at the conclusion of contemplating the three reasons why, at the time of death, nothing other than the Dharma will be of any benefit, you should make a firm determination that you must only practice the Dharma.

Next, regarding meditation on the aspects of death in accordance with the oral instructions of our guru, we imagine [what it will be like to die] by considering the deaths of others we have seen in this life:

When I am at a loss as to what I should do,
The doctor has given up, rituals don't work,
And my companions have abandoned their hopes for my life,
May I recall the instructions of my guru.

Once you are seized by a fatal illness, no matter what you do—such as prayers for longevity, rituals, and so on—it makes no difference, and your illness steadily increases. When it is definite you are dying, even the doctor conceals his true thoughts while he tells you things are okay when they are not, and your family members and friends begin hurriedly packing up your belongings. Moreover, as the connection between your body and mind is about to be severed, you experience intense pain and unbearable suffering as you recall that if you had previously engaged in virtuous actions while you had the free will to do so, it would definitely have benefited your future lives, but you didn't and instead engaged in numerous nonvirtues. [Recalling this] brings great sadness and fear, causing an extraordinarily unbearable suffering. Furthermore, [the following verse describes what happens] at the end of a physical illness that caused prolonged torment:

> Grant your blessing that I may generate a powerful mind of virtue
> As the elements of earth, water, fire, and wind sequentially dissolve;
> The strength of my body is lost, my mouth and nose dry up and change,
> My warmth absorbs, and I gasp and cry out.[365]

Thus, these are the associated signs that emerge with the sequential dissolution of the four elements. Furthermore, while the earth element is dissolving into the water element, you have an appearance as though you are sinking deeper and deeper into this earth, you are being pulled by the hand, and so forth. As a sign of the fire element dissolving into the water element, your mouth and nose dry up and so forth. As a sign that the fire element is dissolving into the wind element, your bodily heat diminishes and so forth. While the wind element is dissolving into consciousness, you gasp for breath, there is a gap before commencing breathing, and so on. When your breathing ceases, you must depart from this body, and this marks the end of this life:

365. This verse is from the First Panchen Lama's *Supplication for Liberation from [Fear of] the Perilous Journey of the Intermediate State, Entitled "A Hero Liberated from Fear,"* translated in Ngulchu Dharmabhadra, *The Blazing Inner Fire of Bliss and Emptiness.*

> At that time, when I fall into the abyss of the three lower realms
> And my unstable mind is carried like feathers in the wind,
> When I am uncontrollably led through my encounter with the bardo
> Through the compassionate objects of refuge,
> May my refuge, my precious guru, come [to my rescue]
> As the supreme Arya Chenrezig and extract me from samsara.

At that point, your power and wealth, your beautiful figure, your close friends and relatives, and so on must all be left behind. Your consciousness is left without a support, and your mere wind and mind are extracted, like pulling a hair from butter; you must go on alone to wander down the perilous path of the intermediate state and on to your next life. Next, someone such as your guru will introduce the intermediate state and so on to your corpse with its head on a pillow. A dimly lit butter lamp is placed next to the corpse to ward off defilements. When [others] use your name, they preface it with "the late" and conclude it with your name; these addendums will make your name unpleasant to hear. After leaving your corpse for a few days, they will take it to the outskirts of town to the charnel grounds and so forth and sequentially scatter your flesh and bones. These meditations also have their source in the *Instructions for a King Sutra*[366] as well as [Shantideva's] *Guide to the Bodhisattva's Way of Life*, which states,

> Having gone to the charnel grounds, sitting
> Amid the bones, I should come to realize
> That my body and the rotting corpses of others
> Are exactly the same, constantly disintegrating.

Therefore, in exactly the same way as the corpses of others are dispersed in the charnel grounds when they die, before too long you will definitely meet with the same fate, and for the first week or two after you die, they will feel the need to say you have departed.

366. Tib. *rGyal po la gdams pa'i mdo.*

Once Pabongkha Rinpoche had taught in detail the contemplations related to the way in which, at that time, other than holy Dharma nothing else will be of any benefit, he restated them in moderate detail and then again in a concise manner.

During the preliminary rituals and the actual meditations, you should consider how you will be separated from the things of this life such as your dwelling, body, enjoyments, friends, relatives, and so on, as well as all your wealth and prosperity of this life. Padampa [Sangye] stated,

> Loved ones are as impermanent as a crowd at market-time;
> People of Dingri, don't argue and fight.

And in the *Great Compassionate Refuge*[367] it states,

> When you die through the force of karma and are seized by virulent illness,
> And the radiance and luster of your flesh disappears
> Like the sun and moon seized by an eclipse,
> May your refuge, the precious guru, come [to your rescue]
> As the supreme Arya Chenrezig and extract you from samsara.
>
> When the pain of disease gives rise to the horrible sound of pain-induced groans,
> And day and night you are endlessly tormented by the disruption of the four elements,
> While they perform divinations and strike at spirits with deity offerings,
> May your refuge, the precious guru, come [to your rescue]
> As the supreme Arya Chenrezig and extract you from samsara.
>
> Surrounded by a retinue of food and drink you can't take with you,
> When even the efforts of medical examinations and ritual are of no benefit,

367. Tib. *sKyabs thugs rje ma*. I was unable to locate any reference to this. I am inclined to think that this is the name of a text, although I can't be certain.

When they've lost all signs of your pulse,
May your refuge, the precious guru, come [to your rescue]
As the supreme Arya Chenrezig and extract you from samsara.

When you've lost all attraction to nutritious food,
Your lips curl, your nose flattens, and plaque forms on your teeth,
And even fresh blue water is no longer pleasurable,
When it's time for the dead and living to part ways and you make your last will and testament,
May your refuge, the precious guru, come [to your rescue]
As the supreme Arya Chenrezig and extract you from samsara.

When your eyes stare straight ahead in a fixed position,
You compulsively grasp at your companions and their clothing,
And your body takes on the scent of the deceased,
May your refuge, the precious guru, come [to your rescue]
As the supreme Arya Chenrezig and extract you from samsara.

When your life is exhausted, your body wears out, and mind and matter separate,
Like an evening shadow and a lamp running out of fuel,
When you are powerless to remain even one instant longer,
May your refuge, the precious guru, come [to your rescue]
As the supreme Arya Chenrezig and extract you from samsara.

Death is like repeatedly pulling on a string until it suddenly runs out.
When body and mind are separated and the movement of your breath ceases,
When you exchange your wealth and companions and go on alone,
May your refuge, the precious guru, come [to your rescue]
As the supreme Arya Chenrezig and extract you from samsara.

Your root guru performs empowerments and cleansing rituals;
Your friends and relatives assemble and give food and drink to your corpse;

When they wail your name and beat at their breasts,
May your refuge, the precious guru, come [to your rescue]
As the supreme Arya Chenrezig and extract you from samsara.

When they bend your neck and hands and bind them with grass rope,
As your closest friends send you off with tears in their eyes,
And they take you from your soft bed and stretch you out on the burial ground,
May your refuge, the precious guru, come [to your rescue]
As the supreme Arya Chenrezig and extract you from samsara.

At present, we find intolerable the slight pain of our body being poked by a needle or even having to wear coarse clothing, due to our immense self-importance. We are unable to bear even something as trivial as whether or not someone attaches honorific particles to our name to signify our rank. When we die, we are powerless to decide something as simple as the place where we will be buried, and our body will be disposed of on the bare ground somewhere like a charnel ground. Moreover, a strong person will make crisscross marks on our body with a sharp knife and cut up all our flesh, skin, nerves, and sinews into tiny pieces, and a mass of vultures and so forth will tear apart our flesh, blood, intestines, stomach, and heart into a bloody mess and then gobble them up. They will finish off your arms, legs, head, and even right down to your bones, and in that very moment this body will be gone without anything remaining. Alternatively, it may happen that your corpse is banished into a body of water or burned in a fire; perhaps it will be buried beneath the ground and so on:

Perhaps it will be carried to the peak of a high mountain.
Your four limbs will be separated by a sharp sword;
Your intestines, lungs, and heart will be spread out over the plains.
When the birds, jackals, foxes, and dogs eat them,
May your refuge, the precious guru, come [to your rescue]
As the supreme Arya Chenrezig and extract you from samsara.

Perhaps your aggregates will be tossed into the clear blue water.
Your blood and pus will mix with the clear blue water;
When your flesh and fat are eaten by the fish-otter,
May your refuge, the precious guru, come [to your rescue]
As the supreme Arya Chenrezig and extract you from samsara.

Perhaps your aggregates will be incinerated within a fire;
When your flesh, bones, and skin are reduced to heaps of ash,
And the male and female gandharva spirits[368] get a whiff,
May your refuge, the precious guru, come [to your rescue]
As the supreme Arya Chenrezig and extract you from samsara.

Thus, you should think, "I must practice Dharma purely, because at the time of my death nothing other than the practice of Dharma is going to be of any benefit." Not only that, but whenever you see anything—such as your sash, your bedding, your corner of the house, or your body, enjoyments, a human skull, a human thighbone trumpet, a corpse in the charnel ground, and so on—use them as stimulus for inducing thoughts of death and impermanence so that you think, "How sad! Before too long I, too, will die, after which this body will be folded in thirds, bound in a sash, wrapped in my bedding, and placed in the corner of the house and left that way."

At present, even if we don't get a delicious meal we argue with our friends and servants, but when we die we will have to wait just to get the scent of burnt food offerings. Even with this body of ours, once the vultures land on our chest, they will carry us off to the eastern, southern, western, and northern peaks of a mountain:

Some other person will even come to live in your house.
As you are being led to the courtroom of Yama's executioner
Because of the negative karma you have accumulated for the
  sake of wealth,
They will scratch and fight over the wealth you have
  accumulated;

368. Gandharvas are a type of spirits that are sustained through scents.

> May your refuge, the precious guru, come [to your rescue]
> As the supreme Arya Chenrezig and extract you from samsara.

Consider with sadness that although you have never been parted from your pleasant possessions, these enjoyments that you have accumulated in so many ways will be carried off in all directions and used up by other people, and get a definite sense of your enjoyments. Whenever you see a human corpse, skull cup, thighbone trumpet, and so on, contemplate, "How sad! Originally each one of these other people was unable to withstand even the most subtle illness, and although they survived by providing [their bodies] with extreme affection, saying 'My head,' 'My limbs,' 'My body,' one day death and impermanence caught up with them such that they could not bring them under control. Likewise, I, too, will definitely end like that one day":

> In short, like the sound of a swiftly flowing stream
> And the passing of the sun's shadow with each passing moment,
> Even a long stick of burning incense is quickly exhausted,
> And the transition of the four seasons . . .

Bit by bit, time passes moment by moment and finally runs out. You should meditate on whatever appears by using them all as metaphors, and continuously contemplate, "My life is running out in just the same way," until you evoke an experience that transforms your mind. As I explained above, it is important that you recall death and impermanence at the beginning, middle, and end to ensure your practice is pure.

Pabongkha Rinpoche gave the following advice:

Although while explaining the lamrim, this meditation on the aspects of death is explained at the conclusion of the three reasons contemplating that at death nothing other than the Dharma will be of any benefit, if you meditate on it at the conclusion of contemplating that death is certain, it will bring great force to your contemplations that the time of death is uncertain.

Day Fifteen

The glorious protector Arya Nagarjuna stated,

> If you wish to attain unsurpassed enlightenment
> For yourself and the world,
> The root is bodhichitta
> As firm as the king of powerful mountains,
> As well as compassion not based on duality.

Query: In what type of path should we train with the wish to attain the state of enlightenment?

Reply: The principal cause of attaining enlightenment is training in the precious bodhichitta and holding it as the main point of your practice. As an aide to that, you need both great compassion and the exalted wisdom realizing nonduality. Those three are the three causes of enlightenment and are indispensable for accomplishing liberation and the state of omniscience. [Therefore, you should think,] "The unmistaken way to practice these three modes of training, which are the unmistaken king-like instructions of our Teacher, is the Dharma of the stages of the path to enlightenment. Therefore, from this very day [I shall practice bodhichitta. With this motivation I will listen to the teachings]."

After giving this introduction, Pabongkha Rinpoche restated the headings. After giving another explanation for developing such a mind recalling death, he explained the effortless means of immortality by recalling death and the cause of being fearless at the time of death.

Although Milarepa's mother had long since passed away when he returned to his homeland, when he saw her corpse—which was at that point just bones—he sang the following song after seeing her body, home, and so forth:

> In my homeland, a prison of demons,
> Impermanent illusory masters appeared;
> Grant your blessing that I may induce confidence
> In this excellent master.

And,

> First there was a father and then no son,
> There is a son and then no father either;
> Even though both may come together, they have no essence;
> The son will now go to meditate at Drakar Taso
> And practice the essential divine Dharma.
>
> There was a mother and then no son,
> When the son arrived, the old mother had died;
> Even though both may come together, they have no essence;
> The son will now go to meditate at Drakar Taso
> And practice the essential divine Dharma.

There are numerous teachings similar to this. Jamgon Tsongkhapa also stated, "If we are assured of impermanence, it's impossible that all functioning things will not reveal impermanence." If we contemplate death and impermanence properly, all appearances will serve as our master to reveal impermanence and enhance our understanding.

Contemplating How the Beings in the Two Types of Migrations Will Have Happiness and Suffering in Their Future Lives in the World

If we don't take the opportunity to close the door to rebirth in the lower realms right now, there will be absolutely nothing we can do at the time

Chandrakirti

of death. If we meditate to evoke an experience as though we have already taken rebirth in the three lower realms, we will develop fear and trepidation. We will need a type of mindfulness seeking the means not to be reborn there, for at the time of our death there will be nothing whatsoever to prevent us from migrating to [the lower realms], and without choice we will have to take rebirth by following our karma. The karmic maturation of virtuous deeds is a happy migration, and from nonvirtue comes rebirth in the lower realms. Furthermore,

From the karma created in samsara,
That which is the heaviest, that which is the closest,
That which is most familiar, and that which was done first [ripen]
With each preceding one reaching fruition.[369]

Thus, you take rebirth by performing a powerful action that derives its capacity of great strength through your nurturing it with attachment and craving. If [two karmic actions] are equal in strength, whichever you are the most familiar with [will ripen first]. If [your virtue and nonvirtue] are equal, whichever you performed first [will ripen] and be nurtured through attachment and craving. Not even the slightest bit of your actions and their effects will transform into something unrelated.

Our virtue is extremely weak in both strength and familiarity. Regarding our nonvirtue, just today alone we have accumulated countless causes for rebirth in the three lower realms; therefore, it is as though it has already been settled that we are going to the lower realms. It is not possible for us to have confidence that we will not be going to the lower realms. To obtain such confidence, it is stated,

Attain forbearance and you won't fall into the lower realms.

Thus, you must attain the [stage of forbearance] on the path of preparation. The Bhagavan Buddha said, "In the future, my shravakas will go to the lower realms like an upturned bag of sand." [One day,] Phuchungwa also saw a similar teaching at about midnight and cried out in a loud voice, "Oh my!" His attendant asked him what was wrong, and he replied, "Today I saw a sutra and it said that when their time is finished, shravakas will be going to a lower rebirth like an upturned bag of sand. That means me, too!" Furthermore, we will go to the lower realms due to the nonvirtue we engage in due to being unable to protect the moral discipline of our spiritual promises. This is not stating that we will go to the lower

369. This means that the karma you have created ripens in the following order: (1) the karma that is the heaviest ripens soonest, (2) that which was done most recently ripens next, (3) that which you are habituated to ripens next, and (4) that which was created longest ago ripens last.

realms through practicing Dharma. For us to not join their ranks, we should have to try to remain like sand in between stitches.[370] Furthermore, if we don't sincerely apply ourselves at this very moment, it will be as the following scripture states,

> What will you do when you suddenly awake in the
> Lower realms from the meaningless disturbing dreams of
> Joy and pain in the short period of sleep that is
> This ephemeral life and you are in a pit of torment?

Having already accumulated the karma for rebirth in the lower realms, being reborn there is not too far off, for as soon as your breathing ceases, the appearances of this life disappear like falling asleep. Once we experience an intermediate state that is like various dreams that correspond to whichever lower realm we are going to be reborn in, we will have already taken rebirth standing upright in those places, just like waking up with no other recourse; therefore, we should make an effort right now to avoid going to a lower realm such as this. We must repeatedly contemplate the suffering of the lower realms for the sake of inspiring us to purify the karmas that will send us to the lower realms. Nagarjuna stated,

> Recall the hells on a daily basis,
> With their extreme heat and cold;
> You should recall as well the hungry ghosts,
> Emaciated by hunger and thirst;
> You should observe and recall animals
> And their numerous sufferings of stupidity—
> Abandon their causes and create the causes of happiness.
>
> A human rebirth in this world is difficult to obtain;
> Once you obtain it, completely concentrate on
> Severing the causes of the lower realms.

370. This is a colloquial expression that is similar to "not fall between the cracks."

For that reason, at this point we contemplate the sufferings of the lower realms in three sections by contemplating the sufferings of the hell beings, animals, and hungry ghosts.

Contemplating the Suffering of the Lower Realms has three sections:

1. Contemplating the Suffering of the Hells
2. Contemplating the Suffering of Animals
3. Contemplating the Suffering of Hungry Ghosts

The Suffering of the Hells has four sections:

1. Contemplating the Suffering of the Great Hells
2. Contemplating the Suffering of the Neighboring Hells
3. Contemplating the Suffering of the Cold Hells
4. Contemplating the Suffering of the Occasional Hells

Contemplating the Suffering of the Great Hells

The "great hells" are hot hells. If you are born there, your body is an object of incineration and is extremely large, like the size of a great mountain. Furthermore, it is utterly unbearable, like raw flesh being roasted over an open fire. That roasting fire is extraordinarily hot and so forth so that it is as though there is no way of enduring it. The heat of the fire is also so hot that, even though the heat at the end of the eon is seven times hotter than the fire in the human realms, the fires of the hells are seven times hotter than even that.

Previously, the Teacher's shravakas Shariputra and Maudgalyayana took just a small fraction of the fire from the hot hells and placed it on the ocean's shore through their magical powers, whereby all of India became so hot that [the Indians] were on the brink of going insane. In India it is extremely hot and to the north it is extremely cold; this is because the hot hells and cold hells are respectively beneath each one, causing surges of [hot and cold] to rise.

From among the eight hot hells, the first is the Reviving Hell. When the beings that are born there see each other, they become angry, and brandishing weapons in their hands battle with each other until they fall to the ground. Next, a loud voice comes from the sky and says, "May you be revived," and the moment a cooling and restoring wind touches their bodies, they are revived and resume their fighting as before. By conventionally designating their falling to the ground and fainting as "death," you could say that they die a hundred times and are revived a hundred times each day. They experience this and other types of suffering. Once you are reborn in the Reviving Hell through a complete disregard for and violation of the pratimoksha vows [just] once, you can be liberated from that so that you don't have to experience that suffering through the duration of your entire life. Through repeated disregard [of your vows] you will have to experience such things throughout the duration of your life in the Reviving Hell.

We can know that we have absolutely no certainty that we won't be reborn in such a place, for we have engaged in numerous violations [of the pratimoksha vows] through our casual contempt [for the precepts]. The defilements incurred by householders burning down forests and other such things, as well as killing wild animals and so forth, down to the ordained incurring an infraction of the five types of downfalls of the pratimoksha, are creating the causes for hot hells right down to the burning sand. Je Gungtang [Jampalyang Rinpoche] stated, "Whatever various faults you engage in, these faults are manifested through the hell realms." As these teachings state, we should be careful with the time that we currently have at hand. In the hell realms, your body is cut into a hundred pieces, and each drop of your blood is scattered on the burning iron ground; they are unable to dry up, [however,] and while they remain there, boiling, you experience the pain and suffering because they have not separated from your consciousness.

Regarding the Black Line Hell, numerous black lines are drawn on your body by a blazing iron cable and then you are cut into small pieces with a blazing saw. In the Crushing Hell there are living beings with faces like the animals that they have killed, such as goats and sheep, and they are squeezed between two iron mountains. The slaughterers of sheep, goats, and so on—and even those who kill lice between their fingernails—will be reborn in the Crushing Hell. In the Wailing Hell, the beings enter into a blazing iron house and so forth and experience suffering. In the

Great Wailing Hell, the beings enter into a two-story iron house and the suffering is twice that of the previous suffering; therefore, it is immense. The *Supreme Dharma of the Application of Mindfulness Sutra*[371] states that if the ordained even drink alcohol they will be reborn in the Wailing Hell, and states,

> Drinking alcohol will result in rebirth in the Wailing Hell.
> Bartenders will be reborn in the [hells] surrounding it.

In the Hot Hell, the beings' bodies are submerged in fiercely boiling water, and when each section of their flesh and bones has been separated, they are spread out on the blazing iron and their bones are reassembled. A cool karmic wind touches their bodies and they are immediately restored to their former state. They are once again submerged and assembled as before, whereby they experience repeated suffering. Some have a blazing iron spear thrust from their anus out through the top of their head, whereby they are incinerated. Their bodies are laid flat on the blazing iron, bound, and so on.

Through the different systems for the way we accumulate negative karma in this life, the specific karma results in limitless varieties of suffering even in the hells. It is extremely stupid to not have fear and trepidation about engaging in the great negative acts of regional customs.[372] When we experience the maturation of karma in our own situation, we find it unbearable. Yet if we are not liberated from samsara, it is definite that we will have to experience these sufferings. Moreover, if we examine this through our way of presenting it, it is as though it is certain that at the end of this life we will be reborn in the lower realms. The suffering of the Extremely Hot Hell is twice as severe as the Hot Hell, and the beings there are impaled by a three-pointed spear. With the exception of the duration of their lives, their experience of suffering is comparable. In the Unrelenting Hell, they are burned by eleven fires coming from the ten directions and [also] from the insides of their own bodies, so that their bodies are like the wick of a butter lamp and are mixed inseparably with

371. Tib. *mDo sde dran pa nyer gzhag*.
372. This means to engage in nonvirtuous actions because it is the custom of a certain place, such as eating live bugs, boiling live lobsters, and so forth.

the flames. Some beings are burning embers, like barley being roasted in a frying pan and so on, as they [suffer] in a multitude of different ways.

Engage in killing numerous beings such as deer and so forth and you will be reborn in the Extremely Hot Hell and Unrelenting Hell. While we are living in the human realm, if we repeatedly commit all sorts of nonvirtuous verbal actions, this will also cause us to be reborn in these places. Even the teachings of the perverted Dharma of the heretic Purna Kashyapa[373] will result in rebirth there. Incurring a root downfall of the mantra or bodhisattva vows, incurring a defeat of the pratimoksha, disparaging your guru, or killing numerous people will be enough for rebirth in the Unrelenting Hell. Even not helping your livestock, having disregard and contempt for your guru, or associating with others who have defiled their spiritual commitments and so on will be enough for you to go to the lower realms as well; therefore, you must be extremely conscientious in this respect as well.

Previously, Drubchen Ling had mastered the attainments of the elements, such as the wind and mind and so on. While he was giving teachings on the *Fifth Commitment* to a large gathering, if there were a couple of people in the assembly with broken tantric commitments, he would immediately send those two persons somewhere else for teachings and would say that the rest were fine. When the Siddha of Ugyen [Drubchen Rinpoche] and his guru Chag Lotsawa were traveling to eastern Nyal, they were approaching the village where someone who had broken his commitments to Chaglo lived. As they were about to encounter this person, Drubchen Rinpoche [went ahead and] reprimanded [the person with broken commitments to Chag Lotsawa] by stating,

> If it is not proper even to look at someone with defiled commitments, then what need is there to mention meeting and conversing with them? I would hang a curtain so that I don't have to see his house. Whatever yogi has broken his commitments, I will not meet or speak with him even for an instant. This should be recited by everyone!

373. Tib. Mu stegs kyi sTon pa rdzogs byed. One of the six heretic teachers alive at the time of Buddha Shakyamuni.

And,

> It is said that even if you drink the water from the same region as someone who has broken their commitments, you will go to the lower realms.

Therefore, although we may not engage in any other magnificent virtues, at the very least we should be sure that we don't sustain a great loss by making sure that the method we are employing is not a means for rebirth in the lower realms. The lifespan [of the hell beings] is also extremely long, and among the beings in the hot hells the Reviving Hell is the shortest. One of their days is equal to nine billion human years and so on, while the lifespan of those in the Reviving Hell is five hundred years. According to [Vasubandhu's] *Treasury of Abhidharma*, the lifespan of the lower hells becomes progressively longer and their suffering becomes progressively greater. We should examine the teachings in the *Supreme Dharma of the Application of Mindfulness Sutra*.

Contemplating the Suffering of the Neighboring Hells

There are four neighboring hells. These are spread out beyond the great hells. There are two ways of being born there: coming there and being there from the beginning. According to the first, when you emerge from whichever of the four doors in the iron fence surrounding the hot hells is appropriate, you are then born there [in the neighboring hell]. The first [neighboring hell] that you come to is the Pit of Embers. The entire region is a blazing pit of embers as deep as [the hell beings'] knees, so that when they step on it everything below their knees is burnt. When they lift up their legs, they are regenerated.

The second is the Swamp of Putrid Corpses, which is filled with human feces that emits a scent like the smell of rotting corpses, which they sink into up to their necks. Numerous insects with sharp beaks like needles bore into all parts of their bodies and eat them from the neck downward.

In the third, the Vast Plain of Razors, beings see something like a blue meadow, and when they go there and step on it, it is filled with sharp razor-like teeth that cut into and split open their flesh, skin, nerves, sinews, and so forth. When they lift up [their legs], they are restored, whereby they repeatedly experience this type of suffering. Regarding the Forest of Razor Leaves,[374] you see a pleasant-looking forest, and when you sit down after reaching it, a karmic wind strikes the leaves of razors, whereby your body is cut to pieces, and you collapse to the ground and iron dogs, jackals, and so on eat your body, causing you suffering. As for the Shalmali garden, the tree trunks are iron and are filled with numerous thorns with extremely sharp tips that [hell] beings climb and descend from. As they ascend the tips point downward, and as they descend the tips point upward, whereby their bodies are pierced and split open and hawks with iron beaks eat them. While beings climb and descend, their friends and relatives who were objects of their attachment of this life call to them from above and below, which causes them to go up and down.

Pabongkha Rinpoche explained that the harm that comes from the weapons in these three directions is included in one heading.

The fourth is the River with No Ford. Through the water merely touching your body, it is capable of disintegrating even your flesh and bones and is like boiling water, giving it the name "a river filled with water without a ford." Once you are free from the previous hell, you escape and fall into this [river], which is like peas being poured into a massive vat of boiling copper, and there [the hell beings] are tossed about, whereby every part of their bodies is cooked. There are guardians of hell with weapons and so forth who beat them and prevent them from escaping. Some of them are pulled out onto the blazing iron ground and are fed blazing balls of molten iron and have molten copper poured into their mouths and so forth.

Contemplating the Suffering of the Cold Hells

The earth underlying all these [cold hells] is solid ice, and there are snow-covered mountains on all sides. They don't receive even the slightest bit of warmth from the sun, are pitch black, and are enveloped in a violent storm of snow and rain. A freezing hard wind blows and strikes [the hell

374. This is a section of the Vast Plain of Razors.

beings'] bodies, whereby their flesh and bones [become so frozen] they are barely discernible as migrating beings. This is the type of freezing circumstances they must live in. What need is there to mention having clothes to wear? They don't even have a flat mat beneath them, and they are born completely naked, whereby they are extremely cold, which causes them extreme torment. These are the shared sufferings of the cold hells. The snow-covered mountains in the cold hells are two thousand leagues high, and Palden Yeshe states that they are at a level equal to the hot hells.

Regarding the causes of being born in the cold hells, these are holding wrong views, tossing living beings into the water or the snow, and throwing lice onto the solid ice in the wintertime. From these causes come [rebirth in] the Blistering Hell and Bursting Blisters Hell, and due to the cold in these two places, although [the beings there] are restricted, they are able to move as they shiver. Those in the Chattering Teeth Hell are not even able to do that but are only able to open and close their mouths. The Weeping Hell and the Moaning Hell are specified by the sound that comes from their palates [there].[375] With respect to the Splitting Like a Blue Lotus Hell, their bodies turn blue and split into a six-petaled lotus. As for the Splitting Like a Red Lotus Hell, their bodies turn red and split into ten [petals] and so forth. In the Great Splitting Like a Red Lotus Hell, their suffering is [even] greater than in the previous [hells], and once they turn red they split into a hundred or thousand petals, whereby they experience suffering.

From among the cold hells, those with the shortest lifespan are the first cold hell, the Chattering Teeth Hell. The lifespan of each of the lower [ones] is twenty times longer than the one above. The lifespan of the Chattering Teeth Hell is measured by the amount of time it would take to remove eighty measures of sesame seeds stored in a barrel from the region of Magadha filled to the brim with sesame seeds by removing a single grain at intervals of a hundred years. When you had exhausted all the sesame seeds, you still would not have exhausted the lifespan in the Chattering Teeth Hell and would have to remain there for that length of time.

375. In Tibetan, these last two hells are literally called *Kihu*, and *Achu*, which have been translated as "weeping," and "moaning," respectively.

Contemplating the Suffering of the Occasional Hells

It is said in the *Narration of Sangharakshita*[376] and the *Captain of Nawache Mountain*[377] that the [occasional hells] are on the banks of the great ocean, in the vicinity of the hot and cold hells, and even in the human realm. We place the physical representations of enlightened body, speech, and mind on the bare ground and toss all sorts of impure things into the room of the Sangha. We use foul and offensive language toward others, we act carelessly and improperly with impure offerings made to us, we take things that are common belongings of the Sangha, we steal things intended for them to eat, we deduct from the money for expenditures [and from] things that are intended for the weak and frail, and so on; these are causes for [being reborn] in hell. Therefore, it is definite that you will be reborn in the occasional hells through accumulating these and other similar actions. Ayushmat saw an occasional hell. Also, previously a Tibetan siddha went to Tsang and [recognized] in a Yardrok lake a powerful person named Tsang Tanak Lama, who had misappropriated and eaten a great many offerings made by the faithful and who had been reborn as a massive living being similar to a fish that was being eaten by numerous worms. This is also an occasional hell. We should be very cautious about [incurring these types of obstructions] from the offerings made by the faithful,[378] and once we eat them we should purify the obstructions from such offerings. Although there are methods for purifying the obstructions from the offerings made by the faithful, there is nothing superior to engaging in studying, contemplating, and meditating on the Dharma.

Also, there was a frog inside a rock being eaten by many other frogs. There was also a manager of Dergé Monastery who was reborn in the trunk of a tree being carried in a river and who was being eaten by numerous frogs. Therefore, if the ordained and officials excessively eat and consume the wealth and possessions of others, in their next life they will have to pay for it with their own bodies.

In [Je Tsongkhapa's] *Great Treatise of the Stages of the Path* and the *Middle-*

376. Tib. *'Phags pa dge 'dun srung.*

377. Tib. *Ded dpon rna ba bye ba ri'i rtogs brjod.*

378. Tib. *dkor.* This term refers not only to the offerings made by the faithful but also to the obstructions that they create if the recipient is not extremely pure or misuses the offerings.

Length Treatise on the Stages of the Path, the [sufferings of] the animals are taught before the hungry ghosts because the animals have a lesser mental and physical basis, so this is taught from the perspective of the status of their physical basis. In the [Second Panchen Lama's] *Swift Path*, the hungry ghosts are taught [first] in terms of the greater degree of their suffering.

Contemplating the Suffering of the Animals

There are two types of animals: those that live in the ocean and those ranging on the surface of the earth. Most live in the depths of the ocean, in the dark recesses between the continents and so on, like a mass of left-over grain at the bottom of a beer vat. Those roaming the surface of the earth live in the human realm as large birds and so on and are the ones that we presently see. They also have various types of suffering, such as eating one another and so forth. Many smaller ones live on the bodies of the larger ones, which are like sea monsters and eat them and so forth. Also, each time the ones like sea monsters swallow many hundreds of creatures that live in the ocean, [the smaller creatures] don't die right away but are still alive and experience the suffering of death when they are in the belly of the sea monster. Not only that, but hawks, fowl, and sparrows eat one another, right down to bees. There is no certainty that we also won't be reborn like that as well. Though we may think, "At present, I have obtained such a human body; therefore, I won't end up like that," the fact that we have currently obtained a human body provides absolutely no certainty that we won't be reborn in such a lower realm in our next life. We have already repeatedly produced numerous causes for rebirth there.

In the lineage of teachings of the previous holy beings, there was a bhikshu from Kham who was reborn as a long red worm. Also, a tribesman had a cow that gave birth to a calf, and when a siddha with clairvoyance saw [the calf], he said, "This is the rebirth of a lama." This frightened [the siddha] and he finished his session in this state. Also, there was a certain lama from Dagpo who was reborn as a female yak that produced a great deal of milk for his [previous] benefactor. We eat and drink the meat, butter, milk, yogurt, and so on that [are offered by the faithful], which are like a loan, and there will come a time when we have to meet with the consequences with our bodies.

Moreover, animals suffer due to being foolish and stupid, having an unattractive shape and color, heat and cold, hunger and thirst, and so on, not to mention pack yaks, dogs, and so forth who suffer from exploitation. Deer, antelope, and so forth suffer from being employed. Previously a non-Buddhist offered animal sacrifices to a deity image, and when the father of that family was about to pass away he made his last will and testament, which stated that the family should continue offering the animal sacrifices. Because of this, the father was reborn six times as a bull belonging to the family that was offered as an animal sacrifice. This being the case, with very little effort we can change rebirths many times from the man of the house to the watchdog. Although at the moment we don't find it difficult to observe [the sufferings of animals] from the outside, as though we are watching a spectacle, once you have actually taken rebirth among the lower realms as something like a fierce dog, [you find that] although you search the entire day for food and drink you don't find any, so that your body is nothing but skin and bones. Our search for food will mostly lead to being beaten and struck, [suffering] broken limbs and so on. And these are only some of the sufferings. We should consider how we load up our pack animals such as donkeys, and the sufferings of other animals as well. The lengths of their lives varies, and the longest an animal is able to live is one eon.

Day Sixteen

The incomparable Atisha the Great stated,

> Life is short and there are many things to learn;
> Since we cannot know just how long we will live,
> We should extract our desires just like
> A swan extracts milk from water.

At this time, we have obtained this life of leisure and endowment just this once. Because this life is as short as the winter sun and will soon be over, if we don't make use of its meaningfulness from this very moment, while we have it, it will soon be over. Therefore, for as long as [this life] lasts, completely abandon your aspirations to the wind. If you don't, at the time of your death you will be full of regret and immense disappointment, as though you had exchanged gold for dirt. Don't let it come to that, and instead [make use of your life] before death comes. It is as though there were a pile of seeds on the banks of a great river, and the water was about to carry off the heap of grain, and you could only get a small amount of the seeds; yet if there were a good method, it would be possible to get the entire pile of seeds. In this example, the vast and extensive river is similar to our forthcoming future death, and the heap of grain is like striving to extract whatever we possibly can to fulfill our ultimate aims: if we do [so, whether to a small or large extent], it will only be of the greatest value and benefit. Furthermore, there is no other way than the practice of Dharma, for which you must also know the way to practice Dharma, for which you must listen [to the Dharma].

Je Rinpoche [Tsongkhapa] also stated, "Initially seek numerous extensive teachings." Furthermore, the degree of detail to which you have studied will determine the size of your mental scope and is not merely a limb of the path but is necessary for a definite understanding of the concise essence of the entire path. The Kadampas also said that the current era is not the time to develop a vast mental capacity; it is the time for the concise meaning. Thus, the teachings that reveal the instructions in their entirety are nothing other than the stages of the path to enlightenment that has the four greatnesses, the three unique qualities, and so on, and that are something we are capable of understanding. Regarding such a unique Dharma as this, as I have already explained, even the Guhyasamaja king of the tantras and teachings, such as the *Perfection of Wisdom in Eight Thousand Lines*, does not possess such qualities. [Set your motivation in this way and think, "For that reason I am going to listen to the stages of the path to enlightenment."]

After Pabongkha Rinpoche gave this general introduction, he covered the outlines. He then explained once again the stages of the path of a small being, which is the actual way of extracting the essence [of this life], and how to develop fear of our next worldly existence by contemplating the happy and suffering migrations.

We must take rebirth through the force of our karma, and as protector Nagarjuna states [in his *Precious Garland*],

> All suffering comes from nonvirtue,
> And likewise all suffering migrations.
> All happy migrations come from virtue,
> As does the happiness in all rebirths.

If you wonder what the suffering in the hells is like, Nagarjuna stated [in his *Letter to a Friend*],

> The suffering of being violently stabbed
> Three hundred times in a single day
> Cannot be compared with—cannot even begin to express—
> The smallest suffering in the hell realms.

Contemplating the Suffering of the Hungry Ghosts

There are limitless unique sufferings and so on in the individual abodes of each of the three lower realms. Regarding the abode of the hungry ghosts, the city of hungry ghosts, Kapila, lies five hundred leagues directly beneath Rajagriha. There, the predominance of covetousness in one's past shapes a resulting environment without any desirable things whatsoever, like grass, water, meadows, and so on. It is copper-red, as if scorched by the sun. Hungry ghosts have a variety of rebirths, such as womb-born and miraculously born. Their heads and bellies are massive and their limbs are thin as needles. They have disheveled hair, emaciated flesh, and their limbs are disproportionate. They can't find a drop of food or water even after a hundred years; therefore, red, violently blazing flames of hunger issue from their mouths. When they go to a place in search of food, as they move about their limbs make cracking sounds and emit sparks, and they find it difficult to move about. Their lives are really pitiable, and when I describe all these things, some people become extremely despondent; however, I shall explain this in three parts:

[Contemplating the Suffering of the Hungry Ghosts has three sections:]

1. Those with External Obstructions to Obtaining Food and Drink
2. Those with Internal Obstructions to Obtaining Food and Drink
3. Those with Obstructions to Food and Drink Itself

Those with External Obstructions to Obtaining Food and Drink

After traveling a great distance, some [hungry ghosts] see something similar to water and go there, causing them great fatigue. When they arrive there, there is not even a drop of water and the banks of the river dry up and turn white. Alternatively, the water looks like pus and blood. Although some find some water, there are guards holding weapons that pierce them and so forth, causing suffering.

Those with Internal Obstructions to Obtaining Food and Drink

Regarding those with internal obstructions, in general hungry ghosts have throats as thin as needles and stomachs the size of mountains. Some have giant goiters on their bodies, which are decaying and emitting pus. Hungry ghosts with small throats have three knots in their throats and so forth, so that even if they find food, they are unable to enjoy it because it can't pass down their throats. Although some [manage to obtain some] food, a fire of hunger emits from their mouths and stomachs, causing even more suffering and so on.

Those with Obstructions to Food and Drink Itself

Regarding those with obstructions to food and drink itself, in a hundred years, although they are about to find food and drink, as they are preparing to eat it, it transforms into foul-smelling things such as feces and urine. They don't have the causes to enjoy nutritious food and drink; therefore, they eat their own flesh, barley chaff, weapons, boiling water, blazing balls of molten iron, and so forth. This adds to their suffering, which they experience in limitless ways as explained in the tale of the *Captain of Nawache Mountain.*

Moreover, in the land of hungry ghosts is Yama's Palace, which is extremely terrifying, and they suffer from panic [there]. Even the moon burns in the summertime, and even the sun is cold in the wintertime. They are constantly hungry and thirsty, and traveling to places in search of food is very tiring and so on, leaving them no choice but to experience these sufferings. Master Buddhajnana gave an extensive account of going to the land of the hungry ghosts. A tormented female hungry ghost had a son who had given birth to five hundred children, and she asked [master Buddhajnana] to deliver a message [to her husband], asking [master Buddhajnana] to look for her husband, who had gone in search of food and drink in the human realm twelve long years before and was able to get some discarded mucus that a morally upright bhikshu dedicated. After a great deal of fighting among numerous hungry ghosts, he was able to get a small piece of dried mucus that he has been guarding in his clenched fist.

Regarding the causes of being reborn as a hungry ghost, even merely calling others bad names or calling them "hungry ghost" is a cause to take rebirth in the body of a hungry ghost a hundred times. By stealing, as well, you will become a hungry ghost, and a strong mind of attachment longing for wealth is also a cause of such a rebirth. Previously, a bhikshu who was attached to his monk's robes was reborn as a hungry ghost wearing monk's robes. Even the mother of the novice monk Uttara was reborn as a hungry ghost after she died because she had extremely strong greed. Once the novice saw her, he asked the Buddha and his shravakas to grant her refuge, and they made dedication prayers and so forth on her behalf. Thus, all the different types of hungry ghosts engaged in miserliness and so on, whereby they were reborn as hungry ghosts. For that reason, if those of us who are ordained monks engage in covetousness and strong mental attachment, clinging to our wealth, possessions, and so on, we establish the cause to be reborn as a hungry ghost.

Pabongkha Rinpoche then explained the following:

Arya Shariputra saw a hungry ghost with a constricted windpipe, which is why during the torma gyatsa we dedicate a drop of water with JALAM IDAM and so on with the object of dedication being hungry ghosts with constricted windpipes and so on.

Regarding the length of their lives, one human month is equal to one day for a hungry ghost, and they live for five thousand, ten thousand years and more, during which time they must experience suffering. Since beginningless time, we, too, have accumulated numerous causes for rebirth as a hungry ghost that have remained unchanged. Still, we continue to produce more, because of which not only do we have absolutely no certainty that we will not be reborn as a hungry ghost after this life, but we have not been able to purify the numerous causes for our rebirth in all three lower realms. If we were to die in this very moment, it is absolutely certain that we would take rebirth in one of the appropriate three lower realms. Therefore, we should meditate until we invoke an experience that understands that, with the exception that we can still draw a breath, we have already arrived in the lower realms with virtually no difference from having already been reborn in the lower realms.

This way of meditating is like meditating on self-generation. When we generate ourselves as our personal deity, if instead we perform a self-generation in the hell realms first, it will have a much more beneficial impact than the former. From this will come very powerful renunciation, whereas although we may meditate on the self-generation as our personal deity, we will not develop renunciation. As [Shantideva states,]

> Through engaging in this type of conduct,
> I will not attain a human body again.
> If I do not attain a human body,
> There will be only negativity and no virtue.

It is certain that we will take rebirth in the lower realms after we die. A multitude of bad actions already exists that functions as the dominant condition for rebirth in the lower realms. If we fall into rebirth in one of the lower realms, we will have no knowledge of the practice of virtue. Nonvirtue, the three poisons, and so on will be our natural state, which we can understand by looking at something such as a dog. Therefore, once we have fallen down into the lower realms, it is as though there will never come a time when we can rise up and be liberated.

By recalling the suffering of the hell realms, even food will not be pleasing, and if it happens that you are unable to eat in that way, it will evoke suffering just as happened to Arya Ananda's two nephews.[379] If you recollect the sufferings of the hell realms properly, it should be like Ananda's two nephews. By meditating on the sufferings of the hot hells, you begin to establish renunciation. During the section of the middle scope, you perfect the skill of renunciation. When you meditate on the sufferings of the lower realms, once you evoke an experience of having already been born there, you should meditate by contemplating that even though you are not actually born there, it is certain that you will be. Je Tsongkhapa stated, "For example, it would be like resting for a while during the descent as soon as you fall into an abyss." Right now our two legs

379. Ananda's sister had two young sons who had become monks and were learning to read at the monastery. Because they were lazy and constantly distracted, they did very poorly in their studies. Ananda asked Maudgalyayana to help, so Maudgalyayana showed them a vision of the hell realms where the two boys would eventually be reborn if they didn't change their errant behavior.

are dangling over the precipice of the lower realms. Because there is no difference [between the aforementioned analogy and our actual situation], we should seek refuge in the Three Jewels to protect us, which is similar to pulling us up by the hand. We need to make a sincere effort in adopting and abandoning according to actions and their effects, as a means to liberate us from the lower realms.

Relying upon the Methods for Attaining Happiness in Our Next Life has two sections:

1. Training in Refuge as the Sublime Door for Entering the Teachings
2. Generating Faith and Confidence in Actions and Their Effects as the Root of Happiness and Excellence

The first has four sections. In the *Middle-Length Treatise on the Stages of the Path* there are four outlines for this section, which do not include teachings on the benefits of going for refuge, which instead are taught separately during the common trainings and not included at this point. These days it is taught according to the *Swift Path*, which has a heading for the benefits. For this, there are five sections.

Training in Refuge as the Sublime Door for Entering the Teachings has five sections:

1. The Causes That Constitute Your Reason for Going for Refuge
2. The Objects You Rely upon When Going for Refuge
3. The Way of Determining You Have Gone for Refuge Properly
4. The Benefits of Going for Refuge
5. The Precepts to Follow Once You Have Gone for Refuge

The Causes That Constitute Your Reason for Going for Refuge

One cause of going for refuge is explaining the suffering of the lower realms during the section on a being of the lesser scope. Another cause is confidence that the Three Jewels have the capacity to protect us. If you don't have a pure act of going for refuge in your mental continuum, you are not included among Buddhists. Although you may meditate on many of the very high practices, such as the generation and completion stages, they won't become a perfect refuge. You need both these causes of going for refuge to be complete, which are, in short, *fear* and *faith*. In addition to that, in the uncommon Mahayana, not only are all living beings tormented by the suffering of samsara but, even though the pratyekabuddhas and shravakas are liberated from samsara, they have not abandoned the obstructions to omniscience. Therefore, with the addition of *great compassion* that is unable to bear [their suffering], we employ three [causes of refuge].

For that to happen, you need a fear of suffering that recalls refuge, which protects us from the lower realms according to what is called "recalling refuge in fear." For that, we must recall suffering; therefore, we begin by recollecting the suffering of the lower realms, which establishes the cause of going for refuge. Refuge is extremely vast, so there is no difference in the causes of going for refuge or in the way of going for refuge among the scopes of beings and in mantra. For this, there are two parts.

The Causes That Constitute Your Reason for Going for Refuge has two sections:

1. Identifying the Objects of Refuge
2. The Reason They Are Suitable Objects of Refuge

Identifying the Objects of Refuge

Only the Three Jewels are objects of refuge. Although there are some who seek refuge in gods, nagas, king spirits, Brahma, and so forth, for the most part, king spirits and so forth are hungry ghosts. As for nagas, they are animals, so they are lower rebirths than humans. They are objects of our compassion but not suitable to employ as objects of refuge. Even Ishvara and so forth are samsaric beings; therefore, they have no power to protect us. For example, if a person falls into quicksand, the one who is going to pull him out of it must not also be stuck in the quicksand himself. If the two are equally stuck in the quicksand, they have no way of helping each other get out of the quicksand. This can also be applied to someone being carried away by water. It is necessary for the one who is going to be pulling someone else from samsara not to have fallen into samara himself. The *Interwoven Praises* states,

> Abiding in the ocean of samsara,
> Which is without end or bottom,
> Devoured by the unbearable sea monsters of attachment
> and so on—
> To whom shall I go for refuge today?

The *Praise of the Exalted One*[380] states,

> I have abandoned other teachers;
> I go for refuge to you, Bhagavan.
> If you ask what the reason for that is,
> It is because you have abandoned all faults and possess all good
> qualities.

The *Hundred and Fifty Praises*[381] states,

> The one in whom all faults are
> Utterly and completely nonexistent
> And in whom all aspects of
> Every good quality abide—
>
> If you have any common sense,[382]
> You will go for refuge in him alone,
> Praise and venerate him, and
> Abide in his teachings.

380. Tib. *Khyad par 'phags bstod.*
381. Tib. *bsTod pa brgya lnga bcu pa.*
382. The Tibetan actually reads, "If you have a mind," which implies having any common sense.

You should seek an unmistaken object of refuge. Furthermore, you should study and contemplate the great scriptures. If you are unable to understand the Dharma presented in the stages of the path, you won't even know the actual objects of refuge. Previously, a smooth-talking tantric practitioner was talking a great deal about Dharma to Zhog Donyon Khedrup. Finally Donyon Khedrup asked the tantric practitioner what he knew about refuge in the Three Jewels. And the tantric practitioner merely pointed his finger toward the sky and said, "In the realm of invisible space is a crystal palace called 'Radiant Light.'" [Donyon Khedrup responded that] that is not the way we should recognize the three supreme objects of refuge.

Furthermore,

> The Buddha, Dharma, and Sangha are
> The objects of refuge for those desiring liberation.

Of the three—Buddha, Dharma, and Sangha—the first is the Buddha. [Maitreya's] *Sublime Continuum*[383] states,

> Unproduced and accomplished spontaneously,
> Not realized through the factor of another,
> Endowed with wisdom, compassion, and power—
> Only a buddha possesses the two aims.

Thus, he is endowed with eight qualities. In short, the Buddha Jewel is the ultimate object of refuge that has perfected the two purposes.[384] If we subdivide that,

> Through that merit all living beings
> Accumulate a collection of merit and wisdom,
> And from merit and wisdom
> Emerge the two holy bodies.

[A buddha] possesses the truth body [dharmakaya] and form body

383. Tib. *rGyud bla ma*; Skt. *Uttaratantra*.
384. A buddha has accomplished his own aims by freeing him- or herself from samsara and perfecting his or her potentiality to work for the welfare of others by becoming omniscient.

[rupakaya]. According to the teaching presented in the *Ornament of Clear Realization*, there are four bodies: (1) a nature truth body, (2) a wisdom truth body, (3) an enjoyment body, and (4) an emanation body. Furthermore, the truth body has two bodies—the nature truth body and wisdom truth body—while the form body is divided into the enjoyment body and emanation body, of which the enjoyment body is like the root of the bodies. Furthermore, [the enjoyment body] possesses five certainties: (1) body, (2) Dharma, (3) retinue, (4) abode, and (5) time.

There are three types of emanation body.[385] For the sake of subduing the King of Gandharvas, [Buddha Shakyamuni] emanated as a musician. For beings like Vishakarma, he emanated as a craftsman. His emanation body takes rebirth in emanations such as Dampa Tokar, a deer, and so on. He emanates as the supreme emanation body in aspects such as our Teacher.

Of the two types of nature truth body, the "naturally pure nature truth body" is the emptiness that has abandoned the imprints of grasping at true existence that is naturally pure and of a truly established nature. The [second], the "pure-of-adventitious-nature truth body," is revealed in the *Commentary on Valid Cognition* when it states,

> The nature of mind is clear light;
> The stains are adventitious.

Previously, in dependence upon that [pure nature of mind], the obstructions are abandoned as the factors of abandonment by employing the power of the antidote. Furthermore, the obscurations and the mind are not permanently linked but are subsequently related; therefore, the stains are adventitious. Stating that the defilements associated with that mind did not previously exist but subsequently arose adventitiously is not the [correct] meaning. The wisdom truth body is the exalted wisdom of a buddha's mind that knows all aspects.

Regarding the Dharma Jewel,

385. Generally there are said to be four types of emanation body: (1) artisan emanation body, (2) birth emanation body, (3) great enlightenment emanation body, and (4) supreme emanation body.

> Inconceivable, free from both, nonconceptual,
> Pure, clear, antidote to the opposite—
> The Dharma is that which is free from attachment
> And defined by the two truths.

These eight [qualities in the aforementioned verse] are included within the two paths of cessation. In short, the truth of complete purification included in the mind of an arya, through any suitable path of cessation, is the Dharma Jewel. For that, there are the two paths of cessation, from which emerge the results related to the true paths as the truth of complete purification that is a true cessation. Furthermore, there are the individual corresponding paths through the wisdom directly realizing emptiness that cause the objects of abandonment to cease and are called "the truth of cessation." The wisdom in the mental continuum of an arya employed to attain the truth of cessation whose result is related to oneself is the true path. These two only exist in the mind of an arya being; therefore, once you attain the stage of forbearance on the path of preparation, you have abandoned the factors for taking rebirth in the lower realms through the force of karma and afflictive emotions. On the peak section of the Mahayana path of preparation, you abandon the factors in your mental continuum that destroy your roots of virtue such as anger, wrong views, and so forth. These are true cessations that are nonanalytical cessations. Regarding the teaching on the true paths on the paths of accumulation and preparation, these are said to be nonanalytical cessations.

Regarding the Sangha Jewel, they are endowed with any of the eight qualities of intellect and liberation of an arya being. Regarding these eight qualities,

> Because of their exalted wisdom of pure perception realizing
> The ultimate truth, conventional truth, and the inner [of both],
> The assembly of wise irreversible ones
> Is endowed with unsurpassed good qualities.

They have three good qualities of intellect, three good qualities of liberation, and two related to each one, making eight in all. There are two types of Sangha: ordinary beings and arya beings. We go for refuge to the

Sangha Jewel that have attained a degree of the path of an arya being of any of the three vehicles of either ordained or lay persons. The Sangha are four or more bhikshus or novices who have yet to attain the path of an arya. If four of those four types of persons are complete, they serve as representatives of the Sangha Jewel and should be recognized as the actual Sangha Jewel. Furthermore, Geshe Potowa and others have stated that even a collection of four ordinary Sangha who have not attained the path of an arya is also posited as the Sangha Jewel. Although any of the eight good qualities of realization and liberation constitute the attainment of the path of an arya, all eight of the good qualities of realization and liberation are not possessed by aryas other than a buddha. Thus, Drom[tonpa] Rinpoche explained how to rely on the Sangha as your assistants when he stated,

> Prepare three or more but less than five assistants.

Thus, you have a balance in the number of assistant Sangha. Furthermore, you should rely upon assistants who will understand the import of a mere look of disappointment and who will act with a sense of concern and conscientiousness, which makes a great difference in assuring that they won't act improperly.[386] If you stay alone or with an unwholesome assistant and so on, it will be difficult to restrain yourself and not to defile your vows.[387]

The Reason They Are Suitable Objects of Refuge

If someone providing protection is not someone who can liberate you from fear, he [or she] is not a capable refuge. However, with respect to the Buddha, he is liberated from all fears, such as the twelve limbs embodied by the lower realms, the twelve limbs embodied by samsara, the twelve limbs embodied by the afflictive obstructions, and the obstructions to omniscience. Although Devadatta hurled a boulder at [the Buddha], he was unable to kill him. Devadatta and King Ajatashatru sent a wild elephant to harm the Buddha, but [the elephant] became pacified and sat in the presence of the Teacher. The householder Shri Gupta intended to

386. Your retreat attendants should be so observant and respectful that by merely giving them a disapproving glance they will adjust their behavior and act properly.
387. In this paragraph, Pabongkha Rinpoche is referring to a retreat setting.

kill the Teacher and invited him for the midday meal as a pretense. He built a fire pit that was set along the path and covered it, yet the Teacher transformed it into a garden of lotus flowers. He also attempted to poison [the Buddha's] food, but the Teacher proclaimed the words of truth "Attachment, hatred, ignorance . . ." to Ananda, whereby no matter how much of the midday meal he ate, it was unable to harm him. Thus, he is **liberated from all fears**.

If you are not skilled in the means of liberating others from every fear, it will be like the child of a blind mother without arms being swept away by water. Buddha is **extremely skilled in the means of subduing others**, which is revealed in the way he subdued Lamchung, Angulimala, Nanda, the king of gandharvas Pramudita, and so on. Regarding his **impartial great compassion for all beings**, without this, you most certainly could not act as a refuge; however, the Teacher brings benefit to the most destitute being. He provided refuge for the repulsive child of a brahman; Svagata, the son of the householder Togden; Vajri, the daughter of King Prasenajit; and so forth. Further, when a bhikshu tormented with illness was staying in the Jetavana Grove, the Tathagata himself went and washed his body with water and so forth, restoring him to health.

Regarding his **working for the welfare of all beings whether or not they have helped him**, although Rahula was his son and Devadatta was his harmful enemy, the Buddha had unbiased love and compassion for them both. The doctor Youthful Physician offered a special medicinal substance worth thirty-two ounces of silver to the Buddha each day, which he accepted. Devadatta, the harmful enemy of the Buddha, also ate some, and when he did his body became wracked with a painful illness, yet the Buddha extended his hand by means of his magical powers and liberated him from his illness through bestowing the power of the truth that there was no difference whatsoever in the degree of his love and compassion for his son Rahula and for Devadatta, and through his blessing Devadatta was immediately liberated from his illness.

Non-Buddhists such as Ishvara, Vishnu, and so forth have themselves not removed even the slightest trace of any of the afflictive emotions. The gods and demons have attachment, anger, and extremely vicious ways, as related in the historical account of Sharu Dragtsen. They don't have any compassion and hold mistaken precepts and Dharma. The Buddha is free from all such faults. He is endowed with all good qualities and is a suitable refuge because he works for the welfare of migrating beings by way of his wisdom, compassion, and capacity. For that reason, the Dharma that the Teacher teaches is also a suitable refuge. The Sangha [members] who properly accomplish that Dharma are also suitable objects of refuge.

The Three Jewels that are already accomplished in the mental continuum of a person who is separate from your own mental continuum are *the causal refuge*. The Three Jewels that are the object that you will attain in the future are *the resultant refuge*. The aryas that train in all three vehicles and those with the Dharmas of scripture and realization in their mental continuum are *the conventional refuge*. The buddha superiors and so forth who have perfected the two purposes are *the ultimate refuge*. There are numerous ways of positing the Buddha and these Dharmas, which amount to four possibilities. Although the Three Jewels on a conventional level [consist of] the form body of the Buddha, the volumes of scripture of the transmitted Dharma, and four groups of monks as the Sangha who have not entered the path [of an arya], if we seek refuge in them with the recognition of them as the actual [Three Jewels], we will receive the benefits of going for refuge to the actual Buddha and so forth.

The Way of Determining You Have Gone for Refuge Properly has four sections:

1. Going for Refuge by Knowing Their Good Qualities
2. Going for Refuge by Knowing Their Distinctions
3. Going for Refuge through Commitment
4. Going for Refuge by Not Proclaiming [Faith] in Another

[Going for Refuge by] Knowing Their Good Qualities has three sections:

1. The Good Qualities of the Buddha
2. The Good Qualities of the Dharma
3. The Good Qualities of the Sangha

The Good Qualities of the Buddha has four sections:

1. The Good Qualities of His Body
2. The Good Qualities of His Speech
3. The Good Qualities of His Mind
4. The Good Qualities of His Enlightened Actions

The Good Qualities of His Body

According to the teachings from the *Red Hat Stages of the Path*,[388] if you sequentially contemplate the good qualities of shravakas, pratyekabuddhas, bodhisattvas, and buddhas, it will serve as a means for you to attain a superior faith. You should learn the extensive presentation of the good qualities of a buddha as found in the *Ornament of Clear Realization*, which explains his thirty-two major marks, such as his hands and feet being marked by wheels, his feet [being as flat as a] tortoise's, and so on, as well as the eighty minor indications, such as his fingernails being copper-colored and so forth.[389] The etymology of the signs and indications and the special causes of the signs and indications are taught in the *Precious Garland of Advice for a King*.[390]

The bodhisattva Vegadhara traveled upward without obstruction to countless pure lands, after which he still could not measure the extent of the Buddha's ushnisha. Within each one of the Teacher's hair pores are buddha lands, and they are simultaneously performing a variety of activities. It is said that in the hair pore of Avalokiteshvara, the Buddha is performing the activity of teaching; the same thing applies to all buddhas. We cannot comprehend their secret inconceivable good qualities. Even [the Buddha's] body performs those activities of his mind and perceives all objects of knowledge. A sutra states,

> The Buddha's head, ushnisha, hair-curl treasure, and so forth perceive all objects of knowledge.

388. Tib. *Zhwa dmar lam rim*. This is a lamrim text by Amdo Shamar Gendun Tenzin Gyatso.
389. For an outstanding presentation of these subjects, see Geshe Acharya Thubten Loden, *The Fundamental Potential for Enlightenment in Tibetan Buddhism* (Melbourne: Tushita Publications, 1996).
390. See Jeffrey Hopkins, *Buddhist Advice on Living and Liberation* (Ithaca, NY: Snow Lion, 1998).

Each of the three lines of the verse is applied to his body, such as "His consummate virtue and excellence . . ." Every aspect of the Buddha's body teaches Dharma and so on. When Changkya Rolpai Dorje became blind, he would direct his finger toward a text and was able to edit texts by seeing with his finger.

The Good Qualities of His Speech

The Buddha's speech has the good quality of the sixty-four limbs of melodious speech and is as pervasive as the sunshine and so on. In short, *An Ocean of Clouds of Praise*[391] states that his gentle and harmonious voice is pleasing to the mind and so on, the meaning of which should be learned from Gyalwang Kelsang [Gyatso, the Seventh Dalai Lama's] commentary on the *Clouds of Praise*;[392] this should also be applied to the *Sublime Virtue and Excellence* and others. Furthermore, he teaches the Dharma appropriate to the mind and capacity of each disciple:

> Although he only speaks with a single voice,
> Each of the numerous beings understands it.

And,

> Although all living beings of every world
> May ask at the very same time about a doubt they have,
> You could simultaneously appear before them in
> Body and speech for as many beings as there are.
> Despite these various deeds, you have pacified your conceptions.

And [Je Tsongkhapa's] *Chapter on a Truth Speaker*[393] also states,

> In this way, if all living beings were to simultaneously ask
> A question in multiple languages, your mind

391. Tib. *bsTod sprin rgya mtsho.*

392. Tib. *bsTod sprin.*

393. Tib. *bDen pa po'i le'u.* This text by Tsongkhapa is also quoted in the immediately preceding verse.

> Could instantly penetrate their meaning
> And even give answers to each one with one melodious voice.

As this states, although each migrating being may ask different questions all at one time, [the Buddha] can answer them with one melodious voice so that they can understand him in their own individual languages. He also taught all nine cycles of the perfection of wisdom sutras at once in various lengths, in accordance with the minds and capacities of each disciple and so on, so that they appeared as nine different [sutras]. It is also not possible to determine the extent of [the Buddha's] speech. Although Maudgalyayana traveled by means of his magical powers to countless other worlds to measure the extent of the Tathagata's speech, he could still hear it as though he were in [the Buddha's] presence. Therefore, it is not possible to determine the extent of his speech.

The Good Qualities of His Mind

The [Buddha's] mind has the two good qualities of wisdom and compassion. Regarding his **good qualities of wisdom**, a scripture states:

> Only your exalted wisdom
> Pervades all objects of knowledge.
> For all others besides you,
> There still remain objects to be known.

Thus, while remaining in the meditative equipoise of the emptiness of ultimate reality, he is able to simultaneously perceive all conventional phenomena like holding a *dhatri* fruit in the palm of his hand, as related in the *Narration of Death of the Shakya Gakye.*[394] In short, although you may take the forests from a hundred thousand regions and burn them, mix the ashes with the ocean, and stir it up for a long time, the Buddha, with his wisdom, would be able to identify each of the ashes from the roots of each tree without mixing them up. Even tenth-level bodhisattvas of the final continuum cannot perceive both conventional and ultimate realities

394. Tib. *Sha kya dga' skyes shi ba'i gtam rgyud.*

simultaneously. It is a unique quality possessed only by a buddha to be able to teach Dharma on the level of conventional reality while remaining in meditative equipoise on ultimate reality.

Previously, at one time when Tuken [Chökyi Nyima] Rinpoche[395] was having a vision of the Teacher, he was able to continue giving a teaching without interruption. If I were to comment on the extensive good qualities of [a buddha's] wisdom, I would explain the twenty-one classes of uncontaminated exalted wisdom, such as the [thirty-seven] harmonies with enlightenment, the [four] immeasurables, and so forth, which you should learn from texts such as the *Ornament of Clear Realization*.[396]

Regarding his **good quality of love**, the Buddha's mind is constantly and uncontrollably bound by great compassion, and there is no time when he is not directly perceiving the suffering of living beings; therefore, there is never a time when the continuity of his mind of love and great compassion for all living beings is ever interrupted. Although we have love for ourselves, the Buddha's love for all living beings is sixteen times stronger.

Pabongkha Rinpoche gave the following advice:

We won't receive any benefit by merely verbally repeating the refuge verses while going for refuge. As it is stated, "The nature of going for refuge is mental." Thus, we should go for refuge by employing a mind that understands that the actual nature of going for refuge is a mental event.

395. Tuken Chökyi Nyima (1737–1802) was one of the principal disciples of Changkya Rolpai Dorje.

396. See Geshe Acharya Thubten Loden, *The Fundamental Potential for Enlightenment*, 191–92.

Day Seventeen

Glorious Chandrakirti stated [in his *Guide to the Middle Way*],

> If while living in harmony and permitted independence
> We don't act with self-restraint,
> When we fall into an abyss and have lost our independence,
> How will we rise up from that in the future?

Pabongkha Rinpoche gave the following introduction to set our motivation:

Contemplate, "At this point, if I don't employ a method to extract the essence of this life while I am free from the eight nonfreedoms and have the independence to practice Dharma, when I fall into the abyss of the lower realms I will be without a means of practicing Dharma or a means of attaining liberation from the [lower realms]. At this moment, while I have freedom in my hands, I must ascertain how to accomplish the ultimate aim of taking rebirth. For that purpose I am going to listen to this commentary on the stages of the path to enlightenment, which is the extracted essence of all the Dharma that the Teacher ever taught."

After this, he covered the headings. He once again explained that training in going for refuge is the sacred gateway to entering the teachings.

The Good Qualities of His Enlightened Actions

A buddha's enlightened actions are effortless and are accomplished spontaneously; therefore, there is not even the most subtle motivation needed to work for the welfare of living beings; his activities are effortless, spontaneous, and ceaseless. Although those on the seventh bodhisattva level require a coarse movement of motivation to work for the welfare of living beings, and those on the three pure levels merely require a subtle [movement of motivation], a buddha does not need such things. For example, a moon is able to cast its reflection without effort or thought process upon the earth's water, even down to a mere drop of water on the tip of a blade of grass. The *Ornament of the Mahayana Sutras* states,

> Just as, without beating the drum,
> The sound always emerges,[397]
> Likewise teachings always emerge
> From the Conqueror without effort.

These examples also serve as reasons for a buddha's spontaneous accomplishment of enlightened actions. Just as Asanga sequentially perceived Maitreya in the aspect of a female dog and so on, in the same way, as the mental continuums of disciples become increasingly pure, the enlightened actions of a buddha become clearer. Although a mother may establish her son as the owner of vast stores of wealth and possessions, that son will become destitute if he is not completely noble. If you sit within a north-facing cave, the sun will never reach that place; in the same way, if you don't have confidence, trust, and so forth in the Buddha, you will not receive the enlightened actions of the Buddha. [Geshe] Potowa stated,

> It is said that we don't even trust the wisdom of the buddha as much as an accurate diviner.

Previously, a man from Phenpo said to [Geshe] Potowa that he doubted the existence of the Buddha, and [Potowa] said, "Well then, your ancestor Teu Nagong never existed, either." The man replied, "He definitely did; I have the contract documents for a house to prove it." "Well then," [replied Potowa], "The Buddha definitely came, because after him there were pandits and siddhas in India and Tibet and they composed commen-

397. This is in reference to Indra's drum, which constantly resounds with the sound of Dharma in the Realm of the Thirty-Three.

Shantideva

taries to his teachings and so forth, as taught in their biographies." Due to this, he developed faith.

Regarding the comparison with Brahma in [Maitreya's] *Sublime Continuum*, this represents the way in which [the Buddha's] body and speech effortlessly enter [the Buddha's] disciples. As for the "sun," this represents the way in which the enlightened activities of [the Buddha's] mind enter. Although the sun does not have a motivating factor and so forth, when the sun shines, the lotus petals open and the night lily closes; in the same way, the Buddha's mind of enlightened actions enters into the pure and impure minds of his disciples. The "sky" is like measuring the secrets of his body and speech. As for "the earth," this exemplifies his mind of love and compassion. In short, [Chandrakirti's] *Guide to the Middle Way* states,

> Just as a bird does not turn back because of a lack of space
> But turns back [only] when its strength is exhausted, [so]
> The disciples and sons of the Buddha [must] not turn back
> When expressing [the Buddha's] good qualities that are limitless like space.

Je Lama [Tsongkhapa] also proclaimed,

> In the same way, the garuda continuously travels through the sky
> And turns back [only] when its strength is diminished;
> He does not turn back because space is exhausted.
> It is just the same with attempting to express your good qualities.

Regarding all the good qualities of the Buddha, even those great bodhisattvas on the tenth level are incapable of expressing them.

If you learn the special good qualities of the Buddha, you will naturally be able to understand the good qualities of the Dharma that came from practicing his Dharma. If this is the case with the Dharma, then you will be able to understand the special qualities of the Sangha who practice it. In general, even just the shravakas on the path of accumulation are the Sangha, yet the modern-day siddhas and mantra-bearers, no matter how good they are, are no comparison.

Going for Refuge by Knowing Their Distinctions

In [Tsongkhapa's] *Middle-Length Treatise on the Stages of the Path*, these are set forth according to the *Compendium of Determinations*, which states that you go for refuge once you have understood the internal correlation between the Three Jewels, which I will not be teaching. Instead it will be combined with the [Second Panchen Lama's] *Swift Path*, for which there are six sections.

The Distinction Based on Their Defining Characteristics

For this we learn the nature of each of the Three Jewels or their causes. Furthermore, regarding the Buddha, he has the characteristic of actualizing enlightenment. He has exhausted all faults and possesses all good qualities and has manifested enlightenment. The Dharma is the result of that enlightenment. The Buddha reveals the teaching of transmission, and beings develop the realizations of Dharma in their mental continuums by practicing [the Dharma]. The Buddha and Dharma are the cause and effect that they should rely upon to transform their mental continuums. The Sangha are those who practice the Dharma.

The Distinction of Enlightened Activities

There are different ways in which the enlightened actions of the Three Jewels enter trainees. For example, the Buddha is similar to a doctor who teaches Dharma by giving a reading transmission; the Dharma is similar to medicine, in that it functions to destroy the causes of the afflictive emotions, the resultant suffering, and the illness of the two obstructions; and the Sangha is similar to a nurse, in that it gives birth to realizations through practicing the Dharma. Having seen it in this way, [trainees] function as enthusiastic assistants for the practice of Dharma.

The Distinction of Devotion

For example, we should be prepared before the doctor arrives, and know what we are going to offer [for his or her services].

The Distinction Based on Practice

With respect to being similar to [nurses] doing the work of presenting the offering themselves after they arrive, this is the distinction based on practice. Furthermore, this is analogous to eating medicine and having reverence and veneration for the doctor. You should regard the nurses as equivalent to assistants. Thus, you should have three different ways of thinking about them.

The Distinction of Recollection

This is taught according to the *Sutra Recollecting the Three Jewels*, its commentary, and so forth, which teaches the recollection of the good qualities of those Three [Jewels]. Regarding the holy Dharma set forth in the *Sutra Recollecting the Three Jewels* and so on, you should learn the distinctions [of the Three Jewels] through the combination of scripture and realization. It is an extremely important essential instruction to go for refuge by recalling the good qualities of each.

The Distinction That Comes from Increasing Merit

When you rely upon the Three Jewels, you should recall the way in which merit increases limitlessly in dependence upon the Dharma and a person. The Dharma that is a true cessation and so forth is not a person, whereas the Buddha and Sangha are persons. For the Dharma there are also numerous different ways of understanding [the word], according to Sanskrit. The translation equivalent for the term *Dharma* is "engaging in that which holds back." Therefore, the Dharma of a being of lesser scope "holds" him [or her] "back" from the lower realms. The Dharma of a being of middling capacity holds him back from samsara. The Dharma of a being of great scope holds him back from all of samsara and nirvana. Furthermore, if you don't generate the path in your mental continuum through sequential training, the Buddha's mind alone will not be able to protect you. Therefore, you must make a sincere effort at the means of gathering the cause of going for refuge in your mental continuum.

Although we are extremely skilled at the trivial things of this life, such as making a pot of tea, we don't undertake a sincere effort in the Dharma; therefore, there is no opportunity for the Dharma to come. We pretend we understand the Dharma well before receiving a commentary on going for refuge, yet once we receive the commentary, we find it too difficult to go for refuge, which is a sign that we never previously understood going for refuge. These days some say, "Once you realize [the nature of] mind, you are enlightened," and so on, which is the fault of the proponent not understanding the qualities of a buddha. We should know what the significance is of the numerous Dharma teachings taught by the Buddha.

Going for Refuge through Commitment

Think that you are requesting the Buddha to provide you with refuge and that you commit to him as the one who teaches you refuge and teaches you the truth of reality as a means of liberation and so on. Think that you are requesting the actual refuge, which is the Dharma, and that you will practice this Dharma. Think that once you generate realizations [of the Dharma] in your mental continuum, it will function to dispel the illness of the afflictive emotions. Think that you are requesting assistance from the Sangha to accomplish that refuge. Further, the Buddha is analogous to a boat captain who takes us across a river, the Dharma is similar to a leather coracle, and the Sangha is similar to good traveling companions. These three are indispensable to be liberated from the ocean of existence.

Going for Refuge by Not Proclaiming [Faith] in Another

The Buddha is the teacher for Buddhists, what he teaches is the Dharma, and the Sangha practices that [teaching]. We do not assert objects of refuge such as non-Buddhist teachers and so on, and we do not go for refuge through our understanding of their superior and inferior distinctions. Buddhists have teachings for liberation that are endowed with happiness, abandon afflictive emotions, and so on. Others don't have such teachings. The non-Buddhists enter into meditative absorption [called] "the peak of existence," which is their substitution for liberation. Yet after this, if they fall into the lower realms in their next life, this is not liberation, and they have developed a wrong view. Therefore, their "liberation" at the peak of existence meditative absorption is a mere deception. Furthermore, *Praise of the Exalted One* states,

> What to engage in and exclude . . .

The *Praise to the One Exceeding the Gods*[398] states,

398. Tib. *lHa las phul byung gi bstod pa.*

> I am not being one-sidedly biased toward the Buddha;
> I also don't have aversion for Kapila and so forth;
> I will thoroughly uphold the teachings of
> Whoever's words are endowed with correct reasoning.

These two praises were composed by the brahman Siddhisvami and his brother.[399] If we rely upon the Bonpo and so forth, we have thrown away our commitment to go for refuge [to the Three Jewels], and if we do so it will bring great harm to our other three sets of vows as well.[400] Although in the middle[-length] and great lamrim texts the precepts of going for refuge are taught after the benefits of going for refuge, according to the oral instructions for the [Second Panchen Lama's] *Swift Path*, it will bring great joyous power to protect your commitments of going for refuge if you extract the precepts of going for refuge from above [and place them after the benefits of going for refuge]; therefore, this teaching will be according to the *Swift Path*.

The Benefits of Going for Refuge has eight sections:

1. You Become a Buddhist
2. Going for Refuge Functions as the Foundation for All Vows
3. You Exhaust Your Previously Accumulated Karmic Obscurations
4. You Accumulate a Vast Amount of Merit
5. You Will Not Receive Harm from Humans or Nonhumans
6. You Will Not Fall into the Lower Realms
7. You Will Accomplish All Your Wishes
8. You Will Quickly Attain Enlightenment

399. The *Praise of the Exalted One* was composed by Siddhisvami, and *Praise to the One Exceeding the Gods* was composed by Samkarapati.
400. The three sets of vows are the pratimoksha, bodhisattva, and tantric vows, which are all based on going for refuge.

You Become a Buddhist

It is taught that we should differentiate the unique features of Buddhists and non-Buddhists going for refuge. If you are without this refuge, it is as Geshe Potowa stated,

> Even the elder sitting with his eyes cast downward may not have entered the gateway of the Buddha's teachings.

If we don't have a pure act of going for refuge in our mental continuum, even the old lama at the head of the row won't receive any benefit; although he is a member of the monastery, he will not be associated with being a Buddhist. If you have a pure act of going for refuge, you will enter the ranks of the Buddhists.

Going for Refuge Functions as the Foundation for All Vows

If you don't go for refuge, there is no need to mention other vows. You cannot even generate the vows of a layperson. They all must be preceded by the act of going for refuge, which is the only way.

You Exhaust Your Previously Accumulated Karmic Obscurations

The son of a god who was on the brink of death and going to be reborn as a pig went for refuge, whereby he diminished the karmic obscurations for being reborn as a pig and was instead reborn in Tushita Pure Land. In the same way, if we engage in a well-founded act of going for refuge, it will have great power to purify our karmic obscurations.

You Accumulate a Vast Amount of Merit

If we accumulate merit through extremely powerful faith in the Three Jewels, it will transform into a powerful potential that will result in attaining vast stores of merit. If the merit of going for refuge were to possess form, even the three thousand worlds would be too small [to contain it].

You Will Not Receive Harm from Humans or Nonhumans

A heretic accomplished the attainment of a "wind noose,"[401] yet was unable to bind a person holding lay vows because that person had gone for refuge. In the same way, a certain person was punished by the king and was sent to the charnel grounds, yet the nonhuman beings there were unable to touch him. Regarding refuge, even merely saying the words has great power, as in the story of the robber who came to steal some cloth from a bhikshu.[402]

You Will Not Fall into the Lower Realms

Although you may meditate on the view of emptiness or the generation and completion stages at the time of your death, I am doubtful that this will prevent you from going to the lower realms. Yet if you engage in a pure refuge, you will most definitely not be reborn in the lower realms. Drogon Sangye Ön proclaimed,

> In short, if I do not generate [a realization of]
> Death and impermanence in my mental continuum,
> Guhyasamaja will not be profound.
> When I generate [a realization] of death in my mental continuum,
> The three verses of refuge are profound.

If you have not repeatedly meditated on practices such as the completion stage, they won't come at the time of your death. Regarding refuge, if you have complete confidence in the Three Jewels [and go for refuge] out of fear and faith without any hypocrisy, that will be sufficient.

401. This is a type of mundane attainment that allows one to manipulate subtle energies to physically subdue and manipulate beings.
402. When the robber arrived, the bhikshu beat him while reciting the refuge formula. Later, the robber slept under a bridge, and by reciting the words he had heard, he was protected from spirit harm.

You Will Accomplish All Your Wishes

Whatever kinds of happiness or suffering, good things or bad things, happen to you, don't place your hopes in nonhuman spirits, local guardians, and so forth. Instead, if the devout make offerings to the Three Jewels for all their needs and practice, they will easily accomplish what they need. Drom[tonpa] Rinpoche also stated,

> Don't let your trust in your personal deity lapse;
> In times of crisis, put less trust in humans.

Past holy beings said that although we need to accomplish a certain aim, we should not engage in deceptive means that are opposed to the Dharma; instead, we should accomplish them by making offerings to the Three Jewels.

You Will Quickly Attain Enlightenment

By going for refuge to the Three Jewels in this life, you will attain another life of leisure and endowment in your future life, come in contact with the Three Jewels, and train in the path, and before too long you will become enlightened and so forth. There are limitless ways in which it is beneficial.

The Stages of Precepts Once You Have Gone for Refuge has two sections:

1. The Individual Precepts
2. The Shared Precepts

The Individual Precepts has two sections:

1. Prohibitive Precepts
2. Prescribed Precepts

Prohibitive Precepts

Regarding the prohibitive precepts of going for refuge to the Buddha, having gone for refuge to the Buddha, you do not entrust yourself to other gods. It is improper to prostrate and go for refuge to the buildings housing statues of non-Buddhist deities such as Ishvara, worldly gods and spirits, nonhumans, king spirits, and so forth, by thinking they will care for you. It is permissible to entrust them with assistance for the sake of dispelling temporary obstructions, as though they were your townspeople, neighbors, and so forth. For example, it is like entrusting your friends and siblings by giving them a payment. Although you may collect alms from your benefactor and so forth, you are merely entrusting them with your temporary aims, and it is not necessary for you to think that you are going for refuge in them.

For the prohibitive precepts of going for refuge to the Dharma, because you have gone for refuge to the Dharma, you abandon harming living beings. The prohibitive precepts of going for refuge to the Sangha indicate that because you have gone for refuge to the Sangha, you should forsake your tirthika friends. Although not actual tirthikas, there is no difference between the [tirthikas] and the Bonpo, and you should not associate with your friends who do not have faith in the Three Jewels and so forth.

Prescribed Precepts

Regard Any Image of the Buddha as the Actual Buddha

Having gone for refuge to the Buddha, you should regard physical representations of the Buddha—including paintings, those composed of good and bad substances, and so forth—as being no different from the actual Buddha. It is inappropriate to be critical about the poor materials used to make a statue that is being sold and so forth. It is an extremely grave misdeed if we ascribe blame to the quality of a statue [itself], as related in the story of Supriyavat.[403] This is very beneficial [to know] in consideration of actions and their effects. There is no fault in assessing the quality of the craftsmanship, [however]. Previously, someone presented a statue of Manjushri to Je Atisha to inspect. [The person] asked [Atisha]

403. See Tsongkhapa, *The Great Treatise on the Stages of the Path to Enlightenment*, 1:195.

about its quality, saying that if it was good he would use the golden coins that Ronpa Gargye had given him to purchase it. Atisha replied, "It is not possible that the body of venerable Manjushri is not good. Regarding the craftsman, he is mediocre." Having said this, he placed it on his head. Atisha the Great also acted the same way toward many other holy images. Yeshe Dondrup, who is in the succession of lineage gurus, would say "Please rest easily"[404] [to holy images] in the evening, and in the morning would ask "How is your health?"[405] and so forth, and this was because he regarded them as actual [enlightened beings].

Regard Even a Single Letter of Scripture as the Actual Dharma Jewel

Having gone for refuge to the Dharma, it is inappropriate to step over any [piece of writing] on the topics taught by the Teacher, such as those written in Sanskrit, Chinese, Mongolian, and so forth, as well as the various forms of writing from Nepal and Tibet. My guru said that as a precept of going for refuge, it is inappropriate to regard even five-star coins and silver as more important [than Dharma texts]. This is quite true! If we dropped some money into a sewer, we would try to retrieve it with a long stick, yet if we dropped some writing in the middle of a cesspool, we would pretend that we didn't see it, even though we did, and keep going.

Geshe Chen-nga-wa would stand up and so forth when a Dharma text was brought into his presence. Later, although he was old and unable to stand, he would join his hands in prostration. When Je Tsongkhapa asked someone if he could borrow the *Stages of the Teachings* by Geshe [Drolungpa Lodro] Jungné, Je [Tsongkhapa] himself lit a stick of incense to welcome the *Stages of the Teachings* when it arrived, as is clearly displayed in the biography of Je [Tsongkhapa] as well as in the tangkha painting of the series of eighty images of Tsongkhapa. Do not wipe your nose on your texts, do not set things such as your eyeglasses on them, and don't step over them and so on. By engaging in acts of disrespect you are accumulating the karma of abandoning the Dharma. By doing so you are

404. Tib. *ga ler bzhugs*. This is an honorific Tibetan colloquial expression used when departing someone's company.

405. Tib. *sku gzugs bde po yin pas*. This is an honorific Tibetan colloquial expression used when greeting someone.

creating the cause to not understand books in all your lives. That being so, establish the recognition of even a single letter being the actual Dharma Jewel.

Regard Even a Patch of Red or Yellow Cloth from a Monk's Robe as the Actual Sangha Jewel

Having gone for refuge to the Sangha, develop the recognition that even the red and yellow worn by someone such as a disrobed monk, which is a mere reflection of a monk, is the actual Sangha Jewel, and don't act disrespectfully. Drom[tonpa] Rinpoche as well would regard even a patch of red and yellow that had fallen onto the ground as the actual Sangha and take it into his hands, shaking off the particles of dirt. He would then say, "It is not possible that there are not a few good qualities from wearing robes such as this on your body," after which he would touch it to the crown of his head, carry it to a clean place, and set it down. The *Sutra of the Ten Wheels of Kshitigarbha*[406] states,

> Even the dilapidated champaka flower
> Is vastly superior to other flowers.
> Even though a bhikshu may engage in derelict and negative
> actions,
> He is superior to all well-behaved tirthikas.

Similarly, like the musk from the corpse of a deceased deer and *giwang*[407] from the corpse of a deceased elephant, even a disrobed monk holding wrong views is superior to a learned and well-behaved practitioner of other [religions]. Therefore, it is inappropriate to despise him with disparaging words; by doing so we are in direct contradiction to our precepts of going for refuge. It is said that even something as insignificant as a patch of red and yellow from the robes of the Sangha should be regarded as the actual Sangha Jewel. The meaning of this is that the actual persons

406. Tib. *Sa'i snying po 'khor lo bcu pa'i mdo.*

407. Tib. *ghi wang.* This is actually a Sanskrit term used in the Tibetan language. It is the bile from elephants (and sometimes bulls) used as a medicinal substance to treat liver and gall-bladder diseases.

wearing such robes are the Sangha; it is not merely the robes that are considered the Sangha.

The Shared Precepts

To Go for Refuge by Repeatedly Recalling the Good Qualities of the Three Jewels

We go for refuge by recalling over and over the good qualities of the Three Jewels according to the previous explanation.

Offering the First Portion of Whatever You Eat or Drink

By doing this you will unceasingly accumulate very powerful merit. It is inappropriate for us to eat the white part of something like cheese and offer the moldy parts. Je Tsongkhapa stated,

> It would be a cause of enormous regret if we didn't take the opportunity to do something similar to what is explained in the sutra when it states, "May I unceasingly sow the seeds of happiness and well-being in the wondrous field of merit with the plow of faith in this ritual in all four seasons."

Lama Rahula explained to Atisha about the enjoyments that would result from offering [even] half a measure of rice and made a prophecy about a man who would send an invitation, who turned out to be the Tibetan king Lha Lama Jangchub Ö. Je Tsongkhapa stated, "Our way of not seeing the supreme field [of merit] even as an ordinary field is not good. Therefore, we should make a sincere effort at all times to make offerings to the Three Jewels."

If we carefully think over the words of the practices that we regularly recite, such as Lama Chöpa, the lamrim preliminary rituals, or the tsok offering , we will complete vast stores of merit with each passing moment. Although we study and listen to the Dharma, we don't understand the meaning of the words and are incapable of developing realizations and so forth. Whatever occurs isn't effective. However, if we earnestly visualize the field of merit and then accumulate merit, purify negative karma, make supplications, and so on, then our listening, contemplation, and meditation will be very beneficial and most effective. Je Rinpoche [Tsongkhapa] also stated,

> When we study, we don't retain the meaning; therefore, we don't understand the meaning when we contemplate. When we meditate, we don't develop [realizations] in our mental continuum and the power of our minds is extremely weak. At such times, it is an oral instruction to rely upon the power of the field of merit.

If we have faith, there will never be a shortage of substances to offer. As [Shantideva's] *Guide to the Bodhisattva's Way of Life* states,

> Clean water not held by an owner . . .

Thus, it is permissible to make such offerings offered in that way. It is unacceptable to not [make actual] offerings if we are wealthy. Je Rinpoche [Tsongkhapa] also stated,

> Some, being incapable of giving even though they have the resources, quote lines such as "I am not endowed with merit; I am very poor. I have no other wealth for offerings." Potowa said, "This is like a blind person trying to trick a sighted person by putting some incense made of weeds into an aromatic conch bowl and saying, 'This is water perfumed with sandalwood and camphor.'"

Although at the moment we have resources, it is the result of the accumulation of merit from a previous life. If we offer the best of whatever we can find from the earlier part of our life to the latter part of our life, the power of our merit will continuously flourish and increase. Geshe Phuchungwa stated,

> In the beginning, I offered incense made of grass that hurt my nose. Next, I obtained long sticks of sweet-smelling [incense] made of the four substances to offer. Now I offer aromatic *akaru*, *turuka*, and so forth.

Thus, you should offer whatever you can, even if it is nothing more than a small lamp offering the size of an eyeball. Bodhisattvas on the first and second levels and so on send forth countless emanations, whereby they engage in immeasurable acts of accumulation and purification. Thinking that we don't need to learn the profound meditations, such as the hand offering and so forth, reveals that we don't know anything about the Dharma.

Encouraging Others to Go for Refuge

There is great benefit in attempting to establish others in the practice of going for refuge by explaining the benefits of going for refuge to your family members, those who share your monk's quarters, and even your traveling companions.

Entrusting Yourself to Go to the Three Jewels as Your Refuge for Whatever Actions You Undertake

You should entrust yourself to the Three Jewels as your refuge for whatever actions you undertake. When there was a lack of favorable conditions while Je Rinpoche [Tsongkhapa] was restoring a statue of Maitreya in his celestial abode, he would supplicate the Three Jewels and entrusted Vaishravana to perform his enlightened actions by making butter torma offerings. Likewise, it is extremely important that, as we are about to accomplish our desired aims, we supplicate, make offerings, and so forth to the Three Jewels.

[Go for Refuge Three Times during the Day and Three Times during the Night][408]

Do Not Forsake the Three Jewels Even as a Joke or at the Cost of Your Life

We should properly protect the precept to not allow ourselves to [forsake] the Three Jewels even temporarily or as a joke.

408. This precept and any related comments are not included in our text. Therefore, I have merely included the heading for clarity. Interestingly, although it is included in the chapter headings in Tsongkhapa's *Middle-Length Treatise on the Stages of the Path,* there is no subheading or related comment. Pabongkha Rinpoche must be following the same structure.

Day Eighteen

The gentle protector, the lord of the Dharma [Tsongkhapa], stated,

> Leisure and endowment are difficult to find and there is no time to waste;
> Familiarize your mind with that fact and overcome craving for the things of this life.
> If you repeatedly contemplate the nondeceptive actions and their effects
> And the suffering of samsara, you will overcome craving for things in your future lives.

Although you may practice either of the two Dharmas of the Mahayana,[409] you absolutely must begin by overcoming your attachment to the things of this life. At the moment, whatever practice you undertake of listening, contemplating, and meditating, none of it becomes Dharma, which is the fault of not abandoning this life. Sachen Kunga Nyingpo also proclaimed, "If you cling to this life, you are not a Dharma practitioner." Although you may have overcome clinging to the things of this life, you still must not strive in any way whatsoever for the welfare of your future lives by wishing to attain the status of a god or human but instead develop an aspiration for liberation. To accomplish that, you must overcome your attachment to the things of your future life by contemplating actions and their effects as well as the faults of samsara. These two means of counter-

409. The two Dharmas of the Mahayana are the perfection vehicle and the mantra vehicle.

action are called "the stages on the path to enlightenment," "the Teacher's king of instructions," and so on.

After giving this introductory discourse, Pabongkha Rinpoche covered the headings and explained once again going for refuge as the gateway for entering the teachings.

There are three different ways of conjoining the causes of going for refuge with the three types of beings. The mind that fears the suffering of the lower realms and desires liberation from that is the act of going for refuge according to a being of small scope. Likewise, the fear of samsara [motivates the act of refuge of] a being of middle scope. Fearing all the disadvantages of samsara and peace [motivates the act of refuge of a being of] great scope or, in other words, the common Mahayana. Thinking "My object of attainment is the Three Jewels, and if I attain that I will be free from all fears; [therefore] that is what I shall attain" is the way of going for resultant refuge and is a unique way of going for refuge of the uncommon Mahayana. If you become the Sangha Jewel and develop the path of cessation in your mental continuum, this will liberate you from some portion of fear. Yet there is a great danger of your making a mistake in the way of going for refuge and generating bodhichitta that is unique to the Mahayana.

While carrying out the visualizations of the suffering of the lower realms and going for refuge, you should combine them as one system of training. With the exception of proper reliance upon the spiritual guide, the other meditations should be carried out after you withdraw the field of merit, visualize the guru on the crown of your head, and employ the descent of purifying nectar. While going for refuge, proceed with a new object of refuge in the space before you. Once you meditate on the suffering of something like the hell realms, recite "I go for refuge to the guru, deity, and Three Jewels" while your mind is imbued with faith in the objects of refuge in the space before you as having the power to protect you from that [suffering].

Although it is suitable to collect a count through this method, you should repeatedly go for refuge purely from the heart. You should recall the unique qualities of the objects of refuge. You can also substitute systems during the breaks in the lamrim preliminary ritual according to the other previous session breaks. Read books about the lower realms, and examine the texts of our Teacher that present [the ways of] going for refuge. There are extensive presentations of our Teacher about the lower realms in the *Supreme Dharma of the Application of Mindfulness*; therefore, you should examine it in detail. The principal precept of going for refuge is accepting and forsaking according to actions and their effects.

Developing Conviction and Faith in Actions and Their Effects as the Root of All Well-Being and Happiness

To develop this, we need to protect our moral discipline striving for the welfare of future lives. For that, we must [practice] accepting and abandoning according to actions and their effects. For that, we must know the methods of abandonment and acceptance. Contemplating actions and their effects is extremely important and is expressed in [Nagarjuna's] *Letter to a Friend*, which states,

> If you wish for higher status and liberation,
> It is imperative that you be familiar with the correct view.

This is stating that you must become familiar with the mundane correct view, which is actions and their effects. Shantideva also stated [in his *Guide to the Bodhisattva's Way of Life*],

> How can I attain certain liberation from
> Nonvirtue, the source of suffering?
> It is proper for me to contemplate only this
> At all times during the day and night.

Furthermore, we should gain the realization of karma through the four means of actions and their effects taught by the Bhagavan, which are (1) karma is certain, (2) karma increases, (3) if you didn't perform a karmic action, you won't meet with [its effect], and (4) a karmic action is never wasted. Some people pretend they have a high view and disregard actions and their effects, which means that they haven't understood the essential point of emptiness. The *King of Concentration Sutra* states,

> Like an illusion, river, mirage, and a flash of lightning,
> All phenomena are like the moon [reflected] in water.
> After death, we move on to another world;
> Although human beings are unobservable [in emptiness],
> The actions they perform will not become nonexistent.
> Karmic maturation functions in accordance with white and black [actions];
> This excellent means of logical reasoning
> Is subtle and difficult to perceive and is [only] the experience of the Conqueror.

And Geshe Potowa stated,

> Although we can understand emptiness through logic,
> Actions and their effects are extremely profound.

Atisha the Great relied upon his guru named Avadhutipa for many years. Sometimes he would engage in great actions of devotion. Although [Atisha] offered a golden mandala to request Dharma, [Avadhutipa] wouldn't teach him much. Sometimes he would teach him Dharma without being requested even though he had no free time. One day, he and Atisha were traveling together, and when they were about to cross a huge body of water on an extremely terrifying and narrow bridge, to stress its great importance, in the middle of the bridge [Avadhutipa] turned, faced [Atisha], and said, "My son, until you are free from self-grasping, you must refrain from even the most subtle ripening of karmic actions."[410]

Thus, if we disregard actions and their effects, although we may be pandits, siddhas, or bodhisattvas, we will go to hell. The *Jataka Tales* state,

> The maturations of karma are inconceivable;
> Even a compassionate person can be reborn as an animal.

410. Tib. *rnam par smin pa phra zhing phra ba la 'dzems.*

Nevertheless, if you are a bodhisattva, although you may be reborn in hell, you would continue to progress. Even there, your perception of the Dharma would not deteriorate. The *Ornament of the Mahayana Sutras* states,

> Even though you go to the lower realms for a long time,
> You will quickly become liberated.

Thus, through the force of that mind [of bodhichitta], you will quickly be liberated into a higher rebirth. Actions and their effects are subtle and precise; therefore, you should be careful with even the most subtle [actions], being sure that you absolutely don't tell lies and so forth. Whatever virtue and negativity you have performed will be clearly revealed in Yama's mirror of karma.

Previously, there was a man from Phenpo in the vicinity of Lhasa who had eaten religious offerings and died. When he arrived in hell, there was no one who could help him. Through the kindness of reciting the names of the buddhas in the *Sutra of a Hundred Invocations and Prostrations*, there is a method for coming back to life after death, yet if you disregard actions and their effects, even though you may be a mantra practitioner who has accomplished attainments, it won't benefit you. Previously, a young brahman man from India named Chanakya was a yogi of Yamantaka and used his power to "liberate"[411] many living beings, whereby he was reborn in hell, as related in the *Manjushri Root Tantra*.[412] This is similar to the story of a yogi of Vajrabhairava from the Pondo region in Phenpo. Drom[tonpa] Rinpoche was unable to bear it when the Tibetans engaged in even the most subtle negative actions, and he said to them, "Followers of Atisha, it is improper to be so bold; dependent relationship is subtle." Geshe Khamlungpa said to [Geshe] Phuchungwa, "Geshe, only cause and effect is important, yet these days no one explains it, listens to it, or meditates on it; I wonder if only this teaching is difficult to practice?" Phuchungwa replied, "It is just as you say."

Although the great shravakas were able to come to a decisive conclusion about emptiness, when it comes to the Vinaya and actions and their

411. Tib. *bskral*. This means to kill others with yogic powers.
412. Tib. *'Jam dpal rtsa rgyud*.

effects, the Buddha didn't teach it to anyone who wasn't capable of developing conviction in it. The expression of worship at the beginning of the texts on the Vinaya states, "I prostrate to the Omniscient One." Therefore, when it comes to these teachings about actions and their effects, we should develop conviction by accepting the validity that only the scriptures taught by the Conqueror contain [teachings] concerning actions and their effects. Even scholars with good qualities will easily go to the lower realms if they do not properly protect actions and their effects. Although Devadatta could read one heap of Dharma,[413] he didn't have faith in the Buddha; therefore, he went to the hot hells. His disciples went to the cold hells. Although the bhikshu Sunakshatra could comprehend the Three Baskets, it did not benefit him, and through his wrong views in the Buddha he went to the hot hells, as taught in the *Nirvana Sutra*.[414] Therefore, there are three contemplations about actions and their effects.

Actions and Their Effects has three sections:

1. Contemplating Actions and Their Effects in General
2. Contemplating the Specifics of Actions and Their Effects
3. The Way to Practice Engagement and Avoidance through Those Contemplations

Contemplating Actions and Their Effects in General has two sections:

1. The Actual Contemplation in General
2. Contemplating Their Individual Distinctions

The Actual Contemplation in General has four sections:

1. The Way in Which Karma Is Definite
2. Karma Increases Greatly
3. You Can't Meet with [the Results of] a Karmic Action That You Did Not Create
4. A Karmic Action Can Never Be Lost

413. Tib. *chos phung gcig*. In the Mahayana, one heap is generally regarded as one thousand verses.
414. Tib. *Myang 'das kyi mdo*.

The Way in Which Karma Is Definite

The feeling of well-being is feeling happiness. Je [Phurchog] Ngawang Jampa stated,

> Although at the moment we say, "The teachings have spread far and wide here in Tibet," as soon as an illness occurs in our bodies, we say we are being harmed by gods, nagas, and so forth. Yet the Buddha said that even something as insignificant as the poke of a thorn is the karmic maturation of similar actions we performed in the past. Therefore, we shouldn't blame harmful spirits, king spirits, and so on.

Sharawa [Yonten Drak] stated,

> The Buddha said that whatever misfortune there is arises only from engaging in a certain action whereby you are born in this life. Do not place the blame on others when things go wrong.

[Nagarjuna's] *Precious Garland* states,

> All suffering comes from nonvirtue,
> [And likewise all suffering migrations.
> All happy migrations come from virtue,
> As does the happiness in all rebirths.]

A sutra states,

> Whatever type of action we engage in,
> We will attain a similar result.

Just as it is not possible for anything other than barley—such as beans, wheat, and so on—to grow once you plant barley in a field, in the same way nothing other than happiness will grow as a result of accumulating virtuous actions, and [nothing other than] suffering will result from nonvirtuous actions. This point can be understood through ancient historical accounts such as the narration of Yashobhadrika who was previously a king, the raksha in India with eighteen heads who was previously a monk, a certain monk who was boiling the monks' robes, the daughter Sakama with thirty-two sons, and so on.[415]

Karma Increases Greatly

For example, although you may plant something as small as the seed of an apricot pit, it will increase so that it forms a trunk, branches, and much fruit, whereby even external cause and effect greatly increases. Likewise, although the cause may be a very small nonvirtue, it will emerge as massive suffering that is its result. Therefore, internal cause and effect increases much more than even external cause and effect. The Teacher made a prophecy that [a certain woman would become] a pratyekabuddha named Legmon. When Bhikshu Samten and a textbook reader got together, Samten would hurl insults at the other bhikshus, saying that they sounded like frogs until they went to bed, whereby he took five hundred rebirths as a frog. The novice monk Kyunté had told a bhikshu who was an arhat, "Your voice sounds like a dog howling," whereby he took rebirth as a dog five hundred times.

You Can't Meet with [the Results of] a Karmic Action That You Did Not Create

Some people say with amazement, "Although I didn't have anything such as a protection amulet, I was in the midst of a rain of bullets on the battlefield, yet nothing whatsoever happened." Yet there is nothing amazing about such situations, because if [the person] didn't create the karma necessary for him to die, then there is no other way for that to happen.

A Karmic Action Can Never Be Lost

Someone said, "You should wear many protection amulets in battle; so-and-so didn't get a protection amulet before going [into battle], and now he has been killed, which is because [the power of] his protection amulet

415. These stories can be found in more detail in Pabongkha Rinpoche, *Liberation in Our Hands*, under the heading "The Results of Karma Are Definite."

deteriorated." In fact, however, at that time [the person] had created the karmic action to die in the war, because [a karmic action] cannot be lost. Likewise, although King Udayana's queen, Shyamavati, and five hundred others had attained miraculous powers, they died by being burned in a fire, which is also because an action can never be lost. Although a female servant named Kubjottara had not attained miraculous powers, she was nevertheless able to escape through a water drain because she had not created the karma [to die] and, therefore, did not meet [with the results]. Moreover, the city of Roruka was overcome by a rain of earth. King Virudhaka and his minister were waging war and attacking the land of the Shakyas, whereby in one day seventy thousand Shakyas were killed, during which time the Teacher himself showed the aspect of contracting an illness in the upper part of his body. Afterward the king and his minister were also burned in a fire and died and so forth. Actions and their effects are extensively portrayed and applied in the narrations of the Teacher's former lives.

Pabongkha Rinpoche gave the following advice:

By contemplating the certainty of karma in this way, you will come to a decisive conclusion to engage in virtuous actions. By contemplating the great increase of karma, you will come to a decisive conclusion to engage in abandonment and adoption in relation to even the most subtle virtue and nonvirtue. By contemplating that you cannot encounter [the results] of an action that you did not create, you will come to a decisive conclusion to properly undertake confession and restraint through applying the four opponent powers to your negative karma. By contemplating how an action performed is never wasted, you will assess the virtuous actions you have engaged in and make completely pure dedication prayers; these four [aforementioned points] are vitally important.

Contemplating Their Individual Distinctions has two sections:

1. The Principal Teachings on the Ten Paths of Actions
2. Coming to a Definitive Conclusion about Actions and Their Effects

The Principal Teachings on the Ten Paths of Actions

If you safeguard the ten virtues through the principal teachings on the ten paths of actions [that is, karma], the *Scripture on Discernment*[416] states,

> If you joyously train in the three paths of actions,
> You will obtain the path taught by the Sage.

All the paths of the three scopes of beings can also be subsumed under going for refuge as well as moral discipline. During the small scope, you engage in the moral discipline of abandoning the ten nonvirtues; during the middling scope, individual liberation; and during the great scope, you engage in the moral discipline of the bodhisattva and tantric [vows]. Moral discipline is an extremely vast subject. Moral discipline is something for everyone from all statuses to safeguard, whether you are a layperson or ordained. If you have mistaken views, you will go to hell, and if you defile your discipline in other ways, you will be reborn as a hungry ghost and so forth. For that reason, it is extremely important that you safeguard your moral discipline. [Chandrakirti's] *Guide to the Middle Way* states,

> There is no cause other than moral discipline for the
> Higher status and definite goodness of ordinary beings,
> For those born from speech, for those definite in
> Self-enlightenment, and for the conquerors' sons.[417]

This is stating that other than moral discipline, there is no other cause for higher states. Whatever virtues you engage in should all be conjoined with moral discipline and performed on the foundation of moral discipline; this is a very practical way of proceeding. Regarding abandoning the ten nonvirtues, this is the cause of a human body of higher status of an ordinary being:

416. Tib. *Lung rnam 'byed.*
417. Those "born from speech" are shravakas, those "definite in self-enlightenment" are pratyekabuddhas, and the "conquerors' sons" are bodhisattvas.

Born from clairvoyance and concentration,
Their cause relies upon moral discipline;
The confused demonic view that they are without a cause
Is itself a broom sweeping away your restraint.

Those without moral discipline who pretend that they have high realizations and are learned are hypocrites. Such confused beings will fall back [into the lower realms] at the time of death. At the very least, it is absolutely necessary that [everyone, from] householders on up, safeguard the moral discipline of abandoning the ten nonvirtues. Regarding the result of the karma that you have engaged in and accumulated, if you have already accumulated nonvirtuous karma through the actual path of black actions, it is something that only you can experience and cannot ripen externally on the earth, stones, and so on.

While we have in our hands a working knowledge of what to adopt and what to forsake regarding virtue and nonvirtue, we must implement it right now. For that, we must learn the ten nonvirtues. There isn't any negativity that is not included within the ten nonvirtues. [Vasubandhu's] *Treasury of Abhidharma* states,

Having assembled the most important of them,
Whichever of the virtues and nonvirtues were appropriate
Were taught as the ten karmic paths.

A rough approximation of the most important actions that were taught by the Buddha about what should be adopted and [what should be] forsaken was compiled as the ten virtues and nonvirtues; therefore, the basis of the activities to be adopted and forsaken is the ten nonvirtues. Langdor Rinpoche also composed a collection of a few of them, after which they were distributed [to the populace]. The imperial rule also contains the sixteen secular purities that are based on the foundation of abandoning the ten nonvirtues; therefore, it is important that we properly safeguard all of these. For [those ten nonvirtues,] a verse states,

The three types of bodily actions . . .

The ten nonvirtues are included in the following: the three physical karmas are (1) killing, (2) stealing, and (3) sexual misconduct; the four of speech are (1) lying, (2) slander, (3) harsh speech, and (4) idle gossip; and the three nonvirtues of mind are (1) covetousness, (2) malice, and (3) wrong views. Each one of those has four aspects: (1) the basis, (2) the intention, (3) the preparation, and (4) the conclusion. The intention has three aspects: (1) discrimination, (2) afflictive emotion, and (3) motivation.

Killing

Regarding the basis of killing, it must be another living being that is an opponent and so on, which is clear in the texts for identifying the ten nonvirtues. If you have the thought of intending to kill a dog and then you kill something [else] like a human, you do not have a complete karmic path of killing. Killing out of attachment would be something like striving to procure flesh; out of hatred would be like killing your enemy; and out of ignorance would be like killing a sheep for the purpose of presenting it as an animal sacrifice through the mistaken Dharma of non-Buddhists such as the non-Buddhist heretics. Killing does not need to be done through weapons, for there is no difference between that and killing with poisons, mantric substances, black magic, and so forth; they are also killing. Even if you are able to kill something through wrathful actions, if you are unable to restore its life, it is not good.

Although someone like a bhikshu may agree with ten people to kill one sheep, each of the ten people will receive the karmic maturation of killing a sheep; therefore, each one must experience the fruit of a complete negativity of killing. If such a thing happens, the bhikshu is a butcher holding a begging bowl and walking staff, and he is no different from a butcher who is a layperson wielding a knife, and they will both meet with the effects of being a butcher. For that reason, there is absolutely no difference between performing the killing yourself or allowing someone else to do it. The Mongolian Ngawang Khedrup composed a narrative of parables about a monk and a goat, a sheep, and a cow.[418] Moreover, [Vasubandhu's] *Treasury of Abhidharma* states,

418. This story is related in Pabongkha Rinpoche's *Liberation in Our Hands.*

> Because in battle and so forth they are fulfilling one purpose,
> They are all similar to the performer [of the deed of killing].

With respect to the person who stays behind yet provided counsel at the beginning of a war, he receives the negative karma of however many people died on the battlefield; therefore, the army commander receives the entire negative karma for however many people were killed by many other people in war.

Killing even lice and bugs is a great nonvirtue through which you will go to hell. If you get lice and lice eggs on your body, take some roasted barley flour and mix it with pure butter, rub it onto some sheep's wool, and place them inside. Don't smear them on something like walls of the temple but set them in a safe place without injuring them, setting them near other creatures that will eat them, and so on. If you have to expel bugs, mice, and so forth from your living quarters, you should gently pick them up and carry them to another place while harming them as little as possible. These teachings have their source in the *Three Hundred Verses of the Vinaya*.

Just as much as you value your own life, and in the same way that you would be terrified and suffering if someone came to kill you, it is the same with others who are killed and those waiting to be executed. In particular, those who are ordained bhikshus and novices make a promise to abandon killing from the outset and must refrain from killing in this life.

Stealing

Stealing out of attachment is the most well-known [sort of theft]; [stealing out of] hatred is robbing from one's enemy; [stealing out of] ignorance is performed by the non-Buddhists and so forth who teach a Dharma of stealing when a brahman is destitute. According to such explanations, it is not a fault to steal; thinking in this way, they steal from others. In general, it is not only sneaking around behind someone's back that is stealing, [thus] acquiring through deceptive means, [but also] stealing by force without being entitled to it. If we borrowed something a long while ago and the owner has forgotten and so forth, whereby we employ means to make it our own, when such things occur we also incur the fault of stealing.

These are very difficult [actions not to commit]; therefore, in the evening when we lie down to go to sleep, we should examine to see whether or not such things have occurred, and if they have occurred, we should perform confession, restraint, and so forth.

Sexual Misconduct

Although the teachings state [that sexual misconduct is] the meeting of the two sexual organs of [yourself and] someone other than your wife, both the correct and incorrect paths constitute sexual misconduct. The ordained are practicing celibacy; therefore, an ordained person not maintaining celibacy constitutes sexual misconduct. Regarding the afflictive emotion, this can be committed through all three poisons. Pretending that a non-dharmic action is Dharma and calling it "the path of skillful means," "the path of attachment," and so on, is completely inappropriate and is sexual misconduct out of ignorance.

Lying

Lying does not necessarily have to be a verbal action; it could be a facial expression and so forth, and if by doing so it becomes a way of displaying a lie, [then] it is also a lie. A bhikshu who says he has perceived the good qualities of the higher realms when he hasn't perceived them or who says he has realized something he hasn't realized and is falsely proclaiming himself to be a guru incurs a defeat.[419] A common lie does not become a defeat.[420]

Slander

While engaging in slander, you could engage in slanderous discussions about the Dharma, which is slander due to ignorance. Slander can be either true or untrue. Lies and slander flow from our mouths continuously. We don't think it is a fault and count it as one of our good qualities.

419. Tib. *pham pa*. A defeat is an offense that causes you to immediately lose your ordination.

420. Lying about one's spiritual attainments by claiming that one has higher realizations than one really does is a defeat. Other types of lies are an offense that can be restored through *sojong*, Tib. *gso sbyong*. Here *gso* means "restoration" and *sbyong* means "purification." The term *sojong* refers to a bimonthly ceremony carried out by members of the Sangha to purify and restore their vows.

Because we do it so often, it is the heaviest of the verbal nonvirtues; therefore, it is a great fault.

Harsh Speech

Harsh speech is spoken out of the vindictive attitude of an unhappy mind. This also has a variety of forms of being true and untrue. Doing something like calling someone a cripple when they are not crippled is both harsh speech and a lie. Many teachers speak this way to their students, their principal attendant, and so forth. Merely moving your lips can propel you into the lower realms through the accumulation of extremely severe karma. Although you may not speak with offensive words out of anger, if a teacher and so forth says to a student that he [or she] didn't do his [or her] work properly and says something like "a-dzig kusho,"[421] and their conversation causes the other person to develop mental suffering, then it is considered harsh speech. The basis of harsh speech can be both sentient and nonsentient beings; when we complain about things by saying things such as "This damn weather is terrible," even though it is not a sentient being, we should still abandon saying such things and worse, because if our mind becomes accustomed to this, [it contradicts] the following verse:

> It is even important to the conquerors' sons
> That negativity does not occur and that virtue increases within.

In this way these [nonvirtues] become easy to possess.

Idle Gossip

This is speaking about a variety of meaningless things. For people like us monks, this means talking about the warmth of the sun during the wintertime and so forth, or when we are doing things like going along the circumambulation path around Lhasa and a few of us get together and talk about how our bag of tsampa is almost empty and discuss the numerous coral ornaments from India and so on. Although idle gossip is the least of the ten nonvirtues, because it bears such a great risk of wasting this

421. This is a derogatory colloquial expression.

leisure and endowment, it is [actually] the worst. With the exception of reading the biographies of the gurus and so forth, it amounts to idle gossip if we do things such as read novels and sing.

Covetousness

Of the three mental faults, covetousness is performed with attachment. It has both a mind attached to one's own wealth and a mind of amassing it. There is a mind [wishing] to experience others' wealth and a mind of competition. When your sense of shame and [understanding the faults] are overcome, together with all five principals [of covetousness],[422] [then covetousness] is complete. Regarding the minds of preparation, actual act, and completion, they determine the degree of strength which that movement of the mind possesses.

Malice and Wrong Views

Malice and wrong views are motivated by a mind of anger and a mind of ignorance, respectively, and when all five principals [of malice[423] and five principals of wrong views][424] are intact, their acts are complete.

422. The five principals of covetousness are having (1) a mind exceedingly attached to your own possessions, (2) a mind of attachment that wishes to accumulate possessions, (3) a mind of longing due to the understanding or experiencing of the wealth and so forth of others, (4) a mind of envy thinking that others' possessions should be your own, and (5) a mind that, due to covetousness, is overcome by shamelessness and oblivious to the determination to be free from its faults.

423. The five principals of malice are (1) hostility reifying the apprehension of the characteristics of the causes of harm and the phenomena related to them, (2) impatience with those doing harm to you, (3) resentment based on repeated inappropriate attention to and mindfulness of the causes of your anger, (4) envy that thinks, "How wonderful if my enemies were beaten or killed," and (5) being dominated by shamelessness and being impervious to the determination to be free from its faults.

424. The five principals of wrong views are (1) confusion due to lacking precise knowledge about the objects of knowledge, (2) a violent attitude due to delighting in harmful actions, (3) an intention that continuously operates in the wrong way due to contemplating improper teachings, (4) an intention that is impaired due to mistaken denial which thinks that things such as gifts, religious offerings, burnt offerings, and correct behavior do not exist, and (5) an intention that is dominated by shamelessness and oblivious to the determination to be free of its faults.

Wrong Views

This is a view like those held by non-Buddhists, the Bon, and so forth, who maintain that the four noble truths, the Three Jewels, actions and their effects, and so on are nonexistent.

Of these ten, there are various factors that determine whether or not it is a karmic path. [Vasubandhu's] *Treasury of Abhidharma* states,

> Although there are three paths, there are seven actions.

The three mental nonvirtues are not paths of actions [that is, karma] because there is no causal [motivation] or timely motivation[425] whatsoever; they are paths because they have the basis for the mental factor of engagement concomitant with oneself.[426] Regarding the actions of body and speech, because there is the timely motivation while engaging in that action, it is an action as well as a path. In this context, the body and speech are the basis of the intended engagement; therefore, the seven [nonvirtues] of body and speech are actions as well as paths.

The Prasangikas and the Vaibhashikas assert that karmic actions of body and speech also possess form. The two terms "action of willing" and "mental activity" are synonymous.[427] The terms "thought-motivated action" and "actions of body and speech" are synonymous.[428] Before finishing an action such as killing through body and speech, it is an "action of willing," and while it is happening it is "thought-motivated action."

425. For every karmic action, there is an initial causal motivation that arises before the action and then a timely motivation that exists at the very moment the action is performed. The causal motivation includes the various preparations to engage in the action, and the timely motivation exists at the very moment the action is performed.

426. The mental nonvirtues of covetousness, malice, and wrong view are not actions that are carried out in relationship to others (although they can be motivating factors). Therefore, they are "paths" but not "paths of actions." The seven related to body and speech are carried out in relation to others; therefore, they are both "paths" and "paths of actions."

427. Tib. *sems pa'i las* and *yid kyi las*, respectively.

428. Tib. *bsam pa'i las* and *lus ngag gi las*, respectively.

Day Nineteen

A teaching of Je Tsongkhapa states,

> Body and life are like bubbles adrift on the water . . .
> Grant your blessing that I may always be extremely cautious.

This quote reveals that although we have now obtained what is difficult to obtain and has great meaning, we will find this excellent physical form just once, and it won't last long, because death is certain and the time of death is uncertain. It is also certain that after death we must take rebirth and that happiness and suffering each follow whatever white and black actions we have performed and will never come after the actions of another.

By contemplating in this way, you must strive to properly accomplish the practice of abandoning negative action and accomplishing virtue. Because of that, it is certain that only virtue will benefit our next life and only negative actions will bring us harm. Someone who properly practices abandoning negative action and accomplishing virtue will be able to shut the door to the lower realms, for which introspection endowed with conscientiousness is indispensable. Thinking along these lines, consider that listening to this excellent profound commentary on the stages of the path to enlightenment, which is the Teacher's king of instructions, perfectly reveals the means of [abandoning negative action and accomplishing virtue].

After giving this introduction to adjust our motivation, Pabongkha Rinpoche restated the headings. He once again explained that the root of all happiness and well-being comes from developing faith and confidence in actions and their effects.

Previously, a scholar from China composed a commentary using the analogy of a snake, where he compared other scholars to a snake, whereby the composer himself transformed into a snake; what need, [therefore,] is there to mention [what will happen to] us?

Not only have arhats directly realized emptiness, but they are able to remain in meditative absorption for up to an eon in the sphere of the complete pacification of pervasive suffering. When you encounter actions and their effects, not even the slightest bit passes beyond karma following whatever white and black actions you have performed, as related in the narrative of Arya Gurchung.[429] Although the corpse of the deceased mother of the arhat Merkye [Fire-Born] was incinerated while he was still in her womb, he wasn't burned in the fire. The Teacher predicted that Merkye had the potential to become an arhat, and later he became ordained in the teachings of the Buddha and attained the state of an arhat.

According to previous accounts, regardless of whether you are a scholar, a siddha, or have had a direct vision of your personal deity and so on, if you disregard actions and their effects you will go to hell. Detailed accounts concerning actions and their effects should be learned from texts such as the *Vinaya Scripture*, the *Sutra of the Wise and Foolish*, the *One Hundred Formal Procedures*, *A Hundred Narrations*, the *[Supreme Dharma of the] Application of Mindfulness Sutra*, and so on. We must do everything possible to refrain from engaging in even the smallest or most insignificant nonvirtue. We should not take lightly even the slightest virtue but should engage in accomplishing as much as we are capable of.

The Distinction in Weight has two sections:

1. The Heaviness of the Ten Paths of Actions
2. A Concise Teaching on the Criteria for Powerful Actions

429. Tib. sGur chung. No matter how hard Gurchung attempted to obtain alms, he could not, and he finally passed away due to starvation.

The Heaviness of the Ten Paths of Actions

The distinctions that determine the weightiness of the ten nonvirtues are explained in *Actuality of the Stages*[430] as six, and when combined with one oral instruction of the guru, there are seven. Also, there are various ways of explaining them in [Nagarjuna's] *Letter to a Friend* and so on, which list five, nine, and so forth. Here, we shall consider seven by way of (1) nature, (2) the intention, (3) the preparation, and (4) the absence of an antidote, as well as (5) the basis, (6) being continuously performed, and (7) heaviness due to the foundation.

By way of **nature**, each of the preceding nonvirtues of body and speech is heavier, and each of the subsequent ones is lighter.[431] Each of the preceding nonvirtues of mind is lighter, and each of the subsequent ones is heavier. Concerning **intention**, it is permeated by powerful afflictive emotions. The **preparation** is carried out through a variety of harmful actions. To use killing living beings, such as a flea, louse, and so forth, as an example, we first rub it and scratch it for a long time and finally kill it, making [the karmic action] heavy. Being heavy by way of **absence of antidote** is when we accumulate negative karma and we continuously and utterly refrain from performing virtue, making it heavy. With respect to heavy by way of **basis**, this is when we accumulate negative karma in dependence upon a special field [such as the buddhas and bodhisattvas]. **Being continuously performed** is someone like a butcher who constantly engages in killing, making it heavy. With respect to being heavy by way of **the foundation**, this refers to the presence or absence of vows and to being engaged in by someone with higher and lower vows. A bhikshu who kills a louse through employing various painful actions, or someone who never performs any virtue such as a butcher and who kills with very strong afflictive emotions, employing horrible methods, [and who] kills [someone] such as his mother, [accumulates very] heavy [nonvirtue] because of completing numbers four, six, and so on [listed above].

430. Tib. *Sa'i dngos gzhi.*

431. This means that killing is heavier than stealing, stealing is heavier than sexual misconduct, and so on.

A Concise Teaching on the Criteria for Powerful Actions

With respect to the **field**, this is your father and mother, the Three Jewels, your guru, and so on. Whatever virtue or negativity you perform [with respect to] these bases, even without powerful intention, is powerful by way of the field. In particular, whatever virtue or nonvirtue you perform in relation to a bodhisattva, such as presenting offerings or acting out of malice, is also powerful by way of field, as taught in the sutras and their related scriptures.

By way of **foundation** is explained in the following verse:

> A wise person's negativity is heavy due to repetitiveness;
> A fool's negativity is heavy due to repetitiveness.

The power of whatever virtue or negativity is performed by [various people]—from an ordinary person without any vows, to a person with lay vows, to the ordained [who are not bhikshus], and to bhikshus, as well as to those [laypersons] holding two vows and holding three vows—increases in sequence from the former to the latter.[432] If a layperson promises to safeguard one vow and so on, then even while that person is sleeping, he [or she] accumulates one type of virtue and so forth, sequentially increasing [according to the number of vows he or she has]. Regarding someone with bodhisattva vows, even while sleeping, that person accumulates merit equal to space. For secret mantra, that person's [merit] increases even more than that. In the same way, through the cooperative cause of an army commander's promise, a hunter's, a butcher's, a prostitute's, and so on, even though they are not vows, they have made a commitment [to their respective professions], so their negative karma unceasingly increases even while they sleep.

By way of **nature** means that giving Dharma has greater power than giving material things, and an offering of practice has more power than an offering of material things. Regarding **intention**, compared to someone who already has bodhichitta, even if each and every living being in

432. This means that the power of the negative and positive action of each person increases sequentially as you move up from a person with no vows to a bhikshu.

the three thousand worlds who doesn't have bodhichitta were to present offerings for an eon to all the physical representations of all the buddhas in the ten directions, as well as stupas and so forth, the merit of someone with bodhichitta who offered one flower would be greater. Someone such as a bhikshu who has bodhichitta and who recites the lamrim preliminary prayers, Ganden Lha Gyama, and so forth has all four powers [listed above].

It makes no difference whether you are reciting in an assembly or in your room; therefore, if your recitation in an assembly is done properly, it performs the function of recitation. Still, there is great benefit in the Sangha reciting in an assembly, gathered together indivisibly. Whether it is in a monastery or village temple, they bear the responsibility of properly maintaining the codes of conduct. You should mentally reflect on the profound meaning of the profound words you are chanting in the group recitations. At the very least, consider how extremely fortunate you are to be reciting the mere words in their entirety and even to be hearing phrases such as "Buddha, Dharma, and Supreme Assembly." Investigate the meaning of method and wisdom, and perform the recitation while recalling the meaning of the words. If that happens, with the mere words you will be able to purify a vast amount of obscurations. Even someone such as a layperson who continuously recites the Mani mantra should recite it very well, without any additions or omissions. Some people first recite the Mani and affix HRIH and pretend it is pure; however, in the *Sutra Designed as a Jewel Chest*[433] and others, it states, "The heart of Avalokiteshvara is the six syllables." It doesn't say there are more than six seed syllables; therefore, we don't need to add the seventh syllable [HRIH].

In general, recitations such as exhortations should be done during things such as restoration and purification rituals;[434] however, combining [exhortations] with other recitations will create a dependent relationship for you to have a short life.[435] At the beginning of the recitation of

433. Tib. *mDo za ma tog*.

434. Tib. *bskang gso*.

435. Restoration and purification rituals have a very precise means of addressing wrathful deities, whereby even if you are very direct with them, using strong language and so forth, it does not offend them or their retinues. Done improperly, these types of rituals can have an adverse effect on your lifespan.

an exhortation, you recite "Listen here," and offer respect as a way of respectfully presenting [the deities] with a seat. Finally you say "Come here," as a means of lengthening to create the auspiciousness for the Buddha's teachings to remain for a long time.

A Teaching on the Effects of Those [Actions] has three sections:

1. The Ripened Result
2. The Result Similar to the Cause
3. The Environmental Effect

If you don't properly avoid nonvirtue, in addition to merely being led to a rebirth in the lower realms, you will have to experience four results.[436]

The Ripened Result

The ripened result of each of the ten great nonvirtues such as killing and so forth is hell; [that of] each of the ten middling nonvirtues is [rebirth as] a hungry ghost; [and] each of the ten lesser nonvirtues [results in] rebirth as an animal.[437]

The Result Similar to the Cause has two sections:

1. The Experience Similar to the Cause
2. The Effect Similar to the Cause

The Experience Similar to the Cause

Despite being born as a human after being in the lower realms, you will experience [the following results, beginning] with killing and so forth, arranged in sequence: (1) [For killing,] you will have a short life. (2) [For stealing,] you will be poor in resources. (3) [For sexual misconduct,] your wife, companion, retinue, attendants, and so forth will not obey you and will leave you for someone else. (4) [For lying,] others will deceive and rob you as well as slander you a great deal. (5) [For slander,] you will not

436. These four results are now enumerated in the next section.
437. The great, middling, and lesser here refers to the way that each of the ten nonvirtues was carried out, which determines its severity, as mentioned above.

have harmony among your retinue, attendants, and so on. (6) [For harsh speech,] others will not have pleasant things to say about you, and even if you try to speak politely, they will not understand you. (7) [For idle gossip,] although you may speak the truth, they will not believe you and your words will not be considered honorable. (8) [For covetousness,] you will have strong desire and no contentment. (9) [For malice,] there will be numerous harms acted out against you. (10) [For wrong views], even in other lives you will be born with perverse views. In the *Precious Garland* Nagarjuna states,

> Through killing come a short life and numerous illnesses.
> Through stealing you are poor in resources.
> Through sexual misconduct come enemies.
> From lying come dislike and slander.
> From idle gossip you have few friends and are separated from
> those dear to you.
> From harsh speech you hear what is unpleasant.
> From idle gossip your words are not trusted.
> Through covetousness your wishes are destroyed.
> Through malice you are bound by fear and trepidation.
> Through wrong view come disturbed views.

The Effect Similar to the Cause

According to the sequence [of the ten nonvirtues of] the various actions such as killing and so forth, you will delight in killing and so forth, and through such actions you will again go to the lower realms. When various undesirable things occur in this life, it is the effect similar to the cause, such as the ten nonvirtues that you performed in a previous life. [Being reborn as living beings] such as cats, mice, and so forth that are skilled at killing and stealing is the effect similar to the cause of having stolen in a previous life. If you have an overabundance of thoughts, this is the karmic maturation of speaking aggressively.

In this life you once again accumulate nonvirtue, after which you will go to the lower realms; therefore, it is very important that in this life you shun them and act with conscientiousness. Several of the holy beings and so forth acted excellently, and they had natural faith and admiration for virtue from the time they were very young, which is the effect similar to the cause of having practiced virtue in a previous life.

The Environmental Effect

Regarding the environmental effect,[438] this ripens as the external worldly environment. Furthermore, through killing, your food, drink, and medicine will have little power, will be difficult to digest, and won't agree with your physical constitution. Through stealing, you will have droughts and floods, your [crops] will yield very few harvests, and your yogurt, butter, milk, and so forth will diminish. There will be heavy snow for the nomads in the winter, and droughts will occur for the local people in the summer. Thus, when people of a certain region engage in stealing, it ripens externally as the environmental effect. Through sexual misconduct, the place where you live will have a multitude [of impurities], such as being muddy, filthy, unclean, and so forth.

Through lying, you will be deceived and very fearful. Through slander, the land will not be level, will be bumpy, will be difficult to traverse, and will not have grass, trees, and so forth. Through harsh speech, there will be numerous unpleasant features such as logs, thorns, gravel, river banks that are at a steep incline, and so on. Through idle gossip, the fruit trees will not develop fruit or they will develop fruit at the wrong time.

Through covetousness, business will be scarce through objects such as food, clothes, and so on, and all the best things in life, such as crops, cattle, and so forth, will progressively decline. Through malice, there will be a great deal of harm and injury from humans and nonhumans, such as battles, epidemics, and so on. Through wrong views, although it is taught that good will overcome evil, there is a saying that states, "The sources of the finest things are waning," and these days it is as if riches such as gold and so forth, which were previously valued, don't have any value, and the source of the jewels is declining.

Presently, whatever happiness and suffering we have in this life are all the result of the virtue and nonvirtue [we performed] in a previous

438. Tib. *bdag po'am dbang gyi 'bras bu*. This is also called the dominant or empowering effect.

life. Therefore, if we wish for happiness in our next rebirth and the lives after that, from this moment onward we must properly perform forsaking [nonvirtuous] and adopting [virtuous] actions and their effects.

Contemplating Virtuous Cause and Effect has two sections:

1. Virtuous Actions
2. Their Results

Virtuous Actions

If you are about to engage any of the ten nonvirtues and immediately stop yourself, that nonengagement is a path of virtuous karma that is in opposition to the ten nonvirtues. For example, abandoning killing is an illustration of a karmic path. The basis is another living being. The intention is the thought not to kill, by observing its faults and [cultivating] the desire to abandon [killing]. The preparation is embodied in the activity of correctly restraining yourself from killing. The completion is the physical karma of not killing that is completed by perfect restraint. You can apply the same reasoning of this system to the [other nine virtues].

Their Results has three sections:

1. The Ripened Result
2. The Result Similar to the Cause
3. The Environmental Effect

The Ripened Result

Great virtuous actions will result in [rebirth as] a god in the higher realms, middling [virtuous actions will result in rebirth] as a desire-realm god, and lesser [virtuous actions will result in] a human rebirth.

The Result Similar to the Cause has two sections:

1. The Experience Similar to the Cause
2. The Tendencies Similar to the Cause

The Experience Similar to the Cause

Through sequentially abandoning killing and so forth, you will have a long life, vast enjoyments, and so on. Although some thieves and butchers have vast resources and long life and so on, this is the result of their [actions] in a previous [life].

The Tendencies Similar to the Cause

You will sequentially delight in abandoning killing and so forth.

The Environmental Effect

Food, drink, and medicine will have great efficacy; these are the opposite of the nonvirtuous environmental effects.

A Presentation of Other Classifications of Karma has two sections:

1. The Distinction between Projecting and Completing Karma
2. Karma Whose Result You Will Definitely or Only Possibly Experience

The Distinction between Projecting and Completing Karma

Although virtue will project you into a happy rebirth and nonvirtue will project you into the lower realms, there is no certainty with respect to completing karma. With respect to being projected through nonvirtuous projecting karma and being completed through virtuous completing karma, this [would result in] births [in forms] such as [those of] a powerful naga or hungry ghost. In short, this also applies to the riding horse or pet dog and so forth of a great lama or official. Being projected by virtuous projecting karma and completed with nonvirtuous completing karma would be to become someone with a human body who is destitute; has a short life, many illnesses, incomplete sense faculties, and poor physique;

is imprisoned; and so forth. If you understand these two, the other two are easy to understand.[439]

Karma Whose Result You Will Definitely or Only Possibly Experience

For this, there is both the karma that you are certain to experience and the karma that you are not certain to experience. A complete accumulation of an action and one that we are certain to experience are synonymous. Even for this [karma that we are certain to experience], there is also one that is definitely purified when powerful and effective confession has been carried out through the four opponent powers. For example, if you have the motivation intending to engage in an act such as killing yet there is no actual basis of killing, you nevertheless accumulate [the karma of killing].[440] [Conversely,] without a mind thinking about the act of killing, even when you kill a bug under your foot while you are walking, you don't accumulate the karma [of killing]. You don't accumulate the karma even if you engage in killing against your will. You don't accumulate [the karma of killing] if it is done in a dream and so forth; therefore, it is not definite that you will experience its results.

If you are willing, have the motivation, and actually engage in an action, then you have a complete accumulation of an action, and you will be certain to experience its results. Regarding the mode of experience, there are actions that you will experience in this life such as great negative actions carried out in relation to a special field. It is a unique quality of this world that noble causes such as studying, contemplating, and so on carried out in the earlier part of one's life can be experienced in the later part of one's life as the state of enlightenment and so forth.

Regarding the experiences once you have taken rebirth, they can be experienced in two lives or experienced over a number of other lives, such as being experienced from the third life onward.

439. The other two would be to have nonvirtuous projecting karma and nonvirtuous completing karma, or to have virtuous projecting karma and virtuous completing karma.
440. For more on these points, see Tsongkhapa, *The Great Treatise on the Stages of the Path to Enlightenment*, 1:241.

Day Twenty

[In his *Songs of Spiritual Experience*,] Jamgon Tsongkhapa the Great stated,

> You will not make an effort if you do not contemplate the faults of the truth of suffering,
> And you will not strive for liberation.
> If you do not contemplate the stages of entering samsara and the true origins,
> You will not know how to sever the root of samsara.
> Therefore, rely upon aversion and renunciation of all existence,
> And cherish the knowledge of what binds us to samsara.

Contemplate, "Thus, if I wish to strive for liberation from samsara, once I contemplate the faults of the truth of suffering, I must develop a mind that has a natural revulsion for samsara; when that occurs, I will easily give birth to a mind striving for liberation. For that, I must consider severing the root of samsara. For that reason, I am going to listen to the stages of the path to enlightenment."

After giving this brief introduction to set our motivation, Pabongkha Rinpoche covered the headings. He once again explained the distinction that determines the heaviness of the black karmic actions.

Contemplating the Specifics of Actions and Their Effects has two sections:

1. The Good Qualities and Function of Karmic Maturations
2. The Cause of Karmic Maturations

SERLINGPA

The Good Qualities and Function of Karmic Maturations

Je Lama [Tsongkhapa] also stated [in his *Songs of Spiritual Experience*],

> Until you attain a physical form with all the characteristics
> For accomplishing the supreme path, you will not make much
> progress;
> Therefore, train in the causes to complete them.

You should not be content through merely obtaining a human body, accomplished by protecting your moral discipline of abandoning the ten nonvirtues. Instead, you must attain a physical form endowed with the eight good qualities of karmic maturation for accomplishing the state of liberation and omniscience. Although we won't understand how to accomplish the eight good qualities of karmic maturation from a teaching on the sadhana of our personal deity, we will definitely attain [the eight good qualities of karmic maturation] if we accomplish the cause to attain an excellent physical form with eight special qualities of karmic maturation on the basis of perfectly protecting our moral discipline of abandoning the ten nonvirtues. If that happens, the amount of ground we can cover on the path of meditation will be like nothing else.

The eight good qualities are (1) a consummate lifespan, (2) consummate color, (3) consummate lineage, (4) consummate power, (5) great renown, (6) trustworthy words, (7) being a male,[441] and (8) being endowed with strength. Regarding the functions of these eight, through a long life, you will perfect whatever Dharma you engage in. Through an excellent form,[442] you will attract many disciples. Through a high lineage, you will be respected and venerated by all people. Through great resources, you will be able to attract a retinue by fulfilling the aspirations of your disciples with material things. Through great power, everyone will automatically listen to what you say. Through trustworthy words, everyone will have high regard for whatever you instruct them to do because they will accept you as being true. Through being born a male, you will have few obstacles to engaging in virtue. Through being endowed with physical and mental strength, you will be able to practice Dharma like Je Mila[repa] and will have the great strength to accomplish attainments.

The Cause of Karmic Maturations

Although it is important to acquire [karmic maturations], you may wonder about not acquiring such [qualities]. For example, to pick fruit in the

441. At the time of Buddha Shakyamuni, especially in what is now India, it was much more advantageous to be born a man than a woman. This is not meant to be discriminatory toward women. If anything, it speaks to the defects of samsara.
442. Here, color is an aspect of form.

fall, you must plant seeds in the spring. Likewise, by its very nature, if you assemble a complete set of causes, they will bear fruit; if you accomplish the causes for these [eight qualities], you will reap the results. Therefore, the causes of the first of the good qualities of karmic maturation are to abandon killing, care for the ill, give medicine, save lives, not engage in harming other living beings in thought or action, and so on. The causes of the second [good quality] are to build statues of the Conqueror, repair them, repair the coloring of their garments, offer butter lamps and so forth, give new garments, meditate on patience, and so forth. The causes of the third one are to abandon pride and to act with respect to your guru, master, father, mother, and so on, as if you were their servant. The causes of the fourth are to benefit those of various social standings with necessities and to engage in generosity. The causes of the fifth are to revere and worship your abbot, master, father, mother, and so on, as well as your teachers and educators, and to make prayers that will lead to various good qualities in your next life. The cause of the sixth is to abandon nonvirtuous speech. The causes of the seventh are to have a dislike for articles of women [such as clothing, jewelry, and so forth], to forsake castrating living beings for the sake of obtaining rebirth in a male body, to recite the names of the five bodhisattvas such as Yeshe Lama Ö Kyi Tog, and so forth. [For example,] if a monk who has a stallion engages in castrating it, this will be the cause not only of going to the lower realms but also, despite the fact that he has obtained a male body [in this life], of taking numerous subsequent rebirths as a woman; therefore, it is utterly inappropriate. The causes of the eighth [good quality] are to accomplish yourself the actions that others are incapable of doing or to assist them [in this], to not engage in beating others, and so forth, as well as to give food and drink [to others].

While accomplishing all eight [good qualities], as explained in the scriptures, if the three aspects of a pure intention, pure preparation, and pure field are also complete [in the actions that produce the eight good qualities], they will become great. Through accomplishing the causes in this way, you will definitely obtain an excellent body endowed with the eight good qualities of karmic maturation in your next life; however, you must also make dedication prayers to direct them so that they don't become a cause of negativity. Otherwise, even after you have accomplished the causes for attaining a human life with eight qualities of karmic maturation, it's possible that you may be reborn as a human such as the king of a border region where the Buddha's teachings don't exist, and thus that excellent human form will become a vessel for negativity. You could have great power capable of accumulating immense negativity that no one else would be capable of. So that you don't become such a vile person, it is extremely important that you make powerful and excellent prayers to become a vessel for the Dharma. Contemplate the general and specific [characteristics] of actions and their effects by thinking over their nature in two sessions, and having contemplated them, practice engagement and disengagement [of virtue and nonvirtue] between the sessions.

How to Practice Engagement and Disengagement once You Have Reflected [on the General and Specific [Characteristics of] Actions and Their Effects

Reflect on actions and effects during the essence of the session. Between sessions, if you place your trust in your practice of adopting virtue and abandoning negativity, you will establish a basis for the Dharma. The very outset of our practice begins with actions and their effects; therefore, we rely upon introspection and conscientiousness with respect to our three doors. We must earnestly strive in adopting and forsaking [virtue and nonvirtue through an appreciation for] the subtlety of the causes and consequences of karmic actions. Je Mila[repa] stated,

> If you don't contemplate the cause and effect of
> Virtuous and nonvirtuous actions,
> It will ripen as the unbearable suffering of the lower realms.
> Please maintain mindfulness that is conscientious
> With respect to karmic maturation in minute detail.

Through merely engaging in recitations, you won't be liberated from the lower realms; therefore, we should engage in authentic Dharma practice like Geshe Ben Gungyal, as explained in his biography.[443] We keep a count

443. Geshe Ben would keep track of his virtuous and nonvirtuous thoughts with black and white pebbles.

with our rosary of whatever slight virtue we engage in, yet we cover up, like a cat with its feces, however many grave nonvirtues we perform. Nevertheless, we will be unable to conceal them from Dharmaraja, the Lord of Death. With the exception of the trivial nonvirtues we engage in, we don't notice in the slightest the negatives that occur or don't occur. A bhikshu, for example, doesn't count even one of the faults he engages in on a daily basis, from the faulty way he drinks a cup of noodles on up, or down to wearing his lower garment incorrectly. Although he recognizes virtue and negativity, it is a fault not to act [appropriately]. [In his *Songs of Spiritual Experience*] Je Lama [Tsongkhapa] proclaimed,

> Saturated by the stains of negativities and downfalls of the three doors,
> There is, in particular, great importance in purifying karmic obscurations;
> Therefore, continuously cherish reliance upon the four complete powers.

No matter how careful we try to be, because of the force of our great familiarity with nonvirtue since beginningless time, we find it difficult not to incur the slightest fault; therefore, we should appropriately apply confession and restraint through the four opponent powers to what we [generally] don't consider or classify as negativity. If we wish to accumulate merit, [we must] conjoin [confession and restraint] with the *Confession of Moral Downfalls*, the Hundred-Syllable Mantra, and so on. Nevertheless, although we engage in negativity, it is inappropriate to think that it is sufficient to engage in confession. It is two different things to not be defiled by negativity [in the first place] and to purify it through confession. For example, this is like the difference between a person who hasn't broken his leg and another person who did break his leg and then had it mended through medicine and so forth, as I taught earlier.[444] In general, there isn't sufficient proof for us to claim, "I haven't accumulated negative karma since beginningless time." We have such a huge number of [negative imprints] that counting each and every one would be endless

444. This was taught during the confession section of the preliminary practices.

and would be like the storehouse of a great and powerful king. Therefore, until we receive the signs of purifying these negativities in this life, we should continue confessing them for the entire length of our lives and continue to sincerely apply ourselves even when the [signs] do occur. Once you practice in that way, if you repeatedly receive clear signs in your dreams indicating that you purified your negative karma, then it has been purified.

Pabongkha Rinpoche gave teachings on the measure of having generated thoughts of a special being of small scope. Next, he explained it again in moderate detail and gave a brief explanation on how to train.

If you don't repeatedly train in something like a scanning meditation once you have listened [to teachings] on the lamrim, then afterward, no matter how many teachings you listen to, it will be of no benefit, and you will become jaded toward the Dharma:

> Even though you use water to control blazing kindling,
> If the water becomes set ablaze, what will extinguish it?

For example, if wood and so forth is blazing, water will extinguish it. But if the water were [somehow made] flammable, there will be no other way to extinguish the fire. Likewise, if you become jaded toward other Dharma teachings, you can be subdued through the lamrim. If you become jaded toward the Dharma of the lamrim, [however,] there is absolutely nothing else that will be capable of subduing you. The *Hundred Verses*[445] also states,

> The monk who has disrobed,
> The woman who has been with three husbands, and
> The jackal that freed itself from a trap;
> You should know these three to be devious types.

Next, combine scanning meditation on the proper reliance on the spiritual guide, leisure and endowment, and so on sequentially for a year

445. Tib. *Tshigs bcad brgya pa.*

or a month. Listen to [teachings] such as those on impermanence in the presence of your guru, gain certainty in the mind through listening, and then go to your separate place, whereby you will attain certain knowledge arisen through meditation that is superior even to that which you previously gained through listening. If you make a sincere effort in that way, you will not become insensitive to the Dharma.

If you don't meditate on the lamrim, it doesn't matter how much you meditate on a deity or how many mantras you recite, you will not be able to elicit an experience. If you develop an experience of the great value and difficulty in obtaining leisure and endowment, it will bring a degree of certainty that is unlike any you previously had in your mental continuum. If you develop an experience of the great value and difficulty in acquiring leisure and endowment and [also] of death and impermanence, it will inaugurate the installation of pure Dharma. Presently, we beginners seek out the very highest paths and a multitude of various experiences right from the very outset, yet we can't reach the higher states. Yet if you are going to build a king's palace, for example, you need a stable foundation; and if you are going to [enter] the assembly hall, you must progress through stages, by [first] crossing the threshold and so forth. In the same way, you must purify your mind properly in the coming path, from proper reliance on the spiritual guide on out.

Thus, despite your efforts in listening, contemplating, and meditating on the method aspect of the path, you will not accumulate a union of the two accumulations [of merit and wisdom].[446] I am willing to bet everything I own that although you may be claiming to follow a profound path, there is no guarantee of enlightenment without the joint accumulation of wisdom and merit. It is enough to examine the Kangyur, Tengyur, and witnesses. Some cite *Reciting the Names of Manjushri*:

> Designating the distinction through a single instant,
> [You attain] complete enlightenment through a single instant.

And [those who cite this also] claim that if you meditate on recognizing one's mind as a buddha in the morning, you will be enlightened in the

446. This is because here there will be no wisdom aspect but only the method aspect.

morning; that if you meditate in the evening, [you will become] enlightened in the evening; and that beings with fortunate karma don't need to meditate on elaborations.

Although they used the term "enlightenment," if you adhere to that view, then the compassionate Teacher and all the Indian and Tibetan pandits and siddhas didn't teach that easy and effortless method of liberation to living beings. Therefore, the holy beings who taught the countless methods for practicing accumulation and purification, and the teachings of the 84,000 heaps of Dharma, either did not have compassion or they were deceiving living beings, and they incur the fault of not being skilled in their methods. [However,] the Supreme Conqueror Kelsang Gyatso [the Seventh Dalai Lama] said, "Although I have compassion for those like myself, you, [Buddha], have unbearable compassion."[447] Although we have compassion for ourselves, the Teacher has compassion for living beings that is trillions of times greater and is incomparable [to what we have for ourselves]. Always and eternally, [the Buddha] does nothing other than work solely at the means of quickly establishing all living beings in the state of enlightenment; therefore, it is utterly impossible that he would confuse or deceive us even for an instant.

Pabongkha Rinpoche explained that during the session breaks we should repeatedly examine the Teacher's scriptures on cause and effect, the Vinaya, the alphabet, and so forth, as well as the Sutra Shasaha *and so forth, and that it is indispensable to practice in that way to develop faith in actions and their effects. Up to this point, he has given a brief explanation of the person of small scope.*

[Training the Mind in the Stages of the Path of] a Person of Middle Scope

As I explained previously, by sincerely applying ourselves to the path shared with the [person of] small scope, we will temporarily not be reborn in the lower realms in our next life; however, that alone is not sufficient. For example, if a person has been put in prison and is certain to be executed but requests a person of influence to grant him temporary

447. This means that although we ordinary beings have self-concern, the Buddha has impartial love and compassion for all living beings.

reprieve from his daily beatings, [the prisoner] is still ultimately not able to escape his eventual execution.

Next, we should train our minds in the path shared with the person of middling capacity, by striving to be permanently liberated from samsara.

[Training the Mind in the Stages of the Path of a Person of Middle Scope] has four headings:

1. The Actual Training in Contemplation
2. The Measure of Having Generated the Thought [Determined to Attain Liberation]
3. Dispelling Misconceptions
4. Developing Certainty about the Nature of the Path Leading to Liberation

The Actual Training in Contemplation has two sections:

1. Identifying a Mind Striving for Liberation
2. The Method for Developing the Mind [Intent on Liberation]

Identifying a Mind Striving for Liberation

In general, we must attain enlightenment, and to attain that, we must develop the renunciation and so on of a person of middle scope. To develop that, it must be preceded by developing the realizations of a person of small scope. To work toward liberation from samsara, we must develop the mind that desires liberation from samsara—in other words, a mind striving for liberation. Liberation is the release from bondage. It is release from the shackles that bind us to the contaminated appropriated aggregates: karma and the afflictive emotions. The term *samsara* refers to the countless contaminated appropriated aggregates, from the peak of existence down to the deepest hell. It is called samsara because it is like a wheel upon which the contaminated appropriated aggregates repeatedly [cycle]. None of the bodies assumed in the abodes of the six classes of living beings has transcended samsara. Furthermore, if we explain this by illustrating it with the example of someone who is bound to the trunk of a tree, for the sake of easy comprehension by persons of lesser aptitude, then the tree trunk is the aggregates, the rope that binds him to the trunk is the afflictive emotions, and the person who is the object bound is oneself. Similarly, you yourself are bound by the afflictive emotions to the contaminated aggregates in samsara; when freed from that, you attain liberation. Wishing to attain that [state] is the mind striving for liberation.

All the teachings of Je Rinpoche [Tsongkhapa] are unlike others; therefore, the intelligent should definitely study, contemplate, and meditate on the teachings of Je [Rinpoche]. If you read *The Great Treatise on the Stages of the Path* seven times, you would develop seven different understandings.[448] Khedrup [Je] had a completely unbiased mind and stated that [the *Great Treatise*] is an object to be eulogized. Dzogchen Patrul also stated,

> Tsongkhapa, the source of eloquence on sutra and tantra,
> You directly encountered Manjushri in the Land of Snows.

The omniscient Buton [Rinchen Drub (1290–1364)] had a very broad perspective and said that his own teachings are incomparable to any other; however [Buton] did not say that [he] himself reached complete certainty about the difficult points. It is said that only Je [Rinpoche's] scriptures expose and come to a definitive conclusion about all the sutras and tantras. Therefore, an Amdo Lama Ga said,

> If you don't see it [elsewhere], inquire into Buton['s writings];
> If you didn't ascertain its meaning, inquire into Je [Tsongkhapa's writings.][449]

The Method for Developing the Mind [Intent on Liberation] has two sections:

1. Contemplating the Faults of Samsara as True Sufferings
2. Contemplating the Stages of Entering Samsara as True Origins

448. This means that Tsongkhapa's *Great Treatise on the Stages of the Path* is so profound that each time you read it your understanding will be different without being contradictory.
449. This means that Buton wrote a huge number of texts concerning many subjects, and Tsongkhapa wrote relatively few about the most difficult points.

Contemplating the Faults of Samsara as True Sufferings has two sections:

1. Revealing the Intention behind Teaching True Sufferings at the Beginning of the Four Noble Truths
2. The Actual Meditation on Suffering

Revealing the Intention behind Teaching True Sufferings at the Beginning of the Four Noble Truths

When the Teacher first turned the wheel of Dharma, he turned the wheel of Dharma of the four noble truths. [The first noble truth] is called "true suffering," and it is also a truth because the aryas perceive suffering and so forth exactly as it is—a truth. Therefore, all four [noble truths] are called "truths for an arya." The suffering of suffering and so forth include all types of suffering and are called "true sufferings." [The second noble truth], "true origins," includes the true origins of actions and true origins of afflictive emotions. The true origins of afflictive emotions are the six root afflictions, the twenty secondary afflictions, and so on. [The third noble truth,] "true cessations," is cessation with merit, without merit, immutable, and so on. [The fourth noble truth,] "true paths," is the wisdom directly realizing emptiness in the mental continuum of an arya in all three vehicles. [Maitreya's] *Sublime Continuum* reveals this by way of an example when it states,

> The illness should be known, the cause of the illness abandoned,
> Well-being should be attained, and the medicine should be relied upon.
> Likewise you should know, abandon, attain, and rely respectively
> Upon suffering, its causes, its cessation, and the path.

Thus, like the cause of illness, true origins are the cause of suffering; by relying upon the medicine as the means of curing the disease, you abandon the true origin, which is similar to well-being. By practicing the true paths as the means to abandon true origins, you attain a true cessation, which is the elimination of true suffering.

With respect to reversing the order of cause and effect and teaching the cause first, this is analogous to experiencing the result of a virulent illness and needing to sever the continuum of its cause. If there is a virulent illness and you know that wellness exists, you will feel the need to strive sincerely in your reliance upon medicine as the cause of curing that illness. Similarly, once you understand that there is a true origin that is the cause of whatever suffering arises, you will have the desire to attain a true cessation, which is the happiness related to that [elimination of suffering]. It is important that you understand the need to meditate on the path for the sake of attaining that [true cessation]. Striving sincerely in that way is the means of attaining a cessation, which is the result of abandoning true origins that are the cause of suffering. During the first turning of the wheel, the Teacher proclaimed,

> You should know suffering;
> You should abandon true origins;
> You should actualize cessations;
> You should meditate on the path.

Through the teaching on the major precepts of practice, the group of five [initial disciples of the Buddha] perceived the truth [of reality]. The three principal aspects of the path are of great importance. Perfecting bodhichitta is the cause of omniscience; perfecting the views of renunciation and emptiness is the cause of liberation. Once you understand those, Je Rinpoche [Tsongkhapa] states, "If you are without any of the three principal aspects of the path, with the exception of relying upon the power of the field,[450] whatever you do will turn the wheel of samsara." Also, Jetsun [Manjushri] said to Je Rinpoche [Tsongkhapa],

> Initially, you should set aside all the other so-called profound oral instructions and employ conceptual meditation on renunciation.

450. Here the term "field" refers to the field of merit. If you don't have any experience of renunciation, bodhichitta, or emptiness, whatever you do will be a cause of the continuation of samsara—with the single exception of any virtuous actions carried out in relation to images of enlightened body, speech, or mind. Because of the power of enlightened beings, any virtuous (and some say even nonvirtuous) actions you perform in relation to such images will ultimately result in your enlightenment.

And,

> Initially, you should definitely set aside any of the so-called profound oral instructions of mantra and so forth and elicit an experience of renunciation and bodhichitta. Develop those [minds], and then all your virtues will effortlessly become a cause of liberation and omniscience. Therefore, not being content with meditating in stages on these points is due to having absolutely no understanding of the essential points of the path.

The phrase "conceptual meditation" means that you should employ analytical meditation.

With respect to training in renunciation and bodhichitta, it is like sharpening a sickle in preparation for cutting the crops. If you have these two, you will make progress on the path like no other, and whatever you do will become the cause of liberation and omniscience. Kadam Phuchungwa said to [Geshe] Chen-nga-wa,

> Between attaining the five types of clairvoyance, being skilled in the five fields of knowledge, obtaining the eight great attainments, or generating Atisha's stages of the path in your mind; which would you choose?

[Geshe] Chen-nga-wa said,

> Let alone generating the stages of the path in my mind, I would even choose an intellectual understanding that wonders about the stages of path. Countless times I have obtained the five types of clairvoyance, been skilled in the five fields of knowledge, and obtained the eight great attainments, yet I have not transcended or risen above samsara. If I gain certainty about the stages of the path, I can say that overcoming samsara exists. Therefore, I would choose a mere intellectual understanding heading in the direction of wondering about the stages of the path to enlightenment.

Merely having the good fortune to have a direct vision of your personal deity, even if you practice something like the king of tantras, Guhyasamaja, for a thousand years, without the lamrim you will not establish the imprints for the complete path to enlightenment. If you have established a good understanding of the lamrim, you will establish special imprints for the complete path.

Previously, through the force of his imprints, King Ajatashatru offered a garment to Manjushri and realized emptiness. A pigeon listened to the *Perfection of Wisdom in a Hundred Thousand Lines* from master Vasubandhu and became Sthiramati [in its next life]. The stages of the path to enlightenment are a means of accomplishing the three principal aspects of the path. Je Mila[repa] stated,

> If you don't meditate as much as possible on the meaning of the
> Hearing Lineage,
> Even staying in a mountain retreat will bring misery.

Thus, it is very important that you first understand the way to practice Dharma. Next, it is important that you put its meaning into practice.

The Actual Meditation on Suffering has two sections:

1. Contemplating the General Sufferings of Samsara
2. Contemplating the Specific Sufferings [of Samsara]

Contemplating the General Sufferings of Samsara has two sections:

1. Contemplating the Eight Sufferings
2. Contemplating the Six Sufferings

Contemplating the Eight Sufferings has eight sections:

1. The Suffering of Birth
2. The Suffering of Aging
3. The Suffering of Illness
4. The Suffering of Death

5. The Suffering of Having to Encounter the Unpleasant
6. The Suffering of Parting from the Pleasant
7. The Suffering of Searching for and Not Finding What You Desire
8. A Teaching on the Suffering of the Five Appropriated Aggregates

The *Great* and the *Middle-Length Treatise on the Stages of the Path to Enlightenment* explain eight, three, and six sufferings.[451] Although the *Swift Path* teaches six [types of suffering], it is a similar system, in that it contains the meaning [of both the eight and three types of suffering]. For the most part, the lamrim needs both analytical and placement meditation. While employing the system of analytical meditation, the *Commentary on Valid Cognition* states,

> Trembling because of desire, fear, and suffering,
> You are deceived by a dream enemy and so forth.

If you properly undertake analytical meditation, you will easily develop a vivid presence and experience. Once you contemplate the eight sufferings, you will realize that for as long as you are reborn within samsara, although you may claim to be a tulku [that is, reincarnate lama], there is no way for you not to experience the suffering of birth, old age, sickness, death, and so on.

The Suffering of Birth

For the suffering of birth, the first [thing to consider] is the way we enter the womb and the five stages of development while in the womb, which are taught in the *Teaching Nanda about Entering the Womb Sutra*[452] and others. At that time [of conception], we enter into a pouch that is filled with impurities, which is like a small bag that has been bound shut. While we are being born and so forth, we experience great suffering.

451. The actual order presented in those texts is eight, six, and three types of suffering.
452. Tib. *dGa' bo mngal 'jug gi mdo.*

The Suffering of Aging

While we age, because the cause of old age is necessarily the afflictive emotions, our memory, intelligence, sense powers, color, and shape all deteriorate, [so that toward the end of our lives] it is as though we have changed human bodies. Eating, lying down, moving about, sitting, and so on bring suffering. [Kadam] Kamapa stated,

> It's a good thing that aging comes bit by bit. If it happened all at once, it would be unbearable.

[Je] Gungtang [Jampalyang Rinpoche] proclaimed,

> These hairs are as white as a conch shell,
> Yet it is not because my defilements have been cleansed;
> They are the arrows of spit from the Lord of Death
> Descending on my head like hoarfrost.

The Great Fifth [Dalai Lama] said much the same thing. Je Mila[repa] also stated,

> First, you stand up as though you are pulling up a stake;
> Second, you move like someone sneaking up on a bird;
> Third, you sit down like a snapped bag of dirt:
> Grandma, the moment has come when these three have been assembled,
> And now you are depressed by the deterioration of your illusory body.

And,

> First, your outer skin has retracted and wrinkled;
> Second, your bones protrude because your inner flesh and blood are depleted;
> Third, in between, you are dim-witted, mute, deaf, blind, and trembling:

> Grandma, the moment has come when these three have been assembled,
> And your wrinkled face is a display of repulsiveness.

Thus, this is how it comes to us.

The Suffering of Illness

Although you may be a powerful young man in the prime of your youth, when sickness strikes you will become weak and helpless, like a baby bird struck by a stone. We lose our strength and are oppressed by the pain of illness day and night in this way until the end. Desirable things are disagreeable, and we must rely upon things we don't enjoy, such as [certain] foods, medical examinations, and so on. We hope we will recover from our illness and in particular worry that we may die, which brings us great suffering. If it is something like leprosy, our bodily health decays, while our [fingers and toes] rot and fall off. If it is something like a stroke, even before we die, half the body becomes paralyzed, which we can directly observe.

The Suffering of Death

As I explained before, during [the section on] how to meditate on the aspects of death, the physicians give up; there are no rituals that will turn away [death], and so on. The earth, water, fire, and wind elements sequentially dissolve. At this point you should apply the explanation that I previously gave of what happens as you are actually dying. Even when our great compassionate Teacher was Prince Siddhartha, he witnessed a sick person, an old person, a dying person, and a bhikshu, after which he became repulsed by samsara. He became ordained and went from one happiness to the next.

The Suffering of Having to Encounter the Unpleasant

All of the unwanted things are going to happen to us from the various types of harms that arise—from the occurrence of a virulent illness to harm from malevolent spirits, the sudden manifestation of enemies and thieves, the punishment of kings, being thrown from a horse, harm from the four elements, and so on.

The Suffering of Parting from the Pleasant

We will be separated from things that are dear to our hearts, such as our pleasing relatives, father and mother, guru and disciple, husband or wife as well as children, and so on. We will suddenly be separated from our powerful status, our fortune, possessions, and so on, producing mental suffering.

The Suffering of Searching for and Not Finding What You Desire

This refers to all those who desire various things and try to obtain them yet don't succeed, such as merchants, farmers, the wealthy, beggars, craftsmen, and so forth, as well as monks who wish for wealth and possessions through things such as village rituals. In addition to that [dissatisfaction], for the most part they develop regret, suffering, and so on and experience limitless types of torments, such as hunger, thirst, and exhaustion, in dependence on their means of livelihood.

A Teaching on the Suffering of the Five Appropriated Aggregates

This burden of the appropriated aggregates is the foundation for generating the aforementioned sufferings, and wherever you are born among the six classes of beings, from this moment onward the suffering will come as an integral component of the [appropriated aggregates]. Therefore, we must develop aversion for samsara, which is the nature of the appropriated aggregates. Moreover, it is said that the place where we stay is also a place of suffering, the friends we associate with are also friends of suffering, and whatever enjoyments we enjoy are also enjoyments of suffering. Also, the Supreme Seventh Conqueror[453] stated,

453. This is an epithet for the Seventh Dalai Lama, Kelsang Gyatso.

Although you may observe the high or low, layperson or monk,
man or woman, they are all the same;
Other than their clothing, appearance, and the degree of their
boasting,
They are all exactly the same in having been born in a life of
misery;
It is said that these friends and loved ones appear to have similar
fortune.

Pabongkha Rinpoche gave an extensive explanation of this quote. He continued by stating the following:

Thus, being oppressed by all these sufferings is the fault of not being liberated from samsara, and if we wish—from this day onward—to be free from having to experience them, then we must employ the means of being liberated from samsara.

Day Twenty-One

Je Tsongkhapa the Great stated [in his *Requesting a Blessing of Strength*],[454]

> The gateway of engaging in all insatiable suffering . . .

Since beginningless samsara until the present, we have taken countless rebirths and have experienced immeasurable suffering, yet there is never a time when we grow weary of it. And although nondeceptive perfections of samsara do not exist, still our attachment increases tremendously, like drinking salt water that never brings satisfaction. Once we contemplate how we are repeatedly oppressed and are constantly tormented by the three types of suffering, we should develop a very powerful mind that wishes for liberation from samsara and a mind that is not attached whatsoever to the best things in samsara. For that we must contemplate the faults of true sufferings, the essential points of which are clarified in what is called "the king of the Teacher's instructions."

After giving this short introduction, Pabongkha Rinpoche covered the headings.

The Way to Contemplate the Six Types of Suffering has six sections:

1. The Fault of Uncertainty
2. The Fault of Not Being Satisfied
3. The Fault of Having to Repeatedly Abandon Our Bodies

454. Tib. *Byin rlabs spungs zhus.*

4. The Fault of Being Repeatedly Born
5. The Fault of Repeatedly Changing from High to Low
6. The Fault of Having No Companionship

Furthermore, after taking rebirth in samsara, nothing transcends being anything but the nature of suffering, for which there are six faults, such as having no certainty and so on. Je Tsongkhapa stated in his *Requesting a Blessing of Strength*, "The gateway of engaging in all insatiable suffering . . ." He goes on to say that [the six sufferings] are included in the three [types of suffering]. From among the six types of suffering, [the first is the fault of uncertainty.]

The Fault of Uncertainty

We act with delight in the best things of samsara, and although we are greatly invested in them, our friends and enemies, benefit and harm, and so on constantly change; therefore, we cannot count on them at all. Nagarjuna stated [in his *Letter to a Friend*]:

> The father becomes the son, the mother becomes the wife,
> And the person who was the enemy also becomes the friend.
> Because the opposite can happen as well,
> There is absolutely no certainty at all in samsara.

A scripture states,

> Eating his father's flesh, he beats his mother;
> He holds his enemy whom he killed in his lap;
> The wife chews on the bones of her husband;
> The things of samsara are laughable.

[This refers to] previously in India, [when it is said that] after a certain father died, he was reborn as a fish in a nearby large lake. After the mother died, although she was unable to take rebirth as a human, due to the power of her attachment to the household, she was born as a pet dog of that family. The enemy whom the dog's owner had killed in a previous life was reborn as his own son. One day, the man of the house caught a fish and killed it and ate its flesh. He tossed out the fish bones, and the female dog had come to eat them, and the man of the house beat the dog while he was holding his son on his lap. While this great spectacle was taking place, Arya Kadyana arrived begging for alms. Having observed through his clairvoyance how they had [all] changed [compared to their relations to one another in their preceding lives], the entire situation became clear in his mind, and he proclaimed the aforementioned four-line verse that begins, "Eating his father's flesh . . ."

Although the householder Palkye was born a king in a previous life, he was next born as a sea monster, and then, by generating a virtuous mind, was born as a householder and so forth. Thus, we have no way of knowing about past and future lives. We have no certainty in this life as well. Shantideva stated [in his *Guide to the Bodhisattva's Way of Life*],

> Even in this life there is no certainty;
> In one instant they become friends,
> And in a brief moment they again become enemies.

From the beginning of life to the latter parts, enemies and friends change. Nor should we place our trust in wealth and resources, either. Friends and enemies change not only over the course of a few years but even after a day or two. Although you may be an ordained [person] or a layperson of high status or low, someone will find fault with you and others will engage in slander. At first they can't bear to be parted from you for an instant and you are their dearest loved one, and then after a while they don't even want to look at you and you have become their enemy. They become hostile toward you, abuse you, and even try to kill you. Such things will happen even in this life. Je Gungtang [Jampalyang Rinpoche] proclaimed,

> Today they are your affectionate friends, [yet]
> Through the conceptions of a single good or bad word
> And superimposition, the next day they are true enemies;
> Sever yourself from adhering to prejudice.[455]

455. This verse utilizes a number of terms generally associated with philosophical texts. "Conceptions" is a translation of the Tibetan term *rnam rtog*, which generally refers to a type of conceptual elaboration or overestimation based on terms and ideas. "Superimposition" is *sgro*

Previously, Desi Sangye Gyatso established a system of Tibetan politics and so forth. He had great influence and great kindness, yet due to a disagreement with King Lhasang, [Desi's] throat was cut, and for a few days there wasn't even anyone to look after his head, and even Desi's acquaintances became destitute.[456]

The Fault of Not Being Satisfied

The *Extensive Sport Sutra* states,

> King, whatever divine sense pleasures there are
> And whatever wonderful human sense pleasures there are,
> Although one person may obtain all these sense pleasures,
> Even so he would not be satiated and would continue searching for more.

Since there is no way to be content with the happiness and well-being of samsara, you will never be satisfied no matter how many enjoyments you have. We bring ruin to ourselves in this life; therefore, in general we must all have contentment in this life. In particular, it is extremely important that we who have become ordained as monks have few desires and conduct ourselves with contentment. If we don't, we will be like the parable of King Mandhata.[457] If we don't have contentment, then even if a solitary monk has twenty-five silver coins he will want fifty, if he has fifty he will want a hundred, and so on, and his desire will continue to increase. Although we may have a pouch full of gold we will not be satisfied because of engaging in commerce, farming, theft, and so on. This is a great fault. Even at the time of his death, King Mandhata was still not

---

btags in Tibetan, and in this instance is specifically related to *rnam rtog* as the reification of the perceived object established by the imputation of the associated conceptual elaborations. "Adhering" is *'dzin pa* in Tibetan and refers to subsequently grasping or apprehending those superimpositions that are imputed upon the perceived object through conceptual elaborations and believing them to be an inherent attribute of an inherently existent object.

456. Desi Sangye Gyatso was the viceroy of Tibet under the Fifth Dalai Lama. For more information, see Glenn H. Mullin, *The Fourteen Dalai Lamas* (Santa Fe, NM: Clear Light Books, 2000).

457. See the *Sutra of the Wise and the Foolish*.

satisfied with this world, and his last testament proclaimed, "There is no greater deception than this life."

If you have contentment, although you may not have more than a pouch of roasted barley flour, you will be wealthy:

> Contentment is the gateway to benefit—
> The gateway where a rich man sleeps
> As he laughs at the desirous who don't notice him.

Nagarjuna declared,

> Always be satisfied! Although you may have no wealth,
> If you know satisfaction you will be truly wealthy.

Once, a poor man found a priceless jewel and gave it to the king, saying that because [the king] lacked contentment he was the poorest of all. If you have few desires and contentment, you will be someone who doesn't work toward anything other than the Dharma. You will not exhaust yourself seeking the greater and lesser riches and enjoyments of this life. If you have results from your merit from a previous life in dependence upon the path, powerful resources will come your way. If you renounce your practice of accomplishing study, contemplation, and meditation on the Dharma and instead strive for food and clothing, you are a "lion lacking two."[458] Completely pure monks should not even have wealth and possessions. Although we think that everything from our dwellings, food, onward are the worst, if we are completely pure monks we should not be conscious of such things, and if we know how to think about things in the proper way, we will dwell within the four preferences of the aryas.[459]

The Bhagavan Buddha was content with merely simple clothing and so on, which is part of those four [preferences of the aryas]. The need to wear inferior and tattered old clothing is also a preference of the aryas, as

458. Tib. *gnyis med sengge*. This is a colloquial Tibetan way to refer to someone who lacks reasoning and learning.
459. The four preferences of the aryas are (1) simple food, (2) simple clothing, (3) a simple dwelling place, and (4) simple possessions.

is simple tea and simple barley flour mixed with butter. Even just a place to sleep or sit is sufficient. As for a fondness of forsaking [worldly things] and [a fondness for] meditation, this is the engagement of studying, contemplating, and meditating on the Dharma. The Teacher Buddha also stated, "There are two activities of the ordained: (1) reading, listening, and contemplating, and (2) being a meditator who has renounced worldly things."

All beings are brought to ruin by their attachment to auditory sounds and bodily tactile sensations:

> A deer, an elephant, a moth, a fish,
> And a bee; all five are destroyed by the five [sense objects].
> If each one can be destroyed by just one of them,
> Why would you not be destroyed by continuous reliance on all five?

And,

> If a butterfly and so on are brought to ruin by forms,
> Each one is also [ruined] by the objects of desire;
> How is it that we who are attached to all five will not end up the same?

The Fault of Having to Repeatedly Abandon Our Bodies

Although we have obtained an excellent physical form, it is excellent if we are capable of practicing Dharma; there is nothing else worthy of our confidence:

> Indra is venerated by the worldly, yet he
> Falls to earth again due to the power of his karma.

We have also been born as Indra and have had the experience of residing in a celestial mansion; however, at the moment it has been of no benefit, and we currently have nothing more than tattered rags:

> Although we have become a chakravartin king,
> Even a chakravartin king will become a servant [one day].

Although you may be born a chakravartin king, you will migrate from that and become the lowest of servants in this world. If a chakravartin king becomes a shepherd, he will have nothing more than a slingshot and a knapsack. Once you experience the happiness and well-being of having been born in the celestial realms, you will fall to the earth and be surrounded by the executioners of the hell realms. [Nagarjuna's *Letter to a Friend* states,]

> You will have to drink boiling water . . .

And,

> Having obtained the extreme great bliss of the desire-realm gods,
> Or the happiness of Brahma that is free from attachment,
> You will once again become kindling for the fires of the deepest hell
> And experience the suffering of unceasing pain.

Thus, [being reborn as] an Indra and Brahma a thousand times each is of no benefit, and after we die we must experience the suffering of being born in the deepest hell.

[Nagarjuna's *Letter to a Friend* states,]

> Obtaining [birth] as the sun and moon,
> The light of your body illuminated the entire world;
> Once again you went into the pitch blackness,
> Where you could not even see your outstretched hand.

Although you were born as the gods of the sun and the moon, that state eventually changed so that not only has that period of assuming the bodies of a chakravartin king, Brahma, Indra, and so on come to an end, but not even the slightest bit of it still remains. You can extract more information about the grandeur of the gods from the *[Supreme Dharma of the] Application of Mindfulness Sutra.*

The Fault of Being Repeatedly Born

Although in general samsara is limitless, it is essential that we strive to end our own samsara. If that doesn't happen, it will be as Nagarjuna stated [in his *Letter to a Friend*]:

> Each of us has drunk more milk than [all the water]
> In the four oceans, yet an individual
> Who follows the ways of ordinary beings
> Still has much more to drink.

[Ashvaghosha's text] *Dispelling Grief*[460] also states,

> Even the water within the ocean
> Cannot equal the amount of molten copper
> That you repeatedly
> Drank in the hells.
>
> The amount of feces you ate
> When you were a pig and a dog
> Would be much greater than
> Mount Meru, the king of mountains.
>
> Even the ocean would not be a sufficient vessel
> To contain the quantities of tears you
> Have shed in samsara due to being
> Parted from your loved ones.
>
> If you heaped up the number of
> Heads you have had severed

460. Tib. *Mya ngan bsal ba.*

Because of engaging in battle,
Their height would excel
Even that of Brahma's realm.

If you filled the ocean of milk with
The amount of manure you have eaten
Out of severe hunger when you were a worm,
It would cause it to expand immensely.

Although we previously experienced such things, if we don't eventually bring an end to samsara, we will have to experience even more [suffering] than before.

The Fault of Repeatedly Changing from High to Low

Although we have been kings of a country and so on, we must eventually stay in a prison. Since this is the situation, although we may have been in a higher state, before too long we will be bugs being squished under someone's foot and so on.

[Je Gungtang Jampalyang Rinpoche proclaimed,]

If you climb progressively higher up
The desiccated tree trunk of name and status,
You'll hurt yourself when its feeble limbs break;
Be content with remaining halfway up!

Geshe Sangphuwa said, "It is disconcerting to think about the many ups and downs we must experience in samsara." Our compassionate Teacher also stated,

The end of elevation is descent;
The end of being born is death;
The end of accumulation is consumption;
The end of meeting is separation.

These are the four conclusions of conditioned phenomena.

Thus, the best things of samsara ultimately decline; therefore, there is nothing [in samsara] that is not included in this classification.

The Fault of Having No Companionship

At first, when you are born, you are born alone. Finally, when you are dying, in the intermediate state, and in your future lives, again you must go on alone. Although at present our father, mother, children, our family, close friends and relatives, teachers and disciples, and so on are [dear to us] like our hearts, yet we are like a crowd at a market that ultimately must part as a natural characteristic of samsara. Shantideva proclaimed [in his *Guide to the Bodhisattva's Way of Life*],

> When you are born, you are born alone;
> When you die, you are again alone.
> Since others cannot share in your suffering,
> What good are these obstructing relatives?

Padampa Sangye also stated,

> Loved ones are as impermanent as a crowd at market-time;
> People of Dingri, don't argue and fight.

For that reason, none of the best things in samsara is trustworthy. Therefore, if you become a person who only practices Dharma and whose only concern is finding food and clothing,[461] that alone will have an excellent conclusion.

If you don't extract the essence of this very moment, you will be carried away like a bubble on a great river and through the great ocean of samsara. If you consider carefully these ways in which samsara cycles, although you may be easily depressed, it will be as the previous Kadampas would say: "Although an arhat engages in a single action, he has great

461. This doesn't mean that as Dharma practitioners we should only be concerned with finding food and clothing. It means that we should not concern ourselves with anything in samsara except obtaining enough food and clothing to survive, and we should then devote the rest of our time to the practice of Dharma.

confidence." We pretend as though we don't have a care in the world, which is the fault of not having thought things over properly. These [sufferings of samsara] are also the faults of being repeatedly born. Furthermore, it is the fault of not liberating yourself from samsara. Also, we are unceasingly tormented over and over by the three types of suffering in samsara, [which are addressed below].

The Three Types of Suffering

With respect to the **suffering of suffering**, this is the suffering we experience when an illness arises, such as when we experience a sharp pain in the kidneys and so forth. When our stomachs are empty, when we have too much food in our stomachs, and so on, this is also considered the suffering of suffering.

Regarding the **suffering of change**, this is like having to stand up after having sat in one place so that you don't suffer from sitting too long and then, if we move around too much, again needing to sit down. Although we may sit in the sun, after a certain point we get sunburn. Once we have gone to a cooler place, we need to warm up, and so on. After getting hungry, we have a pleasurable experience while we are eating, but if we again eat too much we become uncomfortable, and so on. Once we think we are happy, it changes. The same thing applies to all types of happiness.

Regarding the **pervasive suffering** of being conditioned, this is the contaminated appropriated aggregates, and for however long we must appropriate them, our suffering will never end. Geshe Potowa stated,

> As long as you are born in any of the six classes of beings, none of the suffering that occurs, such as sickness, death, and so on, just suddenly appears out of the blue: the person who is sick has the cause to be sick, the person who dies has the cause to die; this is the characteristic or nature of samsara. As long as you remain in samsara, you have not transcended its [characteristics]. If this makes us anxious, we must aban-

don the need to be reborn, and to [accomplish] that, we must abandon its causes.

Furthermore, this is analogous to having a hot wound and sticking it into boiling water, which is like being pierced by a thorn; this is the suffering of suffering. Taking your hot wound and sprinkling it with cold water, which creates a pleasant feeling, is the suffering of change. Having the contaminated aggregates where the wound occurs—in other words, the basis for your suffering to have a hot wound [in the first place]—is the suffering of conditionality. The term "pervasive" is described as being that which pervades the three realms. It is the producer [or creator] of all suffering that serves as a foundation for the suffering of this life. By functioning as the vessel for all our future suffering, it is the worst of all the types of sufferings.

Contemplating the Specific Sufferings [of Samsara]

Of the two contemplations about the suffering of the lower realms and the happy realms, the suffering of the lower realms has already been explained. For the suffering of the happy realms, there are three contemplations.

[Contemplating the Specific Sufferings of Samsara has three sections:]

1. The Suffering of Humans
2. The Suffering of Demigods
3. The Suffering of Gods

The Suffering of Humans

As I explained earlier, these are birth, aging, sickness, death, and so on. Moreover, there are many different types of suffering of all three realms, such as poverty, heat and cold, exhaustion and fear, hunger and thirst, and so on:

> Human beings even have all
> The sufferings of the lower realms . . .

Also, [Aryadeva's *Four Hundred Stanzas* states,]

> Higher persons suffer mentally;
> Ordinary beings develop it physically.
> Every single day beings of this world
> Are overcome by these two types of suffering.

The Suffering of Demigods

The abode of the demigods is in the water at the lower boundary of Mount Meru. [The demigods] are similar to the gods with respect to physical shape, enjoyments, and so on, but they are lesser than the gods in all aspects; therefore, they are constantly jealous of the gods' power and grandeur and do battle with them. However, despite the demigods' attempts, they are defeated by a great elephant that protects the great mountain [of the gods] and that pulverizes them like dust. Also, unless they are able to cut the gods in half at the waist, [the gods] immediately recover from all their other wounds so that the [demigods] are unable to kill them.

In contrast, whatever parts of the demigods' bodies are stuck with weapons becomes the cause of their death and so on. They are constantly defeated; therefore, it is as if the demigods are never victorious. Even their wives experience immense suffering by looking into a lake called All-Seeing, where they can witness their husbands being killed by the gods. Although the demigods have great knowledge, it is obscured by their karmic maturations; therefore, they do not have the good fortune to be able to perceive the truth [of reality] in that physical form.

Although the gods have very little anger, when they dispatch their troops in battle with the demigods, the [demigods] are cleansed in water called "The thicket of roughness," which greatly angers [the gods].

The Suffering of Gods

Contemplate the suffering of the gods by considering the suffering of the desire-realm gods as stated in these verses from [Nagarjuna's] *Letter to a Friend*:

> Their bodies become an unattractive color,
> Their seats are uncomfortable, the flower garlands decay,
> Their clothes develop a bad scent, and their bodies
> Break out in a sweat that was not there previously.
> These are the five signs that they will die and depart from
> heaven.

Thus, there are five signs indicating their deaths. There are also five secondary signs that their death is at hand. The gods are called "beings of the three times" because they can see what karma they engaged in to create rebirth in the following three circumstances: (1) their previous existence that they have transmigrated from, (2) where they will be reborn in their very next rebirth, and (3) their current birth. Once the signs of death occur, they can therefore see with their clairvoyance where they will be reborn in their next life. They have exhausted nearly all their remaining merit that they had [previously] accumulated during their extended consumption of well-being and happiness as a god, so they can see that they will be going to the lower realms when they die, and [as a result] they experience immense suffering for seven days, like a fish being set down on hot sand. Therefore, the mental suffering they experience is immeasurable, exceeding even that in the hell realms.

Compared to being born as such a god, it is preferable to be reborn even as a beggar [because] you would not necessarily exhaust your previous merit and could accumulate [additional] merit to once again attain a human body. The gods only exhaust their merit, and it is difficult for them to accumulate new merit. We, however, do not understand the perfect way to partake of [objects of] enjoyment that is in harmony with any of the three types of vows that we have obtained.[462] Instead, we cur-

462. The three types of vows are pratimoksha, bodhisattva, and secret mantra.

rently consider possessions, wealth, resources, and so on to be valuable, and we place great importance on them; however, they cause our merit to decline. Changkya Rolpai Dorje stated,

> Now is the time to accumulate merit; other than that,
> This is not the time to be intoxicated by consuming our merit.

Trichen Ngawang Chogden also stated,

> If we place great importance on material enjoyments,
> Our merit will deteriorate through their consumption.

Although silk brocade cushions are spread out [for the gods] to sit on, others take them away and say, "You should not sit on that." The gods with lesser fortune threaten those with greater fortune in cowardly ways, and when some of the demigods battle, they are killed by having parts of their bodies amputated and so on. A few of the gods with great power fight those with lesser power, who suffer as they are driven from their homes.

Although the gods in the higher realms don't have manifest suffering, they [also] don't have the freedom to remain there [indefinitely]. When they are born they understand that they have been born in that [god realm], and when they are about to die they have a slight ascertainment through their clairvoyance about where they will be reborn. Between those two periods it is as though they are asleep and they remain in a single state of meditative absorption. In some cases, they abide in a state of blissful concentration that is a mere semblance of enlightenment for the same length of time as it takes others to live out a life in the hell realms and then subsequently attain the state of liberation. Furthermore, as they enter that concentration, they think that they have already attained liberation, so when they rise from that state [of meditation] and see that they are going to take rebirth [after all], they think that this so-called liberation doesn't exist and [thus] develop wrong views about liberation. Mistaking the peak of existence for liberation, they once again go to the deepest hell through their wrong views. Thus, if you are not liberated from samsara, it will be as the previous Kadampas have stated:

> Although you may be reborn at the peak of existence,
> It is not different from taking rebirth in a copper pot of the lowest hell.[463]

The Great Being of Ngari also stated,

> Even while you dwell in the bliss of the gods, you are being misled.

The Supreme Conqueror Kelsang Gyatso [the Seventh Dalai Lama] stated,

> The well-known "three realms of samsara" are a house of blazing iron.
> No matter where you go in the ten directions, you are incinerated by suffering.
> Although it is a pain in my heart, it is the way things appear to me.
> This appearance of wandering in such a horrible place saddens me.

Whether we are born in a high or low station in this abode of samsara, it never transcends being anything but suffering. Therefore, we must be certain to attain liberation from samsara by severing the continuity of contaminated appropriated aggregates.

463. See the text at note 24 above, where this verse is attributed to the Great Being of Ngari.

Day Twenty-Two

The great master Aryadeva stated,

> There is no end to this
> Ocean of suffering. At any time
> You childish being will sink here;
> Why have you not become frightened?

Once you contemplate how we are tormented by the three sufferings in this ocean of samsara, if you do not develop fear of that, you are extremely foolish and [beset by] obscurations. Therefore, by considering the way in which you have fallen into the ocean of samsara, you will develop the desire to be liberated from samsara. The king-like instructions of the Teacher revealing the means of liberation consist of the stages on the path to enlightenment that you are now listening to.

After giving this brief introduction, Pabongkha Rinpoche covered the headings.

In terms of the stages of entering samsara, the Teacher also taught true sufferings and true origins, and in terms of overcoming those stages [of entering samsara], he also taught true cessations and true paths. This is the way in which he turned the wheel of Dharma of the four noble truths. Thus, you must develop a mind wishing for liberation from samsara. For that, you must train your mind. If you don't train [your mind], it will be as [Geshe] Potowa stated when he said, "The guest who never reaches his destination and a sick person who never gets cured . . ." and so on. Still, we will have to stay in samsara for that much longer, which is unacceptable.

After the aforementioned teaching, Pabongkha Rinpoche explained the uncertainty of samsara and so forth once again.

By continuously meditating on the suffering of samsara, Kadampa Langri Tangpa never laughed even once; therefore, the others called him "Black-Faced Langri Tangpa." One day, a close disciple asked him, "Why do people call you Black-Faced Langri Tangpa?" whereby he responded by stating, "If you contemplate the suffering of the three realms of samsara, your face will never be white." [Shantideva's] *Guide to the Bodhisattva's Way of Life* states,

> When their sand castle is destroyed,
> Childish beings weep hysterically.
> Likewise, when praise and fame decline,
> My mind is like a child's.

We are deceived by the meaningless activities of this life. If we took even a small fraction of the hardships we have borne for the worldly activities of this life and applied them to developing the stages of the path to enlightenment, we would already be enlightened. The *[Supreme Dharma of the] Application of Mindfulness Sutra* states,

> Living beings in hell experience the fires of hell;
> Hungry ghosts experience hunger and thirst;
> Animals experience eating one another;
> Human beings experience short lives;
> Gods experience carelessness;
> Samsara is like [sitting on] the tip of a needle
> Where there is never any happiness.

Because you are not liberated from samsara, wherever you are born in the six classes of beings, they all never transcend being the nature of samsara. Although at present we claim to enjoy the objects of desire, in actuality they are suffering; therefore, there is utterly no happiness in samsara whatsoever. This type of disenchantment with the entirety of samsara is the most important [realization] while [training the mind in] the person of middling scope. Je Tsongkhapa states the following about reaching this point:

> If you don't apply yourself to contemplating the faults of true
> suffering,
> You will never develop an authentic yearning for liberation.

The method of striving for liberation is also the means of severing the root of samsara. This is analogous to how we must sever the root of a tree in order to sever the tree [itself]. In our efforts to be liberated from samsara, we must sever the root of samsara, for which we must identify that root. [In his *Songs of Spiritual Experience*, Lama Tsongkhapa proclaims,]

> If you don't contemplate the stages of entering samsara as true
> origins,
> You will not know the way to sever the root of samsara.
> Therefore, cherish the knowledge of what binds you to samsara
> And of definite emergence from samsara and stable
> disillusionment.

Contemplating the Stage of Entering Samsara as True Origins has three sections:

1. How the Afflictive Emotions Are Generated
2. How Karma Is Accumulated through Those [Afflictive Emotions]
3. How We Die and Are Conceived

How the Afflictive Emotions Are Generated has three sections:

1. Identifying the Afflictive Emotions
2. The Stages in Which the Afflictive Emotions Are Developed
3. The Faults of the Afflictive Emotions

The way in which afflictive emotions are generated is explained in the *Commentary on Valid Cognition* when it states,

> The karma of one who has transcended attachment for existence
> Does not have the power to propel him into another [birth]
> Because the cooperative conditions are exhausted.
>
> Because of the existence of craving and grasping,
> Another [rebirth] will occur.

[Karma] is nourished by craving, grasping, and so on. The extensive presentation is combined with the twelve dependent related links in [Je Tsongkhapa's] *Great Treatise on the Stages of the Path to Enlightenment.* If there were no afflictive emotions, even though you would still have karma, it would not be nourished by craving and grasping. Therefore, we must principally apply ourselves to the means of abandoning the afflictive emotions. Therefore, at this point we have three sections.

Identifying the Afflictive Emotions

Attachment

Internal attachment consists of thoughts such as considering your own physical attractiveness, and external attachment is [everything] from delicious tea onward. Attachment is the greatest obstacle to ordained monks and so forth, and even to being a Dharma practitioner. Je Tsongkhapa stated,

> Bound in the prison of samsara by the noose of attachment
> and craving . . .

Although you may be an accomplished practitioner, this is the greatest obstacle. Don't view the afflictive emotions as good qualities but focus on their faults. Accordingly, there is a saying of the Kadampas that states, "Although we are buried by the weight of the afflictive emotions, we should strive to defeat them with clenched teeth, as we would meet an opponent, and battle desire from down in the trenches with the wish that they never occur."[464]

Anger

Although nonvirtues other than anger are not able to completely destroy our roots of virtue, anger and wrong views completely destroy our roots of virtue. These days, many people don't recognize anger, pride, and self-grasping. Therefore, with respect to anger, after focusing on the object of our anger, we find it unbearable, and this vindictive mind thoroughly wishes to inflict harm. With respect to being unable to give to others because of grasping tightly through attachment to wealth and possessions, this is not self-grasping but greed.

Pride

There are seven types of pride, which are arrogant minds regarding your form, voice, youth, hair, and so on, and thinking, "I am better than others." Pride is generated by observing the transitory collection.[465]

Ignorance

[Ignorance] is a lack of knowledge about whatever exists that forms an obscuration between the outer and inner. In short, it is a mental factor that is unaware of the mode of existence of all phenomena. Primarily it does not acknowledge actions and effects, the four noble truths, the Three Jewels, and so on, as well being a mind lacking clear understanding that is similar to closing your eyes.

Doubt

Doubt is a mental factor that is uncertain between two extremes, that observes actions and their effects and so forth, and that lacks confidence in all phenomena.

464. This is a slight variation on Tsongkhapa's presentation in *The Great Treatise on the Stages of the Path to Enlightenment*.

465. Tib. *'jig tshogs la lta ba*. This refers to a view of the transitory collection that observes one or more of the five aggregates and develops the conception of an inherently existent "I."

The View of the Transitory Collection

According to the Prasangikas, there are two views of the transitory collection: (1) the view of the transitory collection that grasps at an "I" that is inherently existent and able to establish itself,[466] and (2) the view of the transitory collection grasping at "mine" that apprehends an inherently existent "I." However, at this point it must conform with the lower tenet systems;[467] therefore, [the view of the transitory collection is defined as] an afflicted wisdom grasping at "I" and "mine" by observing the appropriated aggregates. Although this is an afflicted wisdom,[468] some say that it is not wisdom because it is ignorance, or that it is both wisdom and ignorance; this is something you should examine. In dependence upon the collection of aggregates that are subject to disintegration, we grasp at the thought "I," which is called the view of the transitory collection.

The View Grasping at Extremes

This is a view of a permanent self that is the observed object of the view of the transitory collection, and it is a nihilistic view which thinks that there are no future rebirths after this life; however, it is not the same as the mode of establishing the view of eternalism [in relation to the transitory collection] that occurs during superior seeing.[469]

Grasping at One's Views as Supreme

This is grasping at bad views as being supreme. Regarding grasping at moral discipline and conduct as supreme, this is like non-Buddhist systems which assert that through standing in five fires, impaling oneself on a trident, or imitating a dog you will attain a human body in your next life.

466. Tib. *tshugs thub tu grub pa.*

467. The three lower tenets systems are the Vaibashika, the Sautrantika, and the Chittamatra.

468. Tib. *shes rab nyon mongs can.* This is sometimes translated as "disturbed discrimination."

469. The view of a permanent self that is the observed object of the view of the transitory collection is much coarser than the lack of an inherently existent person that is the object of negation during superior seeing observing emptiness.

Grasping at Bad Religious Disciplines as Supreme

With respect to grasping at these types of bad activities as good and asserting that through them you will attain liberation and so on, this is grasping at bad religious disciplines[470] as supreme. By consolidating the many distinctions into one group and engaging in them, they are called "activities." With respect to thinking that you will not transgress these inferior religious disciplines, if you establish it as "grasping at moral discipline as supreme," then this is easy to understand and also provides a more detailed explanation. The teachings of the Bhagavan Buddha state that from a blissful path comes a blissful result, whereas other systems engage in extreme hardships; however, [by following other systems] you are just purchasing more suffering for yourself.

Wrong Views

This is grasping at the nonexistence of past and future lives, actions and their effects, and so on.

The Stages in Which the Afflictive Emotions Are Developed

The afflictive emotions are developed through the actions performed while circling in samsara. There are six root afflictive emotions and so on. According to Asanga and his brother [Vasubandhu], through ignorance we develop the thought in the view of the transitory collection, thinking "I" on the [basis of] the aggregates, which creates a lack of clarity about the mode of existence of the aggregates. For example, because the darkness produces a lack of clarity concerning the mode of existence of a rope in a house, if we act on that lack of clarity concerning the mode of existence of a rope, we develop the thought "snake." Similarly, through ignorance, we develop the view of the transitory collection, and

470. In Tsongkhapa, *The Great Treatise on the Stages of the Path to Enlightenment*, the Lamrim Chenmo Translation Committee translates the term *brtul zhug* as "religious discipline." I translated *brtul zhug* as "activities" in earlier volumes, but after more consideration I feel their translation is a better choice and hence use "religious discipline" for *brtul zhug* throughout this book. There are various other Tibetan terms that can be translated as "activities," however, so the word "activities" is intentional wherever it occurs herein and is not a translation of *brtul zhug*.

these two are asserted to be one. According to glorious Chandrakirti and so forth, the root of the afflictive emotions is the view of the transitory collection.

In fact, the root of samsara is the ignorance of self-grasping,[471] which is synonymous with "I"-grasping.[472] Through the self-grasping thinking "I, I," you develop attachment, anger, and pride in relation to self and other, and also develop doubts and so forth about the Teacher's scriptures on selflessness. During a concise teaching such as the [First Panchen Lama's] *Path to Bliss*, you identify the afflictive emotions yet don't explain their causes and faults. Based on this, you only explain the way in which the afflictive emotions are developed. Through the view of the transitory collection, you develop the six root afflictive emotions, and from those six, the twenty secondary [afflictions] and so on.

The Causes of the Afflictive Emotions

The *Ornament of the Mahayana Sutras* states,

> Through afflictive emotions you are destroyed, living beings are destroyed, [and] moral discipline is destroyed. They cause defamation, deteriorate your acquisitions and likewise your protection, and the Teachers criticize you. They cause quarrels and disgrace. You will be reborn without freedoms, and through a deterioration of what you have attained and not attained, you will reach a state of great mental suffering.

[Shantideva's] *Guide to the Bodhisattva's Way of Life* states,

> Enemies such as anger and craving
> Don't have arms, legs, and so on,
> And are not brave or wise,
> Yet I am like their slave.

471. Tib. *bdag 'dzin.*
472. Tib. *ngar 'dzin.*

While they dwell in my mind,
They take delight in harming me.
They should not be borne without anger;
It would be slanderous of me to be patient with them.

Even if the gods and demigods
All rose up as my enemies,
Even they are incapable of leading me
Or forcing me into the fires of the deepest hell.

However, this powerful enemy, the afflictive emotions,
Can instantly cast me into the [fires of hell]
Of which not even ashes would remain if
Mount Meru were to encounter it.

My enemies the afflictive emotions
Have endured a long time without limit;
All other enemies do not have
The power to remain for so long.

Everyone is beneficent and brings happiness
If you carry out appropriate service and attend to them,
Yet if you attend to the afflictive emotions,
They will cause you harm and suffering.

To abandon the afflictive emotions, you must view attachment and so forth as your enemies by contemplating their faults. The afflictive emotions bring ruin to yourself and others. The afflictive emotions damage your moral discipline and damage your honor and gain as well. You will become an object of criticism by the Dharma protectors and the Bhagavan Buddha. Although the afflictive emotions don't have form, we are powerlessly bound as their servants, engage in afflictive emotions without conscientiousness, and will henceforth be reborn in the Avici Hell and so on; [the afflictive emotions] are responsible for all of this. [Shantideva's] *Guide to the Bodhisattva's Way of Life* also states,

> This will be my primary goal;
> Out of deep resentment, I will meet them in battle.
> This may appear like an afflictive emotion,
> Yet I am only set on destroying my afflictive emotions.
>
> Even to die in a fire or
> Have my head cut off would be easier
> Than to constantly bow down to
> My enemies the afflictive emotions.

Out of deep resentment, we employ every means to destroy our enemies the afflictive emotions and head into battle against them.

How Karma Is Accumulated [through Those Afflictive Emotions] has two sections:

1. Identifying the Karma That Is Accumulated
2. How Karma Is Accumulated

Identifying the Karma That Is Accumulated

Violantional action[473] can be illustrated by something like killing; it is an act that stirs one's mind to desire to kill. For example, just as iron is involuntarily moved by a magnet, so your three doors are stirred to engage that object involuntarily. The mind is not only stirred thus to engage the object; one may proceed to the actual act of killing, and to undertake to kill someone is a willed action. It is taught that both of these are the mental factor of intention. Regarding actions that are nonmeritorious, there are the well-known ones such as killing, as well as those that appear to be virtues that are employed as a means for attaining happiness up to the point of your death. As for meritorious actions, these are things such as protecting your moral discipline with the intention of striving for future lives. The karma of meditating on mundane tranquil abiding and superior seeing and so forth is a type of contaminated virtuous karma

473. Tib. *sems pa'i las*.

included within the higher grounds that is immutable karma.[474] However, since three[475] are not embraced by the three principal aspects of the path, whatever we do and whatever we meditate on will function as the cause of samsara.

How Karma Is Accumulated

The accumulated actions that are enveloped by the wisdom realizing selflessness do not become phenomena characterized as a cause of samsara. However, they should be posited as being embodied by true origins. The accumulator of new karma that functions to project [a rebirth] in samsara is created by an ordinary being on the great path of supreme mundane qualities and below.[476] Although stream-enterers and once-returners[477] accumulate nonvirtuous karma, they do not accumulate any virtuous or nonvirtuous karma whatsoever that will project a rebirth in samsara. As it is stated, "There is no projection for one who has perceived reality."

How We Die and Take Rebirth

The positive and negative minds at the time of death and their assistant [mental factors], as well as continuously engaging in or not engaging in virtue and so forth, will also become secondary causes. You will have good and bad visions at the time of death due to whatever virtue or nonvirtue you have engaged in. There are great and small interruptions to life that arrive in that way as well.

474. "Mundane tranquil abiding and superior seeing" refers to observing the faults of the lower realms and aspiring to the higher realms with the motivation of attaining the "peak of samsara." According to Buddhism, this peak has still not transcended suffering and is considered "contaminated." Any concentration of the form realm or higher is "immutable" in the sense that, although you may be a human being when you attain it, it is certain that you will attain rebirth in the form realm or higher upon your death and that this cannot be altered.
475. These three are intentional, meritorious, and nonmeritorious actions.
476. The path of preparation is the second of the five Mahayana paths that is sequentially divided into four sections: (1) heat, (2) peak, (3) forbearance, and (4) supreme mundane qualities (or Dharma). The fourth stage is the final stage before becoming an arya bodhisattva, which is synonymous with a direct realization of emptiness conjoined with spontaneous bodhichitta.
477. See Jeffrey Hopkins, *Meditation on Emptiness* (Boston: Wisdom, 1996), 106–7, for a discussion of the Hinayana paths, including stream-enterers and once-returners.

The holy beings and so forth who are endowed with virtue have pure visions. Those endowed with negativity experience the corresponding manifestation of horrible, mistaken appearances as well as terrifying perceptions and so forth. Practitioners of virtue also initially lose their warmth from below, which collects upward to the heart at the time of their deaths; those who engage in negative actions will have the opposite,[478] yet the way both of their consciousnesses leave the heart is the same. The ceasing of the birth of existence and the accomplishment of the intermediate state of existence occur simultaneously.

With respect to the intermediate state, there is a phrase [in Vasubandhu's *Treasury of Abhidharma*] that states, "He will have the form of his previous existence."[479] From the time we die until [the time] we take rebirth is the "intermediate state of existence"; the moment we die in the [intermediate state] and are conceived is "birth existence"; and from that point until we die is the "previous existence." The "death existence" is abandoning the aggregates of a similar type; if it were called "previous existence" because that death existence occurred previous to that [birth existence], it would have the shape and appearance of whatever it had from the time of this life. However, the translation equivalent of the [Sanskrit] term *purva* is "previous," "manifest," and "entering those ahead." Therefore, the term "previous" means "looking ahead at the next life after the intermediate state." Therefore, this means that "going forward" and "previous" must be synonymous.[480]

The color of an intermediate-state being and the way in which it travels, such as upside-down and so on, are in accordance with the individual six classes of beings.[481] The length of their lives is seven days, but if they find the conditions for rebirth, it can be a few days and so on, yet they can [also] take rebirth before a day has passed. If they don't find the conditions

478. This means that their bodily heat will collect from above and move downward.
479. In this instance the term "existence" refers to the four types of existence associated with the process of perpetuating samsara: (1) birth existence, (2) previous existence, (3) death existence, and (4) intermediate-state existence.
480. If we interpret "previous" the way Je Tsongkhapa explains it, it must mean that the intermediate-state being has the shape of his or her next rebirth and not that of the body it just left.
481. Those destined to be reborn as gods move upward; those to be reborn as humans move straight forward; and those to be reborn in the lower realms move with their heads and eyes cast downward.

for rebirth, they will die after seven days and again accomplish an intermediate state; however, after forty-nine days they will definitely find a place of rebirth. The *Compendium of Knowledge* states that they change [their form] in the intermediate state and can be recognized by similar beings in the intermediate state. [Vasubandhu's] *Treasury of Abhidharma* states that they do not change [their form]. After the deceased has entered the intermediate state, if the living accomplish vast amounts of virtuous roots, it will greatly benefit the intermediate-state being. Accordingly, Dromtonpa stated, "The monks of Ratreng pool together all their wealth and possessions, which greatly benefits the deceased by accumulating roots of virtue after they have died." Although there is a great deal of rhetoric about the intermediate state, it should conform to the stainless teachings of the Buddha. Changkya Rolpai Dorje said the same thing.

By nourishing either virtue or negativity at the time of your death, you will accordingly have a good or bad rebirth. Nurses and so forth should definitely not get angry and so on at the time of the sick person's death. Also, it is extremely important to employ methods to nurture karma associated with a virtuous mind at the time of death; although this deserves a detailed explanation, I won't be able to devote more time to it.

Day Twenty-Three

Je Tsongkhapa states, "Induced by a pure mind . . ." As this quote indicates, the sole root of happiness and well-being of migrating beings, including the gods, is only the teachings of the Conqueror; therefore, those who abide in the world—and those that do not—rely upon the pratimoksha [vows]. Furthermore, those who are endowed with the pratimoksha vows safeguard their moral discipline as they would their lives. Adjust your motivation by thinking, "For that reason, by all means possible I will accomplish the supreme long-term aspirations by means of listening, contemplating, and meditating on countless scriptural systems [and] by abiding in a foundation of pure moral discipline. For that reason, I will listen to this king of oral instructions."

After giving this brief introduction, Pabongkha Rinpoche covered the headings and once again explained the contemplation on the stages of entering samsara as a true origin.

As I already explained, we must understand how karma and afflictive emotions function to bind us to samsara:

> Cherish the knowledge of what binds you to samsara . . .

Employing actions striving for the welfare of this life is not meritorious, and the actions that strive for the welfare of our future lives are meritorious actions, through which we are reborn in a happy rebirth in the desire realm. By striving for the internal happiness of concentration, we will be reborn as a god in the higher realms. We cannot have confidence in merely attaining tranquil abiding, since non-Buddhists and so forth also attain all eight levels of thought and form and are reborn as gods in the form and formless realms.[482] There are also many who have even attained superior seeing, yet it is a mundane type of superior seeing; therefore, this is also not worthy of our confidence.[483]

The Measure of Having Generated Thought [Determined to Attain Liberation]

Disenchantment with the mere suffering of samsara is called "a temporary and unstable contrived renunciation."[484]

Query: In that case, what type [of renunciation] should I have?

Reply: If you generate a mind that perceives all the best things in samsara, such as the states of Brahma, Indra, a chakravartin king, and so on, as being the nature of suffering and as being similar to a pit of blazing fire, [then] this is the actual aspiration of renunciation. The foremost great being [Tsongkhapa] also stated,

> However many acts of [devotion] others do for you, such as arranging a high-quality cushion, acting out of veneration, and so on, at that time you don't pay much attention to those actions. Instead, think that they are like illusory deceptions and how it is inappropriate to place any confidence in any of them. From the depths of your heart, abandon this transient appearance with extremely powerful thoughts of disenchantment, and cultivate [such thoughts] for a long time. From the

482. For more information on these mundane states of concentration, see Geshe Gedün Lodrö, *Walking through Walls*, trans., ed. Jeffrey Hopkins (Ithaca, NY: Snow Lion, 1992).
483. This type of superior seeing is based on observing the faults of the various higher realms of samsara and aspiring to attain rebirth in one of the higher realms. For example, after the attainment of tranquil abiding, a yogi contemplates the faults of the desire realm and the good qualities of the form realm. Through increasingly refined states of concentration, he ascends through eight levels of concentration, and finally attains the highest samsaric concentration called "the peak of existence." Since these concentrations are not motivated by renunciation or bodhichitta and are not observing emptiness, they are incapable of serving as a cause for liberation or enlightenment. For these reasons they are not worthy of our confidence.
484. Tib. *nges 'byung bcos ma sna thung spu sud.*

> very beginning [of my practice], such thoughts have naturally occurred for me.

The *Three Principal Aspects of the Path* states,

> When you don't develop even for an instant a mind wishing
> For the best things in samsara through contemplating in this way,
> And when a mind striving for liberation arises
> Both day and night, you have developed renunciation.

Therefore, if you regard the celestial mansions of Brahma and Indra as being no different from a blazing iron house of the hells and perceive them as the nature of suffering, you have developed uncontrived renunciation. If you develop that, it will serve to induce bodhichitta. It states in Je [Tsongkhapa's] lamrim that renunciation is meditating on the suffering of samsara as it applies to oneself, and that great compassion is developed by meditation on how it pertains to others. Accordingly, these two depend on whether you apply them to yourself or others, which is also what my guru Lama Choné Rinpoche said.

Refuting Misconception about the Way to Practice

Misconception: It is a misconception if you have the notion that developing disenchantment with samsara is for shravakas and pratyekabuddhas, but bodhisattvas must voluntarily take on samsara for the welfare of living beings; therefore, they don't need a system for developing disillusionment [with samsara].

Response: Through the force of a bodhisattva's compassion and prayers, he [or she] enjoys entering the abodes of samsara. They must develop disenchantment with being reborn in samsara through the force of karma and afflictive emotions, as explained in the *Sutra on the Inconceivable Secret*.[485] [Nagarjuna's] *Letter to a Friend* states,

485. Tib. *gSang ba bsam gyis mi khyab pa'i mdo.*

> To be reborn holding wrong views, as an animal,
> As a hungry ghost, in hell,
> Without the teachings of the Conqueror, in a border region,
> As a barbarian, as foolish and stupid,
>
> Or as a long-life god—rebirth in any of these places
> Lacks freedom and has eight faults.
> Strive sincerely for the sake of overcoming rebirth,
> So that you can be free and find opportunity.

As this states, we must distinguish ourselves from animals by sincerely applying ourselves to the means of overcoming samsara. Although there is a means of overcoming [samsara], we must apply it ourselves so that samsara doesn't overcome us instead. The supreme basis of overcoming [samsara] is as a human being who has received ordination in general, and it should be a physical basis of a bhikshu endowed with the pratimoksha vows. The Bhagavan Buddha also said that he had perceived the suffering of samsara and took ordination as a support to overcome birth in samsara, and having seen that the very best ordination is that of a bhikshu, he acted accordingly; thus, the Buddha taught the way of progressing to ordination. Atisha the Great also perceived that the supreme basis for accomplishing liberation is that of a monk, so he left behind all the perfections of a kingdom with its power, influence, and resources. It is taught in the *Kalachakra Tantra* that being a bhikshu is also the very best for accomplishing the supreme attainments of secret mantra, that a novice monk is the middling [way], and [that the way of] a householder is the least.

The Type of Path Needed to Overcome Samsara

The actual path for overturning samsara is the three higher trainings. You must develop the wisdom realizing selflessness that serves as a direct antidote to self-grasping and its mode of apprehension to overcome self-grasping, which is the root of samsara. To develop that, you must have excellent single-pointed concentration that abides single-pointedly upon its observed object. For example, to cut down a tree, you need a sharp axe as well as a strong shoulder. Likewise, if you don't have strong concentration, you will not clearly perceive the meaning [of emptiness], so you will not be able to inflict serious harm on your self-grasping.

As a preliminary to developing concentration in your mental continuum, you must train in moral discipline to cease coarse mental distractions. Furthermore, to use a series of metaphors, self-grasping is like the root and trunk of samsara, and training in wisdom is like the sharp axe that is employed for cutting it down. Concentration is like the hand that wields the axe. Moral discipline is like the body [of the axe-wielder]. The term "higher" [or "superior"] in the phrase "three higher trainings" is explained as being superior to non-Buddhists. With respect to the three higher trainings, in Tibet they are view, meditation, and action, and Choné Rinpoche stated that these are also the ways of training in the [three higher trainings]. Nagarjuna stated [in his *Letter to a Friend*],

> If your head and clothes were to suddenly catch fire,
> You should even forsake trying to extinguish them
> And instead strive for the sake of terminating existence;
> Nothing exists that is superior to that.
>
> Through pure moral discipline, wisdom, and concentration,
> You will achieve the state of nirvana that is peaceful, subdued,
> Stainless, ageless, deathless, inexhaustible, and
> Free from earth, water, fire, wind, sun, and moon.

Even if your head was to suddenly catch fire, there is not even enough free time to strive at putting it out; instead, we must apply ourselves with great haste to annihilate samsaric rebirth in samsara through karma and afflictive emotions. Furthermore, according to some non-Buddhists who have a mistaken stance about liberation, they believe that you should rely upon the four elements, the sun, the moon, and so on.

To distinguish ourselves from non-Buddhists who assert that liberation possesses form, we train in the three principal aspects of the path as a necessary means of accomplishing the state of nirvana that is liberation. By relying upon the object of abandonment and result, there is also a definite number of three trainings. In this discourse, while explaining the beings of the three scopes, there is a slightly extensive explanation of the training in moral discipline and the two trainings of concentration and wisdom during [the instructions for training the mind of] a being of great scope. Moral discipline is the foundation for [concentration and wisdom] that gives birth to all good qualities. Nagarjuna stated,

> Discipline is like the earth for the animate and inanimate;
> It is said to be the foundation of all good qualities.

The *[Tantra] Requested by Subahu* declares,

> Just as all crops grow faultlessly
> In dependence upon the earth,
> Likewise the supremely pure Dharma grows in dependence
> Upon moral discipline moistened by the water of compassion.

And,

> Moral discipline is the first source of mantra.

As this states, whether or not all the realizations of sutra and tantra develop depends upon moral discipline. The *Foundation of Medicine [from the Vinaya] Scripture*[486] states,

> If you become accustomed to the moral discipline of a bhikshu, you will dwell for a long time in concentration.
> If you become accustomed to concentration, you will abide in wisdom for a long time.
> If you become accustomed to wisdom, you will become liberated with a mind completely purified of attachment, hatred, and ignorance.

The primary obstacle to accomplishing liberation and omniscience is grasping at true existence, from which develops dualistic mistaken appearances that are factors to be purified as obstructions to omni-

486. Tib. *Lung sman gyi gzhi.*

science, for which the actual antidote is the realization of selflessness as the wisdom of superior seeing. Its primary cause is tranquil abiding, or, in other words, the higher training of concentration. Its primary cause is to have completely perfect restraint with respect to mistaken activities of body and speech, which is the higher training of moral discipline. [Ngulchu] Gyalsé Thogmé also stated,

> If you can't accomplish your own welfare without moral discipline,
> It is laughable to wish to accomplish the welfare of others.

It is a great lie[487] to say that you have stable concentration and excellent realizations without moral discipline. It is extremely beneficial to safeguard your moral discipline, as stated in the *King of Concentration Sutra*:

> Someone with a pure mind may worship the myriad
> Buddhas for as many tens of millions of eons as there are
> Grains of sands in the Ganges, with food, clothing,
> Parasols, banners, and a garland of lamps.
>
> Yet the merit of whomever trains in a single precept for
> A day and night when the holy Dharma is being destroyed
> And the Sugata's teachings are coming to an end
> Will be much greater than that.

Although you may have safeguarded all 253 precepts[488] while the Buddha was alive, there is greater benefit in safeguarding a single precept in this modern era, when the teachings are coming to an end. The principal form of moral discipline is the moral discipline of the pratimoksha [vows]. Master Chökyi Tsongpon proclaimed,

487. A "great lie" is a term used in reference to one of the four defeats of a monk or nun, which states that it is a "great lie" to claim that you have spiritual realizations that you in fact do not have. Here the point is that you are telling a great lie to claim that you have higher concentration or wisdom without training in higher moral discipline.
488. There are 253 vows of a fully ordained monk.

Just as the earth is the foundation for all living beings
From which seeds grow,
Likewise, understand that those who strive in the vows of
The Vinaya are the foundation from which their merit grows.
Moral discipline is the foundation of all good qualities
And is the bedrock of the Vinaya.

The Buddha said that he will appear in the place where a bhikshu adheres to the Vinaya. The *Sutra of Individual Liberation*[489] states,

When I have passed into nirvana,
This will be your teacher.
Out of respect for the ordained,
I earnestly offer praise in the presence of the assembly of bhikshus.

This is saying that the teachings of the Buddha rely upon the Sangha, which means the bhikshus and novices with vows in their mental continuums. This does not only mean great lamas who sit on thrones; even ordinary beings are holders of the teachings, and every novice or bhikshu is a being who is a holder of the teachings; they are upholders of the teachings of realization. Although it is rare to have both concentration and wisdom through teachings of realization, if you safeguard well your moral discipline of the pratimoksha [vows], you are an upholder of the teachings of realization. If the vows of a novice or bhikshu in your mental continuum deteriorate, although the teachings may be spread far and wide, the teachings in your mental continuum have disappeared; therefore, you must ensure that they don't disappear. Geshe Potowa stated,

Although we may not possess the public teachings, if we lose our vows, our share of the teachings has disappeared.

We use the phrase "The teachings have spread to the monasteries and mountain hermitages"; we don't say "temples, luminous offering substances, and many monks." If the Sangha have pure moral discipline,

489. Tib. *So sor thar pa'i mdo.*

then the teachings have spread, and we say they are "people upholding the teachings." The [line in a prayer] that states, "May the teachings of conqueror Losang spread" should refer to spreading in our own mental continuums. In this very moment, we hold in the palms of our hands the means of being counted either as a holder of the teachings or as someone who destroys or damages the teachings. The *Moon Lamp Sutra*[490] states,

> If you don't safeguard your discipline due to pride of listening
> To the various aspects of Dharma on enlightenment,
> Your improper moral discipline will send you to the lower realms,
> Where much learning will not be able to protect you.

Even if you are a scholar upholding sets of scriptures, if you don't protect your moral discipline, it will not benefit you, and you will go to the lower realms. If you don't safeguard your moral discipline, engaging in the purification and restoration rituals of Dharma protectors, receiving a vision of Yamaraja, and so on will not be able to help you. Thus, if your vows deteriorate, other than merely having a bald head, both this life and your future lives will be ruined. The *Manjushri Root Tantra* declares,

> Those who recite [mantras] with defiled moral discipline
> Will not accomplish supreme attainments
> Or the middling attainments either;
> They will not even possess the least of attainments.
>
> Buddha Shakyamuni does not say that those
> With faulty moral discipline will accomplish mantra.
> It is not even a region or direction for
> Those going to the city of liberation.
>
> Where is the attainment of mantra for
> These unfortunate childish beings?
> Where the happy migrations for
> These beings with faulty moral discipline?

490. Tib. *Zla ba sgron me'i mdo.*

> They will not even attain high status,
> Nor will they attain the supreme bliss; therefore,
> What need is there to mention accomplishing
> The mantras taught by the Conqueror?

Also, the *Sutra Cherishing a Bhikshu*[491] states,

> For some, moral discipline is happiness;
> For some, moral discipline is suffering;
> Possessing moral discipline is happiness;
> Corrupt moral discipline is suffering.

Another scripture states,

> If you safeguard moral discipline, what need is there to mention generating other good qualities? By possessing moral discipline, you accomplish your prayers.

It will even be easy to accomplish something as simple as your prayers. For that reason, since there is nothing more important than this teaching of the Bhagavan Buddha, you should at least cherish greatly these four root vows and the fifth, about alcohol. Even among these, alcohol and women are extraordinarily destructive. We must properly apply restraint to safeguard against all five of those imminent [root infractions], by applying introspection and conscientiousness. If we protect our vows and commitments by properly implementing the Dharma, the Dharma protectors will properly guard and protect us through the command of the compassionate Teacher. If we don't protect our moral discipline, even though we may beat drums, play music, and clap our cymbals, it will be utterly impossible for [the Dharma protectors] to protect us; therefore, we should safeguard our vows and commitments properly. With respect to alcohol, this does not pertain only to the ordained; even householder

491. Tib. *dGe slong la rab tu gces pa'i mdo.*

practitioners of mantra must refrain from it, as stated in the *Vajra Peak Tantra*, the *Kalachakra Tantra*, the *Sarvavid Tantra*,[492] and so on.

Query: You may wonder, "Well then, what about the need to utilize alcohol and women [that is taught in the tantras]?"

Response: This permission is given to those lion-like beings who have attained control over the exalted wisdom of bliss and emptiness. This is not permission given to all mantra practitioners. The *Drop of Mahamudra Tantra*[493] states,

> Pretending to be a yogi without yoga,
> Traversing the path to mahamudra
> And the methods of exalted wisdom without exalted wisdom—
> Have no doubt that they will go to hell.

Although donning the victory banner of the saffron robes, it is unsuitable for such people to [even] wear Dharma robes, and if they partake of various types of crude diet and activities, they are a repository of disgrace. The Dharma robes, such as the outer shawl, lower skirt, and so forth, are the attire blessed by the Buddha; therefore, it is inappropriate to use them to clean up garbage, polish vases, and so forth. With respect to disciples spreading out their robes like sitting mats when a lama is approaching to teach Dharma, previously, in India, when arhats assembled for teachings, they would stack their outer yellow robes as a teaching throne and so forth; yet because of the greatness of the Dharma, this was not a fault.

With respect to alcohol utilized during a tsok offering, it is a tantric samaya substance; therefore, it is permissible to merely place a drop on your tongue. There is no tradition of needing to drink it by filling up your drinking cup with alcohol from the tsok offering and saying it gives you strength. It is permissible to drink delicious tea as a substitute for alcohol. Atisha said that tea has [many] good qualities. This was the tradition of my gurus. If someone else needs payment of something like money, they shouldn't say it is for the cost of alcohol. There is a tradition of saying it is [to purchase] substances for flat bread and lunch; even by merely saying

492. Tib. *Kun rig rgyud.*
493. Tib. *rGyud phyag chen thig le.*

it is for the cost of alcohol, one incurs a great fault. For those with high regard for the Dharma of the Vinaya, there is a tradition of not using alcohol for the golden drink offering in the protector temples and so on that are reserved for Dharma protectors, and instead offering tea in its place. It would be excellent if we could do that.

If those who are ordained are unable to abandon alcohol and women, although they may subsequently bestow empowerments and blessing permissions of secret mantra, they should set aside those particular commitments for the time being. It is best if bhikshus and so forth bless their implements, their shoes,[494] and the first portions of their meals and [thereby] become ornaments of the teachings. At the time of the group of five [initial disciples of the Buddha], together with the Teacher there were six bhikshus in all, whose fame spread throughout the celestial realms, and in the *Sutra Endowed with Pure Moral Discipline*[495] it states,

> Although you may not hear it with your ears or see it with your eyes,
> The person who protects the teachings will be going to the higher realms.

Right now, we sit amid the members of the Sangha Jewel; therefore, it is important that we don't remain as a member of those laypeople who wear red robes.[496] If we have pure moral discipline, we will be honored and praised as the Sangha and will be unlike others. If we don't maintain pure moral discipline or live in harmony, and a layperson writes a letter to the monastic community requesting prayers, we should be ashamed of ourselves.[497]

We purify downfalls and so forth through sojong, [so] if we restore vows in our mental continuum and purify the downfall, it is [also] called

494. Bhikshus and bhikshunis must bless their monastic implements, such as their begging bowl, robes, staff, and so forth. There is also a precept for blessing the soles of one's shoes, so as to bless whatever insects may be killed by accidentally stepping on them throughout the day.
495. Tib. *Tshul khrims yang dag par ldan pa'i mdo.*
496. Here Pabongkha Rinpoche is referring to lay lamas who dress in robes and thus look very similar to monks.
497. This means that when laypeople send letters with a mind of faith requesting prayers to be said by the Sangha, yet as a monk you don't keep your vows, you should be ashamed of yourself.

sojong. The confession of [breaches of the] pratimoksha [vows] is done in the presence of the preceptor, instructor, and Sangha; [confession of breaches of] the bodhisattva [vows is done] in the presence of the guru, buddhas, and bodhisattvas; and [breaches of] the secret mantra are confessed in the presence of the guru and assembly of mandala deities. With respect to pure moral discipline, a sutra states,

> A bhikshu endowed with moral discipline is endowed with radiance.

And,

> This bhikshu is a great emporium with merchandise
> In the store of the collection of trainings.

The *Sutra Cherishing a Bhikshu* states,

> This moral discipline is supreme bliss.
> This moral discipline is the path to liberation.
> This moral discipline is the foundation of good qualities.
> This moral discipline is the cause of a buddha.

Je Lama [Tsongkhapa] declared,

> Moral discipline is the water cleansing the impurities of faults,
> The light of the moon dispelling the painful heat of the afflictions,
> Resplendent like the beings in the center of Mount Meru—
> All beings bow to its non-intimidating power;
> Through this knowledge, the holy beings protect
> The discipline of perfect restraint like their eyes.

Moreover, develop (1) the recognition of the Buddha's teachings on the pratimoksha, (2) the recognition of cherishing

> one's own training, and (3) the recognition that the Conqueror's teachings remain for a long time in dependence upon a method such as this.

It is very important that we think about these three [listed in the immediately preceding verse] as one and keep them as an important aspect of our practice. [Je Tsongkhapa's] *Great Treatise on the Stages of the Path to Enlightenment* also [quotes the *Sutra Endowed with Pure Moral Discipline*, which] states,

> Bhikshus, to lose your life and die is easy, yet to violate and destroy your moral discipline is not like that. Why? It is because by losing your life and dying, you only exhaust the lifespan of this very rebirth, but if you violate and destroy your moral discipline, you will experience great downfalls and cause yourself to be separated from your spiritual heritage and happiness over hundreds of thousands of rebirths.
>
> Using logical reasoning, you should safeguard [your moral discipline] even at the cost of your life.

There are four doors to incurring downfalls in the safeguarding of your vows; therefore, you should strive to learn them and close them. **Not knowing [the precepts]** is a door to incurring downfalls; therefore, you should learn the precepts. Furthermore, it would be best if you studied the greater and lesser texts on the Vinaya about the precepts, such as the four sets of scriptures on the Vinaya, the *Ocean Commentary*,[498] and texts by Je Rinpoche [Tsongkhapa], Khedrup Je, Dulzin, Gyalwa Gendun Drup [the First Dalai Lama], Gendun Gyatso [the Second Dalai Lama], and so on. At least you should learn [Geshe] Chen-nga-wa's combined four scriptures, Panchen Losang Chögyan's teachings, the *Binding Words of a Bhikshu's Training*,[499] Tseling Yongzin Rinpoche's teaching concerning the

498. Tib. *mTsho tika*.
499. Tib. *dGe slong gi bslab bya'i sdom tshig*.

three bases, and so on, as well as *A Rosary of Radiant Jewels: Precepts for the Three Vows,*[500] *The Versified Precepts for Novices and Bhikshus,*[501] and so on.

Carelessness is a door to incurring downfalls; therefore, you should safeguard your precepts with self-reproach and introspection. [Shantideva's] *Guide to the Bodhisattva's Way of Life* states,

> For those who wish to safeguard their minds,
> I fold my hands in prayer and say to them,
> "Always apply yourself to safeguarding
> Mindfulness and introspection."

Act out of self-reproach with respect to yourself, and act out of consideration with respect to others.

Lack of respect is a door to downfalls; therefore, you must rely upon the antidotes to the various afflictive emotions. The way to rely upon them is analogous to [how you would deal with] your primary enemy in times of war: you would first subdue [the one] that had the greatest strength.

In the same way, you should rely upon the antidote to whichever **afflictive emotion** is the most prominent. Furthermore, the antidote to attachment is unattractiveness, the antidote to hatred is love, and so on. With respect to unattractiveness, this can be learned from the sutra teachings addressing the perception of the body as a corpse and so on. There are also the conceptual elaborations of the mind that improperly apprehend the negative way of producing attachment as something good. The way to meditate on love as the antidote to hatred occurs during [the instructions on training the mind of] a being of great scope.

The antidote to pride is to meditate on the classifications of the elements[502] that you don't understand, such as an eye consciousness in even a single one of your eyes, the sources, how contact serves as the condition

500. Tib. *sDom gsum bslab bya nor bu'i 'od phreng.*

501. Tib. *dGe tshul slong gi bslab bya ka ri ka.*

502. There is a general breakdown of phenomena into aggregates, elements, and sources. Aggregates are both the five personal aggregates as well as the aggregates not associated with persons. Elements are the various internal and external elements that bind to form aggregations. Sources are the sense powers that are the means of ascertaining those aggregates and elements. See Hopkins, *Meditation on Emptiness*, 219.

for feeling, and so forth. Alternatively, with respect to pride, you can distinguish the elements as the basis of imputation for "I" through generating them in dependence upon apprehending them as whole. Through such investigation, your pride will be pacified. As an antidote to ignorance, you can focus on the incompatible causes, [other] causes, sources, and non-causes for samsara, Shiva, Brahma, and so forth, as well as meditate on the twelve links of dependent relationship. The *Scripture on Discernment* states,

> Whoever takes lightly and even slightly transgresses the
> Teachings of the compassionate Teacher
> Will come under the influence of suffering because of that,
> Just like cutting bamboo ruins the mango grove.
>
> A person in this world can even transgress the great words of
> A king without being subject to punishment,
> Yet if a person transgresses the instructions of the Muni,
> He will be reborn as an animal like the naga Elapatra.

As this states, it is inappropriate to be careless.

> Externally, you are peaceful and subdued through the conduct
> of a shravaka;
> Internally, you are endowed with competence in the yoga of
> the two stages;
> You should progress through the aide of mantra and the Vinaya.
> This intention is an uncommon unique feature of the teachings
> of the old and new Kadampas.

We should be practitioners who combine their practice in this way. In India, when Atisha was acting as the disciplinarian, he expelled Maitripa from the community for accepting alcohol. Khedrup [Je] Rinpoche expelled a siddha-monk from Ganden [Monastery]. Pure moral discipline is an [essential] teaching of the new and old Kadampas, as well as love, compassion, bodhichitta, and so on, which are externally obvious. The realization of clairvoyance, signs of attainment, and so on are not to be externally revealed but should be hidden like a butter lamp in a vase. Atisha stated,

> When I was in India, when things of great importance or unexpected activities arose, we would assemble those who are upholders of the scriptural collections and come to a definitive conclusion about whether these activities were contradictory to the three scriptural collections, in dependence upon which we would come to a decision. In addition to that, we [monks] of Vikramalashila[503] would make certain that there was no opposition to a bodhisattva's conduct and no conflicts. Yet it was the advice of the holders of Vinaya that we would put into action.

The final conclusion about whether or not an activity is permissible should be made by the holders of the Vinaya. The Vinaya is like the root of the other two scriptural collections, and moral discipline is the root of the three higher trainings; therefore, we should safeguard to the best of our ability the individual moral disciplines, from the vows of novices and bhikshus to the one-day precepts. This is also stated in the scriptures on the stages of the path. The *Tantra Requested by Subahu* states,

> Regarding the teachings that I, the Conqueror, taught
> On all of the pure moral disciplines of the
> pratimoksha,
> A mantra householder should abandon the signs[504]
> And practice all the remaining [precepts].

> If a mantra-practicing householder should properly practice the teachings in the Vinaya, with the exception of some of the rituals such as the activity rituals and adopting the signs of the

503. Vikramalashila was one of the two great Sanskrit Buddhist monastic institutions in India. Built by King Dharmapala (782–820), it was intended to compensate for the decline of scholarship at Nalanda, the other great Sanskrit monastery.
504. "Signs" refers to wearing robes, shaving your head, carrying a begging bowl, and so forth.

> ordained, what need is there to mention that those who are ordained should practice them?

Pabongkha Rinpoche once again gave a middle-length and [also] an elaborate explanation, beginning with meditating on impermanence as well as the importance of forsaking this life during [the instructions on training the mind of a being of] the small scope. He also gave a middle-length explanation of perceiving the entirety of samsara as the nature of suffering as an important factor for developing renunciation.

Day Twenty-Four

Tsongkhapa the Great stated,

> Just as I have fallen into the ocean of samsara . . .

As this quote indicates, if we contemplate how we have fallen into the ocean of samsara and have experienced its boundless and extremely fierce suffering for a long time, we will also have a corresponding degree of fear and trepidation for all living beings, who also experience the same type of suffering; the thought that wishes to free them from that [suffering] by oneself alone is bodhichitta.

During the section on a person of middling capacity, you contemplate your own experience of the suffering of samsara and consider how that relates to yourself. You then contemplate the way all living beings are tormented in that way as well and make the determination that thinks, "No matter what the cost, I am going to quickly attain the state of enlightenment for their sake; for that purpose, I am going to [listen to these teachings on the stages of the path to enlightenment]."

After giving this short introduction, Pabongkha Rinpoche covered the headings and once again explained the section on training in the mind striving for liberation.

There are different ways of teaching that state whether or not the mind striving for liberation and the intention of renunciation are synonymous. During the section on the person of small scope, you contemplate the sufferings of the hot hells and initiate renunciation, and during the section [on a person] of middling scope, you complete the foundation. You should not abandon your vows by engaging in a defeat of your vows that constitutes [one or more of] the four root downfalls.[505] If you incur a defeat of your vows through discordant factors or through a root downfall that is concealed and can't be restored[506] then you are not suited to be counted as a member of the Sangha. However, if you don't conceal them, then you are suited [to be a member of the Sangha]. Like the woman who made false claims about Geshe Langri Tangpa,[507] if you blame a bhikshu or novice for not having pure moral discipline it is an extremely grave fault. Although they may have previously been slightly sullied by faults in the past, as [Nagarjuna's *Letter to a Friend*] states,

> Whoever was once nonconscientious
> [And later becomes endowed with conscientiousness
> Is beautiful like a moon freed from clouds, just like
> Nanda, Angulimala, Darshaka, and Udayana.]

As I explained previously, if we properly practice confession and restraint, we will certainly be purified, like the moon freed from clouds.

Training the Mind in the Stages of the Path of a Person of Great Scope

Although you may gain freedom and attain liberation from samsara for yourself alone by contemplating the suffering of samsara during the section on a person of middling capacity, through training in the three higher trainings and so forth as a means of liberating yourself from that [suffering of samsara], just doing that for your own sake does nothing for completing the welfare of others. If you don't also abandon the obstructions to

505. Tib. *pham pa*. A "defeat" is a complete abandonment of your monk's or nun's vows that constitutes violating one of the four "roots"—namely, (1) killing, (2) stealing, (3) sexual contact, and (4) lying about having higher attainments.
506. Tib. *pham pa 'chab bcas*.
507. This most likely refers to a hypothetical situation put forth by Geshe Potowa, who asked Geshe Chen-nga-wa and Geshe Phuchungwa what they would do if a woman made a public statement that they had fathered her child. See Shönu Gyalchok and Könchok Gyaltsen, comps., *Mind Training*, trans. Thupten Jinpa (Boston: Wisdom, 2006), 412.

omniscience for the welfare of others, you haven't attained omniscience for your own welfare either, and so on. Even shravakas and pratyekabuddhas are not even able to accomplish the welfare for their own mothers,[508] as related in the event when Arya Shariputra looked to see where his own mother had taken rebirth. [Unable to locate her, Shariputra asked the Buddha to look,] and the Buddha himself indicated that [Shariputra's mother had been reborn] in the world to the north called Having Light Rays.

The extreme of existence is falling into samsara, and the extreme of peace is falling into the biased peace of a meditative equipoise on a true cessation. Although the buddhas have awakened [the shravakas and pratyekabuddhas] from the extreme of peace to teach the instructions of the Mahayana, it is difficult [for shravakas and pratyekabuddhas] to develop bodhichitta. Although the shravakas think that the path and result of the Mahayana taught by the Buddha are extremely amazing, they respond by stating, "We are like charred tree trunks, and the teachings are too difficult," which is due to the shravakas' own shortcomings. For that reason, it is important that we enter the path of the Mahayana right from the beginning. [Aryashura's] *Compendium of the Perfections*[509] states,

> By permanently abandoning both vehicles,
> We are powerless to accomplish the welfare of the world.
> Enter the vehicle that conqueror Shakyamuni taught
> Out of compassion that naturally only benefits others.

[Geshe] Potowa stated,

> Don't raise your lower garment twice to cross a river once;
> Enter the path of the Mahayana from the very beginning.

Disciples with the lineage of Hinayana will generate wrong views toward the Mahayana Dharma and are reborn in hell; therefore, obtaining the state of a Hinayana arhat becomes a great obstacle to enlightenment. As

508. This is because they have not attained the state of omniscience, so they don't fully know the most effective way of benefiting others.
509. Tib. *Phar phyin bsdus pa*.

related in the *Jeweled Heap Sutra*,[510] previously, Arya Shariputra was about to give instructions on the Hinayana to five hundred bhikshus of the Hinayana lineage when Manjushri gave them instructions on the Mahayana, whereby they developed wrong views. However, they asked the Buddha about this, and he said that Manjushri had revealed skillful means and that the [Hinayana bhikshus] would quickly become enlightened.

For that reason, it is important to enter the Mahayana from the beginning. Furthermore, [Chandragomin's] *Letter to a Disciple* states,

> Like a moving horse, the light of the magnificent sun shines everywhere;
> The earth supports the whole world without concern for the burden;
> This is similar to the nature of great beings who are without self-interest
> And strive solely for the benefit and happiness of the world.

Those who enter the path of the Mahayana must strive only in the means of accomplishing the benefit and happiness of others. Bodhichitta is the only gateway to the Mahayana that is suitable for such a being; therefore, we should train our minds in it.

[Training the Mind in the Stages of the Path of a Person of Great Scope] has three sections:

1. Revealing That Bodhichitta Is the Sole Gateway to the Mahayana, Together with Its Benefits
2. How to Develop Bodhichitta
3. How to Train in the Bodhisattva's Deeds once We Have Developed Bodhichitta

510. Tib. *dKon mchog brtsegs pa'i mdo.*

Revealing That Bodhichitta Is the Sole Gateway to the Mahayana, Together with Its Benefits

Bodhichitta Is the Gateway to the Mahayana

We contemplate the benefits prior to the training to instill enthusiasm for training the mind in bodhichitta, which is also the tradition of my guru. Furthermore, this is not my own fabrication but is conjoined with the oral instructions in *Mind Training: An Ornament of Losang's True Intent*.[511]

Whether you can even be counted as someone who has entered the Mahayana depends on whether you have developed bodhichitta in your mental continuum. If you don't have bodhichitta, then even if you practice something like Guhyasamaja, the ultimate king of the tantras for a thousand years, you will not make the slightest progress toward the causes of enlightenment. Yet if you have taken hold of bodhichitta, then even reciting one Mani will become the cause of enlightenment. Even those of us who are Mahayanists and who may be proud of being top students can find it difficult to recognize bodhichitta as the [sole] gateway to the Mahayana. Although some assert that bodhichitta is merely a prayer that thinks "May I attain enlightenment for the welfare of all living beings," that is a huge error and is mistaken in terms of both prayer and actuality.

It is rare for most of us to investigate just what exactly the term *bodhichitta* means. We must develop great compassion from the outset of developing bodhichitta. Atisha gave a strong reprimand when he stated, "Tibetans regard those who lack knowledge of both love and compassion as bodhisattvas!" Therefore, there is no such thing as a bodhisattva without knowledge of love and compassion. If you either have bodhichitta in your mental continuum or are in the process of developing it, then you have entered into the ranks of the Mahayana. However, if you abandon it, you have been expelled from the ranks of the Mahayana.

Without bodhichitta, enlightenment is impossible. Even all the buddhas of the ten directions first generated bodhichitta in their mental continuums and sequentially became enlightened. Whether or not you have entered the path of the Mahayana is not determined by the view

511. Tib. *Blo sbyong blo bzang dgongs rgyan*. This is a very famous mind-training text by Kachen Yeshe Gyaltsen.

[of emptiness]; instead, it must be determined by engaging in the deeds of a bodhisattva. [Tsongkhapa's] *Great Treatise on the Stages of the Path to Enlightenment* states,

> It is not enough that the Dharma is Mahayana; it is important that the person be someone who has entered the Mahayana.

Atisha the Great also stated,

> Those fortunate beings who wish to enter the gateway of
> The Mahayana Dharma should sincerely and repeatedly generate
> Bodhichitta, which is like the sun and moon
> That dispel darkness and pacify suffering.

Previously, when Atisha was staying in Tibet, an Indian acharya arrived, and [he and Dromtonpa] had a long discussion one evening. The following day, [Atisha] asked Dromtonpa what they had talked about and [Drom] replied, "These days in India, there is a Hevajra yogi who attained the result of a stream-enterer." Astonished, Atisha praised [his own guru,] saying, "My conventional bodhichitta; my guru Serlingpa." At another time in the past, Atisha said to Drom, "Go prepare a red torma," and made dedication prayers. [Atisha] also said, "There was a Yamantaka yogi from India who was reborn as a demon. When this spirit was staying here in Tibet, he was causing great harm, so I gave him a torma and I drove him away." Lodrak Drubchen proclaimed,

> If you aren't embraced by bodhichitta, you will be reborn as a spirit through your numerous recitations.

If you don't have bodhichitta, although you may practice the profound Dharma of secret mantra, you have given up your inclusion in the Mahayana. Some secret mantra yogis are reborn in hell and some, such as the brahman youth Chanakya, are said to be reborn as evil spirits and so on, as well as the historical account of the Bhairava yogi from Phenpo.[512] If

512. These stories were related earlier, under the section on karma.

you have not been embraced by bodhichitta, no matter how excellent the [systems of meditation] may be, such as the generation and completion stages, channels and winds, mahamudra, dzogchen, and so on, they will not be of any benefit. For these reasons, precious bodhichitta is like the life tree for attaining enlightenment. Je Tsongkhapa stated,

> Bodhichitta is the main path of the supreme vehicle,
> The basis and foundation of the vast activities [of a bodhisattva],
> Like an elixir for every one of the two collections,
> A treasury of merit that assembles the limitless virtuous collections.
>
> Through this understanding, the buddhas and bodhisattva heroes
> Take this precious supreme mind as the core of their practice.

The Conqueror and his spiritual sons the bodhisattvas praise and keep bodhichitta solely as their primary spiritual practice. All the buddhas in the ten directions also state that taking this as one's primary spiritual practice is the only way to progress to the state of enlightenment. [Maitreya's] *Sublime Continuum* states,

> Wisdom is the seed of the supreme vehicle,
> The mother giving birth to the buddha qualities.

Bodhichitta is the uncommon cause of enlightenment and is also like the father. The wisdom realizing emptiness is the common cause of all three vehicles, and is like water, manure, warmth, and so forth, and is likened to the mother. Glorious Nagarjuna also stated,

> The sole path to liberation that the buddhas,
> Pratyekabuddhas, and shravakas
> Definitely rely upon,
> And [of which] you proclaim with certainty that there is no other . . .

We Will Be Called a Child of the Conqueror

Thus, with respect to the wisdom realizing emptiness, [the wisdom realizing emptiness] functions as the cause for attaining the "enlightenment"[513] of whomever you meet of the three vehicles. Bodhichitta does not go to any other vehicle and is the sole cause of the Mahayana and the cause of enlightenment. Without training in bodhichitta, although those wishing to attain enlightenment may work to accumulate merit and purify negative karma for many eons, it will not become the cause of their enlightenment. Generating bodhichitta is the cause of bodhisattvas and the cause of buddhas as well. Whoever generates bodhichitta—even something like a dog or a donkey—becomes an object of prostration for migrating beings, including the gods. When a person generates bodhichitta in his or her mental continuum, the thrones of all the buddhas in the ten directions tremble, their minds become joyous, and they extol verses of praise. Furthermore, the buddhas' great joy is analogous to something like each new birth of a son to a king. This sort of thing does not happen even when a shravaka becomes an arhat. Even Maitreya, Manjushri, and so forth perceive you as their bodhisattva sibling. Atisha the Great stated,

> Guru Serlingpa performed the most exalted deed of all my gurus, since whatever degree of bodhichitta I have is due to his kindness.

We Will Surpass Shravakas and Pratyekabuddhas

Even when you first develop the aspiration for supreme enlightenment, you outshine all the shravakas, pratyekabuddhas, and so forth. The *Array of Stalks Sutra* states,

> Child of the lineage, it is like this. For example, there are merchants who have returned from a great ocean holding a priceless precious jewel. When they arrive at the city, their jewel outshines a hundred thousand other jewels through its color and value. Likewise, although they abide in the great ocean of samsara, those who take the boat ride of prayers

513. Sometimes the resultant states of the shravaka vehicle, the pratyekabuddha vehicle, and the bodhisattva vehicle are referred to as small, middling, and great enlightenments, respectively.

for the priceless precious jewel of bodhichitta of omniscience have in their mental continuums a superior intention from the first moment they generate the mind of a bodhisattva. Although they have yet to arrive at the city of omniscience, they outshine the jewel-like shravakas and pratyekabuddhas who have arrived at the city of liberation.

Also, the *Liberation of Maitreya Sutra*[514] states,

> Child of the lineage, it is like this. For example, shortly after someone has taken rebirth as the child of a king, he bears the name of the king. And even though the assembly of ministers may become respected principal elders, the power of this great being of the lineage outshines them all. Likewise, shortly after a bodhisattva first generates bodhichitta, he is born in the lineage of the king of the Dharma the Tathagata, and through the power of his bodhichitta and compassion he outshines the shravakas and pratyekabuddhas who have been practicing the brahman conduct [that is, celibacy] for a long time.
>
> Child of the lineage, it is like this. For example, shortly after [a garuda] is born as the offspring of a great and powerful garuda, whatever good qualities of wing wind power and perfect eyesight it has are not possessed by the entire assembly of other birds that have grown to maturity. Likewise, as soon as a bodhisattva first generates bodhichitta, he emerges in an impeccable lineage of the great and powerful garuda the Tathagata. Through the power of his wing of generating bodhichitta for omniscience, the child of the great and powerful garuda conquers his enemies. Whatever good qualities he has of the eyesight of pure superior intention are not possessed by all the shravakas and pratyekabuddhas who have [practiced] renunciation for hundreds of thousands of eons, and he outshines the shravakas and pratyekabuddhas even through his lineage.

514. Tib. *Byams pa rnam par thar pa'i mdo.*

Also, the same sutra declares,

> Child of the lineage, it is like this. For example, although a diamond may break, it outshines all the superior qualities of golden ornaments, and it still does not relinquish its name "diamond" and even overcomes all poverty. Child of the lineage, in the same way, those who generate bodhichitta for omniscience, although they lack its application, outshine all the golden ornaments that are the shravakas and pratyekabuddhas, do not relinquish even the name "bodhisattva," and even overcome all the poverty of samsara.

Therefore, bodhichitta is like the king post or tree trunk of the Mahayana path. The paths of small and middling scopes as well as secret mantra are like the limbs; therefore, you must sincerely apply yourself to bodhichitta. With respect to those who don't practice bodhichitta yet pretend to be Mahayanist, this is a perfect indication of not having heard the instructions on the Mahayana; if they do not have bodhichitta, they are not Mahayanists. It is said that once we have generated bodhichitta, we produce the paths in stages, beginning with the path of accumulation.

We Will Become a Supreme Object of Veneration

All the great beings such as gods, humans, nagas, and so forth bow to the person who has generated bodhichitta. Even the buddhas are born in dependence upon bodhisattvas; therefore, because bodhichitta is the cause of the tathagatas, the tathagatas also prostrate to bodhisattvas. [As the *Jeweled Heap Sutra* states,] "Kashyapa, [just as beings] prostrate to the new moon and not the full moon . . ." The *Jeweled Heap Sutra* also states,

> Ananda, if a bodhisattva sat in a chariot and enjoyed a feast with the five sense objects and enjoyed the presence of a woman, and there was no one else to pull his chariot, Ananda, [then I,] the Tathagata, would carry that chariot of that bodhisattva on my head. Yet even if the elders Shariputra and Maudgalyayana remained for more than an eon with their three doors

> in a state of complete liberation, the Tathagata would not diligently perform acts of veneration and service.

[Shantideva's] *Guide to the Bodhisattva's Way of Life* states,

> If anyone who repays the kindness shown to them
> Even sometimes is worthy of praise,
> What need is there to mention a bodhisattva
> Who does so perfectly even when not required?

It Is the Supreme Means of Accumulating Merit

If you generate this mind [of bodhichitta], it becomes the supreme means of accumulating merit. Shantideva stated [in his *Guide to the Bodhisattva's Way of Life*],

> Whoever perfectly adopts that mind [of aspiring bodhichitta],
> From that moment on, even while asleep or even [if] careless,
> A continuous stream of powerful merit
> Will flow that is equal to the extent of space.

You attain such benefits even from aspiring bodhichitta. Furthermore, [Shantideva's *Guide to the Bodhisattva's Way of Life*] states,

> If even just the thought to dispel
> The mere headache of living beings
> Is such a beneficial intention
> That transforms into limitless merit,
>
> What need is there to mention wishing to dispel
> The limitless unhappiness of each and every living being
> And the wish to produce limitless good qualities
> In each and every one of them?

If, as this states, even generating just the altruistic intention to merely eliminate the headache of a single living being [produces merit], then if we generate the intention to dispel all the suffering of every living being and establish every living being in every form of happiness, the amount of merit that this would create would be limitless.

Previously, when the compassionate Teacher was born as the brahman youth named Star,[515] due to his strong attachment to a girl, he had to defer practicing celibacy for twelve years, which delayed his accumulation of merit by ten thousand eons. Once again, when he was born as a boat captain with very strong compassion, he killed an evil man named Dungthug Chen and [thus] completed the accumulation of merit that would have taken a hundred thousand eons to accumulate. This was not a nonvirtuous act but instead he completed his collection of merit through the great power of his compassion. Not only that, [but as Shantideva's *Guide to the Bodhisattva's Way of Life* states,]

> If the everyday act of giving a tiny morsel of food
> Even just once to a few beings for half a day and in a
> Disrespectful way is a deed of satiation
> Called "an act of virtue" and respected by beings,
>
> What need is there to mention the eternal gift of
> The unsurpassed bliss of the sugatas
> To countless living beings for a long time,
> Which completely fulfills all of their wishes?

Glorious Nagarjuna stated,

> Even the Conqueror cannot calculate
> The mass of merit of a being
> Who meditates on
> Bodhichitta for just an instant.

The merit of even merely generating bodhichitta is limitless. Even by offering a single bundle of incense for the welfare of all living beings, you obtain merit equal to the merit that would [be accumulated] by each one of those countless beings offering [his or her own] bundle of incense.

515. Tib. sKar ma.

Through being enveloped by bodhichitta, even giving a leftover scrap of food to a dog becomes a bodhisattva's deed; it becomes a cause for the attainment of enlightenment. [Shantideva's] *Guide to the Bodhisattva's Way of Life* also states,

> Like a supreme elixir that transforms [things] into gold,
> Firmly grasp this thing called bodhichitta
> That transforms this impure human body
> We have into the priceless jewel of the Conqueror's body.
>
> Since the immeasurable mind of the sole guide of migrating beings
> Investigated thoroughly and discovered the great value
> Of precious bodhichitta, those with the desire to be free from
> The abodes of migrating beings should firmly grasp this excellent mind.

We Will Quickly Purify Our Negative Karma and Obscurations

Even for purifying negative karma and obscurations, bodhichitta is supreme. Even the negativity that can't be purified through the great force of confession can instantly be purified through generating bodhichitta. [Shantideva's] *Guide to the Bodhisattva's Way of Life* states,

> Our negativity is extremely powerful and enduring;
> Other than perfect bodhichitta,
> What other virtue can overcome it?

And,

> Like the fire at the end of time, [bodhichitta]
> Definitely incinerates great negativities in an instant.

A historical account also states that in India, a yogi of Guru Maitreya was chanting and meditating on mind training while singing vajra songs and sitting on the banks of the Ganges River, and by training his mind in nothing other than bodhichitta, he purified a vast amount of obscurations, as was confirmed by a direct vision of protector Maitreya. Also, Asanga practiced [to see] protector Maitreya for twelve years, whereby he encountered a female dog with a broken hind leg and infested by worms. Moved by his powerful compassion, he purified his severe obscurations and immediately had a direct vision of protector Maitreya. Nyuk-rum-pa said,

> If you give rise to this bodhichitta once,
> You accumulate the collection of merit,
> You purify the obscurations,
> And you dispel obstacles.

Shantideva also stated [in his *Guide to the Bodhisattva's Way of Life*],

> Having considered it for many eons,
> The buddhas perceived that only this is beneficial.

The bhagavan buddhas thought about what is beneficial for all living beings to attain the state of enlightenment, and having considered this for many eons, they perceived that bodhichitta alone is the greatest benefit. Having perceived this, this became what they primarily teach.

We Will Easily Accomplish Our Goals

If you have bodhichitta, you will accomplish whatever you set your mind to; those with bodhichitta will perfect whatever enlightened actions they engage in. If you don't have bodhichitta, you won't be able to do something as insignificant as merely causing it to rain when rain is scarce. If you have bodhichitta, all the collections of ritual actions and knowledge mantras, as well as proclaiming words of truth on down, will be accomplished without obstruction.

Previously, while Je Monlam Pel [1414–1491] was serving as the [Eighth] Ganden Tripa and no one else was able to turn back the overflowing waters of the Tsangpo River in Lhasa, he caused the waters to recede with the words of truth "Monlam Pel is a bodhisattva." Bodhisattva Sadaprarudita also proclaimed words of truth by offering the flesh of his body and so on. Also, the *Array of Stalks Sutra* states,

> Like the king of wish-fulfilling jewels that truly accomplishes all of one's aims,
> Like the excellent vase that thoroughly completes all of your intentions . . .

And,

> If you meditate with great force on bodhichitta, what need is there to mention that this will accomplish all other intentions? You will even effortlessly understand the teachings.

The *Question of Narayana Sutra*[516] states,

> Regarding the radiant stainless Dharma that the great bodhisattvas desire, it is a deep mine of Dharma and is hidden inside trees and even transformed into limitless scriptures that are the gateway to the Dharma that now rests in the palm of your hand.[517]

The *Compendium of True Dharma*[518] states,

> Although the conqueror Buddha may not dwell in the perfect contemplation of the Bhagavan, the Dharma [may even] emerge from the sphere of space, a wall, or a tree. Regarding the contemplations of a bodhisattva, the instructions come from their mental analysis itself, and all subsequent teachings emerge.

Therefore, if we desire enlightenment, we must first apply ourselves to the means of generating bodhichitta. Enlightenment will not be possible through any other means. The *Sutra of the Fortunate Eon* also states, "First generate bodhichitta . . ." There are many such scriptural occurrences

516. Tib. *Sred med kyi bus zhus pa'i mdo.*
517. This is in reference to hidden scriptures that are placed inside trees and so forth by means of magical powers.
518. Tib. *Chos yang dag par sdud pa.*

which state that all the thousand buddhas of the fortunate eon will proceed in this way.

We Will Not Be Damaged by Harm and Obstacles

Since Vajrapani, the [four] great kings, and so forth act as his special guardians, a bodhisattva has twice as many guardians as a chakravartin king; therefore, he cannot be harmed by humans, nonhumans, and so forth. Khamlungpa also states that [wherever] one stays after developing bodhichitta, it would be improper for the humans and nonhumans of that place to inflict harm on such a person, and that they will even come to have affection for him, and so on. The *Array of Stalks Sutra* declares,

> Child of the lineage, it is like this. For example, there is an elixir called "unforsaken"; if you hold on to that [elixir], you will not incur any harm or fear from others. Likewise, if a bodhisattva also holds on to the elixir of bodhichitta, he will not incur any harm or fear from samsara.

There are many scriptures which state that you cannot be affected by harms and obstacles. Bodhichitta is also the very best for purifying the two obstructions together with their imprints.

We Will Quickly Complete All the Grounds and Paths

If you have bodhichitta in your mental continuum, you will quickly complete all the grounds and paths. The *Liberation of Maitreya Sutra* states,

> Bodhichitta is like the seed of all the Buddhadharma,
> Like a field that increases the virtuous Dharma of all migrating beings,
> Like the earth that supports all worlds,
> Like the water that purifies all the stains of the afflictive emotions,
> Like the wind for all worlds without a support,
> Like the fire that incinerates all roots of perpetuating views,
> Like the sun that illuminates the abodes of all living beings,
> Like the moon that completely envelops the mandalas of all virtuous Dharmas,

> Like a lamp that illuminates the Dharma,
> Like eyes that thoroughly perceive what is similar and dissimilar . . .

There are many teachings such as this. Through relying upon the kindness of bodhichitta, you will quickly complete the path as well as the result of the Mahayana.

We Will Become a Field That Produces Every Happiness and Well-Being for Migrating Beings

In short, all the virtue and excellence of samsara and peace arise from the power of bodhichitta. [Chandrakirti's] *Guide to the Middle Way* states:

> Shravakas and middling buddhas are born from the Powerful Able One;
> Buddhas are born from bodhisattvas;
> The mind of compassion, the mind of nonduality,
> And bodhichitta are the causes of the Conqueror's sons.

As this states, all the happiness and well-being of this world arise in dependence upon the kindness of the Buddha, the buddhas also emerge in dependence upon a bodhisattva who is one with his own mental continuum, and the bodhisattva also arises from the teachings on bodhichitta. The middling buddhas are pratyekabuddhas; because they have not perfected their realization of suchness, they are called "middling powerful able ones."

Thus, it is only this precious bodhichitta that is indispensable for the attainment of enlightenment; therefore, we must train ourselves by making this the central focus of our practice. Naljor Chenpo said to [Drom]tonpa Rinpoche, "I offer my realization of perfect concentration." [Drom]tonpa replied,

> You keep your vows well. Although you are not stained by even the most subtle faults of engaging in your vows, and you may have such excellent concentration that you would not be disturbed by someone beating a drum right next to your ear,

> if you don't have my love, compassion, and bodhichitta, you should generate regret and perform confession day and night.

Avadhutipa said to Atisha, "Although you may have concentration as firm as a mountain, you have not reached perfection whatsoever; instead, you should train your mind in love, compassion, and bodhichitta." If you don't have love, compassion, and bodhichitta, no matter how much you meditate on mahamudra, dzogchen, the channels and winds, maintaining the mind's essence, and so forth, you will still be turning the wheel of samsara. Lacking the eye of intelligence to distinguish what is and what is not a path is the fault of not meeting a lama who teaches the path. At Ratreng, Drom[tonpa] asked, "What are the three brothers doing these days?[519] He was told, "Khamlungpa is meditating on bodhichitta and cries." Drom[tonpa] offered his praise, saying, "He is a true Dharma practitioner," and so on.

If, despite our desire to attain enlightenment, we don't have the desire to train our minds in bodhichitta, then no matter how much effort we put into other paths, we will not get anywhere. Therefore, you must see the absolute necessity of doing everything you can to at least establish the imprint of the entire path through [the lamrim]. If you only have bodhichitta yet don't have any other good qualities, you are still a Mahayanist. Whether or not you attain the state of enlightenment strictly depends on whether or not you have bodhichitta; therefore, you must make a sincere effort to elicit an experience of bodhichitta by applying yourself to it for months and years.

The Actual Stages of Training the Mind has three sections:

1. The Way to Train in Bodhichitta
2. Training the Mind by Way of the Sevenfold Oral Instructions of Cause and Effect
3. The Importance of Compassion

519. The three brothers are Geshe Potowa, Geshe Chen-nga-wa, and Geshe Phuchungwa. For more information, see Thupten Jinpa, trans., ed., and comp., *Wisdom of the Kadam Masters* (Boston: Wisdom, 2013).

The Way to Train in Bodhichitta

As Atisha stated, "You must train in stages." The Teacher taught two systems for this: (1) the instructions on the sevenfold cause and effect that come from the *Liberation of Maitreya Sutra* and (2) training the mind by way of equalizing and exchanging self with others, which is taught in the *Sport of Manjushri Sutra*.[520] Atisha is the lord of them both. Equalizing and exchanging self with others contains all [the points of] the instructions on the sevenfold cause and effect, yet these seven do not contain all the points of equalizing and exchanging self with others. Nevertheless, the instructions on the sevenfold cause and effect are an important preliminary, and if you train your mind in these seven, it will give great strength to equalizing and exchanging self with others.

Training the Mind by Way of the Sevenfold Oral Instructions of Cause and Effect

For all seven of these, each of the previous stages functions as a cause for the subsequent stages. To generate bodhichitta in your mental continuum, you take on the burden of others' welfare as [your] superior intention. To generate that [superior intention] in your mental continuum, it must be preceded by compassion that is unable to bear others being tormented by suffering. To generate great compassion in your mental continuum, it must be preceded by a mind of affectionate love for all living beings that is similar to love for one's own child. To generate affectionate love, you must perceive all living beings as benevolent.

As a precursor to that, you must consider all living beings as your mother, recall their kindness, and develop the wish to repay their kindness. If you first recognize all living beings as your mother, the wish to repay their kindness will emerge. Due to the emergence of that, you will develop affectionate love and so on. Thus, each of the previous contemplations induces each of the subsequent [contemplations]. According to the teachings of Atisha, the translation equivalent of "instruction" is *upadesha*

520. Tib. *'Jam dpal rnam par rol pa'i mdo.*

[in Sanskrit], which means "essential practice" and "that which functions to abandon harm."

For this, there are two ways of training the mind. Because the first is generated in a definite sequence, the headings are taught [in that sequence]. [To state them in reverse sequence,] complete enlightenment emerges from bodhichitta; that bodhichitta emerges from superior intention; that [superior intention emerges] from compassion; that [compassion emerges] from affectionate love that cherishes [all beings] like an only child; that [affectionate love emerges] from repaying the kindness of [all beings]; that [repayment] emerges from recalling their kindness; and that [recalling their kindness] emerges from perceiving them as your mother. At this point, there are extensive teachings on how the three components of recognizing [all beings] as your mother, recalling their kindness, and repaying their kindness are the cause of great compassion, as well as on how superior intention and so on are the result of great compassion. Thus, great compassion is extremely important. Although bodhichitta is the sole cause of a buddha, it is born from great compassion; therefore, we must sincerely apply ourselves to [great compassion].

Compassion Is Important in the Beginning

In general, with respect to secret mantra, we must develop an exceedingly special and superior bodhichitta. If you don't have [bodhichitta], although you may practice secret mantra with the desire to become enlightened for yourself alone, you will become a pratyekabuddha. Furthermore, with respect to a bodhisattva of the perfection vehicle, this is similar to a situation where, if a child were to fall into a fire, although others might wish to pull him out, they would not immediately implement a means of extracting him. With respect to a bodhisattva of secret mantra, this is analogous to a situation where the child's father would find it unbearable to leave his son even for a short time in a fire pit and would find it necessary to jump into the fire pit, and once he jumped in he would immediately pull his son out. Therefore, the difference in the bodhichitta of the perfection vehicle and [that of secret] mantra is similar to the [difference in] intensity of the compassion of the father whose son fell into the fire pit and [that of] his other relatives and so forth.

There are five special features that determine the speed with which even a bodhisattva progresses on the path of the Mahayana, as well as how weak the power of your compassion is. If you have very strong compassion, that will result in very powerful bodhichitta and bring great power to everything else, such as your bodhisattva deeds and so on. Through the degree of that [compassion], you will quickly progress to the state of enlightenment. For that reason, within the three commentaries,[521] great compassion occurs at this point. Thus, since great compassion is so important, glorious Chandrakirti stated in [the *Guide to the Middle Way*,]

> Because compassion itself is the seed of the
> Supreme harvest of the Conqueror, as well as
> Water for its growth and the fruit that remains for a long time,
> I begin by praising compassion.

Great compassion is like the seed for the crop of attaining the state of enlightenment. Initially, compassion is important as a cause for entering the Mahayana; bearing the responsibility of liberating migrating beings depends on compassion, and [compassion] is likewise the path and the fruit of the Mahayana for bodhichitta and so forth. Therefore, in the beginning compassion is like the helping hand of migrating beings.

Great compassion is so extremely important that it has a separate heading explaining it as the root of the path. The *Compendium of True Dharma Sutra* states that of all powers, [great compassion] is the life force in the beginning, and draws the analogy of it being like the precious wheel that is the first of the seven precious possessions of a chakravartin king.[522] That same sutra [that is, the *Compendium of True Dharma Sutra*] states,

> If a bodhisattva were to properly grasp and realize a single Dharma, he would hold all the Dharmas of the Buddha in the palm of his hand. What is that single Dharma? It is great compassion! Bhagavan, the Dharma of all buddhas that the

521. This could possibly refer to the *Middle-Length* and *Great Treatise[s] on the Stages of the Path* as well as to Atisha's *Lamp for the Path to Enlightenment*, since the explanation of great compassion appears at this point in those three commentaries.
522. The seven precious possessions of a chakravartin king are the precious wheel, jewel, queen, minister, elephant, horse, and general. For a detailed description of each one, see Kachen Yeshe Gyaltsen, *Manjushri's Innermost Secret*.

> bodhisattvas hold in the palms of their hands is great compassion. Bhagavan, this is analogous to the way in which, wherever the precious wheel of a chakravartin king exists, his army also exists.[523] Bhagavan, likewise, wherever the great compassion of a bodhisattva exists, all Dharmas of the Buddha also exist. Bhagavan, for example, if the life force exists, all other powers also exist. Bhagavan, likewise, if great compassion exists, there will also emerge the other Dharmas of a bodhisattva.

Compassion Is Important in the Middle

You may [develop great compassion] at one time and, if you have great compassion, you can work for the welfare of living beings despite their bad behavior and engage in whatever austerities are required without this ever becoming wearing or causing your bodhichitta to decline. Although Arya Shariputra was initially a bodhisattva, he gave his right hand to an evil mara, whereby the evil mara placed the hand on his head and said, "Don't give me that," which caused him to become discouraged about compassion.

Compassion Is Important in the End

While shravakas, pratyekabuddhas, and so forth are in single-pointed meditative equipoise, they do absolutely nothing for the welfare of living beings, yet no matter how long the Buddha remains in meditative equipoise on peace, he continuously works for the welfare of living beings, which comes from his great compassion. The teacher Shang Nachung asked Atisha for advice, to which [Atisha] replied, "Give up on this life; meditate on love, compassion, and bodhichitta." [The teacher Shang Na-

523. Kachen Yeshe Gyaltsen, *Manjushri's Innermost Secret*, 137, states, "The precious wheel is produced from gold and has a thousand spokes. It is five hundred leagues in width. It is not made by a blacksmith but is produced through the force of the merit of the chakravartin king. It moves through the realms of space like the sun and travels a hundred thousand leagues in a single day. Through the power of the wheel, the chakravartin king and his four branches of soldiers are able to travel through the four continents and heavenly abodes of the four great kings. Anything that he can imagine is able to be produced by the wheel."

chung] said, "Even though I asked for Dharma, he said nothing other than that." Dromtonpa replied, "That was Atisha's innermost instruction."

These instructions are difficult to absorb within your mind, and they are all very difficult to develop; therefore, you must make a sincere effort at the means of accumulating merit, purifying negative karma, and so on.

How [Compassion] Is Either Cause or Effect for the Others in [the Sevenfold Instructions of] Cause and Effect has two sections:

1. How Love Comes from Recognizing All Beings as Your Mother
2. The Actual Stages of Training the Mind [in Bodhichitta]

In general, there are two similar aspects [of compassion]: compassion that is unable to bear living beings being tormented by strong suffering, and great compassion, for which we need affection for all living beings, whether they be enemies, friends, or strangers. Furthermore, the strength or weakness of your great compassion arises in accordance with the extent to which your affection and concern are great or small. To perceive them in an aspect of affection and concern, you must perceive all living beings as your dear mother, who is the ultimate loved one. For that reason, recognizing all beings as your mother, recalling their kindness, and wishing to repay their kindness are causes, while great compassion is the result. The wish that living beings have happiness is love. To perceive all living beings as extremely pleasing and cherish them deeply, like a mother's [love] for her child, is affectionate love. Therefore, the love of the sevenfold cause and effect is affectionate love. If we generate affectionate love for all living beings, we will generate compassion that wishes that they will have happiness and be free of suffering.

Query: If you generate great compassion that not only wishes that all living beings be free from suffering but also wishes to protect them from suffering, wouldn't there be no need to contemplate superior intention[524] in between [generating compassion and then generating bodhichitta]?

524. As we shall see in the instructions that follow, superior intention is a mind that has assumed the responsibility of leading all beings to the state of liberation and enlightenment by oneself

Reply: The bodhisattva has the thought, "I alone will ensure that living beings are free from suffering and come to possess happiness"; therefore, we need superior intention, which is not possessed by shravakas and pratyekabuddhas. If that were not necessarily so, shravakas and pratyekabuddhas would have bodhichitta. You must have the thought that thinks, "Only a buddha has the capacity to establish all living beings in a state that is free from every suffering and that possesses every form of happiness; therefore, I must attain the state of a buddha for the welfare of all living beings."

Pabongkha Rinpoche explained these points again in moderate detail.

alone and that is therefore determined to attain the state of enlightenment as a means of accomplishing that goal.

Day Twenty-Five

The king of Dharma Tsongkhapa the Great stated [in the *Three Principal Aspects of the Path*],

> Carried away by the currents of the four powerful rivers,
> Tightly bound by the chains of karma that are difficult to release,
> Tangled within the iron web of self-grasping,
> Enveloped by the thick all-obscuring darkness of ignorance,
>
> Continuously taking rebirth in boundless samsara, and
> Unceasingly tormented by the three types of suffering—
> Generate the supreme mind [of bodhichitta] by contemplating
> The state of affairs of your mothers who are in such a situation.

As master Jampal Drakpa states, just as it is unbearable for us to be tormented by the sufferings of samsara, so our mother living beings are in the same situation. They are continuously tormented by the four rivers: (1) the river of desire, (2) the river of samsara, (3) the river of ignorance, and (4) the river of [wrong] view. Sometimes they are bound by immutable karma[525] and so forth. In short, they have been thrust into a dark prison of ignorance and so forth. Although living beings are tormented by the suffering of samsara in the same way you are, they have nurtured you with kindness since beginningless time in samsara and are nothing other than your dear mothers. [Set your motivation for listening to the

525. Tib. *mi g.yo ba'i las*. This could also be translated as "unmoving karma." It refers to certain karmic actions that cannot be altered, such as the attainment of the concentration that results in the first formless realm.

teachings by thinking,] "Therefore, I will listen to the stages on the path to enlightenment that is the king of instructions of the Mahayana, so that I alone can liberate [my dear mothers] from the ocean of samsara."

After giving this brief introduction, Pabongkha Rinpoche once again explained from the beginning the section on a person of great scope. He explained the limitless benefits of bodhichitta as explained in [Shantideva's] Guide to the Bodhisattva's Way of Life *and in the* Array of Stalks Sutra. *He explained in a concise manner how bodhichitta ensures that we cannot be damaged by harms and obstacles, and how even Mara was unable to harm the Buddha due to the power of [the Buddha's] love. He explained the importance of bodhichitta in the beginning, middle, and end, as well as how it is like a seed, field, earth, water, manure, and so forth.*

The Actual Stages of Training the Mind [in Bodhichitta] has two sections:

1. Training the Mind in Stages of the Sevenfold Instructions of Cause and Effect
2. Training the Mind in Equalizing and Exchanging Self with Others

Training the Mind in Stages of the Sevenfold Instructions of Cause and Effect

Training the mind to strive for the welfare of others and training the mind to strive for enlightenment are both indispensable for attaining the state of enlightenment. Venerable Maitreya proclaimed,

> Bodhichitta is the desire for perfect and
> Complete enlightenment for the welfare of others.

[Training the Mind in Stages of the Sevenfold Instructions of Cause and Effect has eight sections:

1. Equanimity
2. Recognizing All Beings as Your Mother

3. Recalling Their Kindness
4. Repaying Their Kindness
5. Meditating on Affectionate Love
6. Training the Mind in Great Compassion
7. Superior Intention
8. Meditating on Bodhichitta]

Equanimity

Presently, we don't train our minds in impartiality toward enemies, friends, and strangers. For example, just as we must smooth the surface [of a wall] prior to painting a mural, so we must equalize our minds toward all living beings prior to developing love and compassion in our mental continuums. At this point, the teachings state that there is equanimity from the perspective of other sentient beings and equanimity from our own perspective. Regarding the former [that is, the perspective of other sentient beings], this is the equanimity included in the four immeasurables that are at the beginning of the lamrim ritual preliminaries.[526] Therefore, you will not be completely successful [in the latter aspect] until the attainment of enlightenment. [Regarding] the latter, [that is, your own perspective, this] is the equanimity in which we are currently training our minds. Training the mind in equanimity at this point will be easy to develop if you meditate by visualizing all living beings as being neutral. Regarding living beings that are neutral, because they are neither friends nor enemies, you don't have thoughts of either attachment or hatred. These are thoughts of forsaking; therefore, they are an impediment to equanimity. The *Queries of the Supreme Moon Daughter*[527] states,

> In the past I have killed all of you,
> And you previously cut me into pieces;

526. This is because in the ritual preliminaries it states, "May all living beings abide in equanimity . . . I myself will cause them to abide in equanimity," which you will not be capable of doing until you are a fully enlightened being.
527. Tib. *Bu mo zla ba mchog gis zhus pa'i mdo.*

> Since we have all killed each other as enemies,
> How could you develop such attachment?

This accords with the previous explanations about training our minds in the uncertainty [of samsara] according to a person of middling capacity by considering how neutral living beings have been our enemies and friends, how someone who is currently our friend has been our enemy in the past, and how those who are currently our enemies have previously been our friends. If you meditate by combining this point with the next, you will easily induce confidence with respect to equanimity [that regards all] living beings as those dear to you. Also, once you focus on enemies, friends, and neutral persons and view them with partiality and impartiality, you will generate three distinct thoughts that are conjoined with faults of variance.

Presently, we don't have a mind of equanimity toward enemies and friends. Instead, we classify them into definite friends and enemies. We should not make such [classifications] and instead contemplate how, in all our past and future lives, our enemies have become friends, our friends have also become enemies, and so on. Some people don't see any contradiction in grasping at enemies and friends from the perspective of this life, but they do not recognize friends and enemies according to previous lives. Yet we may have the [mistaken] conception that if the past and future existed, they should be directly observable at this present moment, which is not the case. For example, if someone gave us butter and a brick of tea last year and this year punched us in the head, or if a person punched us in the head last year and gave us butter and a brick of tea this year, there wouldn't be any difference between the two.

If we succeed in developing a mind of equanimity without hatred for enemies, attachment for friends, or forsaking of neutral persons, then we should meditate by focusing on all living beings as pervasive as space. Therefore, it is meaningless for us to be biased, since from our perspective everyone is similar, in that they are our loved ones who have nurtured us with kindness. From the perspective of other living beings, they are alike in that they wish to be happy, don't wish to suffer, and are all equally tormented. If you succeed in developing a mind of equanimity toward all living beings by training your mind so that there are absolutely no thoughts of attachment or hatred for those that are close and distant, then you have generated equanimity, which is the foundation for the sevenfold instructions of cause and effect. Equanimity is very important. As the omniscient Gyaltsab [Je] stated,

> Moistening the ground of equanimity with the water of love,
> The seeds of bodhichitta continually
> Grow into the tree of bodhichitta;
> I prostrate to the supreme resultant fruit of omniscience.

From [equanimity] onward, [the realizations] get even harder to cultivate. Je Tsongkhapa stated, "It is incomprehensible for the ordinary beings of the worlds." Although this hasn't made its way into our minds, it is indispensable for enlightenment; therefore, bodhichitta is the root of the Mahayana path, yet even if you must persist in each of these meditation topics [for generating bodhichitta] for many years and months, it will not be a waste of time. The buddhas of the past and numerous holy beings understood that even recognizing all beings as your mother is to be practiced for many eons. Atisha stayed with Serlingpa for thirteen years for the sake of training in bodhichitta, Drom[tonpa] properly relied upon Atisha for seventeen years, and so on.

Recognizing All Beings as Your Mother

Next is the meditation on all beings as your mother. Although there are limitless different aspects of reasoning to come to a definitive conclusion with respect to emptiness, for recognizing all beings as your mother there is no reason for establishing the infinite bounds of consciousness other than the following quote from the *Commentary on Valid Cognition*:

> When someone takes rebirth,
> His breath, sense powers, and mind
> Are not developed solely from the body,
> Which does not depend upon a [continuum of a] similar kind.

Furthermore, the moment a small child is born, its attributes of awareness come from a preceding mind,[528] because it is awareness. For example, this is similar to your awareness of today. You must establish the infinite bounds of your previous lives through these perfect logical arguments. The definition of the term "mind" is synonymous with "mind," "awareness," and "to know."[529] In this way, the mind of today is a continuity of yesterday's mind. And the mind of this life, which existed the moment I was born from my mother's womb, is the continuity of the mind that existed the moment before I entered the womb of my mother; therefore, this proves its existence prior to rebirth. Next, the mind of my previous life is the continuity of mind of a previous life, and likewise for the time prior to that. If you continue to pursue with "prior to that . . . ," there will never be a beginning to samsara, which establishes that the mind is beginningless and endless. A *Letter Dispelling Suffering*[530] states,

> In hell time and time again . . .

Contemplating in this way also proves the infinite bounds of your previous lives. If they are beginningless in this way, then with the exception of miraculous births as well as births from heat and moisture, you must have had a mother; therefore, this proves that you had limitless mothers in your limitless rebirths when you needed a mother.

To enhance this even further, consider how, just as you had a mother in this life, you also must have had a mother in your previous life, which means you have had two mothers. Not only that, but [this was the case] in the life prior to that, in the life before that, and so on: you had ten rebirths and ten mothers, a hundred rebirths and a hundred mothers, a thousand rebirths and a thousand mothers, and so on. [Using this line of reasoning, you thus] come to the definite conclusion that you have had countless rebirths and countless mothers.

Also, you may wonder, "Although I have had numerous mothers, there are limitless living beings; therefore, all living beings could not have been

528. The Tibetan term *rig pa* is usually translated as "awareness"; however, in this instance it creates some rather awkward sentences, so I have opted for "mind."

529. The three terms being translated are *blo*, *rig*, and *shes*.

530. Tib. *Mya ngan bsal ba'i spring yig*. This is a collection of advice by Nagarjuna.

my mother." But even if we take into consideration the number of all living beings, there are not enough of them to have been our mother only once; instead, each one must have been our mother multiple times. Just in the body of a bull alone, we have been born a hundred times, a thousand times, and so on, until they become countless. The same thing applies to [our previous rebirths] as wild animals such as a deer, antelope, and so forth, and as carnivorous animals, horses, donkeys, yaks, sheep, dogs, pigs, birds, and worms, as well as the living beings that live in water, which have taken rebirth in bodies that don't even resemble living beings. There is no limit to the number of rebirths we have taken in each one of those [types of rebirth]. There aren't any of these places in which we haven't taken rebirth, and there is no limit to the number of times we have taken rebirth there as well. Thus, contemplate, "There aren't any of these living beings that didn't act as my mother. The Buddha, with his clairvoyant perception, could not measure the number of times [they have been my mother]."

If you still don't develop the recognition of all beings as your mother, it is permissible to shift your focus. When you think, "They have absolutely not been my mother," use your mother in this life as direct evidence, [counteracting this mistaken conception]. Next, contemplate how you have been repeatedly born in the past and so forth, as [explained] earlier. Some may disagree, stating, "All living beings are not my mothers; if they were I should recognize them as such." To dispel such obstructing conceptions, think, "What need is there to mention the numerous mothers and children who, when separated from one another from the time of infancy in this life, don't recognize each other later in life, as in the historical account of Bhikshuni Utpala?"

Developing the recognition of all beings as your mother is extremely difficult; therefore, make a concerted effort in accumulation and purification as a means of generating this [realization]. If you develop this, the rest of the [sevenfold instructions of cause and] effect will be easy to develop. Regarding the measure of having developed the recognition of all beings as your mothers in your mental continuum, you have developed it when, upon seeing even the tiniest creatures, you think, "This was previously my mother; she looked after all my happiness and suffering, such as laying me on her belly and so forth," at which time you vividly recall their kindness. You should develop the recognition of all beings as your mother according to Je Atisha.

Recalling Their Kindness

The way to recall the kindness of all living beings is to begin with your mother in this life. The way to recall the great kindness of all is also in regard to your mother in this life in the beginning, middle, and end. Just like holding a jeweled vessel in her hands, she was very careful in all her daily activities of walking, moving around, lying down, and sitting, as well as whatever she shouldn't do that would cause you harm; with great cautiousness she even refrained from eating certain foods and beverages she enjoyed, and so forth. She would rely upon what was beneficial to you and make an effort to forsake those things that were harmful and so on. Thus, in the beginning, your mother looked after you in her womb for nine months and ten days. She refrained from anything she thought might harm her baby, such as foods that are very hot or foods that are very cold. You could easily have died in the womb if your mother hadn't acted in that way.

In the middle [phase with your mother], when you were born you were fragile and weak, and your naked body resembled nothing more than a bug. With the exception of moving your limbs and crying, you didn't know how to do anything other than defecate. Yet for your mother it was as if she had found a wish-fulfilling jewel as she joyously lifted you with her ten fingers, held you against her warm flesh, pleasantly called out your name, looked at you with a loving gaze, welcomed you with a loving smile, and gave you food from the tip of her tongue. Through the power of her love you suckled her breast milk. She wiped the snot from your nose and [cleaned up] your feces with her hands. Although her child was in good health, she could barely sleep and could not bear to lie down out of fear that her child might die.

At that time, you were not physically capable as you are now, and if your mother hadn't constantly protected you, you would have been eaten by a dog, cat, a raven, and so on. Or, you might have fallen to your death in an abyss and would not have been able to survive for even a moment. Each and every day your mother saved your life hundreds of times. She taught you everything, including how to eat, how to walk, and how to talk. From the depths of her heart, given the choice, she would rather have been ill than have her child be ill, she would rather have died than have her child die, and so on; such are the ways that your mother nurtured you with kindness.

In the final [phase with your mother], she gave her son her home and gave her daughter away [in marriage]. She engaged in evil deeds and suffering, spiteful rumors, and scorn for the sake of accumulating food, clothes, wealth, possessions, and so on, without hesitation. In particular, for those of us that became ordained and entered the door of the Dharma, with the exception of giving us empowerments, oral transmissions, and commentaries, she escorted us up to the ends of the path to liberation and omniscience, which is something we would not have been able to do on our own.

Thus, not only in this life but in other lives when we had mothers, such as when we were animals such as birds and deer, our mothers also nurtured us by caring for us and providing whatever is of value, which is something we can directly witness ourselves. Previously, there was a Golog[531] bandit who one day was chasing a large number of horses and chased one in particular a great distance. When he returned to his bandit camp with the pregnant mare that [he had captured because she] was unable to run quickly, he stabbed her with his knife, and after slashing open her belly with his knife, a foal emerged. Although the mare was unable to lift her own body, she nevertheless licked her foal out of her extreme compassion for her offspring. Seeing this, the bandit threw away his knife, escaped [his former livelihood], and entered the Dharma [by becoming ordained].

For the sake of caring for her child, our mother accumulated a plethora of bad karma because of which she will experience a multitude of sufferings in both this and future lives. Our father and others cared for us with compassion in a similar way. If we contemplate the kindness that all living beings have likewise extended to us, [we will see that] there is no difference between the actions of our mother in this life and the activities of all living beings that have been our mother. Their activities

531. Golog is a region in Tibet located in Amdo, approximately 1,200 miles northeast of Lhasa.

as our mother are the same, and the kindness they nurtured us with is also the same.

Repaying Their Kindness

It would be extremely despicable of us not to acknowledge such kindness that living beings have shown us; therefore, we must repay their kindness. There are two instructions with respect to the way to meditate on repaying their kindness. The first is revealed in the following verse [from Chandragomin's *Letter to a Disciple*, which states,]

> While you see that your loved ones are engulfed in the depths of
> Samsara's ocean, as if fallen into its vast expanse,
> It would be deplorable for you to strive for your own liberation
> And abandon those you do not recognize due to the process of
> birth and death.

This is analogous to your own mother being swept away in the middle of a fiercely flowing river while crying for help from those on the river bank; it would be a shameless, wretched, and deplorable act to remain on the banks of the river, idly playing, singing songs, and so forth, while she is calling out for help. In the same way, it would be appalling if we were to strive our best to liberate ourselves alone, without giving a second thought to our mother living beings trapped in the expanse of the ocean of samsara and at this moment calling out to us for help.

Regarding another [or second way to meditate on this], [Shantideva's] *Compendium of Trainings* states,

> Driven insane by the afflictive emotions, blinded by ignorance,
> And stumbling with each step as we walk
> Along the path of many cliffs,
> I and all other migrating beings continuously
> Suffer on a foundation of torment.

This is analogous to your mother being completely blind and without even a guide. She is driven mad and has lost control of her mind. In each and every instant, she is stumbling and is on the verge of falling over a cliff a thousand stories high. Although she cries out for help, if you, her own son, don't save her, there is no one more deplorable than you in this world. Likewise, the wisdom eyes of all mother living beings who have nurtured you with kindness for a very long time are blind to the difference between what is a path and what isn't. They don't even have a spiritual guide to guide them by teaching them which is a path and which isn't. They have been driven mad by the afflictive emotions and have lost control of their minds. Although each of us is also completely insane, we recognize that we are insane. For instance, if one person who is not insane is in the midst of many people who are insane, the insane people will call the person who is not insane "insane," even though [that person] knows that he [or she] is not insane. This is similar to the story about the descent of rain water in a certain region that made people crazy.[532]

Not only that, but they stumble with each step they take through engaging in wrongdoings through their activities. Finally, they fall over the cliff that is more than a thousand stories high and plunge into the lower realms. Thus, although they wish for happiness, they don't know how to accomplish the causes of happiness. Although they don't want to suffer, they incessantly create nonvirtue as the cause of their suffering. They are completely confused about which actions to adopt and which ones to forsake. How could you be so deplorable as to not repay the kindness of these beings who have been so kind to you?

Query: Well then, how do I repay their kindness?

Response: Although there is no doubt that giving food and drink to the hungry and thirsty, such as a little tea and butter, will repay their kindness to a small extent, not only will these acts not bring them long-term benefit, but they have previously done so much more for us than just that. Also, all such deeds only serve as the causes for contaminated happiness and do nothing more than bring them some slight temporary benefit. There could be no greater benefit than to establish in them the cause for becoming endowed with every type of happiness and for becoming free

532. I believe this is in reference to the story of a certain kingdom where everyone became insane by drinking rain water. The king, however, had his own well, so he was the only one not insane. When he heard that his subjects were plotting to assassinate him because they thought *he* was insane, he drank the water and became insane himself, after which he was regarded as "sane."

of every type of suffering; therefore, we should contemplate by thinking, "I shall strive to endow every living being with every type of happiness and to free them from every type of suffering."

Meditating on Affectionate Love

Although, in general, love wishes for living beings to have happiness, and compassion wishes for them to be free of suffering, at this point love is not the love that wishes for living beings to have happiness that is part of the four immeasurables. Instead, it is the effect of the three previous [meditations] in the series of the [sevenfold instructions of] cause and effect, which [subsequently] transforms into great compassion; this is affectionate love. Furthermore, previously an old woman asked Geshe Potowa what affectionate love was, and he replied, "Affectionate love is when you develop loving kindness for all living beings that is just like the love you have for your son Tolekor."

This is the kind [of affectionate love] we need. When that occurs, it will bring forth love that wishes that [all living beings] have happiness. To meditate on that, we visualize our mother of this life and other loved ones before us, and then contemplate by thinking, "Although they presently desire happiness, not only is there no way for them to have uncontaminated happiness, but they don't even have contaminated happiness. Although they presently believe they have happiness, with the exception of the suffering of change, it is not happiness. How wonderful it would be if these mother living beings of mine who grasp at happiness could be free from suffering and endowed with happiness. I shall work to ensure that they have happiness." It is extremely important and highly beneficial to meditate on love in this way. [Nagarjuna's] *Precious Garland* states,

> Giving three hundred dishes of
> Food three times a day
> Cannot compare to a portion of the merit
> Within a mere instant of love.
>
> Gods and men will come to love you,
> And they will also protect you.

> You will have peace of mind and much happiness,
> Poisons and weapons will not harm you,
>
> You will effortlessly accomplish your aims,
> And you will be born in the world of Brahma;
> If you don't attain liberation, you will still
> Be protected by these eight good qualities of love.

Thus, you will obtain these eight good qualities of love. Moreover, by meditating on love, you will come under great protection similar to King Bala Maitreya.[533] If you have the eight immeasurables of love, you will be liberated from all worlds:

> Even the compassionate Teacher
> Could not be captured by your weapons;
> I know of no one other than you
> Who has defeated all ten million demons in battle.

Ten million billion soldier demons were defeated by the [Buddha's] concentration of love. No matter how many or few living beings there are, you will develop dominion over them through the extent of your meditation on love. Furthermore, if you meditate by visualizing the living beings in one continent, you will be reborn as a wheel-turning king of iron. Likewise, if you sequentially visualize living beings in two, three, or four continents, you will be born as wheel-turning kings of copper, silver, and gold, respectively.[534]

According to the teachings in [Vasubandhu's] *Treasury of Abhidharma*, a complete set of the four continents, together with the celestial abodes, is counted as one, functions as the basis for one thousand [worldly realms], and will become the first "thousand" of the worldly realms. Regarding the "three thousand worlds," the first "thousand" are comprised of one thousand similar sets. The second "thousand" is calculated by counting

533. King Bala Maitreya was one of Buddha Shakyamuni's previous lives, in which he offered his flesh and blood to five *yakshas* who later became his first five disciples.
534. The substances of the wheel-turning kings' wheels reflect the number of continents they dominate and are iron, copper, silver, and gold.

those first "thousand" a thousand times, [which would equal one million]. The third "thousand" is calculated by counting the second "thousand" a thousand more times, [which would equal a billion]. If you meditate on love for living beings in three thousand such [worldly realms], you will be reborn in the Great Brahma Realm as "Brahma the lord of the three thousand worlds." If you visualize all living beings reaching the extent of space, you will attain the "great brahma state" of the Bhagavan Buddha; [thus] there are limitless benefits [to meditating on love].

Training the Mind in Great Compassion

Great compassion is the uncommon cause of bodhichitta. The degree of strength of your compassion determines the degree of strength of your bodhichitta, which in turn makes a huge difference in the amount of ground you can cover [in your path to enlightenment]. There are five analogies that show the speed at which you progress along the path, which is determined by the degree of your compassion as follows: a bodhisattva (1) progresses like a chariot pulled by cattle, (2) progresses like a chariot pulled by an elephant, (3) progresses like the sun and moon, (4) progresses like the magical emanations of shravakas and pratyekabuddhas, and (5) progresses like the magical emanations of a buddha.

Although conqueror Maitreya had already developed bodhichitta for eighty thousand eons prior to the time when our compassionate Teacher generated bodhichitta, because of his love, our Teacher achieved great enlightenment before [Maitreya], which was due to the power of extremely powerful bodhichitta that holds others more dear than oneself. Although mantra is said to be extremely swift, even the special feature of secret mantra is derived from the great strength of the compassion that is even more powerful than that of the perfection vehicle of sutra. For example, as I already explained, if your dear child falls into a pit of fire, although his parents and relatives will both have a similar desire to pull the child out of the fire pit, [his parents] will immediately enter the fire pit and attempt to pull him out without hesitation, whether or not they are capable of doing so.

Great compassion is like the precious wheel of the chakravartin king. The precious wheel has the power to go anywhere and carries the four kinds of troops.[535] It is also like a person's life force: if it ceases, other faculties cease as well, and if you have [a life force], you have the others as well. In the same way, great compassion is like the life force and embodies all virtuous Dharmas; therefore, they are like its limbs. Glorious Chandrakirti composed words of praise to great compassion in his *Guide to the Middle Way*, expressing its essential features and its superiority for the attainment of enlightenment. In the beginning, it is important like a seed and serves as the foundation for bodhichitta. In the middle, it is important like water and manure, and ripens and produces the practices of the six perfections and so on without giving up due to difficulties. In the end, it is important like the fruit that turns the wheel of Dharma of the three lineages of disciples and is the fruition of them all.

When training the mind in great compassion, begin by contemplating those such as sheep while they are being killed by the butcher. Their limbs are bound by a rope, and without anyone to protect or assist them, they are turned on their backs facing the sky, their wool is shaved with a sharp blade, they are summoned, and their skin is stripped from their flesh. Their eyes stare straight at the butcher, and before their breathing has ceased, he sticks his hands in their stomachs. Their hearts are burned and ground, and once their aortas are severed, they die and so on. Contemplate in detail this evil system of killing and how they lose their lives in this heart-wrenching way.

Next, meditate on the recognition that this very sheep is your mother, until it becomes unbearable. Although this is not your mother in this current life, she was your mother in a previous life, and she was not only your mother once but served as your mother numerous times. Contemplate the countless times she looked after you in that life and how you had to rely upon her for all of your happiness and suffering, as well as whether you had a good or bad life. Next, meditate on how your mothers will have to experience suffering in the hells as they are surrounded by the minions of the Lord of Death, by considering your own suffering that you previously contemplated during the [sections on] persons of the small and middling scopes. If you develop revulsion for the [suffering of samsara] and shift your focus to others, you will easily generate [compassion]; therefore, you

535. The chakravartin king has four kinds of troops: cavalry, elephants, chariots, and infantry.

should redirect your contemplation to others and meditate on the sufferings of the lower realms in accordance with a person of small scope.

When you develop that, meditate on compassion by contemplating how at this moment in their homeland, they are creating very severe negative karma, such as the ten nonvirtues, abandoning Dharma, being deceptive, and so on, which are the causes of [rebirth in] the lower realms, whereby they will have to experience the boundless suffering of the lower realms. When your mind has been trained in that, you should shift your focus to samsara in general and all living beings as extensive as space, and meditate by thinking, "How wonderful it would be if they were free from those sufferings; I will cause them to be free." According to historical accounts, after Jonang Taranatha [1575–1634] saw a hunter kill a deer, his compassion grew exponentially, whereby he developed compassion in his mental continuum. Throughout this section you must also contemplate recognizing all beings as your mother, remember their kindness, and develop the wish to repay it.

With respect to the measure of having developed great compassion, [Kamalashila's] treatise the *First Stages of Meditation* states,

> When you develop a naturally occurring compassion that spontaneously wishes to completely purify all living beings from their suffering, which is similar to the affection a mother feels when her child is unhappy, at that time your [compassion] is complete and therefore receives the name "great compassion." The mere compassion that a mother develops when her small child whom she greatly loves experiences very painful suffering is a mere fraction of that mind of [great compassion]. It becomes fully qualified great compassion when you generate spontaneous compassion for all living beings.

The occurrence of an uninterrupted powerful desire to liberate all living beings from suffering is the measure of developing great compassion. Through this, you should also understand the measure of generating great love. Thus, generating a sequential experience of compassion and so on is the way to develop actual bodhichitta. Merely making a prayer of bodhichitta, as is done at the beginning of a ritual, and calling it "bodhichitta" is an extremely grave error.

Superior Intention

Meditate on superior intention that takes on the burden of [liberating and enlightening all living beings] by thinking, "I will strive to endow all living beings with every form of happiness and free them from all suffering. Furthermore, the state of enlightenment is endowed with every form of happiness and is free from every type of suffering; therefore, I alone will ensure that all living beings are endowed with every form of happiness and become free of every type of suffering without depending upon anyone else." This is called "superior intention" because it is superior to the minds of shravakas and pratyekabuddhas.

Query: Well then, what is the difference between the wish to repay the kindness of our mothers and superior intention?

Reply: With respect to this point, my refuge and protector Dagpo Lama Rinpoche stated that although you have the wish to repay the kindness of your mothers [and generate] love, compassion and so forth while merely thinking, "I shall endow living beings with happiness and free them from suffering," it is the thought, "I alone shall accomplish such things," which occurs during superior intention, that the previous [thoughts] don't possess and that is distinguished by whether or not you are carrying the burden of accomplishing such intentions. For example, it is like the difference between deciding and not deciding to sell something while engaging in business.[536]

Meditating on Bodhichitta

Although during superior intention we have the intention to guide all living beings, at the moment we are incapable of guiding all living beings in that way.

Query: Well then, who is capable of such a thing?

536. The general sense of love and compassion is like trying to decide whether or not to engage in business and superior intention is similar to having made the determination to engage in business.

Response: In general, shravakas and pratyekabuddhas have a limited [capacity] to benefit others, and from the very beginning of generating bodhichitta until the end of samsara, bodhichitta has a vast altruistic intention to benefit others; however, only a buddha is incomparable in perfecting the welfare of others. If you attain that state, you will have great capacity to guide living beings without difficulty. Even each light ray [from a buddha] accomplishes the welfare of countless living beings by teaching Dharma in perfect accordance with the realms of living beings, their intentions, and potentials. [Buddhas] are also capable of revealing an emanation body in the presence of each and every living being. While in meditative equipoise on suchness, they are able to understand and display all conventional phenomena. Without relying upon effort or conceptual thought processes, they spontaneously accomplish their enlightened actions, engage in them unceasingly, and so on, as I explained previously during the section on going for refuge. For example, previously a famine broke out in a country and a father found one piece of discarded sheep carcass. If he were to divide it into portions for his family, it would immediately be consumed, so after careful consideration the father ate the entire piece of sheep carcass and went in search of more food. By eating the sheep carcass himself, he was able to free his entire family from the famine. Likewise, before working for the welfare of living beings, you must attain the state of enlightenment. Not only that, but [Je Tsongkhapa's] *Lamp Illuminating the Five Stages*[537] states that just as in the case of carrying water you must first find a container, in the same way, to work for the welfare of living beings you must first attain the state of enlightenment for yourself. The thought "For the sake of all living beings, I shall attain the state of enlightenment to perfect the two aims of myself and others" is the perceived aspect of bodhichitta in its entirety.

With respect to the measure of having generated bodhichitta by meditating in that way, just as a mother feels great sorrow in her heart when her only child is ill and constantly recalls her wish to free her child from his suffering in all her daily activities, such as eating, lying down, walking, and sitting, so if we experience an effortless recollection of the attainment of enlightenment by merely seeing and recalling living beings by

537. Tib. *Rim lnga gsal sgron.*

thinking "I shall attain complete enlightenment for their welfare," we have generated bodhichitta. When you develop that, you have entered the Mahayana path of accumulation, and in the practice of mantra, it forms an auspicious condition for enlightenment in the intermediate state. However, that is only the preliminary development of bodhichitta and is like tasting the bark of sugarcane. As a verse states,

> Bodhichitta is the wish for full enlightenment
> For the welfare of others.

Assembling the two minds of striving for the welfare of others and striving for enlightenment is like establishing two legs for the attainment of enlightenment and living beings; therefore, bodhichitta must possess the two aspirations.

Query: Is it possible for people like us to attain a state like that?

Reply: If you attain the state of enlightenment, you will most definitely attain [the ability to work for others in that way].

[Chandragomin's] *Letter to a Disciple* states,

> With a human life you attain great mental strength; it is the basis of the
> Path of the sugatas and equips you to guide migrators.
> Such a path is not attained by gods, nagas, demigods,
> Garudas, knowledge-holders, kinnaras, or snakes.

A human life is necessary in general as a basis of generating bodhichitta, and even among human beings there is no migration superior to the human body in this world for generating bodhichitta. With respect to the Dharma, you have met the Dharma of the Mahayana, and even within that, you have encountered the unexcelled secret mantra, which is the quick path to enlightenment in one short human life in this degenerate age. In particular, by relying upon the oral instructions of the Ganden Hearing Lineage, and if you practice from the very depths of your heart, as Milarepa and Gyalwa Göstangpa[538] did in the past, it will not take more

538. Gyalwa Göstangpa was a famous lama of the Drikung Kagyu lineage.

than three years and three cycles of the moon[539] [to attain enlightenment] through listening to such an unmistaken Dharma as this. It would be difficult to find a teaching such as this even in the limitless pure lands of the buddhas. It is said that bodhisattvas in Sukhavati make prayers to be reborn in this world with a physical form suitable for the practice of mantra.

539. Tib. *lo gsum phyogs gsum*. This is usually translated as "three years and three months" but it actually means "three years and three phases (or sides) of the moon," which would be roughly six weeks. A phase of the moon is from the new moon to the full moon or from a full moon to a new moon. See also note 709 below.

Day Twenty-Six

The great bodhisattva Shantideva stated [in *Guide to the Bodhisattva's Way of Life*],

> I prostrate to the body of those who have
> Generated the precious holy mind;
> I go for refuge to the sources of happiness
> Who unite even those who harm them with happiness.

The supreme method for leading migrating beings to the state of omniscience is none other than the precious mind of bodhichitta. Even the tathagatas will venerate the person who has generated it in his mental continuum. If you also develop bodhichitta in your mental continuum, any contact with you will become meaningful, and those persons [who interact with you] will attain the supreme state [of enlightenment]. Therefore, feel, "I am going to listen to the king of instructions called the stages of the path to enlightenment so that I can train in bodhichitta."

After giving this brief introduction, Pabongkha Rinpoche once again covered the headings. He once again explained the way to train the mind in stages.

When you have trained your mind in the bodhichitta of a person of great scope by training the mind in [the instructions of] a person of small scope, the time has come when you should unite it with the instructions for training the mind through equalizing and exchanging self with others. If you are engaging in an extensive practice, this is a system of explanation that combines it with mind training. With respect to this, although there are numerous mind-training [texts], the main ones among them all are [Dharmarakshita's] *Wheel of Sharp Weapons*, the *Peacock Destroying Poison*,[540] and so forth.[541] The complete oral instructions are presented in [Geshe Chekawa's] *Seven-Point Mind Training*; therefore, this will be explained from the beginning, and I will give the oral transmission and commentary from the beginning, based on an old publication of the root verses of [his *Seven-Point*] *Mind Training*.

Seven-Point Mind Training

The [root verses] contain an offering of praise that contains a prostration to great compassion stating, "**I prostrate to great compassion as the cause**." This is similar to glorious Chandrakirti's praise and prostration to great compassion at the beginning of *Guide to the Middle Way*. It is taught in this way because the state of enlightenment is born from great compassion. Attaining the state of enlightenment depends solely upon the precious mind of bodhichitta. Nagarjuna stated,

> If you desire the attainment of unsurpassed
> Enlightenment for yourself and the world,
> Its root is bodhichitta as stable
> As the King of Mountains.

As previously explained, we treat deity meditation and mantra recitations as the root and regard bodhichitta as though it were the limbs:

> Everyone has a deity body to meditate on,
> Everyone has a mantra to count,
> Yet no one has a Dharma to contemplate.

540. Tib. *rMa bya dug 'joms*.

541. English translations of both of these commentaries are found in Dharmarakshita, *Peacock in the Poison Grove*, trans. Geshe Lhundub Sopa, with Michael Sweet and Leonard Zwilling (Boston: Wisdom, 2001).

This is the fault of not understanding that even the unique speed and unique profundity of mantra must be drawn out through bodhichitta. Shantideva stated [in *Guide to the Bodhisattva's Way of Life*],

> If living beings have never before even
> Dreamt about such a mind for
> Their own welfare, how could
> They generate it for the welfare of others?

When our hair pores don't tremble upon contemplating the way in which we experience suffering in the lower realms, we will never reach a level of compassion that cannot bear other living beings being tormented by suffering; therefore, we must sincerely engage in [training our minds in the path] of a being of lower scope and so forth and sequentially train the mind, from the proper reliance upon the spiritual guide onward. If we understand this point, we will understand the way to progress along the path of the complete teachings. We should apply these meditations on the lamrim by combining them in this way for many months and years. If we don't apply ourselves in that way, it will be as the Kadampas of old said when they stated,

> You say nothing comes from your contemplations when you meditate. Don't lie! During the day you are constantly distracted, and you spend the night sleeping.

This is how things go for us. Atisha the Great spent twelve years in the presence of Serlingpa, and Geshe Chekawa spent fourteen months on mind training in the presence of Sharawa. When Je Tsongkhapa the Great was alive, he also had a system for giving a commentary on mind training for eight months. As I already explained yesterday, the origins for the system of mind training through the sevenfold instructions of cause and effect are the *Liberation of Maitreya Sutra* and the lineage of oral instructions that Maitreya gave to Asanga. Although you are definitely able to develop bodhichitta in dependence upon [the sevenfold instructions of cause and effect], still for the sake of bringing about an extremely strong and powerful bodhichitta, if you combine [the sevenfold instructions of cause and effect] with the instructions for mind training through equalizing and exchanging self with others that originate from the *Sport of Manjushri Sutra*, it will be particularly sublime.

Furthermore, at this point I will offer a combination of [equalizing and exchanging self with others] and the seven-point instructions on mind training. For this, there are (1) the greatness of the composer, (2) the greatness of the Dharma, (3) the actual instruction, and (4) attaining stability in bodhichitta together with the conclusion.

[Seven-Point Mind Training has three sections:

1. The Greatness of the Composer
2. The Greatness of the Dharma
3. The Actual Instructions]

The Greatness of the Composer

[The root text of Geshe Chekawa's *Seven-Point Mind Training* states,]

> **The lineage of this nectar-like**
> **Instruction comes from Serlingpa.**

In general, the two main disciples of the Teacher are Maitreya and Manjushri, and the lineages for both the oral instructions of the vast and profound come from these two. The incomparable Atisha the Great combined them together in a single stream of transmission and mastered the instructions in their entirety. In particular, these oral instructions for equalizing and exchanging self with others were given to bodhisattva Shantideva by venerable Manjushri and were passed down in stages, and Atisha the Great received that lineage of instructions for bodhichitta from three lamas.[542] He received these [instructions on the seven-point mind training] from Serlingpa, and [Atisha] in turn gave them to Geshe Drom[tonpa] as a sealed-in-secrecy teaching by stating, "Other than you, I have not found anyone else to offer these teachings to," which was the way

542. Atisha's three gurus from whom he received teachings on bodhichitta were (1) Dharmarakshita, (2) Kusali the Younger, and (3) Serlingpa Dharmakirti. For a brilliant synopsis of the lineage of the mind-training genre, see Gyalchok and Gyaltsen, *Mind Training*.

things actually were. Next, the lineage continued on to [Geshe] Chekawa as a secret Dharma that could not be set into writing. The necessity of keeping these teachings secret is revealed in [Shantideva's] *Guide to the Bodhisattva's Way of Life* when it states,

> You should practice this holy secret
> Of exchanging self with others.

As this states, having forsaken consideration for your own welfare, you contemplate exchanging self with others. These days, the scope of ordinary beings' activities does not lie beyond their selfish concerns. [These teachings] will not enter their thoughts or be absorbed in their minds; therefore, they are kept secret. The *Narration of the Daughter of Dzawo* and so forth are sources of these instructions on equalizing and exchanging self with others presented in the discourse of these oral instructions. This is in accordance with [Tsongkhapa's lamrim], which relays the events of Captain Dzawo's daughter as well as when our Teacher was previously born in hell as the strongest wagon-puller and generated bodhichitta by cherishing others and so forth.[543]

Je Lama [Tsongkhapa] praised these instructions by calling them "Chekawa's special lineage for bodhichitta," and [Chekawa] was among Geshe Sharawa's four most well-known disciples of the oral lineage.[544] Geshe Chekawa's family was Nyingma. He was extremely bright and had memorized around a hundred volumes of teachings, their texts on the five sciences, and so forth. He traveled to Nyang to meet [the Kadampa Geshe] Chakshingwa[545] and saw Langri Tangpa's *Eight Verses of Mind Training* [in Geshe Chakshingwa's room]. His mind was captivated by that Dharma

543. In one of Buddha Shakyamuni's previous lives, he was reborn in hell and was given the task of pulling a wagon of the denizens of hell. At this point he developed compassion for another, weaker being and developed the intention to take the responsibility of pulling his wagon as well. This was the Buddha's first act that set him on the path to enlightenment. He suddenly died and was reborn in the higher realms as he began his accumulation of merit and wisdom for three incalculable eons, which ultimately resulted in his enlightenment under the bodhi tree in India.
544. It's possible that his four most important disciples are the four mentioned in Thupten Jinpa's *Wisdom of the Kadam Masters*, 85, which lists Chekawa, Tapkapa, Tumtön Lodro Drak, and Naljorpa Sherap Dorje.
545. Geshe Chakshingwa was a disciple of Geshe Gya Chakriwa, who was a disciple of Langri Tangpa, thus placing Chakshingwa in the twelfth century.

and when he asked whose teaching it was, he was told "Langri Tangpa." Having gone to meet Langri Tangpa, [Geshe Chekawa] was unable to meet him because Langri Tangpa had passed away. Two of his disciples at the monastery were arguing because they did not get along; therefore, [Geshe Chekawa] didn't develop faith. Those two were not engaged in a nonvirtuous dispute; they were arguing over who would attain high status at the monastery and so forth. Being aggravated, one of them said, "I did not do that, you did," in the debate.

[Chekawa] asked who else possessed that Dharma and was told that Sharawa did. When he went to see him, Sharawa was engaged in a philosophical discussion and teaching the *Shravaka Levels*. After listening to him, [Chekawa] felt no inspiration at all and instead became despondent and confused. At a point between discourses, he ask about the teaching that states, "All our good qualities are due to the kindness of gracious living beings, and all our faults are due to cherishing ourselves," and Sharawa said, "Others didn't have the slightest uncertainty about this teaching, yet you [Chekawa] had some doubts." One day, when Sharawa was circumambulating a stupa, [Chekawa] approached him and, setting out a cushion on a platform, requested him to please have a seat since he had a question for him, to which [Sharawa] replied, "What do you want? I was perfectly clear when I was upon the Dharma throne; what didn't you understand?" [Chekawa] said, "I saw a text that said,

> Offer profit and victory to others;
> Take all loss and defeat upon yourself.

When I am despised by humans and can't find lodging, is this beneficial for my mind? Is this profound or not? Is it suitable to practice or not?"

[Sharawa replied,] "There is no doubt whatsoever that this is appropriate for your mind. If you have no desire for complete enlightenment, you can forget about it. But if you do [want to become enlightened], it is indispensable."

"Well then," [Chekawa inquired,] "Where can I find the scriptural reference for this Dharma teaching?"

[Sharawa responded,] "Who would not recognize it as the valid teachings of Nagarjuna? These teachings are from the *Precious Garland* of the Middle Way, which states,

> May their negativities ripen upon me
> And may my virtues ripen upon them."

[Having inspired his confidence, Chekawa said,] "I have faith in this teaching; please bestow the instructions upon me."

[Sharawa accepted by stating,] "If you are capable of staying with me for a long time and practicing, I will teach you."

After listening to an experiential commentary for fourteen months, an uncontrived experience of bodhichitta was born in Chekawa's mental continuum. He gave these instructions to one of his disciples with leprosy, and his leprosy was cured by meditating on them. From that time onward, many lepers came from all over, and by receiving these teachings and meditating on them, they were all cured of their leprosy; therefore, this teaching became famous as "the leper's Dharma."

One day, one of [Geshe Chekawa's] angry relatives came to see what he was up to, and after seeing that he was practicing mind training, he was able to subdue his anger. When this happened [Geshe Chekawa] decided to abandon the restricted nature of these teachings and began giving them to large assemblies of disciples. He also composed the root verses on mind training, which spread far and wide. Nevertheless, mind training was declining, and there were many variations on the root verses of this teaching; therefore, many of his students took notes during Chekawa's teachings, which resulted in a variety of commentaries.

The Greatness of the Dharma

The root text states, "**Like a diamond, the sun, and a medicinal tree** . . ." The famous diamond can destroy a rocky mountain and so forth as well as dispel poverty; therefore, what need is there to mention fulfilling our wishes? Even a small portion of that [diamond] can overcome poverty and does not even lose the name "diamond." It outshines all other special ornaments such as gold and so forth, and that small portion of the vajra jewel still functions as a diamond. Likewise, although we may only develop a small portion of the meaning presented in this text, it will overcome the poverty of samsara and we will not lose the name "bodhisattva." Therefore, what need is there to mention developing these instructions in their entirety within our mental continuum?

Although shravakas and pratyekabuddhas are like golden ornaments, they are outshone [by a bodhisattva]. Just as the sun dispels darkness, so, although we may develop only a portion of the meaning contained in this text, it will dispel the darkness of our afflictive emotions such as self-cherishing and so forth. What need is there to talk about a complete medicinal tree when each and every part, such as the leaves, is capable of dispelling illness? In the same way, what need is there to mention the entire meaning of this text when even developing a small fraction of it in our mental continuum will [work] like medicine to dispel the illness of the afflictions, such as self-cherishing and so forth? In particular, if we don't possess this Dharma during this era of the five degenerations, when we are seized by adverse circumstances, it will be difficult to continue with our Dharma practice unimpeded. If we sincerely apply ourselves to the mind training, adverse circumstances will arise as supportive elements, and we will be able to transform unfavorable conditions and favorable conditions by bringing them into the path for enlightenment, and so forth. Such are the unique benefits possessed by this teaching.

The Actual Instructions

This is presented in the following seven points, which contain the complete path in its entirety.

[The Actual Instructions has seven points:

1. Point One: Teaching the Dharma of Preliminary Foundation
2. Point Two: Training in the Two Types of Bodhichitta
3. Point Three: Transforming Adverse Conditions into the Path to Enlightenment
4. Point Four: Presentation of a Lifetime's Practice in Summary

5. Point Five: The Measure of Having Trained the Mind
6. Point Six: Presenting the Commitments of Mind Training
7. Point Seven: The Precepts of Mind Training]

Point One: Teaching the Dharma of Preliminary Foundation

The root text states, "**First, train in the preliminaries**." Furthermore, if I were giving a commentary on mind training alone, as a preliminary I would give a commentary on the paths of a person of small scope and a person of middling scope. However, I have already given a detailed commentary earlier, and that will perform the same function; therefore, I don't need to give a new commentary.

[Point Two: Training in the Two Types of Bodhichitta]

Training in the Two Types of Bodhichitta has two sections:

1. Training the Mind in Ultimate Bodhichitta
2. Training the Mind in Conventional Bodhichitta

This order is according to the ancient texts on the root verses of mind training of the old Kadampas and is intended for bodhisattvas with sharp faculties. The system for bodhisattvas with sharp faculties employs the realization of emptiness prior to generating [conventional] bodhichitta. Next, although they have perfected the other paths, in general during this degenerate era you first internalize the method aspects [such as love, compassion, bodhichitta, etc.], after which you are taught the view of emptiness. If emptiness is taught from the beginning, there is an extremely great potential for error through misunderstanding and negating the necessity of karma, as the story of the Indian mahasiddha Mantangipa [illustrates]. For that reason, it is important that the commentary is given according to the order presented in the stages of the path to enlightenment in conqueror Tsongkhapa's teaching tradition of the new Kadampas. The way to meditate on ultimate bodhichitta will come later, during the final perfection [of wisdom] by conjoining it with superior seeing, when I give a detailed explanation.

At this point, I will give a brief explanation according to the root verses, which state, "**Teach the secret once they have attained stability.**" The ultimate secret should be taught once [the disciple] attains stability in the method aspect of conventional bodhichitta. The root verses state,

> **Regard phenomena as being like a dream,**
> **Analyze the ultimate reality of unborn awareness;**
> **Even the antidote is liberated in its natural state;**
> **Remain in the state of the basis of all as the nature of the path.**

The subsequent Kadampas combined this with the view of the previous Tibetan scholars. The *Thog Commentary*[546] and the *Compendium of Eloquence*[547] are great oral lineages that represent the tradition, which accords with the view of the previous scholars. These systems of explanation are on the verge of being like the Chittamatra system. During meditation, you do not analyze anything whatsoever in the mind and just let it settle. Ngulchu Gyalsé Thogmé [Zangpo] also stated,

> The mode of existence of objects of knowledge is utterly not established,
> And whatever is apprehended is mistaken.

Although the learned have a variety of different ways of reaching their conclusions, most of them end up leaning toward Hvashang Mahayana's view. Through the reasoning of persons who are great bodhisattvas, he used illogical reasoning that was influenced by valid teachings. Therefore, through this you should also understand the need to examine pure visions and phenomena. The words and meaning of this root verse of mind training say that the mind is without color, shape, and so forth, and is a vivid

546. Tib. *Thogs 'grel*. I was unable to locate this text, although it may refer to Ngulchu Gyalsé Thogmé Zangpo's autocommentary on his *Thirty-Seven Practices of a Bodhisattva*, entitled *rGyal sras lag len so bdun ma dang de yi mchan 'grel yid kyi mun sel*.

547. Tib. *Legs bshad kun 'dus*. This is a famous mind-training text by the Fifth Dalai Lama, Ngawang Gyatso.

empty state, which is the way of being deluded about emptiness.[548] Furthermore, [Hvashang] states that all external phenomena arise through the force of imprints on consciousness; therefore, there are no external phenomena and they are only mind. Nevertheless, with respect to the perception of solidity and hardness that is similar to being nonexistent, these arise from powerful imprints.

Previously, a girl in Varanasi meditated on her body as a tiger, whereby her body actually transformed into a tiger, and once she had eaten people there, [the town] became vacant;[549] a bhikshu meditated on his body as a skeleton, whereby he actually turned into a skeleton, and so forth. There are other similar stories which show that all worlds and their beings, which are externally perceived objects, are like a dream, and other than mistaken appearances of the mind's nature, they are not separate from the mind. Thus, the mind of the apprehender does not exist anywhere inside or outside the body; it is free from arising, ceasing, and abiding.

[Hvashang states] that you place your mind in its true nature that is not truly established whatsoever. In fact, the external environment and internal living beings are like a dream and like an illusion. They do not have a truly established nature whatsoever. This is called "resting the mind within the state of nonconceptuality that does not grasp anything." Although that is its meaning, it is observing the conventional nature of the mind. Therefore, when resting in the view of normal condition, the mind does not grasp at anything whatsoever; therefore, this is equivalent to Hvashang's view of nihilism and is the cause of going to hell and has thereby digressed into an erroneous path.

If we explain it according to our own tradition, just as the externally apprehended entities contained within a pleasant dream are nothing other than mere appearances to the mind that do not have even an atom of true existence and the phenomena contained with the internally apprehending [consciousness] are not inherently existent, so if we grasp at that emptiness which is the absence of inherent existence as being truly

548. This means that the way it is worded could lead to misunderstandings (which are explained in the following paragraph).

549. This may be a scribal variant of an example quoted from the *Manjushri vikurvana sutra* by Ngorchen Konchog Lhundrub in his *Beautiful Ornament of the Three Visions*, trans. Lobsang Dagpa and Jay Goldberg (Ithaca, NY: Snow Lion, 1991), 180.

established, our view has become incurable.[550] Accordingly, the phrase, "the emptiness of emptiness" is intended to assist you in ascertaining not only the ultimate nature of subject but [the fact] that oneself as well is not truly existent. If you realize emptiness by coming to a definitive conclusion in that way, you will attain nirvana. If you don't realize it, you will not overturn samsara; therefore, emptiness is the basis of all of samsara and nirvana which teaches both emptiness and dependent arising.

The root text states, "**Between sessions be a creator of illusions**"; during subsequent attainment, we should think of [appearances] being like illusions.

Training the Mind in Conventional Bodhichitta has five sections:

1. Meditation on Equalizing Self with Others
2. [Contemplating the Numerous] Faults of Self-Cherishing
3. [Contemplating the Numerous] Benefits of Cherishing Others
4. [The Actual Contemplation of] Exchanging Self with Others
5. How to Meditate on Giving and Taking [in Dependence upon That]

Meditation on Equalizing Self with Others

[Shantideva's] *Guide to the Bodhisattva's Way of Life* states,

> If I don't exchange my happiness
> For the suffering of others,
> I will not attain enlightenment,
> And there won't be any happiness in samsara.
>
> Whoever wishes to quickly protect
> Themselves and others

550. In other words, we are left without an antidote because at this point emptiness, which is intended to be the remedy to grasping at true existence, is being conceived of as inherently existent.

Should practice the holy secret
Of exchanging self with others.

Thus, we should begin by meditating on equalizing self with others; without meditating, equalizing self with others will not [naturally] arise in our minds [of its own accord]. Once we say "I," we grasp at it and cherish it strongly, even [with respect to something as insignificant] as only having a single cup of tea.[551] When we say "others," we automatically abandon them; therefore, we are unable to exchange [self with others]. For that reason we must [work hard to] equalize self with others; thus, from this moment onward we should meditate by contemplating, "From this moment on I will not view myself as being precious and others as undesirable. Instead I will consider how both I and others are equal in our desire for happiness and [also how] we are equal in not wishing to suffer." Meditate on the equality of those two [states of happiness and suffering for self and others] by contemplating that there is no sense in making distinctions between good and bad by using the terms "self" and "others."

Contemplating the Numerous Faults of Self-Cherishing

[Shantideva's *Guide to the Bodhisattva's Way of Life* states,]

If whatever difficulties there are in the world
And however much fear and suffering there is
All come from grasping at self,
What use is this great demon to me?

However much unhappiness and suffering exists in the world, it all originates from self-cherishing. [This is the origin of] the disharmony between the kings and their subjects of this world and the disharmony kings have among each other, as well as the disharmony that subjects have among each other. Likewise, the disharmony between ministers and servants, the disharmony ministers have among each other, the disharmony between

551. In other words, when we are visiting others, we get offended due to our strong self-cherishing when we are served only one cup of tea rather than having our cup constantly refilled.

patrons and ritualists, and the disharmony ritualists, gurus and disciples, parents and their children, and so on have among each other [are all due to self-cherishing]. Even for monks, the disharmony between teachers and students, among teachers themselves, among students themselves, among housemates, with the person sitting next to you in the prayer hall, and so forth [are due to self-cherishing]. Whatever harms exist, such as the wars that break out between countries, lawsuits, and so on, all arise from self-cherishing. Not only that, but even though it is thieves, robbers, and so forth who accumulate wealth out of self-cherishing, it is their self-cherishing that should be accused of being the bandit. Even a cat or a mouse eating our meat, butter, and so forth are all an encounter with our self-cherishing. All the conditions for an untimely death such as indigestion-related illnesses, poisonous concoctions, harm from fire, water, or wild animals, enemies stabbing us with weapons, or an animal being deprived of its life, right down to interruptions to our studies, are all actions [that are the karmic result] of our self-cherishing.

If we don't act on our self-cherishing, we will be able to bear it even if someone punches us in the head, in a way that is similar to what occurred in the following story: Previously, someone trespassed on the field of the daughter of a certain family by constructing a pathway, but it didn't upset her mind because she thought, "When I am born in that place in my next life, I will be able to walk on it," whereby she was able to bear it. Even harm from nonhuman beings comes from our self-cherishing. As it states, "The arising of the enemy of superstitions is like a 'thief in an empty house.'"[552] Je Milarepa's *Hundred Thousand Songs* also states,

> If the evil spirit of superstitious thoughts does not arise,
> The obstacles of obstructing spirits will not enter;
> The yogi purifies his mental continuum within
> By possessing conduct that is not suspicious.

552. Tib. *khang stong rkun ma dra*. "A thief in an empty house" is a colloquial expression for something that is meaningless.

Although we become angry at others for whatever unfortunate things befall us, such behavior is irrational. [Shantideva's] *Guide to the Bodhisattva's Way of Life* states,

> Whatever suffering there is in the world
> All comes from the desire for our own happiness.

Lama Chöpa states,

> Seeing that this chronic disease of maintaining self-cherishing
> Gives rise to all unwanted suffering,
> I seek your blessing to destroy this great demon of self-cherishing
> By despising it as the object of blame.

The root verses of mind training also state, "**Drive all the blame on one**." This is analogous to seeking the ringleader in a criminal court case; if we investigate the root cause of whatever misfortune comes our way, we will discover that it is self-cherishing and that there are no grounds for blaming others. For this reason, since self-cherishing is the source of the entirety of whatever awful things happen to us in this life and the next, we should view self-cherishing as our enemy.

You should contemplate the extensive way of viewing this according to teachings presented in *Mind Training: Rays of the Sun*.[553] Self-cherishing and abandoning others are like holding the sharp spear of wrong views as well as [like being] the evil butcher who kills higher status and liberation. It is also [like] a thief carrying a bag of the three poisonous afflictions who steals the crops of everything virtuous. It is also [like] the owl-headed[554] creator of destruction who brings the various things we don't want through accumulating the noxious substance of nonvirtue within our hearts. This means that we accumulate the owl-headed noxious substances and then engage in rituals to destroy curses while the curse is in the center of our hearts; therefore, if we are going to cast spells, it should

553. Tib. *Blo sbyong nyi ma'i 'od zer*. An English translation is available as Namkha Pel, *Mind Training Like the Rays of the Sun*, trans. Brian Beresford (Ithaca, NY: Library of Tibetan Works and Archives, 1992).
554. In Tibetan culture, an owl is considered an omen that portends disaster.

be directed toward this [self-cherishing]. This is also a shameless and cowardly mind that would even blame others—from our gurus down to our parents—to avoid a major loss for ourselves. This is also the harvester of suffering of the twelve dependent related links by planting the seeds of karma in the field of our consciousness.

Although previously both we and our Teacher were equally circling in samsara, our Teacher embraced cherishing others, whereby he became the Buddha, through which he ripened and liberated numerous living beings. We embraced our self-cherishing, whereby even at this present moment we still dwell in samsara; this enactor of laziness that stems from indolence is also [due to self-cherishing]. This is also the agent of covetousness that is constantly attached to samsara despite the fact that nothing in samsara, such as our wealth and friends, has any essence. It is also the agent of our hopes and fears; it has hopes for things that are hopeless and worries about things that are not to be feared. With respect to this last metaphor, this is analogous to how we even worry about a pile of rocks when it is dark, as when we go for a walk at night, and how we have hopes of gaining a profit even when buying meat with one silver coin. This is similar to a hunter who developed fear of Milarepa.[555] [Self-cherishing] is also responsible for us freely expressing our afflictive emotions like a wild animal without a bridle, such as the competitiveness between higher and lower lamas or a louse and a tiny bug, our jealousy, and disparaging comments, on up.

This is also the agent of wrong views that are incompatible and contradictory. For instance, although we want to be happy, we don't create virtue, which is the cause of happiness, and although we don't want to suffer, we don't forsake the causes of suffering. [Self-cherishing] is also responsible for not seeing the faults that the afflictive emotions have caused since beginningless time until the present even though they have led us to suffering, which is like being completely blind and eating dried food because we don't have eyes to see the food supply. Our self-cherishing is also like the ill omen of a blue-headed sparrow, which is a foreboding of all the harm that will come our way in this life and the next. We should

555. See Tsangnyön Heruka, *The Life of Milarepa*, trans. Andrew Quintman (London: Penguin Books, 2010), 138.

sincerely apply ourselves to the means of overcoming our self-cherishing by contemplating it faults. According to the texts, a "blue-headed sparrow" is a screech owl, and when one appears it is a sign of impending inauspiciousness. [Shantideva's] *Guide to the Bodhisattva's Way of Life* states,

> If you had formerly acted that way,[556]
> Such a condition as this, which is lacking
> The perfect bliss of a buddha,
> Could not have come into existence.

We can determine that we would already be enlightened if we had been able to recognize ourselves as the enemy and had dedicated whatever we have done for the welfare of others. However, we currently remain enveloped in suffering, and the various adverse things that happen are the fault of embracing our self-cherishing in this life. Shapowa[557] stated, "At this very moment we should do whatever we can to tame the bewitching spirit in this short life." Langri Tangpa also stated,

> No matter how many profound texts I open, I can't find any that don't say that all faults are one's own and all good qualities come from brother sentient beings. Their essential instructions are to offer all profit and victory to others and take all loss and defeat upon oneself. They don't have any other meaning.

If we load all loss on others, we will definitely have to experience the results of that, which will be a great loss. A poem that I wrote myself states,

> Accepting the burden upon myself is the way of great gain,
> Yet I load the loss upon others, whereby
> It will in turn descend upon me;

556. Here, "that way" means cherishing others and forsaking self-cherishing.

557. Shapowa (dates unknown) was a disciple of the Kadam master Gonpawa Wangchuk Gyaltsen.

> Grant me your blessing that I may be able to
> Take all loss upon myself.

[Dharmarakshita's] mind-training [text] the *Wheel of Sharp Weapons* states,

> When an unbearable illness occurs in my body,
> This is definitely the weapon of my evil deeds
> Returning to me for harming the bodies of living beings;
> Now I will take all illness upon myself.
>
> When suffering arises in my mind,
> This is definitely the weapon of my evil deeds
> Returning to me for disturbing the minds of others;
> Now I will take all suffering upon myself.

This same reasoning can be applied to whatever happens to us.

[The *Wheel of Sharp Weapons* continues,]

> Since that's the way things are, I have apprehended the enemy;
> I have apprehended the thief who ambushed and deceived me,
> The fraud who disguised himself as me and then deceived me.
> Eh ma! Have no doubt that this is self-grasping,
> The savage called bewitching self-grasping;
> Corner the samaya-breaker who brings ruin to self and other.
>
> Wrathful Yamantaka, summon him, summon him,
> Beat him, beat him, and pierce the heart of the enemy self;
> Roar down upon the head of this ruinous conception and
> Slaughter the heart of the butcher, the enemy self.[558]
>
> HUM HUM great yidam, produce your miraculous emanations.
> DZA DZA, bind the enemy with an oath.
> PHAT PHAT, please liberate me from all bonds.

558. The Tibetan verses present various components of wrathful mantras. In this verse the syllables MARAYA are used, which literally mean "kill." In this verse I have rendered those syllables into English as "slaughter."

According to the extensive explanations, although we are entreating wrathful actions, they should be directed toward our self-cherishing. If we kill dear mother living beings, it is like killing a corpse. Shantideva also states [in *Guide to the Bodhisattva's Way of Life*],

> Those who have disregarded all suffering to
> Destroy the enemies of anger and so on
> Are conquerors and actual heroes;
> The rest are killing corpses!

As this states, if we destroy the ultimate enemies such as anger, we will gain victory over all three realms, whereby we become the ultimate heroes. The actions of the rest of them, such as assassins and so on who are determined to kill others, such as humans, by stabbing them with their swords and so on, are no different than chopping up a corpse with a knife. The previous holy beings have said that when [assassins' victims] die, [the assassins] have [not vanquished their enemies but have actually] killed their own parents, they have killed their deity and guru, and they have killed their wish-fulfilling jewel, and therefore, such persons [as assassins] should not be called heroes. They should be called insane!

The wrathful deities who have wrathful facial expressions, with their mouths gaping and fangs bared, are not angry at living beings; they are angry at the self-grasping and self-cherishing in the mental continuums [of those living beings]. The teachings in [Dharmarakshita's] *Wheel of Sharp Weapons* are only directed at the faults of self-cherishing; therefore, it would be excellent if you were able to contemplate extensively the points presented in it. Previously, a geshe from Dagpo established a tradition of reciting the *Wheel of Sharp Weapons* during group [protector *pujas*], whereby an aura of great turbulence[559] would arise, and he was henceforth called "Lama Rinpoche." [Those at the monastery said,] "Previously we did not recognize our enemy with our incantations, so [this type of] turbulence did not arise. Once we recognized this enemy, turbulence emerged through our evocations."

559. Tib. *'tshub chen po*. This is a type of atmospheric disturbance like a twister or sudden gusts of violent wind and rain.

Previously, Drukpa Kunleg [1455–1529] revealed to his younger brother Drukchen Chögyal his magical powers; he hung his robes on a sun ray, which became workable, and Kunlegpa's bow, arrow, and knife became unworkable. Drukchen became violently ill, and although others performed longevity rituals for him, they did not help him; therefore, they invited Kunleg, and he hurled a throwing torma[560] into the lap [of his younger brother], striking the illness, which was the conception of self-cherishing, and thereby dispelling his illness. The daughter of Machig Labdron and others stole the cow of a *ngagpa*, so the ngagpa used his powers and the others died. However, according to the teachings of Labdron, Labdron's daughter stated, "The thief is self-cherishing; therefore, may its power be placed upon me" and so forth. Having accomplished that, the power of the ngagpa was unable to harm her.[561]

Trichen Tenpa Rabgye [1759–1815] stated,

> I offer this mountainous torma made of flesh and blood
> For the sake of pleasing oath-bound Dharmaraja and to be liberated from all
> The enemy conceptions of attachment to the excellence of this life's appearances,
> As well as to destroy the massive heap of bones that are my negativities and downfalls.
>
> I offer this mountainous torma of conceptions
> Apprehending the suffering of attachment to the wealth of samsara
> As happiness that resulted in all of the transgressions and
> Downfalls of my three vows to the great kings and Vaishravana.
>
> I offer this ocean of completely pure nectar of lesser intention
> As flesh, blood, and bones for the sake of generating delight in
> Glorious six-armed Mahakala and to be liberated from
> The enemy self-cherishing. Please accept it!

560. This is a type of torma that is physically tossed in the direction of a malignant force. By throwing it in the lap of his brother, Drukpa Kunleg was showing that the real malignant force was his brother's self-cherishing that resided within his brother's own mind.
561. In Pabongkha Rinpoche's *Liberation in Our Hands*, this is said to be Machig Labdron's son.

Having visualized the torma as the appearances of this life and so forth, you then offer it to the protectors of the beings of the three scopes.[562] If such a thing occurs, it will be a very effective way to offer tormas; therefore, it is a very special way of accomplishing the enlightened actions of the Dharma protectors.

From this moment onward, we must cease the processes that bring about this evil mind of self-cherishing. Now, "self-grasping" is when I think "I" and cling to the fact that, from my own perspective, I exist and am self-sufficiently real. "Self-cherishing" is something conditioned by grasping at my existence and self-sufficient reality; it means cherishing myself and clinging to myself as something valuable. Therefore, the two are not synonymous, but they do accompany one another and function as obstacles to the correct view and to developing bodhicitta. That is why it is taught that the two seem to alternate. [There is a verse from *Lama Chöpa* illustrating this point] which states,

> Seeing that this chronic disease of maintaining self-cherishing
> Gives rise to all unwanted suffering,
> I seek your blessing to destroy this great demon of self-cherishing
> By despising it as the object of blame.[563]

Contemplating the Numerous Benefits of Cherishing Others

The root text states, "**Meditate on the great kindness of all**." Furthermore, we should contemplate the benefits of cherishing others. [Shantideva's] *Guide to the Bodhisattva's Way of Life* states,

> Whatever happiness there is in the world
> All comes from wishing for others to be happy.

562. Dharmaraja is the protector of a person of small scope, due to his association with death and impermanence. Vaishravana is the protector associated with a person of middle scope, due to his association with pure moral discipline. Mahakala is the protector associated with a person of great scope, due to his association with compassion.
563. Pabongkha Rinpoche only quoted the first and third lines of the verse. I have included the entire verse to give a more thorough understanding.

Lama Chöpa states,

> Cherishing mother beings is the basis of all good qualities.

All the prosperity and well-being that we currently enjoy, such as having obtained a human body of leisure and endowment, a long life free of illness, abundant enjoyments, and so forth, are the good qualities of cherishing others. Accordingly, there is a verse [from Nagarjuna's *Precious Garland*, quoted earlier,] that states,

> Enjoyments come from generosity, happiness from moral discipline . . .

Things such as generosity and moral discipline depend upon living beings as the objects of generosity. [To practice moral discipline,] you have to refrain from harming others, who are also the basis. Although we contemplate each of the [sevenfold instructions of] cause and effect in the same way, there is a great distinction [between that and equalizing and exchanging self with others].

Here, we accept others as being worthy of being cherished. For example, just as we instinctively cherish the field that produces abundant crops in the fall, despite whatever hardships we may have to endure while working in a field, so we should think that whatever hardship we have to endure is for ourselves alone and not for the sake of the field. In the same way, we must rely upon the kindness of all living beings for whatever good things happen to us. I am able to wear my upper monk's shawl in dependence upon the kindness of numerous living beings. Even the fact that my bag of roasted barley is full depends upon the kindness of numerous living beings. The seeds were planted in the field, and [everything that occurred] from the time [the field] was plowed until the point where [the roasted barley] reached the inside of my barley pouch was all due to the kindness of living beings. Not only that, but just knowing how to eat roasted barley and butter mix[564] is due to the kindness of living beings.

564. Tib. *spag*. This is a mixture of roasted barley flour and butter that is sometimes mixed with water.

Likewise, all the happiness and well-being that we have in this life, such as food, clothing, and resources, including a place to live, were all produced through the great hardship of numerous living beings; therefore, they came from their kindness.

Although there are two instances when we contemplate the kindness of living beings—namely, (1) contemplating the kindness of living beings during the sevenfold instructions of cause and effect, and (2) contemplating the kindness of living beings during [equalizing and exchanging self with others] in mind training—there is a great distinction between the two.[565] Without even mentioning the happiness and well-being of this life, from an ultimate standpoint there is the higher status and definite goodness. From the development of bodhichitta up to the bodhisattva's deeds and the attainment of enlightenment, all [these] come from the kindness of all living beings. Even the buddhas became enlightened solely by relying upon living beings during the beginning, middle, and end. For that reason [Shantideva's] *Guide to the Bodhisattva's Way of Life* states,

> Since living beings and buddhas equally
> Produce the Buddha's qualities,
> Why would you not venerate
> Living beings as you do the conquerors?

[Geshe] Chen-nga-wa stated,

> The Dharma and the world are incompatible. It is not enough to merely avoid taking a wife.[566] Between those who harm and those who help, worldly people choose those who help. We [as Dharma practitioners], on the other hand, should like those who cause us harm. Likewise we should cherish living beings more than buddhas.

565. Of the two systems utilized—namely, the sevenfold cause and effect and equalizing and exchanging self with others—the latter creates a much greater depth in your recognition of the kindness of others, making equalizing and exchanging self with others much more powerful and effective.

566. Geshe Chen-nga-wa is implying that it is not enough to merely remain celibate without doing anything further; your way of thinking must become completely opposed to ordinary beings.

The *Eight Verses of Mind Training* state,

> With the intention to accomplish the supreme purpose
> Which surpasses even a wish-fulfilling jewel,
> May I regard all living beings
> As extremely precious.

Although we should cherish living beings more than a wish-fulfilling jewel and regard them as our foundation for accomplishing all temporary and ultimate excellent accumulations, we instead revere our wallets! It is utterly stupid to abandon living beings. Although for the moment living beings are not acting as our mothers, we should contemplate the great kindness [they extended to us when they were our mothers] and offer them the profit and victory. This way of contemplating the great kindness of living beings despite the fact that they are not *currently* acting as our mothers greatly increases our affectionate love. In short, [Shantideva's] *Guide to the Bodhisattva's Way of Life* states,

> What need is there for a lot of explanation?
> The childish work for their own welfare,
> And the munis work for the welfare of others;
> Just look at the difference between these two.

Lama Chöpa states,

> In short, since the childish work for their own welfare
> Whereas the buddhas work for the welfare of others,
> I seek your blessing to be able to realize
> The faults and qualities and thereby exchange myself for others.

We have experienced various sufferings since beginningless time, but in the end we haven't accomplished a single beneficial thing for our own welfare and have instead distanced ourselves from the welfare of others. We must also experience the suffering of the lower realms, which is due to the activities of our self-cherishing. Therefore, once we see that self-cherishing is like a thieving dog, we should apply the methods to expel it. According to the *Jataka Tales*, our Teacher was previously reborn in hell as the strongest chariot puller, a rabbit, a woodpecker, a turtle in the ocean, and so on, and also as King Bala Maitreya, Chandraprabha, Shirsena, Shiwai Gyalpo, Tsugna Norbu, Prince Nyingtob Chenpo, and so on. While our teacher the Powerful Able One (Munindra) was on the path of training, he abandoned [all concern for] himself and embraced cherishing others, and he underwent great hardships such as offering his head, eyes, and even his life. Therefore, once we contemplate the way in which even enlightenment is a good quality of cherishing others, we should exchange self with others.

The Actual Contemplation of Exchanging Self with Others

The phrase "exchanging self with others" is not like thinking "I am them and they are me." *Lama Chöpa* states,

> Since no one desires even the most subtle suffering
> Or is ever content with the happiness he has,
> There is no difference between myself and others;
> Seeing this, I seek your blessing that I may delight in the happiness of others.

[Shantideva's] *Guide to the Bodhisattva's Way of Life* also states,

> Thus, for the sake of pacifying the harm to self
> And to pacify the suffering of others,
> I will give myself to others
> And regard others as I do myself.

Until now we have regarded "self" as something to be cherished, yet this has produced great torment. We have forsaken "others" without giving them any consideration whatsoever. These two should change places, so that from now on you should embrace cherishing others just as you previously cherished yourself, and offer others the gain and victory. To the extent that your mind forsook others, it now forsakes yourself and takes the loss and defeat upon yourself. If you meditate by repeatedly contemplating the faults of self-cherishing and the benefits of cherishing others, it will naturally bring strength to the mind for exchanging self with others.

How to Meditate on Giving and Taking in Dependence upon That

For the sake of increasing the aforementioned contemplations on exchanging self with others,[567] you engage in giving and taking[568] to dispel obstacles and enhance your experience. The root verses state, "**Train by alternating giving and taking.**" Although the teachings place giving first, when you are putting them into practice, in the oral tradition we begin with taking, followed by giving in accordance with the phrase, "Therefore, the compassionate venerable guru . . ."[569] While practicing the affectionate love of a great-scope being of the lamrim, we contemplate the faults and benefits of attachment and apply giving and taking directly to love and compassion. Once you have induced the compassion of the sevenfold instructions of cause and effect, you will develop a much more powerful compassion than you did previously [through the practice of taking and giving]. Once you develop proficiency in the visualizations associated with compassion, you meditate on taking. Once you develop proficiency in the visualizations associated with love, meditate on giving.

567. In the heading "How to Meditate on Giving and Taking in Dependence upon That," "that" refers to the previous four sections of (1) the equality of self and others, (2) the faults of self-cherishing, (3) the benefits of cherishing others, and (4) exchanging self with others.

568. Tib. *gtong len*. Although English translations of the Tibetan term *tonglen* often render it as "taking and giving," in Tibetan the phrase is presented as "giving and taking." Perhaps the reason for translating the phrase as "taking and giving" is a reflection of the oral tradition, which states that you should begin by taking the sufferings of others upon yourself and then give them your happiness, virtues, and so on. If you were to give others your happiness while they are still overwhelmed with suffering, it would be less effective than first removing their suffering and then giving them happiness.

569. This is in reference to the verse from *Lama Chöpa* that states, "Therefore, great compassionate Venerable Guru, / I seek your blessing that all the negative karma, obscurations, / And suffering of mother living beings without exception / May ripen upon me right now, and may all / My happiness and virtue be delivered to others /So that all living beings may be endowed with happiness."

Taking

Furthermore, think, "Although mother living beings do not wish for suffering, they are unable to abandon negativity, which is the cause of suffering." If you think about what harms living beings, they are harmed by suffering; therefore, you should contemplate, "I will take their suffering upon myself as well as the causes of suffering, together with the negative karma of all living beings." Imagine that [all] this is conglomerated into a black heap, similar to the way hair is trimmed, at which time you should think, "I shall take the suffering of these beings."

Next, think, "Although these living beings wish for happiness, they don't create the cause of happiness. If living beings are helped, they are helped through happiness; therefore, I shall give them all my happiness, virtue, and enjoyments."

The root text states, "**Begin the sequence by taking from your own side**." While practicing taking, you can also train the mind in stages. First, take the causes of negativity and suffering of tomorrow [onto yourself] today. Likewise think, "May I take on the causes of negativity and suffering from next month, next year, and my next life in this month, this year, and this current life"; if you practice in sequence like this, your self-confidence will increase. When you train your mind in that way, sequentially train your mind in taking on the negativity and suffering of your friend and then your enemy. Train your mind by taking on the negativity and suffering from the upper part to the lower part of your region and from the lower part to the upper.

From time to time, take on the suffering of all living beings in the ten directions embodied by the four types of rebirth,[570] from the hells below up to the peak of existence above. If fear arises, making you unable to think like that, it is because it is striking your self-cherishing and has penetrated the essential point. It would be excellent if you had the sealed-in-secrecy oral instructions for generating bodhichitta at this point; however, beause of its strict nature, it is bound by an oath, and there is no tradition of bestowing it indiscriminately to those who will not practice it continuously.

570. The four types of rebirth are (1) from a womb, (2) from an egg, (3) from heat and moisture, and (4) miraculously.

Giving

While giving your body, transform your body into a wish-fulfilling jewel, and then, from the depths of your heart, imagine that you give all living beings your abode, body, and enjoyments of the three times, together with your roots of virtue, whereby all living beings become endowed with consummate enjoyments and happiness. From time to time, also give [the aforementioned excellence] to hell beings, hungry ghosts, animals, and so on. From time to time, practice giving to those who have not entered the path, the ordinary and arya beings who have entered the path, and your guru and the buddhas. Also, for both taking and giving there are extensive ways of practicing taking and giving with respect to the outer environment and the living beings within it, where you are capable of actually benefiting human beings, dogs, and so forth. Although you may not be able to benefit them directly, you can do so indirectly and benefit them through your roots of virtue and so forth.

If [the beings you are visualizing] are gods and demons, you should contemplate, "With this I shall repay my karmic debt to you, through consuming your flesh and blood with no apparent end in sight." While practicing chö, you mentally dissect your body before these [gods and demons] and offer it in a continual stream without any reservations while saying, "Eat as much of my flesh, blood, bones, and so forth as you wish." Next, imagine that by consuming that flesh and blood, their bodies and minds are completely satiated by bliss. Practice the same way with all the other gods and demons.

Thus, by practicing giving and taking with respect to all living beings, you transform their environments into pure lands, and the living beings themselves who are their inhabitants transform into a physical form of leisure and endowment that has all the possible favorable conditions required for the practice of Dharma. Imagine that by abandoning true suffering and origins in their entirety, their mental continuums become the truth body endowed with bliss.

In your practice of giving, you give your present body and enjoyments and those of the future, but you don't give those of the past. While practicing taking, it is taught that buddhas don't have faults and that your guru's nature is also that of a buddha; therefore, you do not practice taking with respect to these two. While practicing giving, it is permissible to imagine that they accomplish a long life and the fulfillment of their wishes and attain all the favorable conditions for enacting the welfare of migrating beings. Thus, for higher objects, your practice of giving takes on the aspect of offering substances, and for lower beings it becomes whatever is needed by each of the six classes of beings, such as clothes worth a thousand gold coins, food with a hundred flavors, five-hundred-story houses, and so forth.

The benefits of meditating on taking and giving are related in the biography of Guru Maitri Yogi, who would chant his vajra songs on mind training while sitting on the banks of the River Ganges, whereby he had a direct vision of protector Maitreya, after which he composed a praise to [Maitreya].

Mounting Giving and Taking upon the Breath

It would be excellent if you were to combine taking and giving with your breath when you become proficient [in the previous meditations]. The root text states, "**Mount these two upon the breath**." Furthermore, you don't mount them upon the breath from the beginning, yet [if you] mount them upon the breath when you gain mental proficiency [in the previous meditations], it will reach the same essential point as bodhichitta; therefore, this has great significance for training in bodhichitta. *Lama Chöpa* states,

> I seek your blessing that I may [generate] perfect bodhichitta by
> Dispatching the wind mounted by taking and giving,
> [And liberate living beings from the great ocean of existence
> With the mind of love, compassion, and superior intention.]

The root text states, "**The three objects, the three poisons, the three virtuous roots** . . ." When we generate attachment for pleasing objects, we contemplate by thinking, "How wonderful it would be if all the attachment of all living beings would ripen upon this attachment of mine, whereby the attachment of all living beings would become endowed with the virtuous root of their attachment being nonexistent." You can apply the [same] reasoning to anger for things unpleasant, ignorance for things of indifference, and so on. This way of practicing taking and giving when developing attachment, anger, and so on was explained by Maitri Yogi when he stated,

> Calling forth all father and mother migrating beings,
> I shall summon all five poisons of living beings,
> So that I may come to possess their five poisons;[571]
> I shall distribute whatever virtues of nonexistence[572] I possess, such
> As attachment equally to the six classes of migrating beings.

According to historical accounts, Dagpo Kelsang Tenzin Rinpoche[573] would generate bodhichitta in dependence upon singing this vajra song and meditating on it. The root verses state, "... **are the brief instructions for subsequent attainment. For the sake of stimulating remembrance, train by means of words in all actions.**"[574] This is the practice of subsequent attainment between sessions. As before, train at all times, whether eating, sleeping, walking, or sitting, by imagining that from the depths of your heart you take upon yourself the three poisons and so forth of living beings. You should also train by unifying your practice with verbal incantations of teachings from texts such as [Shantideva's] *Guide to the Bodhisattva's Way of Life*, [Nagarjuna's] *Precious Garland*, the *Sutra of Golden Light*, and so forth. You should recite lines such as "How wonderful it would be if the suffering of migrating beings [would ripen upon me]," "May their negative karma ripen upon me," and so forth. It would also be excellent if we additionally recited verses from *Lama Chöpa* such as "Therefore, Venerable Guru ..." The first line of this verse was requested by Damchö Gyatso[575] and was subsequently added by Je [Losang] Chögyan. Lama Chöpa was the main practice of Je Serkhangpa,

571. The five poisons are desire, anger, delusion, pride, and envy.
572. The "virtues of nonexistence" are virtues from having eliminated certain faults—in this case the poison of desire.
573. This is Pabongkha Rinpoche's root guru's guru. Pabongkha's root guru was Dagpo Jampal Lhundrup. I was unable to locate the exact dates for Dagpo Kelsang Tenzin Rinpoche. However, he was obviously somewhat older than Jampal Lhundrup, placing his birth somewhere in the early nineteenth century.
574. This quotation from the root verses begins with "... are" because it is a continuation of the previous line ending in "the three virtuous roots."
575. Tib. Dam chos rgya mtsho. He was an important lama from Tashi Lhunpo. Although the

and he would accumulate numbers of recitations [of this verse as though it was a mantra]. It is said that if you practice giving and taking separately, it will be easier.

Point Three: Transforming Adverse Conditions into the Path to Enlightenment

It is impossible that adverse inner and outer conditions won't occur while practicing Dharma in this degenerate age. *Lama Chöpa* states,

> When the world and its beings are completely filled with
> The results of nonvirtue and unwanted suffering pours down
> like rain,
> I seek your blessing that I may see this
> As a cause to exhaust the results of bad actions
> And transform adverse conditions into the path.

This is an encouragement to [transform] adverse conditions into virtue and [to think] that we should be able to regard suffering as happiness. If we don't, we will be like so many living beings who abandon the Dharma no matter what happens—whether it is happiness or suffering, good or bad. Some people postpone the Dharma if something like an illness happens to them. Likewise, many give up the Dharma when their wealth and possessions are snatched or stolen; when others become jealous, criticize them, unjustly and falsely accuse them of something, or there are extenuating lawsuits; when they come into possessions, wealth and enjoyments, or an increase in prosperity, power, and fame; or when they attain a high and influential status, and so on. If any of these happen, they will say, "Now the Dharma is pointless" and will abandon their practice. Therefore, we must not abandon the Dharma and instead transform whatever happens—whether happiness or suffering, good or bad—into the path.

There are two ways of transforming [adversity] into the path: **(1) transforming through thought or action**, and **(2) transforming through view.**

---

date of his birth is not known, he died in 1651. He became the abbot of dGon lung monastery in 1609.

Transforming Unfavorable Conditions through Thought or Action

[Gyalwa] Yang Gönpa stated,

> If you don't destroy faults of self-grasping,
> Even if you build a fortress, it will not keep you safe.
> Wherever you run, you will not be free of the enemy.
> Right now, endowed with the armor that knows the nature of his faults,
> Extract the master of ruin from deep within his roots.
> You currently practice mistaken meditation that does not flee from this bandit.
> Instead, train in the illusory body on the basis of the eight worldly concerns that occur,
> Develop the experience of terminating disputes within yourself,
> Practice offering with faith and devotion,
> And rob the two occurrences with malice.
> Dry rhetoric is of no use and similarly
> Appears to have no distinctive depth;
> [Therefore, feel,] "Whatever happens is fine; my mind is happy."
>
> Although sudden experiences are good, they are a mere reflection;
> Without severing the clinging that is attached to the conception of self,
> Even minor mistakes are not seen by the mind.
> Roaming through mountain dwellings full of conceit,
> Living beings of the degenerate era engage in bad actions
> That are carried out fully in a mountain retreat.
> Frightened, they flee and run away the next morning.
> Instead, you should engage directly the equal taste of whatever you encounter
> Without handing yourself over to conceptual thought.

You must use this as encouragement to take whatever adverse conditions arise and bring them into complementary factors for your spiritual practice. Instead, we place the blame on others and say, "So-and-so said something improper."

[Dharmarakshita's *Wheel of Sharp Weapons* states,]

> In short, the undesirable things that descend upon me
> Are the weapons of my own bad actions returning to me,
> Like a blacksmith killed by his own sword;
> Now I shall be very cautious about my negative actions.
>
> Even experiencing the suffering of lower states
> Is the weapon of my bad deeds returning to me,
> Like an archer killed by his own arrow;
> Therefore, I shall be very cautious about my negative actions.

The root of blame lies in the fault of not recognizing what is created by self-cherishing. Therefore, whatever suffering occurs, such as an illness when we are engaging in something like study, contemplation, and meditation, we should think, "In dependence upon this, great stores of negative karma and obscurations will be purified, and whatever negative karma and obscurations I possess will all ripen upon me in this life and be purified. Also, when adverse conditions such as sickness, harm from spirits, and so on occur, this is definitely the karmic retribution for the bad actions I previously accumulated catching up with me, and I am encountering the consequence of my previous actions." We should think, "These sufferings such as illness are no different from the Dharma teachings that my lama gave, and they are an excellent teaching as a message exhorting me to the Dharma." Lama Serlingpa gave Je Atisha a teaching that stated,

> Adverse conditions are the spiritual guide.
> Demons and spirits are manifestations of the Conqueror.
> Illness, negativity, and obstructions are brooms.
> Suffering is the natural display of the Dharmata.[576]

576. Tib. *chos nyid*. This can be translated in numerous ways, such as "the true nature of being," "the very nature of things," "intrinsic nature," and so on.

Geshe Karagpa [eleventh century] stated,

> Adverse conditions are the spiritual guide;
> Obstacles are an exhortation to spiritual practice;
> Suffering is the broom sweeping away negativity—
> Don't view them as an unpleasant misfortune!

According to the historical accounts of Milarepa and Bhikshuni Lakshmi,[577] adverse conditions are exhortations to [practice] Dharma. It is excellent when suffering befalls us. It has the good qualities of purifying negative karma, obscurations, and so forth.

If we enjoy happiness and well-being and consummate prosperity, it is exhausting our merit and has the great fault of increasing our pride, arrogance, and so forth. Dza Patrul Rinpoche stated,

> Don't be pleased when you are happy; be pleased when you suffer:
> If you are happy, it ignites the five poisonous afflictive emotions;
> If you suffer, it exhausts your previously accumulated bad actions.
> Suffering is the compassion of the lama.
>
> Don't be pleased when you are praised; be pleased when you are disparaged:
> If you are praised, your pride and arrogance increase;
> If you are disparaged, it dispels the demon of faults.
> Slander is your inheritance from the deity.

And,

> We Dharma practitioners should view the excellences of this life as the enemy. Although we may be poor in resources, when we Dharma practitioners rely upon austerity as our livelihood, we should not despair.

577. Bhikshuni Lakshmi is the founder of the nyungné fasting practice. She contracted leprosy, went into retreat, practiced fasting in conjunction with bodhichitta, and received a vision of Avalokiteshvara that taught her the nyungné practice.

> Don't be pleased with riches; be pleased when they decline:
> If we have riches, our suffering increases by protecting our accumulations;
> If they decline, our hardships accomplish the sublime Dharma.
> It is directing us toward this lowly life of a Dharma practitioner.

Although our compassionate Teacher held the kingdom of a chakravartin king in the palm of his hand, the next day he enthroned the chakravartin king, [and then] he escaped [his kingdom] that very evening and became ordained.[578] Carrying his begging bowl, he relied upon an austere life as his livelihood. He was content with simple places to sleep, clothes to wear, and alms. Delighting in being a renunciant and meditator, he dwelt within the four preferences of the aryas[579] and actualized complete enlightenment.

Jamgon Tsongkhapa the Great was displeased when a Chinese minister for the king of the Taming dynasty invited him to be the head guru [of the king and his subjects], and he instead left for Olga Chölung to live the life of a renunciant and engage in single-pointed practice. Together with his retinue of eight, they decided to establish the conditions to restore the Maitreya statue at Dzingchi Temple; however, they didn't even have eight pennies[580] to purchase the ritual water-offering set. They offered very special butter tormas to Vaishravana[581] as a way of accomplishing his enlightened actions.

Je Mila[repa]'s sister went to Dingri and saw Bari Lotsawa with umbrellas above him, wearing fine silk robes, and practicing Dharma with a vast collection of prosperity. Having seen this, she traveled to the foot of Mila[repa] and said, "He has another kind of excellent Dharma.

578. A chakravartin king is the ruler of our present world system. The Buddha had enough merit to become a chakravartin king but instead forsook the position in favor of becoming ordained.
579. Tib. *'phags pa'i rigs bzhi*. As mentioned in note 459 above, the four preferences of the aryas are (1) simple food, (2) simple clothes, (3) a simple dwelling place, and (4) simple possessions.
580. Tib. *zho*. This is a coin that is of very little value.
581. Vaishravana is one of the four great celestial kings ruling the northern direction. Worshiping him is said to lead to financial prosperity.

My brother practices a kind of Dharma that doesn't even give him enough food to eat or enough clothes to cover his back. You are only purchasing the cost of suffering staying here and trying to endure whatever you can. If you check and see if Bari Lotsawa will accept you as his servant, then even if you become the lowest of them, it will still make you happy." Jetsun replied,

First, the upper part has a parasol topped with a golden vase;
Second, the lower part is draped with Chinese silk;
Third, the middle part has a canopy of peacock feathers;
Fourth, [it is] painted with five types of color:
I could also have those four hoisted above me,
But I have abandoned the eight worldly concerns and I am happy.

First, a small pretty monastery on the outskirts of a village;
Second, a new young teacher expounding the Dharma;
Third, the dexterous hands of happy young monks; and
Fourth, a stovetop for making Indian butter tea:
I could also get these four if I wanted to care for them,
But I have abandoned the eight worldly concerns and I am happy.

First, a fine horse with its head held high;
Second, an ornamented saddle glittering with jewels;
Third, a warrior in his brightly shining iron armor; and
Fourth, the passion for subduing enemies and protecting friends:
I could also get these four if I wanted to subdue them,
But I have abandoned the eight worldly concerns and I am happy.

First, the abbess and priestess as the tsok-offering masters;
Second, making a tsok offering while greedily wishing for food;
Third, a little song of a young woman meant to deceive; and
Fourth, village rituals of divinations, chanting, and astrology:
I could also get these four if I wanted to care for them,
But I have abandoned the eight worldly concerns and I am happy.

Thus, to reduce the extent of the influence of the eight worldly concerns while abiding in the four preferences of the aryas is very important, and if such a thing comes about, we will be following the example set in the biographies of our Teacher and his successors. Ordained monks who have promised to abandon the seven [nonvirtues],[582] along with their retinues, are also dwelling in the four preferences of the aryas. If we renounce the eight worldly concerns, we won't need anything more than contentment, even though we have worn-out clothing and miserably insipid food:

> Don't be pleased with high status; be pleased with low status.
> High status gives birth to jealousy and pride;
> Low status increases your openness to spiritual practice.
> A low profile is the superior position.

Wrap your nose-rope around your neck.[583] We should maintain such a low position that nothing, with the exception of water, can pass beneath us. Drom[tonpa] Rinpoche also stated,

> Even if I am respected as authentic by all,
> I think, "May this reduce my pride."

And,

> Even if there is no one else who is greater than me,
> May I assume a lower position and remain happy.

According to [Dromtonpa's] biography, by assuming a lower position, Drom[tonpa] made prostrations to Shang Trangka Berchung, and when Lo Gonpa invited Drom and [Drom] was on the road [to visit Lo], Drom encountered a ngagpa and voluntarily made prostrations to [the ngagpa's]

582. The seven nonvirtues are the three of body and four of speech from the ten nonvirtues.

583. This is a Tibetan colloquial expression that refers to a yak or other domestic animal that has a ring in its nose with a rope tied to it that a herdsman uses to lead it around. The analogy is used to indicate that you shouldn't give someone or something else control over your life but should instead take the rope out of his hand and wrap it around your own neck.

shoes. If we conduct ourselves in this way, it will be possible for adverse conditions to the Dharma to manifest as happiness.

When all the shravakas of our Teacher were invited to travel to a border region, the Teacher said that [the people] in the border region were faithless, were vile, and maintained a bad livelihood. [The shravakas] thought, "If they slander us but don't beat us it would be best, and if they beat us and we don't die, that would be best." [The Buddha replied], "If such a thing happens by going to the regions without Dharma, and if you follow these instructions, you will not degenerate; therefore, you have permission to go." In the same way, whatever happens to us, such as suffering, poverty, and inferiority, we will be able to bring it into the path. For example, when merchants head out on the road in the summer and it rains, they say that the thieves will not come. If it snows in the wintertime, they say it is beneficial to the horses' hooves. In these ways they transform [these adversities] into supportive elements.

Transforming Adverse Conditions into the Path through View

The lines

> Viewing mistaken appearances as the four [buddha] bodies
> Is the unsurpassed protection of emptiness

are in accordance with the [interpretation of] earlier Tibetan [Buddhist traditions]. By perceiving the essential nature of adverse conditions, such as illness, harm from spirits, and so forth, as not being born in any way whatsoever from the beginning, they are the unborn truth body. Since they are ultimately free of cessation, they are the unceasing enjoyment body. Since they are unceasingly born and do not abide in between, they are the nonabiding emanation body. Their inseparable essential nature is the nature truth body, and so on.

In our own tradition, we consider them illusory-like dreams, while remaining in a state that views the nontrue existence of every adverse condition that could possibly arise, such as sickness, suffering, and so on.

The root text states, "**The fourfold practice is the supreme method**." These four are (1) accumulating merit, (2) purifying obstructions, (3) offering tormas to spirits, and (4) entrusting Dharma protectors with enlightened actions.

Accumulating Merit

When suffering befalls us, once we present offerings to the Three Jewels, we should pray, "Since this is exhausting my previously accumulated negative karma and is coming from taking on the suffering of father and mother living beings, may such things continue to occur. If it is best that I am ill, grant your blessing that I may be ill. If it is best that I die, grant your blessing that I may die. If it is best that I live, grant your blessing that I may live."

Purifying Obstructions

Employ confession and the four opponent powers completely, by understanding that negative karma is the cause of suffering.

Offering Tormas to Spirits

If you are practitioners of mind training, you should dedicate the collection of flesh and blood from your body by commanding them,

> The harm and so forth that you previously caused me functioned to encourage me to practice Dharma. The occurrence of suffering purified numerous negativities and enhanced [my mind training]. Continue to send even greater illness and suffering.

Offering Tormas to Dharma Protectors

Offer tormas to the Dharma protectors and make supplications, thinking,

> Engage in your enlightened actions so that, in dependence upon being able to bring whatever suffering and harm befalls me into the path, I will be able to generate the conventional bodhichitta that has not been generated, maintain that which has been generated, and increase even more that which is being maintained in dependence upon that [suffering].

If there are some people whose minds are not developed enough to be able to bring such training into the path, they should offer a torma and entrust [the Dharma protectors] with their enlightened actions to pacify unfavorable conditions to bodhichitta and accomplish favorable conditions. You can also offer a torma to the spirits and ask them not to send obstacles to training in bodhichitta. You can also consider how, whenever sickness, suffering, and so forth emerge, it is definitely purifying your karmic debt.

Likewise, such meditations are the essential point of practices such as chö as well as purification and restoration rituals of Dharma protectors. If you are also going to practice chö, you should do so at this point. Although the term *chö* is expressing that we should sever our self-grasping and self-cherishing, these days it isn't used as an antidote; instead, it has become a means of traveling around villages and begging for roasted barley. Dza Patrul Rinpoche expressed his thoughts on the matter when he stated,

> Although you beat your small drum, it is for mere enjoyment;
> Although you carry flesh and blood, it is out of self-cherishing;
> Although you play your small cymbals, it is without reference point:
> Abandon your deceptively nice-looking ostentatious display!

If we engage in the hundred torma offering while reciting the *Confession of Moral Downfalls*, we will be accomplishing an extensive practice with the essential meaning of these four practices of mind training. The root text states, "**Apply meditation to whatever you encounter**." Thus, you should employ the meditations for applying the antidotes to whatever adverse conditions you encounter. For example, previously in Tibet, during the outbreak of a large battle, a mind-training practitioner named Kyorlung Geshe was frightened at first, but after recalling the instructions, he experienced happiness; we should be that way as well.

Day Twenty-Seven

The great bodhisattva glorious Shantideva stated [in *Guide to the Bodhisattva's Way of Life*],

> Like the supreme elixir that transforms into gold,
> [Firmly grasp this thing called bodhichitta,
> Which transforms this impure human body
> We have taken into the priceless jewel of the Conqueror's body.]

Although we were born amid the swamp of samsara and are uncontrollably bound by karma and afflictive emotions, with the mind of precious bodhichitta we can transform this impure body into the priceless jewel of a buddha's body adorned with the signs and indications, which is analogous to an elixir that can transform base metals into gold. Set your motivation by thinking, "For the sake of enacting that transformation, I am going to listen to this king of instructions."

After giving this short introduction, Pabongkha Rinpoche covered the previous headings. Next, from the actual meditation on two types of bodhichitta, he explained once more the way to meditate on conventional bodhichitta, as well as the benefits of exchanging self with others and the faults of not exchanging them.

"Self" and "others" are analogous to making distinctions between "this mountain" and "that mountain" in dependence upon the ground from which we are making such observations.

Query: Well then, is there no difference between myself and others with respect to this body?

Reply: This body is also others' since it was born from the sperm and ovum of your father and mother. For that reason, if you train by shifting your position between the two perspectives of cherishing self and [cherishing] others, you will be able to develop [the transference]. In general, if we contemplate results that come from the functioning of the two types of cherishing [self and others], we will develop conviction. As I explained earlier, we focus on the benefits and faults by observing the difference between the Buddha and ourselves. [Shantideva's *Guide to the Bodhisattva's Way of Life*] states,

> [What need is there for a lot of explanation?]
> The childish work for their own welfare,
> [And the munis work for the welfare of others;
> Just look at the difference between these two.]

The way to train is to stress the visualization of love and compassion with respect to giving and taking. When giving a brief explanation according to the other general preliminary rituals, you recite, "I supplicate you, Tubwang Dorje Chang,[584] whose nature is the four buddha bodies." Here, you can substitute it with the supplication "I supplicate you Guru Avalokiteshvara," through which purifying [lights and nectar] descend. Next, you meditate on equanimity, recognizing all beings as your mother and recalling their kindness and the wish to repay their kindness. Although these meditations are *not* different [from the sevenfold cause and effect system], the love and compassion of the sevenfold instructions of cause and effect and those of equalizing and exchanging self with others *are* different. By considering the faults of self-cherishing and the benefits of cherishing others, your recollection of their kindness will be much stronger. From that, you will develop a very powerful affectionate love. From that, you will develop a much more powerful bodhichitta. You can also meditate on giving and taking according to the dedication and so forth from [Shantideva's] *Guide to the Bodhisattva's Way of Life* and then [develop] superior intention.

If you are going to engage in an extensive practice for developing those

584. On Tubwang Dorje Chang, see note 202 above.

minds, train in stages utilizing the following thirteen headings: (1) practicing equanimity, (2) recognizing all beings as your mother, (3) recalling their kindness, (4) wishing to repay their kindness, (5) contemplating the equality of self and others, (6) contemplating in numerous ways the faults of self-cherishing, (7) contemplating in numerous ways the benefits of cherishing others, (8) contemplating the reason it is necessary to cherish others, (9) actually exchanging self and others, (10) practicing taking by placing emphasis on the meditations on compassion, (11) practicing giving by placing emphasis on the meditations on love, and at the conclusion of that, supplementing it with (12) superior intention and the (13) actual bodhichitta.[585] Alternatively, you can dispense with equanimity and have twelve cycles of meditation. Either way you train, it will result in bodhichitta.

Point Four: Presentation of a Lifetime's Practice in Summary

The root text states,

> **The essential instructions, briefly stated,**
> **Are the application of the five forces.**

This reveals the practice of one life within a twenty-four-hour period and how to combine that in the five forces. For that, there are two applications: **(1) the continual practice of the five forces**, and **(2) the practice of the five forces at the time of death**. Of those [five forces], the first is the following:

The Force of Intention

All Dharma [activities] and worldly activities, as well as whatever virtuous or negative actions we undertake, depend upon the way in which intention is formed. From something as substantial as war between countries to something as minor as a simple monk making a pot of tea, [every

585. In *Liberation in Our Hands*, Pabongkha Rinpoche lists eleven stages. Here, he has added numbers 8 and 9 to make thirteen stages.

action] depends upon forming an intention. Although from the beginning we form the intention to have profit and success, pleasant conversation, fame, and so forth, we should not [do so]. Instead, from the moment we awaken in the morning, we should form our intention by thinking, "At the very least, I am going to practice some Dharma." However, setting such a limited intention is inappropriate for practitioners of mind training. Instead, after arising early each day they should think,

> Today I am so fortunate that I have not died thus far. Therefore, right now in this life in general, and within that, in this year, in this month, and on this day in particular, I am going to do everything possible to subdue this insidious demon of self-cherishing and strive to elicit as much as possible an experience of the two types of bodhichitta, thereby extracting the essence of this life of leisure and endowment.

It is extremely important that we repeatedly recall the motivation we formulated in the morning for the day.

The Force of Familiarity

Employ familiarity through training the mind in the two types of bodhichitta. Furthermore, [Shantideva's *Guide to the Bodhisattva's Way of Life*] states,

> There is nothing that is not easy to accomplish
> If we have familiarity with it.

And,

> There isn't any phenomenon whatsoever that
> Is not easy once you familiarize your mind with it.

For example, whether or not a tangkha painter is skilled at artistry depends on the degree of his familiarity. Through repeated and stable visualization of the objects of attachment and so forth, they will arise as though they are directly perceptible before us. In the same way, if the mind is familiar through repeated contemplation, the object will appear clearly. If we become familiar with the lamrim, mind training, or even the generation and completion stages, they will become easy. According to their biographies, some of the previous holy beings could complete a scanning meditation on the entire lamrim while putting one of their feet in the stirrups:

> The path of meditation is reflecting again and again,
> Fathoming and gaining a definite understanding.

As this states, we should improve our mind's familiarity.

The Force of the White Seed

Engaging in accumulation and purification as the causes of developing the two types of bodhichitta is the embodiment of everything that exists in this force of "the white virtue of Dharma."

The Force of Destruction

We should see that self-cherishing is the true enemy and then meditate on the two types of bodhichitta as the antidote that is the only means of destroying it, which is called the "destruction of self-cherishing."

The Force of Prayer

Substitute the dedication prayers [to accommodate] your roots of virtue. Furthermore, in the evening, when going to bed, look back on the day's activities and observe whatever virtue or negativity you have engaged in, such as study, memorizations, gathering in the debate courtyard, and so on, and examine whether or not you improved your intellect and practiced virtue. If you engaged in virtue, meditate on joy and then make extensive and pure prayers that these actions may become the cause of your complete enlightenment. If you didn't engage in wholesome acts, engage in the appropriate confession and restraint, together with the four opponent powers, and apply them to the negative karma you have accumulated since beginningless time in samsara. For example, if a traveler is leaving early the next morning, he should make preparations to depart that evening. Likewise, when the previous Kadampas would go to their sleeping quarters in the evening, they would say, "Even if we die right now, we are going to stick to this aspiration." And deciding that there was a very good chance that they wouldn't wake up the next morning, they would even turn their teacups upside down.

When you are not separated from all five of these forces, it is called "equalizing your life and your practice."

Applying the Practice of the Five Forces at the Time of Death

The root text states, "**Cherish the conduct of the five forces alone as instructions of transference of consciousness of mind training.**" Although there is a great deal of bragging about the oral instructions for transference of consciousness at the time of death,[586] this is the most profound. For that, there are [also] five points.

The Force of Intention

When you are approaching the time of death, think, "Now is the time of my death; therefore, I shall practice the transference of consciousness from within the state of bodhichitta by equalizing and exchanging self with others." Also, repeatedly formulate an extremely powerful intention by thinking, "I am not going to forget my bodhichitta at the moment of my death and even in the intermediate state."

The Force of the White Seed

When it is time to die, once you forsake your mind of attachment, you should perform acts of generosity to the fields of accumulating merit by making offerings upward to the Three Jewels and by giving offerings downward to evil spirits. It is a great fault if you develop a mind of attachment to your wealth and possessions. Previously, a bhikshu had attachment to his begging bowl, and when he died he was reborn as a snake inside his begging bowl. A merchant had a pouch of gold that he was attached to, and when he died he was reborn as a snake wrapped around the gold. A woman was attached to her own body, and when she died

586. Here Pabongkha Rinpoche is stating that there are a lot of so-called profound practices for transference of consciousness that people brag about, saying that they are the most profound instructions ever. However, in Pabongkha's (and the Kadampas') opinion, this system is the most profound.

she was reborn as a snake within her [previous] aggregates. A bhikshu was attached to some silver and was reborn as a frog after his death. We also are in danger of being reborn in such situations through polishing our teacups out of attachment. Previously, an old monk from Tashi Kyil Monastery in Amdo[587] who was attached to the type of butter mixed in his tea found it difficult to stop breathing at the time of his death. Thus, if we develop attachment and craving for our possessions at the time of death, we will be like a bird with a rock strapped to its legs trying to fly in the sky; therefore, it is very important that we abandon our attachment for our loved ones, wealth, enjoyments, and so on.

The Force of Destruction

You should engage in confession right down to your friends whom you may have offended. Engage in confession and restraint for your previous negative actions through various avenues while employing confession and restraint. If your lama is available, you should request an empowerment, and if he isn't, you should perform self-initiation on your own to restore your bodhisattva vows, mantra vows, and so forth.

The Force of Prayer

Combine with great sincerity whatever prayers you know for quickly developing precious bodhichitta in your mental continuum and so forth.

The Force of Familiarity

Make an effort to recognize in advance the stages of dissolution at the time of death. If you are practitioner of the generation and completion stages of mantra, once the elements sequentially dissolve, you should practice transference through bringing the three bodies into the path. Mind-training meditators should practice transference within a state of practicing giving and taking while meditating on bodhichitta. Although we have well-known practices of reciting HIK and PHAT for projecting us upward to the pure lands and the higher realms, I am concerned that they may project people down to the lower realms. [However,] if we

587. Tashi Kyil is one of the six great monasteries of the Gelug tradition and was founded in 1708 by the great Jamyang Shepa Ngawang Tsondru.

practice transference while in a state of meditating on bodhichitta, we will not go to the lower realms, and there is no doubt that we will be reborn in the pure lands and so forth.

Geshe Chen-nga-wa said, in reference to giving and taking, "Even as I am now dying, I don't practice anything other than this." While [Geshe] Potowa was uttering a teaching on equalizing and exchanging self with others, he departed from this throne [that is, he died]. If we meditate properly on mind training, although we may wish to be reborn in the lower realms we won't be reborn in the lower realms. Geshe Chekawa gained complete mastery of bodhichitta. When he was about to pass away, he said, "In this world there is no more melodious sound than the sound of mind training; therefore, make that sound in my ear." Also, to a close disciple [Geshe Chekawa] said, "Make offerings; it seems I am not going to accomplish what I had in mind." His close disciple inquired, "Lama Rinpoche accomplished the Dharma in one life; therefore, what intention did you not accomplish?" [Chekawa responded,] "Although I have been praying to be reborn in the lowest hell for the welfare of living beings, I have been receiving signs that I am going to the pure lands; therefore, I am [continuing] to make prayers to be reborn in hell for the welfare of living beings." What need is there to mention [what will happen] if we meditate on bodhichitta? Even if we [simply] have a benevolent mind at the time of death, we won't go to the lower realms.

Previously, in Jasa, on the Yarlung River, there was a boat with many people on board, including six monks and one layperson, so that the leather coracle was too heavy; therefore, it capsized. When this happened, a messenger decided to jump in the river despite risking death; however, he did not die and instead auspicious signs occurred, such as a rainbow emerging from the place where he crossed and so forth. Also, according to a historical account, a mother and her child were swept away by the water's current, and [as this occurred] they developed loving thoughts for each other. Both of them died in the water and were reborn in the god realms. Therefore, although there are many famous oral instructions for the time of death, none is more profound than this Mahayana mind-training transference of consciousness.

Regarding our physical posture, since our compassionate Teacher practiced transference while lying in the lion posture when he passed into nirvana, this physical posture alone is sufficient for transference. Next is developing the three intentions and so forth, as presented in the lamrim scriptures. Thus, you will definitely develop bodhichitta through a ritual if you have reached a point where you have developed a mere partial experience of bodhichitta through meditating according to the previous explanations. If it is ripened through a ritual for adopting bodhichitta, you will definitely develop bodhichitta. However, whether or not you adopt bodhichitta through a ritual depends upon whether or not you have developed it [through experience] and not through words alone. If you adopt bodhichitta through a ritual, it will be stabilized and increased, you can receive instructions on the precepts, and so on; thus, it is extremely vast.

This should be explained during the actual section on how to adopt bodhichitta through a ritual. Once you are dismissed from your current preparations, you should prepare offerings for the development of bodhichitta tomorrow and sweep the floor of the temple, set out an arrangement of flowers to adorn the master's throne, arrange rows of offerings, and so forth. It is said that the offerings should be [so vast that] your friends would be astonished and that you should offer one sixth of your belongings.

[Ritual for Receiving the Bodhisattva Vows]

While bestowing bodhichitta at Samyé and Mangyul,[588] Atisha the Great said that those in attendance would not generate bodhichitta because their offerings were inferior. If I had not previously given a discourse on the lamrim, at this point during today's preparation I would have to bestow a complete commentary on the lamrim as a preparation once the preliminary rituals were completed. However, at this point I have already given a detailed explanation on the lamrim; therefore, I do not have to explain it again at this point. Tomorrow we will assemble twice. The lama does not need to attend during the earlier gathering. Once the Dharma-assembly gathers, recite the preliminary rituals. The best would be to read aloud the entire Kangyur. If that is not possible, read sections of the

588. Mangyul is located in western Tibet near the Nepalese border.

teachings such as the *Buddha Ornament Sutra*, the *Sutra of the Fortunate Eon*, and so forth. Offer the three-sectioned torma offering. To practice the hundred torma offering, those who have the lineages should gather to one side and practice the hundred torma offering extensively and so forth to accumulate merit as extensively as possible.

After the next session, the lamas and students should all wear the three sets of monk's robes and so forth very elegantly, for engaging in the actual bodhichitta [ceremony]. It is the tradition of the guru that after the master performs confession himself, he takes the bodhisattva vows and so forth. Right now I am giving the detailed system of teaching according to the ritual tradition of the [six] preliminary ritual practices.[589] Next are the extensive preparations for generating bodhichitta and the lamrim prayers. From the point when that is finished, the guru initiates the ceremony by reciting, "Buddha, Dharma, Supreme Assembly . . ." three times, "The supreme mind of bodhichitta . . ." three times, "May all father and mother living beings be endowed with happiness," and so forth, together with "May our glorious guru have a long life. . . ." The chanting master then leads the recitation, "In short, may the glorious guru have a long life. . . ."

After this explanation, we were free to leave.

589. Tib. *sbyor chos.*

Day Twenty-Eight

For the actual bodhichitta ceremony, we recited prayers for averting demons and so forth as before. We offered the six extensive preliminary rituals and offering verses, together with collecting numbers of mandala offerings. At the conclusion of reciting the Muni mantra[590] *during the preliminary rituals, we made dedications such as "Through this merit . . ." up to "May I establish . . ." Next we offered a mandala to the guru as a request for bodhichitta, at which point we held up [special offering] substances [that each disciple brought to facilitate the generation of] bodhichitta. Once that was completed, the guru led the ceremony by reciting teachings from conqueror Tsongkhapa the Great that state, "Bodhichitta is the main path of the path of the supreme vehicle. . . ."*

We must enter the path of the Mahayana to attain the state of enlightenment. For that, we must generate bodhichitta. Generating the mind of supreme enlightenment of the Mahayana is like the seed of a buddha; therefore, it determines whether or not we progress toward the state of enlightenment. Also, whether we are heading toward or away from [enlightenment] depends solely on whether or not we have the precious mind of bodhichitta. If we don't have it, although we may have other good qualities, such as the divine eye, the six types of clairvoyance, and so forth, we cannot even consider the possibility of attaining enlightenment, and we have not entered the ranks of the Mahayana.

In contrast, if you have bodhichitta, because you have accomplished that mind, even something as insignificant as giving a scrap of food to something like a dog or a hawk becomes a cause of enlightenment and

590. This is the mantra of Buddha Shakyamuni: OM MUNI MUNI MAHA MUNIYE SVAHA.

becomes a deed of a bodhisattva. If you have not accomplished that mind [of bodhichitta], even practicing something like Guhyasamaja, the king of tantras, for a thousand years will not be included within the Dharma of the Mahayana. If you generate this mind in your mental continuum, even animals such as dogs and pigs that are born in the same place as [you] will become worthy objects of veneration by gods and humans.

According to the previous explanation, at this point, even though we are newly generating bodhichitta in our mental continuum, because of that we [already] possess good qualities, like a mountain of gold that overpowers shravakas and pratyekabuddhas. For example, this is comparable to the way in which even when a prince is very young he overpowers the assembly of elder ministers, and the newborn offspring of a garuda overpowers the assembly of elder birds [from other species]. When you generate bodhichitta, various signs occur, such as the thrones of the buddhas trembling and so forth. It is as though you have been born as a new son, as a universal king of all the buddhas in the ten directions, whereby they are delighted and fulfill your wishes. A verse describes the benefits as follows:

> Through churning the milk of the holy Dharma,
> The essence of butter overflows.

[Bodhichitta] is the only thing that emerges from the heart practice of all the buddhas and bodhisattvas. Although we may generate an authentic bodhichitta in our mental continuum, if we sequentially train our minds according to the stages of the path of the three types of beings, we will generate it without difficulty.

At this point, Pabongkha Rinpoche said that we should formulate our motivation of the complete path in its entirety, and he once again gave a detailed discourse on how to cultivate an uncontrived motivation through training the mind in the three types of beings.

During the section on superior intention, we should generate bodhichitta by thinking, "I will accept the responsibility of ensuring that all living beings are endowed with every type of happiness and free of every type of suffering; however, presently I am unable to do such a thing. The Buddha has perfected the two purposes [of self and other]; therefore, so that I am able to accomplish such a state as quickly as possible, I shall attain the state of enlightenment." It is important that once you experience even a slight experience of these two aspirations, you generate aspiring bodhichitta, and when you elicit an uncontrived experience of them, [then] you have generated engaging bodhichitta.[591] With respect to the distinction of aspiring bodhichitta, [Shantideva's *Guide to the Bodhisattva's Way of Life*] states,

> Just as you understand the distinction
> Between wishing to go and going,
> Likewise, the wise should know
> The distinction between these two [bodhichittas].

Aspiring bodhichitta is analogous to making a wish to go to India once you have considered going, and engaging bodhichitta is like actually setting out on the path. Therefore, aspiring bodhichitta is the thought, "I shall attain the state of enlightenment for the welfare of all living beings." The mind that promises to train toward that attainment, receives the bodhisattva vows, and then trains in the deeds [of a bodhisattva] is engaging bodhichitta. The teachings in [Asanga's] *Bodhisattva Levels*[592] state that someone with a powerful capacity who is incapable of training in the [bodhisattva's] deeds takes aspiring bodhichitta vows. According to [Shantideva's] *Guide to the Bodhisattva's Way of Life*, you receive bodhisattva vows from the perspective of being able to train in the deeds [of a bodhisattva]. These two traditions should not be mixed together.

For the actual acceptance of aspiring bodhichitta through a ritual, the disciples kneel on their right knee and hold their hands in prayer at the heart. Visualize that to your left are the six classes of mother living beings in the aspect of your tormented dear mother of this life, and to your right are the six classes of father living beings in the aspect of your tormented father of this life. Think, "No matter what the cost, I shall attain the precious state of enlightenment for the welfare of these beings. For that

591. A slightly different explanation is presented below.
592. Tib. *Byang sa*.

purpose I will take the bodhisattva vows." Also, your guru appears in the aspect of the teacher Buddha Shakyamuni upon a jeweled throne, and in the cardinal and intermediate directions of space are the buddhas and bodhisattvas of the three times like billowing heaps of clouds. At the sides and gateways are directional protectors, wrathful beings, and so forth dwelling in their appropriate directions, who are protecting and assisting you so that you can develop bodhichitta in your mental continuum.

At this juncture there should be a detailed presentation for identifying the ways of gaining conviction in the mind of refuge and so forth. In accordance with the *Middle-Length Treatise on the Stages of the Path to Enlightenment* text, as a preliminary you recite, "Master please listen to me . . ." three times after the guru. You also recite, "Master please listen to me . . ." three times when going for refuge and [when] the precepts of going for refuge are recited [by the master] and so forth. Also, according to the texts about the actual [ceremony] for bodhichitta, you generate bodhichitta by reciting [the verses] three times [after the master]. Although [Asanga's] *Bodhisattva Levels* does not teach developing delight [in having received the bodhisattva vows], the ceremony will be amended from the teachings in [Shantideva's] *Guide to the Bodhisattva's Way of Life*, which [contains verses for developing delight,] beginning with "Now my life has borne great fruit . . . ," up to "and have become a bodhisattva." Next, with respect to the trainings, you recite, "All my actions . . ." up to "shall never bring disgrace." In between [the verses], you recite each one after the master.

Thus, there are great benefits in generating bodhichitta, and we should dedicate the vast stores of virtuous roots in the three times symbolized by that bodhichitta. Furthermore, [think,] "In the future, when conqueror Maitreya comes to this world, may I be reborn as the first of his retinue as a conquerors' son, a bodhisattva with intellect and courage. For that purpose, I am requesting with my current roots of virtue to be entrusted to the regent protector Maitreya in the Yiga Chözin Palace in Tushita." Recite the dedication verse that begins, "One day, above the mountain of Bodhgaya . . . ," along with "One day, elevated to the mountain . . ." [Next,] recite each four-lined verse (*shloka*) beginning from "Je . . ." onward one time, and then begin again from the start, and thereby recite it twice; after this [the assembly] completes the third recitation while the lama's attendants toss flowers into the air. Imagine that your current objects of meditation, such as generating the mind of supreme enlightenment and so forth, appear in the aspects of clouds of offering that are your roots of virtue of the three times, which descend all around protector Maitreya in Tushita. Regarding the precepts of the mantra vows during the section on precepts, you are not permitted to listen to or see those that you haven't already received. With respect to the bodhisattva vows, prior to taking the vows, you should check to determine whether or not you are capable of keeping them, and you should learn the precepts before requesting the vows and then take them from that perspective.

Although you may only be taking [the precepts] of aspiring bodhichitta, there are four causes for not deteriorating bodhichitta. So that bodhichitta does not deteriorate in our future lives, abandon the four black Dharmas, which are not to (1) deceive your guru through telling lies, (2) cause others to develop regret for the virtue they have performed, (3) disparage bodhisattvas out of anger, or (4) cause deception without a special intention. The opposite of these four are to rely upon the four white Dharmas, which are to (1) be vigilant in not telling a lie even through a slight smile, (2) practice to the best of your ability the means of ripening the mental continuums of others and the means of generating bodhichitta, (3) develop the recognition that all living beings are the Teacher, [593] and (4) remain honest without deceiving others.

We should learn the precepts taught for engaging bodhichitta from [Shantideva's] *Compendium of Trainings*, [Chandragomin's] *Twenty Verses on the Bodhisattva Vows*,[594] and so forth. Once we accept the bodhisattva vows, we should take them three times during the day and three times during the night without forgetting. The mind forsaking living beings is the [main] cause of deteriorating bodhichitta. We do not need to forsake all living beings; if we have a mind forsaking even one living being, we have immediately forsaken our bodhichitta. [Therefore,] even though it is not appropriate to be close with our body and speech to those who have [a bad relationship] through having broken their spiritual bond to our guru

593. In Pabongkha's *Liberation in Our Hands* and Tsongkhapa's *Great Treatise on the Stages of the Path*, it says that we should recognize bodhisattvas as being the Teacher.

594. Tib. *Byang chub sems dpa'i sdom pa nyi shu pa*.

and so forth, we should not mentally abandon them. Once we accept aspiring bodhichitta through a ritual, we should strive in the means of accumulating the two types of accumulations for the sake of increasing our bodhichitta.

Day Twenty-Nine

To give a scriptural citation, the *Prayer to Maitreya* states,

> Turning away from the path of the lower realms . . .

If we generate bodhichitta of the Mahayana, we temporarily turn away from the lower realms and attain the excellent physical form of a god or human. Ultimately, we easily attain the state of omniscience without having to wait too long. In that way, the supreme means of training in that mind [of bodhichitta] is this king-like instruction.

After giving this short introduction, Pabongkha Rinpoche covered the headings.

The Measure of Having Generated That Mind [of Bodhichitta] and the Measure of Having Generated Great Compassion

With respect to the measure of having generated great compassion, as I already explained, [you have attained it when,] by merely remembering or seeing any type of living being, you naturally develop affectionate love and regard them as extremely precious and pleasing in aspect, like the compassion a mother feels for her only child when he is suffering.

With respect to the measure of having generated bodhichitta, it is not immeasurable love and compassion, since even shravakas and pratyekabuddhas have that; in this context just that is not sufficient. Instead, in addition to that, you must generate superior intention that assumes the responsibility for accomplishing the benefit and happiness [of all living beings], after which you must develop an uncontrived aspiration to attain complete enlightenment for the welfare of all living beings. Therefore, as I explained earlier, if each time you see a living being you spontaneously give rise to a mind thinking, "I shall attain enlightenment for their welfare," then you have generated bodhichitta.

The [root text of *Seven-Point*] *Mind Training* [by Geshe Chekawa continues and] states the following:

Point Five: The Measure of Having Trained the Mind

The root text states, **"The intent of all Dharmas converges into a single point**." There aren't any scriptures of the Conqueror contained within the Hinayana and Mahayana that are not embodied by the methods presented in mind training or, in other words, the means of subduing self-grasping. Therefore, a Dharma practitioner is someone who progresses toward the means of subduing self-cherishing, and a mind-training meditator must be able to harm self-cherishing. If you are Dharma practitioners, there should be indications that your afflictive emotions are not increasing in size. For example, at Drag Yerpa, Je [Tsongkhapa] saw with his own eyes two retreatants who were staying above and below each other [yet] who would criticize each other. We must make sure we don't become like that.

In particular, if our meditation on bodhichitta through equalizing and exchanging self with others is effective, there should be a reduction in our self-cherishing. Mind training is like a scale weighing the effectiveness of the Dharma practitioner to determine whether or not [he or she is reducing our self-cherishing]. We profess how utterly amazing clairvoyance and miraculous powers are, and if a person can fly through the sky or go underwater or under the ground, we treat him [or her] as though he [or she] is actually the Buddha. However, there is nothing particularly amazing about these things at all. We do not need to be anything more than a hawk, a mouse, a fish, and so on to be able to do such things. With respect to clairvoyance, this is something that worldly nonhuman beings have, such as gods, nagas, king spirits, evil spirits, and so forth. If we propitiate malignant spirits,[595] they can easily deceive foolish worldly beings

595. Tib. *the'u rang*.

Geshe Chekawa

by accomplishing some minor things. If we train in illusions and optical illusions, poisonous substances, evil mantras, and so forth, we will receive similar signs of attainment and be able to engage in sudden miraculous displays and deception. However, these days most people who engage in such things have mentally forsaken their next lives[596] in the world and deceive many others by employing numerous ways of devoting themselves to the means of accomplishing food and clothes for this life. Previously,

596. This means they are only concerned with the things of this life such as wealth, fame, power, and so forth.

through the power of the dependent relationship of substances and mantras, an acharya from India could make finger tormas out of rocks[597] by relying upon a familial lineage of employing numerous evil mantras and the blood of a rock-eating frog. Even the sheep and goats that would eat the grass where he lived were able to leave their hoof prints in stone and so forth, which comes from nothing other than the nature of dependent relationship.

Even miraculous signs and clairvoyance do not contribute even a fraction to our progression along the grounds and paths of sutra and tantra and are without essence. [Geshe] Potowa asked Geshe [Drom]tonpa, "What is the demarcation line between Dharma and non-Dharma?" [Drom]tonpa replied, "If it serves as an antidote to the afflictive emotions, it is Dharma. If it doesn't, it is not Dharma." If that is what Dharma is, whether or not we cut our hair and change our clothes, whether or not we perform recitations, and so forth is not the determining factor. Practicing Dharma depends on the mind and serves as an antidote to the afflictive emotions. Previously, many Tibetans said, "We are going to investigate Panchen Shakya Shri." Geshe Ben Gungyal said, "Although he is a great scholar, if you must investigate, don't go with such an intention. If you are going to make preparations to go, once you turn your intentions around, your application of studying and contemplating the Dharma should serve as an antidote to destroy the afflictive emotions. You should go because you are on the verge of lessening your afflictive emotions. I don't need to go into the presence of Panchen Shakya Shri because my afflictive emotions have already been diminished. After consideration, I am not going. The sign of having studied is being pacified and subdued; the sign of attainment is the lessening of afflictive emotions."

If our practice of Dharma reduces the imprints of our afflictive emotions and self-cherishing, then the Dharma has become Dharma and this is a sign that we have penetrated the essential meaning of mind training and is the real sign of attainment.

The root text states, "**Uphold the principal of the two witnesses**." Regarding the two witnesses, as Dharma practitioners we need the wit-

597. Tib. *chang bu*. These are small tormas used in rituals such as obstacle-dispelling tormas, the three-part torma offering, and so forth. This is stating that the acharya attained the worldly attainment of being able to mold solid rock with his bare hands.

nesses of both self and others. Therefore, although we may not be despised by others, from the two witnesses of self and others, the principal one is to be able to serve as your own witness. If we examine from an unbiased perspective, it is not necessary to be ashamed of ourselves. For example, although another person may consider you an excellent Dharma practitioner, [just ignore him,] for he has no way of knowing. However, you [also] shouldn't have thoughts such as "I am the worst person; I have all these various faults." Furthermore, [Nagarjuna's] *Letter to a Friend* states,

> Understand that the actions of human beings are like mangoes:
> They can be unripe and yet appear ripe,
> Be ripe yet appear unripe,
> Be unripe and appear unripe, or appear ripe and be ripe.

Thus, there are four permutations, such as being ripe on the outside and ripe on the inside and so on, using a mango as a metaphor for the best, middling, and worst persons.

Therefore, like a mango fruit that is both ripe on the outside and ripe on the inside, it is important outwardly to have pure conduct that is subdued and internally to abide in pure view and the conduct of moral discipline, view, meditation, compassion, and so forth. Je Gungtang [Jampalyang Rinpoche] stated,

> Tether your experiences of compassion and hide them deep
> within,
> And be as sly and cunning as a cat.

Thus, keep any honor and gain or fame and glory that come your way in your innermost heart. Although internally you may be a Dharma practitioner, if your conduct is crude, it will serve as a cause for the many others who rely upon you to go to the lower realms. In particular, [Chandragomin's *Twenty Verses on the Bodhisattva Vows*] states [that the fifteenth secondary bodhisattva vow downfall states], "Not avoiding a bad reputation . . ." Thus, we should conduct ourselves in a peaceful and subdued manner and avoid the type of behavior that will cause others to disparage us. If our actions are faulty and improper, all the buddhas in the ten directions as well as the Dharma protectors onward, and even the virtuous gods, will know and understand; therefore, we should be very careful.

In short, we don't need to despise ourselves, and from the point of view of the perception of exalted wisdom of the gurus, buddhas, and bodhisattvas, they also won't despise us. However, some think that even if you are incapable of practicing Dharma, you will not accumulate negative karma, and that it is best to sit around idly, which is also inappropriate. Presently, we have obtained a human body of leisure and endowment, we have encountered a guru who is like an actual buddha, and we have met the complete teachings of sutra and tantra. This is not something to be wasted; instead, we should make use of this meaningful life of leisure and endowment and accomplish something that is necessarily superior to [being like something inanimate such as] the earth or rocks.

Furthermore, according to Indian [culture], your actions should be carried out according to the trainings in the exact way that your disciplined elder monk, reading teacher, and so forth asked you to perform them. Also, in the same way, at the great monastic seats of Lhasa, you must rely upon your teacher who is responsible for you, your textbook teacher, and so forth. From the time you are a youth [and] rely upon your excellent teachers, it is extremely important that you carry out whatever they say to do, such as study, contemplation, and so forth. If things don't happen this way, it is extremely regretful, because as the saying goes, "The young monk with a great deal of intelligence; a senior monk with few good qualities . . ."

The root text states, "**Always rely upon a happy mind alone**." A practitioner who has trained his [or her] mind properly in giving and taking should not be overpowered by whatever happens, whether it is happiness or suffering as well as good or bad conditions. The Kashmiri Pandit[598] stated,

> If you are happy, dedicate the collections of happiness:
> "May benefit and happiness fill space."
> If you are suffering, bear the responsibility of everyone's suffering:
> "May this dry up the ocean of suffering."

598. Tib. Kha che pan chen. His full name was Kha che pan chen zla ba mngon dga'.

Thus, when happiness comes our way, we should not have attachment to it for our own welfare and instead pray that our happiness, and happiness like it, will come to all living beings. When suffering befalls us, as in the story of Mrgara's daughter,[599] we should pray, "May this sever the suffering experienced by all living beings." Learn how to bring it into the path by thinking, "I am enduring this suffering for the sake of all living beings." Also, even when physical suffering befalls us, we should not become depressed but be capable of relying solely upon a happy mind. Therefore, as I already explained, the name *mind training* means the source of the City of Happiness, which is another way of saying Sukhavati, Abhirati, and so on. Once we think in this way, it will be as Gyalwa Yang Gönpa also stated,

> This exercise of self-reliant naked introspection—
> One that forgoes healing rituals or medical treatment
> For a sickness caused by a disturbance of the four elements
> And avoids performing auspicious visualizations—
> Is a quality of spiritual practice that can purge illnesses.
> This technique that avoids seeing physical imbalances
> And fluctuating states of mind as obstacles or interferences
> And turns faults into benefits that bring great progress
> Through the instruction whose key element is spontaneous
>   warmth
> Is a quality of spiritual practice that dispels obstructions.
>
> Without calling for medicine or Bon practices, I maintain great
>   tolerance of illness.
> By remaining free of doubt, I am skilled at integrating death [into
>   my practice].
> Invoking the Buddha throughout the day is an important
>   undertaking.
> Since my tenure as abbot is over, these diverse experiences
> That cause both pleasure and pain make no difference to me
>   at all.

599. For the details of this story, see Pabongkha Rinpoche, *Liberation in Our Hands*, 2:233.

This ability to maintain great joy inwardly when meeting others,
Even if it should be a person stricken by the blisters of leprosy,
Is my beggar's way of remaining at ease.
This ability to bear up unexpectedly when needed,
Even if I should meet with a death-bringing executioner,
Is my beggar's way of integrating [every experience] into the path.

The former spiritual lords' example was to persevere in the face of hardship.
Not being subject to the worldly person's sign of desiring [this life's] happiness,
I do not worry about food or clothing.
Abandoning all concern for life or limb, I go about however I please.
I have succeeded in bringing my practice of the path to its culmination.

With an attitude that finds everything acceptable,
I do not fret about the three sources of concern and keep my mind relaxed.
Without inviting dissatisfaction to any great extent,
I ignite great bliss in my mind and go about however I please.
I have dispelled the turbulence of discursive thoughts from my mind.[600]

The root text states, "**If you can do this even when distracted, you are trained**." For example, even if the mind of someone who is skilled at riding a horse is distracted, the horse will not be able to throw him. Likewise, if our minds are trained properly, we will be able to practice equalizing and exchanging self with others during adverse conditions, no matter how distracted our minds are. When that occurs, it is said that your mind is trained. Even to a lesser degree, you should be able

600. These verses were translated by Art Engle, based on a previous translation by David Gonsalez.

to [practice exchanging self with others] through recollection when various conditions arise. Even if that happens, it is a sign of having developed a partial experience.

The root text states, "**The measure of having trained is reversal.**" The measure of having trained the mind is that you have renounced self-cherishing, so that where you previously cherished yourself, you now cherish others. If a person of the highest mental capacity trains his [or her] mind, he [or she] will eventually obtain what is called "the concentration of overcoming all phenomena with happiness." At that point, even if someone were to cut an ounce of flesh from the body of that bodhisattva, he wouldn't experience the slightest mental suffering whatsoever and instead would experience joy and bliss.

The root text states, "**The sign of having trained is possessing five greatnesses.**" (1) By forsaking self-cherishing and voluntarily taking on the welfare of others, you are a great bodhisattva. (2) By not violating the precepts you have promised to maintain, you are a great holder of the Vinaya. (3) By enduring the difficulties in applying the methods for destroying self-cherishing, you are a great ascetic. (4) By continuously employing diligence day and night in the yoga of bodhichitta through equalizing and exchanging self with others, you are a great yogi. (5) Through the ability to utilize the path of the Mahayana through the activities of your three doors, you are a great spiritual practitioner. However, it is just as valid if you practice this Mahayana mind training.

Point Six: Presenting the Commitments of Mind Training

[1.–3.] The root text states, "**Always train in the three general points.**"

1. With respect to not violating the commitments of mind training, if we abandon our other commitments and vows, such as those of the Vinaya and so forth, with the pretense of being a mind-training practitioner, it is in complete opposition to mind training. Therefore, so that such a thing doesn't happen, strive to not contradict the boundaries of whatever precepts and vows you have promised to maintain.

2. Do not let your mind training cause reckless behavior. This is doing things such as saying, "I am a mind-training practitioner; therefore, I

don't have any self-cherishing," and then digging [the earth], cutting down trees where spirits live, disturbing the water where spirits dwell, associating with people who have infectious diseases, and so forth—[that is,] to give the impression that we are mind-training practitioners and then engage in all sorts of crazy behavior. Instead, we should conduct ourselves in a peaceful and subdued manner. In our incomparable tradition, we should train according to the teaching tradition of the great Atisha and Jamgon Tsongkhapa the Great.

3. Don't let your mind-training practice fall into partiality. [Partiality] means being patient with those who don't harm us and not being patient with gods and demons that do harm us. [Thus, it means] being patient with friends and not being patient with enemies, or being able to practice mind training when we are at the monastery but not being able to do the same in the city. This is stating that we should not let our mind training come to this and should instead have equanimity for all living beings and in every situation, whether at the monastery or in the city.

[4.] The root text states, "**Change your aspiration but remain natural**." Although we may reach high levels of realization within, through training the mind in the stages of the path of sutra and tantra in dependence upon the mind, the previous Kadampas stated, "We should practice Dharma with very little outward display of the amount of spiritual ground we have covered." As this states, under no circumstance should we make an outward display, by acting as though we have a high level of spiritual attainment. Instead, we should remain natural and keep our good qualities hidden like a butter lamp inside a vase, which is a special quality of the old and new Kadampas.

This is like [the case of] Bodhisattva Shantideva and others in India. The other pandits only saw him engaging in eating, sleeping, and defecating, without showing any other good qualities, whereby he was given the names "Bhusuku" and "The Three Conceptions." One day, the pandits said that Shantideva should give a discourse on the Dharma according to the established tradition, with the intention of publically humiliating him. While Shantideva was teaching the *Guide to the Bodhisattva's Way of Life*, the throne he was sitting upon elevated into space. During the chapter on wisdom, his body gradually disappeared. Although he had traveled a great distance, due to the pandits' ear clairvoyance and attainment of nonforgetfulness, they were able to mentally retain the *Guide to the Bodhisattva's Way of Life* that they had heard.

Even though our realizations may be similar to [those of] a deity, our actions should be comparable to [those of] humans, and we should not profess [our realizations] to worldly persons. We should not act like those who broadcast every little realization that they generate and pretend to be pious. Our outer conduct should be peaceful and subdued, according to the previous tradition. As the saying goes, "The best practitioners should develop inner experiential realizations of Dharma in a day, the middling [should develop them] in a month, and the inferior, in a year."

As this states, we should produce an increase in our experience of the unmistaken noble path of the sutra and tantra in our mental continuum. Otherwise, our minds will be the same as they were before we became ordained and we will not produce any special qualities in our minds. If there has been absolutely no improvement in a person's mind between when he came from his homeland and today, then his mental progress has stagnated.[601] If you have failed to make any progress in your qualities—without even mentioning being a Mahayana mind-training practitioner—then you haven't even entered the ranks of a Dharma practitioner and should apply the means of producing progress in your mind. Although glorious Chandrakirti attained union[602] and others didn't see his good qualities and thought of him as nothing special, he milked a drawing of a cow. At one time, when the Dhuruka war broke out at Nalanda, glorious Chandrakirti struck the head of a stone lion with a rosewood mace. [The stone lion came to life] and averted the war. Previously, at Ratreng, one day when Drom[tonpa] Rinpoche, Palden Gonpa[wa], and so forth were staying together, they ran out of sustenance; therefore, a close disciple said, "After that, we don't have any food to offer." [Palden] Gonpawa said, "Eat this which comes out from my nostril," and a benefactor emerged from his nostril carrying a full horse-load of provisions. When this was perceived by [Dromtonpa's] clairvoyance, Drom reprimanded him [for displaying his magical powers].

Thus, in India as well as here in Tibet, the great scholars and siddhas

601. This is in reference to someone who left his homeland to come to Lhasa and enter one of the monasteries.

602. This is in reference to a high realization of the completion stage.

maintained a common external appearance and did not show anything beyond being an ordinary person. In the same way, although we may develop realizations of the lamrim, we are not permitted to proclaim them to anyone other than our lama, and instead we should keep our inner realizations hidden like a butter lamp within a vase. Nevertheless, it is also not appropriate to carry out our practices in secret and not have any inner good qualities whatsoever. Therefore, even someone like a monk at a monastery should not wish for things such as a colorful storage cabinet, an altar, and so forth, and instead he should have the desire to study, contemplate, and meditate on the Dharma. We should strive with whatever means we can to increase our good qualities of realization, [so as to progress] from generating them in a month to generating them in a day.

[5.] The root text states, "**Do not express degenerate limbs**." Whether or not someone has faults such as corrupt moral discipline or has incomplete sense faculties such as being crippled, deaf, and so forth, we should nevertheless not express [anything about] his [or her] faults.

[6.] "**Do not contemplate others' shortcomings**." Do not analyze others' faults. We do not have clairvoyance, and like a bodhisattva covered in ash from a fire pit, we don't know what good or bad aspects someone [may] have assumed. Therefore, although we see others' apparent faults, it is utterly inappropriate to place our trust in those perceptions and deprecate those persons. Previously, a person heard that a monk he disliked had incurred some serious faults; therefore, he invited a friend he liked a great deal and said, "Today you should make a very special unparalleled tea for me, and I shall tell you some good news." When asked what the news was, he replied, "I heard Monk So-and-So has disrobed." Having said this, he was as happy as a child. Geshe Potowa heard this and said, "Although [the person who disrobed] incurred some serious faults, the person who meditated with joy incurred much greater negative karma."

[7.] "**Purify your greatest afflictive emotion first**." Purification is crushing the afflictive emotions by relying upon the antidotes to whichever of the afflictive emotions is the greatest, such as meditating on the unattractiveness of the object for which we have an excessive amount of attachment and so forth.

[8.] "**Abandon all expectation of reward**." Do not entertain expectations of results in this life through meditating on mind training—

DROMTONPA

[namely, results] such as honor and respect, fame, and so forth. Also, do not have any expectations of fulfilling your desires for your future lives—not even regarding [actions done] solely for the welfare of living beings, [your desire] not to attain liberation for your own welfare, and ultimately even [your desire to attain] omniscience [itself].

[9.] "**Abandon poisonous food.**" Just as it is inappropriate to partake of food that has been mixed with poison, so we should not contaminate whatever virtue we perform with the eight worldly concerns or the conception of self-cherishing.

[10.] "**Do not maintain [inappropriate] loyalty**." Do not maintain that which only brings us harm, and do not maintain loyalty to the afflictive emotions; instead, we should apply whatever is the very opposite of it.

[11.] "**Do not engage in malicious banter**." This is similar to not responding to harmful language with harmful language. We should practice the four Dharmas of a spiritual ascetic: (1) do not respond to anger with anger, (2) do not respond to abuse with abuse, (3) do not respond to criticism with criticism, and (4) do not respond to being beaten with a beating.[603] If we practice in this way, we will be following the instructions of mind training to offer the gain and victory to others. We will even be able to put into practice the advice to "accept loss and defeat."

[12.] "**Do not wait in ambush**." This refers to thinking thoughts such as "I am going to wait in a back alley holding a knife, so that I can harm the person that harmed me." It also [refers] even to someone like a monk with thoughts such as "When I am the monastic disciplinarian, I am going to pay close attention to him." These kinds of thoughts are in direct opposition to practicing mind training; therefore, it is inappropriate to respond with harm to the harm we encounter.

[13.] "**Do not strike at the vital point**." This refers to revealing the faults of a person's defects. Once we strike the mind of our adversary, he [or she] becomes discouraged, depressed, and so on. Also, it is inappropriate to recite life mantras toward nonhumans wrathfully and to recite the wrathful mantras of personal deities to subdue spirits, since these actions create an enormous amount of suffering in their minds.

[14.] "**Do not place the load of a *dzo* on an ox**."[604] If we see that we have a big responsibility coming our way, we should not quickly shift the responsibility to someone else or place the blame on someone else for something we ourselves should be doing.

[15.] "**Do not engage in corrupted practices**." We must not let our mind training become [defiled] by the thought "I will immediately accept defeat and bear the loss so that others will not have to do so," out of our deepest desire to be thought of as someone noble for the sake of wealth, fame, and so forth, nor should we train the mind for the sake of pacify-

603. These four Dharmas of a spiritual ascetic are basic commitments accepted by those who receive monastic ordination.

604. A dzo is a cross between a yak and a cow and is much stronger than an ox.

ing sickness, harm from spirits, and so forth. [This is true] even while practicing chö: if we practice chö out of contempt for gods, demons, and so forth, with the wish to bind them into servitude and the wish that, once we subdue them, we will have subjugated them and will serve as their master and so forth, that is a perverted practice of *tochö*.[605] So that it doesn't come to that, at every turn we should have love and compassion and make sure that it only be used as a means of enhancing the two types of bodhichitta.

[16.] "**Do not sprint to win the race**." This refers to striving to quickly obtain something that is a shared object of enjoyment or public property, such as an outer monk's shawl,[606] for yourself, out of fear of losing it to someone else. It also refers to hoping to take all the credit yourself for some benevolent deed that was done in common with others, by saying "I did that myself." These are called "unacceptable actions that are contradictory to the practice of equalizing and exchanging self with others."

[17.] "**Do not turn a god into a demon**." If your reliance upon a god becomes a means of harming yourself, it is called "turning a god into a demon." In the same way, once mind training becomes a factor assisting our afflictive emotions—by our ostentatiously pretending to be meditating on mind training so that others will say we are good Dharma practitioners, as well as using mind training to serve our pride and so forth—this is like turning a god into a demon and is something we should not do. Meditation on mind training should be used as an antidote to our self-cherishing and should become a means of abandoning our self-cherishing.

[18.] "**Do not seek misery as a means to happiness**." This refers to striving or wishing to obtain others' means of happiness for ourselves. For example, once we hope that we will receive personal gain by seeing others' relationships, neighbors, housemates, and so on and thinking, "If he were to die, I would obtain these various things," we are meditating on suffering befalling others, such as their death and so on. Thus, up to this point we have covered the eighteen commitments of mind training.

605. Tib. *lto bcos*. This is a ritual to avert obstacles.

606. A monk's robes are often distributed to the general population at the monastery when he dies.

Point Seven: The Precepts of Mind Training

There are twenty-two precepts of mind training.

[1.] "**Perform all yogas through a single means**." All of our yogas of daily actions performed by body and speech—such as those related to food and clothing, our sleeping quarters, walking, moving around, lying down, and sitting—as well as the yogas of whatever spiritual practices we perform should be embraced solely by bodhichitta equalizing and exchanging self with others, as taught in the *Completely Pure Sphere of Conduct Sutra*.[607] We should also practice according to the compositions of Chusang Lama Yeshe Gyatso [Rinpoche] and other previous holy beings that are arranged in a blend of verse and prose.

[2.] "**Apply all countermeasures by one**." Like a doctor using a medicine as a countermeasure to pacify an illness that does not help the illness, if someone is engaged in spiritual practice and an illness and so forth occurs while he [or she] is resting after meditating on mind training, and that person thinks, "Through my meditation on mind training, things did not go well for me and have gotten progressively worse. Favorable conditions are rare; illness, harm from spirits, and afflictive emotions are plentiful; and people act hostile toward me," then through this it is possible to develop the mistaken heartfelt wish not to meditate on mind training. Therefore, if something like this happens, you should know that this is an obstacle of Mara. Think,

> This is the result of the mistaken evil minds that I have developed and have generated up to this point, which are the result of my former nonvirtues. Limitless living beings in the world have definitely accumulated bad deeds similar to this. Therefore, may everything that did not go well for them, such as all their sickness and harm from spirits, afflictive emotions, and misfortune, ripen upon me through this action.. How wonderful it would be if all living beings were endowed with the most excellent bliss and virtue and if their mental continuums were to blend with the Mahayana Dharma.

607. Tib. *sPyod yul yongs dag gi mdo.*

After this heartfelt contemplation, meditate on giving and taking, which you should merge together with bodhichitta. Dharma practitioners who are on the verge of developing good qualities should be able to bring into the path the various dangers that arise, as Mila[repa] and Drubkangpa Geleg Gyatso were able to do. Whatever kinds of dangers arise for a mind-training practitioner, they should be used solely as a means for destroying self-cherishing through equalizing self with others, and as nothing else; therefore, we should not employ other means, such as rituals and so forth, [to avert them].

[3.] "**There are two activities: at the beginning and end**." Whatever spiritual practices we undertake, we should formulate our motivation at the beginning and seal it with a pure dedication at the end. These two are indispensable; therefore, all our virtuous activities should be embraced by these two.

[4.] "**Be patient with whichever of the two occurs**." Some [abandon the Dharma] when they become too happy because of affluence, attaining high status, and so forth; others [abandon the Dharma] when they experience suffering like illness, criticism, theft, and so on. There are many people who permanently abandon their practice of the Dharma when either of these two situations arises; therefore, Ngulchu Gyalsé [Thogmé] proclaimed,

> Looking like a Dharma practitioner when their stomachs are full
> and warmed by the sun,
> And an ordinary person when adverse conditions befall them . . .

To ensure that this doesn't happen, whenever better or worse conditions arise as happiness or suffering, good or bad, [you should] think, "There is no other more productive cause for me to meditate on bodhichitta." You should be able to bring adverse conditions into productive factors for the accomplishment of bodhichitta without relinquishing your practice of mind training.

[5.] "**Protect the two even at the cost of your life**." You should make a concerted effort in the methods for not becoming defiled by the faults of breaking the general Dharma commitments that you promised to maintain together with the three sets of vows, as well as [in the methods for not becoming defiled by] natural nonvirtues. In particular, you should protect as you would your life all nineteen[608] of the special commitments of mind training that I have already explained, by keeping them pure without any conflicts.

[6.] "**Always train in the three difficulties**." The three difficulties are (1) the difficulty of learning or recognizing the development of afflictive emotions such as attachment, (2) the difficulty of overcoming them, and (3) the difficulty of terminating their continuity. Therefore, we strive to recognize the afflictive emotions as soon as they are developed, and train sincerely in the means of overcoming them by recalling their faults.

[7.] "**Adopt the three principal causes**." The three principal causes for the practice of dharma are (1) encountering a fully qualified guru as your spiritual guide, (2) having a mind that is suitable for meditation on bodhichitta, and (3) having all the favorable conditions for the practice of Dharma. We will not be able to become authentic Dharma practitioners if those three are incomplete; therefore, we should make a sincere effort with pure prayers to be able to intentionally assemble those in the future by accumulating the causes for the practice of mind training like a waxing moon.

[8.] "**Meditate on the three undeteriorated aspects**." These three are (1) undeteriorated devotion for your guru, (2) undeteriorated conscientiousness with respect to the precepts, and (3) undeteriorated delight in mind training. The first is the foundation for developing all good qualities. The second closes the door to faults and transgressions. The third gives power to your effort to wholeheartedly meditate on bodhichitta.

[9.] "**Be endowed with the three factors you should not be separated from**." Your body, speech, and mind should not be separated from the application of virtuous conduct. Sincerely apply yourself to prostrations, offerings, service, mantra recitations, meditating on bodhichitta, and so forth. Even while we are sitting during teachings, if you sit with the essential physical postures, such as the vajra position and so forth, it is included within the twelve good qualities of ascetic practice;[609] therefore,

608. There are eighteen commitments of mind training. I am uncertain whether there is an extra commitment that Pabongkha Rinpoche is referring to here or whether this is a scribal error.

609. The twelve ascetic virtues are (1) wearing the dress of a dung sweeper, (2) owning only

it is important for spiritual practice. It would be excellent if you could sit without a back support and sit upright without sleep as a way of supreme transformation.[610]

[10.] "**Train in impartiality toward objects**." [Being biased] is being able to meditate on patience for friends but being unable to [meditate on patience] with respect to enemies, as well as being able to be patient with inanimate objects but being unable to be patient with living beings. Instead, you should train your mind to be impartial to all, whether they are living beings or inanimate objects.

[11.] "**It is crucial to train in everything deeply and pervasively**." Mentally examine everything that arises. All activities, such as eating, drinking, lighting a fire, and so forth, should be pervaded by training the mind in equalizing and exchanging self with others. In particular, don't be biased toward living beings, and instead train in bodhichitta with respect to all living beings as pervasive as space. Furthermore, don't merely pay this lip service, and instead apply the training methods deeply and from the bottom of your heart.

[12.] "**Always meditate on chosen objects**." There are five chosen objects: (1) our companions who are equal to us, such as our housemates whom we live with; (2) those who have become our opponents; (3) those whom we have benefited but who have inflicted harm on us in return; (4) those who, although we have not harmed them, through the force of karma dislike us as soon as they see us. It is difficult to develop mind training toward these four types. Because we are extremely close to (5) our guru and parents, there is a very grave danger of creating serious negative karma through becoming angry with them, despite the fact that it is not the least bit appropriate; therefore, we should meditate separately on this fifth chosen object.

[13.] "**Do not rely upon other conditions**." When people are practicing other Dharmas and unfavorable conditions occur or the favorable conditions are incomplete, they abandon their practice. When practicing

---

three robes, (3) wearing poorly colored clothes, (4) begging for food, (5) eating only one meal a day, (6) restricting the quantity of food, (7) staying in isolation, (8) sitting under trees, (9) sitting in exposed places, (10) sitting in charnel grounds, (11) sitting without sleep, and (12) begging in turns.

610. Sitting upright without sleeping is number 11 in the twelve ascetic virtues.

mind training, although there are unfavorable conditions, you transform them into favorable conditions and are thereby able to bring them into your mind training as supportive elements. Furthermore, there are those who put off their mind training due to conditions of happiness or suffering, saying things such as "I cannot practice mind training right now due to severe sun and wind." They are unable to withstand heat and cold for the sake of Dharma, but they can withstand austerities of heat and cold to receive a financial contribution; we mustn't allow ourselves to become like such people.

[14.] "**Engage in the principal practices right now.**" Having made the three lower realms our homeland since beginningless lives, we have repeatedly wandered throughout samsara, yet at this moment we have obtained, just this one time, a human life of leisure and endowment through fortunate circumstances. Therefore, our primary Dharma practice should be for the sake of our future lives more than for the sake of this life. From among the Dharmas of the three vehicles, our principal practice should be the Mahayana. Within that, between explanation and practice [of the Mahayana], our primary aim should be practice. Of all other practices, our exclusive emphasis should be meditating on bodhichitta in conjunction with equalizing and exchanging self with others, by combining it into one package through the practice of training the mind.

[15.] "**Do not apply mistaken understanding.**" There are six mistaken understandings:

1. *Mistaken compassion* is not having compassion for those for whom we should have compassion, such as unwholesome wealthy people who are accomplishing the causes of suffering by accumulating various negative actions that are incongruent with the Dharma, and instead pretending to have compassion for someone like a simple monk who endures hardships for the Dharma or an ascetic who voluntarily accepts the suffering associated with austerities endured for the sake of Dharma. Previously, someone said, "Poor Je Mila," to which Jetsun [Milarepa] replied,

> I also have disgust for you;
> If you pity me, I pity you.

2. *Mistaken forbearance* is being able to endure whatever suffering and

difficulties occur while pursuing the aims of this life, such as subduing enemies, carrying burdens for friends, and so forth, yet being unable to bear the austerities associated with studying, contemplating, and meditating on the Dharma, as well as being unable to meditate on patience with respect to even the most insignificant harm from others.

3. *Mistaken savoring* is when we have encountered the Mahayana Dharma at this point, yet we don't savor it, enjoying the taste of the fully qualified teachings of lamrim and mind training through studying, contemplating, and meditating on this sacred Dharma. Instead, being motivated by attachment and so forth, we are deceived by experiencing amusements and savoring all the worldly deceptions through discussion, work, and so forth, such as the means for acquiring happiness for this life and the methods for enjoying the objects of desire, subduing our enemies, caring for friends, and so on.

4. *Mistaken aspiration* is admiring those who study, contemplate, and meditate on the Dharma, yet not having the wish or aspiration to practice the Dharma by thinking, "I should also act like that." In contrast, we have a dislike for the austerities required for the practice of Dharma and take delight in and aspire to worldly activities associated with this life, such as prosperity, riches and honor, fame, and so forth.

5. *Mistaken concern* or sympathy is not practicing the means of accomplishing the Dharma for the sake of attaining enlightenment for someone who is your rival and so forth but instead partaking of worldly abundance that is contradictory to the Dharma. Although a king is placed upon a throne, if he engages in the activities of this life and doesn't practice Dharma, he will go to the lower realms.

6. *Mistaken rejoicing* is not rejoicing in the virtues performed by yourself and others. We should not be pleased when someone such as our enemy experiences some suffering, nor should we rejoice in negative actions performed by others.

Thus, you should strive sincerely to reverse those six mistaken understandings and transform them into the six nonmistaken understandings.

[16.] "**Do not act sporadically**." This means acting fickle in our spiritual practice due to conditions such as unstable renunciation with [only] occasional perseverance or going to the other extreme and meditating on mind training without even lying down to sleep, while at other times we are distracted by the activities of this life and barely engage in spiritual practice at all. Sometimes we meditate; sometimes we don't meditate. If we are sporadic in our practice, we will not make any progress. For example, when a flea and a louse travel together, each time the flea jumps, he then rests and stays still. The louse does not need to rest, and by going at a slow and easy pace, he arrives first. We shouldn't be like [the flea]; instead, our spiritual practice should be continuous, maintaining a balance between tight and loose with breaks in between and combining our three doors with mind training.

[17.] "**Train with decisiveness**." When a physician performs bloodletting, he cuts the flesh and the veins simultaneously. In the same way, like the way a walnut is split open, we should not have a two-pointed mind about our spiritual practice; instead, all our aspirations should be combined as one, and our mind should completely surrender itself to mind training. We should make a sincere effort, see our practice through to the very end, and probe the depths of bodhichitta through equalizing and exchanging self with others.

[18.] "**Be released by two: investigation and analysis**." This means that we should apply analytical meditation to mind training. We should repeatedly analyze our body, speech, and mind with great frequency. We should apply the methods for blocking whatever powerful afflictive emotions occur, such as self-cherishing and so forth. We should make a sincere effort in mind training by developing the good qualities, such as cherishing others, and by continually increasing them until it is refined.

[19.] "**Don't be boastful**." We should not be boastful by continually telling others about the Dharma practices we have done to make the other person feel guilty, as though he [or she] is indebted to us. Instead, we should consider the kindness of living beings and work for the welfare of living beings through our practice of mind training and so forth. Once we have promised to work for the welfare of all living beings, it is only proper that we devote ourselves to it. Therefore, we should not be boastful about the long list of things we have done, such as studying texts, practicing generosity, meditating on mind training, and so forth.

[20.] "**Do not be irritable**." When others do not respect us and so forth, despite the fact that we are engaging in mind training, we should not become irritable by considering the various types of activity they engage in. When others discredit and criticize us in front of many others and do things such as inflicting the most severe type of humiliation on us, we should not become angry but instead diligently ensure that it becomes part of our mind training, as an antidote to our afflictive emotions. There are two things we should not do even for an instant:

1. [We should not] become angry in dependence upon the slightest condition and remain with an unpleasant facial expression, or complain after having gone a short distance by saying things such as "This is so difficult."[611] If we demonstrate a multitude of changing facial expressions, oscillating between happiness and sadness, we will create uneasiness in the minds of our companions and so forth. We should not act like the sky in springtime that is constantly undergoing change.

2. We should not act like someone who meditates on something like the lamrim at first and then dispenses with it after one session. Our enthusiastic perseverance should be like the flow of a river.

[21.] ["**Do not be fickle.**"][612]

[22.] "**Do not wish to be thanked**." This refers to thinking, "I am meditating on mind training, so I deserve honor, gain, and fame," or [wishing for others to say things] such as "Thank you so much" and "You are extremely compassionate." Therefore, you should not have any hopes of receiving benefit in return for hardships you endure during your Dharma practice or for the slight benefit you bring others, or of receiving the slightest renown applauding your compassion. For example, you should not even [wish that] someone will say, "You were compassionate to me." Therefore, you should not have even the slightest hope of being thought of as a mind-training meditator, like someone saying whether or not you were helpful.

Next, the teaching [from the *Seven-Point Mind Training*] is concluded with the bodhisattva [Geshe] Chekawa saying, "I attained confidence in bodhichitta and attained stability in mind training":

611. Tib. *a kha kha*. This actually means "How sad" or "Alas" and is used as an expression of dismay.

612. Number 21 is absent from our list in the Tibetan text, so I have included it for clarity and consistency.

Because of my numerous aspirations
I have overcome the sad tale of suffering and,
Having received the instructions for subduing
self-grasping,
Now, even at death, I will have no regrets.

Bodhisattva Chekawa is saying that he has obtained self-confidence by stating that he has received numerous instructions on mind training and that by meditating on them he gave birth to realizations in his mental continuum, due to which his mind is delighted and he will have no regrets even at death.

Day Thirty

The king of the Dharma Tsongkhapa the Great stated in one of his compositions,

> Although you may develop this mind alone, the three types of moral discipline . . .

It is not sufficient for us to attain the temporary state of higher status or the definite goodness of mere liberation. Instead, we must attain the state of omniscience. The intelligent cause for accomplishing that is to develop the precious mind of bodhichitta. However, it is not sufficient to merely develop that [bodhichitta]; instead, we must also train in the deeds of a bodhisattva. The bodhisattva's deeds consist of the six transcendent perfections and the four ways of gathering disciples.[613] If we condense those even further, they are embodied in the three types of moral discipline, so these three are important. For that reason, after we develop bodhichitta we definitely need to train in the vast deeds of a bodhisattva. Therefore, think, "No matter what the cost, I shall attain the precious state of complete enlightenment for the welfare of all living beings. For that purpose I am going to listen to these king-like instructions on the stages of the path.

613. These four ways of gathering disciples were explained later, on day thirty-one. In short, they are (1) attracting a retinue through generosity, (2) speaking pleasantly, (3) applying the meaning, and (4) being consistent.

Having given this short introduction, Pabongkha Rinpoche covered the headings.

Once we have developed bodhichitta, we are permitted to train in the deeds of a bodhisattva and so forth. If we meditate on love, compassion, and bodhichitta for a long time and with great intensity, it will not be a hardship to train in the deeds of a bodhisattva. According to the repeated explanations I have already given earlier about the means of training in bodhichitta, if we don't make a sincere effort in the oral instructions of Atisha's Kadampa tradition, such as the stages of the path of the three types of beings, there is no way that it will be effective. Kagyu Dagpo Lhaje [Gampopa] stated,

> If you wish to truly understand, whatever Dharma you practice will be profound;
> If you don't wish to truly understand the meaning, whatever Dharma you practice will not be profound.

Geshe [Drom]tonpa knew the inconceivable Dharma of secret mantra and gained certainty in the three scopes of beings; therefore, he was constantly engaged in meditation on love and compassion. Because of that, all migrating beings developed faith [in Dromtonpa]. Presently, the teachings of the Kadampas are being propagated, which is due to his work on the three scopes of beings. Likewise, Lotsawa Rinchen Zangpo had already met sixteen panditas, yet he didn't have the instructions on love and compassion. Once he met the great Atisha, he truly understood love and compassion, and he became a mahasiddha. Likewise, from the three yogis on down and from Geshe Atisha on up, all the Kadampas truly understood the beings of the three scopes in their minds, which came from their meditations on love and compassion. For that reason it is stated,

> Conventional bodhichitta is of great importance. It is the principal part in the beginning, since if we don't have it we won't enter the path of the Mahayana. It is the principal part in the middle, since without it we will fall into the [paths] of the shravakas and pratyekabuddhas. It is the principal part

> at the conclusion, since without it the two bodies[614] will not emerge.

And,

> [So-and-So said,] "In a dream I found a leather amulet,"[615] to which Gonpa Tray-yung said, "Show it to me." To this So-and-So replied, "No, I am not going to show it to you," [to which Gonpa Tray-yung replied,] "In there are the relics of Atisha Je that contain the teachings of the Kadampas; therefore, you should open it." So I dreamt. Currently, whatever small amount of benefit there is for others is dependent upon the Kadam [teachings]. Naropa taught many instructions but was of very slight benefit because he lacked a connection with Kadam. If it is not related to the teachings of the Kadam, then the benefit will be very little.

This is saying that we should abide in an honest mind. At this point I am not going to give a detailed explanation on how to train in the vows of engaging bodhichitta. Instead, you should learn them in combination with Je [Tsongkhapa's] commentary on the chapter of moral discipline from [Asanga's] *Bodhisattva Levels.* Make a concerted effort in practice during the *beginning* of the chapter of the *Ornament of Clear Realization* and engage in the practice of the Mahayana at the *end* of the first chapter.

Furthermore, once we accept the vows, we should learn their precepts, and for that purpose we should learn how to accomplish the practice of understanding, the practice of entering, the practice of accumulating [merit and wisdom], and the practice of definite emergence.[616] Although, in general, there was a monk from China named Hvashang, the proper Hvashang did not hold wrong views.[617] With respect to the teaching of

614. The two bodies are the truth body and the form body.
615. Tib. *ga'u.* This is a protective amulet usually containing relics, blessed substances, and so forth.
616. These are sections of the seventy sections of the perfection of wisdom sutras.
617. There were two monks from China named Hvashang. One taught wrong views about emptiness, and the other was a very pure monk who did not have or teach wrong views.

Hvashang we are discussing from this point onward, [however,] he is called "Hvashang Mahayana" [and is the improper Hvashang] who established an evil system of wrong views in Tibet. This person holding wrong views appeared in Tibet as Shantarakshita was about to die, and [Shantarakshita] gave a prophecy stating, "If you invite my disciple Kamalashila, he will be able to subjugate him." This is the historical background of Hvashang [Mahayana].

> Only the Buddha is free from both extremes of samsara and
> peace;
> Knowing this, do not abide in peace.

Thus, we should not even grasp at the attainment of nirvana, [or peace].

Day Thirty-One

Glorious Chandrakirti stated [in his *Guide to the Middle Way*],

> The king of geese spreads his broad white wings of conventional [truth] and thatness
> And soars ahead of the geese of living beings.
> Then, through the force of the winds of virtue, they travel to the supreme
> And reach the other shore of the ocean of the Conqueror's good qualities.

The mode of existence of the conventional is the conventional truth of all phenomena, and "thatness" is the mode of existence of the ultimate truth. The king of geese endowed with the two wings [of conventional truth and ultimate truth] can travel through the sky without obstruction. In the same way, we absolutely must work to reach the other shore of the ocean-like good qualities of the Conqueror, by way of being skilled in the essential points of the two truths and being endowed with method and wisdom, whereby we accumulate the union of the two accumulations. In that way, the unmistaken key features of the two truths are commonly referred to as "the supreme instructions of the Teacher."

After giving this introduction, Pabongkha Rinpoche covered the headings.

With respect to training in the general [bodhisattva] deeds, with the exception of tranquil abiding and superior seeing, there is no need for me to explain it again.

[Pabongkha] Rinpoche gave the oral transmission of the third section, "The Stages of Training in the Precepts," and so forth.

An Explanation of the Stages of Training in the Precepts

Although you may generate bodhichitta, if you don't learn the precepts, you will not be able to attain complete enlightenment; therefore, it is not sufficient to merely develop bodhichitta. Instead, you must train in the activities of a bodhisattva. Furthermore, if you possess the vows of mantra in addition to the common six transcendent perfections, even the paths of the generation and completion stages are included within the six perfections. You don't need much more than the six transcendent perfections for all the activities of a bodhisattva; they are also not contained in any fewer [than six]. Their specific enumerations, benefits, and so forth are explained clearly in Je [Tsongkhapa's] *Great* and *Middle-Length Treatise[s] on the Stages of the Path [to Enlightenment].*

Beginners are traditionally not given an extensive explanation, other than those who have an extremely vast and well-established foundation in the six transcendent perfections; therefore, at this time I am going to teach little more than the essential meaning of the six transcendent perfections and so forth. Most of the rest [of the section on the six transcendent perfections] will be transmitted through the power of the oral transmission alone; the sections on tranquil abiding and superior seeing will be explained in a little more detail. For that, we employ the six transcendent perfections to ripen our own mental continuums, and the four ways of gathering disciples to ripen the mental continuum of others.

The Six Transcendent Perfections

[The Six Transcendent Perfections has six sections:

1. Generosity
2. Moral Discipline
3. Patience
4. Joyous Perseverance
5. Concentration
6. Wisdom]

Generosity

With respect to the essence of generosity, it is an act of body and speech induced by a mind of giving. The essence of the transcendent perfection of generosity is being thoroughly familiar with the mind of giving that does not have the least bit of stinginess and gives everything that one possesses of body and enjoyments, including the roots of virtues of the three times. Therefore, there are two special features of generosity. Through that [explanation] you should also understand moral discipline and so forth. Thus, [Shantideva's] *Guide to the Bodhisattva's Way of Life* also states,

> The perfection of giving is said to be
> A mind of giving all one's possessions
> Together with their results to all beings;
> Thus, it is the nature of mind itself.

We should recollect the benefits of generosity, which will give rise to a very powerful, joyful desire to practice the transcendent perfection of generosity. Of the three types of generosity, **giving material things** is giving articles and includes giving to ants and other creatures. If we sequentially train to give as much as we possibly can, from the very small, such as water and wood, on up, eventually we will even be able to give our life and our actual physical possessions and will have the benefit of not going to waste. Atisha's disciple Shangtsun of Yerpa[618] said, "Once you offer your drinking cup on up to someone else, it is on loan until you die; when you die, they can keep it." The *Sutra Requested by Vishnu*[619] states,

> Child of the lineage, a bodhisattva—a great being—should generate bodhichitta in this way: "If I give completely even my body to all living beings, what need is there to mention my external possessions? However many living beings there

618. Also known as Ölgöpa Yeshe Bar, Shangtsun of Yerpa was a disciple of Atisha and later became a disciple of the three Kadampa brothers. His exact dates are uncertain. However, since Atisha lived from 982 to 1054, we can assume that Shangtsun lived during the eleventh century.
619. Tib. *Sred med kyi bus zhus pa'i mdo.*

> are and whatever they need, I must give them these various things."

While we are training in the bodhisattva vows, once we are placed under the power of the conquerors' sons, we make a promise to give our body, life, and so forth; therefore, we must not deceive them.

With respect to **giving protection from fear**, this is protecting the life of another. We should train in stages, beginning with the very small, by rescuing a bug that has fallen into a stream or a watermill, saving a small fish being scorched by the sun, and so forth.

With respect to **giving Dharma**, this should be motivated by your own desire to teach and for the other person to have the desire to listen, and includes teaching as little as one verse. Even reciting a scripture, learning texts, or discussing Dharma as part of a conversation with a beneficial intention that includes employing methods for subduing the minds of others becomes giving Dharma and is a practice of the bodhisattvas.

A householder principally gives material things. Bodhisattvas who are ordained primarily give Dharma. Everyone should practice giving the protection of fearlessness by protecting humans and nonhumans from the fear of being harmed. *Inappropriate giving by way of material substances* refers to [giving] things such as your three Dharma robes as material things, since they are like weapons against fear caused by the accumulation of negative karma, [or giving] texts that contain commentaries revealing bad views, religious disciplines, and so forth. With respect to *inappropriate giving by means of time*, this refers to giving an afternoon meal to those who are ordained[620] and so forth. Therefore, instead of presenting [external] offerings to the ordained, the best thing is the offering of practice [after noon].

Although you should train your mind in giving your body, it is inappropriate to actually give away your body until you have thoroughly perfected your meditation on compassion. Once your mind is acquainted with the mind of giving, if you can give your body without any more difficulty than you would have with the idea of merely giving a vegetable, it is time to give [your body], which is the most supreme form of giving. [Shanti-

620. A monk or nun incurs a downfall if he or she eats after noon.

deva's] *Compendium of Trainings* states, "Giving, protecting, purifying, and increasing." Je Tsongkhapa also mentioned at Olga [retreat facility] that although there are difficult tasks to be carried out for training the mind in the deeds of a bodhisattva in dependence upon the *Flower Ornament Sutra*,[621] there are ways of attaining the confidence that is not frightened of giving. It is not appropriate to give scriptures to someone such as a non-Buddhist who has the wish to seek out something to criticize.

With respect to the benefits [of generosity], the *Summary of Meanings*[622] states,

> Generosity is the wish-fulfilling jewel that fulfills the hopes of migrating beings;
> It is the supreme weapon for annihilating the demon of miserliness.
> Develop bravery that is not discouraged by the deeds of a bodhisattva;
> It is the foundation of your fame resounding in the ten directions.

Moral Discipline

With respect to the nature [of moral disciple], it is a mind that has abandoned harming others together with the basis [of such harm]. Of its three divisions, with respect to the **moral discipline of restraint from misdeeds**, for the ordained this is abandoning that which is discordant with the three vows of moral discipline,[623] and even for a householder it is refraining from the ten nonvirtues and so forth and protecting the moral discipline of the ten virtues.

With respect to the **moral discipline of gathering virtuous Dharmas**, this is generating those we have not yet generated and increasing those that we have already generated.

With respect to the **moral discipline of working for the welfare**

621. Tib. *mDo phal po che*; Skt. *Avatamsaka sutra*. Lama Tsongkhapa made a special effort to study the *Avatamsaka Sutra* while in retreat at Olga.

622. Tib. *bsDus don*.

623. The "three vows of moral discipline" are the pratimoksha, bodhisattva, and secret mantra vows.

of living beings, all the methods of working for the welfare of living beings are done within the context of already having bodhichitta. Those three [types of moral discipline] include the deeds of a bodhisattva in their entirety; therefore, they also embody the six transcendent perfections, and it is for that reason that Je Rinpoche [Tsongkhapa] said they are a heap of blessings. Even though you have merely generated bodhichitta, while training in the general deeds [of a bodhisattva] such as the three types of moral discipline and so forth, the other transcendent perfections are not taught separately from the three types of moral discipline.

With respect to the benefits [of moral discipline], this was already explained in a fair amount of detail during the section on the being of middle scope. In short, [in his *Songs of Spiritual Experience*] Je Lama [Tsongkhapa] declared,

> Moral discipline is the water cleansing the impurities of faults,
> The light of the moon dispelling the painful heat of the
> afflictions;
> Resplendent like the beings in the center of Mount Meru,
> All beings bow to its non-intimidating power.
> [Through this knowledge, the holy beings protect
> The discipline of perfect restraint like their eyes.]

Patience

Regarding the nature [of patience], it is a mind of virtue that does not become agitated [by suffering or harm inflicted by another]. Of its three divisions, with respect to the **patience of enduring harm**, this refers to not becoming angry even if all living beings rise up as your enemies. [As a line in *Lama Chöpa* states], "Become angry, humiliate, criticize, threaten, or even kill me. . . ." Furthermore, it will not be beneficial if you become angry and patience does not come easily. Previously, the disciple of a lama was only told that he should meditate on patience for others continuously. One day, a thief appeared and [the disciple] started beating [the thief] to the point of almost killing him. Even when his lama came, he couldn't help his [disciple to calm down], so the lama put his finger on [his disciple's] nose and said "Patience, patience!" three times. As this states, you should recall patience from the beginning. It is absolutely necessary that this is an object of your meditation.

The object of your anger is the foundation for the development of patience. Atisha Je had one crude and annoying person in his presence named Acharya Manu, whom [Atisha] described as "the foundation of my meditation on patience." Such things become a cause for our meditation on patience; therefore, our enemy is very kind. If we have patience, all beings will see us as attractive. Even if you are a holy being, if you don't have patience, you are not attractive. Of the three types of patience, the patience of enduring harm is the most important of all.

There are also reasons why anger is unacceptable and patience is necessary. For example, if the sky is obscured by clouds, we don't blame the clouds but instead blame the sky, yet it is not the fault of the sky but the fault of the clouds. Therefore, it is inappropriate to blame the sky; we should blame the clouds. This is like when the monastery disciplinarian hits you on the head with a stick; if you are going to get angry with the actual inflictor of harm, you should be angry at the stick. If you consider the actions performed by the monastery disciplinarian, the monastery disciplinarian is not to blame. The person who makes the monastery disciplinarian restless is [actually just] the afflictive emotions in his mental continuum. Therefore, if you are angry, it is inappropriate to be angry with the monastery disciplinarian, with the exception of his afflictive emotions. For that reason, if you are going to be angry with the agent of harm, it should begin with the stick, then the anger, and then your own karma that you should be angry at, since the monastery disciplinarian wields his stick after you reveal your body, whereby the harm occurs. Their root [cause] also lies within your engagement in unwholesome acts.[624]

Furthermore, in an ultimate sense we are meeting with our self-cherishing; therefore, we should view our self-cherishing as our enemy and apply the methods to subdue it. Also, if our mother becomes insane and tries to kill us, it is inappropriate for us to be angry with her. We can utilize this means of applying metaphors [to assist us in developing patience].

624. Namely, these are being hit by the club, the disciplinarian being angry, having a body of appropriated aggregates, and so on.

Also, it is the nature of fire to burn; therefore, when we are burned by fire, it is due to not using caution when dealing with fire, so we do not get angry with the fire. Likewise, if [the disciplinarian] gets angry, since it is his nature to inflict harm, it is not appropriate for us to be angry at his nature, either. This is illustrated in the story of Kshantivadin.[625]

With respect to the **patience of accepting suffering**, [Shantideva's] *Guide to the Bodhisattva's Way of Life* states,

> If a remedy exists,
> What use is there in being unhappy?
> If no remedy exists,
> What benefit is there in being unhappy?

Whatever happens while practicing Dharma, such as a lack of food and clothing, illness, harmful and interfering spirits, and so on, we should accept them by thinking, "Previously, I accumulated powerful karma through my experience of the suffering of samsara and the lower realms, and I am currently experiencing the result of those [actions], through which they are being eradicated." When physical suffering manifests, we should mentally develop joy. Not only that, but [Shantideva's *Guide to the Bodhisattva's Way of Life*] states,

> How is it unfortunate when a person sentenced to death
> Is freed by having his hand cut off instead?
> [Likewise,] how is it unfortunate if a person is freed
> From hell through experiencing suffering?

If we had our hand cut off instead of being killed, we would need to be patient with that and think, "It is excellent that, although I had my limb cut off, I wasn't killed." Likewise, if instead of having to experience the suffering of something like the hells, [our negative karma] were to ripen in this physical form that we are currently utilizing for the practice of Dharma as something as insignificant as a bad headache, and if this were

625. Kshantivadin was one of Buddha Shakyamuni's previous incarnations as a bodhisattva, as told in the *Jataka Tales*.

to substitute [for being reborn in the lower realms], then we should think, "Whatever suffering I am currently experiencing is excellent." In the root text, becoming discouraged[626] is called "being disheartened."[627]

Moreover, with respect to the good qualities of suffering, [Shantideva's *Guide to the Bodhisattva's Way of Life*] states,

> Arrogance is dispelled by disenchantment;
> You avoid negative actions and delight in virtue.

There are numerous benefits in the occurrence of suffering; therefore, it is excellent when suffering occurs. As I explained briefly before, during the previous section on mind training, even not lying down to sleep and so forth and instead engaging in meditation with an excellent sitting posture is the patience of accepting suffering.

Regarding the **patience of gaining firm conviction in the Dharma**, this is the patience of training in memorizing and reciting religious texts and so forth and, once we have made a comparison, gaining an ascertainment of their meaning and contemplating those phenomena that are objects of attainment, such as the qualities of a buddha and so forth. It is also studying and contemplating the twelve limbs of scripture as well as coming to a definite understanding of what is to be adopted and forsaken, such as virtuous and nonvirtuous actions and so forth. In short, the faults of not meditating on patience and the benefits of meditating on it are [stated in Shantideva's *Guide to the Bodhisattva's Way of Life*,]

> There is no evil like anger;
> There is no fortitude like patience;
> Therefore, you should meditate in earnest
> In a variety of ways on the benefits of patience.

Geshe Chen-nga-wa stated, "Striving to be the leader once you are worried about being weak, patience is the supreme [protection] against sarcasm;

626. Tib. *yid zhum pa*.
627. Tib. *sro shi ba*.

therefore, striving to be the leader is meaningless." Je Lama [Tsongkhapa] also stated [in his *Songs of Spiritual Experience*],

> Patience is the supreme ornament for the powerful,
> The austerity to offer when overcoming the delusions,
> The garuda bird that destroys the enemy-snake of anger,
> And the armor to protect oneself from the weapons of harsh speech.

The *Compendium of the Perfection of Wisdom Sutra*[628] states,

> Patience leads to the attainment of the vast excellent form [of a buddha],
> With its golden color that is worthy for migrating beings to behold.

Even the attainment of the perfect and faultless body of the Conqueror is primarily due to the mental imprint of meditating on patience.

Joyous Perseverance

With respect to the nature of joyous perseverance, [Shantideva's *Guide to the Bodhisattva's Way of Life*] states,

> What is effort? It is delighting in virtue.

Thus, it is a mind that delights in virtuous actions. Of its three divisions, with respect to **armor-like joyous effort**, this is like thinking, "I am capable of practicing for the numerous eons required to accomplish even the good quality of a single hair pore of a buddha. Furthermore, even if we calculate each day of each great eon as consisting of the beginningless time spent in samsara until the present, [I am still able to] accomplish it." In this way you will not act out of shortsightedness. *Lama Chöpa* states,

628. Tib. *Sher phyin sdud pa*.

> [I seek your blessing to complete the perfection of effort
> By striving for supreme enlightenment with unwavering
> compassion,
> Even if I must remain for an ocean of eons dwelling within
> the flames]
> Of the lowest hell for the sake of each living being.

This is like thinking, "Even if I must remain for a hundred eons in hell for the sake of each and every being, it is appropriate for me to be patient." Even while a pupil is studying religious texts, he [or she] needs to remember this.

With respect to the **joyous effort of collecting virtue**, this is the perseverance involved in assembling [virtuous qualities] such as the six perfections, which function to ripen our own mental continuums; the four ways of gathering disciples, which function to ripen the minds of others; and so forth.

With respect to the **joyous perseverance of working for the welfare of living beings**, it accomplishes the welfare of living beings without weariness. The benefits of joyous perseverance are presented in [Chandrakirti's] *Guide to the Middle Way* when it states,

> All the good qualities follow from joyous perseverance.

Je Rinpoche [Tsongkhapa] stated in his *Songs of Spiritual Experience*,

> If you wear the armor of steady and irreversible effort,
> Qualities and insights will increase like a waxing moon,
> All your actions will become meaningful,
> And all works begun will reach completion.

Also, the *Prayer to Maitreya* states,

> Through the joyous perseverance of commencing joyous
> perseverance,
> You have stable joy, laziness does not exist,

And you are endowed with strength of body and mind;
May I complete the perfection of joyous perseverance.

Thus, however much joyous perseverance you have is the degree to which your desire for joyous perseverance will increase. There are three types of laziness that are contrary to joyous perseverance.

With respect to *the laziness of procrastination*, this is simply postponing [a virtuous] activity. We should meditate on the uncertainty of the time of death as its antidote. This laziness is also the greatest obstacle to practicing Dharma. The *Supreme Dharma of the Application of Mindfulness Sutra* states,

Whatever afflictive emotions there are have
Laziness as their sole basis.
Wherever a lazy person exists,
All Dharmas do not exist in that place.

With respect to *the laziness of discouragement*, this is like thinking, "How could such an inferior person as I attain such great good qualities of a buddha?" As an antidote to that, think, "If the Tathagata said that even ants and flies can become enlightened if they develop joyous perseverance, then since I have attained this excellent physical form, complete with the eight freedoms and ten endowments, I am certainly able to also accomplish the state of enlightenment."

Query: Well then, how exactly am I able to accomplish the countless vast good qualities of a buddha?

Reply: We should contemplate this by thinking, "I am capable of accomplishing such things because there are countless various miraculous transformations of common and uncommon skillful means within the paths and deeds of a bodhisattva for accomplishing that; therefore, accomplishing enlightenment will not be difficult." Also, if we think, "I am not able to practice the difficult deeds of a bodhisattva," [consider the passage from Shantideva's *Guide to the Bodhisattva's Way of Life*, which states],

> Because they have abandoned negative actions, they have no
> suffering;
> Because they are learned, they are not unhappy.

At that point, it is not the same as our present situation of circling in samsara through karma and afflictive emotions; rather, they intentionally enter [into a samsaric rebirth] for the welfare of others out of great compassion, so they do not have suffering and instead are endowed with joy and happiness.

With respect to *the laziness of being attached to bad actions*, this is engaging in hardships associated with meaningless activities with perseverance. Although we consider that this is joyous perseverance, following these activities with fortitude does not make them joyous perseverance. In fact, we have great familiarity with them in this life because they are associated with the worldly activities of a human life. Therefore, as an antidote to [this form of laziness], we should contemplate how samsaric activities are meaningless.

Concentration

With respect to the nature of concentration, it remains single-pointedly on the observed object of a virtuous mind without distraction. When divided, it is divided in terms of nature and in terms of its perspective and function.

Wisdom

With respect to the nature of wisdom, it analyzes individual meanings or investigations. It is called wisdom because it thoroughly differentiates its object through knowledge. When divided, it is a wisdom that realizes the ultimate, realizes the conventional, and realizes the activities for the welfare of living beings.

Tranquil abiding is not the culmination of the perfection of concentration, and superior seeing is not necessarily the perfection of wisdom. Instead, [their culmination occurs] through the combination of tranquil abiding and superior seeing in terms of their existing concurrently.

According to tradition, it is necessary to give the explanation on the benefits of concentration and wisdom later, during the sections on tranquil abiding and superior seeing.

Ripening the Minds of Others through the Four Ways of Gathering Disciples

With respect to **attracting a retinue through generosity**, all ordinary beings find joy in material possessions; therefore, you first bestow actual gifts of material goods to gather a circle [of disciples]. With respect to **speaking pleasantly**, this is explaining Dharma by teaching the points of accepting and rejecting. Speaking pleasantly also refers to a situation such as that with a teacher and his disciple in which [the teacher] uses rough language without getting angry as a means of benefiting [the disciple]. Regarding **applying the meaning**, this is [encouraging your disciples] to engage in the activity of accepting and rejecting in exact accordance with the teachings of the points of accepting and rejecting by training in the precepts and so forth. **Being consistent** means that if you don't act in accordance with the precepts you have taught others, they will not have confidence. Not only that, but as the colloquial expression goes,

> Whatever is spoken by a lama is a teaching,
> Yet the lama does whatever he likes.[629]

So that we don't end up that way, we must be sure to conduct ourselves properly.

629. This means that the lama doesn't act in accordance with the teachings and advice he gives others.

Day Thirty-Two

[In the *Songs of Spiritual Experience*] Jamgon Tsongkhapa the Great states,

> Concentration is the king with dominion over the mind.
> [If set, it will not waver like a powerful mountain;
> When focused, it enters into all virtuous objects
> And leads to the bliss of physical and mental pliancy.]

If we attain a stable concentration that can abide single-pointedly upon its mental object of focus, we will attain a stability of mind that can be employed for whatever virtuous object we desire. While the mind is in that state, we have serviceability of body and mind. This is indispensable for attaining the good qualities that come from meditation. Therefore, we should set our motivation by thinking, "If I rely upon the incomparable teachings for accomplishing that, they are the extracted heart essence of the oral instructions set forth in the texts of the regent Maitreya, such as [those recorded by Asanga in Maitreya's] *Distinguishing the Middle from the Extremes*[630] as presented in the stages of the path to enlightenment." Therefore, [we should set our motivation by] thinking, "I will properly listen to these teachings and then put them into practice."

After giving this brief introduction, Pabongkha Rinpoche stated the headings. In particular, he gave the oral transmission for training in the last two perfections.

630. Tib. *dBus mtha' rnam 'byed*.

During the teachings on the [Second Panchen Lama's] *Swift Path*, the way to train in the last two perfections is presented as follows:

[The Final Two Transcendent Perfections has two sections:]

1. Training in Tranquil Abiding as the Essence of Concentration
2. Training in Superior Seeing as the Essence of Wisdom

[Training in Tranquil Abiding as the Essence of Concentration has three sections:

1. How to Train in Tranquil Abiding as the Essence of Concentration
2. Relying upon the Conditions for Tranquil Abiding
3. The Actual Way to Attain Tranquil Abiding]

How to Train in Tranquil Abiding as the Essence of Concentration

Regarding the nature of tranquil abiding, it is a quality common to Buddhists and non-Buddhists. In this context, if it is embraced by refuge, it merely becomes a Buddhist Dharma; if it is embraced by renunciation, it is a Dharma that bestows liberation; if it is embraced by bodhichitta, it becomes a Dharma of a being of great scope; therefore, you need the wisdom realizing selflessness to abandon ignorance. You need a stable concentration to perceive clearly the meaning of the absolute nature by the wisdom realizing selflessness. If you don't have tranquil abiding, there will be no way of developing any of the realizations that come from meditation. Not only that, but although you may generate bodhichitta in your mental continuum, you cannot progress beyond the middle section of the path of accumulation.[631] [Without tranquil abiding,] you can only attain

631. The path of accumulation has three sections simply named small, middling, and great. The small section of the path of accumulation is attained once one attains spontaneous bodhichitta. The middle section is attained when one accomplishes tranquil abiding. The great is attained when one progresses to meditating on emptiness with tranquil abiding motivated by bodhichitta.

Geshe Sharawa

the coarse generation stage of secret mantra; it is not possible to attain the subtle [generation stage] or the completion stage. If you attain tranquil abiding, you will cover vast amounts of ground in an instant with tranquil abiding, compared to meditating for a year on the common path without tranquil abiding. However, these days there are many people who wish to become enlightened through tranquil abiding alone by focusing on the mind, yet if you don't have renunciation, bodhichitta, and so forth, it is impossible to attain enlightenment.

Thus, with respect to the objects of desire, there are teachings that reveal the true characteristic of things that are not recognized, such as the objects of abandonment, the abandonment of [nonvirtuous] friends, the grounds, paths, and results, and so forth. Therefore, at this point there are six ways of training in tranquil abiding.

Relying upon the Conditions for Tranquil Abiding

For the attainment of tranquil abiding, it is very important that the place have the prerequisites for tranquil abiding from the beginning. Regarding accumulating the causes for that, they are (1) being in an isolated place, (2) having few desires, (3) relying upon contentment, (4) having few activities with few goals, (5) maintaining pure moral discipline with respect to our commitments, and (6) abandoning distracting activities and stopping coarse conceptions associated with craving objects of desire.[632] Furthermore, the *Ornament of the Mahayana Sutras* states:

> The intelligent practice in a place that has
> Good facilities,[633] a wholesome environment,
> Good grounds, good companions,
> And the articles for comfortable yoga.[634]

As this states, there are five characteristics needed for a favorable **[isolated] place** in which to engage in practice: (1) [With respect to *good facilities*,] it should be easy to find good sustenance, clothing, and so forth favorable to Dharma. It is unacceptable if, although they are easy to acquire, they come from a cause for accumulating negative karma. (2) *A wholesome environment* means a place where wild beasts, adversaries, and so forth do not live. It should be a place where others who have broken their spiritual commitments or have defiled their spiritual commitments have not stayed and where the great holy beings of your own tradition have stayed and gained experiences. This [last point] is extremely important; if the place is defiled with broken spiritual commitments or the possessions utilized are defiled by broken spiritual commitments of possession, you

632. These six ways of training in tranquil abiding appear below in boldface type.
633. Tib. *legs par rnyed*. This is a place where the necessities for survival such as food and clothing are easily obtained.
634. These five characteristics of a place favorable for practice appear below in italics.

will not develop any new good qualities in your mental continuum and those that you have already attained will also deteriorate slightly. (3) *Good grounds* refers to a place where you will not become ill due to inappropriate soil, water, and so forth. (4) *Good companions* refers to companions who have similar conduct and views. The place should also be very isolated—that is, free of activities of humans and free of noise such as the clamor of water, dogs, and so on. The Bhagavan also stated,

> Noises are the thorns of concentration.

Therefore, while attaining tranquil abiding, it is extremely important that you only live in a place that is completely isolated. (5) With respect to a suitable place with *the articles for comfortable yoga,* according to the tradition of oral instructions, this is explained in our tradition as meaning that we should have removed our doubts through study and contemplation for remaining in the practice. If we haven't, at first we pretend we know [how to practice] and head off to an isolated place. Once we have left, while we are engaging in practice, we realize we don't know what we are doing, and all we can do is send letters from our retreat house to our guru, spiritual companions, and so on and wait for a response. We must make sure we are not such a person.

With respect to **few desires**, this means abandoning the coarse conceptions associated with aspiring for objects of desire. If you don't, there is a great danger of getting sidetracked into numerous activities for multiple goals; therefore, **rely upon contentment** with few desires [and **have few activities with few goals**]. [Maintaining] **pure moral discipline** is very important. If we don't stop coarse external distraction through moral discipline, there is no way that we will accomplish concentration through stopping subtle internal distractions.

With respect to **abandoning distracting activities**, this means not engaging in such things that cause us preoccupation, such as listening to sounds [such as music, pursuing] medicine and astrology, and so forth. While we are attaining tranquil abiding—with the exception of using cooking utensils for eating and drinking, taking the time to eat food, dispensing with our feces and urine, and taking a little time to sleep—if we don't devote ourselves continuously to meditation, we won't accomplish [tranquil abiding]. If we meditate in this way consistently with all the effective factors in place, it is said that we will attain stable tranquil abiding in six months.

The Actual Way to Attain Tranquil Abiding

Thus, in dependence upon having assembled the conditions for tranquil abiding, you should sit upon a comfortable cushion in the seven-point posture of Vairochana, eliminate the stale winds [through the nine-round breathing], and meditate.

The Object of Observation

[Bhavaviveka's] *Heart of the Middle Way*[635] states,

> The wayward elephant of the mind
> Is securely bound to the stable pillar of
> Visualization by the rope of mindfulness
> And gradually controlled with the hook of knowledge.

As this states, that place to fasten [your mind] should be a single object of observation for which there are four: (1) objects of observation for scholars, (2) pervasive objects, (3) objects which serve as antidotes, and (4) objects of observation for abandoning afflictive emotions. In general, if something that is the observed object for accomplishing tranquil abiding is an established base [that is, existent], then it is a visualized basis, so non-Buddhists use a stone or a stick as their perceptual object of observation, the Bon and a few Nyingma visualize the letter A̲[636] for their practice, and so on. These days, some people of other traditions use visual objects of observation for accomplishing tranquil abiding. However, whatever the characteristics of the observed object, meditation is not accomplished through an eye consciousness. Therefore, because of not understanding this essential point, they are even stupider than the non-Buddhists.

635. Tib. *dBu ma'i snying po.*

636. The underscore is meant to signify that it is pronounced "AH."

Although it is permissible to place [your mind] upon any object of observation for tranquil abiding, until you attain tranquil abiding, you should not change your object of observation. Instead, you should remain fixed on one object of observation. [Atisha's] *Lamp for the Path* states,

> You should place the mind upon any
> One suitable virtuous object of observation.

Furthermore, this is analogous to when you are trying to set fire to a stick by rubbing; if you switch to another stick, the heat will dissipate and you won't get a flame. Just as you will get a fire if you continue rubbing the fire stick without interruption, in the same way, if while accomplishing tranquil abiding you practice for a prolonged period without interruption, you will definitely generate it.

If you haven't already developed realizations of the path in your mental continuum, it would be excellent if you were to meditate on the body of Buddha Shakyamuni as the focus of your attention while you are accomplishing tranquil abiding. If you do, then even if you die [while attempting to attain tranquil abiding] you will be accumulating merit, it will be easy to attain realizations of the generation and completion stages and so forth of mantra, you will recall the Buddha, and so on. If you practice in this way, you should either visualize the body of Buddha the size of a pea at the level of your navel, or alternatively, once you dissolve the Buddha into the crown of your head, focus your attention upon yourself appearing clearly in the body of Buddha Shakyamuni.

Also, if you wish to practice without observing any external form, you can practice by focusing internally on the mind. According to the teachings in the [First Panchen Lama's text on] Ganden Mahamudra, [while meditating on the mind] you should rely upon three special features: (1) clarity, (2) awareness, and (3) emptiness. Furthermore, it is unacceptable if you don't keep anything in mind and slip away from the clarity and awareness into unconsciousness and sleep, because [if this occurs] your meditation has become a nihilistic view similar to the view of Hvashang [Mahayana]. If you are going to meditate in dependence upon the mind, you must definitely rely upon [the teachings on] mahamudra. As I already explained, you should meditate upon a single underlying support according to the mantra system, in dependence upon either the generation stage or a subtle drop of the completion stage. Thus, it is permissible to use whichever of those objects of observation you find it easiest to give rise to.

Query: How do I meditate in dependence upon the body of Buddha Shakyamuni?

Reply: Once you have recited the lamrim preliminary rituals, at the end of making the supplication called "planting the stake,"[637] light rays radiate from the heart of the Buddha on the crown of your head like a spider's web on the tips of which are variegated lotuses with sun and moon mandala seats, upon each of which is a conqueror Shakyamuni with a body like refined gold and so forth, according to the general presentation. Each one sits with his legs in the vajra posture and is the size of a pea. Having emanated them, they [dissolve into a single Shakyamuni who] comes to sit in the sky before you at the level of your navel, and once you focus your mind, meditate single-pointedly upon him. Furthermore, because clarity doesn't arise from the very beginning, if you only get an approximation of his head or hands and feet, or a bit of golden color, you have found your object of observation. Although the ultimate essential instructions for attaining tranquil abiding are taught in texts such as the *Shravaka Levels*, [Asanga's] *Bodhisattva Levels*, [Maitreya's] *Distinguishing the Middle from the Extremes*, and so forth, these days without knowing that these texts possess the instructions for accomplishing single-pointed concentration, people seek them out from somewhere else, which is like someone wishing for water who doesn't go to the ocean but instead seeks water from a dried-up spring.

Regarding the principal [teaching] set forth in those aforementioned texts, [Maitreya's] *Distinguishing the Middle from the Extremes* states,

> Abandon the five faults through
> Cultivating the eight types of application.

637. Tib. *phur tshugs*. In the lamrim preliminary ritual entitled *Adorning the Throats of the Fortunate*, planting the stake is represented by repeated requests to Tubwang Dorje Chang (see note 202 above) on the crown of your head just prior to the actual meditation.

For that reason, in this instance there are two: (1) abandoning five faults, and (2) relying upon the eight applications as the antidotes to those. For the first, there are faults when engaging in single-pointed concentration. That very [text, Maitreya's *Distinguishing the Middle from the Extremes*,] states,

> Laziness, forgetting the instructions,
> Mental sinking and excitement,
> Nonapplication, and application
> Are asserted to be the five faults.

The First Fault: Laziness

Furthermore, engaging laziness is a fault when the yogi initially engages in concentration.[638] With respect to "laziness," in this instance it is the heartfelt desire not to engage in concentration. From the eight applications of abandonment that are antidotes, there are four antidotes to laziness: (1) *faith* that perceives the good qualities of concentration, (2) *aspiration* that strives for concentration, (3) *effort* that seeks concentration, and (4) [mental and physical] *pliancy* that is the result of seeking concentration. Among these four, the most important is pliancy. If they arise from anywhere, they come from effort, that [effort] comes from aspiration, and that [aspiration] comes from faith. Thus, the latter are developed in dependence upon the former. If we attain pliancy, it is like an assistant who incites a type of bliss that induces you into whatever type of [virtuous] work makes you capable of single-pointed concentration, allowing you to visualize whatever you desire. Jamgon Tsongkhapa stated in his [*Songs of Spiritual Experience*,]

> If set, [the mind] will not waver, like a powerful mountain;
> When focused, it enters into all virtuous objects.

638. In the following paragraphs dealing with the five faults, the eight antidotes are italicized within the paragraphs themselves. The eight antidotes are (1) faith, (2) aspiration, (3) effort, (4) pliancy, (5) mindfulness, (6) introspection, (7) application, and (8) nonapplication.

Query: Well then, since we don't have pliancy, what do we do?

Reply: Although we beginners don't have pliancy, it is important to develop faith in it. We should perceive the good qualities of concentration in developing it. As I explained earlier about tranquil abiding, generally speaking by way of its essence, it doesn't belong to any of the three vehicles because even some of the non-Buddhists have [tranquil abiding] as well. Without [tranquil abiding] you won't accomplish any of the mundane or supramundane good qualities that come from meditation, whereas if you have [tranquil abiding], progression on the paths of all three vehicles is easy. The primary necessity of attaining tranquil abiding is expressed in [Shantideva's] *Guide to the Bodhisattva's Way of Life* when it states,

> Through realizing that superior seeing endowed
> With tranquil abiding destroys the afflictive emotions,
> You should seek tranquil abiding from the outset.

Thus, once you attain a stable tranquil abiding, you will develop realizations that come from meditation observing emptiness. With that, once you directly realize emptiness, it will function to sever the root of samsara. Once you perceive the good qualities of tranquil abiding, you will sequentially develop faith, aspiration, effort, and then pliancy.

The Second Fault: Forgetting the Instructions when Engaged in Meditative Concentration

"Forgetting" is not like forgetting the Dharma teachings of your lama; it is losing the observed object of concentration. Furthermore, once you become distracted while abiding single-pointedly upon the body of Buddha Shakyamuni, this is the fault of losing the observed object. With respect to the antidote to this, it is the fifth [antidote], *mindfulness*. Therefore, we need a continuous apprehension of the observed object, which is analogous to holding a cup of tea in our hands.

With respect to mindfulness, in the *Compendium of Abhidharma* it is described as having three special qualities: (1) being acquainted with the visualization, (2) not forgetting the object of observation once you have continuously apprehended it, and (3) functioning to prevent distraction. With it, you develop an uninterrupted, continuous, and powerful mode of apprehension.

The Third Fault: Mental Sinking and Excitement

When you have placed your mind in meditative concentration, the third fault is mental sinking[639] and excitement; therefore, you need the sixth antidote, *introspection*, as its antidote, which not only interrupts mental sinking and excitement but checks to see whether they are about to occur. Excitement is mental scattering to an object of attachment. For example, if you are attached to tea and meat, once you think of eating meat while you are drinking tea, [your mind] subsequently switches to that [meat], which is [a case of] both scattering and excitement. With respect to excitement about [an object of] anger or virtue, although it is scattering, it is not excitement [because it is not distracted by an object of attachment]. If it is scattering, it does not follow that it is [also] excitement. [However,] if it is excitement, it is necessarily scattering.

Query: Well then, if it occurs when it is applied to concentration, why is it not said to be excitement?

Reply: It is principally taught that excitement occurs primarily through the force of scattering to an object of attachment that happens continuously.

There are two types of excitement: coarse and subtle. Once you stray from the observed object, this is coarse excitement. With respect to scattering that occurs without straying, this is subtle excitement; therefore, it is easy to understand excitement. Mental sinking is difficult to recognize. The cause of mental sinking is mental dullness.[640] With respect to mental dullness, this is similar to sleepiness, where the observed object becomes unclear and the body and mind become heavy. Furthermore, it can be either a nonvirtuous or a neutral mental obscuration. If it is mental dullness, it does not follow that it is mental sinking. If it is sinking, it also does not follow that it is mental dullness. Mental sinking must be either virtuous or neutral.

With respect to mental sinking, it is as if darkness has settled over the mind so that it is without a factor of clarity or a factor of lucidity. For this, there are two aspects: (1) although the mind remains on the observed object, it does not have a factor of clarity or a factor of lucidity, in which case it is coarse mental sinking, or, (2) although it has a factor of clarity,

639. Tib. *byings ba*.
640. Tib. *rmugs pa*.

a factor of lucidity, and a factor of stability, the factor of lucidity does not have intensity, in which case it is subtle mental sinking. This factor of clarity is not a factor of clarity in relation to the object; [rather,] it is necessarily a factor of clarity in relation to the mind. Therefore, at present, if we beginners can get clarity on merely an upright golden image similar to the body of the Buddha, this is [our object of meditation]. Until it is free of subtle mental sinking and the faults of concentration, there won't be any difference between whether you do or do not have a factor of clarity with intensity. Therefore, you need an extremely firm mode of apprehension. Once the mode of apprehension becomes slack, a slackness will occur in the mind, at which point you have arrived at subtle mental sinking.

These days, when it comes to subtle mental sinking and unmistaken meditation, there are many meditators who make the mistake of meditating with subtle sinking. If we meditate with subtle mental sinking, it is an enormous fault. If you accumulate mental sinking, whatever degree to which you increase that accumulation is the extent to which it will be difficult to develop unmistaken concentration. [As a result,] your wisdom will become dull, and this functions as a cause for you be reborn as an animal in your next life. Sapan stated,

> Most fools who meditate on mahamudra
> Are creating the cause to become an animal.[641]

In fact, if although you have a factor of clarity and a factor of stability, your mind has become slack, it is subtle mental sinking.

If you have a finely tuned mode of apprehension, there will be an intensity to the factor of clarity. The tradition of Tsongkhapa and his disciples is to delight in a mode of apprehension that is as firm as possible. With a firm mode of apprehension, you will elicit a factor of clarity that is free from the fault of mental sinking; however, the danger of mental excitement will increase. If your mode of apprehension is lax, it will be easy to develop a factor of stability; however, it will become subtle mental

641. This is not a criticism of mahamudra meditation but of those who meditate on it incorrectly.

sinking. Therefore, you will not be aware of the fact that subtle mental sinking has set in.

Because they knew that it was easy to develop a factor of stability [with a lax mode of apprehension], in dependence upon this, some previous Tibetans said, "The best relaxation is the best meditation." And although they knew that they would develop a factor of stability with a relaxed mind, they didn't know that they would slip into subtle mental sinking. Still, they confirmed it with scriptural sources such as Saraha, who stated,

> The nature of mind is bound by over-conceptualization.[642]
> Have no doubt that if you relax it, you will be liberated.

Although they cite this, this scripture is intended for someone who has reached the eighth mental abiding;[643] therefore, to apply it at this point [in your training] is a huge mistake.

In short, if you employ a mode of apprehension that is as firm as possible without mental wandering, the lack of mental wandering will sever mental excitement. Firmness will sever mental sinking; therefore, it is the extremely essential point that is the heart treasure of great meditators. For that reason, if you are applying a certain amount of firmness and you think that you are developing mental excitement, loosen it a little. When you think that this amount of looseness is becoming mental sinking, tighten it a little bit; this is an extremely skillful way to practice. Furthermore, as each factor of clarity arises, seek out a factor of stability once you are cautious about mental sinking. As each factor of stability arises, be cautious about mental sinking. Once you induce an intense factor of clarity, you should apply skill in sustaining it, as in the examples that the Bhagavan told Ananda about the lute[644] and the bird catcher.

Regarding faultless concentration, this has a factor of stability and a factor of clarity. Furthermore, the mind experiences both sinking through

642. Tib. *'jur bu*.

643. This is explained below in the subsection "The Fifth Fault." Suffice it to say for now that the eighth mental abiding is an advanced stage in the attainment of tranquil abiding.

644. This is the famous analogy used by the Buddha about meditation, in which he suggests that meditation should be neither too loose nor too tight, just like the proper tuning of the strings on a lute.

becoming too elevated and sinking from being too low. Therefore, once you recognize mental sinking and excitement through introspection, you instantly hold the object of observation through mindfulness. You should stand guard with introspection for the onset of either mental excitement or [mental] sinking. Use introspection from time to time; it doesn't need to be constant. Mindfulness is something that you always need. [The First Panchen Lama's text on Ganden] Mahamudra states,

> Keep watch from afar with undistracted mindfulness;
> Prepare introspection by knowing discursive thoughts.

This occasion is exemplified by the way in which you hold a cup of tea in your hand and states that you need to utilize a tight grip to separate laxity from all your meditations.[645]

The Fourth Fault: The Fault of Not Applying the Antidote When Mental Sinking and Excitement Occur

You must rely upon the intention to apply the application of the antidotes, as an antidote to that [fault of not applying the antidotes]. For example, it is like [being in the midst of] preparing for battle when you receive a tip and realize that an enemy is [already] approaching. Likewise, you need the seventh antidote, *application*, when you realize that mental sinking and excitement are approaching and you are not paying heed to them. Furthermore, with great wisdom you will recognize mental sinking and excitement before they come; with middling [wisdom] you will recognize them as soon as they arise; and those with the least [wisdom] will recognize them after they have arisen.

If your mind is distracted away from the object of observation but doesn't lose it, this is subtle mental excitement. This is the fault of the mode of apprehension being too tight; therefore, it should be loosened a little. If it still does not pass, it is middling excitement; therefore, you should set aside your visualization. With respect to excitement, since it

645. When holding a cup full of tea, we use mindfulness to maintain our grip on the cup and introspection to ensure that we do not spill the tea. In the same way, we employ mindfulness to maintain the object of observation and introspection to ensure that we have not succumbed to laxity.

occurs when the mind is uplifted and taut, you should relax the mind. The three terms "uplift," "taut," and "tight" are synonymous.[646] And "lower," "loosen," and "deflate" are synonymous.[647] The Teacher said to King Shuddhodana, "Once you are taught the method for relaxing the mind, only then will you realize emptiness."

With respect to the antidote to mental excitement, you should deflate the mind by contemplating impermanence, the sufferings of the lower realms, and the sufferings of samsara, and then once again engage [in meditation]. If even that does not dispel it, you have coarse mental excitement; therefore, the instructions state that you should forcefully eliminate it by visualizing a black drop at the navel or the coming and going of your breath. For this [latter method], when you exhale you should think, "One breath is going outward," and as you inhale, think, "I am inhaling." With this, think, "That was one [count]," ["That was two,"] and so forth. Don't count them on your rosary. The best practitioners can eliminate mental excitement with one count; even a middling person can do it in either five or seven. If even that doesn't eliminate it, you have reached a point of extremely coarse mental excitement; therefore, you should set your session aside for a short while, rest, and then resume your session.

With respect to eliminating mental sinking, if it occurs while you are concentrating, it is subtle mental sinking, so once you tighten [your mode of apprehension], continue meditating. If that doesn't dispel it, it is coming from the mind being either depressed or deflated; therefore, you should apply methods to uplift the mind. Therefore, you should contemplate the leisures and endowments, the good qualities of the Three Jewels, bodhichitta, and so forth, and resume meditating. With respect to the forceful methods [to use] when even that doesn't dispel it, Padampa [Sangye] stated,

> If there is sinking, eliminate it with PHAT.

Visualize your mind in the aspect of a white letter A, and imagine that you shoot it out through the crown of your head by reciting "PHAT,"

646. Tib. *'phangs mtho ba*, *grims pa*, and *dam pa*, respectively.
647. Tib. *dma' ba*, *lhod pa*, and *zhum pa*, respectively.

and as it goes higher and higher it becomes increasingly bigger, until it mixes with space. This is called "mixing space and awareness." If even that doesn't dispel it, you should stop your session and go for a walk in a place that is filled with light, has an expansive view, and so forth. The glorious Sakyapas also state,

> If there is clarity, end your practice with clarity;
> If there is no clarity, end your practice without clarity
> [And it will remove the poison from your concentration].

Thus, [too,] if your visualizing is coming along well, you should have the wish to prolong your meditation technique but [nevertheless] end it while it is going well and resume it again later. For example, you should depart from your meditation while it is still going well; therefore, in the beginning, each session should be short. If you meditate by ending your session while there is some slight clarity to the visualization, eventually the length of your meditative state will naturally increase, at which point you should extend the duration slightly. Furthermore, if a disciple has extremely crude behavior, his teacher will postpone subduing him, and when [the disciple] becomes a little pacified through his own accord [due to remaining in the presence of his teacher,] the teacher should then apply methods for training him. Je [Tsongkhapa's] *Great* and *Middle-Length Treatise[s] on the Stages of the Path [to Enlightenment]* also state,

> In the beginning, if your [sessions] are long, it will be easy to come under the influence of sinking and excitement. If you meditate on that, it will be difficult to repair the mind; therefore, you should have many short sessions. If you stop your session while you still wish to meditate, later you will have the heartfelt wish to engage in meditation. If not, you will feel nauseous when you see your meditation cushion.[648]

This is an extremely important pith instruction.

648. I was unable to locate this exact passage in either of Je Tsongkhapa Rinpoche's two lamrim texts; therefore, this seems to be a paraphrase.

The Fifth Fault: The Fault of Applying the Antidote When You Are Free from Mental Sinking and Excitement

Thus, when we are dwelling single-pointedly upon the observed object, free from mental sinking and excitement due to skillful training, and we are supervising with introspection to determine whether or not mental sinking or excitement are developing despite the fact that our factor of stability is not being harmed by [sinking or excitement], we should rely upon the compositional factor of equanimity as the [eighth] antidote, [*nonapplication*,] to that [unnecessary application]. This occurs when we have attained the eighth mental abiding. The phrase "bound by overconceptualization"[649] should be applied at this point. Furthermore, once you loosen your efforts [in applying] introspection, do not slacken your mindfulness. Those in other philosophical traditions do not understand the demarcation line at which you should slacken [introspection], and in addition to relaxing their [introspection] they also slacken their mindfulness, which is the fault of an excessive lack of knowledge.

With respect to mindfulness, it should not be slackened but continuously developed and increased, whereby through its expansion it will become the wisdom of a buddha; we don't need mindfulness higher than that.

With that, I have completed the actual way to accomplish tranquil abiding. When you have such an excellent system as this, even if you are meditating according to the concentrations of the generation and completion stages, this is like the life pillar of such practices.

How to Accomplish the Nine Mental Abidings in Dependence upon That [Instruction]

You will accomplish the nine mental abidings by employing a skillful means of practice by continuously apprehending the visualization through mindfulness. With respect to the nine mental abidings, they are (1) placing the mind, (2) continual placement, (3) patched placement, (4) close placement, (5) subdued placement, (6) pacified placement, (7) completely pacified placement, (8) single-pointed placement, and (9) placement in equipoise.

649. This phrase occurs in the quote by Saraha above, in the subsection on "The Third Fault."

With respect to the first mental abiding, **placing the mind**, this is striving to repeatedly place your mind on the object of observation, even though you will not be able to do so continuously. At this stage, it is as though you have a multitude of conceptions appearing; however, there are not any more [than usual] at this point—rather, you are [simply now] experiencing the recognition of your conceptual thoughts. Furthermore, this is analogous to the way in which a traveler investigates the highway he is on. At this point [our conceptual thoughts] are like water in a narrow ravine.[650] Furthermore, you need to practice with the six forces.[651] Therefore, at this stage you practice through *the force of listening* to the meaning of the instructions from your guru.

With respect to the second mental abiding, **continual placement**, when you are able to repeatedly place the mind on the object of observation and maintain a slight continuation through familiarity with visualization, you have attained the second mental abiding through *the force of contemplation*. At this point you experience a respite from your conceptual thoughts, which is said to be analogous to the [settling] of agitated waves on the water.

With respect to the third mental abiding, **patched placement**, the term "renew"[652] means to "patch" or to "mend" [a piece of fabric]. Therefore, this is the basis of mending and patching together. When you are able to maintain a continuation slightly longer than the second [mental abiding], you have attained the third [mental abiding]. With the third [mental abiding], patching comes from having developed *the force of mindfulness*, which does not allow [your mind] to wander [for too long] from the observed object. The difference between the second mental abiding and the third is that on the third mental abiding you have less wandering from the object of observation and a greater degree of concentration. The distinction can also be made in that on the first [mental abiding] you are merely placing the mind, and on the second you are able to lengthen the duration a little, although you still have a great deal of wandering from

650. In other words, they are noisy and without much substance.

651. The six forces are (1) the force of listening, (2) the force of contemplation, (3) the force of mindfulness, (4) the force of introspection, (5) the force of perseverance, and (6) the force of familiarity.

652. Tib. *blan*.

the state of abiding. On the third [mental abiding, in contrast], although there is [still] a slight amount of wandering from the object of observation, the wandering is less.

With respect to the fourth mental abiding, **close placement**, by developing the force of mindfulness, although you have some slight mental sinking and excitement, due to mindfulness you try as much as you can to remain collected within the object of observation. The difference between the third and fourth [mental abidings] is whether or not you lose the object of observation. With the third, you lose the object of observation by wandering. Although there is mental wandering on the fourth, you do not lose the object of observation. Those two [that is, the third and fourth mental abidings] are accomplished through the third [force], the force of mindfulness.

With respect to the fifth mental abiding, **subdued**, although there is subtle mental sinking and excitement, once you perceive this fault, you develop the force of mindfulness. This is called "being endowed with the force of mindfulness" and is the measure of having completed mindfulness. From this point, you must develop [the fourth force], *the force of introspection*. From the very beginning [of the fifth mental abiding], you do not engage in mental wandering, but you have subtle mental sinking; therefore, [the fifth mental abiding] must be accomplished by developing an awareness endowed with the force of introspection. Furthermore, the mind was withdrawn inward forcefully during the fourth mental abiding, and as a result there is a danger of subtle mental sinking; therefore, that is made perceptible. From here onward, with the exception of the danger of subtle mental sinking, there is no danger of coarse [mental sinking].

With respect to the sixth mental abiding, **pacified**, since you were cautious about subtle mental sinking during the fifth mental abiding, there is a danger of subtle excitement. Therefore, you abandon it through recognizing it. Both the fifth and the sixth mental abidings are accomplished through the force of introspection. From this point, this force [of introspection] is completed through having become endowed with the force of mindfulness. The difference between the [fifth and sixth mental abidings] is determined by the presence or absence of faults. On the fifth you have [subtle] mental sinking, and on the sixth there is the danger of subtle excitement.

With respect to the seventh mental abiding, **completely pacified**, during this state you have completed the power of both mindfulness and introspection; therefore, at this point mental sinking and excitement are like wounded enemies. Although their coarse aspects are intangible due to being injured, the powers of both mindfulness and introspection have become *the force of effort* due to having abandoned subtle sinking and excitement.

With respect to the eighth mental abiding, **single-pointed**, although you are able to continue faultless concentration for one-sixth of a day free from mental sinking and excitement, you still need effort. At this point [your mind] is said to be like waves on a great ocean.[653] The seventh and the eighth mental abidings are accomplished through the force of effort.

With respect to the ninth mental abiding, **placement in equipoise**, this is accomplished through *the force of familiarity*. It is called the force of familiarity because not only is it free from sinking and excitement but you don't need even the slightest effort, and instead it is carried out continuously.

The Four Types of Attention

For the [attainment of tranquil abiding], there are four types of attention. On the first two mental abidings, there is an intense awareness that is tight and that is called *engaged attention*. On the five middle stages [that is, the third through the seventh mental abidings], although we are cautious about mental sinking and excitement, our concentration is interrupted, so this is *interrupted [attention]* and engaged attention.

Query: Well then, since the first and second mental abidings have a great deal of sinking and excitement, why don't we also call them interrupted [attention] and engaged attention?

Reply: Since during those two mental abidings there is, for the most part, very strong sinking and excitement, they do not conventionally exist as interruptions.[654] During the eighth mental abiding, you are free of sinking and excitement due to the force of effort; therefore, it is *unin-*

653. From the shore, the waves on a great ocean seem to be slow and slight.
654. This means that there is not even enough mental stability for obstacles to count as interruptions.

terrupted attention. On the ninth mental abiding, you don't need to exert any effort whatsoever; therefore, it is *spontaneous attention*.

Although you may attain the ninth mental abiding with the mind in single-pointed equipoise, you have not actually attained tranquil abiding. Upon that attainment, you have attained a mind that is included in the "infallible access"[655] of the first concentration included in the higher realms. If you attain tranquil abiding, you attain the good qualities associated with the higher realms.

With respect to the way in which tranquil abiding is attained from there, although you abide effortlessly [upon the object of observation] once you have attained the ninth mental abiding, it is included with the level of the desire realm, and you haven't actually attained tranquil abiding. However, it is permissible to posit it as a similitude of tranquil abiding. Next, you obtain the bliss of mental and physical pliancy through sincerely applying yourself to meditating single-pointedly. Furthermore, it is called "pliancy"[656] because an internal energy-wind associated with dysfunctional tendencies that make your body and mind unserviceable for virtue is pacified, whereby your dysfunctional tendencies are purified, and your body and mind become serviceable for virtue, and you are capable of utilizing them for whatever you wish.

Therefore, at the end of the ninth mental abiding, a heaviness and numbness is felt upon the top of the person's head as a sign that you are about to attain pliancy. Furthermore, this heaviness is not uncomfortable but is analogous to a warm hand being placed on the center of a person's head as soon as it is shaven. Regarding this, a wind of serviceability flows through all parts of your body, and the wind of dysfunctional tendencies leaves through the crown of your head. Next, your mind is freed from dysfunctional tendencies, after which you develop mental pliancy first. In dependence upon that, you develop physical pliancy as the wind courses through your body. With that, you are free from physical dysfunctional tendencies and develop physical pliancy. With respect to pliancy, it is mental as well as bliss which is a bliss that is a tactile sensation of the body; therefore, it is called "physical pliancy." The tactile sensation that

655. Tib. *nyer bsdogs mi lcogs med*. This is a concentration that is a preparatory stage for the first level of concentration of the form realm of the mundane path.
656. Tib. *shin sbyangs*.

is generated within the body is mentally pleasing but is not said to be a mental factor.

Thus, once you attain physical pliancy, you generate a very blissful experience within the body through the power of energy-wind, whereby it is called "the bliss of physical pliancy." In dependence upon attaining the bliss of physical pliancy, there also occurs the most wonderful experience of bliss and joy within the mind, which is called "the bliss of mental pliancy." For that reason, from among the two types of pliancy, you develop mental pliancy first. From among the two types of bliss, you develop the bliss of physical pliancy first. There are vast differences in both the pliancy and the bliss associated with those two. Once you attain physical pliancy, at that point the ecstasy of pliancy slowly fades and diminishes [slightly], so that the mind is not disturbed by the ecstasy or bliss. When you attain a stable bliss [as just explained], you have completed the bliss of physical and mental pliancy and have attained fully qualified tranquil abiding. This is called the "infallible access" of the first concentration, and its attainment is indispensable to being included within [the first concentration].

When you attain a fully qualified tranquil abiding, while you are in meditative equipoise, the experience of the appearance of all worlds and their beings seem to dissolve into your own body, and it is as though you have attained a new body in post-meditation. Moreover, you don't engage in the ten mental designations,[657] your afflictive emotions are reduced, sleep and concentration mix, you have special dreams while dreaming, your mind is so clear that it is as though you could divide the atoms in a wall, your factor of clarity greatly increases, and you will be able to see through mountains. If you have tranquil abiding observing the mind, it should possess the three special features of clarity, awareness, and vacuity once the mind seems to have become utterly empty; this is how to attain the bliss of pliancy explained earlier.

These days, there are some who don't understand this, and because of the complete empty state [of the mind], they mistakenly think they have discovered the view [of emptiness], and having mistaken that bliss for the simultaneously born bliss [of highest yoga tantra], they say that

657. The ten mental designations are the five associated with the five sense objects, the three associated with the three poisons, and the two of male and female.

enlightenment is something that is within our grasp. Once they think they have actualized the natural face of the primordial mind, they say that it has good qualities of the primordial mind that are expressed in the *dohas*.[658] There are many who have made this kind of mistake by applying the former [realization of highest yoga tantra] to the latter [view of the mind]. With respect to this, this is like thinking that a genital worm on a female dog is a lion and then trying mix all the good qualities of a lion [with those of a worm].

With respect to actualizing the primordial mind, if you generate a special exalted wisdom of bliss and emptiness at the time of the basis when you are dying or during the dissolution of the winds at the time of the path so that they occur exactly as they do at death, then you will attain the example clear light that is actualizing the nature of the primordial mind. This is also the state that is being compared to the good qualities of primordial mind in the dohas. The "primordial mind" is difficult to realize through latent tendencies. For that, you must realize up to the point of and including the [three subtle minds of] white appearance, red increase, and black near-attainment. You do not need to perceive something like the clarity, awareness, and utter vacuity of the nature of mind, which should be able to be understood based on my previous explanation.

If you attain concentration in that way [as described in the previous explanation about fully qualified tranquil abiding], you will have the foundation for attaining superior seeing, the ten arya bodhisattva levels [that is, bhumis], the Mahayana and Hinayana, the generation and completion stages, and so on. This is the gateway to all these types of concentrations. In dependence upon this you will quickly develop all the realizations of the higher paths.

658. Tib. *do ha*. Dohas are songs of spiritual realization that were common among Indian tantric mahasiddhas, most notably Saraha.

Day Thirty-Three

The teachings of the gentle protector Tsongkhapa the Great state,

> Without being endowed with the wisdom realizing the mode of existence . . .

Although we may strive toward bodhichitta and its limb of renunciation, which are the causes of the Mahayana, if they are divorced from the wisdom realizing suchness we will not be able to sever the root of samsara. Therefore, it is utterly indispensable that we sincerely strive at realizing the unmistaken ultimate view that is profound and perfect. Furthermore, it is very important that we engage in a fully qualified scriptural tradition of our Teacher that presents the view [of emptiness]. Thus, the unmistaken profound view according to the intention of the Conqueror is the stages of the path to enlightenment, which are the king of instructions of the Teacher . . .

After giving this brief introduction, Pabongkha Rinpoche covered the headings and gave the oral transmission for each of the headings for the superior seeing section of the Middle-Length Treatise on the Stages of the Path *without providing an elaborate explanation.*

The profound and deep summation of the meaning of each of the scriptures is combined in the instructions [within the Middle-Length Treatise on the Stages of the Path*], but we were unable to arrange the notes; therefore, what follows is being set forth according to the teachings given during the teachings on the* Swift Path.

The Way to Train in the Superior Seeing That Is the Nature of Wisdom

To make it easy to understand for those of lesser intelligence, I shall present this in concise fashion, combining the essential points for which there are two headings:

1. Relying upon the Collection of Causes for Superior Seeing
2. How to Actually Meditate [on Emptiness]

Relying upon the Collection of Causes for Superior Seeing

For this, there are three: (1) relying upon a skilled lama to teach the meaning of the definitive meaning, (2) purifying negative karma and accumulating merit, and (3) making supplication to your lama while regarding him as inseparable from your personal deity.

Furthermore, [superior seeing] is tranquil abiding that observes emptiness which has attained the physical and mental pliancy induced through engaging in placement meditation observing emptiness. With respect to the observed conventional objects of superior seeing, [on the mundane path] they are the eight mental stabilizations of concentration. Once you are dwelling within tranquil abiding, you induce pliancy through the force of analysis which is a conventional superior seeing that is common to Buddhists and non-Buddhists. We are not striving for such a thing. Instead, through abiding single-pointedly in tranquil abiding we analyze emptiness, whereby we attain the bliss of physical and mental pliancy. For that reason, if we haven't already attained the view of emptiness, from the point at which we attain tranquil abiding, we need to strive to ascertain the view [of emptiness]. For that to happen, we must follow an unmistaken scripture.

Furthermore, from the four tenet systems of the Bhagavan, there are the two higher tenet systems of the Madhyamaka, which are the Prasangika and the Svatantrika. Therefore, although all phenomena lack true existence, the Svatantrikas assert an inherent existence. The Prasangikas assert the absence of inherent existence and the absence of true existence.[659] Although each one of the tenet systems states that its view is the definitive meaning and that the others are the interpretive meaning, the Conqueror himself prophesied that no one other than the two great trailblazers[660] would be able to discern the meaning of the interpretive and the definitive; therefore, we should emulate those two. Furthermore, Asanga the charioteer founded the Chittamatra system following the *Sutra Unraveling the Intent*,[661] and Nagarjuna [founded the Prasangika system] following the *Sutra of Inexhaustible Intellect*.[662] [Nagarjuna] explained that the first and the last turnings of the wheel [of Dharma] are the interpretive meaning and the middle [turning of the wheel is] the definitive meaning. Furthermore, a sutra states,

> Four hundred years after I pass
> Into the sphere of peace,
> A glorious and renowned bhikshu
> Will appear in the southern land of Vedali.
>
> Addressed by the name Naga,
> He will destroy the views of existence and nonexistence
> And will perfectly explain the unsurpassed vehicle
> Of my teachings in this world.
>
> He will attain the ground of Very Joyful
> And go to Sukhavati.

As this states, [Nagarjuna] will destroy the bias of existence and nonexistence. According to the Conqueror's own prophecy, the great charioteer glorious protector Arya Nagarjuna will perfectly elucidate the intention of the Conqueror with the unmistaken view of the profound Madhyamaka that is free from the extremes of existence and nonexistence as well as permanence and annihilation. Therefore, we should strive to follow his

659. Tib. *rang bzhin gyis grub* and *bden par grub*. These two are seen as synonymous in the Prasangika system.

660. The two great trailblazers were Nagarjuna and Asanga.

661. Tib. *mDo sde dgongs 'grel*; Skt. *Samdhinirmochana sutra*.

662. Tib. *Blo gros mi zad pa'i mdo*; Skt. *Akshayamati nirdesha sutra*.

actual definitive meaning. Since there is absolutely no one else who has appeared with the unmistaken view, glorious Chandrakirti stated [in his *Guide to the Middle Way*],

> There is no means to peace outside of the
> Path of master Nagarjuna-pada.
> Others depart from the truth of the conventional and thatness;
> Because they stray from them, they cannot attain liberation.

For that reason, you must absolutely rely upon his texts. If you don't rely upon [Nagarjuna], you will not attain even mere liberation through either sutra or tantra. Therefore, you will not find another method or door to attain the peace of nirvana. Aryadeva stated,

> Two doors to peace do not exist.

Bhavaviveka, Shantarakshita, their spiritual descendants, and others have commented upon the intention of Arya Nagarjuna. Although many have appeared, for the most part they did not [properly identify] Nagarjuna's true intent. With respect to the composers [of philosophical treatises] that perfectly elucidate [Nagarjuna's] true intent, they are Buddhapalita and Chandrakirti. We should follow the texts of Nagarjuna Father and Sons in our search for the unmistaken view of the Middle Way. With respect to the composers [of philosophical treatises] that perfectly elucidate the unmistaken intent of [Nagarjuna], there is only the gentle protector Tsongkhapa the Great. During the earlier propagation of the teachings, the great master Padmasambhava was a Prasangika; however, other than a few fortunate beings who were liberated through his teachings, the texts of the Madhyamaka were not able to become established and were not proliferated extensively.

Afterward, Hvashang Mahayana came and spread his view that the mind should not focus on anything at all. Many of the earlier generations of Tibetans, and even today all those who have not encountered the perfect explanations of Je Tsongkhapa, for the most part hold that view [of Hvashang Mahayana]. Although [Je Tsongkhapa] composed numerous excellent ways explaining how to identify the differences in Hvashang's system right from the very beginning, everyone is in agreement that the actual conclusion [of Hvashang's view] states, "The mind should not grasp at anything whatsoever since ultimate nature is not produced in the slightest," which means that you should not focus your mind on anything at all and place your mind on just that. Therefore, no matter how skillfully [the aforementioned wrong views] are explained, there is no other choice than to admit that they are Hvashang's view. According to the teachings of the omniscient [Jamyang Shepa Ngawang Tsondru's] *Great Treatise on Tenets*,

> There are well-known teachings in the Bon that have descended from Tibetan gods and demons, called (1) the *shen* of prediction, (2) the shen of existence, (3) the shen of appearance, and (4) the shen of magic,[663] which are substitutes for the four classes of tantra. The Vinaya and the perfection of wisdom are not different [in Buddhism and Bon].[664] They also have substitute lay vows, intermediate monk's vows, novice vows, and bhikshu vows. [In addition,] there are (1) the layperson's vows, (2) novice monk's [vows] of the Bon, (3) rishis [or seers], (4) the white AH,[665] and (5) the especially great vehicle, which are well known as the Bon of the four causal vehicles of the five resultant vehicles.[666] The first four [of the second group] engage primarily in view and conduct. With respect to the [fifth, which constitutes the] ninth [overall], this is primarily concerned with view.[667] Therefore, in their completion stage, they also don't focus the mind on anything at all. They uphold the tradition of Hvashang by disparaging virtues of body and speech.[668]

663. Tib. *phya gshen*, *'dur gshen*, *snang gshen*, and *'khrul gshen*, respectively.
664. These days, the Bon rely on the Vinaya and perfection of wisdom sutras of the Buddhists without any alterations.
665. Tib. *a dkar pa*.
666. The five Bon of the fruit (or resultant) vehicle are (1) *dge bsnyen theg pa*, (2) *drang srong theg pa*, (3) *a dkar theg pa*, (4) *ye gshen theg pa*, and (5) *yang rtse bla med theg pa*. See Thuken Losang Chökyi Nyima, *The Crystal Mirror of Philosophical Systems*, 328–29.
667. The ninth is Bon Dzogchen.
668. For more information on Bon, see Thuken Losang Chökyi Nyima, *The Crystal Mirror of Philosophical Systems*.

Also, the *Treasury of the Natural State* [by Longchen Rabjam (1308–1364)] states,

> In the definitive essence of the ultimate meaning,
> Just as you are equally bound by a golden chain or by a [grass-woven] rope,
> So the mind is equally bound by Dharma and by non-Dharma;
> Just as the [sky] is [equally] obscured by black or by white clouds,
> [So] you are equally obscured by conceptions of both virtue and nonvirtue;
> In this way, the yogi who realizes this
> Transcends all virtue and nonvirtue, as well as cause and effect.

And in the autocommentary to that, it states,

> Although at the time of the great master Hvashang, those of feeble minds were unable to grasp these points, in fact this is how things exist.

With respect to such teachings, Je [Tsongkhapa's] *Stages of the Path [to Enlightenment]* states, "It is unacceptable in all aspects to rely upon the Bon and so forth." Therefore, his perspective is that the view of such a system is an extremely great point of error.

Previously, the views of Marpa and Mila[repa] Father and Sons of the Kagyu tradition and Atisha Father and Sons of the Kadam tradition had the unmistaken view of the Prasangika; however, after a while even their followers had divergent ways of identifying each of their own traditions with meanings that were influenced by Hvashang's view. Later, the Sakyapas identified the illusory-like mind; however, this is like meditating on an illusory affirming negation, so in fact it has become an extreme of permanence.

Je Lama [Tsongkhapa] composed a number of texts concerning the view [of emptiness] that rely upon the texts of the Arya Father and Sons, such as his great commentary to the *Root Text on Wisdom*, his commentary to the *Guide to the Middle Way*, the *Essence of Interpretive and Definitive*, and so forth. These teachings of Je Lama are incomparable in their eloquence and are so clearly composed that they are like the jewels of the three worlds; therefore, we should follow these texts by examining them with an unbiased mind. To search somewhere else once something like this has been set forth is like trading gold for rocks. If you don't apply yourself well to this view, you are in extremely great danger. Nagarjuna stated,

> If there are faults in your view of emptiness,
> Those of little wisdom will be ruined.

And,

> Those who [believe] in existence will go to happy rebirths;
> Those who [believe] in nonexistence will go to miserable rebirths.

Here "existence" is the extreme of permanence and "nonexistence" is the extreme of nihilism; therefore, through meditating on the view of permanence we will not be able to free ourselves from samsara. If we meditate on the view of annihilation, we will go to hell. For that reason, we definitely must rely upon Je Rinpoche [Tsongkhapa's] perfectly explained scriptures. If we rely upon these, and if we enthusiastically meditate, there is no way we will be deceived. At present, even people such as we have the knowledge to distinguish paths from non-paths, which is not due to our own cleverness. Instead, it is [due to] the kindness of Je Tsongkhapa the Great.

How to Actually Meditate [on Emptiness]

This is not merely the mundane superior seeing of the peaceful and the coarse;[669] instead, we meditate on the supramundane superior seeing for which we need the decisive view of selflessness and stable concentration. For example, when viewing a mural at night, you need a lamp that has the qualities both of being an extremely bright lamp and of not being

669. This is in reference to the mundane paths of superior seeing followed by non-Buddhists. In these systems, you meditate on the coarse and undesirable aspects of the realms such as the desire realms and the peacefulness and good qualities of the higher realms such as the form and formless realms.

disturbed by the wind. In the same way, you need the lamp-like emptiness and the undisturbed-by-the-wind-like tranquil abiding to perceive clearly the meaning of reality. At this point, for a person who has already attained tranquil abiding to come to a definitive conclusion about selflessness, even though he may strive for many thousands of years with a concentration and so forth of the mundane path, if he doesn't have a special wisdom that apprehends the path of selflessness that is in direct opposition to self-grasping and its mode of apprehension, he can forget about it ever becoming an antidote to the afflictive emotions; instead, it becomes an aid to them! The *King of Concentration Sutra* states,

> Although you may meditate on mundane concentrations,
> It will not destroy the conceptions of a self,
> Because [the conception of self] is an affliction and very intensely
> Meditating on this is similar to Lachö's[670] concentration.

Thus, if you practice on the mere essence of the clarity and awareness of the mind, it is similar to the meditative concentration of Lachö. The wisdom realizing selflessness is the actual path to overcome the afflictive emotions. That very *[King of Concentration] Sutra* states,

> If the selflessness of phenomena is analyzed
> And if you cultivate this analysis,
> It causes the effect of attaining nirvana;
> Through no other causes does one come to peace.

This scripture states that this must be realized through meditative analysis, with the individual analysis on the meaning of selflessness, and also reveals that one will not be able to realize [selflessness] according to Hvashang [Mahayana's] system called "meditating by not focusing the mind on anything at all." Therefore, the only door to attaining nirvana is the view of selflessness. You will not attain liberation no matter how much you strive in other practices, such as the other five perfections;

670. Tib. lHag spyod. Lachö was one of the six brahman ascetics and a teacher of the Buddha before his enlightenment.

identifying the nature of mind; Shijé mahamudra;[671] channels, winds, and drops; generation and completion stages; and so forth. Because of that, the way to meditate once you reach a definitive and unmistaken conclusion with respect to the meaning of selflessness has three sections.

[How to Actually Meditate on Emptiness has three sections:]

1. Ascertaining the Selflessness of Persons
2. Ascertaining the Selflessness of Phenomena
3. The Way to Develop Superior Seeing from That

Ascertaining the Selflessness of Persons has two sections:

1. How to Practice the Space-like Meditative Absorption
2. How to Practice the Illusory-like Subsequent Attainment

For that, we must first understand their distinctions; therefore, [we must understand its associated terminology]. A compounded phenomena and a functional thing[672] are synonymous. An uncompounded phenomena and a permanent entity[673] are synonymous. There are three compounded phenomena: form, consciousness, and nonassociated compositional factors. For form, there are color and form and the shape of the form. For consciousness, there are mental consciousness and sense consciousness. For mental consciousness, there are primary consciousness and the fifty-one mental factors and so on. For sense consciousness, there are five. For nonassociated compositional factors, there are those that are persons and those that are not [persons]. With respect to those that are persons, there are living beings and buddha-superiors. For those that are not persons, there are years, months, days, and so forth. With respect to nonassociated compositional factors, there are those that are existent and those

671. *Shijé* is translated as "holy Dhamra that pacifies suffering." It was founded by Padampa Sangye. For more information, see Thuken Losang Chökyi Nyima, *The Crystal Mirror of Philosophical Systems*, 157–68.

672. Tib. *'dus byas* and *dngos po.*

673. Tib. *'dus ma byas* and *rtag pa.*

that are not subject to disintegration.[674] For those who have not trained in the scriptural tradition, by coming to know these [it will assist you] in ascertaining selflessness.

The selflessness of persons ascertains the selflessness upon the person which is its subject and basis [for establishing selflessness of persons]. The selflessness of phenomena ascertains their non[inherent] existence in dependence upon phenomena which are its subject and basis [for establishing the selflessness of phenomena], such as forms, sounds, and so forth. Although there is not any distinction with respect to the subtleness or coarseness of those two, it is definitely easier to [understand] in dependence upon the person as the basis and subject of emptiness, and definitely more difficult in dependence upon phenomena. Therefore, because it is easier in the beginning to [understand] the selflessness of persons, I shall explain that first.

With respect to the teachings for ascertaining the absence of inherent existence of persons, they are ascertaining the absence of inherent existence of the "I." There is a list of synonyms for the object of negation, such as truly established, established from its own side, inherently established, existence able to establish itself, established by way of its own characteristics, established through its own entity, established from the side of the object, established without conceptual imputation, and so forth. They are the objects of negation by way of reasoning. [Regarding the synonyms for emptiness, they are] not truly established, not established from its own side, not inherently established, not having an existence that is able to establish itself, not established by way of characteristics, not established through its own entity, and so forth.

Although there are a multitude of synonyms for the reasoning ascertaining the absence of inherent existence, the primary ones are the reasoning refuting the absence of sameness and difference, the reasoning of the diamond slivers, the reasoning of production and cessation from existence and nonexistence, the reasoning of production and cessation from the four alternatives, and the logical argument of dependent arising which is the king of reasoning. Although there are five mentioned, it is easier for beginners to use the first and last [logical arguments]. Even within that,

674. Tib. *'jig rgyu med pa.*

the first of these is the easiest to grasp; therefore, it is important. For that, we need an explanation that combines the four essential ways of analysis. Therefore, the first essential point is ascertaining the object of negation.

[How to Practice the Space-like Meditative Absorption has four sections:

1. The First Essential Point: Ascertaining the Object of Negation
2. The Second Essential Point: Ascertaining the Pervasion
3. The Third Essential Point: The Self Is Not Truly Identical to the Five Aggregates
4. The Fourth Essential Point: The Self Is Not Truly Separate from the Aggregates]

The First Essential Point: Ascertaining the Object of Negation

First, we must ascertain the generic image of the object of negation. If we don't ascertain that, it will destroy dependent relationship and become the extreme of nihilism. We must identify either the causal self which is empty in the realization of emptiness or the causal self which is nonexistent in the understanding of selflessness. Furthermore, [Shantideva's] *Guide to the Bodhisattva's Way of Life* states,

> Without coming into contact with the imputed entity,
> You cannot identify the nonexistence of its mode of being.

If we do not identify the causal self which is nonexistent in ascertaining selflessness, we will not be able to negate it. For example, to apprehend an enemy and thief, you must identify him. Although the thief may be a layman, be youthful, and have a mole on his face, you still will not recognize him. To recognize him, you must actually see him. Likewise, although the object of negation is not inherently existent, does not exist as a self-supporting entity, and does not have true existence, if you are not able to identify the object of negation, it will be extremely difficult to realize this [aforementioned] view of nonexistence. Furthermore, it will be difficult to realize the generic image as the subtle object of negation. If you realize this [object of negation], it will not be difficult to realize the view [of emptiness].

The object of negation is known by other terms as well, but we should not emulate others by merely reading them and instead come to realize them by identifying them through our own experience. For that [object of negation], there are two: the object of negation of the path and the object of negation of reason. With respect to the object of negation of the path, this is the two obstructions. The principal object of negation of reasoning is the true existence. This is called "the object of negation of reasoning" and is asserted to be established from its own side without depending upon names and concepts. [Chandrakirti's] *Commentary on the Four Hundred Stanzas* states,

> That which is called "self" is that which [is believed to] have its own inherent entity that does not depend upon other functioning things; its nonexistence is selflessness.

Thus, the object of negation is a truly established "I" that does not depend upon another to impute it. The act of grasping at that is called "self-grasping," "dualistic grasping," "conception of [an inherently existent] 'I,'" "grasping at true existence," and "grasping at characteristics."[675] In general, from among the two—[namely,] (1) the conception grasping at true existence, and (2) innate self-grasping—it is the latter which is the root of samsara. It is possessed by living beings right down to ants. With respect to this [first] conception, it does not exist in the minds of those not affected by tenets. The conception that something such as a dog is inherently established is not the view of the transitory collection that comes from grasping at persons. The conceived object of "I"-grasping that comes from the mode of grasping of an innate "I"-grasping with the thought "I, I" is the self of the object of negation.

When meditating, begin by doing the lamrim preliminary rituals, and after making supplication to your guru inseparable from Manjushri, from

675. Tib. *bdag 'dzin*, *gnyis 'dzin*, *ngar 'dzin*, *bden 'dzin*, *bden 'dzin*, and *mtshan 'dzin*, respectively. *Ngar 'dzin* is also translated as "'I'-grasping" at various points in the text.

among self and others, you should examine just how the "I" exists by observing the "I" in your own mental continuum. Furthermore, if someone accuses you of stealing and you respond by stating, "You accused me of being a thief; I did not do that," then as soon as you think, "You accused me of being a thief" and "I cannot accept this," a self-supporting "I" emerges that appears vividly, even though it does not exist anywhere within the external body or the internal mind.[676] When it is praised, you are happy; when it is criticized, you are unhappy; when it is frightened, you are frightened; when it suffers, you suffer. In these instances, the grasping mind is the root of samsara.

Also, with respect to occasional practices such as accumulating virtuous Dharmas due to your fear of going to the lower realms and so forth, these will bring you benefit; therefore, the previous Kadampas and others were also said to [make confessions to] the relics of the Buddha. The "I" exists in two ways: (1) there is an "I" that is merely conventional, and (2) there is an "I" that is grasped by the innate self-grasping. With respect to the conventionally existent "I," this is the mere thought "I did not do such a thing" when we are accused of stealing. For example, this is similar to an illusory horse or elephant, the moon in water, or a form reflected in a mirror, which arise as mere appearances. After that, you say very strongly, "I did not do such a thing," and the thought "I, I" vividly appears, and that is the nonexistent causal "I" which is the "I" of the innate "I"-grasping. When you are observing that, once you place your mind upon the sphere of the majority of the mind and with one subtle corner of the mind examine it, it is like someone trying to catch a small bird. When observing it with [one corner of the mind], if we say, "The "I" is not my body and mind," and a vividly appearing sense of it appears, then that is the self which is the object of negation.

This search for the object of negation is very difficult and also very important. If we don't take it far enough, we will fall into the extreme of permanence, and if we take it too far, we will fall into the extreme of nihilism. In this way, we should not be satisfied with examining in dependence upon ourselves but should analyze others as well, and the way

676. This is because to a mind of self-grasping it appears to be an inherently existent "I" that exists independent of the body and mind.

they become puffed up when they are referred to as "Bhikshu" and "him." Furthermore, if the mind that is the analyzer is too forceful, we will lose the object and it will disappear. Therefore, the mind should examine the mind for [the false conception of an inherently existent "I"] by utilizing great care. The conventional "I" is not nonexistent but is an existent phenomena. The way in which it is existent can be expressed with the following analogy: The terms "lama" and "kind sir" that are imputed upon the basis of imputation are mere imputations of the mind that are factually concordant. [In contrast], the "I" that possesses an existence able to establish itself[677] is not an existent phenomenon but is nonexistent.

For example, if we use the term "horse," it is not the body and mind of a horse but a horse that is able to establish itself that arises vividly [to our minds], and that is the object of negation of that inherently existent horse. Furthermore, the body of the horse is not the horse. If it were the horse, then we could also ride the corpse of a horse; however, it is not possible to ride on such a thing [as a dead horse]. If its mind were the horse, then once it died it should also exist as something to be ridden in the intermediate state. It is not possible to ride that, either; therefore, the mind of the horse is also not the horse. Although there is more to explain, if we [think of] it this way, it will be easy to understand.

Query: Well then, just what is the horse?

Reply: The term "horse" is a mere mental designation of conceptual imputation upon the mere collection of body and mind that is the basis of imputation of a horse: that is the horse. That is an existent phenomenon and is the conventionally existent horse. That is the person.[678] For that reason, the horse that appears as being able to establish itself is not a mere appearance to our minds when we use the term "horse"; instead it is the object of negation. Such a horse [that appears as though it is truly existent] is nonexistent, just like in the example that "my body is not the 'I.'" If it were [inherently existent], then when we died, this body would not transform into a corpse but would become the "I." And if that were the case, the self would have to be form. If the "I" were my mind, consequently the mind would not be the basis of imputing the "I," and numerous faults

677. Tib. *tshugs thub tu grub pa'i nga*.

678. Tib. *gang zag*. Here the term "person" does not refer to a human being but to a living being—in this case a horse.

would be incurred, such as that while I was riding a horse, my mind would assume the shape and color of riding a horse.[679]

By observing that conventionally existent "I" which is a mere imputation and mere appearance, we develop the wish "If I attain liberation, I will not need to concern myself with my body and mind," and we worry "Will I fall down into the lower realms?" When the "I" is praised we are happy, when it is criticized we are unhappy, and so on; this concrete self-substantiating ["I"] is the object of negation.

At present, once we mix the object of negation and the conventionally existent object, it then appears as various objects, such as a vase and pillar and so forth. Furthermore, this is analogous to when we think, "I am meditating on emptiness": if we ask, "Who is 'I'?," saying "I, I" in that way is nothing other than the appearance of the object of negation. Whenever we grasp at "I" through innate self-grasping, it is apprehended in dependence upon the conventionally existent ["I"]. When we grasp in that way, we are grasping at true existence. The mere sound of the phrase "mere appearance" refutes inherent existence.

679. If the "I" were the mind, then if you were riding a horse and you were to say, "I am riding a horse," this would be equivalent to saying, "My mind is riding a horse," and therefore, your mind would have to assume the color and shape of someone riding a horse. The mind doesn't have color or shape, so this becomes an unwanted consequence.

Day Thirty-Four

The gentle protector Tsongkhapa the Great stated,

> Pacifying wandering to mistaken objects . . .

It is indispensable to develop the special realization of the union of tranquil abiding and superior seeing, to fulfill whatever wish we may have for the state of liberation and omniscience. If we manage that, we will be able to easily accomplish the state of liberation and omniscience. For that purpose, [we should think,] "I am going to listen to the stages of the path to enlightenment, which are the king of instructions of our Teacher and contain the complete and unmistaken oral instructions for accomplishing that [union of tranquil abiding and superior seeing]."

After giving this short introduction, Pabongkha Rinpoche covered the topics.

The Second Essential Point: Ascertaining the Pervasion

If the vividly appearing self-instituting thought "I, I" exists according to the appearance of innate self-grasping to a mind that grasps at a self-instituting "I," then it must exist as either one with or separate from the five aggregates. It is utterly impossible that there is a third way of existing other than existing in those two ways.[680] The phrase "utterly impossible" is synonymous with "nonexistent."[681] To express this through an analogy

680. These two ways are being either (1) inherently one with or (2) inherently separate from the five aggregates.
681. Tib. *gtan nas mi srid* and *med pa*, respectively.

Geshe Potowa

that is easy to understand, when we search for something like a wallet after we have lost it, it must exist inside our room, or alternatively, it must exist outside our room. In the same way, a phenomenon must be one or the other—it either has one aspect or it has many aspects; there are no possibilities other than those two. This point is important. Since [a truly existent "I"] is either truly identical to or truly separate [from the five aggregates] and there isn't a third possibility, if the "I" doesn't exist in that way, it is necessarily nonexistent.

The Third Essential Point: [The Self] Is Not Truly Identical [to the Five Aggregates]

If the "I" were truly one with the five aggregates, then it would incur many faults, such as that there would be many selves, the "I" would be subject to birth and destruction, and so forth. The aggregates, which are that which is appropriated, and the "I," which is the appropriator, would become one. The self from a previous life would come into this life and would go on to the next life. They [that is, the selves from a previous life] would be fastened to the aggregates of this life. The aggregates have a material cause; therefore, there is no way that these two have one mode of existence. Also, there are five aggregates and no more than one self; therefore, even through mere calculation we can understand that those two [the self and the aggregates] are not one. If these two were one, then as [Chandrakirti's] *Guide to the Middle Way* states,

> For that reason, if the aggregates were the self,
> Because there are many [aggregates], the self would also become many.

Just as there are five aggregates, so it would be necessary for the "I" to have five distinct continuums. Alternatively, if the aggregates were truly one, so would the "I" [have to be], and even the five aggregates could not have parts and would become a singular entity. While the aggregates are subject to production and destruction, the "I" would also have to be subject to production and disintegration. The *Root Text on Wisdom* states,

> If the self were the aggregates,
> It would be subject to production and disintegration.

If the "I" and the aggregates were one, when you carried the aggregates to the burial ground, the "I" would also arrive in the burial ground. If you are presently a bhikshu, for instance, then when your "I" arrived in the intermediate state, a bhikshu would necessarily also arrive in the intermediate state, and if you were reborn as a dog, that dog would necessarily be a bhikshu. When leaving a human life and taking rebirth as an animal, that animal body would have to simultaneously be one with a human body, and when that [animal] took rebirth as a god, there would have to be three bodies—of a human, an animal, and a god—simultaneously. Therefore, however many times you take rebirth, you would have that many bodies existing simultaneously, and in that way the six classes of beings would necessarily have a common substratum. Not only that, but there would be the fault of encountering [the results of] actions that one did not perform and so forth. [Chandrakirti's] *Guide to the Middle Way* states,

> It is untenable that whatever entities have their own
> Characteristics can be included in the same continuum.

If the two selves of past and future lives are unrelated distinct entities, then the "I" of a previous life and the "I" of this life would necessarily have unrelated distinct continuums. If that were the case, you would incur many faults, such as actions performed would be wasted and so forth. Therefore, [the self and the aggregates] also cannot be established as being truly one.

The Fourth Essential Point: [The Self] Is Not Truly Separate [from the Aggregates]

If the "I" and the aggregates of the "I" were not related, they would have to be truly different. If that were so, you would be able to remove each of the five aggregates from the ones before it and identify each one separately and say, "This is the aggregate of consciousness," for example. And with respect to something such as a horse and an elephant, for instance, you could separate the horse, set it aside, and afterward point out [the elephant as a separate thing] and say, "This is the elephant." In the same way, [if the "I" were truly separate from the aggregates,] you would be able to separate it from each one of the aggregates such as form, and afterward point your finger at the illustration of the "I" and say, "This is the 'I.'" You should contemplate [this] by thinking, "Since there isn't even an atom that can be identified in this way, the "I" cannot be established as being distinct from the five aggregates either." Nagarjuna also stated [in his *Precious Garland*],

> The person is not earth, not water,
> Not fire, not wind, not space,
> Not consciousness, and not all of them;
> What person is there other than that?

Thus, if [your sense of an inherently existent "I"] completely disappears by thinking "Such an 'I' is utterly nonexistent," in dependence upon analyzing the fourth essential point and negating that concrete self-supporting ["I"] that is placed deep within your mind, then you have discovered the view of the Middle Way, and you should place your mind within that state.

Those with no previous experience of emptiness [from a previous life] are frightened, and those with such an experience [from a previous life] are as delighted as if they had found a treasure. Of the two similar systems of explanation—[namely,] (1) the extreme of nihilism that destroys dependent arising and (2) the absence of being one or many[682]—if we don't properly identify the object of negation, there is the danger of our [meditation] becoming the extreme of nihilism that destroys dependent arising. Therefore, we must properly identify the object of negation. We must negate [the mistaken conception of] the self-supporting "I" that is deep within the recesses of our minds. Furthermore, the "I" that appears to be a truly existent self-supporting "I" in the innate view of the transitory collection is not the object of negation. The object of negation is the *taking* of said appearance—a truly existent, self-supporting "I"—*to be real.*[683] This is the area that is a potential pitfall for our minds with respect to emptiness. If we don't work properly at accumulating merit and purifying negative karma during our [efforts to realize] the view, there is a great danger of our straying into such pitfalls.

Furthermore, although we may think that the empty nature of the mind's clarity and knowing are emptiness, they are not emptiness. If that were so, then sound, space, and so forth, which have the characteristic of being empty [of obstructive contact], would necessarily be emptiness. In

682. These are similar, in that the negation of an inherently existent self that is neither inherently one with nor inherently different from the aggregates could easily lead to the mistaken conception that the "I" doesn't exist at all. Therefore, properly identifying the object of negation becomes essential to avoid falling into the extreme of nihilism.

683. Thanks to Gelong Losang Tenzin (Sean Price) for his helpful contribution to this last line.

this case we are meditating on an object that is actually conventional, and [so this] is a meditation on the extreme of permanence. With respect to the emptiness dependent upon mind, once we negate the truly existent mind, it becomes an utter vacuity that establishes its absence of true existence. This is meditation on the ultimate [truth]; therefore, these two are as different as heaven and earth.

Also, positing that the mind should not be focused on anything whatsoever and that its essential nature is utterly nonexistent is the view of nihilism. For the absence of an inherently existent "I," the mind is not the observed object of negation. The "I" is not the body and mind. For that reason, if we state that [the mind] is the absence of inherent existence, we destroy dependent arising, which is the view of annihilation. At the point when that [mind] becomes totally empty, the conventionally existent "I" also becomes nonexistent, and the view [of emptiness] becomes an utter vacuity, whereby it becomes the view of annihilation. By meditating on that, we will be reborn in the lowest hell. A verse states, "They go to the lowest hell upside down, on their heads." Among non-Buddhists, the very worst of all are the Charvakas, with the view of nihilism that says that the future lives do not exist because they are unable to see them. However, even *they* don't say that those who can directly perceive [future lives] don't exist; therefore, the former[684] are even worse than the Charvakas. Choné Lama Rinpoche stated,

> [Those with] the view of nihilism become firewood in hell.

Once that truly existent "I" is refuted through meditating that the truly existent "I" also does not exist as one nor does it exist as being different, and it becomes completely empty, this refutes that truly existent "I." That functions as the cause to guide one to liberation, whereby there is an enormous distinction between this and the former [mistaken meditation on the mind].

The conventional "I" is the observed object of grasping at a truly existent ["I"] and is the conceived object of grasping at a truly existent self-

684. The "former" refers to those who err in the meditation on emptiness and fall into the extreme of nihilism.

supporting "I." Once you discover the view [of emptiness] and you think, "The [inherently existent] 'I' does not exist at all," a completely empty state dawns. You are not refuting the conventionally existent "I" by refuting the self-supporting ["I"]; therefore, you do not need to worry that you have fallen into the view of nihilism. Panchen [Losang] Chögyan stated,

> When we meditate on mahamudra, we are not merely refuting mental engagement. Instead, the very person who is engaged in meditation, his [or her] mind, and so forth are ascertained as being non[inherently] existent, and one continuously sustains that by applying it to the object—emptiness. The appearance of true existence that appears to the awareness of an ordinary person is the object of negation of true existence according to such an appearance. Therefore, by apprehending nonexistence according to appearance, it does not become the view of nihilism. All phenomena of cause and effect, such as the self and so forth, are like illusions that exist as mere nominal imputations, and [this] is the meaning of conventional existence. This is also the way to practice the view of illusoriness during subsequent attainment. Therefore, there is no point in resisting [appearances] during subsequent attainment. Those appearances do not disappear in meditative stabilization. Ascertaining through reasoned analysis that all phenomena are mere name is the definitive method for ascertaining the emptiness of true existence. Through the power of such ascertainment, you sustain that ascertainment of emptiness which is the perfect practice of mahamudra.

[Kachen Yeshe Gyaltsen's] *Mind Training: An Ornament of Losang's True Intent* states,

> Through the innate "I"-grasping, the "I" is apprehended as an object that is established from its own side. The ultimate object of negation is the "I" as an object that exists from its own side as the object of the mode of apprehension of this very mind [of innate self-grasping]. Furthermore, there are

three ways that the mind apprehends [the "I"]: (1) apprehending the "I" to exist from its own side, (2) apprehending the "I" as lacking true existence, and (3) a mind that apprehends the mere "I" without making a distinction between either of those [first] two. For that, grasping at the mere "I" is not the same as grasping at "I" and all appearances to the mind, thinking that "I" is not the object of negation. If you negate all thoughts thinking "I" that are apprehending self-grasping, this will annihilate the basis of actions and their effects; therefore, it is important that you make this hair-splitting distinction of conceptions very precisely.

[Shantideva's] *Guide to the Bodhisattva's Way of Life* states,

> However, visual awareness and auditory awareness
> Are not the objects of negation.
> The object to be overcome is the conception
> Of true existence of those, which is the cause of
> suffering.

It is inappropriate to block these mere appearances to the mind that are left unexamined and unanalyzed. Also, a very clear distinction should be made between the appearance of true existence and blocking or grasping at [those appearances].

And [the same text states],

> Once you have properly identified the way in which the object of negation appears to a mind [apprehending] true existence grasping at appearances, establish that in your mind. And once you analyze it using those lines of reasoning which I explained earlier, establish the absence of true existence. Being uncertain about what the object of negation is, and following mere words such as "Does it exist inside or outside my body and mind?" as your means of investigation, and then analyzing whether or not it exists [based] upon the object and sense powers, and when you can't find it, thinking, "The mind does not exist!"—[all this] is not the appropriate mode of appre-

> hension. If you apprehend it in that way, you are apprehending the mind as being utterly nonexistent, whereby [your meditation] becomes the view of nihilism! Moreover, with respect to not identifying the object of negation and employing analysis of observing the way conventional realities appear, this is the analysis of a fool who is not skilled in the essential points of both, and harms the appearance of dependent relationship, which has been repeatedly explained by master Chandrakirti in *Guide to the Middle Way* and his commentary to the *Root Text on Wisdom*. Master Shantideva also stated, "It is improper to block these mere appearances of conventional phenomena," as I have already cited.

Moreover, we should strive for further understanding by making a mutual comparison of the view [of emptiness] that is very clearly explained in the *Swift Path*, revealing numerous important points that are potential causes of error with respect to the view; Baso [Chökyi Gyaltsen's] commentary on the view, which perfectly explains self-grasping; and [Je] Gungtang [Jampalyang Rinpoche's] *Meaningful Praise*,[685] as well as his commentary to the *Root Text on Wisdom* and so forth.

Some say that when they attain a subsiding of appearances by meditating on the view, this constitutes discovering the view; therefore, when they think they are meditating [on emptiness properly], this is called "being overconfident with the view of emptiness." Also, when [appearances] totally disappear, if they reflect that this is not nothingness, the actual conventional object is appearing.

Query: Well then, what can I do?

Reply: When [conventional objects] have totally disappeared for a long time, there is a great danger of the mind not engaging in anything whatsoever; therefore, you should not let other [wrong] systems interfere with your practice. In that way, when the strength of your ascertaining consciousness that is ascertaining an utter vacuity that is empty of self-existence is about to diminish, the essential point is that you should once again employ the four essential points of analysis. Furthermore, once you

685. Tib. *Tsong kha pa'i bstod pa don ldan rgya cher 'grel pa.*

first have performed the complete fourfold analysis, for the remaining [instances of employing the fourfold analysis,] analyze the exact way in which the innate self-grasping apprehends the "I." Through the force of ascertaining that such an [inherently existent "I" apprehended by innate self-grasping] is nonexistent, induce an ascertaining consciousness realizing the absence of its true existence. Once you have assembled the two special features of (1) a finely tuned ascertaining consciousness ascertaining the absence of an inherently existent "I" for the ascertaining factor and (2) a mere negation of the truly existent object of negation for the factor of appearance that is an utter vacuity, you should sustain a space-like meditative equipoise that sustains [these two points] single-pointedly.

How to Practice the Illusory-like Subsequent Attainment

In our state of subsequent attainment that has refuted a self-supporting "I," or in other words, when [our meditative equipoise] diminishes and we perceive whatever remains—we realize that all phenomena, such as the "I" and so forth, that seem to be vividly self-supporting are in fact nonexistent and are mere bases of imputation upon which we impute—and that the "I" is a mere appearance of a mere conventional designation of the mind and is merely nominal. We should train ourselves [to realize that all phenomena and the "I"] are like an illusory horse and elephant that, though they appear to have true existence and appear as manifestations, are [in fact] false, like illusions. The Prasangikas also explain this by saying that they exist as mere nominal imputations. Once we are satisfied with the fact that their way of existing is as mere nominal imputations, we should remain in that state. If [phenomena] are conventionally existent, they are capable of performing the function of an existent [phenomenon], and all principals of actions, agents, and objects are admissible.

With respect to their being unable to perform functions if they lacked true existence [because of being falsely thought of as] nonexistent, only if they were nonexistent from the perspective of a mind analyzing the ultimate truth would they be nonexistent and unable to perform functions. It is said that although we may have mere doubts tending toward the factual with respect to emptiness, it will tear samsara to shreds. [Aryadeva's *Four Hundred Stanzas* states,][686]

> Those of little merit do not even
> Have doubts about this Dharma.
> Merely entertaining doubts [about it]
> Will tear samsara to shreds.

With respect to that fact that although the "I" does not inherently exist, conventional [phenomena] do exist, [we refer to] the conventionally existent "I" by saying "I am going," "I am sitting," "I am hungry," "I am full," and so on, in which it does not exist as more than a mere appearance and mere name. Therefore, that which is conventionally existent is the mere appearance of "I." With that [understanding] we [need to] establish that the "I" lacks inherent existence. If we understand that the "I" lacks inherent existence with that approach using a single basis, it will be possible to transfer [this understanding] to all other phenomena. [Aryadeva's] *Four Hundred Stanzas* states,

> Whoever is a viewer of one thing
> Is proclaimed to be the viewer of all.
> That which is the emptiness of one thing
> Is the emptiness of all.

Thus, once we have established the selflessness of persons first, we then establish the selflessness of phenomena, which has two parts.

[Ascertaining] the Selflessness of Phenomena has two sections:

1. Establishing the Absence of Inherently Existent Compounded Phenomena
2. Establishing the Absence of Inherently Existent Uncompounded Phenomena

686. Aryadeva's *Four Hundred Stanzas* has been translated in Aryadeva and Gyaltsab, *The Yogic Deeds of Bodhisattvas* (Ithaca, NY: Snow Lion, 1994), which contains Gyaltsab Dharma Rinchen's commentary with additional commentary by Geshe Sonam Rinchen and translation by Ruth Sonam.

Establishing the Absence of Inherently Existent Compounded Phenomena has three sections:

1. Establishing the Absence of Inherently Existent Form
2. Establishing the Absence of Inherently Existent Consciousness
3. Establishing the Absence of Inherently Existent Nonassociated Compositional Factors

Establishing the Absence of Inherently Existent Form

Furthermore, when we say "my body" or "my form," a vivid form appears that seems to exist through its own power; that form is the object of negation. Once that is established deep within our minds, our five limbs, such as our head and so forth, must exist as a truly existent single entity or as [five] distinct [entities]. If they exist as one, then just as there are five limbs such as our head and so forth, so form must exist as five [distinct entities], yet this is not the way it exists. If it existed as truly distinct, we should be able to separate each one of our limbs and subsequently find [our complete body in each one,] by saying, "This is my form." Not even a mere atom can be found to exist in this way, and instead, when [the appearance of an inherently existent] form dissipates into a complete vacuity, that is the emptiness of form.

Query: Well then, isn't the form utterly nonexistent?

Reply: That is also not correct. We use the term "form" in dependence upon the basis of imputation that is a collection of the five limbs and so forth, whereby it exists as a mere imputation or mere appearance. If we are not satisfied with that and undertake a search [for an inherently existent form], we will not find anything whatsoever that is form. Moreover, with respect to it being a mere imputation upon a collection that is its basis of imputation, this is analogous to saying "I am going" or "I am sitting" when it is the body that is doing such things. With respect to the "I" that is suitable to be a similar entity to mind, when we say "I am sick" or "I am hot," it is a mere imputation projected upon a collection and is a symbol. Apply that same reasoning to your [other limbs, such as your] hand and so forth. Not only that, but [you should apply it to] all forms, including their directional aspects.

If two of the smallest atoms meet, they touch a part [of each other], and if they don't touch, they exist as one part. If the partless touch, even a mountain would become an atom. If those with parts touch, there would be one part that touches and one part that doesn't touch, whereby there would be two parts; therefore, they could not become partless. In general, if it is an established basis, it has parts; therefore, we assert a pervasion.

Establishing the Absence of Inherently Existent Consciousness

If we use something like today's consciousness as an example, if today's consciousness from this morning and the consciousness of this afternoon were not mere conceptual imputations, and instead the consciousness of today were truly existent, then these two [consciousnesses from this morning and this afternoon] would exist either as [inherently] one with or [inherently] different from [each other]. If they were [inherently] one, the consciousness of this afternoon would also exist together with the consciousness of this morning. If they were [inherently] different, today's consciousness of this morning and the consciousness of this afternoon could be separated from each other, after which you should be able to reveal each one, saying, "This is the consciousness of today." The fact that [consciousness] does not exist [in this way] is the emptiness of consciousness.

Query: Well then, what is a nonexistent consciousness?

Reply: A [nonexistent consciousness] does not exist. The consciousness of this morning and the consciousness of this afternoon that are the consciousness of today exist as mere conceptual imputations. [Shantideva's] *Guide to the Bodhisattva's Way of Life* states,

> The things we call continuums or collections
> Are false, similar to rosaries, armies, and so forth.

Establishing the Absence of Inherently Existent Nonassociated Compositional Factors

Examples of nonassociated compositional factors that are not persons are, for instance, the time period of one year. When we say "one year," it appears to be self-supporting; therefore, if this were in fact so, month and year would be either [inherently] one or separate. If they were [inherently] one, then just as one year contains twelve months, so there would necessarily also be twelve years. Since one year has three hundred sixty days, the first month would necessarily also have three hundred sixty days. [Yet] if they were truly different, then after you separated each of the twelve months, you would be able to reveal each one, saying, "This is that year." Because it is not possible to reveal them in this way, you sustain an ascertaining consciousness thinking, "Such a self-supporting year does not exist in any way whatsoever."

Query: In what way *does* a year exist?

Reply: A mere collection of twelve months is the basis of imputation for a year. In dependence upon that, we apply the term "year," and this mere conventional imputation is a year. Since it exists conventionally, it is able to perform functions. Apply the same reasoning to a month and a day. If we search for the object imputed in the name "year," we also will not find it. [Nagarjuna's] *Precious Garland* states,

> Because the entity of form is mere name,
> Space is also a mere name.
> How could form exist without the elements?
> Therefore, even mere name does not exist.

Although that selflessness pervades all phenomena, because sustaining the mind's essence is not emptiness, it does not pervade all phenomena.

Establishing the Absence of Inherently Existent Uncompounded Phenomena

If we take something like space as an example, space does not [inherently] exist among its parts of the cardinal directions, intermediate directions, and the center of space. Therefore, if a space did exist that was truly existent and not a mere conceptual imputation in dependence upon those [directions], it would be either [inherently] one or [inherently] different. If it existed as one [with its directions], those [directions] and the partless would necessarily be one. Therefore, although there is the eastern direction of space and the western direction of space, they would become one. If that were so, many faults would occur, such as when clouds gathered and rain fell in the sky in the eastern direction, clouds would necessarily also gather and rain would fall in the western direction and so on. Therefore, these also cannot [inherently] exist as one. If they existed as [inherently] different, you could necessarily separate each one of the parts of space and subsequently reveal each one and say, "This is space." Since they cannot be revealed in that way, analyze by thinking, "Therefore, there is no way whatsoever that space can be [inherently] established from its own side," and sustain a finely tuned consciousness ascertaining its lack of true existence.

Query: Well then, I wonder how *does* space exist?

Reply: Space is conventionally existent as a mere conceptual imputation that imputes the term "space" upon a nonaffirming negation that is the lack of obstructive contact. If you think that emptiness itself is most likely truly existent, that is also not the case because it exists dependently as a subject that is the basis of emptiness, because of which it also does not exist as a substantially existent entity. It is an extremely grave fault if you view [emptiness] as [inherently] existent. A sutra states,

> Kashyapa, it would be better to grasp at the view of a self the size of a mountain
> Than to view emptiness as being truly existent.

Asserting that emptiness is truly existent is an incurable view. Therefore, truly existent emptiness is the object of negation based upon emptiness. For that, you employ analysis of the absence of being [inherently] one, [inherently] different, and so forth, and when [the appearance of a truly existent emptiness] becomes an utter vacuity, you have discovered the view based on emptiness. The term "emptiness" necessarily pervades all objects of knowledge. Since all phenomena are imputed upon their individual bases of imputation in dependence upon names and terms, they are not established from their own side, and because they are not [inherently] established, this occurs due to the validity of dependent relationship. For example, if a seed were truly existent, it could not transform during the [stage of] a sprout and during the [stage of] ripening. It is an indication of its absence of inherent existence that, in dependence upon water, manure, warmth, moisture, and so forth, a seed transforms during the [stage of] being a sprout and during the [stage] of its fruition. Therefore, it is through the "kindness" of the absence of inherent existence that happiness results from engaging in virtuous causes and so forth. This occurs due to the nondeceptive dependent relationship of cause and effect.

Although some people claim, "I have realized emptiness," and engage in perversions of actions and their effects, this is a perfect indication that such people do not understand the essential point of emptiness. When we penetrate the key points of understanding the view, our regard for actions and effects will become even greater. This has been stated in numerous valid scriptures and has also been taught by Je Mila[repa] and others.

With respect to the way to dispel the two extremes, in our own uncommon system of tenets, appearances dispel the extreme of existence and emptiness dispels the extreme of nonexistence. Although the sentence "Thus, the extreme of nonexistence [is dispelled] through appearances" dispels the view of nihilism and the sentence "The extreme of existence [is dispelled] through emptiness" dispels the view of permanence, in our own uncommon tradition, it is asserted that appearances dispel the extreme of existence and emptiness dispels the extreme of nonexistence; this is extremely important. Through the dependent relationship of appearances emerging in dependence upon others, the extreme of existence [is dispelled]. Through the causal process of being empty by nature, you develop a definite conviction in the nondeceptive [functioning] of actions and their effects, through which the extreme of nonexistence is [dispelled].

The Measure of Having Developed Superior Seeing

Once we have studied emptiness, we contemplate the meaning of that which has arisen from study. By analyzing that, we gain an understanding of its meaning, which has arisen from contemplation. By repeatedly meditating on that, we develop realizations arisen from meditation. The gentle protector Tsongkhapa the Great stated [in his *Songs of Spiritual Experience*],

Wielding the sharp weapon of the Madhyamaka reasoning
Will completely destroy the view holding extremes.
With vast wisdom examining in this way,
Enhance your knowledge realizing suchness.

As I already explained, you will not be liberated from samsara with mere tranquil abiding. To perceive clearly the true nature of emptiness, you must accomplish a stable tranquil abiding and, from within that state, sustain suchness single-pointedly with an ascertaining consciousness ascertaining that not even an atom exists [inherently] from its own side. [This serves as an opponent to the mistaken view] that all phenomena within samsara and nirvana, such as self, the aggregates, mountains, houses, and so on, are not mere conceptual imputations. This is space-like meditative equipoise.

In the state of subsequent attainment, once again all objects of perception emerge as non–truly existent in dependence upon other [phenomena] and are understood to be the nature of illusions. In dependence upon training in these two excellent yogas, you will induce a factor of stability through the force of analysis through analyzing emptiness. When you attain the perfect bliss of pliancy induced through the [aforementioned analysis], you focus on emptiness and establish the attainment of fully qualified superior seeing conjoined with tranquil abiding. Hereafter, you attain the patience level of the path of preparation.[687]

687. Tib. *'di nas*. "Hereafter" is a bit vague. Generally the initial attainment of the union of tranquil abiding and superior seeing marks the third "great" section of the path of accumulation, which is followed by the path of preparation.

Day Thirty-Five

The foremost great being [Tsongkhapa] stated in his *Destiny Fulfilled*,[688]

> In the beginning I sought much learning . . .

Pabongkha Rinpoche quoted this and other scriptures.

We should seek an unmistaken path as the factor of attainment for attaining the state of enlightenment. Furthermore, we must eliminate doubts through listening to and contemplating the Dharma, and practice in dependence upon a wise and fully qualified spiritual guide. Furthermore, the best [practitioners should study] the five great subjects,[689] and at the very least we should listen to the stages of the path to enlightenment, which are like a key that opens a hundred doors of scripture. However, merely listening is not sufficient; instead Je [Tsongkhapa's *Prayer for the Beginning, Middle, and End*[690]] states,

> Through perfectly analyzing day and night the meaning
> of exactly
> What was heard with the four types of reasoning,
> May I eliminate the doubts with a mind of reasoning
> That comes from a reflection on the objects of contemplation.

688. Tib. *rTogs brjod 'dun legs ma.*

689. The five great subjects are (1) Logic, (2) Madhyamaka, (3) Perfection of Wisdom, (4) Phenomenology, and (5) Vinaya.

690. Tib. *Thog mtha' ma.*

MANJUSHRI

Thus, you should gain a state of certainty arisen from contemplation. This is the way to develop an authentic realization through repeated meditation. Initially while you are engaged in study, you also employ listening to and contemplating whatever Dharma is the object that is to be practiced. If you conduct yourself in this way, you have entered the unmistaken path. If not, you will not have transcended straying from the [correct] path and proceeding down mistaken paths. Therefore, think, "After listening to this excellent system of these stages on the path to enlightenment that is the noble and unmistaken path, I am going to put them into practice."

After giving this brief introduction, Pabongkha Rinpoche covered the outlines and explained the individual distinctions of the two truths in accordance with the Middle-Length Treatise on the Stages of the Path, *after which he gave an explanation of the complete distinction of superior seeing, combined with the oral transmission and interspersed with the essential points. However, the compilation of [the notes from those teachings] was not completed.*

Day Thirty-Six

The teachings of the gentle protector Tsongkhapa the Great [in his *Three Principal Aspects of the Path*] state,

> Thus, the three principal aspects of the path . . .

We should strive to attain an everlasting happiness, for which we should strive to perfectly realize the essential points of the three principal aspects of the path through initially listening to and contemplating the lamrim, through which [we accomplish] renunciation, bodhichitta, and the correct view [of emptiness]. We will attain union[691] in this life through forcefully severing our attachment to this life, through constant application and striving with intense application while abiding in four preferences of the aryas and staying in an isolated place conducive to the Dharma, being content with few desires, and having few desires and things. If [attaining enlightenment] does not happen, having set out on the path, we should at least be free of any regrets at the time of death. Additionally, we should strive to attain the state of enlightenment before too long and without disrupting the succession of leisure and endowments in our future lives.

For the sake of working toward attaining that [state of enlightenment], we should think, "Presently, I have attained a human body with leisure and endowment, I have met the general teachings of the Buddha, and in particular I have met the completely pure and stainless teachings of the

691. Tib. *zung 'jug*. There are two primary types of union: (1) union of the pure illusory body and meaning clear light, which is the fifth of the five stages of the completion stage, and (2) union of body and mind, which is synonymous with enlightenment and is the direct result of the first type of union.

gentle protector Tsongkhapa the Great. I have assembled all the favorable conditions without exception for the practice of Dharma, such as having met a fully qualified spiritual guide. At this time, I am not going to return empty-handed [by wasting my time on] the meaningless things of this life but will instead listen to this excellent commentary on the stages of the path to enlightenment which is the essence of Jamgon Lama [Tsongkhapa's] teachings."

After giving this brief introduction, Pabongkha Rinpoche covered the headings and the actual way to meditate on superior seeing in dependence upon tranquil abiding.

As I have already explained, if we need a teacher when it comes to learning even the [mundane] activities of this life, we cannot possibly learn the practice of Dharma without a teacher. Therefore, from the beginning we absolutely must rely upon a lama to teach us the Dharma. If that lama is also not fully qualified, it is analogous to a blank mold that can make a clay image in the shape of either an enlightened being or a scorpion.[692] If the lama doesn't know how to properly guide students on the complete path, the disciple will not be able to develop any more than a mere portion of the good qualities of the complete path in his [or her] mental continuum. Therefore, it is important that we rely upon a fully qualified lama who is capable of guiding the disciple on the complete path of sutra and tantra.

Next, once you are mindful of his [or her] teachings on the difficulty of obtaining [a life] of leisure and endowment, its great meaning, and death, you should then renounce this life, generate certainty in actions and their effects, and so forth, which constitutes the path of a being of lesser capacity. Next, if you don't have an extremely forceful mind that perceives the suffering nature of the entirety of samsara, how could you possibly have the means of striving for progressively higher states of the Dharma? You would also be expelled from the ranks of those striving for liberation. Renunciation is also the first of the three principal aspects of the path; therefore, sincerely apply yourself to this.

692. This means that a faithful disciple is like a blank mold that can be formed into a scorpion or a buddha, depending on whether or not he or she meets an unqualified teacher or a fully qualified teacher.

Once you have developed the path of the beings of the small and middle scopes in that way, develop an extremely powerful contemplation of renunciation, and on the basis of that train in the three higher trainings. In particular, you must work primarily at the means of [maintaining] pure and faultless moral discipline. Next, train in bodhichitta which is the path of a being of great scope. Even if you develop a mere understanding of the complete path by training in the paths of the three types of beings in that way and amend it with the generation and completion stages of mantra, you will have established special imprints in your mental continuum, which is far superior to perceiving the face of your personal deity, accomplishing many hundreds of millions of retreats, attaining clairvoyance and miraculous powers, or being an expert in the five sciences.[693]

If you are able to establish the mere imprints of the complete path, even if you die before you develop any realizations, through having established the imprints of the complete teachings, you will have the good fortune to develop the complete path in your mental continuum in your next life. If you die without being able to manage even that much, you will be incapable of meeting the complete teachings of the current buddha, and what need is there to mention developing the complete path in your mental continuum? Even if you develop a mere understanding, it will establish the imprints. If you are able to establish the imprints [of the complete path], once you awaken those imprints in your future lives, you will easily develop realizations, just as King Prasenajit developed realizations.[694] [Also,] after five hundred geese listened to the Buddha teach the Dharma, they were born as gods and realized the truth [of emptiness]; moreover, [there is] the historical account of master Sthiramati.[695] Even if you only establish imprints by merely listening to the sound of the Dharma, what need is there to mention [what will happen] through meditation? For that reason, you should strive sincerely to establish special imprints.

Although initially you won't understand the teachings of your lama,

693. Tib. *rig pa'i gnas lnga*. The five sciences are grammar, dialectics, medicine, arts and crafts, and religious philosophy.

694. Previously, through the force of his imprints, King Prasenajit offered a garment to Manjushri and realized emptiness.

695. This refers to the story that a pigeon listened to the *Perfection of Wisdom in a Hundred Thousand Lines* from master Vasubandhu and became Sthiramati in its next life.

once you employ wisdom and method, you must follow the outlines properly so that you are not merely meditating on the emptiness of the ultimate essence. While you are meditating, the best would be if you [recited] *Lama Chöpa* as the preliminary. If that isn't possible, once you recite the lamrim preliminary ritual, spread out the headings for the lamrim and perform a scanning meditation on the entire path. The phrase "scanning meditation"[696] is referred to as "repeatedly scanning the meaning in one's mind." Furthermore, it is best to complete a scanning meditation each day. At the very least you should [perform a scanning meditation] on the entire path every seven days. In addition to that, engage in a scanning meditation of secret mantra according to the generation stage of your personal deity. With respect to the completion stage, do that in the evening in combination with guru yoga.

If you are unable to develop realizations through scanning meditation and mere imprints, don't spend your entire human life on scanning meditation; instead, you should emphasize one section of the headings as a means of developing realizations. It would be excellent to continue on the perceived aspect by practicing it as much as possible until you develop effortless experience, after which it is permissible to employ scanning meditation for the other [topics in the lamrim].

Furthermore, in the beginning it will be difficult to develop [realizations] on proper reliance on your spiritual guide; therefore, by using this as one topic from the beginning and leisure and endowment as one topic from the beginning, you will elicit an experience by applying yourself to these two topics. After you have generated as much of a realization of both of those topics as you can as a preliminary, you should practice until you elicit a sequential experience of each one of the topics that follows. Furthermore, if you don't develop realizations of each of the preceding [topics], you won't penetrate the subsequent [topics].

With respect to easily developing realizations [of a certain topic], this [will happen in] only one day; if it is difficult, [however,] it will take two years, three years, and so on [to develop realizations]. If even that is difficult, continue with great fortitude until you develop realizations. If you develop realizations easily after one day, you do not need to repeat the

696. Tib. *bshar sgom*.

meditation [extensively] but can contemplate it for a short while. When you elicit an experience of proper reliance upon your spiritual guide, with the exception of tranquil abiding and superior seeing, you sequentially elicit an experience from leisure and endowment up to bodhichitta without inserting the two limbs [of tranquil abiding and superior seeing]. Tranquil abiding and superior seeing should not follow a linear sequence.

If you divide each day into three sessions, the first should be a scanning meditation on the complete [path]. In one [session] you should meditate on the stages of the path of the profound [view], and in another you should practice the mental abidings [of tranquil abiding]. This is the practice tradition for an experiential commentary on the lamrim. If you have a little faith in your spiritual guide, train the mind in proper reliance upon your spiritual guide and so forth. For example, a foolish person builds a corral of dust for irrigating water from [the spot] where the water escapes. Afterward he still needs to make something [more substantial], like piling up earth to block it; scanning meditation is similar. We should establish imprints through scanning meditation and elicit experiences through analytical meditation.[697]

If the best person practices in that way, he [or she] applies himself [or herself] to listening to and contemplating [Je Tsongkhapa's] *Great* and *Middle-Length [Treatise(s) on the] Stages of the Path to Enlightenment* in the presence of his [or her] lama. Even the least of persons should apply whatever teachings he hears from his lama, such as the *Swift Path* lamrim, by bringing this into his mental continuum repeatedly. If not, listening to vast numbers [of teachings] and doing very little meditation is said to become the cause of becoming jaded to the Dharma.[698] Becoming jaded to the Dharma is one of the worst things that can happen. It is like the saying,

697. Scanning meditation is a temporary means of establishing imprints, much like building an irrigation system from dust. Analytical meditation is the means of eliciting a substantial experience of the lamrim, much like reconstructing the irrigation system out of rocks and earth.

698. Tib. *chos dred*. This literally means "Dharma demon" and refers to those who listen to and study a great deal of Dharma but don't meditate and thereby become hardened to the Dharma, so that they begin to get sick of hearing about it. Conversely, those who regularly practice and meditate on the lamrim will find constant inspiration from studying and listening. Trijang Rinpoche remarked that he had read Je Tsongkhapa's *Great Treatise on the Stages on the Path to Enlightenment* more than one hundred times, and each time it was like reading the book for the first time.

> Although hardened leather can be softened with oil,
> You cannot soften a butter pouch with butter.
> Although an evil person can be tamed by the Dharma,
> Someone jaded to the Dharma cannot be tamed by the Dharma.

Moreover, although you can be subdued by the stages of the path to enlightenment if you have slipped into being jaded to the Dharma through other teachings, if you become jaded to the lamrim you cannot be subdued by other teachings. The way to not be swayed into becoming jaded to the Dharma is to immediately meditate on whatever you are currently listening to in the presence of your lama and apply it to your practice.

[Also,] developing a slight degree of faith and so forth in your spiritual guide the very moment you listen to your lama is a realization of correct assumption arisen from listening, or [in other words,] through the force of another. Therefore, it is not stable and is subject to change if we abandon it through the reasoning of another who may say, "You are wrong." If we repeatedly meditate on the meaning arisen from listening,[699] [however,] we will develop a stable ascertainment which is superior to that [which arises from mere studying and listening without also meditating on the meaning]. With respect to this [stable ascertainment], it is a valid realization arisen from contemplation, or [in other words,] through one's own power. With respect to the welling forth of realization through repeated meditation, this is the realization arisen from meditation.

The demarcation line of whether or not you are swept away by the "Dharma demon" [of being jaded to the Dharma] is also determined by [gaining experience] arisen from hearing and arisen from contemplation; therefore, everyone should sincerely apply himself [or herself] to practicing in four daily sessions, so as not to fall sway to becoming jaded to the Dharma. Furthermore, engage in scanning meditation, from proper reliance upon your spiritual guide up to the completion stage.

There are three ways of [gaining experience]: (1) penetrating [the meaning] after gaining experience in meditation, (2) doing so with effort, and (3) doing so effortlessly. With respect to the first, although one reflects on things he [or she] doesn't properly understand, when he [or

699. Tib. *thos*. This term encompasses both studying and listening.

she] is meditating and these [thoughts] fade away in his [or her] mind, he [or she] thinks about what he [or she] has learned and develops an understanding of their meaning. With respect to the second, once he ponders over subjects such as impermanence, he develops a vivid experience in meditation, and if he doesn't meditate, he doesn't develop [experiences]. With respect to the third, he develops [experiences] effortlessly, which is analogous to suffering related to the death of one's mother: we don't have to ponder it; instead, we develop a vivid experience.

With respect to the view, during a separate session, according to whatever is convenient, train by combining supplications, accumulation of merit, and purification, through practices such as the guru yoga of Ganden Lha Gyama or the guru yoga of Guru Manjushri. "Striving in that way, the best Dharma practitioner will develop [realizations] in a day, the middling will develop them in a month, and the lesser will develop them in a year." In accordance with this saying, you should strive to be someone who reaches the demarcation line and crosses the threshold where they advance in dependence upon the stages of the path to enlightenment in this life.

That which is called "the complete path of sutra and tantra" is striving [to realize the various subjects,] from proper reliance upon the spiritual guide up to the union of no-more-learning. In striving to attain to the state of union of Vajradhara, one part of the pair that is the cause of union is the pure body that is the illusory body of complete enjoyment, and the other part of the pair is the pure mind that is the exalted wisdom meaning clear light, which is the exalted knower of all aspects. The union of those two is the union of no more learning. For the attainment of that, you must attain the union of learning, [which contains the following two aspects:] (1) you must attain the union of learning which is the pure illusory body accomplished from the extremely subtle mere wind and mind that has a cause of a similar type of entity,[700] and (2) [you must attain] the meaning clear light directly realizing emptiness that comes from actualizing the essence of the primordial mind. To attain that, you must: (1) actualize the primordial mind through the dissolution of all the winds into your heart [channel wheel] exactly the way it occurs at the time of

700. Tib. *dngos kyi rigs 'dra'i rgyu.*

death, whereby you attain the example clear light that realizes emptiness through a generic image, and (2) attain the impure illusory body.

[The illusory body] is distinguished as being pure or impure with respect to the obstructions of the afflictive emotions.[701] To attain that, you must attain isolated mind. To attain that, you must first attain the concentration of vajra speech of isolated speech for the sake of completely loosening the channel knots at the heart. To accomplish that, you must attain vajra recitation. To attain that, you need to attain isolated body. To attain that, you must loosen the channel knots at the navel which are easy to loosen. In that way you must produce a completely qualified practice of the completion stage.

Prior to that, you must attain the four complete purities of a fully qualified generation stage, with all the essential features of bringing the three bodies into the path. If your practice of bringing the three bodies into the path is incomplete, you will not make progress on the generation stage. If you think that meditating on the deity is the generation stage [of highest yoga tantra], that is not correct, since you must also meditate on the deity in the lower classes of tantra, and you would be forced to say that they also have the practice of the generation stage.[702] The generation stage is an uncommon feature of the highest yoga tantra vehicle. In our efforts to accomplish a fully qualified generation-stage practice, we must obtain the authentic four empowerments of highest yoga tantra and properly safeguard the vows and commitments that we promised to keep at the time of the empowerment.

For that, we must first train our minds in the common general path and the precious mind of bodhichitta in particular. If we enter secret mantra without those, we will be a like small child riding an untamed stallion or wild elephant. It would not be appropriate for us to be thrown off and cast into Vajra Hell. Having considered this point, Geshe Dromtonpa said to [Geshe] Potowa,

701. Tib. *nyon sgrib*. The afflictive emotions are also known as the obstructions to liberation.

702. In highest yoga tantra, you generate yourself as the deity through the process known as "bringing death, intermediate state, and rebirth into the path as the truth body, enjoyment body, and emanation body." In the three lower classes of tantra, you do not generate yourself as a deity through utilizing death, intermediate state, and rebirth; therefore, it does not qualify as "generation stage."

> For you to enter the path of mantra in this life
> Is like [riding] an untamed stallion that tries to kick you
> without aim.

If he needed to say something like that to Geshe Potowa, if people like us are not extremely careful, there is more danger than profit. Also, Drom[tonpa] Rinpoche stated,

> Those who are disingenuous about the pratimoksha merely engage in worldly deeds. Bodhisattvas who engage in worldly deeds are not [necessarily] disingenuous; yet for the most part they are disingenuous. Mantra is not disingenuous, and mere actions are not worldly.

And,

> The path of the perfections is easier and swifter than secret mantra.[703] Secret mantra is like a wheel of sharp weapons. It is like a venomous snake that has entered your pant leg.

Manjushri said to Je Rinpoche [Tsongkhapa],

> In addition to possessing the three essential points of the vehicle of defining characteristics,[704] meditate on the short path of the mantra path. With respect to mantra without the three essential features, the path of the vehicle of defining characteristics becomes greatly weakened. You will never attain enlightenment that way. Enlightenment is attained through the path of the vehicle of defining characteristics.

703. Many Kadampas were opposed to the practice of tantra due to Dromtonpa's influence. Dromtonpa repeatedly requested Atisha not to teach tantra due to the misuse of tantra in Tibet prior to Atisha's arrival, and he discouraged his own disciples from practicing tantra, which is reflected in these statements. For various views on this point, see Atisha and Dromtonpa, attrib., *The Book of Kadam*, 6.

704. Tib. *mtshan nyid theg pa*. The vehicle of defining characteristics is synonymous with the sutra vehicle.

With respect to the "three essential features," these are renunciation, bodhichitta, and the correct view of emptiness. Therefore, strive to properly train your mind in the common path as a preliminary [to the practice of mantra]. To strive at training in the common path as a preliminary [to tantric practice], you should develop bodhichitta in your mental continuum that strives for complete enlightenment for the welfare of all living beings. To develop that, you must develop superior intention that bears the responsibility for others' welfare. To develop that, you must develop compassion that is unable to bear living beings being tormented by suffering. To develop that, you must develop renunciation that sees that all of samsara is utterly meaningless during [the section of the lamrim dealing with the path of] a being of middle scope. To develop that, you must develop aversion for the suffering of the three lower realms in dependence upon the path of a being of small scope. To produce that, you must develop a realization of death and impermanence in your mental continuum. To develop that in your mental continuum, you must recall the great value of leisure and endowment and the difficulty of obtaining them.

In that way, strive to understand the entire path. Having searched for a fully qualified spiritual guide as the root of the path, contemplate the benefits of relying upon him [or her] and the faults of nonreliance; through this, you will properly understand the proper way to rely upon him in thought and the proper way to rely upon him in deed, and then [actually] rely upon him properly in thought and deed. Listen to and contemplate his instructions on the complete path. If you wish to attain the exalted state of Vajradhara, begin by training in the common path from the great value and difficulty of obtaining leisure and endowment, and train in stages by utilizing each of the previous [topics] to induce each of the following [topics], up to bodhichitta. Then, perfectly obtain the four empowerments into any suitable mandala of the great highest yoga tantra. In addition to safeguarding your vows and commitments taken at that time [of the empowerment] as you would your own eyes, train in the generation stage. If you elicit an experience of the coarse generation stage, it is permissible to enter the completion stage.

Next, apply yourself to the meditations on isolated body, isolated speech, and isolated mind. During isolated mind, you actualize the very subtle wind and mind. With the impure illusory body, you substitute the three countless great eons required to accumulate merit in the perfection vehicle.[705] With extremely subtle primordial mind, you directly realize emptiness as meaning clear light, the continuity of which becomes the truth-body mind of a conqueror. With the wind that is the mount for meaning clear light acting as the substantial cause, you attain the pure illusory body which has an uninterrupted continuity of a similar type and transforms into the form body of a conqueror.[706] By augmenting method and wisdom in that way, you attain the state of union of no more learning.

Striving in that way is analogous to the necessity of having a stable foundation for constructing a king's palace. If we sincerely strive in stages, as I have already explained, [and] if we stabilize each of the lower paths, it will not take too long to attain the state of the union of Vajradhara, which is actually quite close at hand and [a potential] that you already possess; therefore, you should strive with everything you have.

How to Train in the Vajrayana

The gentle protector Tsongkhapa the Great stated [in his *Foundation of All Good Qualities*],

> Having become a suitable vessel by training my mind in the common path,
> Grant your blessings that I may easily enter the
> Sacred gateway of the fortunate beings,
> The Vajrayana that is the pinnacle of all vehicles.

Having trained our minds in the paths of the three types of beings, we should develop uncontrived renunciation, bodhichitta, and the correct

705. In other words, once you attain the impure illusory body, you can emanate thousands upon thousands of bodies that can make offerings to the buddhas, receive teachings, and work for the welfare of living beings, thereby accumulating in a very short period of time the merit required to become enlightened, which would take three countless eons to accumulate in the sutra path.
706. Simply put, the pure illusory body is similar to the form body of a buddha, and without needing to cease, it directly transforms into the enjoyment body of a buddha, which in turn emanates the emanation body, thereby being directly responsible for both the form bodies of a buddha.

view in our mental continuum. At the very least we should have attained certainty in those three, or if we develop just the beginnings of an experience, this [counts] as becoming a suitable vessel through training in the common path. Therefore, at that point we should enter the Vajrayana. If we haven't trained in the common path, we are not suitable vessels; therefore, we are not fit to enter secret mantra. If we don't have renunciation, there is no way we can develop bodhichitta. If we don't have bodhichitta, although we may work at meditation and recitation in a consummate practice of secret mantra, it will not become a Mahayana Dharma. If we don't have the view of emptiness, we don't have more than half of the path of mantra; therefore, this is like loading one side of a wild yak and letting it loose or like the lack of benefit that comes from not having more than half of something such as furnishings in a monk's room.

Therefore, with respect to the three principal aspects of the path, they are like the life tree of the paths of both sutra and tantra; therefore, all three are indispensable. There are common and uncommon types of bodhisattva conduct. The common is the practice of the six transcendent perfections, and the uncommon is entering the path of secret mantra and training in the paths of the generation and completion stages. In this respect, if we attain stability in the common religious disciplines, although from our own side we could bear remaining in the lowest hell for a hundred eons for the welfare of each living being, from the perspective of living beings we find it unbearable to have to wait even one instant while they experience suffering. Instead, we enter the Vajrayana out of our bodhichitta motivation to attain enlightenment extremely quickly for the welfare of living beings, which is our reason for entering [the Vajrayana].

In general, the occurrence of the Buddha's teachings in this world is difficult. Even among that, the occurrence of the secret mantra teachings is extremely difficult in this world. [Lama Tsongkhapa's] *Destiny Fulfilled* states:

> There are two types of vehicle for progressing to complete
> enlightenment:
> The profound Vajrayana and the perfection vehicle.
> Secret mantra is said to be vastly superior

To the perfection vehicle;
This is renowned everywhere, like the sun and moon.

While accepting these words to be true,
There are those who accept the responsibility of
Being scholars; they do not strive to find out why
By asking, "Just what is the profound vehicle?"

If even such people are supposed to be learned,
Then where are the people with dull faculties?
How amazing that anyone would not cherish such
An unsurpassed path that is so difficult to meet.

For that very purpose, I have trained for a long time in many ways
To enter the Vajrayana, which is even rarer than the buddhas
And the supreme vehicle of the conquerors,
And which is a profound treasury of the two attainments.

We should definitely enter the quick path of Vajrayana now that we have met the teachings of secret mantra that have appeared in this world this one time. For [the Vajrayana], there are four classes of tantra: (1) action tantra, (2) performance tantra, (3) yoga tantra, and (4) highest yoga tantra. Of these, although in the first three there are methods for becoming enlightened in one life by attaining the ability to live for about a thousand years, they do not have a means of becoming enlightened in one short life in this degenerate age. In the ultimate class of tantra, the highest yoga tantra vehicle, there are methods for becoming enlightened in one short life in this degenerate age.

For that [class of highest yoga tantra], in general there are many personal deities; however, by relying upon the glorious Guhyasamaja, which is the king of all father tantras, you will attain the illusory body, and by relying upon glorious Chakrasamvara, which is the king of all mother tantras, you will attain the clear light. You must train in these two, which primarily reveal [the means of attaining the illusory body and the clear light]. In the uncommon tradition of Je [Tsongkhapa], in addition to the two personal deities of Guhyasamaja and Heruka, we practice glorious

Vajrabhairava, who is vastly superior to other personal deities with respect to pacifying obstacles to practicing a path such as [Heruka and Guhyasamaja], through the five special features of a supreme deity.[707] We should practice these three inseparably. If we are able to do that, it will not be difficult to attain enlightenment; therefore, we should definitely rely upon these three deities. We should enter the gateway of highest yoga tantra in dependence upon them. For that, once we receive the four

707. In Ngulchu Dharmabhadra's thirteen deity commentary, translated in his *Roar of Thunder*, 25–27, he states, "Furthermore, this supreme deity has five great unique qualities, not possessed by other deities, that were taught directly to the Foremost Great Being [Tsongkhapa] by Manjushri himself:

> **The first unique quality:** Furthermore the modern era is a time when the power of the five degenerations are on the increase, the Dharma practice of living beings is plagued with adverse conditions, and favorable conditions are at a minimum. Therefore, if you don't have a deity such as this with incomparable power and strength to overcome external and internal obstacles, you won't be able to complete the Dharma practice you began, and for that reason we absolutely must rely upon this deity.
>
> **The second unique quality:** He also holds the hand implements of intestines and a brazier that symbolize that he contains the explanations from Guhyasamaja of the father tantras for the path of the illusory body and clear light.
>
> **The third unique quality:** He also has the hand implement of a *katvanga*, which exists only in the mother tantra, and although it is not found in the father tantra, in this practice there is a katvanga hand implement. This reveals that [the practice of Yamantaka] contains the explanations of the mother tantra of Hevajra and Chakrasamvara for blazing [the inner fire], dripping [the bodhichitta], and so forth as the paths of bliss and emptiness.
>
> **The fourth unique quality:** One of Yamantaka's own unique features is that he holds the hand implement of a brazier; therefore, the wisdom of the practitioner increases much more than through other [practices]. The right hand is the method factor, and [Yamantaka] holds his threatening mudra in the sky as if he were saying, "I have the entire pith instructions of father tantra!" and says to the transcendent beings, "Swiftly bestow attainments on practitioners, and if you don't, I will threaten you," which symbolizes that attainments are much swifter [with Yamantaka practice] than with other [deities]. The left hand is the factor of wisdom, and with the threatening mudra facing downward, it is as if he were saying, "I have the complete pith instructions of mother tantra!" and says to the worldly beings, "Don't create obstacles for my practitioners, and if you do, I will threaten you," which symbolizes that the [practitioner] will be unharmed by obstacles. Holding the hand symbol of a person impaled by a spear reveals that regardless of whether you have engaged in the most nonvirtuous activities such as the ten nonvirtues, or the five actions of immediate retribution, and so forth, if you practice this path with great force, you will attain enlightenment.
>
> **The fifth unique quality:** As already explained, this practice simultaneously accomplishes the sole father of the conquerors, Manjushri—which is something not possessed by red and black [Yamantakas]."

complete empowerments from a fully qualified vajra master, even if we don't practice the two stages, if we perfectly safeguard our commitments that we promised during the time of the empowerment, those with the highest capacity will attain the state of Vajradhara without having to wait more than seven lives, and even those who are least fortunate will not take longer than sixteen lives.

If we don't properly safeguard our commitments, we will go to Vajra Hell. Despite whatever other great negativities we have engaged in, they cannot cause us to take rebirth in Vajra Hell, yet if we don't safeguard our commitments [we promised to keep] upon receiving a great empowerment of highest yoga mantra, there will be no other place for us to go. The principal commitments [of highest yoga tantra] are root downfalls. Therefore, once we can recognize the root downfalls, gross downfalls, and so forth, we should protect against them. If we strive sincerely in the yogas of the two stages, those of the highest capacity will become enlightened in this life, and even those of the least capacity will become enlightened in the intermediate state. In particular, according to the Hearing Lineage of Jamgon Tsongkhapa the Great, in addition to obtaining a proper commentary on the two stages, once we request the pure four empowerments as the gateway of mantra, we should properly safeguard the vows and commitments that we promised to keep during the empowerment.

If you are capable of striving to obtain a proper commentary on the two stages and the stages of the path common to sutra and tantra, and of practicing with enthusiastic perseverance and engaging in hardships like Je Mila[repa] and Gyalwa Götsangpa, and [if you also] practice Guhyasamaja, Heruka, and Yamantaka inseparably, then it will not take longer than a mere twelve human years to attain enlightenment. If you are extremely effective, you will be able to [become enlightened] even much more quickly than that—in fact, you will definitely be able to attain the state of the union of Vajradhara in just three years and three phases of the moon.[708] It was not necessary for the previous mahasiddhas of the Geden [that is, Gelug Tradition] to undergo such hardships [as Milarepa and others], and instead countless beings actualized with extreme expediency

708. Tib. *lo gsum phyogs gsum*. For more information, see note 539 above and Jamgon Kongtrul, *Jamgon Kongtrul's Retreat Manual*, trans. Ngawang Zangpo (Hugh Leslie Thomson) (Ithaca, NY: Snow Lion, 1994).

the state of union in just a few short years, like a soaring garuda. The oral instructions of the Ganden Hearing Lineage are unimaginably profound, which we would be able to understand by directly studying the numerous valid biographies of the [previous siddhas of the Geden tradition].

Even the lamrim scriptures teach numerous important oral instructions, complete with the important pith instructions about how to train in mantra, as well as the general points of the path on up; therefore, you should definitely study them. Moving upward from there, you should perfectly receive a step-by-step commentary[709] on the stages of the path to enlightenment in the practice tradition of your lama. Therefore, this is like a young and intelligent person at one of the higher seats of learning undertaking study and contemplation of the great texts. Although you may be unable to manage something like that, you should strive at studying, contemplating, and meditating, in accordance with your mental capacity, on such [works] as the *Great* and *Middle-Length [Treatises on the] Stages of the Path to Enlightenment*, the *Swift Path*, and so forth.

In addition to pure view and conduct of monastic discipline, develop the experiences and realizations of the stages of the path that you have not yet developed, and increase those that you have developed. Strive to abandon negativity and practice virtue to the best of your ability, and extract each unique essence of this life of leisure and so forth, as I have already repeatedly explained. There are numerous extremely cherished general and specific trainings that are all necessary for establishing a practice. We should dedicate the roots of virtue from listening to and teaching the Dharma. With great happiness I have fully given you all the teachings with great clarity and in extensive detail.

709. Tib. *khrid rim*. This is a type of commentary where you receive the instructions on a small section at a time while you practice what you have received. Once you have gained sufficient experience, you move on to the next subject.

Colophon

The meditative equipoise in the sphere of great bliss of the buddhas'
Abandonment and realization emerges at this time in the guise of a spiritual guide,
Appearing as a perfect transformation of a protector increasing the essence of the teachings;
Again and again I recall the kindness of the incomparable guru.

Your courageous incomparable name is like a water lily
With a thousand glorious and noble bangles;
Gautama, the supreme incomparable guide during the time of five degenerations,
Only you can express what you perceive in the three times.

The wish-fulfilling jewels of the Conqueror's valid teaching on sutra and tantra [are
Unlike] the impure teaching of false teachers that seems sufficient from a distance,
While the three types of supreme training—namely, view, meditation, and action—
Are praised by numerous scholars who proclaim, "This is the perfectly educated Geden tradition."

All 84,000 heaps of Dharma are explained as the
Definitive means for a single person to attain enlightenment through
The Abode of Nectar revealing how to practice them without contradiction,
And as a path with the unique quality of being easy to practice.

The producer of all protection, the mother of the lord Vajradhatu Ishvari,
In a dance of passion reveals the Hearing Lineage of the Gentle Protector
Whose mere guidance is the unrivaled medicine that restores the
Feeble vital life force of explanation and practice.

Whatever you say is in accordance with the disposition and capacity
of the three types of beings,
A composition in the clear blue sky with lightning clouds that cleanses
forgetfulness
In the wondrous form of the mother. The sprouting incomparable
clouds are diffused
To the conscious beings on earth as delightful saffron.

These lecture notes on the stages of the path to enlightenment are entitled *Essence of the Vast and Profound*. While Lama Dorje Chang the Great[710] was imparting this ripening commentary, it was as though the second conqueror Jamgon [Tsongkhapa] had once again appeared, and there is no way I could express its benefit. It was arranged in accordance with the *Great Treatise* in general, in such a way that the difficult points were easy to understand, set forth as a system for putting the meaning of the scriptures into practice, and so forth.

[Pabongkha Rinpoche] bestowed the complete stages of the path in conjunction with oral instructions as an explicit commentary of experience of the *Swift Path*, with the sole intention of gaining an intense experience to tame the minds of disciples such as I, with little familiarity with textual tradition, whose innate and learned knowledge is like a moon-offering of a sky lotus.[711] Therefore, I was unable to write extensively most of what was taught about the great scriptures and even those teachings concerning the explicit commentary. Nevertheless, for the sake of those of lesser intelligence similar to my own, I was able to collect some scattered notes, and included only the things I was sure that the lama taught without adding any fabrications of my own.

To sustain the uninterrupted great kindness that the Pervasive Lord Vajradhara Pabongkha had for his followers, including the common people, the monk from Den Chökor Monastery, Losang Dorje, compiled the notes from the teachings once again in the Iron Tiger Year (1950). Previ-

710. This is a term often used by particularly faithful disciples as an epithet for their guru. It means "Guru Vajradhara" and reveals their pure perception of their guru as being inseparable from Vajradhara.

711. This means that it is like something nonexistent.

ously, I had received a commentary on the other paths from the Foremost Being; therefore, I added a few bits of notes that I had collected from previous commentaries. In this day and age, disciples don't request extensive teachings on the lamrim as they used to, and instead they rush for tantric teachings and for the most part request major empowerments. Although they want to know how to train in mantra, very few request extensive teachings.

Many of the teachings [by Pabongkha] merely begin with the opening verse of scriptural quotations because the students are expected to be familiar with the teachings. However, I took the liberty of filling in the rest of the quotations. Although I assume that it is all correct, due to my inferior intelligence I request the wise to be patient with whatever mistakes I have made. May whatever merit I have attained through my excellent endeavor cause the stainless essence of the teachings to spread and increase in every direction in all times and remain for a very long time.

OM SVATI.

These teachings were given by Pervasive Lord Pabongkha Dorje Chang Palsangpo, who is kinder to us even than the Buddha. These teachings were compiled during a profound commentary based on Je [Tsongkhapa's] *Middle-Length Treatise on the Stages of the Path*. Losang Dorje compiled the notes in the presence of Lama Dorje Chang the Great, by serving and attending him for a long time as his scribe. These instructions of the vast and profound grow rich in the mind; I arranged the notes from Losang Dorje-la's [notes] and entitled the composition *The Essence of the Vast and Profound*. Having attained indestructible faith through my understanding of the long-standing tradition of Jamgon Lama [Tsongkhapa], I venerate the guru who is the embodiment of the buddhas with the crown of my head at the soles of your feet. I received your blessing from serving you with the three ways of pleasing, just as in the biography of Jayulwa Shönu Ö. The Honorable Katsab Shankha Gyurmé Sonam Tobgyé Gyechog, who naturally possesses faith in and superior intention toward the spiritual guide and the precious teachings—which are unrivaled in all directions—sponsored the printing of this text with the most wondrous armor of patience and fortitude and without any miserliness;

therefore, we dedicate the merit of his virtuous practice. This text was arranged and composed by the special assistant tutor [to His Holiness the Fourteenth Dalai Lama], the tulku Ganden Trijang [Rinpoche].

May virtue increase.

Outline of the Text

The outline of this text is presented exactly as it appears in the Tibetan text— with the exception of the words and headings in square brackets, which have been supplied for continuity and the reader's convenience. *Although this does not match Western academic standards, this style is intended to be memorized and used as a teaching and meditation aid. Once the outline is memorized, a practitioner can recall the entire structure of the lamrim without the need of a text. Also, when teaching, you will be able to maintain the integrity of the internal structure of the commentary without the need for a text.*

[Trijang Rinpoche's Opening Verses of Praise]

[Trijang Rinpoche's Introduction]

The Commentary on the Stages of the Path to Enlightenment has four sections:

1. The Greatness of the Author to Show the Authentic Source of the Dharma
2. The Greatness of the Dharma to Generate Faith in the Instructions
3. How to Listen to and Explain the Dharma Endowed with Those Two Greatnesses
4. How to Sequentially Guide the Disciple with the Actual Instructions

The Greatness of the Author to Show the Authentic Source of the Dharma

The Life of Atisha has three sections:

1. How He Took Rebirth in an Excellent Lineage
2. How He Practiced and Attained Good Qualities of Realization through Proper Practice
3. How He Worked on Behalf of the Teachings

How He Worked on Behalf of the Teachings has two sections:

1. His Activities in India
2. His Activities in Tibet

The Greatness of the Dharma

[The Three Unique Features has three sections:]

1. [The First Unique Feature:] It Embodies the Essential Points of Both the Sutras and Tantras
2. [The Second Unique Feature:] The Stages Are Primarily Composed to Subdue the Mind, Therefore, They Are Easy to Put into Practice
3. [The Third Unique Feature:] It Is Adorned with the Instructions of the Two Gurus Skilled in the Tradition of the Two Great Trailblazers, Therefore, It Is Superior to Other Traditions

[The Four Greatnesses has four sections:]

1. The Greatness That You Will Come to Realize That All the Teachings Are Not Contradictory
2. The Greatness of All the Scriptures Appearing as Personal Instructions
3. The Greatness of Easily Discovering the Ultimate Intention of the Conqueror
4. The Greatness of Stopping the Great Misdeed

How to Listen to and Explain the Dharma Endowed with Those Two Greatnesses has three sections:

1. How to Listen to the Dharma

2. How to Teach the Dharma
3. How to Conduct Their Common Ending

How to Listen to the Dharma has three sections:

1. Contemplating the Benefits of Listening to the Dharma
2. Developing Reverence for the Dharma and the Dharma Teacher
3. The Actual Way to Listen to the Dharma

The Actual Way to Listen to the Dharma has two sections:

1. Abandoning the Unfavorable Condition of the Three Faults of a Vessel
2. Cultivating the Six Recognitions

Relying upon the Six Recognitions as Favorable Conditions has six sections:

1. Establishing the Recognition That You Are a Sick Person
2. Establishing the Recognition That the Dharma Teacher Is Like a Doctor
3. Establishing the Recognition That the Dharma Teachings Are Medicine
4. Establishing the Recognition That Persistent Practice Will Cure the Illness
5. Establishing the Recognition That the Tathagata Was a Holy Being
6. Establishing the Recognition That the Dharma May Remain for a Long Time

How to Teach the Dharma has four sections:

1. Contemplating the Benefits of Teaching the Dharma
2. Cultivating Respect for the Dharma and Its Teacher
3. An Explanation of What Type of Thought and Behavior You Should Have [when Explaining the Dharma]
4. Making a Distinction between Who Should and Should Not Be Taught

An Explanation of What Type of Thought and Behavior You Should Have [when Explaining the Dharma] has two sections:

1. What Type of Thoughts You Should Have
2. What Type of Behavior You Should Have

[How to Conduct Their Common Ending]

How to Sequentially Guide the Disciple with the Actual Instructions has two sections:

1. A Slightly Elaborate Explanation for the Sake of Attaining Certainty
2. The Characteristics of the Relying Disciple

How the [Disciple] Properly Relies upon Him has two sections:

1. How to Rely through Thought
2. How to Rely through Action

How to Rely through Thought has two sections:

1. How to Apply It to the Root of Faith
2. Generating Devotion by Recalling His Kindness

How to Rely [upon Your Guru] through Action

A Concise Way of Practicing [the Preliminary Rituals] during the Meditation Session

Offering the Seven Limbs Together with the Mandala has seven parts:

1. The Limb of Prostration
2. The Limb of Offering
3. The Limb of Confession
4. The Limb of Rejoicing
5. The Limb of Requesting Them to Turn the Wheel of Dharma
6. The Limb of Making Supplications Not to Pass into Nirvana
7. The Limb of Dedication

Accomplishing a Definitive Integration between Your Mind and the Supplication

The Actual Practice has two sections:

1. How to Carry Out [the Meditation] in General
2. How to Carry Them Out at this Point [in Particular]

How to Carry Out [the Meditation] in General has three sections:

1. Identifying Meditation
2. The Faults of Improper Meditation
3. How to Carry Out Proper Meditation

Relying upon the Spiritual Guide has four sections:

1. The Benefits of Reliance [upon the Spiritual Guide]
2. The Faults of Not Relying and the Faults of Improper Reliance
3. How to Rely in Thought
4. How to Rely in Action

The Benefits of Relying Properly upon the Spiritual Guide has eight sections:

1. You Will Come Closer to the State of Enlightenment
2. You Will Delight the Conquerors
3. You Will Not Be Harmed by Demons and Bad Companions
4. All Your Afflictive Emotions and Unwholesome Behavior Will Naturally Cease
5. All Your Realizations of the Grounds and Paths Will Continuously Increase
6. You Will Not Be Deprived of Spiritual Guides in All Your Lives
7. You Will Not Fall into the Lower Realms
8. You Will Accomplish All Temporary and Ultimate Aims

You Will Come Closer to the State of Enlightenment has two sections:

1. By Practicing the Instructions Taught to You by Your Guru, You Will Come Closer to the State of Enlightenment
2. By Worshiping and Respectfully Honoring Your Guru, You Will Come Closer to the State of Enlightenment

The Faults of Not Relying upon Your Spiritual Guide [has eight sections:]

1. If You Disparage Your Guru, You Criticize All the Buddhas
2. If You Generate an Angry Mind toward Your Guru, You Destroy the Roots of Virtue Equal in Number to the Instances of That [Anger] and Will Be Reborn in Hell for [That Number of] Eons
3. You Will Not Accomplish Supreme [Attainments] despite Your Reliance on Mantra
4. Although You May Apply Yourself to the Meaning of Tantra, It Will Be as though You Are Accomplishing the Hells
5. You Will Not Develop Your Previous Good Qualities of the Grounds and Paths or Develop New Ones, and Those You Have Developed Will Deteriorate
6. In This Life You Will Be Tormented by Undesirable Things such as Illness
7. In Your Next Life You Will Wander Endlessly in the Lower Realms
8. You Will Be Deprived of Spiritual Guides in All Lives

The Actual Way to Rely in Thought and Action has two sections:

1. How to Rely in Thought, or Training in Faith as the Root
2. The Way of Recalling His Kindness

How to Rely in Thought, or Training in Faith as the Root [has three sections:]

1. The Reason You Must Perceive Your Guru as a Buddha
2. The Reason You Are Able to Perceive Your Guru as a Buddha
3. How to Regard Your Guru as a Buddha

How to Regard Your Guru as a Buddha has four sections:

1. Vajradhara Said That the Guru Is a Buddha
2. The Guru Performs the Enlightened Actions of All the Buddhas
3. In These Degenerate Times, Buddhas Continue to Work for the Welfare of Living Beings
4. Our Perceptions Are Unreliable

The Way of Recalling His Kindness has four sections:

1. The Guru Is Kinder than the Buddhas
2. His Kindness in Teaching Us Dharma
3. His Kindness in Blessing Our Mental Continuum
4. His Kindness in Assembling Disciples through Material Gifts

The Guru Is Kinder than the Buddhas has two sections:

1. He Is Kinder than All the Buddhas in General
2. He Is Kinder than Buddha Shakyamuni in Particular

[Pleasing Him through Action]

[A Repeated Explanation and a Concise Teaching on How to Sustain That According to the Previous Explanation]

The Session Breaks

You Should Understand the Appropriate Diet

How to Train the Mind once You Have Relied [upon the Spiritual Guide] has two sections:

1. Encouragement for the Sake of Extracting the Essence of This Human Existence
2. How to Extract Such Essence

Encouragement for the Sake of Extracting the Essence of This Human Existence has three sections:

1. Identifying Leisure and Endowment
2. Contemplating Their Great Value from a Temporary Perspective and Contemplating Their Great Value from an Ultimate Perspective
3. Contemplating the Great Difficulty in Obtaining [a Life of Leisure and Endowment]

Contemplating Their Great Value from a Temporary Perspective and Contemplating Their Great Value from an Ultimate Perspective has two sections:

1. Their Great Value from an Ultimate Perspective
2. Contemplating the Great Difficulty in Obtaining [a Life of Leisure and Endowment]

Contemplating the Great Difficulty in Obtaining [a Life of Leisure and Endowment] has three sections:

1. The Great Difficulty in Obtaining It by Way of Its Cause
2. The Great Difficulty in Obtaining It by Way of Its Nature or Result
3. The Great Difficulty in Obtaining It by Way of Example, Expanded with the Oral Instructions of the Gurus

How to Extract Its Essence has two sections:

1. Developing Certainty in the General Presentation of the Path
2. The Actual Means of Extracting Its Essence of Leisure and Endowment

[Developing Certainty in the General Presentation of the Path]

The Reason Beings Are Guided through the Stages has two sections:

1. The Actual Reason
2. The Need to Lead through the Stages in That Way

The Actual Means of Extracting Its Essence of Leisure and Endowment has three sections:

1. Training the Mind in the Path Common to a Person of Lesser Capacity
2. Training the Mind in the Path Common to a Person of Middling Capacity
3. Training the Mind in the Path Common to a Person of Great Capacity

Training the Mind in the Path Common to a Person of Lesser Capacity has three sections:

1. The Actual Training of the Mind of a Person of Lesser Capacity
2. The Measure of Having Generated such an Intention
3. Dispelling Misconceptions about That Intention

The Actual Training of the Mind of a Person of Lesser Capacity has two sections:

1. Developing a Mind Striving for Future Lives in the World
2. Revealing the Means of Attaining Happiness in Future Lives in the World

Developing a Mind Striving for Future Lives in the World has two sections:

1. Being Mindful of Death and That You Will Not Remain Long in This World
2. Contemplating How the Beings in the Two Types of Migrations Will Have Happiness and Suffering in Their Future Lives in the World

Being Mindful of Death and That You Will Not Remain Long in This World has four sections:

1. The Faults of Not Cultivating Mindfulness of Death
2. The Benefits of Cultivating Mindfulness of Death
3. How to Cultivate Mindfulness of Death
4. The Way to Meditate on Mindfulness of Death

How to Cultivate Mindfulness of Death has three sections:

1. [The First Root:] Contemplating That Death Is Definite
2. [The Second Root:] Contemplating That the Time of Death Is Uncertain
3. [The Third Root:] Contemplating That, at the Time of Death, Nothing other than Our Practice of Dharma Will Be of Any Benefit

The First Root: Contemplating That Death Is Definite has three reasons:

1. The Contemplation That the Lord of Death Is Definitely Coming and That There Are No Circumstances That Can Turn Him Away
2. Our Lifespan Cannot Be Extended and Is Constantly Decreasing
3. Even While You Are Alive, There Is No Time to Practice Dharma

The Second Root: Contemplating That the Time of Death Is Uncertain has three sections:

1. Contemplating That in General the Lifespan in This World System Is Uncertain
2. Contemplating That the Time of Death Is Uncertain Because There Are Many Causes of Death and Few Causes of Life
3. Contemplating That the Time of Death is Uncertain Because Our Bodies Are Extremely Fragile

The Third Root: Contemplating That at the Time of Death Nothing other than Our Practice of Dharma Will Be of Any Benefit has three reasons:

1. Our Wealth and Enjoyments Are of No Benefit
2. Our Friends and Loved Ones Are of No Benefit
3. Even Our Body Will Be of No Benefit

Contemplating How the Beings in the Two Types of Migrations Will Have Happiness and Suffering in Their Future Lives in the World

Contemplating the Suffering of the Lower Realms has three sections:

1. Contemplating the Suffering of the Hells
2. Contemplating the Suffering of Animals
3. Contemplating the Suffering of Hungry Ghosts

The Suffering of the Hells has four sections:

1. Contemplating the Suffering of the Great Hells
2. Contemplating the Suffering of the Neighboring Hells
3. Contemplating the Suffering of the Cold Hells
4. Contemplating the Suffering of the Occasional Hells

Contemplating the Suffering of the Animals

Contemplating the Suffering of the Hungry Ghosts [has three sections:]

1. Those with External Obstructions to Obtaining Food and Drink
2. Those with Internal Obstructions to Obtaining Food and Drink
3. Those with Obstructions to Food and Drink Itself

Relying upon the Methods for Attaining Happiness in Our Next Life has two sections:

1. Training in Refuge as the Sublime Door for Entering the Teachings
2. Generating Faith and Confidence in Actions and Their Effects as the Root of Happiness and Excellence

Training in Refuge as the Sublime Door for Entering the Teachings has five sections:

1. The Causes That Constitute Your Reason for Going for Refuge
2. The Objects You Rely upon When Going for Refuge
3. The Way of Determining You Have Gone for Refuge Properly
4. The Benefits of Going for Refuge
5. The Precepts to Follow Once You Have Gone for Refuge

The Causes That Constitute Your Reason for Going for Refuge has two sections:

1. Identifying the Objects of Refuge
2. The Reason They Are Suitable Objects of Refuge

The Way of Determining You Have Gone for Refuge Properly has four sections:

1. Going for Refuge by Knowing Their Good Qualities
2. Going for Refuge by Knowing Their Distinctions
3. Going for Refuge through Commitment
4. Going for Refuge by Not Proclaiming [Faith] in Another

[Going for Refuge by] Knowing Their Good Qualities has three sections:
1. The Good Qualities of Buddha
2. The Good Qualities of the Dharma
3. The Good Qualities of the Sangha

The Good Qualities of the Buddha has four sections:
1. The Good Qualities of His Body
2. The Good Qualities of His Speech
3. The Good Qualities of His Mind
4. The Good Qualities of His Enlightened Actions

Going for Refuge by Knowing Their Distinctions

Going for Refuge through Commitment

Going for Refuge by Not Proclaiming [Faith] in Another

The Benefits of Going for Refuge has eight sections:
1. You Become a Buddhist
2. Going for Refuge Functions as the Foundation for All Vows
3. You Exhaust Your Previously Accumulated Karmic Obscurations
4. You Accumulate a Vast Amount of Merit
5. You Will Not Receive Harm from Humans or Nonhumans
6. You Will Not Fall into the Lower Realms
7. You Will Accomplish All Your Wishes
8. You Will Quickly Attain Enlightenment

The Stages of Precepts Once You Have Gone for Refuge has two sections:
1. The Individual Precepts
2. The Shared Precepts

The Individual Precepts has two sections:
1. Prohibitive Precepts
2. Prescribed Precepts

The Shared Precepts

Developing Conviction and Faith in the Actions and Their Effects as the Root of All Well-Being and Happiness

Actions and Their Effects has three sections:

1. Contemplating Actions and Their Effects in General
2. Contemplating the Specifics of Actions and Their Effects
3. The Way to Practice Engagement and Avoidance through Those Contemplations

Contemplating Actions and Their Effects in General has two sections:

1. The Actual Contemplation in General
2. Contemplating Their Individual Distinctions

The Actual Contemplation in General has four sections:

1. The Way in Which Karma Is Definite
2. Karma Increases Greatly
3. You Can't Meet with [the Results of] a Karmic Action That You Did Not Create
4. A Karmic Action Can Never Be Lost

Contemplating Their Individual Distinctions has two sections:

1. The Principal Teachings on the Ten Paths of Actions
2. Coming to a Definitive Conclusion about Actions and Their Effects

The Distinction in Weight has two sections

1. The Heaviness of the Ten Paths of Actions
2. A Concise Teaching on the Criteria for Powerful Actions

A Teaching on the Effects of Those [Actions] has three sections:

1. The Ripened Result
2. The Result Similar to the Cause
3. The Environmental Effect

The Result Similar to the Cause has two sections:

1. The Experience Similar to the Cause
2. The Effect Similar to the Cause

[The Environmental Effect]

Contemplating Virtuous Cause and Effect has two sections:

1. Virtuous Actions
2. Their Results

Their Results has three sections:

1. The Ripened Result
2. The Result Similar to the Cause
3. The Environmental Effect

The Result Similar to the Cause has two sections:

1. The Experience Similar to the Cause
2. The Tendencies Similar to the Cause

[The Environmental Effect]

A Presentation of Other Classifications of Karma has two sections:

1. The Distinction between Projecting and Completing Karma
2. Karma Whose Result You Will Definitely or Only Possibly Experience

Contemplating the Specifics of Actions and Their Effects has two sections:

1. The Good Qualities and Function of Karmic Maturations
2. The Cause of Karmic Maturations

How to Practice Engagement and Disengagement Once You Have Reflected [on the General and Specific Characteristics of] Actions and Their Effects

Training the Mind in the Stages of the Path of a Person of Middle Scope [has four sections:]

1. The Actual Training in Contemplation
2. The Measure of Having Generated Thought [Determined to Attain Liberation]
3. Dispelling Misconceptions
4. Developing Certainty about the Nature of the Path Leading to Liberation

The Actual Training in Contemplation has two sections:

1. Identifying a Mind Striving for Liberation
2. The Method for Developing the Mind [Intent on Liberation]

The Method for Developing the Mind [Intent on Liberation] has two sections:

1. Contemplating the Faults of Samsara as True Sufferings
2. Contemplating the Stages of Entering Samsara as True Origins

Contemplating the Faults of Samsara as True Sufferings has two sections:

1. Revealing the Intention behind Teaching True Sufferings at the Beginning of the Four Noble Truths
2. The Actual Meditation on Suffering

The Actual Meditation on Suffering has two sections:

1. Contemplating the General Sufferings of Samsara
2. Contemplating the Specific Sufferings [of Samsara]

Contemplating the General Sufferings of Samsara has two sections:

1. Contemplating the Eight Sufferings
2. Contemplating the Six Sufferings

Contemplating the Eight Sufferings has eight sections:

1. The Suffering of Birth
2. The Suffering of Aging
3. The Suffering of Illness

4. The Suffering of Death
5. The Suffering of Having to Encounter the Unpleasant
6. The Suffering of Parting from the Pleasant
7. The Suffering of Searching for and Not Finding What You Desire
8. A Teaching on the Suffering of the Five Appropriated Aggregates

The Way to Contemplate the Six Types of Suffering has six sections:

1. The Fault of Uncertainty
2. The Fault of Not Being Satisfied
3. The Fault of Having to Repeatedly Abandon Our Bodies
4. The Fault of Being Repeatedly Born
5. The Fault of Repeatedly Changing from High to Low
6. The Fault of Having No Companionship

The Three Types of Suffering

Contemplating the Specific Sufferings [of Samsara] has three sections:

1. The Suffering of Humans
2. The Suffering of Demigods
3. The Suffering of Gods

Contemplating the Stage of Entering Samsara as True Origins has three sections:

1. How the Afflictive Emotions Are Generated
2. How Karma Is Accumulated through Those [Afflictive Emotions]
3. How We Die and Take Rebirth

How the Afflictive Emotions Are Generated has three sections:

1. Identifying the Afflictive Emotions
2. The Stages in Which the Afflictive Emotions Are Developed
3. The Faults of the Afflictive Emotions

The Causes of the Afflictive Emotions

How Karma Is Accumulated [through Those Afflictive Emotions] has two sections:

1. Identifying the Karma That Is Accumulated
2. How Karma Is Accumulated

[How We Die and Take Rebirth]

The Measure of Having Generated Thought [Determined to Attain Liberation]

Refuting Misconception about the Way to Practice

The Type of Path Needed to Overcome Samsara

Training the Mind in the Stages of the Path of a Person of Great Scope [has three sections:]

1. Revealing That Bodhichitta Is the Sole Gateway to the Mahayana, Together with Its Benefits
2. How to Develop Bodhichitta
3. How to Train in the Bodhisattva's Deeds Once We Have Developed Bodhichitta

The Actual Stages of Training the Mind has three sections:

1. The Way to Train in Bodhichitta
2. Training the Mind by Way of the Sevenfold Oral Instructions of Cause and Effect
3. The Importance of Compassion

Compassion Is Important in the Beginning

Compassion Is Important in the Middle

[Compassion Is Important in the End]

How [Compassion] Is Either Cause or Effect for the Others in [the Sevenfold Instructions of] Cause and Effect has two sections:

1. How Love Comes from Recognizing All Beings as Your Mother
2. The Actual Stages of Training the Mind [in Bodhichitta]

The Actual Stages of Training the Mind [in Bodhichitta] has two sections:

1. Training the Mind in Stages of the Sevenfold Instructions of Cause and Effect
2. Training the Mind in Equalizing and Exchanging Self with Others

Training the Mind in Stages of the Sevenfold Instructions of Cause and Effect has eight sections:

1. Equanimity
2. Recognizing All Beings as Your Mother
3. Recalling Their Kindness
4. Repaying Their Kindness
5. Meditating on Affectionate Love
6. Training the Mind in Great Compassion
7. Superior Intention
8. Meditating on Bodhichitta

Seven-Point Mind Training has three sections:

1. The Greatness of the Composer
2. The Greatness of the Dharma
3. The Actual Instructions

The Actual Instructions has seven points:

1. [Point One:] Teaching the Dharma of Preliminary Foundation
2. [Point Two:] Training in the Two Types of Bodhichitta
3. [Point Three:] Transforming Adverse Conditions into the Path to Enlightenment
4. [Point Four:] Presentation of a Lifetime's Practice in Summary
5. [Point Five:] The Measure of Having Trained the Mind
6. [Point Six:] Presenting the Commitments of Mind Training
7. [Point Seven:] The Precepts of Mind Training

Training in the Two Types of Bodhichitta has two sections:

1. Training the Mind in Ultimate Bodhichitta
2. Training the Mind in Conventional Bodhichitta

Training the Mind in Conventional Bodhichitta has five sections:

1. Meditation on Equalizing Self with Others
2. [Contemplating the Numerous] Faults of Self-Cherishing
3. [Contemplating the Numerous] Benefits of Cherishing Others
4. [The Actual Contemplation of] Exchanging Self with Others
5. How to Meditate on Giving and Taking [in Dependence upon That]

[Point Three: Transforming Adverse Conditions into the Path to Enlightenment]

[Point Four: Presentation of a Lifetime's Practice in Summary]

[Ritual for Receiving the Bodhisattva Vows]

[The Measure of Having Generated That Mind of Bodhichitta and the Measure of Having Generated Great Compassion]

[Point Five: The Measure of Having Trained the Mind]

[Point Six: Presenting the Commitments of Mind Training]

[Point Seven: The Precepts of Mind Training]

An Explanation of the Stages of Training in the Precepts

The Six Transcendent Perfections has six sections:

1. Generosity
2. Moral Discipline
3. Patience
4. Joyous Perseverance
5. Concentration
6. Wisdom

Ripening the Minds of Others through the Four Ways of Gathering Disciples

The Final Two Transcendent Perfections has two sections:

1. Training in Tranquil Abiding as the Essence of Concentration
2. Training in Superior Seeing as the Essence of Wisdom

[Training in Tranquil Abiding as the Essence of Concentration has three sections:]

1. How to Train in Tranquil Abiding as the Essence of Concentration
2. Relying upon the Conditions for Tranquil Abiding
3. The Actual Way to Attain Tranquil Abiding

The Object of Observation

How to Accomplish the Nine Mental Abidings in Dependence upon That [Instruction]

The Four Types of Attention

The Way to Train in the Superior Seeing That Is the Nature of Wisdom has two sections:

1. Relying upon the Collection of Causes for Superior Seeing
2. How to Actually Meditate [on Emptiness]

How to Actually Meditate [on Emptiness] has three sections:

1. Ascertaining the Selflessness of Persons
2. Ascertaining the Selflessness of Phenomena
3. The Way to Develop Superior Seeing from That

Ascertaining the Selflessness of Persons has two sections:

1. How to Practice the Space-like Meditative Absorption
2. How to Practice the Illusory-like Subsequent Attainment

How to Practice the Space-like Meditative Absorption has four sections:

1. The First Essential Point: Ascertaining the Object of Negation
2. The Second Essential Point: Ascertaining the Pervasion
3. The Third Essential Point: [The Self] Is Not Truly Identical [to the Five Aggregates]
4. The Fourth Essential Point: [The Self] Is Not Truly Separate [from the Aggregates]

How to Practice the Illusory-like Subsequent Attainment

[Ascertaining] the Selflessness of Phenomena has two sections:

1. Establishing the Absence of Inherently Existent Compounded Phenomena
2. Establishing the Absence of Inherently Existent Uncompounded Phenomena

Establishing the Absence of Inherently Existent Compounded Phenomena has three sections:

1. Establishing the Absence of Inherently Existent Form
2. Establishing the Absence of Inherently Existent Consciousness
3. Establishing the Absence of Inherently Existent Nonassociated Compositional Factors

[Establishing the Absence of Inherently Existent Uncompounded Phenomena]

The Measure of Having Developed Superior Seeing

[How to Train in the Vajrayana]

Colophon

Glossary

acharya: A Sanskrit term indicating a high degree of scholarship that is usually associated with a degree. *Charya* means "training" and is prefixed by the negative particle *a*, indicating that such a person is beyond need of further training.

analytical meditation: Usually juxtaposed to stabilization meditation, analytical meditation uses reasoning and inference to reach a determined conclusion about the subject of meditation. Once such a conclusion is reached, one engages in stabilization meditation on the subject under analysis.

Ananda: Buddha Shakyamuni's foremost disciple, who was responsible for recording most of the Buddha's teachings during the First Buddhist Council due to his spiritual attainments, which endowed him with a remarkable memory.

arhat: Literally meaning "foe destroyer," an arhat has destroyed the "foe" of afflictive emotions, thereby gaining liberation from samsara.

arya: A superior being who has gained a direct intuitive realization of emptiness—the ultimate nature of realty—through a combination of tranquil abiding and superior seeing.

aspiring bodhichitta: A mind that aspires to attain enlightenment for the welfare of all living beings, due to being motivated by universal love and compassion.

Avalokiteshvara: Known as "Chenrezig" in Tibetan, he is the manifestation of the compassion of all the buddhas appearing as a white deity in various aspects. The most common aspect has one face and four arms; another has eleven faces and one thousand arms.

bhagavan: An epithet for an enlightened being that means "having destroyed the obstructions to omniscience and endowed with all good qualities, he or she has transcended samsara and attained enlightenment."

bodhichitta: The intention to become enlightened for the welfare of all living beings, motivated by love and the compassion that sees the suffering nature of samsara and seeks to liberate all living beings from it.

Buddha Shakyamuni: The historical Buddha who lived approximately twenty-five hundred years ago and is the founder of the Buddhism practiced today.

Chakrasamvara: A highest yoga tantra deity that is a manifestation of Buddha Shakyamuni as a countermeasure to powerful worldly spirits that increase afflictive emotions.

Chittamatra: See Mind Only.

chö: A term that means "sever," indicating that the practitioner offers his or her body to malignant spirits as a means of severing his or her self-grasping and self-cherishing.

clear light: The extremely subtle mind that becomes manifest during the completion stage of highest yoga tantra, it is utilized to realize emptiness.

compassion: A mind that feels a sense of distress upon observing the suffering of others and wishes to relieve them of that suffering. Great compassion observes *all* living beings without exception.

completion stage: The second stage of highest yoga tantra that utilizes channels, winds, and drops to cause the winds to enter, abide in, and dissolve into the central channel, whereby one manifests subtle levels of consciousness while conjoining them with bliss.

dependent relationship: A phrase that reveals the nature of conventional reality as being interdependent upon causes and conditions, parts, and conceptual imputation for its existence. It also refers to the causal relationship between karma and the afflictive emotions that propels samsaric existence.

Dharma: The teachings of the Buddha that lead one through spiritual paths that culminate in varying degrees of happiness, from the happiness of this life to the happiness of liberation and enlightenment.

dzogchen: A highly advanced and profound practice mainly found in the Nyingma tradition of Tibetan Buddhism that means "great completion." The Nyingma tradition asserts that through the practice of dzogchen one is able to remove the obstructions to both liberation and omniscience from the most subtle level of mind.

eight worldly concerns: Eight attitudes that determine many of the motivations and actions undertaken under the domination of samsaric existence. They are wishing for gain and avoiding loss, wishing for praise and avoiding blame, wishing for happiness and avoiding suffering, and wishing for fame and avoiding disrepute.

emanation body: A coarse physical body of a buddha that provides guidance and assistance to living beings in accordance with their various dispositions and potentialities.

empowerment (Tib. *wang*): A ritual utilizing a mandala that transmits the blessing of a particular buddha in the aspect of a deity and establishes the imprints to attain the resultant body, speech, and mind of that deity.

emptiness: The ultimate nature of reality. Emptiness is the absence of a falsely imagined sense of inherent existence that is not in accord with reality. Through gaining a realization of emptiness, one progressively removes the afflictive emotions and their imprints, resulting in the state of complete enlightenment.

engaging bodhichitta: A mind wishing to attain enlightenment for the welfare of living beings after taking bodhisattva vows and undertaking the practice of the six transcendent perfections.

enjoyment body: A subtle body of a buddha that is only visible to arya bodhisattvas and is the basis for the emanation body.

equalizing and exchanging self with others: A method for generating bodhichitta consisting of the following five stages: (1) equalizing self and others, (2) recognizing the faults of self-cherishing, (3) recognizing the benefits of cherishing others, (4) taking and giving, and (5) having bodhichitta.

field of merit: A visualization consisting of either a single enlightened being or an assembly of enlightened beings. They are referred to as "a field of merit" because, just as we use a field of soil to plant seeds that will ripen as a harvest, the field of merit is a field in which we sow our virtuous actions, such as offerings and praises, which will ripen as the harvest of realizations.

five paths: The framework through which both Hinayana and Mahayana practitioners progress. Both traditions posit them as the paths of (1) accumulation, (2) preparation, (3) seeing, (4) meditation, and (5) no more learning. The resultant state of no-more-learning for a Hinayana practitioner is either a shravaka or pratyekabuddha. For a Mahayana practitioner, it is the state of full enlightenment.

generation stage: A term unique to highest yoga tantra, where one imagines transforming the basic experiences of ordinary death, the intermediate state, and rebirth into the truth body, enjoyment body, and emanation body, respectively.

Guhyasamaja: The first highest yoga tantra taught, it provides the framework for all subsequent tantras. In particular, the completion stage consists of five stages: (1) isolated speech, (2) isolated mind, (3) illusory body, (4) clear light, and (5) union. These five stages are a natural progression that any practitioner will embark upon, regardless of which deity he or she is practicing. For that reason, these five stages are often used in other tantras to draw parallels with the indigenous systems of each tantra to facilitate a more comprehensive understanding.

highest yoga tantra: The highest of the four classes of tantra that emphasizes internal actions and utilizes embracing a physical consort as a means of generating the most subtle mind of clear light as a blissful subjective awareness that is capable of penetrating the nature of reality.

illusory body: The subtle body that is actualized during the completion stage. There are two divisions of the illusory body: pure and impure. The impure illusory body is attained after the attainment of ultimate example clear light, and is so called because the wind from which it is composed is still impure in the sense that the mind from which it arose has yet to directly realize emptiness. The pure illusory body is so called because it arises from meaning clear light that has directly realized emptiness.

intermediate state: The transitional state between the end of one life and the beginning of the next. The intermediate state can last up to forty-nine days, consisting of seven minor transitional periods each resulting in a "small death," after which one either takes rebirth or assumes another intermediate-state body.

isolated body: A preliminary to the five stages of the completion stage of Guhyasamaja as presented by Nagarjuna. It is so named because the wind that gives rise to the body as being ordinary is isolated from its movement by dissolving it into the central channel, which gives rise to the pure conceptions of the body as being the deity body.

isolated mind: The second of the five stages of the completion stage of Guhyasamaja as presented by Nagarjuna. It is so named because the wind that gives rise to the mind as being ordinary is isolated from its movement by dissolving it into the central channel, which gives rise to the pure conceptions of the mind as being the deity's mind.

isolated speech: The first of the five stages of the completion stage of Guhyasamaja as presented by Nagarjuna. It is so named because the wind that gives rise to the speech as being ordinary is isolated from its movement by dissolving it into the central channel, which gives rise to the pure conceptions of the speech as being the deity's speech.

Kangyur: The original spoken words of the Buddha about both sutra and tantra, which were subsequently translated into Tibetan.

karma: A Sanskrit word meaning "cause and effect." It indicates the relationship between an action created and its corresponding result. In its most basic presentation, whatever we experience is a result of our previous actions. Pleasant experiences stem from virtuous actions, and painful experiences stem from nonvirtuous actions.

Lama Chöpa: A ritual consisting of prayers, praises, and supplications to one's spiritual guides, who are appearing in the aspect of Lama Losang Tubwang Dorje Chang, which consists of Je Tsongkhapa with Buddha Shakyamuni at his heart, Buddha Vajradhara in the heart of Buddha Shakyamuni, and a syllable HUM in the heart of Buddha Vajradhara. It contains all the practices contained in both sutra and in the generation and completion stages of highest yoga tantra.

lamrim: Meaning "the stages on the path to enlightenment," the lamrim presents the entire Buddhist teachings in a systematic format designed for an individual's progress to enlightenment.

Losang Tubwang Dorje Chang: Also known as Lama Losang Tubwang Dorje Chang, this is a title given to the central figure of the Lama Chöpa field of merit. When prefaced with "Lama," this refers to one's personal guru. "Losang" is in reference to Tsongkhapa, whose proper name was Losang Drakpa. "Tubwang" is Tibetan for "Powerful Able One" and is an epithet for the Buddha Shakyamuni, and "Dorje Chang" refers to Vajradhara. The title is given because the outer aspect of the central figure of the field of merit is in the aspect of Tsongkhapa with Buddha Shakyamuni in his heart, who in turn has Vajradhara in his heart. All three are seen as inseparable from your own root guru, hence the name "Lama Losang Tubwang Dorje Chang."

Madhyamaka: The "Middle Way" school of Mahayana philosophy founded by Nagarjuna. There are two primary divisions of the Madhyamaka: the Prasangika and the Svatantrika. The Prasangika utilizes consequential syllogisms and presents a slightly more subtle interpretation of emptiness than the Svatantrika. The Svatantrika utilizes autonomous syllogisms and presents emptiness in a slightly coarser interpretation than the Prasangika.

mahasiddhas: Tantric adepts of varying degrees of realization who have attained a degree of realization far beyond that of an ordinary being. They are most often associated with ancient India.

Maitreya: In a general sense, as a deity Maitreya embodies the love of all the buddhas. As a personal figure, he is said to be the successor to Buddha Shakyamuni, appearing as the fifth of the thousand buddhas of this fortunate eon.

merit: A type of good karma that functions as a catalyst for our spiritual attainments.

Milarepa: Tibet's most famous yogi, who lived 1052–1135. Milarepa spent the earlier part of his life engaged in nonvirtuous actions and finally killed thirty-six people through the use of black magic. Repenting his nonvirtuous actions, he sought out his guru, Marpa, who famously put him through extreme hardships as a means of purifying Milarepa's negative karma. In the latter part of his life, Milarepa devoted himself to solitary retreat, eventually attaining enlightenment and establishing numerous disciples on the path to enlightenment. His teachings were adopted by his disciple Gampopa, who combined them with the teachings of the Kadam lineage, resulting in the Kagyu lineage.

Mind Only: The Chittamatra school of philosophy within Mahayana Buddhism, which asserts that there are no external objects and that all phenomena are mere appearances to the mind.

muni: Meaning "Able One," this epithet refers to enlightened beings, indicating that they have fully actualized the innate potential.

Nagarjuna: The founder of Mahayana Buddhism, who is said to have traveled to the subterranean land of the nagas to obtain the perfection of wisdom sutras.

nagas: Serpent-like beings who have varying degrees of power and can be either malevolent or benign.

ngagpa: A lay tantric practitioner most commonly associated with the Nyingma and Kagyu traditions.

Nyingma: A Tibetan word meaning "ancient" or "old." This term was coined during the second wave of translations, which were made largely under the guidance of Rinchen Lotsawa and which were called the Sarma, or "new," translations. Thus, the Nyingma tradition largely follows the translations from the first wave of translations, which were produced under the guidance of King Songsten Gampo (sixth to seventh century) and implemented by Padmasambhava, Shantarakshita, and their twenty-five first disciples.

Padmasambhava: An eighth-century Buddhist master who was invited to Tibet by King Trisong Detsen at the request of Shantarakshita to assist in the construction of Samyé, Tibet's first monastery. Under the direction of the king, Padmasambhava and Shantarakshita began a massive translation program that was later recognized as the Nyingma, or "ancient," translations.

placement meditation: A type of meditation that utilizes the capacity for the mind to focus single-pointedly on a topic of meditation to deeply imprint and transform the mind. It is often preceded by analytical meditation that develops the observed object of placement meditation.

pratimoksha: A Sanskrit word meaning "individual liberation" that commonly refers to a set of vows taken with the motivation of attaining liberation from samsara.

pratimoksha vows: Vows of individual liberation: a set of vows taken with the motivation of attaining liberation from samsara.

pratyekabuddha: A state of arhatship that is distinguished by its practitioners, who spend numerous lives accumulating merit and wisdom, thereby resulting in a state of arhatship that is superior to that of a shravaka.

renunciation: Literally, "definite emergence." This refers to the definite determination to be liberated, or "emerge," from samsara through a proper understanding of its shortcomings.

root downfall: A violation of one of the root vows associated with either the pratimoksha, bodhisattva, or tantric codes of discipline.

samsara: A cycle of uncontrolled rebirth that occurs through the force of afflicted actions and delusions.

scanning meditation: This type of meditation moves from one topic of meditation to another in a sequence that is intended to create an overall perspective on a particular topic of meditation.

secret mantra: A synonym for tantra, the term "secret mantra" implies that tantra should be practiced under the strictest secrecy.

self-cherishing: An exaggerated sense of self-importance based on the mistaken interpretation of oneself as inherently existent, which causes one to think of one's happiness as more important than that of everyone else.

self-grasping: Grasping at an inherently existent self, based on a mistaken interpretation of the nature of reality, which is the cause of samsara and all the suffering within it.

sevenfold cause and effect: A method for generating bodhichitta based on the following seven steps: (1) recognizing all beings as your mother, (2) remembering their kindness, (3) wishing to repay their kindness, (4) developing affectionate love, (5) developing great compassion, (6) attaining the superior intention, and (7) bodhichitta.

seven limbs of embrace: The seven qualities unique to the enjoyment body of an enlightened being: (1) the complete enjoyment body, (2) union, (3) great bliss, (4) the absence of inherent existence, (5) being completely filled with great compassion, (6) unbroken continuity, and (7) ceaselessness.

shravaka: A state of arhatship in which an arhat has not attained the same degree of wisdom or merit as a pratyekabuddha.

six transcendent perfections: Enumerated as (1) generosity, (2) moral discipline, (3) patience, (4) enthusiastic perseverance, (5) concentration, and (6) wisdom. They become transcendent when they are conjoined with bodhichitta and the realization of emptiness.

superior intention: The universal responsibility to liberate and enlighten all living beings, which is preceded by meditation on love and compassion. When the practitioner realizes that he or she is incapable of accomplishing the goal of superior intention in his or her current unenlightened state, he or she determines to attain full enlightenment so as to be capable of fulfilling his or her superior intention. This determination to attain complete enlightenment is the actual mind of bodhichitta.

superior seeing (Skt. *vipashyana*): Insight meditation. There are both mundane and supramundane paths of vipashyana. The supramundane path consists of a union of tranquil abiding and the realization of emptiness.

sutra: A series of public discourses given by the historical Buddha.

Tengyur: The indigenous Indian commentaries to the Buddha's sutra and tantra teachings translated into Tibetan.

Three Baskets (Tib. sDe snod gsum; Skt. Tripitaka): Broad divisions of the Buddha's teachings—namely, the basket of moral discipline (Vinaya Pitaka), the basket of discourses (Sutra Pitaka), and the basket of wisdom (Abhidharma Pitaka).

three doors: Body, speech, and mind. The name comes from the fact that these are the doorways through which we accumulate and experience karma.

three higher trainings: Necessarily motivated by either renunciation or bodhichitta, these consist of (1) moral discipline, (2) concentration, and (3) wisdom.

three vehicles: (1) The Hinayana, or "individual vehicle," (2) the Mahayana, or "universal vehicle," and (3) the Mantrayana, or "indestructible vehicle."

tranquil abiding: A mind of single-pointed meditative equipoise that is enhanced by a special pliancy of body and mind, allowing the practitioner to remain absorbed in meditation upon a desired object with utter unwavering focus for as long as desired.

transference of consciousness (Skt. '*pho ba*): A method to intentionally separate the subtle wind and mind from the coarse aggregates at the time of death, as a means of taking rebirth in a pure land of a buddha.

truth body (Skt. *dharmakaya*): The extremely subtle mind of an enlightened being that is completely free from the obstructions to omniscience and that serves as the foundation for the enjoyment and emanation bodies.

tsok offering (Skt. *ganachakra*): A tantric feast involving ritual music and sacred substances for invoking the blessing of the dakas and dakinis and strengthening one's tantric commitments.

Tsongkhapa: A Tibetan lama who lived from 1357 to 1419. He is responsible for the formation of the Gelug tradition of Tibetan Buddhism. He was a great nonsectarian teacher who assembled various practices and lineages that resulted in the Gelug tradition.

ultimate reality: The ultimate reality of all phenomena is their being empty of inherent existence.

union: There are several types of union, such as the union of bliss and emptiness, the union of the illusory body and clear light, and the union of body and mind. When used in reference to the five stages of Guhyasamaja, it refers to the fifth stage, simply called "union." At this stage there is the union of meaning clear light and the pure illusory body, which is referred to as "a learner's union." At the resultant state of enlightenment it is called "the union of no more learning" or "the union of body and mind" and is synonymous with enlightenment.

Vajrabhairava: A wrathful highest yoga tantra deity who is a manifestation of Manjushri, the embodiment of all the buddhas' wisdom.

Vajradhara: An emanation of Buddha Shakyamuni who appeared as a blue-colored deity and taught the various tantras.

wisdom truth body: The exalted wisdom of a buddha's mind that knows all aspects.

yoga: Meaning "unify with the true nature of reality," yoga appears in numerous forms as a means of unifying with the ultimate nature of reality, such as deity yoga, guru yoga, and so forth. In Buddhism, the physical yogas are merely a preliminary to prepare the body and mind for the means of unifying with reality.

Bibliography

Works in English

Aryadeva and Gyaltsab [Dar-ma-rin-chen]. *The Yogic Deeds of Bodhisattvas: Gyel-tsap on Aryadeva's "Four Hundred."* Commentary by Geshe Sonam Rinchen; translated and edited by Ruth Sonam. Ithaca, NY: Snow Lion Publications, 1994. (Reprinted as Aryadeva and Gyel-tsap, *Aryadeva's Four Hundred Stanzas on the Middle Way with Commentary by Gyeltsap*, Snow Lion, 2008.)

Atisha and Dromtonpa, attrib. *The Book of Kadam: The Core Texts.* Translated by Thupten Jinpa. Library of Tibetan Classics, vol. 2. Boston: Wisdom Publications, 2008.

Buddha Shakyamuni. *Sutra of the Wise and the Foolish.* Translated by Stanley Fry. Dharamsala: Library of Tibetan Works and Archives, 1981.

Cleary, Thomas, trans. *The Flower Ornament Scripture: A Translation of the Avatamsaka Sutra.* Boston: Shambhala Publications, 1993.

Dharmarakshita. *Peacock in the Poison Grove: Two Buddhist Texts on Training the Mind.* Translated by Geshe Lhundrub Sopa, with Michael Sweet and Leonard Zwilling. Boston: Wisdom Publications, 2001.

Gedün Lodrö, Geshe. *Walking through Walls: A Presentation of Tibetan Meditation.* Translated and edited by Jeffery Hopkins. Ithaca, NY: Snow Lion Publications, 1992.

Hopkins, Jeffrey. *Buddhist Advice on Living and Liberation.* Ithaca, NY: Snow Lion Publications, 1998.

———. *Meditation on Emptiness.* Boston: Wisdom Publications, 1996.

Jamgön Kongtrul Lodrö Tayé. *Buddhist Ethics.* Translated by the International Translation Committee. Ithaca, NY: Snow Lion Publications, 1998.

———. *Jamgon Kongtrul's Retreat Manual.* Translated and introduced by Ngawang Zangpo (Hugh Leslie Thomson). Ithaca, NY: Snow Lion Publications, 1994.

Kachen Yeshe Gyaltsen. *Manjushri's Innermost Secret: A Profound Commentary of Oral Instructions on the Practice of Lama Chöpa.* Translated by David Gonsalez. Seattle: Dechen Ling Press, 2014.

Loden, Geshe Acharya Thubten. *The Fundamental Potential for Enlightenment in Tibetan Buddhism.* Melbourne: Tushita Publications, 1996.

Mullin, Glenn H. *The Fourteen Dalai Lamas: A Sacred Legacy of Reincarnation.* Santa Fe, NM: Clear Light Books, 2000.

Nagarjuna. *Nagarjuna's Letter to a Friend: With Commentary by Kyabje Kangyur Rinpoche.* Translated by the Padmakara Translation Group. Ithaca, NY: Snow Lion Publications, 2005.

Namkha Pel. *Mind Training Like the Rays of the Sun.* Translated by Brian Beresford. Ithaca, NY: Library of Tibetan Works and Archives, 1992.

Ngorchen Konchog Lhundrub. *The Beautiful Ornament of the Three Visions.* Translated by Lobsang Dagpa and Jay Goldberg. Ithaca, NY: Snow Lion Publications, 1991.

Ngulchu Dharmabhadra. *The Blazing Inner Fire of Bliss and Emptiness: An Experiential Commentary on the Practice of the Six Yogas of Naropa.* Translated by David Gonsalez. Seattle: Dechen Ling Press, 2014.

Ngulchu Dharmabhadra and the Fifth Ling Rinpoche, Losang Lungtog Tenzin Trinley. *The Roar of Thunder: Yamantaka Practice and Commentary.* Translated by David Gonsalez. Ithaca, NY: Snow Lion Publications, 2012.

Pabongkha Rinpoche. *Liberation in Our Hands.* Translated by Sermey Khensur Lobsang with Artemus B. Engle. 3 vols. Howell, NJ: Mahayana Sutra and Tantra Press, 1990–2001.

Shönu Gyalchok and Könchok Gyaltsen, comps. *Mind Training: The Great Collection.* Translated and edited by Thupten Jinpa. Library of Tibetan Classics, vol. 1. Boston: Wisdom Publications, 2006.

Thuken Losang Chökyi Nyima. *The Crystal Mirror of Philosophical Systems: A Tibetan Study of Asian Religious Thought.* Translated by Geshe Lhundub Sopa with E. Ann Chávez and Roger R. Jackson; special contributions by Michael Sweet and Leonard Zwilling; edited by Roger R. Jackson. Library of Tibetan Classics, vol. 25. Boston: Wisdom Publications, 2009.

Thupten Jinpa, trans., ed., and comp. *Wisdom of the Kadam Masters.* Tibetan Classics, vol. 2. Boston: Wisdom Publications, 2013.

Tsangnyön Heruka. *The Life of Milarepa.* Translated by Andrew Quintman; introduction by Donald S. Lopez, Jr. London: Penguin Books, 2010.

Tsongkhapa [Tsong-kha-pa]. *The Great Treatise on the Stages of the Path to Enlightenment.* Translated by the Lamrim Chenmo Translation Committee. 3 vols. Ithaca, NY: Snow Lion Publications, 2000–2004.

———. [rJe Tsong Khapa]. *The Ocean of Reasoning: A Great Commentary on Nagarjuna's "Mulamadhyamakakarika."* Translated by Geshe Ngawang Samten and Jay L. Garfield. Oxford and New York: Oxford University Press, 2006.

Willis, Janice D. *Enlightened Beings: Life Stories from the Ganden Oral Tradition.* Boston: Wisdom Publications, 1995.

Yangsi Rinpoche. *Practicing the Path: A Commentary on the Lamrim Chenmo.* Translated by Tsering Tuladhar; edited by Miranda Adams. Boston: Wisdom Publications, 2003.

Tibetan Texts

Kachen Yeshe Gyaltsen. *An Instruction Manual on Mahayana Mind Training Entitled "The Essential Nectar"* (Theg chen blo sbyong gi khrid yig bdud rtsi'i snying po). TBRC W1022. 19: 9–352. New Delhi: Tibet House Library, 1974–1977. http://tbrc.org/link?RID=O01DG04|O01DG04d1e2970$W1022.

———. *An Instructional Manual on Mind Training Entitled "Adorning the True Intent of Losang [Drakpa]"* (Blo sbyong gi khrid yig blo bzang dgongs rgyan). TBRC W1022. 25: 15–846. New Delhi: Tibet House Library, 1974–1977. http://tbrc.org/link?RID=O01DG04|O01DG04d1e3892$W1022.

Losang Yeshe, The Second Panchen Lama. *An Explicit Commentary on the Stages of the Path to Enlightenment: A Swift Path for Reaching the State of Omniscience* (Lam rim dmar khrid thams cad mkhyen par bgrod pa'i myur lam). TBRC W1174. 3: 129–290. [bkra shis lhun po?]: [bkras lhun chos sde tshogs pa], [199–?]. http://tbrc.org/link?RID=O00EGS105883|O00EGS1058835926$W1174.

Pabongkha Rinpoche. *Liberation in Our Hands* (Lam rim rnam grol lag bcangs / byang chub lam gyi rim pa'i nyams khrid kyi zin bris gsung rab kun gyi bcud bsdus gdams ngag bdud rtsi'i snying po). TBRC W3834. 11: 3–784. Lhasa: [s.n.], [199–]. http://tbrc.org/link?RID=O01PD4|O01PD4d1e3711$W3834.

Sonam Gyatso, the Third Dalai Lama. *A Guide to the Stages on the Path to Enlightenment Entitled "The Essence of Refined Gold"* (Byang chub lam gyi rim pa'i khrid gser gyi yang zhun) (ka). In Gsung 'bum/_bsod nams rgya mtsho. TBRC W1CZ2856: 19–70. Dharamsala: Library of Tibetan Works and Archives, 2000. http://tbrc.org/link?RID=O1GS139111|O1GS1391111GS139115$W1CZ2856.

Index

What to Read Next
from the Dechen Ling Practice Series

Manjushri's Innermost Secret
A Profound Commentary of Oral Instructions on the Practice of Lama Chöpa
Kachen Yeshe Gyaltsen
Foreword by Ganden Tripa Lobsang Tenzin
Now available from Wisdom Publications

The Extremely Secret Dakini of Naropa
Vajrayogini Practice and Commentary
Pabongkha Dechen Nyingpo

The Chakrasamvara Root Tantra

The Roar of Thunder
Yamantaka Practice and Commentary
Ngulchu Dharmabhadra
and the Fifth Ling Rinpoche, Losang Lungtog Tenzin Trinley

Source of Supreme Bliss
Heruka Chakrasamvara Five-Deity Practice
Ngulchu Dharmabhadra,
and the First Panchen Lama, Losang Chökyi Gyaltsen

Secret Revelations of Chittamani Tara
Generation and Completion Stage Practice and Commentary
Pabongkha Dechen Nyingpo

The Blazing Inner Fire of Bliss and Emptiness
An Experiential Commentary on the Practice of the Six Yogas of Naropa
Ngulchu Dharmabhadra

The Melodious Drum of Dakini Land
A Commentary to the Extensive Dedication Prayer of Venerable Vajrayogini
Yangchen Drupai Dorje

Healing Nectar of Immortality
White Tara Healing and Longevity Practices and Commentary
Trijang Rinpoche and Aku Sherab Gyatso

The Ecstatic Dance of Chakrasamvara
Heruka Body Mandala Practice and Commentary
Trijang Rinpoche
Foreword by Gen Lobsang Choephel

About Wisdom Publications

Wisdom Publications is the leading publisher of classic and contemporary Buddhist books and practical works on mindfulness. To learn more about us or to explore our other books, please visit our website at wisdomexperience.org or contact us at the address below.

Wisdom Publications
199 Elm Street
Somerville, MA 02144 USA

We are a 501(c)(3) organization, and donations in support of our mission are tax deductible.

Wisdom Publications is affiliated with the Foundation for the Preservation of the Mahayana Tradition (FPMT).